THE JEWISH EXPERIENCE
IN AMERICA

V

AT HOME IN AMERICA

36095

THE JEWISH EXPERIENCE
IN AMERICA

Selected Studies From
The Publications of The

AMERICAN JEWISH
HISTORICAL SOCIETY

Edited with Introductions By
ABRAHAM J. KARP

V

AT HOME IN AMERICA

AMERICAN JEWISH HISTORICAL SOCIETY
WALTHAM, MASSACHUSETTS

KTAV PUBLISHING HOUSE, INC.
NEW YORK

This book is printed on acid-free paper.

SBN 87068-025-0

Library of Congress Catalog Card Number: 72-77150
Manufactured in the United States of America

Contents

Volumes 1-50 (1892-1961) were published as the
*Publications of the American Jewish Historical
Society.* Since 1961 the *Publications* are titled
the *American Jewish Historical Quarterly.*

AT HOME IN AMERICA

Those Who Came

Well into the twentieth century immigration continued to be the single most important factor in the American Jewish historic experience. Some 600,000 Jews came to the United States in the last two decades of the nineteenth century. Three times that number arrived in the first two decades of the twentieth. This great immigration wave was temporarily halted by World War I, 1914–1918, and was brought to a virtual end by the restrictive immigration laws of 1924. Some ninety-five percent of the immigrants originated in eastern Europe. Most came directly to America: some had remained for shorter or longer periods in West European countries. The rise of Hitler in 1933 precipitated a migration of German Jews to America in significant numbers, and some 150,000 came here in the years which followed World War II.

The 50,000 Jews of America in 1850 constituted one percent of world Jewry. The million Jews in 1900 were ten percent of the world's Jews. America's five million Jews were almost half of world Jewry in 1945. At the turn of the century the Jews constituted some one percent of the population of the United States. Within two decades it had risen to three percent where it has remained to date.

The increase in immigration from eastern Europe was due not so much to worsening conditions in that part of the world as to other factors. The Jews of Russia were far more disadvantaged, discriminated against, and oppressed in the half-century before 1870 than in the half-century which followed. But in the later years, America had more opportunities for urban, artisan immigrants; increased communication spread the knowledge about America and its opportunities to the remotest villages; improved means of transportation made the journey seem less fraught with danger; and the earlier immigrants were now subsidizing the later emigration. A good deal of the later immigration consisted of families which were being reunited— wife and children joining the head of the family, younger brothers and sisters brought over by the first to arrive. In the years 1900–1925, almost one-half of the Jewish immigrants were women, though women constituted no more than one-third of the non-Jewish immigrants. In the same years, children comprised one quarter of the immigrants, twice as many as among non-Jews. The traditional Jewish emphasis on family found expression in immigration practices.

The high percentage of women and children among Jewish immigrants was due to another factor. The Jew came to America to stay. Among other European people, a man would go to the New World to "make his fortune" and then return home to his town in Russia, Poland, Italy or Hungary. The dollars he brought back enabled him to establish a firm economic base for himself and his family. In the years 1908–1925 the remigration percentage was more than fifty percent for Romanians, Magyars, Italians and Russians. At that same time the percentage of Jews returning to the Old Country was only five percent relative to those arriving in the New World. Even more striking is the percentage of returnees to Poland between 1919–1922, when that nation had been restored to independent sovereignty: Poles, 369.5%; Ukranians, 56.5%; Jews, 0.5%. The statistics speak eloquently in evidence that for the immigrant Jew America was "home at last"!

It was only in comparison to conditions in eastern Europe that America was considered home and haven. In truth, the Jew was beset here by economic discrimination, social exclusion and a pervasive anti-Semitism usually genteel but on occasion overt and blatant. Many neighborhoods, hotels, clubs, and jobs were closed to him. In the first decades of the century the specter of the rapacious Jewish international financial conspiracy to dominate the world was raised. After World War I, the fear of the Jewish Bolshevik conspiracy to subjugate the Christian world was widely disseminated and discussed by some very "'respectable" persons and groups. "The International Jew and his satellites, as the conscious enemies of all that Anglo-Saxons mean by civilization . . ." was "exposed" in Henry Ford's *The Dearborn Independent,* and reprinted in pamphlets, under the title *The International Jew,* which received the widest circulation. The notorious *Protocols of the Meetings of the Zionist Men of Wisdom* (also called *The Protocols of the Elders of Zion*) was published in 1920 to alert America to the Jewish plot, fostered by Bolshevists and Zionists, to control the world. The American Jew came to know the Protestant minister and Catholic priest spewing anti-Semitism. He was not even spared the "ritual murder" charge, when in 1928 after the disappearance of a little girl in Massena, a small town in upstate New York, the rabbi of the town was brought in for questioning about Jews offering human sacrifice on the Day of Atonement.

Discrimination and accusations were of course not new experiences for the Jew. But here in America, more than anywhere else they could be countered and fought in the press, in the court of public opinion and in the courts of law as well. Individual Jews and Jewish leaders stood ready to enter the fray. Jewish organizations were formed to protect the Jew and defend Judaism. The American Jewish Committee, the Anti-Defamation League of B'nai B'rith, the American Jewish Congress, the Jewish Labor Committee, the Jewish War Veterans, all made "Jewish defense" a major part of their program and activities. They were able to invoke the American tradition of rights and freedom, to quote the classic American documents and the words of American greats, and to enlist the friendship and help of leading Americans who stood vigilant against the importation of Old World prejudices to the New World.

Exerted pressure forced Henry Ford to issue a public apology in 1927, addressed to Louis Marshall, asking the American Jews "as fellow men and brothers" to forgive him and pledging "henceforth they may look to me for friendship and good will."

With all its problems and imperfections, America was still the best bright hope in all the world for full rights, freedom, and opportunities for the Jew. The immigrant Jew lived to see overt discriminatory practices prohibited by law and proscribed by public opinion. He experienced ever widening economic opportunities for himself and educational openings and professional acceptance for his children. For the immigrant America was a haven; for his children's children it became home.

Making a Living

Fully two-thirds of the immigrants in the first quarter of the century came from Russia. In the last decades of the nineteenth century Jewish economic life in Russia had undergone a revolution. The traditional Jewish middleman was being replaced by the Jewish worker. The demographic movement was from the small town to the large city. In the small town, the Jew was the storekeeper serving the peasants who lived in surrounding villages. With the industrialization of eastern Europe, the cities grew, attracting a labor force. Many young men grew up in the small towns, and then left for the industrial cities of Lodz, Bialystok, Warsaw, Odessa to seek employment. Once on the way, a great number continued on to America. In the Russian cities they had acquired a trade, and this skill they brought with them to these shores. In the years 1900–1925, sixty percent of the Jewish immigrants were in industry, the very great majority as workers, as compared to fifteen percent of non-Jewish immigrants. Only ten percent of Jewish immigrants were engaged in trade, but two and one-half percent in agriculture (against twenty-six and one-half percent of non-Jewish immigrants). Of the workers, over sixty percent were employed by the clothing industry. It is also interesting to note that almost half of the immigrant labor force in the clothing industry was Jewish, as were jewelers and watchmakers. Jews were also very heavily represented as employees in printing, as leatherworkers and storekeepers. In all, in the first quarter of the century, Jewish immigrants were ten percent of the total immigration, but comprised twenty-five percent of the industrial immigrants. The Jewish immigrant then was a very important factor in the industrial life of early twentieth-century America.

The clothing worker never looked for his son to join him in the factory, nor did the small storekeeper expect to turn over the store to his descendants. They labored long and hard at machine and counter, to make it possible for their sons to escape their economic status.

S. M. Melamed wrote in 1927:

The labor unions of the needle industry in America are daily growing less Jewish. In the year 1919 . . . the unions were all packed with Jewish labor. Then the decline began. . . . The Jewish laborer . . . is not a tailor by choice but by chance . . . he gets out of the trade himself as soon as he possibly can, [and] he never teaches his son his trade. . . .

The Jewish garment and cloak manufacturer will keep on, but it is doubtful if his children will continue the tradition . . .

Entry into the professions was the dream of the immigrant Jew for his children. Medicine and law for the son, teaching for the daughter, were on the highest rung of aspiration. Higher education became a passion with second-generation Jews. Many found that quotas were set by colleges and universities for the number of Jews to be admitted, the smallest of all set by the medical schools. Certain professions, like engineering and college teaching, offered few opportunities for employment to Jews.

Jewish disabilities were widespread in America in the first decades of the century. Advertisements for jobs in the daily press often stated: "Christians only" or "No Jews need apply." In a survey conducted in 1926, discrimination was justified on such grounds as: "We find Protestants . . . more trustworthy than Catholics or Jews"; "Everyone in the office is a Christian . . . it would be more convenient to continue on that basis"; "Sometime ago we had the Bolshevik class of Jews in our place who caused a strike"; and, "We have only Christian men working here, and they would not work with Jews or Negroes."

Undisguised discrimination against the Jews in business, industry, education and social life continued till World War II.

The Ku Klux Klan, the Silver Shirts, the Christian Front, the German-American Bund felt free to carry on anti-Jewish propaganda. Overt acts of anti-Semitism were not uncommon. Social discrimination in community club, and campus were an accepted phenomenon on the American scene. The Jewish community expended vast energies and resources in its efforts to stem anti-Semitism and promote good will and understanding. For a time it was the chief preoccupation of organized American Jewish life.

Zionism and the Religious Communities

Zionism shared with Jewish "defense" a place of central concern and enterprise of the American Jewish community. From the perspective of the American Jew, they both addressed themselves to the same problem, the insecurity of Jewish existence in a non-Jewish world. Both recognized that the status of the Jew needed strengthening, but they differed in their analysis of the cause of the problem and in the proposed solution. The Zionist saw the Jewish problem as the result of statelessness which made the Jew an anomaly in the modern world. What one doesn't understand one fears; what one fears one hates. A Jewish state would remove the cause of mystery, fear, and hate. It would provide a haven for the driven and persecuted, and would give new status, strength and security to all Jews everywhere. Those engaged in "defense," saw the root of the Jews' plight in the ignorance of the non-Jew about the Jew, and in the Jews' lack of integration and assimilation into the fabric of civic and communal life. The solution, then, was to teach the non-Jew about Judaism and acquaint him with the worth and merits of the Jew. The Jew then must become a loyal member of the nation, a valued member of his community, and a source of strength for all civic endeavor. He should be the exemplar of a patriotic, virtuous, philanthropic American.

To those who proposed that full acceptance of the Jew must be preceded by evidence of the Jew's political patriotism and social integration, Zionism was an evil to be denounced and a threat to be fought. In the nineteenth century, leaders of Reform Judaism had declared: "America is our Zion, Washington is our Jerusalem." As an ideological expression, it was based on the conviction that Judaism is a religion pure and simple, whose mission is to spread the knowledge of the one God to all. Dispersion is not a calamity to be reversed, but a God-ordained opportunity to be seized. As a practical program it proclaimed the need of the Jew to make America the "center of his joy," to become fully and wholly part of the American landscape, take on its coloration, breathe to its rhythm, and eschew prayerful hopes for the restoration and resettlement of the ancient homeland—a Holy Land to be sure, but a foreign, alien land. What was practical consideration to religious leaders in the nineteenth century became the ideological posture of the defenders of the Jewish community in the twentieth century. The early "Lovers of Zion" accused the Reformers of espousing views which would inevitably lead to assimilation and apostasy. Later Zionists leveled grave charges of cowardice and callousness against anti-Zionist leaders of the American Jewish establishment who countered with accusations of dual loyalty. It was only when the community became established, the status of the Jew in America was more secure, and the American Jew felt no special need to proclaim his patriotism or demonstrate his loyalty that the two groups recognized the integrity of both programs and the sincerity of those who espoused them. They then could and did join in common effort, realizing that the two are not antagonistic but mutually helpful and complementary.

Zionism was high on the agenda of American Jewish interests and concern in the first half of the twentieth century. For many American Jews it served as the vehicle for Jewish identification and expression. For others it loomed as a challenge to their ideological position and as a threat to the status of the Jew in America. Reform Jewry opposed it (some few notables taking exception) as a denial of the "Mission of the Jew." The Socialist camp, which looked to and labored for the World Revolution, condemned it as a parochial, retrogressive, reactionary force, a handmaiden of Western imperialism. The Jew whose chief obsession was to be accepted as a full, loyal, patriotic American denounced Zionism as a dangerous libel upon the American Jew's undivided loyalty and unqualified patriotism.

The Zionist ranks were filled largely by East European immigrants and their children of traditional religious bent. Reform
Jewry and the Jewish socialist camp comprised the anti-Zionist
force.

At the turn of the century Zionism was the passion of a few
leading American Jews, Bernhard Felsenthal, Richard Gottheil,
Stephen S. Wise and a coterie of East European immigrants. By
and large American Jewry and its leaders and organizations
were indifferent or antagonistic. With each decade adherents
were added and activity increased. Elsewhere (*The Jewish
Journal of Sociology*, Volume VIII, No. 2, December 1966) I
have sketched the changes which took place in American religious Jewry's reaction to the three premier moments in Zionist
history: the First Zionist Congress, 1897; the Balfour Declaration, 1917; the State of Israel, 1948. The changes have much to
say about Jewish communal and religious life in twentieth-
century America.

In the half-century between the First Zionist Congress in
1897 and the establishment of the State of Israel in 1948, the
attitude of the American Jewish religious community changed
from vigorous opposition—with but a few religious spokesmen
dissenting—to full, formal, even joyous approval by organized
religious life; only small fringe groups on the extreme left and
right protested.

What brought about the change in view and reactions were
the changes which took place in the world, and in the Jewish
world, particularly, during this half-century; in the changed
American nation and the changed American Jewish community
in the years 1897–1947; and in the developments in the religious ideology of the American Jew.

The world became more cosmopolitan and more interdepen-
dent. The optimistic world view current in the late nineteenth
century that the world's problems were on the way to permanent
solution was shattered by two World Wars and the rise of
totalitarianism which dominated so large a part of the world.

The rise of anti-Semitism in the twentieth century culminating
in a holocaust unprecedented in Jewish history and the experience of man, wiped away the roseate hope that the problem

of the Jew would find final solution in a world of peace and brotherhood which was believed to be imminent.

In 1897 the Russian Jewish emigrant could choose between the United States, Canada, England, the Argentine, South Africa, Australia and Palestine. Some two million Jews came to the United States in the next half-century. In 1917 and in the post-World War I world it was believed that the countries of Europe could and should be a home and a haven for its Jews through the enactment of minority rights legislation. In the post-World War II world all doors were closed to Jewish immigration. Only those who lacked sensitivity could suggest that the Jew ought to rebuild his life in a Europe which was the mass graveyard of his community and family. Palestine alone could offer the hope of a haven.

Fifty years of Zionist education by the Zionist Organization of America, Hadassah, Labor Zionists, Mizrachi, etc., and a half a century of practical accomplishment in Palestine implanted the dream in the heart of the Jew, and convinced him that the dream could indeed become a reality. At the turn of the century every anti-Zionist speaker had pointed to the utter impracticability, if not the impossibility, of the fulfillment of the Zionist program.

At the end of the nineteenth century America was a young giant flexing its muscles, preparing itself physically and psychologically to venture into the wide world. It was a time of heightened and unenlightened nationalism, marked by self-centeredness and a sense of self-importance. American Jewry was caught up in this mood and sentiment.

In the next half-century America moved into the world—into Latin America, then Europe in World War I, and the world in World War II. It became legitimate and desirable in the service of the national interest to become concerned and involved in all manner of endeavor anywhere and everywhere. Interest in, concern for, involvement in Zionism, Palestine, and Israel was therefore a legitimate and even desirable activity for the American Jew as an American. American Presidents and the Houses of Congress declared for Zionism. Could the patriotic American Jew do less?

In 1897 America was viewed as a great melting pot. Each ethnic group was to lose its own distinctiveness and identity to become fused into the American nation. The Jews felt that America called upon them to give up their identity as a national group, to erase their ethnic uniqueness.

In 1917 the Jew perceived the beginning of a new view of America—cultural pluralism. It became a virtue and a service to America for the ethnic group to retain its distinctiveness and foster its own unique identity. America was, in the phrase of Louis D. Brandeis, a "nation of nationalities." Zionist cultural activities would no longer be considered alien to the spirit of America, but a welcome contribution to American culture. By 1948, multiplicity of loyalties was accepted as legitimate. America was a nation in which cultural pluralism held sway, and in which nationalism was not monolithically exclusive. The spectre of dual loyalty frightened only a small though influential segment of the Jewish community.

In 1897, organized religious Jewry was almost wholly Reform. The leading Seminary, the largest congregation, and the most influential rabbis were of that group. The twentieth century saw the rise of Conservative and Orthodox Jewry, and the beginnings of their institutional organization. Their numbers had swelled through mass immigration. The bulk of the Zionist constituency and workers were from these groups. By 1948, American religious Jewry was a tripartite group composed of well-organized and institutionally conceived Orthodox, Conservative, and Reform bodies. The fastest growing movement, Conservative Judaism, was also the most Zionistically committed. The rise of Conservative Judaism with its emphasis on Jewish peoplehood, culture, history, and national experience and aspirations, and its influence on both Reform and Orthodox Judaism did much to change the Zionist climate in American religious Jewry.

At the end of the nineteenth century the membership in Reform Congregations was almost exclusively of Jews who came from Germany and Central Europe. By 1948, American Jewry was eighty percent of East European origin, and most Reform congregations were composed largely of East European immigrants or their sons and daughters. For half a century, from 1885 to 1937, Reform Judaism was ideologically committed to the anti-nationalist, anti-Zionist Pittsburgh Platform. In 1937 *Guiding Principles of Reform Judaism* were adopted by the Central Conference of American Rabbis. The first principle reads: "Judaism is the historical religious experience of the Jewish people."

Classic Reform's anti-Zionism was ideologically rooted in the concept of the "Jewish Mission." Exile was not a punishment. It was necessary for the Jews to be dispersed throughout the world in fulfillment of their God-ordained role to spread the truth of religion throughout the world. In time, the Mission concept was pressed into Zionist service. Zionist proponents now claimed the "'Jewish Mission" to the nations to be the establishment of a state which would serve as a guide and model to the nations of the world, of a commonwealth devoted to the service of God through love of one's fellowman, of a nation motivated by prophetic ideals and directed by the Jewish passion for social justice and human brotherhood.

But prudent and practical considerations of anti-Zionism outweighed the ideological. American Jews were afraid of being accused of dual loyalty. The leading ideologist of classic Reform in America, Kaufman Kohler, concludes an impassioned anti-Zionist plea in 1897:

> Let us in unmistakable terms protest against the insinuation that we are not with every fibre of our hearts American citizens, that we have for us and our children any land dearer and holier to us, one to which we are allied with closer ties than to America . . .

Reform anti-Zionists were ever avid to point out that Zionism in America was confined to the immigrant Jews. In a "Statement to the Peace Conference" in 1920 they stated:

> We feel that in so doing we are voicing the opinion of the majority of American Jews born in this country and of those foreign born who have lived here long enough to thoroughly assimilate American political and social conditions . . .

The sons of East European immigrants who began to occupy the pulpits and pews of the Reform temple did not use such arguments or make such distinctions. By 1948 American Jewry had grown mature and secure enough to risk accusations of dual loyalty in its concern for fellow Jews and in its commitment to the great dream of Return and Redemption. But the most significant change of all occurred not in America but in Palestine— the founding of the State of Israel.

The Jewish Community

In 1905 "during the Russian massacres . . . a general desire was expressed for the creation in the United States of a[n] . . . organization to deal with Jewish questions at large . . ."

The Anglo-Jewish Association in Great Britain, the Alliance Israélite Universelle in France, the Hilfsverein der deutschen Juden and the Verband der deutschen Juden and similar organizations in Austria and Italy were held up as challenge and example. Early in the month of February, 1906, a conference to consider the matter was held. The fifty-eight representatives agreed that "it was advisable and feasible to establish a General Jewish Committee in the United States." An attempt was made to make the proposed Committee a democratically constituted Congress, elected by the Jews of the United States affiliated with congregations. The plan was rejected because it was feared that,

> . . . unless such an organization consisted of the most prudent and discreet elements the standing of the Jews might be seriously affected for the worse; and according to the plan of election proposed, it was probable that the organization would not be so constituted.

The upshot was that a small committee was formed, constituted of "persons who, while representative of American Jewry, need not necessarily be formally accredited representatives of any organization." It took the name, American Jewish Committee.

The divisiveness which characterized American Jewry in the last decades of the nineteenth century spilled over into the twentieth. In local communities and on the national scene there were two distinct communities, the German and the East European. Not even philanthropy could unite them. Thus after the outbreak of World War I there were *three* national relief committees.

Early in the war, the belief was strong that hostilities would end in a few months and that the belligerent powers would soon meet in conference to discuss the questions the war had raised. It was felt that "the Jews of America should take some action at once in order to prepare for bringing the Jewish question prominently to the attention of the Powers." The proposal was put forth that "the Jews of America should meet in a Congress which should formulate their requests and decide the manner in which these should be presented to a future Peace Conference." The suggestion quickly won many adherents and a democratically constituted Congress of American Jews seemed imminent. Protracted negotiations then ensued between the American Jewish Committee representatives and the forces favoring a Congress. It was the beginning of a struggle for power between the communities of German origin, emboldened by wealth and prestige, and largely anti-Zionist, and that of East European origin, strong in numbers, zeal and ambition, and Zionist.

It was soon apparent that the American Jewish Committee would not agree to an American Jewish Congress, and the pro-Congress forces met in a preliminary conference at Philadelphia on March 27–28, 1916. Stephen S. Wise set the tone:

> The Jewish people must create their own organ through which after earnest deliberation and discussion to express their convictions touching the needs and demands of the Jewish people. . . . This Conference is to labor solely to the end that there be devised and perfected such agencies as may bring about a completely democratic organization of all the forces of American Israel save for such as may will to exclude themselves. A people is not worthy of respect which does not insist upon the right to be heard touching its own affairs, but surrenders the right of judgement and decision to a company of men, however wise and benevolent, who substitute their own opinions and wishes for the convictions and determinations of the whole people.

After negotiations and renegotiations with the organized labor elements, which now opposed, now favored a Congress, elections finally took place in June, 1917. Some 335,000 votes were cast electing three hundred representatives. Another hundred were appointed by thirty national Jewish organizations.

The Congress met in Philadelphia, December 15—18, 1918. A list of demands was drawn up to present to the Peace Conference and a delegation was appointed to represent the Congress at the Peace Conference.

In May, 1920 the Congress convened again to hear the report of its delegation, and having done so it dissolved, its function fulfilled. Hardly had one Congress come to an end when the Zionist representatives met and began plans for a permanent American Jewish Congress. Philadelphia, in 1922, was again the scene of the birth of a Congress. In composition it was made up of Zionist and pro-Zionist groups and some *landsmanschaften*.

Defense of Jewish rights at home and abroad became, and still is the program of both the Committee and the Congress. Early aspirations of being representative of American Jewry are now only memories, if that.

Another war and the prospects of *its* peace conference gave birth to the most recent and most ambitious attempt at national Jewish unity, the American Jewish Conference. The vision was that of Henry Monsky, the president of B'nai B'rith. He brought to it organizational skill and consummate diplomacy. With the stipulation that the convened body be called Conference and not Assembly and that it be disbanded on the accomplishment of its mission, the American Jewish Committee and the Jewish Labor Committee assured the Conference of the participation of all major Jewish organizations.

One remembers so well the great activity and expectancy that surrounded this communal enterprise. The elections in the local communities opened many old communal wounds and created new ones, but it also placed on the communal agenda the great problems confronting American and world Jewry. It challenged individual communities to rise to new heights of Jewish maturity, responsibility and concern. Above all it brought

together all the elements of the Jewish community for cooperative communal activity. In a very real sense it laid the foundation for the many community councils and united welfare
funds which unify so many of our communities. Nationally it
made possible the united philanthropic efforts of postwar
American Jewry, efforts in scope, intensity and effectiveness unparalleled in the history of charitable endeavor.

One also remembers the thrill of seeing the leadership of
American Jewry taking counsel together on behalf of persecuted brethren. There were those who dared hope that this
mighty organization welded together by the needs of European
Jewry might also address itself to the problems confronting the
American Jew. But the American Jewish Committee, outvoted
in the Conference, withdrew. Others resigned in protest against
the withdrawal. When it was suggested in 1946 that the American Jewish Conference be made a permanent body, its doom
was sealed. Some of the large national Jewish organizations,
ever zealous for their sovereign independence, dissolved the
Conference in 1947.

The early attempts at union tried to encompass wider areas
of concern. As the American Jewish community grew in size
and complexity and as needs fashioned organizations and institutions each with its own program, interests and staff, the
field for united communal effort became ever smaller. A great
world crisis could bring American Jewry together for a common
effort, but only for endeavors that did not touch the areas
already staked out by an organization or an institution.

For His Country And For His People

In the political arena at the turn of the century the Jew represented a vote to be won. Blatant ethnic appeals were used by
both parties. In 1899, for example, a circular in Yiddish was
distributed by "Jewish members of the Republican State Committee." A vote for the gubernatorial candidate, Theodore
Roosevelt, was solicited because through him and his Rough
Riders, "the long felt Jewish desire to see Spain fall was finally
fulfilled. . . . Every vote for the COLONEL OF THE ROUGH
RIDERS is approval of . . . the war. Every vote for Roosevelt's

opponent . . . is a vote for Spain . . ."

The appeal to Jewish self-interest continued and continues still in a subtler manner, to be sure, and denied by political managers and Jewish leaders. The Jews constitute an important part of the electorate and their feelings and wishes are reckoned with. But with the increasing integration of the Jew into American economic, social and civic life, the Jew more and more expresses the political preferences of his economic or social group rather than his Jewish feelings and interests.

In twentieth-century America, the Jew has served his nation and community in the whole gamut of political offices. He has been and is found in City Council chambers and in the mayoralty, on state legislatures, and in the gubernatorial mansion, in halls of Congress and on the floor of the Senate, in embassies and in the Cabinet. It is perhaps particularly noteworthy that five Jews have now served as Justices of the United States Supreme Court. What is perhaps most noteworthy of Jews in high office in twentieth-century America is that, unlike their nineteenth-century predecessors, they have by and large been and remained loyal and active Jews. The example was set by the first Jew appointed to the Supreme Court, Louis D. Brandeis, who, while carving a career as a great lawyer and judge in America, entered Jewish history as a noted Zionist leader.

In no endeavor did the American Jew distinguish himself more than in philanthropy. The children's homes, hospitals and homes for the aged which the Jewish community established became models of their kind. United, organized charitable efforts were pioneered by the Jewish community. In the nineteenth century, charity was individual or congregational, dispensed as the need arose. In the twentieth century it became communal and national, ongoing, structured, professionalized. The institutions to help the immigrant were followed by organizations to aid the Jew abroad. Political help came from influential individuals and from organized bodies as well—the American Jewish Committee, B'nai B'rith, the Zionist Organization of America. But the proudest page in the story of the American Jew is the one on which his efforts to save, support and reestablish his suffering brethren is writ.

As soon as the plight of the Jews in the war zones of Europe in 1914 reached the ears of the American Jew, he began to organize relief agencies. The community was still a divided community between German and east-European, between labor and the middle class. Small wonder then that three agencies were established. But it soon became apparent that the efforts must be united and common concern and compassion erased old divisions and prejudices. The American Joint Distribution Committee was established and "became one of the conspicuous landmarks in the story of the Jews in America and even more in that of Jewish communities in many other parts of the world, wherever distress called for relief and the havoc wrought by war or persecution called for rehabilitation." Jews from all communities joined in the relief efforts, led by such outstanding figures as Jacob H. Schiff, Felix M. Warburg, Louis Marshall, Cyrus Adler, Herbert Lehman and Julius Rosenwald. In 1917, the sum of ten million dollars was raised, and in following years surpassed. This was the single largest philanthropic endeavor ever undertaken by any group.

The efforts and accomplishments of the United Jewish Appeal in the years following World War II set new heights in man's philanthropic efforts for fellowman. By 1967 some one billion seven hundred million dollars had been collected and disbursed.

The efforts of such American Zionist leaders as Stephen S. Wise, Louis Lipsky, Louis D. Brandeis and Abba Hillel Silver in laying the foundation and helping in the establishment of the State of Israel should also be recorded. It should be mentioned, too, that non-Zionists joined Zionists in supporting institutions and projects in Palestine.

A phase of philanthropy which is often overlooked is that of the various *landsmanschaften* which sent large sums of money to their European home towns. The personal concern and the ongoing communication with the Jewish communal organizations and institutions in post-War I Europe did very much to lift the morale and strengthen the life of those communities. Nor should the most personal and persistent philanthropic endeavor be left unrecorded. There was hardly an immigrant who did not send money home to parents, brothers, family friends on a regular, continuous basis. Many European families were supported by their American relatives. The Jewish immigrant to America left family and friends behind, but concern for their welfare and well-being never left him. Those who would come, he brought to join him. Those who stayed behind remained his concern and responsibility.

The Hitler period produced a traumatic impact upon American Jewry. Many whose ties to the Jewish community were tenuous, now asserted their Jewishness through pronouncement and activity. The national Jewish organizations sponsored protest rallies; relief activity was intensified; political pressures were exerted; Zionist ranks swelled; a new urgency stepped up the tempo of Jewish activity. Jewish refugees from Germany were welcomed and integrated into the community.

The great depression and growing anti-Semitism notwithstanding, the plight of brethren in greater need and more immediate danger claimed the concern of the American Jewish community. Anti-Jewish excess in Germany, economic oppression in Poland, anti-Jewish acts in Romania and anti-Semitic organizations in Central Europe united the American Jewish community in common endeavor. The war clouds rapidly gathering over Europe dissipated the prejudices, antagonisms and rivalries which had sundered American Jewry. The outbreak of World War II found American Jewry united in and through one overriding purpose—to attempt to save their brethren in peril of their lives. At the same time Jewish rights and status in America had to be defended and protected. For all of America the 1930's were an era of economic depression, for the American Jew it was a time which demanded of him a heightened concern for his own rights at home and for his brother's plight abroad.

The Jew in America

In answer to his own question, "What is an American?" Michel Guillaume Jean de Crèvecoeur wrote in 1782:

He is an American, who leaving behind him all his ancient prejudices and manners, receives new ones from the new mode of life he has embraced, the new government he obeys, and the new rank he holds. . . . Here individuals of all nations are melted into a new race of men . . .

The concept of America as a melting pot is then as old as these United States. It had its pronounced affect on the Jewish community during the decades which formed the turn of the century. This was America as hailed by the hero of Israel Zangwill's *The Melting Pot*:

Celt and Latin, Slav and Teuton, Greek and Syrian, black and yellow—Jew and Gentile—Yes, East and West, and North and South, the palm and the pine, the pole and the equator, the crescent and the cross—how the great Alchemist melts and fuses them with his purging flame! Here shall they all unite to build the Republic of Man and the Kingdom of God.

America welcomes all peoples; all nationalities. It extends to them the privileges of political freedom and the promise of economic opportunity. In turn it asks that peoples and nationalities cast off their folkways, their traditions, whatever made them distinct and distinguishable, and that they adopt the way of life which was emerging from the fusing fires. This was the price one had to pay for the prize of being an American. Most thought the prize well worth the price.

Within the Jewish community there ensued a mighty endeavor to accommodate the Jew to this vision of America. America was looked upon as a monolith, a jealous god admitting of no diversity in loyalty.

The strong assimilationist program and practices of Radical Reform were in response to America the Melting Pot. The early history of East European Orthodoxy in the United States, its withdrawal and self-imposed ghettoization was in reaction to such an America. This jealous crucible admitted of no middle ground. You surrendered or you withdrew, and the Jewish community became two communities as a result.

It was the day of the "Americanizing" agencies, the settlement houses, the churchlike temple and the *shtibl;* the day when the door to Jewish leadership was opened only by the key of acceptance or accomplishment in the general community.

Those were the days when sensitive Jews despaired for the future of the American Jewish Community.

In the second decade of the twentieth century there was a new look at the Melting Pot. The product which comes out of the Melting Pot is a dull, drab, lackluster metal. Was this to be America? Was it to the benefit of America to cast in the cauldron the glittering gold, the shimmering silver, the supple copper, even the hard-stoked iron of national characteristics and ethnic distinctiveness and thus remove from the landscape of America these precious metals—because their uniqueness and distinctiveness gave color and glow to America? The lilting song which was America was in danger of becoming a monotonous hum.

Horace Kallen sounded the alarm and proposed a solution. "Democracy Versus the Melting Pot" he called his pronouncement which appeared in *The Nation* in 1915. His was a new image of America.

> Its form is that of the Federal republic: its substance, a democracy of nationalities, co-operating voluntarily and autonomously in the enterprise of self-realization through the perfection of men according to their kind. The common language of the commonwealth, the language of its great political tradition is English, but each nationality expresses the emotional and voluntary life in its own language, in its own inevitable aesthetic and intellectual forms. . . . As in an orchestra, every type of instrument has its specific timbre and tonality, founded in its substance and form; as every type has its appropriate theme and melody in the whole symphony, so in society each ethnic group is the natural instrument, its spirit and culture are its theme and melody, and the harmony and dissonances and discords of them all make the symphony of civilization. . . .

On the fourth of July of the same year, Louis D. Brandeis described "True Americanism" in an address at Faneuil Hall, Boston.

The new nationalism adopted by America proclaims that each race or people, like each individual, has the right and duty to develop, and that only through such differentiated development will high civilization be attained.

Adhering to the Melting Pot concept thus would be a disservice to America. America would be best served, its people find greatest fulfillment through Cultural Pluralism.

This new image of America was seized upon as a "democratic imperative" by individuals and groups of men committed to Jewish survival and Jewish cultural creativity. Mordecai M. Kaplan gave it philosophical exposition in terms of modern Jewish experience and needs. Milton Steinberg wrote beautifully of living in "two civilizations." It helped create interest in all forms of Jewish cultural expression.

In terms of practical implementation, it turned settlement houses into Jewish Community Centers; it made of the House of Worship a synagogue-center (whether called by that name or not); communal *Talmud Torahs,* Yiddish Schools, Hebrew culture and Zionist activities all benefited from this new image of America.

The Jew now looked upon himself (now, as before, through his American spectacles) as a member of an ethnic minority of whom America asked ethnic distinctiveness, loyalty to its culture, and creativity in its "aesthetic and intellectual forms," as its *contribution to American civilization.* The Jew felt that America asked of him to participate in the enterprise which is America, as a member of his ethnic group. And the Jew formed organizations and founded institutions in response to this felt demand.

The "second generation" was largely a generation of rejection. The children of the immigrants threw out the cultural and spiritual baggage which their parents brought with them.

The historian Marcus L. Hansen argued a thesis which has been given the status of a sociological law, namely:

What the son wishes to forget, the grandson wishes to remember.

C. Bezalel Sherman points out that:

> Alone of all the white ethnic groups do American Jews
> supply proof for the correctness of the Hansen thesis.
> Only among them do the grandchildren manifest a greater
> desire to be part of the community than the children of
> immigrants.

The third generation of Italians are not anxious to be identified as Italians, nor does the third generation Pole return to the
language, customs and cultural forms of his immigrant grandfather. "But the third generation of American Jews," writes Will
Herberg, "instead of somehow finally getting rid of their Jewishness, as the Italians were getting rid of their 'Italianness' and
the Poles of their 'Polishness' actually began to *reassert* their
Jewish identification and to *return* to their Jewishness. . . ." He
offers an explanation:

> We can account for this anomaly by recalling that the
> Jews came to this country not merely as an immigrant
> group but also as a religious community; the name "Jew-
> ish" designated both. . . . When the second generation
> rejected its Jewishness, it generally, though not univer-
> sally, rejected both aspects at once. . . . The young Jew
> for whom the Jewish immigrant-ethnic group had lost all
> meaning because he was an American and not a foreign-
> er, could still think of himself as a Jew, because to him
> being a Jew now meant identification with the Jewish
> religious community.

Oscar Handlin's observation is similar:

> As their immigrant antecedents receded, their identifica-
> tion remained most meaningful in the area of diversity
> which America most clearly recognized—that of religion.

What the third generation Jew returned to was not the mores
and folkways of his immigrant grandparents, but the faith of his
forefathers. To be sure the return has been tentative, groping,
probing, but it is important to know that this is the door at
which the returnee stands and sometimes knocks—and not at

any other.

The American Jew is now beginning to react to a new image of America: America as a land of "ethnic assimilation and religious differentiation." America as a nation demands political unity and civic concern, but it also fosters religious diversity. The Jew sensing this has made synagogue affiliation his expression of Jewish association. Salo Baron, in discussing "Religious or Ethnic Community?" pointed out: "In western Europe and America, the religious factor has retained its preeminent position in the scale of communal values . . . the religious congregation has continued to attract the relatively most constant and active participation of a large membership. . . . [The work of the Jewish Federations of Charities] can never hope to attract the same intensity of allegiance or even the same extensity of effort as has so long been the case with the Synagogue. . . . total congregational membership in the United States vastly exceeds, numerically, Jewish membership in purely philanthropic undertakings. . . . "

The famed Riverton Study disclosed that eighty percent of the *parents* interviewed considered religion to be one of the principal attributes of the Jew, but the percentage of their *children* who believed so was *ninety-seven percent.*

Clearly, America considers the Jew to be a member of a religious community, and the Jew believes so, too. There is much promise for good in this new imaging, but great danger as well. Marshall Sklare points to the danger:

> There is, then, a strong predilection among members of the Jewish group for synagogue affiliation in spite of considerable secularization and of consequent wide departures in attitudes and life patterns from religious norms. Such a predilection presents a challenge of considerable proportions for a religious institution; its very success may serve to mask its failure.

Religion, Culture, Education

The tripartite division of the American Jewish religious community into Orthodox, Reform and Conservative Judaism continued and became institutionally concretized in the twentieth century. Each group had its rabbinical seminary, lay and rabbinic organizations. Each movement also underwent change. Reform continued its drift away from tradition for the first two decades of the twentieth century. A return to traditionalism then began, at first hardly perceptible, then slowly developing, and finally bursting into great activity in the years which followed World War II. An increasing number of rabbis ordained by the Reform seminary, the Hebrew Union College, came from East European traditionalist background. A significant number came under the influence of Zionism, which turned their attention and interest to Jewish peoplehood and Jewish culture. This interest became a commitment that they brought to their movement and their individual congregations. A comparison of the Pittsburgh Platform of 1886 and the Columbus Platform of 1936 discloses a redefinition of Judaism which transferred the emphasis from the credal formulation to the ongoing historic, spiritual experience of the Jewish people. The mass influx of sons and daughters of East European immigrants into the Reform congregations permitted and stimulated a return to traditional forms in the temple and a reintroduction of ritual into the home. The Sabbath eve service on Friday night replaced the Sunday service as the main service of worship. The use of Hebrew in the liturgy increased. *Bar* and *Bat Mitzvah, kiddush* and even *havdalah* became part of Reform practice. The formerly proscribed head covering for men was made optional in many congregations, and some reintroduced a form of the *tallit* for pulpit wear. The return to tradition continues, with committees and commissions now charged with the responsibilities of revitalizing the Sabbath, and preparing new prayer books and a new *Hagaddah,* with all indications that they will be far more traditional in form and content than those currently in use.

Conservative Judaism in the era of Solomon Schechter, 1902–1915, was an ideological reaction to Reform. It was a reaffirmation of the authority of *halacha,* as a living albeit changing system of laws, usage, customs and traditions. It placed emphasis on the total historic experience of the Jewish people, and held precious all Jewish cultural and spiritual creations. In later decades, it came into competitive confrontation with Orthodoxy. Many Orthodox congregations turned Conservative in the hope of retaining the interest and loyalty of the rising generation. Graduates of the Jewish Theological Seminary founded Conservative congregations which drew their membership from the Orthodox camp.

The Conservative emphasis on Zionism and Jewish culture won for it the adherence of elements of the Jewish community which heretofore were content to permit themselves to be accounted part of Orthodoxy. The chief influence on the movement in the years betwen the wars when it stood in ideological and practical contention with Orthodoxy was Mordecai M. Kaplan, who espoused a liberal theology, urged a reinterpretation of traditional belief and a reconstruction of traditional forms. His definition of Judaism as a total civilization—"the evolving religious civilization of the Jewish people"—became the basic position of the movement. In consequence Jewish culture in its totality, language, literature, art, music were stressed. The synagogue was turned from a House of Worship into a spiritual, cultural, educational, social center for congregation and community.

The earliest experiences of East-European Orthodoxy in America were calamitous. The immigrant transplanted Old World synagogal forms to the New. They answered his own spiritual needs, but could not win the interest or allegiance of his children. The reaction was a withdrawal from the American scene, into self-contained communities and spiritual and cultural isolation. Forward-looking leaders, taking example from the neo-Orthodoxy of Samson Raphael Hirsch of Frankfurt am Main, launched an attempt at making the traditional faith at home in the modern world. It took the form of a yeshiva-university, where young men would receive modern high school and college training while studying the sacred texts in the traditional manner in an orthodox religious atmosphere.

The Yeshiva University and Rabbi Isaac Elchanan Theological Seminary has now put forth a generation of rabbis, teachers and lay leaders who have given great vitality to Orthodoxy.

Orthodox Jews are found on college faculties, in the laboratories and in communal and cultural life. The Orthodox congregations have taken on new life, though the price has sometimes been the adoption of new forms borrowed from coreligionists on the left—mixed seating and English prayers and readings at services, the *Bat Mitzvah* ceremony and others. In the post-World War II years there has been a growth of a reemphasis on traditionalism in certain sectors of Orthodoxy, occasioned by the immigration of *Hassidim* from Central Europe, and a new militancy on the part of native-born Orthodox leaders as they stand in confrontation to what they term the "deviationist" movements of Conservative and Reform Judaism.

In recent decades Reform has been characterized by an attempt to rediscover tradition and to grope with the challenge it presents. The majority of rabbis and laymen are committed to the ever-widening influence of traditionalism, but a few have sounded the alarm that this is a reactionary and retrogressive tendency. Orthodoxy has discovered the world outside, and most leaders and committed laymen are grappling with its implications and demands—with a small but significant number advocating great caution or actual withdrawal. Conservative Judaism continues to stress the total Jewish civilization, placing its emphasis on Jewish cultural creativity, educational enterprise and communal activity.

The new century opened with the publication of a landmark of Jewish scholarship, the twelve-volume *The Jewish Encyclopedia*. Scholars of the whole world joined in the enterprise. It enlisted the participation of American Jewish scholars and stimulated their scholarly activity. Outstanding among these was Professor Louis Ginzberg, who became America's premier Jewish scholar. He was not alone. Scholars came to these shores to fill faculty positions. But until recent years Jewish scholarship in America has been a European product. Of late America has begun to produce its own Jewish scholars, and they bid fair to make their mark in world Jewish scholarship in such fields as Talmud, Bible, History and Theology. The output of scholarly works continues to increase year by year. The *Jewish Quarterly Review,* the *Hebrew Union College Annual,* the *Proceedings* of *American Academy for Jewish Research, Historia Judaica, Jewish Social Studies* and the *American Jewish Historical Quarterly* are scholarly publications of first rank. *The Menorah Journal, Judaism,* and *Commentary* among others have contained significant contributions to Jewish thought. Books on Jews and Judaism, many of high quality and lasting worth, increase in number annually. Significant contributions to Jewish scholarship and culture have already been made and all indications point to an even more creative future.

At the turn of the century, Jewish education was carried on in the congregational Sunday School, the communal *Talmud Torah,* and in private *hadorim* of *melamdim.* The private enterprise education was sporadic, of short duration, and generally had the utilitarian aim of preparation for *Bar Mitzvah* or mechanical reading of the prayers. The Sunday school with its weekly two hours of instruction by volunteer teachers proved both inadequate and ineffective. The communal *Talmud Torahs,* with instruction five days a week and a professional corps of teachers, for a long time was the only effective institution of primary Jewish education. Its shortcomings were serious. Few if any girls attended, attendance rarely continued beyond *Bar Mitzvah,* and both the curriculum and instructors bore little relationship to the world beyond the classroom walls. The Conservative congregational school, which combined elements of the *Talmud Torah* and the Sunday school, began to become a factor in Jewish education in the 1920's. It was congregation-associated, oriented toward Jewish communal life and aware of the world of the public school in which the child received his basic education, but it also stressed the Hebrew language and held classes during the week as well as on Sunday mornings. This type of education spread to Orthodox congregations in the 1930's and 1940's, and to Reform in the 1940's and 1950's. It is today the basic Jewish educational unit. Of very great significance was the rapid growth of Jewish All Day schools in the post-World War II community. Some nine percent of all religious students attend these schools of intensive Jewish instruction. Initially fostered by the Orthodox community, they have spread to Conservative Jewry and have become an issue for discussion and debate in Reform.

At present, the Day School movement continues to grow and has become the chief educational interest of Orthodoxy. In Reform, the afternoon school is being added to the Sunday school. Conservative Judaism is placing great emphasis on formal education for the high school students and vacation study in a string of summer camps. All three groups have active youth movements for informal education and sponsor youth pilgrimages to Israel.

Almost totally gone are the Yiddish afternoon schools which, as late as the 1940's, still flourished in many communities throughout the country. Their dwindling was due to the unwillingness of the generation born and raised in America to foster the Yiddish language and culture. This went hand in hand with the diminution of the number of Jews in the labor force and in the labor unions.

The vitality and creativity of Yiddish culture in America during the first half of the century was most noteworthy. The American Jewish community supported a newspaper and periodical press of wide circulation and of high quality. Newspapers and journals reflected the whole variety of community interests and configuration—from ultraradical to ultraorthodox. Novelists, playwrights, essayists, poets and journalists of first rank produced cultural creations of lasting value. The Yiddish stage, up till World War II, was a potent cultural force, and vied in caliber with the finest in the American theater. But time took its toll of Yiddish writers, readers, playgoers. Of late there has been a renewal of interest in the language and culture, but it would be foolhardy to expect a blossoming which would even approximate the cultural activity and accomplishments of the past.

Of signal importance is the Jewish contribution to the trade-union movement in America. The labor force in the soft goods industry which was centered in the large cities was largely Jewish. The unions established, notably the Amalgamated Clothing Workers of America and the International Ladies' Garment Workers' Union, became models of their kind. The caliber of leadership was of the highest. Real statesmanship was exerted by these unions which in time came to be esteemed by the entire industry. Some of the earliest and most enlightened social welfare benefits for its members were pioneered by these unions, including cooperative housing, cultural and social centers, banking and insurance. They also became important factors in the political life of their cities, states and the nation.

But, as mentioned earlier, the son never joined his father in the shop. The once predominantly Jewish unions are no longer so. They wrote an important chapter in the story of organized labor in America and in the struggle for economic and social justice.

And Now

The six million Jews constitute three percent of the American population. Almost all live in the urban centers. Well over two-thirds of America's Jews are in the ten metropolitan centers, New York, Los Angeles, Philadelphia, Chicago, Boston, Miami, Cleveland, Detroit, Baltimore and San Francisco. They are almost entirely of the middle class. Increasingly they concentrate in the professions. Education remains a top priority, with some three of every four Jews of college age on campus. The dream of the immigrant has been realized. His sons are not in a shop or factory, but in an office or laboratory, his grandchildren in college classrooms. Almost all professions are fully open to the Jew, and but few neighborhoods remain closed to him. He is not overly concerned that country clubs exclude him for he has built his own, every bit as luxurious and often more so. Settlement houses have become community centers. Synagogues are architectural landmarks on the American landscape, and have taken their place in American religious life. The community remains divided into the three religious groupings, Orthodox, Conservative, Reform, but most congregants view these as institutional distinctions rather than as religious schisms. Although there is no overall American Jewish representative body, American Israel is largely united in sentiment. Common concerns and joint efforts unite, where institutional differences and organizational competitiveness tend to divide.

The American Jew has entered the cultural life in all its aspects, has made important contributions and exerts signal influence. Initially the Jewish participation and contribution was in the field of entertainment. More recently and increasingly it has been in the arts and literature. A good deal of American culture today has taken on a kind of Jewish coloration. The Jewish novel, by Jews and about Jews, has been dominant in the literary scene. Being Jewish is no handicap today in American cultural life or in American life in general. The Jews seem vividly, firmly and permanently incorporated into the American landscape.

But problems there are, and they are serious.

Sociologists point with concern to the low Jewish birthrate, a rate below the survival level. Religious leaders speak with alarm of the rising rate of intermarriage, particularly among the intellectually gifted and the economically favored. Integration is good and desirable. But at which point does integration become assimilation? In sum, the central question facing the American Jew is: Can a minority group survive in a free and open democratic society? More pointedly, can Jew and Judaism survive and flourish in America?

The Jew has exerted vast energies and expanded great sums in fashioning institutions to assure his survival and foster his faith, but the question remains. The answer will have to be recorded by a historian of a future generation.*

AMERICAN VIEWS OF THE JEW AT THE OPENING OF THE TWENTIETH CENTURY*

By Oscar Handlin

In the portentous period between 1913 and 1920, years which brought so many other changes to the United States and to the world, anti-Semitism became a factor of considerable importance in this country. As the years went by between the Frank case and the publication of Henry Ford's version of the forged Protocols of the Elders of Zion, great numbers of Americans became obsessed with fear of the Jew. Ominous hatreds began to take form in economic and social discrimination and even in political action. Shortly, the Klan would draw for part of its armory upon those hatreds.[1]

These hostile sentiments were quite new to American society. Indeed the favorable prevailing temper of tolerance had produced a great willingness to accept the Jew as a desirable and equal participant in the emerging culture of the nation. The steady disappearance of political disabilities early in the century and the opening of all sorts of political and social places as the immigrant Jews adjusted to the New World were the signs of that acceptance.

It is possible to find occasional slurs such as those in General Grant's Order Number 11; there are instances of exclusion as when Joseph Seligman was refused accommodations at Saratoga's fashionable Grand Union Hotel; and a handful of

---

* In the preparation of this essay I have profited from the helpful suggestions of Arthur Mann, of Barbara M. Solomon, and of Rowland T. Berthoff.

[1] See John M. Mecklin, *Ku Klux Klan* (New York, 1924); C. Vann Woodward, *Tom Watson Agrarian Rebel* (New York, 1938) pp. 435 ff.; *Jewish Activities in the United States* (Dearborn, 1921).

1

obscure pamphlets were explicitly hostile.[2] But the shocked public repudiation of the slurs and the exclusion indicated how exceptional such instances were. It would be a mistake to treat them as the same in meaning with the anti-Semitism that did emerge after 1913. After all, in 1899, Tom Watson, later of the Frank case, was still vigorously condemning medieval prejudices against the Jews.[3]

The factors that produced anti-Semitism in the twentieth century are well known and have been abundantly discussed. Competition for places generated economic discrimination. The movement to restrict immigration gave rise to a chain of arguments in which Jews, like other newcomers, were blamed for pauperism, vice, crime, and every other social evil. The growth of racist thinking allowed men like Madison Grant and Lothrop Stoddard to foster the Aryan myth. Most important, perhaps, the xenophobia of the war years and after led many Americans to reject every kind of tie with Europe.[4]

There was, in addition, another factor that has not been as well evaluated, the disappointment of many radicals and reformers who somehow came to blame the Jews for their failure after 1900. The great populist, Tom Watson, was only the most striking of many figures who felt the world was plunging hell-ward and who held the Jews responsible for the descent.[5] And significantly the mass of decent folk who joined the Klan

[2] Although it may not even have had an anti-Semitic intent, the most important of these was Joseph Pennell, *The Jew at Home. Impressions of a Summer and Autumn Spent With Him* (New York, 1892), pp. 6, 7. See also Leonard A. Greenberg, "Some American Anti-Semitic Publications of the Late 19th Century," *Publications of the American Jewish Historical Society,* no. 37 (1947), pp. 421 ff.

[3] Thomas E. Watson, *The Story of France* ... (New York, 1899), vol. I, pp. 171, 177, 189, 190, 204. See also Morris U. Schappes, *Documentary History of the Jews in the United States, 1654–1875* (New York, 1950), pp. 472 ff.; Carey McWilliams, *A Mask for Privilege* (Boston, 1948); Oscar Handlin, "Prejudice and Capitalist Exploitation," *Commentary,* vol. VI (July, 1948), pp. 79 ff.

[4] See in general Oscar and Mary F. Handlin, *Danger in Discord* (New York, 1948), pp. 13 ff.

[5] See Woodward, *Watson, supra,* pp. 332 ff., 400 ff., 411, 422, 431 ff.

and who read the *Dearborn Independent* came from areas that had in the 1890's been strongly moved by radicalism.

Yet these later prejudices were not inscribed upon a tabula rasa. They were overlaid on attitudes toward the Jews that had already taken form before the turn of the century. An examination of those anterior conceptions will throw light both on the general American view of the Jew in the 1890's and on the nature of radicalism in that decade.

The ten years after 1890 were not only free of anti-Semitism; they were actually marked by distinct philo-Semitism. The picture of the Jews I am about to reveal existed in the minds of people who were horrified by the Dreyfus Case, people who condemned pogroms in Russia, ritual murder charges in Hungary, and the distorted propaganda of the Stoeckers and Drumonts in France and Germany.[6]

To a certain extent that picture was based on real contacts with Jews. As the number of Jews in the United States grew through the nineteenth century, they became familiar figures in every part of the country. From dealings with them emerged a distinct stereotype, the features of which were dictated by the condition of the Jews as immigrants.

Like other immigrants the Jew was a strange and easily recognized character in American society. He could be distinguished from the mass of his fellow citizens physically, in visual or auditory terms. In mid-nineteenth century, there was still a good deal of vagueness about his particular features however. What seemed then to mark off the Jew most prominently was language and accent. Yet to untutored American

[6] On Stoecker, see Walter Frank, *Hofprediger Adolf Stoecker und die christlich-soziale Bewegung*, 2nd ed. (Hamburg, 1935), pp. 70–123. On Drumont, see Robert F. Byrnes, *Anti-Semitism in Modern France* (New Brunswick, N. J., 1950), pp. 137 ff., 327. See also Salo Wittmayer Baron, *Social and Religious History of the Jews* (New York, 1937), vol. II, pp. 285–298. On the American attitude see, for example, *The Nation* (New York), Oct. 2, 1890, p. 271; *ibid.*, Dec. 29, 1898, p. 480; *The Jewish Question and the Mission of the Jews* (New York, 1894), pp. 4 ff.

ears, his sounds were quite like those of the generality of Germans; often he was counted simply a kind of German.

In the writings of the New England humorist Charles Follen Adams are the most characteristic expressions of this early image. The central personage of these popular poems bore the unmistakable name, Yawcob Strauss and spoke an outlandish dialect in which the humor seemed to lie. But Yawcob was not recognizably different from any other German. A shopkeeper, he was pictured in a wholly kindly light, sentimental and goodhearted, preoccupied with his beer and his pipe.[7] The same lack of differentiation was evident in such minor characters as Shonny Schwartz "mit his hair so soft und yellow und his face so blump und mellow."[8]

By the 1890's however, the stereotype was much more clearly delineated. In the comic magazines of the decade it appeared fully drawn in all its lights and shadows. Occupationally, the Jew was more distinctive than ever. He had by then been identified as a peddler, as an old clothes dealer, and as a pawnbroker; indeed the three-ball sign and the title "uncle" were synonymous with him. Distinctive names also set him off; Isaacs or Cohen, Ikey, Jake, or Abie. His appearance was familiar too, pack on back, or holding a basket, or pushing a cart. His garments were either old and shiny with an inevitable black derby hat, or else they were ludicrously new and flashy. His hooked nose stood prominently forth from his bearded face and his accent was thick. Finally he was invariably concerned with money; the words put into his mouth dealt always with finance and reflected a stingy, grasping temperament. Some Jews were just on the edge of dishonesty like the Bowery shysters, Katch & Pinch. But even a likeable chap like

[7] Charles F. Adams, *Leedle Yawcob Strauss, and Other Poems* (Boston, 1878), pp. 11, 12. See also Charles F. Adams, *Dialect Ballads* (New York, 1888) and the series of illustrated booklets published by L. Prang & Company, Boston.

[8] Adams, *Leedle Yawcob Strauss, supra,* p. 47. But see also "A Tale of a Nose," *ibid.,* p. 50.

Old Isaacs from the Bowery, in the popular play, tells his daughter,

Vhy, I vould trust you mit my life, Rachel. But vid mein money, ach, dot vas different.[9]

There are undoubtedly antecedents of this figure in the older Shylock image. But its specific form came from the contemporary scene. A dispute over closing hours could bring the charge from a labor leader that the "hoggish Jews" were always after "their pound of flesh."[10]

Whatever its source, by the end of the century the stereotype was clear. Repeated in popular novels, in the press, on the dramatic and vaudeville stage, it made Americans acquainted with a distinctive pattern of physical features, clothing, forms of expression, and language associated with the Jews. Most important, it ascribed to that figure a pervasive concern with money.[11]

These caricatures in the perspective of their later uses have the appearance of anti-Semitic insults. But there is evidence that they were not meant and not taken as such. In the first place, no such intent was involved. A public school teacher in New York could affectionately give *Oliver Twist* to a little Jewish boy as a reward.[12] And as late as 1913, Maurice Levy

[9] Charles E. Blaney, *Old Isaacs from the Bowery. A Novel Founded upon the Melodrama of the Same Name* (New York, [1906]), p. 19. See also *Judge* (New York), July 3, 1897, pp. 7, 9; July 17, 1897, p. 34; Aug. 7, 1897, p. 90; Aug. 21, 1897, p. 119; Aug. 28, 1897, pp. 132, 134; Sept. 11, 1897, p. 166; *Puck* (New York), vol. XXXIII, April 19, 1893, p. 138; vol. XXXVI, Feb. 21, 1894, p. 3; vol. XXXVI, Nov. 14, 21, 28, 1894, pp. 202, 211, 230, 232, 234; also [Harold Roorbach], *Rebecca and Rowena or the Triumph of Israel* (New York, [1883]), p. 7; Howard Holmes, *Plush Velvet, the Prince of Spotters* (Beadle's Dime Library, no. 817, New York, 1894), cited by Albert Johannsen, *House of Beadle and Adams* (Norman, 1950), vol. I, p. 239.

[10] *Labor Standard* (Fall River), Sept. 24, 1881.

[11] See, for instance, Pennell, *Jew at Home, supra*, pp. 33, 34; Harold Payne, *The Grand Street Gold-Dust Sharpers; or, Shadowing Sheeny Sam's Silent Seven* (Beadle's Dime Library, no. 806, New York, 1894), cited in Albert Johannsen, *House of Beadle and Adams* (Norman, 1950), vol. I, p. 239.

[12] W. L. White, *Bernard Baruch, Portrait of a Citizen* (New York, [1950]), p. 17.

would unreflectively be described in like terms in Booth Tarkington's popular Penrod stories without derogatory intent.[13]

Here was the critical departure from the Shylock image;
the American stereotype involved no hostility, no negative
judgment. In a popular story, repeatedly reprinted throughout
the century, Moloch, a money-lender thirsty for revenge, plots
to compel a duke's son to marry his niece. The duke's response
is not anger, but compassion. In the denouement, he declaims:

> Take her my son and wear her close to thy heart, for she is a jewel
> worthy of thy high position . . . . Moloch where is now thy revenge!
> "Thou hast conquered it, my noble Duke," answered Moloch,
> overcome with surprise and admiration.

And everyone lived happily ever after.[14] Indeed, a Jew detective with "the stamp of his race, indelibly traced on the features
of all his blood" could, in another romance, win the beautiful
Anglo-Saxon heroine, who in assenting declares, "to you I now
turn for happiness in life, for your people shall be my people,
your creed my creed, and your God my God."[15]

The stereotype of the Jew is more comprehensible when we
recall that it was, in the 1890's, only one among many. The
notion that physical appearance was a sign of national identity
was so widely held that a dime novel could speak, as a matter
of course, of the New York detective who disguised himself as
an Englishman.[16] In the comic magazines the Jew was joined

[13] Booth Tarkington, *Penrod, His Complete Story* (New York, [1938]), pp. 25, 72, 87 ff.

[14] Professor [Joseph H.] Ingraham, *The Clipper Yacht; or, Moloch the Money-Lender! A Tale of London and the Thames* (Boston, 1845), p. 54. Reprinted as *Moloch the Money-Lender* (DeWitt's Ten Cent Romances, no. 38, New York, 1869), and occasionally, thereafter. For the Shylock image, see, by contrast, Leslie A. Fiedler, "What Can We Do About Fagin?," *Commentary*, vol. VII (1949), pp. 411 ff.; "The Jewish Writer and the English Literary Tradition," *ibid.*, vol. VIII (1949), pp. 209 ff., 361 ff.

[15] Col. Prentiss Ingraham, *The Jew Detective* (Beadle's New York Dime Library, no. 662, New York, 1891), pp. 2, 12, 14, 27. See also Oll Coomes, *Vagabond Joe, the Young Wandering Jew; or, Plotting for a Legacy* (Beadle's Half-Dime Library, New York, 1877, no. 5), cited in Johanssen, vol. I, p. 257.

[16] Tony Pastor [Harlan Halsey], *Tom and Jerry; or the Double Detectives* (Secret Service Series, no. 15, New York, 1889), pp. 76 ff.

by the drunken, shiftless Irishman,[17] by the sinister Catholic priest,[18] by the gaudy or ragged Negro,[19] by the stupid, soggy German,[20] and by the avaricious Yankees, Mandy and Aminadab.[21] Identified in outward aspects and in dialect as decisively as the Jew, these were intended to be as funny, but no more hostile, than the Mr. Dooley of the same period.[22] Significantly, the Jews themselves accepted the caricature: *Der Yiddischer Puck*, a comic magazine edited and published by the well-known journalist N. M. Schaikewitz, often sketched the identical picture of the Jew as its English counterparts.[23] In neither case, did the picture reflect a depreciatory attitude.

In the 1890's, an additional element took a place in the American picture of the Jew. The conception of Jewish interest in money deepened into the conviction that Jews controlled the great fortunes of the world. Although the Jews are still sometimes miserly Shylocks, more often they are princes wielding power through their gold.

In part the newer image was a shadow cast by the prominence of certain Jewish banking houses in Europe. Every American had heard of the Rothschilds and of Lazard Frères. If they had not, an English edition of Drumont's *La France juive*, published in the United States, gave them long lists of names, even if its conclusions were rejected.[24]   Articles in

---

[17] *Judge*, July 10, 1897, pp. 18, 19; *Puck*, vol. XXXIII, April 19, 1893, p. 135.

[18] *Judge*, Sept. 11, 1897, p. 167.

[19] *Ibid.*, July 3, 1897, pp. 6, 10; *Puck*, vol. XXXVI, Feb. 21, 1894, p. 10.

[20] *Judge*, July 3, 1897, p. 7; July 10, 1897, p. 26.

[21] *Ibid.*, July 3, 1897, p. 5.

[22] For Germans, Irish and Yankees, see also Adams, *Leedle Yawcob Strauss*, *supra*, pp. 27, 36, 55, 123.

[23] See, for example, the character, חיים שמואל [Ḥayyim Shmu'el], the peddler, the butchers, the pawnbrokers, and Cohn and Levy in Coney Island, דער יודישער פאק [The Jewish Puck], Nov. 29, 1894, pp. 1, 13; Dec. 14, 1894, p. 1; Dec. 28, 1894, p. 69; Jan. 25, 1895, p. 129; March 15, 1895, p. 259.

[24] Byrnes, *Anti-Semitism in Modern France*, *supra*, p. 153.

popular magazines devoted considerable space to Jewish millionaires.[25]   The exotic figure of Disraeli, "the Empire-making
Jew" seemed large in significance; and travelers in England,
like James Russell Lowell, were quite ready from what
they saw, to believe Jews were coming to control the whole
world.[26]

By a variety of means, the notion of limitless Jewish wealth
gained wide currency. Already in Henry Adams' anonymous
novel of 1880 there appeared the opulent Hartbeest Schneide-
koupon "descended from all the kings of Israel and . . . prouder
than Solomon in his glory."[27] In dime novels, the fabulously
rich Jew was a stock character.[28] In the midst of depression
in 1894, the notion was so commonplace that a magazine
seriously suggested that the unemployed of the United States
would be relieved if only "the trustees of the magnificent fund
that Baron Hirsch entrusted to a band of Wall Street bankers"
would "loosen the cords about . . . [their] money bags."[29]

The wealth of the Jews was ascribed to the fact that they
were

> a parasitical race, who, producing nothing, fasten on the produce
> of land and labor and live on it, choking the breath of life out of
> commerce and industry as sure as the creeper throttles the tree that
> upholds it.[30]

Like the American Jew in a serialized novel, who stayed at
his telephone speculating while the world was threatened with

[25] W. Freeman Day, "Foreign Millionaires," *Munsey's Magazine*, vol. VIII (1893),
pp. 665 ff.

[26] *Labor Standard*, Aug. 9, 1879, May 1, 1880; Henry Cabot Lodge, *Early Memories*
(New York, 1913), p. 339.

[27] Henry Adams, *Democracy, An American Novel* (New York, 1908), pp. 41, 44.
For the subsequent development of Adams' ideas, see Edward N. Saveth, *American
Historians and European Immigrants, 1875–1925* (New York, 1948), pp. 68–89.

[28] See, for example, Pastor, *Tom and Jerry, supra*, pp. 60 ff.

[29] *Illustrated American* (New York), Jan. 6, 1894, p. 22.

[30] "Russian Jews and Gentiles from a Russian Point of View," *The Century*, vol.
XXIII (1881–82), p. 919.

destruction, these people were credited with the capacity for profiting from every contingency.[31]

Again, such judgments were not intrinsically hostile. So a tract that warned "you should not be prejudiced against any race," went on to point out the Jews were naturally money changers through no fault of their own, but simply "on account of their excessive shrewdness."[32] Even laudatory accounts praised the Jews' ability to make money. One of the books to defend the group boasted:

> In finance the Jew has for four hundred years been the factor that supplied the nations of the earth with money. The financial system of the world, its inventions and perfection, we owe to the Rothschilds.[33]

A little later, a compilation published by the American Hebrew Publishing Company casually remarked:

> Of all the nations, which the world has known, the commercial instinct is strongest and most fully developed in the Jew. He never sacrifices future opportunity for present gain.[34]

If an occasional commentator did point out that the great American bankers were Christians, that only seemed to stress the internationalism of the Jews.[35]

To some extent, the lines of socialist thinking that connected capitalism with the Jews strengthened these conceptions. So,

[31] See Camille Flammarion, "Omega; the Last Days of the World," *Cosmopolitan*, vol. XV (1893), p. 200.

[32] *Up to Date Coin's Financial School* (Chicago, March, 1895, vol. II, no. 6), p. 68.

[33] Madison C. Peters, *The Jew as a Patriot*. With an Introductory Essay by Oscar S. Straus (New York, 1902), p. 192. See also the comments on the German Jews, Ezra S. Brudno, "The Russian Jew Americanized," *Worlds Work*, vol. VII (1903–04), p. 4556. For other laudatory articles emphasizing money-making ability, see Herbert N. Casson, "The Jew in America," *Munsey's Magazine*, vol. XXXIV (1906), pp. 381 ff.; Anna Laurens Dawes, *The Modern Jew; His Present and Future* (Boston, [1886]), p. 24; Zebulon B. Vance, *The Scattered Nation* ... (New York, 1904), p. 30.

[34] S. B. Goodkind, ed., *Prominent Jews of America* ... (Toledo, [1918]), p. 119. See also the picture of the Baron de Hirsch trustees on the cover of דער יודישער פּאָק, Jan. 11, 1895.

[35] *The Jewish Question, supra*, pp. 265 ff.

the foremost exponent in this country of revisionist socialism in a widely-read volume pointed out:

> Our era may be called the *Jewish age*. The Jews have indeed, had a remarkable influence on our civilization. Long ago they infused in our race the idea of one God, and now they have made our whole race worship a new true God: the Golden Calf . . . . "Jewism," to our mind, best expresses that special curse of our age, *Speculation*.[36]

Even more important, the growing preoccupation of many Americans with the money question fixed the tie between Jews and finance. In a period of falling prices disaster was close at hand for great numbers of farmers who, despite mounting production saw their situation deteriorate steadily, particularly after the depression of 1893. The temptation was well-nigh irresistible to seek a solution in terms of monetary reform. There were still some calls for greenbacks, but increasingly those who agitated for a change in the currency thought of silver, demanded bimetallism, the free coinage of silver in some established relationship with gold.

In the 1890's these wishes met with an uninterrupted succession of defeats. The rate of silver coinage was not expanded but contracted. President Cleveland's arrangement with J. P. Morgan strengthened the hold of gold and the election of 1896 confirmed the trend. What was more, silver in that decade was abandoned by almost every other country that still used it, — Tunis in 1891, Austria-Hungary in 1892, China in 1896, Japan and Russia in 1897.[37]

Frustrated, the reformers acquired a sense of religious intensity about their cause; their speeches became profuse with Christian images.[38] Unable to see any flaw in the rationality

---

[36] Laurence Gronlund, *The Cooperative Commonwealth in Its Outlines. An Exposition of Modern Socialism* (Boston, 1884), p. 50.

[37] See Henri Rollin, *L'Apocalypse de notre temps. Les dessous de la propagande allemande d'après des documents inédits* (Paris, [1939]), pp. 175, 286.

[38] See, for example, William Jennings Bryan, *Speeches Revised and Arranged by Himself*. With a Biographical Introduction by Mary Baird Bryan, His Wife (New York, 1909), vol. I, pp. 78, 230, 231.

of their arguments, they could explain their defeats only by the intervention of some external power. The blame was not in themselves, nor in the people in whom they had faith; it must be outside, in England, among the international bankers, or — with growing frequency — among the Jews.

The prominence of Montefiore Levi and Alfred de Rothschild in the Brussels Monetary Conference gave the silver men one ground for their suspicion; the activity of Perry Belmont among the gold Democrats gave them another.[39] But they hardly needed evidence. By 1894, the famous *Coin's Financial School* included a map entitled, "The English Octopus. It Feeds on Nothing but Gold." Where England belonged was the simple inscription, Rothschild.[40] In a novel, William Harvey traced the monetary difficulties of the whole world to a plot by "Baron Rothe" to demonetize silver for the sake of English world mastery.[41] In 1895 a silver tract noted as a fact that the Rothschilds owned "one-half the gold in the world, available for use as money, and their aids and satellites own nearly all the remainder."[42]

What could have been in the minds of the delirious audience at the Democratic national convention the very next year when Bryan ascended to his blood-stirring peroration, "You shall not crucify mankind upon a cross of gold!"[43] There is an indication of the answer in the explanations advanced by the silver men in the next few years to explain their defeat.

They had been beaten, they explained, by the power of an "invisible empire," an "oligarchy" centered in the "mysterious money power," which had bound "the hands of the United States" and had then "proceeded ... with marvellous rapidity

[39] See E. Benjamin Andrews, "Notes on the Brussels Monetary Conference," *Cosmopolitan*, vol. XV (1893), pp. 243 ff.; William Jennings Bryan, *Commoner Condensed* (New York, [1902]), pp. 377, 378.

[40] William H. Harvey, *Coin's Financial School* (Chicago, 1894), p. 124.

[41] *Idem, A Tale of Two Nations* (Chicago, 1894), p. 9.

[42] *Up to Date Coin's Financial School*, p. 173.

[43] Bryan, *Speeches, supra*, vol. I, p. 249.

to enslave the human race." Although there was a vagueness
in identifying the members of the oligarchy, the Rothschilds
are often mentioned and occasionally Shylock openly reveals
himself. Thus, one of the reformers, J. C. Ridpath, has Shylock
confess his fear of the radicals, and has him point out that the

> insurgents will presently turn upon me and my tribe and destroy
> our business. I must keep my influence with these contemptible
> Christian nations, else they will cease to support me and my enter-
> prises. My business is to live by the labor of others.[44]

The use of such terms was perhaps figurative to begin with,
but they certainly received a more literal reading as time went
on.

The radicals' suspicions of the designs of the financial oligarchy gained strength from the sense of mystery within which
Americans had long enveloped the Jew. The elements of the
conviction in the United States that there was a strangeness
to the Jew were quite different from those of the demoniac
character that persisted into nineteenth century Europe from
its medieval past.[45] The emphasis in this country was upon
interpretations of the mission of Israel which went back at
least two hundred years to the reflections of Cotton Mather on
the subject.[46]

The visible evidence of mystery was the persistence of Jewry
itself. Wonderful in their past achievements, the Jews were
"still more wonderful in their preservation." Scattered among
the nations they held to their identity. Like the gulf stream

[44] The quotations are from John Clark Ridpath, "Plutocracy and War," *Arena*,
vol. XIX (1898), pp. 97 ff., 98, 100; James R. Challen, "True Reasons for the Apparent
Failure of the Bimetallic Conference," *ibid.*, vol. XIX, pp. 199 ff.; William Jennings
Bryan, "Foreign Influence in American Politics," *Arena*, vol. XIX, pp. 433, 434;
Senator William M. Stewart, "Great Slave Power," *ibid.*, vol. XIX, pp. 577, 580;
John Clark Ridpath, "Invisible Empire," *ibid.*, vol. XIX, pp. 828 ff.

[45] See Joshua Trachtenberg, *Devil and the Jews; The Medieval Conception of the
Jew and Its Relation to Modern Anti-Semitism* (New Haven, 1943).

[46] See Lee M. Friedman, *Jewish Pioneers and Patriots* (Philadelphia, 1948), pp. 95 ff.

in the ocean of mankind, endless movement did not alter their essential quality; found throughout the world, they were everywhere alien.[47]

The strangeness discernible in Jewish ritual and belief might extend to many unknown realms. The rabbi initiate in the lore of the kabbalah might possess the power of divination.[48] By the same token the detective with a Jewish name might uncover a murderer with the aid of "second sight."[49] All sorts of practices might have hidden significance. "The Jewish people don't believe in taking life," testified a social worker, "so to all sorts of vermin they use a whisk brush and out it goes out of the window."[50] The functionings of their institutions were likewise obscure. *The Century Magazine* exposed the practices of the Kahal through which Jews

> have always succeeded in driving alien elements from the town . . . where they have settled to get into their hands the capital and immovable property of those places.[51]

There was a purpose to the survival of the group and to the persistence of these differences. In one sense, the Jew retained his identity to serve as the eternal witness of the truth of Christianity. To one Christian advocate of the Jewish return to Palestine, these people were "Jehovah's ever present answer

---

[47] Richard Hayes McCartney, *That Jew!* (Chicago, 1905), p. 9; Dawes, *The Modern Jew, supra*, pp. 11, 12; A. W. Miller, *The Restoration of the Jews* (Atlanta, 1887), p. 3; Zebulon B. Vance, *The Scattered Nation, supra*, pp. 9, 10.

[48] M. W. Macdowell, *Tempted of the Devil. Passages in the Life of a Kabbalist. A Story Retold from the German of August Becker* (Boston, 1889), pp. 35, 44, 107, 184.

[49] W. I. James, *Heller's Pupil or Seligman the Second-Sight Detective* (Old Cap Collier Library, no. 4, New York, 1883). In another such story, in a vague conflation of Orientals the detective Isaac Lazarus proves to be an Egyptian. See Gilbert Jerome, *Isaac Lazarus the Egyptian Detective* (Old Cap Collier Library, no. 114, New York, 1884).

[50] Robert W. DeForest and Lawrence Veiller, *Tenement House Problem* (New York, 1903), vol. I, p. 410.

[51] "Russian Jews and Gentiles," *Century*, vol. XXIII, p. 910. Yet the article as a whole was not hostile. Its recommended solution was that the Jews be treated as equals to induce their improvement. By contrast, see Pennell, *Jew at Home*, p. 9.

to the innuendoes against the absolute credibility of the Inspiration of the Old Testament."[52]

But there was a larger purpose still, one involved in the whole Christian conception of salvation. For it was in the whole scheme of things that the mass conversion of the Jews would herald the second coming. While practical efforts to induce Jews in the United States to change their religion seem to have fallen off in this period, their Christian fellow-citizens were still eager to read about such conversions and looked forward with anticipation to ultimate total success. The Reverend Joseph Ingraham dedicated three of his immensely popular novels to "the daughters of Israel," to the "Men of Israel," and to "all American Hebrews" in the hope they would see the light.[53]

In a more rationalistic form, the mission of the Jews was sometimes described as the task of disseminating among all mankind their own peculiar cosmopolitan spirituality and sense of ethics.[54] But that still left a distinctive purpose to their strangeness. If Americans then continued avidly to read Sue's *Wandering Jew* it was in part at least due to the hold on their minds of its very title.[55]

The vogue of popular novels with a biblical setting added to the atmosphere of mystery that surrounded Jews. Lew Wallace's *Ben Hur* was only the best known of an enormous

---

[52] McCartney, *That Jew!*, *supra*, pp. [3], 39 ff.

[53] Rev. Professor J. H. Ingraham, *Prince of the House of David; or Three Years in the Holy City. Being a Series of the Letters of Adina, a Jewess of Alexandria, Sojourning in Jerusalem in the Days of Herod, Addressed to Her Father, a Wealthy Jew in Egypt and Relating as by an Eye-Witness all the Scenes and Wonderful Incidents in the Life of Jesus* . . . (New York, 1855); Rev. J. H. Ingraham, *The Throne of David; from the Consecration of the Shepherd of Bethlehem to the Rebellion of Prince Absalom* (Boston, 1868); Rev. J. H. Ingraham, *Pillar of Fire or Israel in Bondage* (Boston, 1899); Miller, *Restoration of the Jews*, *supra*, p. 3; Aunt Friendly [Sarah S. T. Baker], *Jewish Twins* (New York, 1860).

[54] Eugene F. Baldwin and Maurice Eisenberg, *Doctor Cavallo* (Peoria, 1895), pp. 20, 41 ff.; *The Jewish Question*, pp. 58 ff., 67.

[55] William Allen White, *Autobiography* (New York, 1946), pp. 101, 106.

number of books the scenes of which were set in ancient
Palestine or Babylonia, books which took their readers back
in everyday language through the incidents of the bible. In
these stories, Jewish characters appeared in a variety of forms,
generally sympathetically portrayed, but in any case, in close
connection with the most sacred and most mysterious events.[56]

The attributes of mystery were naturally transferred to the
present since Jews had retained their identity from the most
ancient times and since their strangeness gave continuing evidence of inexplicable characteristics. This mysterious strain
explains the beautiful Jewess who appears so often in the
novels of these years. She has antecedents of course in Scott's
Rebecca and in Shakespeare's Jessica; but she is no mere copy.
The American heroine is exquisitely beautiful and distinguished
by great nobility of character. Some taint, curse, or fateful
misfortune involves her in intricate difficulties which however
lead to a happy ending. Often she is juxtaposed with a mean
and miserly father, who is, in a sense, her taint, the source
through his paternity of her troubles. The mysterious element
here is hereditary, in a way, racial.[57]

These mysterious racial ties can also take other forms. In
1872 Lynn Linton, a popular English writer of romantic stories,
described in a novel the life of a revolutionary who attempted
in modern times to pattern his acts upon those of Jesus. To
heighten the analogy, the author gave her hero the English

[56] Ingraham's novels (cited above, note 53) went through numerous editions in
these years. See also Wilson Barrett and Robert Hitchens, *Daughters of Babylon*
(Philadelphia, 1899); Edward Payson Berry, *Leah of Jerusalem, a Story of the Time
of Paul* (New York, 1890); Lew. Wallace, *Ben-Hur, a Tale of the Christ* (New York,
[1880]).

[57] Noel Dunbar's *Jule the Jewess*, the story of a bankrupt millionaire who sold
his beautiful daughter, went through at least five novel and magazine editions,
1881–1898 (Johannsen, *House of Beadle*, vol. I, pp. 195, 247, 313, 442, 467; vol. II,
p. 90). See also Arthur M. Grainger, *Beautiful Jewess* (*ibid.*, vol. I, p. 169); Roor-
bach, *Rebecca and Rowena, supra,* p. 27; Harriette Newell [Woods] Baker, *Rebecca
the Jewess* (Boston, 1879); Berry, *Leah, supra,* p. 36; Barrett and Hitchens, *Daughters
of Babylon, supra,* pp. 100 ff.

version of the name of Jesus, Joshua Davidson. The novel
was well-known in the United States.[58]

Twenty years later, Jesse Jones, a radical New England
minister who had his own doctrines of social reform to expound,
labored on a novel that used the same device. However Jones
felt the compulsion to secure for his protagonist a Jewish
ancestor, one of "Israel's sacred race," a grandfather, from
whom Joshua could learn "as a 'son of the Law,' the sacred
Lore of Israel." The injection of this element was significant
for it suggested that there was a mysterious body of knowledge
available only to "one of the blood."[59]

In this review of the American image of the Jew, I have
attempted to isolate three elements, the stereotype of the
immigrant Jew, the relationship to finance, and the sense of
mystery. In the writings of the populist leader, Ignatius
Donnelly, one may trace the combination of those elements
into a pattern that markedly influenced many of the earnest
radicals of the period. In *Caesar's Column*, a utopian novel,
Donnelly looked ahead to a period when

> the task which Hannibal attempted, . . . to subject the Latin and
> mixed-Gothic races of Europe to the domination of the Semitic blood

had been accomplished

> by the cousins of the Phoenicians, the Israelites. The nomadic chil-
> dren of Abraham . . . [had] fought and schemed their way, through
> infinite pains of persecution . . . to a power higher than the thrones
> of Europe.

[58] [E. Lynn Linton], *True History of Joshua Davidson* (London, 1872). All
references are to this edition. See also [E. Lynn Linton], *True History of Joshua
Davidson, Communist* (Philadelphia, 1873); E. Lynn Linton, *Life of Joshua Davidson;
or, the Modern Imitation of Christ. A Theoretical Novel* (New York, 1882).

[59] For the circumstances of composition, and for the quotations, see Jesse H.
Jones, *Joshua Davidson Christian. The Story of the Life of One Who, in the Nineteenth
Century was "Like Unto Christ"; as Told by His Body-Servant. A Parable.* Edited
by Halah H. Loud (New York, 1907), pp. v, 1, 2, 5, 16, 21, 23.

At that future date, "survival of the fittest" had made the aristocracy of the world "almost altogether of Hebrew origin." Christians had earlier subjected the Jews

> to the most terrible ordeal of persecution .... Only the strong of body, the cunning of brain ... the men with capacity to live where a dog would starve, survived the awful trial .... Now the Christian world is paying, in tears and blood for the sufferings inflicted by their bigoted and ignorant ancestors upon a noble race .... The great money-getters of the world ... rose from dealers in old clothes and peddlers of hats to merchants, to bankers, to princes. They were as merciless to the Christian as the Christian had been to them.[60]

Under the leadership of Prince Cabano, born Jacob Isaacs, the Jewish oligarchy was pushing the world toward destruction.

In this anticipation of things to come is a tone of fear. The radical urging changes yet dreads the effects of change. For Donnelly was no facile optimist as to the possibility of reform. His revolution degenerates into an orgy of destruction in which the whole civilization is consumed.

Significantly, the brains of the revolutionary organization was "a Russian Jew, ... a cripple, driven out of his synagogue in Russia, years ago, for some crimes he had committed." With the success of the uprising, he fled to Judea, taking with him one hundred million dollars of public funds, with this vast wealth intending to "re-establish the glories of Solomon, and revive the ancient splendors of the Jewish race, in the midst of the ruins of the world."[61]

There were specific reasons for the distrust of revolutionary violence. The labor rioting at Homestead, at Coeur d'Alene, and at Pullman in these years, the activities of the anarchists at home and in Europe had the substantial citizens eager to

[60] [Ignatius Donnelly], *Caesar's Column. A Story of the Twentieth Century* (Chicago, 1891), pp. 36, 37, 111, 112.
[61] *Ibid.*, pp. 147, 172, 331.

build armories in the middle of the cities and had even the radicals worried about the dangers of unrestrained socialism.[62]

But more interesting for our purposes is the implication in *Caesar's Column* that there were hidden organizations, conservative and radical, working toward hidden Jewish ends. To that suspicion would later be added confused impressions of what the Zionist Basle Congress of 1897 was up to, hazy recollections of European charges, and the explicit accusation of the *Protocols of Zion* that the gold standard was the Jewish tool of world domination.[63] The sum total would be the conspiracy of the international Jew. Millions of well-intentioned Americans would find the later anti-Semitic libel credible because they had already accepted its ingredients in a form that was not anti-Semitic.

There still remains the task of accounting for the sense of fear from which the idea of conspiracy grew, a sense that was repeatedly expressed in other connections as well. The apocalyptic visions of the radicals in these years were often stated in terms of imminence of doom. They envisaged great eras of ruin and destruction that would precede the final redemption and reconstruction of society. The conviction that suffering was inevitable was fed by memories of the commune of 1870, by scientific descriptions of lost worlds or of the end of this one, by the analogy with the reign of anti-Christ that was to precede the second coming, and by the figure of Christ himself.[64]

Thus in both the English and the American *Joshua Davidson* the martyr hero is killed by the very people to whom he

[62] See J. C. Cowdrick, *Broadway Billy and the Bomb-Throwers* (Beadle's Half-Dime Library, New York, 1894), cited in Johannsen, *House of Beadle*, vol. I, p. 293; Woodward, *Watson, supra*, pp. 404–406; Rollin, *L'Apocalypse, supra*, pp. 407 ff.

[63] See, Rollin, *L'Apocalypse, supra*, pp. 32 ff., 37 ff., 175, 279, 286.

[64] See Ignatius Donnelly, *Atlantis the Antediluvian World*, 7th ed. (New York [1882]), *passim*; Flammarion, "Omega," *Cosmopolitan*, vol. XV, pp. 15 ff., 185 ff., 468 ff.; also McCartney, *That Jew!, supra, passim*; Ignatius Donnelly, *Ragnarok: the Age of Fire and Gravel* (New York, 1883).

preached and for whom he suffered.[65] Donnelly's novel of revolt ended in disaster as did Jack London's a few years later.[66]

These uneasy conceptions of the future were judgments of the unhappy nature of the present in which they were written. Certainly in the unhappy decade of the 1890's there was much that seemed to be changing, — and for the worse. For the class in which Edith Wharton grew up, the changes appeared to be a deterioration of culture and the reaction of that class was fastidiousness in speech and manners. But for the mass of Americans, change took another form.[67]

Through the period change centered in the city, an object of dread and fascination. To the city, and particularly to New York, whole regions of the South and West felt themselves in bondage.[68] Yet to the people of those regions, the metropolis was altogether strange; often their only source of information was the lurid detective story. The farmers' view of the city was therefore based less on knowledge of it than on its impact upon them.

The cities were unnatural. They worshipped Mammon, not God. They could all burn down, Bryan declaimed, and the great heart of America would still beat.[69] "Embodied paganism," the city was "composed of the people of this world ... seeking the ends of this world, ... satiating the animal man with the riches, with the lavish luxury of things." The city,

Babylon the great, the mother of the harlots and of the abominations of the earth ... drunken with the blood of the saints, and with the

---

[65] Linton, *True History, supra,* pp. 250 ff., 261 ff.; Jones, *Joshua Davidson, supra,* pp. 300 ff.

[66] Jack London, *Iron Heel* (1907) (New York, 1932).

[67] Edith Wharton, *A Backward Glance* (New York, 1934), pp. 48 ff.

[68] *Letter of Henry R. Jackson of Georgia to Ex-Senator Allen G. Thurman,* with Explanatory Papers (Atlanta, 1887), p. 7.

[69] Bryan, *Speeches, supra,* vol. I, p. 248; Jones, *Joshua Davidson, supra,* pp. 201 ff. See also Donnelly's vision of the ideal society without cities, *Caesar's Column, supra,* p. 360.

blood of the martyrs of Jesus . . . reigneth over the kings of the earth

and feeds off peoples and multitudes and nations.[70]

This literal fear of the city was not altogether surprising in a period which, despite its rationalism, still found the occult, spiritualism, mesmerism, theosophy, astrology, mental healing popular, even among the intellectual reformers.[71] Nor is it unexpected that some men should transfer the blame for their tribulations to these alien places. In the same years, others were blaming the Pope or secret societies, and one ingenious author even demonstrated that the Jesuits had infiltrated the Masonic societies in order to spread atheism in the United States.[72] The city was indeed a likely butt for the hatred and resentments of disappointed people.

In the United States, the Jews were particularly connected with the city through commerce which was its lifeblood. Coming back in 1907, Henry James was impressed by the alien quality of American cities. He noted "the extent of the Hebrew conquest of New York," a new Jerusalem, and felt a certitude that the culture of the future in this country might be beautiful in its own right, but would inevitably be totally strange.[73]

This was the opinion of a widely-traveled man of the world. But what did the farmers think in the populist areas while the mounting burden of debt loosened their hold on the land? In the years of populism's mounting strength, William Allen

[70] Jones, *Joshua Davidson, supra*, pp. 302, 303; James G. Clark, "Fall of New Babylon," *Arena*, vol. X (1894), p. 110.

[71] Woodward, *Watson, supra*, pp. 182, 416 ff.; Heinrich Hensoldt, "Occult Science in Tibet," *Arena*, vol. X (1894), pp. 181 ff., 366 ff.; James R. Cocke, "Value of Hypnotism as a Means of Surgical Anaesthesia," *ibid.*, vol. X, pp. 289 ff.; B. O. Flower, "In the Psychic Realm," *ibid.*, vol. X, pp. 684 ff.; T. E. Allen, "Experimental Telepathy," *ibid.*, vol. XI (1895), pp. 227 ff.; *ibid.*, vol. XIX (1898), pp. 632 ff.; Rollin, *L'Apocalypse, supra*, p. 345.

[72] J. M. Foster, "Secret Societies and the State," *Arena*, vol. XIX (1898), pp. 229 ff.

[73] Henry James, *The American Scene* . . . (W. H. Auden, ed., New York, 1946), pp. 117–120, 132, 135, 138, 139.

White was reaching maturity in Eldorado, Kansas. The children of the few Jews in town mixed freely with the adolescent elite of which White was himself a member, just as Maurice Levy was one of the boys.[74] When White thought of the Jew he thought of the wealth of the tradespeople, of the luxury of their weddings.[75] Himself well off, his impressions were favorable.

But there were others, many others, who believed "all trade is treachery," who believed that commerce "by the manipulation of Satan" has become "a curse to humanity" dominating all the people of the earth. To those people every Jewish storekeeper was in the advance guard of the new civilization, bore the standard of all the dread forces that threatened their security.[76]

Two decades later, a boy who had grown up in Donnelly's Minnesota, who had come to New York and never adjusted to the change, gave explicit statement to that sentiment. Down the street, the hero of his novel

> read a dozen Jewish names on a line of stores; in the door of each stood a dark little man watching the passers from intent eyes — eyes gleaming with suspicion, with pride, with clarity, with cupidity, with comprehension. New York — he could not dissociate it now from the slow upward creep of this people — the little stores, growing, expanding .... It was impressive — in perspective it was tremendous.[77]

In those formative years of the 1890's, the injured groups of American society, in agony, had issued the cries of an infant that has no words to express its pain. Searching vainly for the means of relief, they could scarcely guess that the source

[74] White, *Autobiography*, *supra*, p. 75; Tarkington, *Penrod*, *supra*, p. 375.

[75] White, *Autobiography*, *supra*, pp. 109, 150, 164 ff.

[76] Jones, *Joshua Davidson*, *supra*, pp. 201, 203; McCartney, *That Jew!*, *supra*, p. 46; Donnelly, *Caesar's Column*, *supra*, pp. 116 ff.

[77] F. Scott Fitzgerald, *The Beautiful and the Damned* (New York, 1926), p. 283 (Bk. 2, ch. 3). See also for the later period, Irving Howe, "The Stranger and the Victim," *Commentary*, vol. VIII (1949), pp. 147 ff.

of their trials was a change in the world in which they lived. And groping toward an understanding of that change, some perceived its instrument, the Jew. If all trade was treachery and Babylon the city, then the Jew — stereotyped, involved in finance, and mysterious — stood ready to be assigned the role of arch-conspirator.

It was this suspicion that transformed the conception of the Jew after 1900, replaced the older images with that of the Elder of Zion.

In Defense of the Jewish Immigrant (1891-1924)

By Esther Panitz

INTRODUCTION*

This paper is a conclusion to a previously published study, entitled "The Polarity of Jewish Attitudes to Immigration," which stated that from 1870 to 1891, when America as a whole was pro-immigrant, American Jewry was restrictionist in its approach.[1] The current monograph deals with the period from 1891 to 1924, when a complete reversal of attitudes prevailed. During this time, when the country generally moved in the direction of tighter controls upon alien entry, representative American Jews battled for a more liberal approach to immigration.

That battle then became a delaying action. From 1891, until the passage of the Johnson-Reed "national origins" bill of 1924, acknowledged Jewish spokesmen such as Simon Wolf, Max J. Kohler, Abram Elkus, and Louis Marshall, to mention but a few, tried to demolish, or at best modify, every piece of restrictive legislation as it arose. Their prime concern was the threatened loss of inalienable human rights occasioned by administrative misinterpretation of immigration law. These men were convinced that certain Federal applications put upon the terms "assisted immigrants" or "public charges" trespassed on liberties constitutionally due both alien and citizen alike. Governmental decisions to create arbitrary distinctions amongst aliens via literacy tests or by means of racial or religious qualifications were likewise deemed to be derogations of democratic principles. In correspondence with immigration officials, before Con-

* The author wishes to acknowledge with many thanks the following for making their resources available to her: the American Jewish Archives, [=AJA], the Archives of the American Jewish Committee [=AAJ Committee], the American Jewish Historical Society [=AJHS], the Manuscript Division of the New York Public Library [=NYPL], the National Archives [=NA], and Mrs. Marjorie Bloomberg of Larchmont, New York. The author is especially grateful to Dr. Isidore S. Meyer for the aid and encouragement offered her in the preparation of this paper.

[1] *American Jewish Historical Quarterly* [=AJHQ], vol. LIII, no. 2 (Dec., 1963), pp. 99-130.

gressional committees, and in courts of law, these champions of the immigrant propounded their courses of action.[2]

Unlike the restrictionists who took a circuitous road to achieve their goals,[3] representatives of the American Jewish community trod a direct path towards a liberal interpretation of immigration policy. Despite privately voiced misgivings concerning the wisdom of admitting thousands of their brethren,[4] leaders of American Jewry consistently espoused the cause of the immigrant in their midst.

I

PUBLIC CHARGE AND ASSISTED IMMIGRANT PROVISOS OF THE LAW

In March, 1891, Congress passed a comprehensive immigration bill, which, among other features, banned the admission of all assisted immigrants.[5] This law signalled a new departure in American

---

[2] See, for example, the following two letters of Simon Wolf to Terence V. Powderly, dated Nov. 25, 1901, *Twenty-eighth Annual Report of the Board of Delegates on Civil and Religious Rights, Proceedings of the Union of American Hebrew Congregations*, pp. 4479–4480, and Wolf to Robert Watchorn, dated Oct. 19, 1906, *Thirty-third Annual Report of the Board of Delegates, supra*, pp. 5648–5654. See also *Ellis Island Investigating Commission* in *ibid.*, pp. 5036–5042; *United States Industrial Commission, Reports*, vol. XV, "Immigration and Education," House Doc. no. 184, 57th Congress, First Session, pp. 245–249; *American Jewish Yearbook* [= *AJYB*], vol. XI (1909–1910 — 5670), pp. 19–98, and vol. XII (1910–1911 — 5671), pp. 344–349; "Protecting Immigrant Rights," *American Hebrew*, vol. LXXXV, no. 12 (July 22, 1909); *Recommendations Respecting Revision of the Immigration Laws Made by the American Jewish Committee, the Board of Delegates on Civil and Religious Rights of the Union of American Hebrew Congregations, the International Order B'nai B'rith to the United States Immigration Commission* (New York, 1910), *United States Immigration Commission, Reports* [= *USICR*], vol. XLI (Washington, D.C., 1911), pp. 141–157; "The Galveston Case, Correspondence Between Simon Wolf and Secretary Benjamin W. Cable, Legal Aspect by Max J. Kohler," *Jewish Exponent*, vol. LI, no. 17 (Aug. 5, 1910), pp. 1–2, and 8; Max J. Kohler and Abram J. Elkus, "Brief in the Matter of Hersh Skuratowki" (New York, 1909) in *USICR*, vol. XLI, pp. 161–180; Max J. Kohler, "The Injustice of a Literacy Test for Immigrants," (New York, 1912); *idem*, "Memorandum In Opposition to Classification of Immigrants as Hebrews," in *USICR*, vol. XLI, pp. 265–278.

[3] See *AJHQ*, vol. LIII, no. 2 (Dec., 1963), p. 130.

[4] *Eighteenth Annual Report of the Board of Delegates*, pp. 2820–2821; Moritz Ellinger, "Concerted Efforts for the Relief of Distressed Jews in Galicia," *Menorah Journal*, vol. XXVIII, no. 3 (March, 1900), pp. 136–137; "Transactions of the Convention," *ibid.*, vol. XXVIII, no. 4 (June, 1900), pp. 375, 381–383; M. Ellinger, "The Relief Work," *ibid.*, vol. XXIX, no. 2 (Aug., 1900), p. 72; Leo N. Levi to Simon Wolf, Oct. 7 and Oct. 23, 1902, Simon Wolf Papers, *AJHQ*; John V. H. McMurray to Alvee A. Adee, Nov. 22, 1911, State Department File, 861.111/94, NA.

[5] *United States Statutes At Large, 1879–1895, Fifty-first Congress, Second Session*, ch. 551, pp. 1084–1085; Henry Pratt Fairchild, *Immigration* (New York, 1926), p. 115.

immigration policy. Previous legislation of the 1880's, directed against the immigrant pauper and the contract laborer, had been the immediate result of economic unrest which periodically punctured America's expanding industrial wealth. Despite repeated cycles of depression, employers still looked for new sources of labor supply and various geographical sections of the country still welcomed the foreigner. By 1891, however, new attitudes to the immigrant were burgeoning. American nativism was growing more vocal and more virulent in its expressions. The frontier as a locale for immigrant settlement had begun to close, and early labor organizations were beginning to view the alien as a potential threat to economic stability and financial responsibility.[6]

In the face of this growing public mood, Jewish groups pressed for the admission of their brethren because they responded to the plight of the oppressed, because they now possessed more adequately structured philanthropic organizations to aid the immigrant, and because they had developed a readier acceptance of the newcomer. For the following two decades these factors intensified in the Jewish community. The number of newcomers grew prodigiously,[7] while American Jewry became increasingly aware of the need for a Jewish exodus from Eastern Europe. At the same time, institutions geared to receive the alien achieved national status by learning to cope efficiently with immigrant problems.[8]

The problems posed by a mass immigrant influx were sufficient to require intercession with the Government. Several Jewish groups, represented by Simon Wolf and Lewis Abrahams of the Board of Delegates of the Union of American Hebrew Congregations, prevailed upon Charles Foster, the Secretary of the Treasury then in charge of immigration, to remove from the category of assisted immigrants all aliens who were aided by private, charitable agencies, since they were not in fact charges upon the public welfare. The Secretary saw the justice of this contention, provided that the Jews in accordance with their own predetermined plan would disperse the immigrants throughout the land.[9]

For their part, the Jewish groups tried — even if with little success — to redistribute the newcomers. Numerous accounts have detailed the results of these various schemes. Efforts were made to

[6] *AJHQ*, vol. LIII, no. 2 (Dec., 1963), pp. 103–104.

[7] *AJYB*, vol. XXI (1919–1920 — 5680), pp. 610–613.

[8] See Mark Wischnitzer, *To Dwell in Safety* (Philadelphia, 1948), pp. 120–130, 154–157; *idem*, *Visas to Freedom: The History of HIAS* (Cleveland and New York, 1956), pp. 38–72.

[9] Simon Wolf, *Presidents I Have Known* (Washington, D.C., 1918), pp. 159–162.

direct Jews into farming, although only a few of these agricultural experiments survived in New Jersey, New York, and Connecticut.[10] By 1910, industrial and vocational resettlement in cities away from the Eastern seaboard accounted for 50,000 Jewish immigrants, representing 221 different callings out of a total entry of more than 1,186,000 such aliens since 1891.[11] Jacob H. Schiff's contribution of several hundred thousand dollars to the Galveston Plan notwithstanding, that project to divert Jews from the Eastern cities ceased at the beginning of the First World War due largely to the intransigeance of petty immigration officials.[12] However, the Industrial Removal Office, created with the aid of the B'nai B'rith in 1901 to facilitate Jewish immigrant employment throughout the land, lasted until 1922.[13]

These attempts at immigrant distribution were weakened by Federal action which countermanded Secretary Foster's decision on an administrative level. Not only in the Galveston situation, but elsewhere as well, many immigration officials continued arbitrarily to deport Jewish immigrants on a variety of pretexts. By 1909, a solicitor for the Department of Commerce did confirm the Jewish interpretation of the words, "liable to become a public charge,"[14] but in actual practice, the frequent Federal resorts to an increasingly stricter application of the pauper clause nullified this opinion.

Such procedures stemmed from the stringent attitude to aliens taken by Commissioner of Immigration at the Port of New York, William Williams. Williams was a well-known restrictionist who, in 1902, told President Roosevelt that aliens had "no inherent right whatsoever to come here," and that America ought to take steps, "however radical and drastic," to exclude "all below a certain physical and economic standard."[15] Upon Williams' appointment to office in 1902,[16] the more moderate approach to immigrants held

[10] *AJYB*, vol. XXXVII (1935–1936 — 5696), pp. 100–103 and 112.

[11] David M. Bressler, *The Removal Work, Including Galveston, delivered on May 17, 1910*, published by the National Conference on Jewish Charities (St. Louis, Mo.), p. 11.

[12] Max J. Kohler to Mortimer Schiff, Oct. 14, 1925, Kohler Papers, *AJHS.*

[13] M. Wischnitzer, *To Dwell in Safety*, p. 300.

[14] Solicitor Charles Earl to Secretary of Commerce Charles Nagel, Dept. of Commerce File no. 3991, July 28, 1909, "In Re the meaning of the term 'public charge' as used in section 20 of the Immigration Act of 1907," in the communication of Asst. General Counsel for the Dept. of Commerce, Bernard A. Stol to Mr. Irving Bloomberg, of Katz and Bloomberg, attorneys at law, which was made available through the courtesy Mrs. Marjorie Bloomberg, Larchmont, New York.

[15] William Williams to Theodore Roosevelt, Nov. 25, 1902, William Williams Papers, Box I, NYPL.

[16] Frank P. Sargent to William Williams, Oct. 10, 1902, Williams Papers, NYPL.

by other officials in the Department of Commerce and Labor was diminished. Even Williams' superior, Commissioner-General of Immigration, Frank P. Sargent, whom Wolf praised continuously as a humane and just administrator,[17] now agreed with Williams' definition of the public charge category. In a memorandum to Williams, Sargent had proposed a double standard: People immigrating from Southern or Eastern Europe, on the one hand, were to be admitted only if their appearance, financial assets in hand, or firm assurance of employment guaranteed their non-public charge status; newcomers from Scotland and Ireland, on the other hand, were to be welcomed regardless of these criteria.[18]

Simon Wolf was unaware of the distinctions agreed to between Williams and Sargent for determining the admissibility of different immigrants. Accordingly, in testimony before an Ellis Island commission, investigating conditions at that point of entry in 1903, Wolf complained of the harsh legal tendency to dismiss aliens as public charges by ruling on the amount of cash they had on their persons.[19] The Chairman of the Ellis Island Commission, Arthur van Briesen, then justified the Federal attitude when he insisted that the alien's ability to earn a living wage was the issue and not the number of dollars he possessed.[20] Years later, two Jewish attorneys used the recommendations of the Ellis Island Commission, that employability was more important than money, to the advantage of certain immigrants.[21] More immediately, in concluding his testimony before the Commission, Wolf simply emphasized that to his knowledge, no Jew admitted by the United States had ever become a public charge.[22] Both Foster in his answer of 1891 to the Jewish groups and a United States Industrial Commission in 1901 had earlier acknowledged the Jewish genius for never permitting its own to become charges upon the public welfare.[23] Yet, used too often, these words lost their magic.

It must be remembered that Wolf had spoken against a background of national concern with immigration, in which President Benjamin Harrison, though affirming the special Hebrew talent for

[17] *Twenty-eighth and Twenty-ninth Annual Reports of the Board of Delegates*, pp. 4474 and 4662.

[18] Sargent to Williams, Oct. 10, 1902, Williams Papers, NYPL.

[19] *Thirtieth Annual Report of the Board of Delegates*, p. 5039.

[20] *Ibid.*, pp. 5039-5040.

[21] M. J. Kohler and A. Elkus, "Brief in the Matter of Hersh Skuratowski," *USICR*, vol. XLI, p. 166.

[22] *Thirtieth Annual Report of the Board of Delegates*, p. 5040.

[23] United States Industrial Commission, *Reports* (Washington, D.C., 1901), vol. XV, *Introduction, Review and Digest of Testimony*, pp. xi and 648.

providing for its poor, had first warned in 1891 that a large influx
of aliens to this country would seriously affect the labor market.[24]
More than a decade later, Secretary of State John Hay, in his
famous Roumanian note urging a naturalization treaty with that
country, cautioned against the effects of a flight of pauperized
foreign Jews to this country. Naturally, Hays made sure to welcome
those who came in full possession of such "mental and moral qualifications as made for good leadership."[25] Yet both statesmen felt
that the admission of those made "double paupers" by economic or
religious deprivations abroad and by attendant industrial or social
misfortunes here, was not to be countenanced without some re-
monstrance.[26]

Wolf again, in 1906, had occasion to protest against Federal
tendencies to deport on the public charge basis. In correspondence
with Robert Watchorn, a Commissioner of Immigration for the
Port of New York, Wolf revealed a growing sense of desperation
at the increasing number of exclusions which he was unable
to halt.[27] Having earlier, in 1900, written a sympathetic report of
the plight of the Roumanian immigrant,[28] Watchorn pointed with
pride to his past record, and now refuted Wolf's accusations of unwarranted Federal harshness in pressing the public charge matter.
Watchorn thereupon cited the many occasions he had seen fit to
admit aliens who legally ought to have been deported. But Wolf's
dismay at Watchorn's attitude was heightened when the Commissioner marshalled statistics to prove that the public charge
cases amongst Jewish immigrants were indeed increasing.[29]

This was not to be wondered at. The hastened tempo of Russian-
Jewish persecutions abroad accounted for a growing number of
arrivals here,[30] so that proportionately more Jewish immigrants,
subjected to a strict interpretation of the pauper clause might
conceivably have been regarded as charges upon the public welfare.
Meanwhile, in his official capacity as Chairman of the Board of
Delegates of the Union of American Hebrew Congregations and as
Washington representative of the B'nai B'rith, Wolf duly protested

---

[24] S. Wolf, *Presidents I Have Known*, p. 157.

[25] *Twenty-ninth Annual Report of the Board of Delegates*, pp. 4676–4677.

[26] *Ibid.*, p. 4680; S. Wolf, *Presidents I Have Known*, p. 157.

[27] *Thirty-third Annual Report of the Board of Delegates*, Appendix B, pp. 5648–5652.

[28] "Mr. Watchorn's Report on Roumania," *American Hebrew*, vol. LXVII, nos. 23
and 24 (Oct. 19 and 26, 1900), pp. 647–648, 679 and 682.

[29] *Thirty-third Annual Report of the Board of Delegates*, Appendix B, pp. 5651–5652.

[30] Simon M. Dubnow, *History of the Jews in Russia and Poland* (Philadelphia, 1920),
vol. III, chaps. 35–37; *AJYB*, vol. VI (1904–1905 — 5665), p. 24; *Thirty-third Annual
Report of the Board of Delegates*, pp. 5640 and 5646.

the results of Russia's anti-Semitic policies, and was concerned with their effects on Jewish immigration to this country.[31]

Not only did his efforts appear futile, but his privilege of repre- senting his co-religionists to the Federal Government had now to be shared with others. No longer would he reign supreme as liaison agent for American Jewry to the executive and legislative branches of the Government. In 1906, a new organization of younger men had been formed, a group which justified its existence by virtue of the changing needs of American Jewry, molded in no small part by the immigrant Jewish masses flooding this country.[32] Henceforth, the American Jewish Committee, represented by such leading in- tellectuals and members of the bar as Cyrus Adler, Louis Marshall, Judge Mayer Sulzberger, and others, was prepared to busy itself precisely in those matters which had hitherto been the exclusive domain of the B'nai B'rith and the Board of Delegates of the Union for whom Wolf was accustomed to speak. Though duplication and rivalry sometimes rent the effectiveness of the American Jewish Committee and those older organizations in certain areas of common concern,[33] to their credit they all saw the need for united action against restrictive immigration legislation. By 1906-1907 the need for such action was quickly shaping up.[34]

Here, in America, there was a recrudescence of economic ex- pansion, and once again, the business community beckoned to the immigrants. Yet, at the same time, a seasoned core of restrictionists, re-invigorated by their earlier demands to halt the anarchist peril from abroad, and abetted by organized labor, fearful of foreign competition, continued to look askance at the new immigration.[35] They introduced legislation in Congress, which, aside from its literacy requirement, endowed immigrant inspectors with sufficient arbitrary power to deport aliens deemed to be of "poor physique"

[31] *Thirty-third Annual Report of the Board of Delegates*, p. 5641; *Thirty-second Annual Report of the Board of Delegates*, Appendices B, pp. 5525-5528, and C, pp. 5529-5532; Andrew D. White to S. Wolf, May 12, 1905, AJA.

[32] *Nineteenth Council of the Union, Proceedings of the Union of American Hebrew Con- gregations* (1907), pp. 54 and 72; *Twenty-first Council of the Union, Proceedings* ... (1909), pp. 6155 and 6159.

[33] S. Wolf to Dr. David Philipson, April 25, 1907, AJA; see file on "The Boston Sailor Case," AAJ Committee; S. Wolf to M. J. Kohler, Dec. 21, 1909, Wolf Papers, AJHS; S. Wolf to Cyrus Adler, Oct. 21, 1907, AAJ Committee.

[34] Mayer Sulzberger to Herbert Friedenwald, to Simon Wolf and to Adolph Kraus, Nov. 20, 1909, Sulzberger Papers AAJ Committee; "Memorandum of a Conversation by Cyrus Adler with Simon Wolf, March 5, 1908"; H. Friedenwald to M. J. Kohler, Dec. 15, 1909, with enclosures; Cyrus Adler to M. Sulzberger, Jan. 30, 1910, Adler Papers, AAJ Committee; *AJYB*, vol. XIII (1911-1912 — 5672), p. 301.

[35] J. Higham, *op. cit.*, pp. 113-116; *AJYB*, vol. VII (1905-1906 — 5667), p. 537.

and liable to become public charges.[36] Here apparently were the logical consequences of Williams' and Sargent's concern with the physical appearance of the immigrants. Wolf strenuously sought a more liberal construction of those terms. In his correspondence with Sargent, Wolf observed that the immigrant Jews' physical suffering abroad, accentuated by an arduous ocean voyage under steerage conditions, would tend to obscure their true earning capacities, and make the aliens appear physically weaker than they really were.[37]

Politics, in the form of the Republican Party, eager to husband immigrant votes, intervened to modify the 1906–1907 immigration bill. Astutely handled in its passage through the legislature by the Republican Speaker of the House, Joseph Gurney Cannon, the bill, as it finally emerged, proved more amenable to immigrants.[38] Henceforth, aliens would not be examined at points of embarkation, an issue to which Louis Marshall had earlier taken strenuous exception.[39] Furthermore, arriving immigrants, charged with poor physique, would be granted the privilege of posting bonds.[40] The fort had been held against the restrictionists, but only temporarily. By 1908, with Commissioner Williams' imposition of an additional cash requirement of $25.00 upon all aliens,[41] immigration officials were more loath to take bonds in alleged public charge cases. In fact, in the following years, two attorneys, Max J. Kohler and Abram Elkus, representing the Board of Delegates of the Union and the American Jewish Committee, protested that eleven out of fifteen Jewish immigrants awaiting deportation were shipped out of the country even before application for posting bonds could be made. The remaining four became the subject of an interesting brief, whose outcome was not heard in court.[42]

Prepared by Kohler and Elkus in July, 1909, the "Brief in the Matter of Hersh Skuratowski" ably summed up the attitudes of Jewish agencies to the Federal approach to immigration legislation. Since the matter of the three other cases was similar to the Skuratowski issue, all four were included in the same brief.[43]

[36] *AJYB*, vol. VIII (1906–1907 — 5667), p. 98.

[37] *Thirty-third Annual Report of the Board of Delegates*, Appendix C, p. 5654.

[38] Blair Bolles, *Tyrant From Illinois: Uncle Joe Cannon's Experiment with Personal Power* (New York, 1951), pp. 71–77; J. Higham, *op. cit.*, pp. 128–129.

[39] Charles Reznikoff [ed.], *Louis Marshall, Champion of Liberty; Selected Papers and Addresses* (Philadelphia, 1957), vol. I, p. 114.

[40] *AJYB*, vol. IX (1907–1908 — 5668), p. 537.

[41] *Ibid.*, vol. XII (1910–1911 — 5671), p. 99.

[42] "Brief in the Matter of Hersh Skuratowski," pp. 162–163.

[43] *Ibid.*, pp. 160–181.

Skuratowski, aged twenty-nine, a butcher by trade, and literate, had reached New York on July 23, 1909. He was described as of "Russian nationality, Caucasian in race, and Hebrew by religion." Though he had only $2.75 in cash on hand, his home and other property abroad represented an estimated cash value of $3,000. He could have secured more money had it been necessary, but was prevented from telling this to the Board of Special Inquiry. He had planned to reside with his cousin, a painter by trade, who earned $30.00 a week. One of the inspectors made the motion to deport, since the alien had little cash on hand, and his relatives were not legally bound to support him. While the second member of the Board moved to admit the alien, the third corroborated the earlier viewpoint, and Skuratowski was ordered deported.[44] As he and the other immigrants were being placed upon a departing steamer, their attorneys filed writs of habeas corpus in the United States District Court for the Southern District of New York. The Court took jurisdiction before a rehearing could be submitted to Commissioner Williams.[45]

In this brief Kohler and Elkus charged that the Commissioner had shown an unwarranted abuse of executive power.[46] Though Congress had refused to establish Williams' cash qualification for immigrants, the Commissioner nevertheless ruled that its absence would make the aliens inadmissible. The lawyers contended that by treating the money requirement as one to be legally exacted, Commissioner Williams had created a new means of exclusion.[47] Williams further compounded the legal difficulties for the immigrants when he discounted the value of the aliens' foreign assets and refused to consider any proffers of aid from friends or relatives as sufficient evidence that the immigrants would not become public charges. Accepting bonds would have made such assurance as sworn aid legally justifiable, but the Commissioner would not follow this procedure on the grounds that none of the American associates of the immigrants was legally bound to support them. Kohler and Elkus thereupon noted that the statute did not limit exclusion to those people who had relatives or kin here, but merely limited admission to those who might become public charges by virtue of age, lack of occupation or physical disability.

All these contentions proved valueless. The Commissioner, in recommending deportation, omitted any evidence of aid offered the

[44] *Ibid.*, p. 161.
[45] *Ibid.*, p. 163.
[46] *Ibid.*, pp. 160–176.
[47] *Ibid.*, pp. 165–166 and 169.

aliens by American citizens and neglected to reckon the value of the immigrants' cash or property abroad. The results of the Commissioner's policy of omission were compounded, when a colleague of his, in proposing deportation, relied on statements that had not been part of the original inquiry. Acting Commissioner Byron F. Uhl, in communicating with the Secretary of Commerce Charles Nagel, maintained that one alien would be going to a congested area, that another had no decent residence, and that still a third did not appear sufficiently robust. In this way, local officials could knowingly have prejudiced the views of the Secretary of Commerce, whose decision in such matters was final.[48] In having thus been denied the semblance of a fair hearing, the defendants' rights of due process had been abridged, and the attorneys urged that public charge accusations against their clients be dropped on habeas corpus proceedings.[49]

Judge Learned Hand, before whom the Skuratowski brief was to have been presented, never heard the case. Instead, the four aliens were given a rehearing before the Ellis Island Board of Inquiry and admitted on the basis that work had been found for them. Any investigations concerning the administration of Ellis Island which the brief might have uncovered were thereby abandoned. This was in conjunction with the Court's earlier decision that a hearing would be granted only on condition that habeas corpus proceedings were quashed.[50]

In the Skuratowski brief, Jewish attorneys had settled for the rescue of specific aliens. As matters stood, no principles had been enunciated by the Court, no statutes so amended as to clarify the entire issue of those who arrived under the suspicious shadow of the public charge or assisted immigrant provisions of the law. One year after filing the Skuratowski brief, Jewish spokesmen for immigrant rights had another opporunity to test their contentions. This time the results were more promising in theory, but ultimately failed in practice.

In the summer of 1910, the Department of Commerce and Labor strictly enforced the ban on assisted immigration against Jewish immigrants coming to Galveston.[51] Part of an immigrant re-distribution system established by Jacob H. Schiff back in 1907, the Galveston Movement had become both the shining hope of American

---

[48] Ibid., p. 162.

[49] Ibid., pp. 166–167 and 175.

[50] "Protecting Immigrant Rights," American Hebrew, vol. LXXXV, no. 12 (July 22, 1909), pp. 296–297.

[51] AJYB, vol. XII (1910–1911 — 5671), pp. 129–131.

leaders who sought to deflect Jewish immigration from the Eastern
cities, and the goal of European committees of immigration who
wished to further Jewish settlement in the American Southwest.[52]
But neither of these intended aims fully materialized.[53] The depression of 1907 and its aftereffects resulted in fewer Jewish arrivals.[54]
By 1909, any increase in Jewish newcomers was shortlived, for soon
thereafter, the Department of Commerce and Labor applied its
provisions against assisted immigrants and public charges with
particular vigor in the Galveston area.[55] This action was taken
despite an opinion obtained from Solicitor Charles Earl of the
Department of Commerce and Labor, at Wolf's behest, which indicated that an immigrant would not be liable to become a public
charge were he dependent upon private rather than public charities.[56]

Having aroused the ire of Jewish public opinion in the Galveston
matter,[57] the Department of Commerce and Labor then called on
Simon Wolf to intervene in its controversy with the Jewish Information Bureau[58] of the Galveston project. In a letter to Assistant
Secretary of Commerce and Labor, Benjamin W. Cable, who himself had originally lodged complaints of illegal activities against the
Bureau, Wolf rebuked those Anglo-Jewish journals representing
"ardent advocates of immigration" who flouted immigration regulations. Wolf was certain that the Department of Commerce and
Labor had liberally and justly construed the immigration laws of
this country. Yet, at the same time, Wolf adroitly reminded Cable
of the basic Jewish position on the public charge and assisted immigrant aspects of the law.[59]

Such diplomatic hedging was absent from Kohler's legal memorandum which accompanied Wolf's communication to Cable. Instead, Kohler emphasized the organized efforts of the Jewish com-

[52] M. Wischnitzer, *To Dwell in Safety*, pp. 127-129; *AJYB*, vol. IX (1907-1908 —
5668), pp. 538-539.

[53] D. M. Bressler, *op. cit.*, pp. 16-18.

[54] *AJYB*, vol. X (1908-1909 — 5669), pp. 191-192.

[55] M. J. Kohler to Mortimer Schiff, Oct. 14, 1925, Kohler Papers, AJHS.

[56] *Thirty-sixth Annual Report of the Board of Delegates*, p. 6394; *Selected Addresses
and Papers of Simon Wolf* (Cincinnati, 1926), p. 301; see *supra*, p. 60, note 14.

[57] *AJYB*, vol. XIII (1911-1912 — 5672), pp. 129 ff.; *Thirty-seventh Annual Report of
the Board of Delegates*, pp. 6529-6530.

[58] M. J. Kohler to Mortimer Schiff, Oct. 14, 1925, Kohler Papers, AJHS; *Thirty-
seventh Annual Report of the Board of Delegates*, p. 6529; S. Wolf to M. J. Kohler, Feb. 9,
1910, Kohler Papers, AJHS.

[59] "The Galveston Case, Correspondence between Simon Wolf and Secretary Benjamin
W. Cable. Legal Aspect by M. J. Kohler," *Jewish Exponent*, vol. LI, no. 17 (Aug. 5,
1910), p. 1.

munity to fulfill the Government's intention of preventing immigrant employment in depressed areas. The purpose of the Jewish Information Bureau, Kohler maintained, was to deflect immigrants to other ports of entry so as to ease the competition with native American labor in Eastern cities. Kohler argued that the whole purpose of the 1907 Immigration Act was precisely the prevention of such unwholesome competition. The provisions of that bill, in expanding and consolidating the earlier Alien Contract Labor Laws included a ban on the importation of foreign labor, brought here either on a contractual basis, abetted by advertising abroad, or by means of paid transportation to this country. In this connection Kohler stressed that no inducements of any kind had been offered to Jewish immigrants. They had determined to migrate to America in any event, unsolicited by offers of specific employment, or by having others pay their fares for them. Under no circumstances had there ever been any evidence that the Jewish Information Bureau resorted to advertising abroad to recruit Jewish aliens for particular tasks. Kohler sustained his argument by citing several analogous opinions of Attorney General George W. Wickersham who claimed that only a specific promise of employment constituted a violation of the Alien Contract Labor Law. On the contrary, Wickersham observed that the law clearly distinguished between contract laborers deemed an economic menace to the society they were entering, and such morally fit immigrants as were needed to develop the resources of unsettled areas. The Attorney General was certain that this distinction was likewise inherent in the Immigration Act of 1907.

The second half of Kohler's memorandum included a Supreme Court opinion which stressed the desirability of such aliens who upon arrival were helped financially by friends or private agencies. This was the basis of Kohler's assumption that in determining whether a person was or was not likely to become a public charge, all the agents at his disposal, including such representatives as may not have been legally bound to support him were to be taken into account. To prove this point Kohler then cited the ruling by Solicitor Earl, previously referred to, that private or personal aid would not subject aliens to public charge or assisted immigrant accusations.[60]

In his response, Cable refused to commit himself to any legal interpretation, but insisted that Jewish aliens were entering Galveston both as assisted immigrants and as public charges.[61] At a conference on the matter before Jewish representatives and Federal

[60] *Ibid.*, pp. 2 and 8; see *supra*, p. 60, note 14.
[61] "The Galveston Case . . .," p. 8.

immigration officials, Jacob H. Schiff wasted no words. In marked contrast to Wolf's deferential communication to Cable, Schiff frankly observed that neither he nor the Jewish Information Bureau were on trial, but that the Secretary of Commerce and Labor, Charles Nagel, the Assistant Secretary, Benjamin W. Cable, and the entire department were. Schiff cautioned Nagel that America would rue the day were the Galveston project

> so conducive to the best interests of the country ... throttled by the Department's unreasonable obstacles.[62]

Secretary Nagel and Attorney General Wickersham overruled Cable in favor of the course taken by the Jewish Information Bureau.[63] Unlike the Skuratowski brief, where the Jewish view of the assisted immigrant and public charge had gone unheeded, here it had been vindicated. But it proved to be an empty victory. As late as 1921 Jewish representatives had to refute charges that Jewish institutions were engaged in illegally assisting immigration to this land.[64] More immediately, Kohler complained that after the decision in the Galveston matter immigration officials at that port of entry resorted to illegal methods for enforcing exclusions, by applying overly stringent standards of admission. Kohler admitted there was nothing in the immigration record to bear out his contention,[65] but he was convinced that the practice of rejection by petty immigration officials was such as to discourage Jewish immigrants from hazarding a longer, costlier voyage to the Southwest. When World War I began, the work of the Jewish Information Bureau was finally abandoned.[66]

The outcome of the Galveston controversy was still pending, when, in November, 1910, representatives of the B'nai B'rith, the American Jewish Committee, and the Board of Delegates presented their written recommendations for the revision of the existing immigration laws to the Congressional Immigration Commission, a body which had been called into being by the Immigration Act of 1907. Led by Senator William P. Dillingham of Vermont, its purpose was to investigate all matters pertaining to immigration. In their memoranda, Jewish societies contested many proposed restrictions and

---

[62] M. J. Kohler to Mortimer Schiff, Oct. 14, 1925, Kohler Papers, AJHS.

[63] *Ibid.*

[64] C. Reznikoff, *op. cit.*, vol. I, p. 196.

[65] M. J. Kohler, "A Vital Immigration Decision," *American Hebrew*, vol. XCVII, no. 26 (Oct. 29, 1915), p. 710; see also David M. Bressler to Jacob Billikopf, Feb. 20, 1914; S. Wolf to M. J. Kohler, Jan. 2, 1914; S. Wolf to Jacob H. Schiff, Jan. 5, and April 25, 1914, Schiff Collection, AJA.

[66] M. J. Kohler to Mortimer Schiff, Oct. 14, 1925, Kohler Papers, AJHS.

again emphasized the need for a more just interpretation of the
public charge statute, a matter which would need no further clarification were the rights of aliens to certain procedures in law secured.
Specific reference was had to the privileges inherent in the due
process and religious liberty clauses of the Constitution. These
included the right to the advice of counsel, to the proper use of
evidence, to greater liberties in the taking of bonds, and to the
abandonment of any racial or religious classification system for
incoming aliens.[67]

These written statements were the distillation of arguments presented before the Commission the previous spring. Those who had
appeared to give testimony in March, 1910, included Wolf, Kohler,
Elkus, Cyrus Sulzberger, Louis Marshall, Harry Cutler, representing the B'nai B'rith, the Board of Delegates, and the American
Jewish Committee, and Leon Sanders, President of the Hebrew
Immigrant Aid Society. Wolf again extolled the wise discretion
practiced by Federal officials in executing the law, though at one
point he did admit that immigration statutes frequently were administered in a drastic manner. He then proceeded from this para-
dox of a Federal department engaged in the maladministration of
immigration statutes whose officials practiced a wise discretion, to a
general plea for a more liberal immigration policy.[68] He described
the assets of immigration to this land, and protested such intended
legislation as a literacy bill, an increase in the head tax, and the
extension of time in which it would become feasible to deport alien
criminals.[69] The others, in their presentations, pursued different
aspects of the problems created by an intensified restrictionist
policy. Cyrus Sulzberger proved by statistics that Jewish immigrants neither engaged extensively in the white slave traffic nor in
other criminal activities.[70] Marshall expatiated on the progress
Jewish immigrants had made towards Americanization, and praised
their achievements in the art of agricultural and industrial retrain-
ing.[71] Sanders issued general statements opposing the same restrictive policies referred to by Wolf.[72] Cutler reiterated the benefits to
be derived from immigration to this country,[73] while Elkus, in
testifying upon the construction of the term "public charge,"

[67] *AJYB*, vol. XIII (1911–1912 — 5672), pp. 315–334.
[68] *USICR*, vol. XLI, pp. 183–184.
[69] *AJYB*, vol. XII (1910–1911 — 5671), pp. 19–20.
[70] *Ibid.*, pp. 21–37.
[71] *Ibid.*, pp. 39–47.
[72] *Ibid.*, p. 61.
[73] *Ibid.*, pp. 86–88.

strengthened Kohler's specific recommendations for amending existing law.[74] These called for eliminating an indiscriminate use of the public charge accusation, a process which hitherto had led to unjust applications of the assisted immigrant proviso, had curtailed the use of bonding facilities, and had hampered opportunities for fair hearings.[75]

The response of the Immigration Commission to all this testimony was harsh. Public charge provisions were retained, while various means for limiting immigration by quota systems, increases in the head tax, and discriminatory levies were suggested.[76] Such proposals were based on the Commission's interpretation of economic conditions drawn from the panic year of 1907-1908, when inadequate wages and an oversupply of workers made the furor to decrease the number of newcomers seem even more urgent. In preparing its report, the Commission overlooked the fact that hard times normally were accompanied by a decline in immigration, with a comparable increase in those departing these shores. Instead, the Commission sought to justify a continuing relationship between an industrial or economic malaise and an augmented influx of aliens.[77] The tenor of its conclusions, published by 1911, denied most of the suggestions made by Jewish and other minority groups given in testimony before it. The generally repressive tone of the proposed legislation was relieved only by suggestions that hearings before a Board of Special Inquiry ought not to be secret, and that an office of an additional Assistant Secretary of Commerce and Labor be created to aid in reviewing appeals.[78]

The efforts expended by Jewish representatives on a brief that was not heard, on principles agreed to but not practiced, and on recommendations that were largely ignored, were indeed discouraging. This, then, was the background for a confrontation in 1911 between Max Kohler and Charles Nagel, Secretary of Commerce and Labor.[79] In an unguarded moment, Wolf let old inter-Jewish organizational rivalry get the better of him. Having obtained Secretary Nagel as a speaker for a convention of the Union of American Hebrew Congregations, he confessed, was a decided

---

[74] *Ibid.*, pp. 61–64.

[75] *Ibid.*, pp. 70–86.

[76] *Thirty-ninth Annual Report of the Board of Delegates*, Appendix A, pp. 7164–7174.

[77] M. J. Kohler, "Immigration" *American Israelite*, vol. LVIII, no. 32 (Feb. 8, 1912), p. 1.

[78] *Thirty-seventh Annual Report of the Board of Delegates*, p. 6536.

[79] Max J. Kohler, Charles Nagel and Jacob H. Schiff, *The Immigration Question* (New York, 1911).

"scoop" over the American Jewish Committee.[80] But he need hardly have gloated. Seen in retrospect the dialogue between Kohler and Nagel was frank and painful. Kohler again repeated his old contentions of immigration statutes poorly administered, and of arbitrary decisions with no foundations in law indulged in by doctrinaires in office.[81] Kohler claimed that much bureaucratic pettifogging in the immigration system even extended to inspectors on the line, who, upon disagreeing with Williams' old ruling of a $25.00 cash minimum, were deemed guilty of insubordination and summarily dismissed. The newer aspects of Kohler's charges against the whole Federal immigration apparatus amounted to an almost personal attack on Commissioner Williams and his subordinates, who, he alleged, were motivated by an anti-Semitic bias.[82]

In the light of Kohler's criticism Secretary Nagel observed how unprepared he was for the welcome extended to him by the Chairman of the session, Jacob H. Schiff. Then, responding to Kohler, Nagel cited his own personal record with its inclinations to frequent revocations of deportation orders, and asked to be allowed sufficient latitude to interpret immigration cases without relying on past written opinions, opinions which Kohler felt were absolutely necessary to safeguard legal ethics. Nagel, however, was fearful lest such established precedents would lead to unduly conservative immigration rulings.[83]

Having explained the differences in approach between Kohler and himself, Nagel wryly noted that Jewish societies, acting as counsel for the immigrants, ought not to expect him always to accede to their demands. He marked Wolf as the immigrants' advocate par excellence, who, in contrast to the attitudes taken by Jewish agencies, would, upon defeat, graciously accept the Government's point of view.[84]

Nagel had accurately described the manner in which Wolf approached those in command. While they undoubtedly pleased Nagel, Wolf's methods were reminiscent of the operations of the court Jew. Since Wolf always bargained in delicate terms and by means of muted comparisons, he was frightened by the candidness of Kohler's charges against Williams. Not only did Wolf deem them impolitic,[85] but they also sullied Williams' reputation, which Wolf

---

[80] S. Wolf to Max J. Kohler, Jan. 9, 1911, Wolf Papers, AJHS.

[81] M. J. Kohler et al., *The Immigration Question*, p. 6.

[82] *Ibid.*, pp. 6–7.

[83] *Ibid.*, pp. 33–34 and 39–42.   [84] *Ibid.*, p. 42.

[85] S. Wolf to M. J. Kohler, Jan. 9, 1911, Wolf Papers, AJHS; *Thirty-sixth Annual Report of the Board of Delegates*, p. 6394.

was prepared to defend.[86] Williams' methods of immigrant administration had drawn the fire of other critics for many years, including the powerful German-American Alliance,[87] but Wolf placed "no stock" in such "wholesale" accusations against the Commissioner. Instead, Wolf urged spokesmen for immigrant rights to effect closer contacts with Federal representatives of Ellis Island.[88]

His opinion of the Commissioner having been what it was, it was natural for Wolf to have viewed the problem of increasing deportations differently from Kohler. Wolf did acknowledge an upsurge in the number of aliens accused of being public charges, or possessing poor physiques,[89] characterizations which produced the same results. But in his analysis of immigration statistics, he noted that the proportion of Jewish exclusions to admissions, was less than that of the total number of exclusions to admissions. Accordingly, Wolf proudly pointed to the success he and his Board of Delegates had achieved in reversing deportation orders for as many as eighty-five per cent of the cases brought to their attention.[90] Kohler, relying on the same statistics, reached a different conclusion. The matter of increasing deportations on an overall basis from 1907 to 1910 he viewed as sufficient reason to amend the laws. If the Jewish group had proportionately fewer exclusions, then here was ample proof that it formed a better than average class of immigrants. Instead of agreeing to Wolf's suggestion that the Board of Delegates be credited for its success in reversing deportation orders, Kohler merely noted the Board's opposition to more stringent application of immigration statutes. His plans for liberalizing the immigration laws were far more radical than any Wolf would have envisaged.[91]

Ultimately, neither Wolf's penchant for stance, nor Kohler's concern with substance altered Federal policy on immigration. Wolf's policy of personal diplomacy did result in the revocation of many deportation proceedings. Through his efforts during the First World War, there were instances when the Department of Labor relented

[86] S. Wolf to Charles Nagel, Oct. 19, 1911; Charles Nagel to S. Wolf, Oct. 18, 1911, Wolf Papers, AJHS.

[87] United States Immigration and Naturalization Committee (Sixty-second Congress, First Session, *Hearings on House Res. no. 166, Authorizing Committee on Immigration and Naturalization to Investigate Office of Immigration Commissioner of the Port of New York*, May 29, 1911, pp. 4–11 and 16–26; Elting E. Morison [ed.], *The Letters of Theodore Roosevelt* (Cambridge, Mass., 1951–1954), vol. III, p. 659, note 1.

[88] *Thirty-sixth Annual Report of the Board of Delegates*, pp. 6394–6395.

[89] *Thirty-seventh Annual Report of the Board of Delegates, supra*, p. 6525.

[90] S. Wolf to M. J. Kohler, Jan. 9, 1911, Wolf Papers, AJHS.

[91] M. J. Kohler et al., *The Immigration Question*, pp. 3–4.

sufficiently to admit aliens not on bond, but merely on assurances given by Jewish charitable agencies.[92] Such occasions were to be reckoned as exceptions to the law; no principles had been modified.

At one time, in 1915, Kohler's impassioned appeal for sound legal ethics received justification in the courts. In the matter of Gegiow vs. Uhl, Kohler's view that the courts have the right to review cases of immigrant exclusion, provided the question at issue was one of law, and not a statement of fact, was unanimously approved by the Supreme Court. The highest court of the land, in the same case, also sustained Kohler's theory that economic conditions prevailing at an immigrant's destination need have no bearing on his liability to become a public charge.[93] But by 1917, Congress so worded its Immigration Act as to nullify that portion of the decision dealing with the economic nature of the area to be settled by the immigrant.[94]

The inexorable march to restrictionism continued apace. The formation of a separate Department of Labor to be responsible for immigration matters confirmed the worst fears of Jewish leaders. Publicly Wolf unqualifiedly praised the new Secretary of Labor's methods for administering the immigration law,[95] but privately he, together with Schiff and Kohler, were disheartened at the stringency with which Secretary William B. Wilson interpreted the public charge or assisted immigrant provisos.[96] On one occasion Wolf himself even admitted the hopelessness of his hitherto well-tried methods. Accompanying Secretary Wilson to a B'nai B'rith convention, or engaging him in private pourparlers on the immigration issue was of no avail.[97] The Secretary was convinced that a liberal immigration policy intensified employment problems and was prepared to adhere to the letter rather than the spirit of the law.[98]

[92] *Thirty-ninth Annual Report of the Board of Delegates*, p. 6968; *Fortieth Annual Report ...*, p. 7344; *Forty-first Annual Report ...*, p. 7647; *Forty-second Annual Report ...*, p. 7935; *Forty-third Annual Report ...*, p. 8006; *Forty-fourth Annual Report ...*, p. 8269, and *Forty-fifth Annual Report ...*, p. 8425.

[93] Gegiow vs. Uhl, 239 U. S. Reports 8 (1915), cited in Abbott, *op. cit.*, pp. 254–256; "A Vital Immigration Decision," *American Hebrew*, vol. XCVII, no. 26 (Oct. 29, 1915), p. 710; M. J. Kohler to Mortimer Schiff, Oct. 14, 1925, Kohler Papers, AJHS.

[94] E. Abbott, *op. cit.*, p. 216, note 2; Roy L. Garis, *Immigration Restriction: A Study of the Opposition to and Regulation of Immigration into the United States* (New York, 1927), p. 126.

[95] *Fortieth Annual Report of the Board of Delegates*, p. 7346.

[96] S. Wolf to M. J. Kohler, Jan. 2, 1914, to Jacob H. Schiff, Jan. 5, and 8, 1914; Jacob H. Schiff to S. Wolf, Jan. 6, 1914 and March 7, 1914, Schiff Collection, AJA.

[97] S. Wolf to J. H. Schiff, Jan. 8, 1914, Schiff Collection, AJA.

[98] *Ibid.*, and S. Wolf to J. H. Schiff, Feb. 11, 1914; S. Wolf to M. J. Kohler, Jan. 2, 1914, Schiff Collection, *supra* AJA.

II

LITERACY TESTS AND IMMIGRANT CLASSIFICATION

Though World War I witnessed a diminution in the number of immigrant arrivals, the effects of a depression in 1914, coupled with America's involvement in the conflict later on, released a whole set of nationalist values to plague the alien. With fewer newcomers reaching these shores during the war years, American xenophobists vented their spleen on Jews and Catholics, on Americans of German origin and other so-called hyphenates, and on native American radicals whose image was linked to foreign ideologies.[99] Even the movement to Americanize the stranger, which had its impetus in the progressivism of the early twentieth century, lost some of its humaneness. No longer was the doctrine of immigrant contributions, of cultural diversities forming a unified America applicable. In its place, whole-hearted conformity, a complete sloughing off of old-world customs, became the requisite for undying allegiance to the United States.[100]

This zeal for fashioning a monolithic America, prepared to exclude the outsider reached its peak after the War. Such a passion was exacerbated by industrial upheavals which pitted an alienated capital class against a rising labor movement and both ultimately against the stranger in their midst.[101]

In this atmosphere, first of frenetic loyalties exercised during the War, and of sharpened inter-group conflict emerging after it, the two main weapons of the restrictionists were at last successfully forged. In 1917, after many attempts, Congress passed a literacy test over the President's veto.[102] Four years later, a quota system of immigrant admission, itself the outcome of classifying immigrants by race or religion became the law of the land.[103]

---

[99] J. Higham, pp. 208-214; Louis L. Gerson, *The Hyphenate in Recent American Politics and Diplomacy* (Lawrence, Kansas, 1964), pp. 64-68; Gustavus Myers, *History of Bigotry in the United States* [revised edition, Henry M. Christman, ed.] (New York, 1960), pp. 199-225; Edward H. Flannery, *The Anguish of the Jews* (New York, 1965), pp. 255-256; *AJYB*, vols. XIX (1917-1918 — 5678), pp. 471-472, and XXI (1919-1920 — 5680), pp. 641-648; George M. Stephenson, *A History of American Immigration* (New York, 1926), pp. 209-214.

[100] J. Higham, *op. cit.*, pp. 197-199, 207-215 and 219-227; G. M. Stephenson, *op. cit.*, pp. 217-221, 225-231 and 235-237.

[101] Kate Holladay Claghorn, *The Immigrant's Day in Court* (New York, 1923), pp. 271-281; G. M. Stephenson, *op. cit.*, p. 161; J. Higham, *op. cit.*, pp. 225-226.

[102] *Congressional Record*, Sixty-fourth Congress, Second Session, pp. 316, 2443, 2456 and 2629; R. L. Garis, *op. cit.*, p. 125; *AJYB*, vol. XX (1918-1919 — 5679), pp. 377-378.

[103] R. L. Garis, *op. cit.*, pp. 142-149; E. Abbott, *op. cit.*, pp. 240-242.

From the earliest days of their concern with the Federal aspects of immigration policy, Jewish leaders had to contend with these two pet theories of the restrictionists; the literacy test, and the matter of immigrant classification. Their struggle with these restrictive aspects of immigration law had of necessity to be different from their battle on the public charge issue. Seeking a just interpretation of the latter statute was as much a matter of principle as delaying or finally attempting to overthrow educational requirements for immigrants, and rejecting the practice of tabulating them by race or religion. Yet there was always the possibility that the urgent threat to deportation posed by the assisted immigrant or public charge accusations could have been overcome by posting bonds or securing a reversal of deportation orders without a continuous recourse to abstract concepts of justice and ethics. Literacy and classification requirements, however, presented conditions whose future implications had always to be refuted by reference to principle. There may never have been sufficient proof that categorizing immigrants as "Hebrew" or requiring them to read a passage in some recognized language resulted in mass exclusions, yet Kohler, Elkus, Marshall, and Wolf could easily have sustained their arguments that immigrant tabulation lead to prejudice and that educational tests made for discriminatory practices.

Interestingly enough, the literacy measure did have racial connotations. Its sponsors viewed it as an inoffensive but adequate means of limiting unwanted races from coming to these shores.[104] Led by Senator Henry Cabot Lodge of Massachusetts, the early attempts of the 1890's to pass restrictive legislation by means of a literacy test failed for the same reasons that were to make successive ventures miss the mark until nationalism reached its crest with America's entry into the war. Up to that time, whenever the literacy question arose in Congress, either the economics of the times were not propitious, or immigrant pressures combined with political considerations successfully hindered its passage. This was true in 1897, in 1906–1907, and again in 1914–1915.[105]

In 1897, immigrant groups themselves, led in part by the German language press,[106] helped defeat the literacy bill. Republican leaders

[104] *Selections from the Correspondence of Theodore Roosevelt and Henry Cabot Lodge* (New York, 1925), vol. II, p. 158; Henry Cabot Lodge, "The Restriction of Immigration," Speech before the Senate (March 16, 1896), pp. 3–5; R. L. Garis, *op. cit.*, pp. 131–132; G. M. Stephenson, *op. cit.*, pp. 161–162; *Congressional Record*, Sixty-second Congress, Second Session, pp. 3536 and 4794; Third Session, pp. 2035–2036; Sixty-third Congress, Second Session, p. 2597.

[105] J. Higham, *op. cit.*, pp. 128–129, 162–163 and 192; see also L. Gerson, *op. cit.*, p. 68.

[106] *Congressional Record*, Fifty-fourth Congress, Second Session, p. 376.

realized that President William McKinley's success was due in no small measure to the midwestern immigrant vote,[107] a force more powerful in the last analysis than the combined efforts of Senators Lodge, William Chandler of New Hampshire, and the Immigration Restriction League, created in Boston in 1894 by native New Englanders. The League had been borne hard on the heels of a vast depression accompanied by an increasing antipathy to immigrants. But Lodge and his colleagues were unable to capitalize on this event. Despite a Republican majority in Congress in 1897, Lodge's literacy bill in its final conference report won by a narrow margin,[108] and President Grover Cleveland, because of his own attitude to immigration, vetoed the educational qualification.[109] In those years Wolf duly recorded his opposition to any literacy proposals and claimed that both his discussions with Senator Jacob Harold Gallinger of New Hampshire and his meeting with the President helped sway the course of events in favor of the immigrants.[110]

During the 1906–1907 Congressional season, Jewish rejection of any literacy requirement was both more detailed and more determined. This time, the newly formed American Jewish Committee under Marshall's tutelage, and the Liberal Immigration League, organized on a non-sectarian basis, but with Jewish leadership at its helm,[111] joined with Wolf and his Board of Delegates to defeat Lodge's latest attempt in the literacy field. This time, a combination of circumstances, themselves quite separate from any specifically Jewish interests, helped save the day for the immigrants and their allies.

Spurred on by the demands of organized labor, Senators Lodge and Dillingham introduced a literacy bill in the Senate, while Lodge's son-in-law, Representative Augustus P. Gardner of Massachusetts, brought its counterpart to the House. But those who opposed an educational test now found their chief champion in Joseph Gurney Cannon of Illinois, the powerful Speaker of the House. Cannon was first and foremost an able politician, keenly

[107] *Ibid.*, pp. 372–373.

[108] J. Higham, *op. cit.*, p. 104.

[109] Cited in E. Abbott, *op. cit.*, pp. 199–201; Grover Cleveland denied that he ever regretted his veto action. See *The Letters of Theodore Roosevelt*, vol. V, p. 294.

[110] *Twenty-fourth Annual Report of the Board of Delegates*, pp. 3777–3778; S. Wolf, *Presidents I Have Known*, pp. 151–152.

[111] *AJYB*, vol. IX (1907–1908 — 5668), p. 537; James H. Patten to Cyrus Adler, Feb. 11, 1914, Adler Papers, AAJ Committee; see also C. Adler to H. Friedenwald, Jan. 30, and Feb. 18, 1907, and H. Friedenwald to C. Adler, Feb. 20, 1907, Adler Papers, AAJ Committee.

attuned to the needs of the mining district which he represented. Midwestern employers of foreign workers were among Cannon's constituents. He was not likely to disappoint his followers, particularly those business and industrial leaders who in the midst of revived commercial activities were pressing for easily controlled immigrant labor. By the summer of 1906, Cannon successfully outwitted Representative Gardner in a legislative manoeuver by which the House of Representatives supported an amendment to the 1906 Immigration Bill which would provide for an investigative commission in lieu of a literacy test.[112] For the ensuing conference on the bill with the Senate, which had already endorsed Lodge's proposals, Cannon selected two members of the House Committee on Immigration and Naturalization who had been opposed to the literacy bill from the outset. Representatives William S. Bennett and Jacob Ruppert, Jr. of New York represented large immigrant populations; political considerations for these legislators were sufficient to prevent them from following the dictates of the restrictionists. Their presence at the conference was to disallow any attempts by representatives of the Senate to restore the literacy test to the House version of the bill. The bill then remained conveniently deadlocked in conference until the beginning of February, 1907.[113] By then Representative Gardner re-introduced his proposal, only to have it buried in the Rules Committee,[114] while protagonists for the immigrant, including members of the American Jewish Committee bent all their efforts to prevent the measure from coming to the floor.[115] It was during this period that Wolf received assurances from the Speaker of the House that no literacy bill would pass.[116]

At this juncture, the Executive branch of the Government intervened in the immigration scene for reasons of state. As the head of his party, President Theodore Roosevelt was likewise aware of capital's renewed demands for workers,[117] and knew well the political

---

[112] B. Bolles, op. cit., p. 73; Henry P. Fairchild, "The Making of the Literacy Test," *Quarterly Journal of Economics*, vol. XXXI (1917), p. 455; *Congressional Record*, Sixty-second Congress, Third Session, p. 862.

[113] C. Adler to H. Friedenwald, Jan. 10 and 28, 1907; H. Friedenwald to C. Adler, Jan. 23 and 29, 1907; J. Hampton Moore to Isador Sobel, Jan. 28, 1907; Arthur Bates to Isador Sobel, Jan. 28, 1907; Julius Kahn to Cyrus Adler, Feb. 2, 1907, Adler Papers, AAJ Committee; B. Bolles, op. cit., pp. 72-75.

[114] B. Bolles, op. cit., p. 76; C. Adler to H. Friedenwald, Feb. 3, 1907, Adler Papers, AAJ Committee.

[115] C. Adler to H. Friedenwald, Jan. 28 and Feb. 3, 4, 5, 6, 12, and 18, 1907; Lucius N. Littauer to C. Adler, Feb. 11, 1907, H. Friedenwald to C. Adler, Feb. 7, 1907, Adler Papers, AAJ Committee.

[116] H. Friedenwald to C. Adler, Jan. 23, 1907, Adler Papers, AAJ Committee.

[117] *The Letters of Theodore Roosevelt*, vol. V, pp. 285-286.

lesson of retaining the good will of the foreign-born among the electorate.[118] But a more immediate objective outweighed even these considerations. On the West Coast, the forced segregation of Japanese children from the San Francisco public schools had prompted the Mikado's Government to hint at demands for retaliation. Since there was no Japanese vote of any consequence in America, the President and his Secretary of State realized the benefits of a voluntary agreement with Japan by which that country would, seemingly of its own accord, bar its nationals from reaching the continental United States via Hawaii. In return, Japanese children resident in San Francisco would be permitted to attend school with their white colleagues. In this way, the Japanese Government, by controlling its own emigrants would avoid a national loss of face, while Japanese children in the States would not be discriminated against. At the same time, native American clamor against Japanese entry to this country would be stilled.[119] Secretary of State Elihu Root thereupon asked the Speaker of the House to add a Japanese exclusion amendment to the general immigration bill. Cannon was prepared to comply only on condition that the literacy bill for European immigrants be abandoned.[120] Under the circumstances, it was understandable that William Loeb, the Presidential Secretary, should have suggested to Wolf that he write a letter to President Roosevelt urging the appointment of an investigative commission as a substitute for the educational requirement.[121] Wolf's request and those of other anti-restrictionists[122] were granted, not because the President himself may have had a change of heart concerning the literacy test, and now opposed what he had previously favored,[123] but simply because here was a diplomatic im-

---

[118] *Ibid.*, vol. III, pp. 254-255, 411-412, 524 and 659-660; vol. V, pp. 360-361, 393, 439-440, 453-454 and 461b.; vol. VI, pp. 1247n., and 1276n.

[119] B. Bolles, *op. cit.*, p. 75; Evelyn Tupper and George McReynolds, *Japan in American Public Opinion* (New York, 1937), pp. 32-37; *The Letters of Theodore Roosevelt*, vol. V, pp. 530, 532-533, 537, 541-542, 589, 608-615 and 618-619; Stephenson, *op. cit.*, pp. 269-271; Garis, *op. cit.*, p. 314. Despite his annoyance at the injustice accorded the Japanese in California, Roosevelt himself was vigorously opposed to any mass Japanese immigration to this country.

[120] B. Bolles, *op. cit.*, pp. 76-77; H. Friedenwald to Mayer Sulzberger, Feb. 13, 1907, Sulzberger Papers, AAJ Committee.

[121] C. Adler to H. Friedenwald, Jan. 28, 1907, Adler Papers, AAJ Committee.

[122] See Manoel F. Behar, *Our National Gates, Shut, Ajar, Or Open?*, National Liberal Immigration League Publication, no. 204 (May, 1916), p. 6, for indication that the League petitioned President Roosevelt in January of 1907 to create a commission in place of the literacy amendment.

[123] R. L. Garis, *op. cit.*, p. 102; *The Letters of Theodore Roosevelt*, vol. V, pp. 285-286

passe to be avoided through the introduction of an extraneous element in the general issue of Southeastern European immigration into the United States. Cannon did not yield in his demands that the educational issue be waived, but Senator Lodge agreed to Secretary Root's request that a Japanese exclusion agreement take precedence over any literacy measure.[124] The bill, as it finally passed, met Cannon's conditions. Yet Cannon's victory was not complete. His tactics earned him the enmity of Samuel Gompers,[125] himself an immigrant Jew, who, as President of the American Federation of Labor saw eye to eye with Senator Lodge on the issue of immigration restriction.[126] Nor had Lodge failed his followers completely. President Roosevelt's promise to Wolf to appoint an investigative commission merely postponed the inevitable. Some four years and forty-seven volumes later, the recommendations of the Immigration Commission centered around a proposal for

> a reading and writing test as the most feasible single method of restricting undesirable immigration.[127]

During the course of those four years several factors contributed to the growing popularity of the literacy test. As the effects of the 1907–1908 depression wore off,[128] more immigrants from Southern and Eastern Europe again came streaming to these shores. Though the majority remained in the northern and midwestern industrial areas, those newcomers who trekked to the South and West encountered increased racist and nationalist hostilities in both locales.[129] In the South, the foreigners intruded an element of doubt

---

and 360–361; B. Bolles, *op. cit.*, p. 70; *Congressional Record*, Sixty-second Congress, Second Session, p. 3536.

[124] B. Bolles, *op. cit.*, pp. 76–77; see *The Letters of Theodore Roosevelt*, vol. V, pp. 556–557, for the view that in 1907, the South acceded to administration demands for Japanese exclusion only because the terms of the 1907 Immigration Act as they applied to contract labor would be so interpreted as not to harm the South economically, which then was witnessing a brief industrial revival.

[125] William Rea Gwinn, *Uncle Joe Cannon, Archfoe of Insurgency* (New York, 1947), pp. 113–115, 129, 133–135 and 150–151; B. Bolles, *op. cit.*, pp. 112 and 133–137. Besides the matter of immigration restriction, Cannon and Gompers opposed each other on many political and economic issues, including the use of the injunction against labor unions.

[126] Samuel Gompers, *Seventy Years of Life and Labor* [revised edition] (New York, 1957), p. 37; *Selections from the Correspondence of Theodore Roosevelt and Henry Cabot Lodge*, vol. II, p. 204; B. Bolles, *op. cit.*, pp. 68–70, 71 and 73; *Congressional Record*, Fifty-ninth Congress, First Session, pp. 9171 and 9189.

[127] Cited in E. Abbott, *op. cit.*, p. 210; in *Thirty-seventh Annual Report of the Board of Delegates*, p. 6539.

[128] *AJYB*, vol. X (1908–1909 — 5669), pp. 191–192.

[129] *Congressional Record*, Fifty-ninth Congress, First Session, pp. 551–555, 7293–7295

into the pattern of white supremacy established after the Civil War. By being white, but working side by side with Negroes, immigrants from Southeastern Europe, whose own Caucasian purity was frequently called into question, were contributing to a revolution in hitherto accepted racial standards.[130] Such standards had earlier provided the bases for Populist and Democratic agrarian reformers to re-enforce the southern white farmers in their morbidly anti-alien attitudes.[131] Meanwhile, that interest in immigrant labor displayed by southern industrialists and state bureaus of immigration centered around the introduction of foreign workers from Northern and Western Europe.[132] Southern legislators went so far as to demand exclusion for all immigrants from Southern and Eastern Europe, even if such a condition would hamper the industrial and economic development of the South.[133] By 1912, Southern representatives in Congress provided the mainstay for a literacy test.[134] So eager were they for its passage that Congressman John L. Burnett threatened more stringent legislation were the literacy test and certain other restrictive features not to become law. Louis Marshall took strong exception to this stand.[135]

Anti-foreign attitudes in the West, emerging from a dislike for Orientals and a penchant for national pride, were equally as intense as those in the South. On the West Coast, anti-Japanese agitation, which was manifested in discriminatory legislation and almost threatened an international crisis, was first resolved by the aforementioned Gentlemen's Agreement of 1907 and by a later Japanese note of February 18, 1908, which together were to provide the basis for an effective restriction of immigration.[136] But the West insisted

and 9174, and Second Session, pp. 2941, 2945, 3028, 3222, 3224 and 3228; Sixty-second Congress, Second Session, pp. 5023-5024 and 5029; Sixty-third Congress, Second Session, pp. 2623-2627; E. Tupper and G. McReynolds, *op. cit.*, pp. 31 and 73; J. Higham, *op. cit.*, pp. 166-168.

[130] *Congressional Record*, Fifty-ninth Congress, First Session, pp. 9155 and 9174; Rowland T. Berthoff, "Southern Attitudes Toward Immigration, 1865-1914," *Journal of Southern History*, vol. XVII (1951), pp. 352-353.

[131] G. Myers, *op. cit.*, pp. 193-194 and 211-217; S. E. Morison and H. S. Commager, *op. cit.*, pp. 239-243 and 254-256; Higham, *op. cit.*, pp. 174-175; R. T. Berthoff, *op. cit.*, pp. 343-347; Oscar Handlin, *Adventure in Freedom* (New York, 1954), pp. 184-191.

[132] R. T. Berthoff, *op. cit.*, pp. 350 and 355.

[133] *Ibid.*, pp. 352-353.

[134] E. Tupper and G. McReynolds, *op. cit.*, pp. 72-73; *Congressional Record*, Sixty-second Congress, Second Session, p. 5023; Third Session, p. 864; Sixty-third Congress, Third Session, pp. 3000, 3002; G. M. Stephenson, *op. cit.*, pp. 162-163. By 1915, the South supported the literacy measure wholeheartedly.

[135] C. Reznikoff, *op. cit.*, vol. I, pp. 118-119.

[136] E. Tupper and G. McReynolds, *op. cit.*, p. 52; R. L. Garis, *op. cit.*, pp. 325-327;

that the Japanese had not kept their word, and cited statistics to show yearly increases in Japanese immigration to this country.[137] Much of this anti-Oriental attitude was intensified by the alarm with which residents of the West Coast viewed Japanese imperialist expansions.[138] At the same time, Roosevelt's display of naval power for Asiatic consumption augmented such feelings of American patriotism, nationalism, and jingoism as had had their original impetus during the years of America's involvement in the Philippines and in Cuba.[139] This native pride of race and country with which much of the West was taken from 1907 on produced an atmosphere scarcely conducive to the gracious reception of the foreigner; Western dislike of the Oriental was easily transferred to arrivals from Eastern Europe.[140] In a reciprocal mood, the South detected an allegedly inferior quality common to Asiatics in peoples inhabiting the Mediterranian area, and sympathized with the West in its tribulations over the Orientals.[141] In common with their colleagues from the South, Congressmen from the Western States supported the literacy provision in the 1912 immigration proposal.[142]

In addition to regional anti-alien attitudes dominant in the South and the West, organized labor continued effectively to muster public opinion against the immigrant. We recall that in 1907 Samuel Gompers had seen only justice in Senator Lodge's demands to limit alien entry.[143] By 1912, as for other restrictionists, so too for the Federation, the literacy test appeared to offer the most efficacious method of controlling unwanted immigration.[144]

G. M. Stephenson, *op. cit.*, pp. 271–272; *The Letters of Theodore Roosevelt*, vol. VI, pp. 611–615, 851–853.

[137] G. M. Stephenson, *op. cit.*, pp. 272–273; *The Letters of Theodore Roosevelt*, vol. VI, pp. 1477–1479, 1481, 1483–1486, 1502–1505 and 1509–1510.

[138] *The Letters of Theodore Roosevelt*, vol. V, pp. 709, 724n., 729–730; vol. VI, pp. 918–921.

[139] *Ibid.*, vol. V, pp. 717, 725; vol. VI, pp. 950–952, 956, 981 and 1342, note 2; E. Tupper and G. McReynolds, *op. cit.*, pp. 41–42; James Ford Rhodes, *The McKinley and Roosevelt Administrations, 1879–1909* (New York, 1922), pp. 368–377; S. E. Morison and H. S. Commager, *op. cit.*, pp. 337–341.

[140] E. Tupper and G. McReynolds, *op. cit.*, pp. 52–53 and 73; *Congressional Record*, Fifty-ninth Congress, First Session, p. 9174; J. Higham, *op. cit.*, pp. 173–174, O. Handlin, *op. cit.*, p. 191.

[141] *Congressional Record*, Sixty-second Congress, Second Session, pp. 5023 and 5029–5031.

[142] E. Tupper and G. McReynolds, *op. cit.*, p. 73; *Congressional Record*, Sixty-third Congress, Second Session, p. 2911.

[143] G. M. Stephenson, *op. cit.*, pp. 159–160; W. R. Gwinn, *op. cit.*, pp. 113–115 and 129; *Congressional Record*, Fifty-ninth Congress, First Session, pp. 9171 and 9181; *Selections from the Correspondence of Theodore Roosevelt and Henry Cabot Lodge*, vol. II, pp. 158 and 204; B. Bolles, *op. cit.*, p. 71.

[144] *Congressional Record*, Sixty-second Congress, Second Session, pp. 3533–3534, 3538–3539, 3543, 5023 and 5029; *USCIR*, vol. LXVI, pp. 103, 111 and 124 ff.

The recommendation of the Immigration Commission that an educational test was the most "feasible" of restrictive measures had taken hold. Foremost amongst the proposals introduced by Senator Dillingham in August of 1911 was a literacy requirement.[145] In other particulars, the bill codified existing legislation, barred persons not eligible for naturalization from these shores, and subjected aliens to possible deportation were they to become public charges at any future time due to causes existing prior to their arrival here. New classes of excludable persons were established and the Commissioner General of Immigration was granted unprecedented power in establishing rules for enforcing this act.[146] Significantly, the counterpart in the House to the Dillingham resolution, the Burnett Bill, was devoted entirely to the educational test.[147]

In January and February, 1913, the combined Dillingham-Burnett Bill passed both Houses of Congress, but when President William Howard Taft vetoed it, he gave the literacy test as the reason for his rejection. He explained his action to Congress by referring to an enclosed letter from Secretary Charles Nagel, confirming the need to invalidate any literacy requirements.[148] Taft's veto, motivated though it was by basic democratic ideals, did not negate the fact that now too, as in previous years, political representatives from cosmopolitan centers were careful not to alienate voters of foreign origin. On occasion, principles and political expediency fitted neatly together.[149]

By 1914, leadership on the immigration committees of both Houses was bestowed on those legislators from the South and the

[145] *Congressional Record*, Sixty-second Congress, Second Session, pp. 3536, 4794 and 5025; Third Session, pp. 2034–2036.

[146] M. J. Kohler, L. Marshall and A. Elkus, "Objections to Dillingham Immigration Bill," *Jewish Exponent*, vol. LVI, no. 18 (Feb. 23, 1912); *Thirty-ninth Annual Report of the Board of Delegates*, Appendix A, pp. 7164–7174; M. J. Kohler "Sees Injustice in Immigration Bills," *New York Times*, Jan. 27, 1912; and an editorial, entitled "Administering the Immigration Acts," *New York Evening Post*, Jan. 24, 1912 (National Liberal Immigration League Reprint).

[147] *Congressional Record*, Sixty-second Congress, Third Session, p. 2025; Fulton Brylawski to Cyrus Adler, June 6, 1912, Adler Papers, AAJ Committee; *AJYB*, vol. XIV (1912–1913 — 5673), pp. 212–214 and 294–295; vol. XV (1913–1914 — 5674), pp. 236–237 and 443–444.

[148] *Congressional Record*, Sixty-second Congress, Third Session, pp. 3268–3270; Sixty-third Congress, Second Session, p. 2911; E. Abbott, *op. cit.*, p. 211, note 2.

[149] *Congressional Record*, Sixty-second Congress, First Session, pp. 3709–3710, 3536 and 10417–10418; L. Gerson, *op. cit.*, pp. 12–13; J. Higham, *op. cit.*, pp. 189–191; G. M. Stephenson, *op. cit.*, pp. 153, 157–158, 162 and 166. When President Taft vetoed the literacy bill he had already lost the election. Nevertheless, in rejecting the Dillingham-Burnett bill, he carried out his party's campaign promise to foreign-born voters.

West. These men, by virtue of the larger native population in their areas, were not as overly concerned with the power of the naturalized voter as were their colleagues from the northern and midwestern industrial sections of the country. Heartened by their now more powerful representations in Congress and by the general temper of the times, restrictionists returned emboldened to the fray. Rising unemployment strengthened the clamor for greater controls over immigration.[150] Features of the Dillingham Bill were revived in the newly called Burnett Bill, with the emphasis again put upon an educational test.[151] In addition, provisions against contract labor were now extended to include menial workers, while people with "constitutional psychopathic inferiorities" were to be excluded. Vagrants were added to the public charge lists, and a percentage scheme based on ethnic origins to regulate the number of arriving newcomers was introduced. In February, 1914, the Burnett Bill passed the House, but the European war broke out shortly thereafter,[152] and with an impending election the following fall, the bill dragged along. Once again, the voting potential of naturalized immigrants was sufficient to halt debate in the Senate until after election.[153] The Senate then passed the bill, but President Woodrow Wilson, like Taft before him, vetoed it because it contained a literacy measure, and because it violated the historic right of asylum which this country had been wont to offer those seeking freedom.[154]

Through all these years Jewish leaders fought the literacy proposals with all the powers at their command. Marshall, Kohler and Wolf were particularly active. They appeared before Congressional committees,[155] issued statements to the press and to persons in high station,[156] and unabashedly used whatever influence they

[150] J. Higham, op. cit., pp. 191-193.

[151] E. Tupper and G. McReynolds, op. cit., p. 73; Congressional Record, Sixty-third Congress, Second Session, p. 2596.

[152] M. F. Behar, op. cit., pp. 7-9.

[153] J. Higham, op. cit., p. 192.

[154] Congressional Record, Sixty-third Congress, Third Session, pp. 2481-2482.

[155] AJYB, vol. XV (1913-1914 — 5674), p. 443; Forty-first Annual Report of the Board of Delegates, p. 7650, and Forty-second Annual Report . . . , p. 7935; AJYB, vol. XX (1918-1919 — 5679), p. 378.

[156] C. Reznikoff, op. cit., vol. I, pp. 113-115, 118-120, 123-125, 137-146, 149-150 and 155-159; S. Wolf to James A. O'Gorman, Feb. 11, 1914, Schiff Collection, AJA; Report of a Special Committee of the National Jewish Immigration Council Appointed to Examine into the Question of Illiteracy among Jewish Immigrants, M. J. Kohler, Chairman (Sixty-third Congress, Second Session), Senate Doc. no. 61 (Washington, D. C., 1914); M. J. Kohler, "The Immigration Question," Proceedings of the Twenty-fourth Council of the

possessed to prevent the passage of such measures.[157] By 1912, Kohler capped the campaign with a brochure entitled, "The Injustice of a Literacy Test for Immigrants." Interestingly enough, Kohler now found a champion for his anti-literacy views in Secretary Nagel, and dedicated the work to him. But Nagel, still smarting from the sharpness of Kohler's earlier charges against him and his department, hinted to Wolf that matters might not have gone so badly for Kohler on the immigration picture had he proved himself more conciliatory in the past.[158]

Basically, Kohler's contentions in his pamphlet were repeated by him with slight variations, and also by Wolf and Marshall. They maintained that a literacy test would arbitrarily discriminate against good immigrant stock through no fault of its own, but because of religious and economic discrimination abroad.[159] They cited the absence of any relationship between illiteracy and such undesirable character traits as would tend to exclude an alien. They were well aware that only a clever, highly literate alien would be able to commit anarchy and fraud in a variety of languages.[160] Not only was it heightened irony that the hardships of a literacy test would therefore fall upon the innocent, but since Jewish immigrants tended to underestimate rather than overstate their rate of illiteracy,[161] they would

Union (1915), pp. 7727–7734; M. J. Kohler, A. Elkus and L. Marshall, "To Regulate Immigration of Aliens" *Jewish Exponent*, vol. LIV, no. 20 (Feb. 23, 1912), p. 8; M. J. Kohler, "Objections to the Immigration Bill," *Jewish Exponent*, vol. LIV, no. 18 (Feb. 7, 1913), p. 6; Kohler, "The Restriction of Immigration," *American Israelite*, vol. LVIII, no. 27 (Jan. 4, 1912), p. 1; "Max J. Kohler Condemns Literacy Test," *American Hebrew*, vol. XCI, no. 2 (May 10, 1912), p. 36.

[157] See Cyrus Adler correspondence with Herbert Friedenwald for 1907, 1908, and Friedenwald correspondence with Mayer Sulzberger and Fulton Brylawski for 1911, Adler and Sulzberger Papers, AAJ Committee. Examining these communications shows that on several specific occasions in 1907 and 1911 Wolf had received written and verbal assurances from Speaker Cannon that no literacy bill would pass. See especially, Adler to H. Friedenwald, Jan. 23 and 28, 1907, and Feb. 3, 1907; and H. Friedenwald to Mayer Sulzberger, Jan. 16, 1911. For other examples of attempts to delay immigration measures concerned with literacy provisos see also H. Friedenwald to C. Adler, Feb. 19, Feb. 21, Feb. 25, April 17, and May 3, 1912; F. Brylawski to C. Adler, June 6, 1912; H. Friedenwald to M. Sulzberger, March 6, 1912, and same to same, July 19, 1912; Sulzberger to Friedenwald, March 2, 1912, Adler Papers, AAJ Committee.

[158] Charles Nagel to S. Wolf, May 2, 1912, Wolf Papers, AJHS.

[159] M. J. Kohler, "The Immigration Question and the Right of Asylum for the Persecuted," *Jewish Comment*, vol. XLII, no. 5 (Oct. 31, 1913), Part II, p. 38; C. Reznikoff, *op. cit.*, vol. I, pp. 115, 119–120 and 131–142; *Thirty-ninth Annual Report of the Board of Delegates*, pp. 7166–7167.

[160] *USCIR*, vol. XLVI, p. 183; C. Reznikoff, vol. I, *op. cit.*, p. 139.

[161] *Thirty-ninth Annual Report of the Board of Delegates*, p. 7166; M. J. Kohler, "The Injustice of a Literacy Test," pp. 3–7; idem, "The Immigration Question," *Proceedings of*

suffer more than others from the effects of such a bill. To make matters worse, a literacy requirement was a denial of individual liberties since it blurred the distinction between permission to enter this country and the right to acquire citizenship through the process of naturalization, a method dependent in part on being literate.[162] Last, but far from least, these Jewish representatives felt that Congress, by exempting refugees fleeing religious persecution from the operations of a literacy requirement had not really created any worthwhile dispensation. It would be impossible, they contended, for an alien always to prove that his flight to this country stemmed solely from religious rather than from economic, social, or political persecution abroad.[163]   In this connection, Marshall scored that irony of fate in which the immigrant would not even have recourse to the persecution he endured, since the illiteracy it engendered would prevent his entry here.[164]

All such protests were of no avail. In 1917, after the usual delay because of a pending election,[165] the literacy bill was passed. This time it finally overrode Wilson's veto.[166] It had taken a war to make the fears of the restrictionists seem real. Here at last was a bill whose educational requirement was intended to bar dangerous foreigners and whose other provisions strengthened the exclusionist principles enunciated in its 1913 forerunner.[167]

After the armistice, as Wilson's ideals of a federated, harmonious world waned, American nationalism waxed hotter than before. Industrial unrest and labor agitation coupled with an alleged Bolshevik menace gave renewed strength to American nativists. Their seeming need to close America's doors crystallized, when, after a brief flurry of prosperity, a reconversion to peacetime pursuits re-

the Twenty-fourth Council of the Union, pp. 7727-7729; C. Reznikoff, op. cit., vol. I, pp. 158-159.

[162] M. J. Kohler, "The Immigration Question," p. 7730; M. J. Kohler, A. Elkus and L. Marshall, "To Regulate Immigration of Aliens," Jewish Exponent, vol. LIV, no. 20 (Feb. 23, 1912), p. 8.

[163] M. J. Kohler, "The Immigration Question and the Right of Asylum for the Persecuted," Jewish Comment (Oct. 31, 1913), p. 38; Thirty-ninth Annual Report of the Board of Delegates, pp. 7167-7168; C. Reznikoff, op. cit., pp. 124, 138-141, 151-152 and 157-158. Senator Lodge, however, was adamant about limiting exemptions to the literacy clause solely on the basis of religious persecution. See Congressional Record, Sixty-second Congress, Second Session, p. 5021.

[164] C. Reznikoff, op. cit., vol. I, p. 131.

[165] Congressional Record, Sixty-fourth Congress, First Session, pp. 12767 and 12923-12930; J. Higham, op. cit., p. 203.

[166] R. L. Garis, op. cit., p. 125; Congressional Record, Sixty-fourth Congress, Second Session, p. 316, 2443, 2456 and 2629.

[167] E. Abbott, op. cit., pp. 214, note 1, and 215-225.

sulted in the inevitable fear of rising unemployment.[168] Kohler's pre-war calculations that the end of hostilities would see a decrease in the number of incoming immigrants proved true for only a brief period after 1918.[169] By the summer and fall of 1920, transatlantic steamers were reaching Ellis Island with thousands of aliens each month.[170] A goodly proportion of these were Jews fleeing the horrors of renewed East European persecution. Upon landing, such refugees encountered an increasingly vociferous anti-Semitic movement here,[171] itself the ultimate product both of small town regional revolt against urban society, and of a heightened distrust of the immigrant or hyphenate community.[172]

In America, dislike for the Jew had begun to swell with the onset of the First World War and would shortly reach its crest under the xenophobic isolationism of the Harding Administration. American racists took the lessons taught by their European counterparts well to heart. Madison Grant's book, for example, *The Passing of the Great Race*, published in 1916, placed great reliance on the vitriolic statements concerning a supposed Jewish racial inferiority that had appeared in the work of Houston Stewart Chamberlin, a well-known British anti-Semite.[173] Not only did Grant's work set the pattern for other diatribes against presumably inferior races of which the Jews were allegedly a part, but it also reached the high water mark of Judeophobia for intellectual consumption. Contemporaneously, the publications of Tom Watson, a southern agitator, supplied the ammunition for Jew baiting on a popular level. Somewhat earlier, Watson's hysterical rantings had provided the impetus for that internationally known travesty of justice, the lynching of Leo Frank, in 1915.[174]

---

[168] J. Higham, *op. cit.*, pp. 255-261 and 267-270; *Hearings: Prohibition of Immigration*, House Committee on Immigration and Naturalization, Sixty-fifth Congress, Third Session (Washington, D. C., 1919), pp. 31-35, 157-158 and 286-287; *Hearings: Emergency Immigration Legislation*, Senate Committee on Immigration and Naturalization, Sixty-seventh Congress, First Session, *Digest of Statements before Senate Committee*, Sixty-sixth Congress, Third Session, (Washington, D. C., 1921), pp. 39, 44-45, 56-57 and 59.

[169] M. J. Kohler, "Effects of the War on Immigration," *American Israelite*, vol. LXI, no. 27 (Dec. 31, 1914), p. 4.

[170] E. Abbott, *op. cit.*, p. 234.

[171] *AJYB*, vol. XXII (1920-1921 — 5681), pp. 410-411; vol. XXIII (1921-1922 — 5682), pp. 313-328 and 367-369; C. Reznikoff, *op. cit.*, vol. I, pp. 353-355.

[172] O. Handlin, *op. cit.*, pp. 191-202; J. Higham, *op. cit.*, pp. 198-203; G. M. Stephenson, *op. cit.*, pp. 225-228; L. Gerson, *op. cit.*, pp. 9-14, for a current estimate of the hyphenate community.

[173] E. Flannery, *op. cit.*, pp. 255 and 319; O. Handlin, *op. cit.*, p. 196; *AJYB*, vol. XXIX (1927-1928 — 5688), p. 400; J. Higham, *op. cit.*, pp. 271-273.

[174] G. Myers, *op. cit.*, pp. 199-208.

From the time that Frank lost his life to an infuriated mob until 1920, when Henry Ford gave his blessings to the publication of a whole series of defamatory articles based on the notorious *Protocols of the Elders of Zion*,[175] anti-Semitism in America was acquiring much of that specific racial distinctiveness that had hitherto characterized its European variety. To the other stereotyped notions of Jewish domination on the economic level and of Jewish aggressiveness on the social level had been added the dangers of Jewish racial defilement.[176] What could have been more logical in this context than that individuals embodying such negative characteristics were the forerunners of revolutions. The view that Jews would herald such upheavals as had recently convulsed the Czarist Empire was becoming current in public opinion and found its echo in the halls of Congress.[177] What had hitherto been an immigration policy of restriction was scheduled to become one of exclusion.

Inspired by the demands of organized labor and led by a restrictionist, Albert Johnson, as Chairman of its Committee on Immigration and Naturalization, the House of Representatives was prepared to suspend all immigration for a varying number of years.[178] Marshall, horrified at the notion, contended that such a suggestion violated the very premises upon which this country was founded and sustained.[179] Shortly thereafter, Wolf, in marked contrast to Marshall's adamant opposition, advocated halting immigration temporarily as a means of safeguarding the character of America's institutions and of narrowing the influx of aliens to a land suffering from unemployment. Wolf softened the harshness of his proposal by requesting exemptions from the suspension law for relatives of American citizens.[180]

---

[175] *AJYB*, vol. XXIII (1921–1922 — 5682), pp. 313–329 and 367–369.

[176] *Hearings: Biological Aspects of Immigration*, Senate Committee on Immigration and Naturalization, Sixty-sixth Congress, Second Session, (Washington, D. C., 1920), pp. 7–14 and 17–19; *AJYB*, vol. XXIV (1922–1923 — 5683), pp. 53–54; vol. XXIV (1924–1925 — 5685), pp. 634–635; E. Flannery, *op. cit.*, pp. 255–258; O. Handlin, *op. cit.*, pp. 194–196.

[177] *AJYB*, vol. XXIII (1921–1922 — 5682), pp. 313–329; *New York Times*, Nov. 19, 1917, p. 2; O. Handlin, *op. cit.*, pp. 202–203; *The Letters of Theodore Roosevelt*, vol. VIII, p. 1304; C. Reznikoff, *op. cit.*, vol. I, pp. 323–330; *Hearings: The Ku Klux Klan*, House Committee on Rules, Sixty-seventh Congress, First Session, (Washington, D. C., 1921), pp. 19–20; G. Myers, *op. cit.*, pp. 221–224; L. Marshall to S. Wolf, Feb. 15, 1919, Louis Marshall Correspondence, AJA; *Temporary Suspension of Immigration*, House Report no. 1109, Sixty-sixth Congress, Second Session (Washington, D. C., 1920), pp. 39 and 57.

[178] *Hearings: Prohibition of Immigration*, pp. 1–4; *Temporary Suspension of Immigration*, pp. 1–6; J. Higham, *op. cit.*, pp. 304–309.

[179] *Temporary Suspension of Immigration*, pp. 4–7; C. Reznikoff, *op. cit.*, vol. I, pp. 159–162.

[180] *Forty-seventh Annual Report of the Board of Delegates*, p. 8763.

Neither Wolf's attempts to succeed through ingratiation nor Marshall's overriding concern with principle brought the desired results. In the fall of 1920, the House of Representatives passed a bill suspending immigration for a period of one year.[181] Its action was preceded by a strongly worded anti-Semitic description of the then current migration to America. This report was allegedly attributed to American consuls abroad who sent their negative evaluations of the contemplated alien arrivals here to the Director of the Consular Service of the State Department, Wilbur J. Carr. Carr then paraphrased the views of his agents and made them available to Congressman Johnson.[182] Only the protests of American employers of foreign labor,[183] and Senators themselves such as Le Baron Colt of Rhode Island, who represented a state with a large foreign-born population, prevented the Senate from agreeing to the Johnson plan to halt immigration.[184] In its place Senator Dillingham, encouraged by public stipulations that immigration be radically restricted,[185] reproduced his earlier quota scheme, first suggested by the Commission he headed in 1911, put forth in his 1913 legislative proposal,[186] and endorsed by an American missionary to Japan, Dr. Sidney L. Gulick. The latter wanted to admit a certain annual percentage of each ethnic group of immigrants based not on any census, but on the number of naturalized citizens and American born children of that immigrant stock.[187]

Implicit in any quota arrangement was the arbitrary evaluation of different groups or nationalities. The notion of racial or religious classification against which Jewish spokesmen had contended for well nigh two decades had at last formed the basis for a Federal immigration policy.

As early as 1899 Wolf claimed he had convinced Terence V. Powderly, Chief of the Bureau of Immigration at that time, of the

[181] *Congressional Record*, Sixty-sixth Congress, Third Session, pp. 285–286; G. M. Stephenson, *op. cit.*, p. 176.

[182] *Temporary Suspension of Immigration*, Appendix A, pp. 9–12; C. Reznikoff, *op. cit.*, vol. I, pp. 174–191; *Forty-eighth Annual Report of the Board of Delegates*, p. 9018; *AJYB*, vol. XXIV (1922–1923 — 5683), p. 365.

[183] *Hearings: Emergency Immigration Legislation, supra*, pp. 15–26, 28 and 39; G. M. Stephenson, *op. cit.*, p. 182.

[184] *Ibid.*

[185] *New York Times*, Feb. 9, 1921, p. 8; Feb. 10, 1921, p. 15; Feb. 18, 1921, p. 3; G. M. Stephenson, *op. cit.*, pp. 171–172, 175 and 180.

[186] E. Abbott, *op. cit.*, p. 210; *AJYB*, vol. XV (1913–1914 — 5674), p. 236; R. L. Garis, *op. cit.*, pp. 123 and 142–149; G. M. Stephenson, *op. cit.*, pp. 177–180.

[187] *Hearings: Proposed Restriction of Immigration; Statement of Sidney L. Gulick*, House Committee on Immigration and Naturalization, Sixty-sixth Congress, Second Session (May 22, 1920), pp. 4 and 8–10; G. M. Stephenson, *op. cit.*, pp. 176–177.

necessity to abandon such categorization.[188] But Frank P. Sargent, Powderly's successor, refused to accept Wolf's point of view, and by 1903, tabulating all immigrants by race and requiring religious identification for Jews had become standard practice.[189] Eager to prove the unconstitutionality of Federal inquiries concerning the nature of the faith professed by Jewish immigrants, Wolf wrote to any number of leading Jews of the day and asked the age old puzzler, whether the Jews were a race.[190] Since all immigrants had been required by law to reveal their racial origins, any affirmative answers Wolf would receive would vindicate the Immigration Department's contention that such an inquiry was not prejudicial to the Jewish group. American Federal agencies were not to blame for the fact that as far as the Jews were concerned, both their race (if they did constitute a race) and the faith they practiced bore the same name.[191] As matters finally turned out, the answers Wolf received in his poll of Jewish opinion did more to reveal the personalities of his respondents than to shed light on the problem. It would indeed have been very difficult for Wolf to bolster his argument that designating an immigrant as "Hebrew" was an invasion of one's religious privacy, when such eminent Jews as Dr. Solomon Schechter, Lewis Dembitz, and Rabbi Bernhard Felsenthal informed him that in their view the Jews were indeed a race.[192] An Undersecretary of State, Alvee A.

---

[188] *Twenty-sixth Annual Report of the Board of Delegates*, p. 4121.

[189] *Thirtieth Annual Report of the Board of Delegates*, pp. 5031 and 5042–5043.

[190] *Ibid.*, pp. 5043–5050.

[191] See W. W. Husband to William R. Wheeler, Dec. 15, 1908, p. 3, Kohler Papers, AJHS.

[192] Dr. Solomon Schechter was fully aware that the term "race" might be construed negatively, in the manner in which racists hastened to define different groups as possessing inferior or superior racial characteristics. He nevertheless referred Wolf to his well-known essay, "Epistle to the Jews of England," in which he expressed the opinion that the Jews are a race by virtue of its "common origin" and "common blood." Schechter was prepared to retain this doctrine "at the risk of being misunderstood." For he observed that the "contrary standpoint leads to assimilation, which is more dangerous to Judaism than any device the anti-Semites may invent." See S. Schechter to S. Wolf, Aug. 27, 1903, *Thirtieth Annual Report of the Board of Delegates*, p. 5050.

In his correspondence with S. Wolf, L. Dembitz made no reference to any negative consequences which might possibly ensue upon designating the Jews as a race. Instead, he was very glad that the Commissioner of Immigration in his report classified the Jews as a race, since that is what they "are for all practical purposes." Dembitz was certain that such categorization would produce much needed information concerning the Jewish alien. See L. Dembitz to S. Wolf, Sept. 5, 1903, *Thirtieth Annual Report of the Board of Delegates*, p. 5050.

Rabbi Bernhard Felsenthal, a leading Reform rabbi, informed Wolf that all immigrants, including the Jews, ought to be identified racially, religiously, and in terms of their former political allegiances. Since he felt that the Department of Commerce was absolutely correct in classifying the Jews as a race, the additional information he requested was in the interests of statistics and ethnology. Religiously, though most Jews

Adee, then tried to settle the issue for Wolf by taking note of that racial quality which permitted the Jewish group as a unit to survive centuries of persecution. Adee maintained that such historical evidence provided ample justification for the State Department to consider the Jews as a race.[193] The Department of Commerce and Labor, who by 1903 had acquired jurisdiction over matters of immigration and naturalization, thereupon concurred in the opinion of the Department of State, and was prepared to classify Jewish immigrants by race.[194] The term "nationality" was used in reference to the alien's country of origin; exceptions to this procedure, however, occurred in the matter of classifying various immigrant ethnic groups who originally may have jointly inhabited large territorial empires.[195]

Though the Government sought to justify the racial classification of Jewish immigrants both on historical grounds and in the interests of gathering pertinent statistical or ethnological information[196] Wolf's primary concern was that in the process of identifying Jews by race, the Government was indulging in unconstitutional, and hence unwarranted inquiries into the faith of these aliens.[197] He further affirmed that it was an invidious distinction to require Jews to state their religious persuasion when no such demands were postulated for immigrants of the various Christian denominations.[198]

This was the burden of the testimony presented by Wolf and Julian W. Mack of the American Jewish Committee to the Immigration Commission in December of 1909,[199] when it was feared that the Commission, in publishing the results of its investigation, would

---

would bear the same identification as their racial classification, there were those — either converts to Christianity or Jewish proselytes — who would not. And Felsenthal was most concerned with classifying these people properly. As an example, he referred to Lord Beaconfield as one who, had he been an immigrant, would be known racially as a Jew, religiously as an Episcopalian, and politically as an Englishman. Felsenthal, similarly, was prepared to classify Warder Cresson, a nineteenth century American consul in Palestine, who had become a Jew, as a Scotchman racially, a Jew religiously, and an American politically. Like Dembitz, Felsenthal made no reference in this correspondence to any possible anti-Semitic utilization of the term "race." Nor did he deem it illegal to classify Jews either racially or religiously. In fact, from his reply to Wolf it is apparent that he was prepared to resort to both racial and religious identities whenever the occasion warranted such procedures. See B. Felsenthal to S. Wolf, Aug. 7, 1903. *Thirtieth Annual Report of the Board of Delegates*, pp. 5047–5048.

See the Appendix for the reaction of other leading Jews to Wolf's query [infra, pp. 96–97].

[193] *Ibid.*, p. 5051.   [194] *Ibid.*

[195] *USCIR*, vol. XLVI, pp. 269–270; W. W. Husband to William R. Wheeler, Dec. 15, 1908, p. 2, Kohler Papers, AJHS.

[196] *USCIR*, vol. XLVI, p. 273.   [197] *Ibid.*, p. 274.

[198] *Ibid.*, p. 268.   [199] *Ibid.*, pp. 266–278.

persist in classifying Jewish immigrants as "Hebrew," with no reference either to their birthplace, or country to which they may have first sworn allegiance.[200] But neither Mack nor Wolf were able to sway Senator Lodge, a member of the Commission, from his conviction that the Government, in tabulating most immigrants on an ethnological basis, was therefore justified in categorizing Jewish immigrants as "Hebrew," since they were, in fact, members of a distinct race.[201] The Senator vigorously denied Wolf's and Mack's allegations that the Federal practice of labeling Jewish arrivals in this fashion was merely an illegal means of inquiring into their personal profession of faith. Lodge insisted that the Government never intended any religious classification of immigrants, but that it had every right to tabulate them on the basis of racial origins.[202] An Assistant Secretary of Commerce and Labor, William Walter Husband, agreed with Senator Lodge, and in a letter to a colleague indicated that it was indeed unfortunate if the terms, "Hebrew" and "Jew" referred both to a race and a religious group.[203] Certainly, the Government was not to be taken to task, if in the process of eliciting racial information, the religious identity of Jewish immigrants were to become known.

Shortly after Wolf and Mack had engaged Senator Lodge in the matter of immigrant classification, members of the American Jewish Committee felt that in the light of more urgent immigration problems facing them, there would be little advantage to any prolonged contentions with Government over racial and religious issues. They then informed Wolf of their decision to abstain from further discussions on the question of immigrant tabulation.[204] But Wolf, throughout his life, persisted in the view that inasmuch as Jews were bound together only by principles of faith, any governmental inquiry into their religious belief violated their constitutional privileges.[205]

Like Wolf, Kohler had originally insisted upon the illegality of immigrant classification when based on race or religion. Such a procedure, he thought, would be tantamount to a denial of the due process and religious liberty clauses of the Constitution.[206] In his

[200] Ibid., p. 269-272.   [201] Ibid., pp. 272-275.   [202] Ibid., pp. 271-272.

[203] Ibid., p. 271; W. W. Husband to William R. Wheeler, Dec. 15, 1908, p. 2, Kohler Papers, AJHS.

[204] Minute Book, American Jewish Committee Executive, Dec. 28, 1909, AAJ Committee.

[205] Selected Addresses and Papers of Simon Wolf, pp. 296-298. As late as 1922, shortly before his death, Wolf still contended that if Jewish immigrants were to be classified as "Hebrew," all other aliens coming as immigrants to the United States must then be identified in terms of their religious affiliations.

[206] "Memorandum in Opposition to the Classification of Immigrants as Hebrews," in USCIR, vol. XLVI, p. 277; "Brief in the Matter of Hersh Skuratowski," pp. 175-179.

famed "Brief in the Matter of Hersh Skuratowski," Kohler cited Wolf's correspondence with the near and the great on the question of race to show that the different values applied to the term "race" by knowledgeable Jews made any racial categorization seem absurd.[207] Many years later, in 1927, Kohler still maintained that such means of tabulating aliens were conducive to discrimination. By then, however, he had modified his view sufficiently to affirm that historically and intellectually there may have been good reason to regard the Jews as a race or ethnic group.[208]

Unfortunately, such justification did not alleviate the practical effects of classifying immigrants according to their national origins. By May, 1921, despite President Wilson's earlier pocket veto, Congress had reintroduced and passed a law limiting immigration to three per cent of the members of each nationality based on the census of 1910.[209] Marshall protested against the statute's arbitrary means of distinguishing between different races and nationalities. Coming as it did, after Europe's map had been redrawn, it would be well nigh impossible to determine which peoples were to be ascribed to what lands. The Jews, not being considered a nationality in their own right, would then find it doubly difficult to enter this country. Marshall contended that the bill would further separate families already torn asunder because of the war,[210] while Kohler maintained similar views on behalf of the Board of Delegates of the Union.[211] In addition, Marshall emphasized that the bill was discriminatory both in exempting from its operation those aliens who resided in lands contiguous to the United States for one year, and in its application to foreigners living in the United States, who made only temporary visits abroad. Marshall also insisted that no such emergencies existed as would necessitate further restrictions upon immigration.[212] Kohler, for his part, noted that the practical effects of the quota system resulted in hundreds of illegal deportations, created situations which violated America's treaties with foreign countries, and led Federal authorities to bar judicial review of immigration decisions. Kohler was irked by the inconsistent regulations of the

[207] *Ibid.*, p. 178.

[208] M. J. Kohler to W. W. Husband, March 21, 1927, Kohler Papers, AJHS.

[209] Cited in E. Abbott, *op. cit.*, pp. 240–242; R. L. Garis, *op. cit.*, pp. 142–149; *AJYB*, vol. XXIV (1922–1923 — 5683), p. 345; G. M. Stephenson, *op. cit.*, pp. 178–180.

[210] *AJYB*, vol. XXIV (1922–1923 — 5683), pp. 346–354; C. Reznikoff, *op. cit.*, pp. 166–169; *Hearings: Proposed Restriction of Immigration*, House Committee on Immigration and Naturalization, Sixty-sixth Congress, Second Session (Washington, D. C., 1920), pp. 4–65.

[211] *Forty-eighth Annual Report of the Board of Delegates*, p. 9022.

[212] C. Reznikoff, *op. cit.*, vol. I, pp. 166 and 182.

Department of Labor in enforcing the law. He also charged that at Ellis Island counsel for the immigrants found it difficult to resort to writs of habeas corpus, or to put up bail in order to present appeals to the courts.[213] Another difficulty created by the bill, to which Kohler, Wolf, and Marshall referred, was the matter of the excess monthly quotas of immigrants, dumped here partly through the ignorance of American consuls overseas, who would visa passports of aliens with no regard for the basis of the fixed quotas. Contentions would then multiply as to whether or not these aliens were to be charged against the succeeding month's quota, or were to be deported.[214] Sometimes, these matters would be resolved not in terms of principles, but simply on the basis of expediency. In December, 1921, because it was the Christmas season, Secretary of Labor James P. Davis reversed his order for the deportation of 1,000 Polish and Hungarian immigrants at Ellis Island who had arrived in excess of their respective quotas.[215]

So strong was the Federal decision to hamper immigration in those days, that Marshall confirmed his inability to persuade President Harding to veto the "odious" Quota Act. Marshall was certain that had Harding acceded to his request, the President would be acting counter to prevailing public opinion. Marshall complained that even the employers of immigrant labor had been "cowed into silence" by America's penchant for exclusion.[216] The American policy of welcoming the foreigner had just about ground to a halt.

By the middle of 1923, Simon Wolf was dead, and the Board of Delegates which, in a sense, had been his creation, would not long survive thereafter.[217] Kohler and Marshall, however, continued to battle for a more liberal immigration policy. Their task was to become progressively harder, because by 1924, the presumably temporary 1921 law had become permanent. Modifications of the original provisos now reduced the nationalities percentages from three to two per cent and took the 1890 rather than the 1910 census as the basis for the quota.[218] This new arrangement favored the immi-

[213] Forty-eighth Annual Report of the Board of Delegates, pp. 9022–9023.

[214] Ibid., pp. 9018, 9022; AJYB, vol. XXIV (1922–1923 — 5683), p. 354; vol. XXV (1924–1925 — 5685), pp. 644–645; vol. XXVII (1925–1926 — 5686), p. 429.

[215] Fiftieth Annual Report of the Board of Delegates, pp. 9471–9473; Forty-eighth Annual Report of the Board of Delegates, pp. 9018–9019 and 9022; Selected Addresses and Papers of Simon Wolf, pp. 292–293; C. Reznikoff, op. cit., vol. I, pp. 197–201; AJYB, vol. XXVII (1926–1927 — 5686), p. 429.

[216] C. Reznikoff, op. cit., vol. I, p. 191.

[217] M. J. Kohler, "Letter to the Editor," American Hebrew, vol. CXVIII, no. 3 (Nov. 27, 1925), p. 60.

[218] AJYB, vol. XXV (1923–1924 — 5684), pp. 58 and 376; vol. XXVI (1924–1925 —

grants coming from Northern and Western Europe as opposed to those from the southern and eastern portions of the continent.[219] Since the proponents of the 1924 arrangement believed it closely approximated the proportion of each national stock to America's total population, it was known as the "national origins" plan.[220] In reality, framers of the 1924 national origins bill looked to the 1890 census as the base by which to regulate the ethnic makeup of entering aliens, so that they would more closely resemble the immigrants who had settled America in the mid-nineteenth century. Congressman Albert Johnson and Senator David A. Reed hoped to strengthen the Nordic and Teutonic components of America's population.[221]

For over three decades, representatives of the Jewish community had fought a long, delaying action to prevent a contingency such as this. But by 1929,[222] the 1924 Immigration Act, with only slight modifications, had become a condition which was to extend well into the middle of the twentieth century. Wolf, Kohler, and Marshall were to be credited not only for helping to postpone this ultimate state of affairs, or for the untold numbers of people they helped save from deportation, but also because they constantly reminded policy makers of the basic principles upon which this republic was founded.

5685), pp. 56–57 and 645–646; vol. XXVII (1925–1926 — 5686), p. 427; *Selected Addresses and Papers of Simon Wolf*, p. 293; R. L. Garis, *op. cit.*, pp. 171–202; House Report no. 1621, Sixty-seventh Congress, Fourth Session (Washington, D. C., 1923).

[219] G. M. Stephenson, *op. cit.*, pp. 184–185 and 191; *AJYB*, vol. XXVII (1925–1926 — 5686), p. 427 and 431–434; vol. XXVI (1924–1925 — 5685), pp. 56–57 and 645–646.

[220] *Congressional Record*, Sixty-eighth Congress, First Session, pp. 5467–5471; *AJYB*, vol. XXVI (1924–1925 — 5685), pp. 645–646.

[221] See J. Higham, *op. cit.*, pp. 396–397 for an interesting reconstruction of the origins of the "national origins" plan by its proponents; R. L. Garis, *op. cit.*, pp. 157 and 256–257; G. M. Stephenson, *op. cit.*, pp. 185 and 187–191. The "national origins" amendment to the immigration law of 1924 differs from the quota base arrangement in that the former scheme would allow an annual total of approximately 162,000 immigrants, whereas the latter would permit no more than 150,000 aliens in any one year. This was the result of a proviso in the 1924 law which authorized that until 1927 quotas would be limited to two per cent of the foreign-born of each nationality resident in the United States according to the census of 1890, with the minimum quota being fixed at one hundred. After 1927, however, the annual quota was to be fixed at the same ratio to 150,000 as the number of persons of foreign extraction were to the white population of the United States according to the 1920 census. For an insight into Senator David Reed's views on immigration, with their emphasis on national origins, see *AJYB*, vol. XXVII (1925–1926 — 5686), p. 448; vol. XXIX (1927–1928 — 5688), pp. 400–402.

[222] Richard B. Morris [ed.], *Encyclopedia of American History* (New York, 1950), p. 449.

APPENDIX

Included below are the responses of different leaders in the American Jewish community to Wolf's query concerning race.

Mayer Sulzberger, a prominent Philadelphia attorney, who later held a judgeship and was President of the American Jewish Committe, felt that any governmental inquiry into one's religious belief was unconstitutional. He was certain that the term "race" applied to Jews in Federal legislation was a "periphrastic method of denoting their religion." As Sulzberger understood the term "race," it had hitherto been used in the Constitution

> or laws . . . to designate marked physical diversity of color such as the red or Indian Race, the yellow or Mongolian.

He was certain that no one would

> contend that the Jews belong to any other than the group called Caucasian . . .

Nor did he see any relationship between the various subraces which may have been included in the Caucasian group and specific functions of Government. (See ·M. Sulzberger to S. Wolf, Aug. 5, 1903, *Thirtieth Annual Report of the Board of Delegates*, p. 5043.)

Marcus Jastrow, a leading scholar and rabbi, told Wolf that the Jews were "neither a nation or a race in a political sense" but that they did "represent a race for anthropological and sociological purposes." He therefore suggested that if the Department of Commerce recorded all immigrants not only by country of origin, but also by race, the Jews would then find it impossible to take exception to such classification. However, he did agree with Wolf that any method wherein Jewish immigrants were the only ones to be identified racially would be discriminatory. (See M. Jastrow to S. Wolf, Aug. 5, 1903, *Thirtieth Annual Report of the Board of Delegates*, p. 5043.)

Leo N. Levi, the President of the B'nai Brith refused on practical grounds to inject the question of Jewish racial classification into the councils of his organization, lest it open a Pandora's box. But he did observe that if such classification was deemed necessary, then the term "race" had to be defined properly, and the reason for its application extended to all immigrants. By the same token, if keeping records of individual aliens was a requisite, then such files ought to include racial identification, religious affiliations and national origins for all immigrants. Singling out the Jewish group racially or religiously he felt, was "invidious" and prejudicial. (See L. N. Levi to S. Wolf, August 6, 1903, *Thirtieth Annual Report of the Board of Delegates*, p. 5044.)

Emil G. Hirsch, a well-known Reform rabbi, insisted that the Jews were not a race and that such governmental classification, though not "intended as a piece of anti-Semitic chicanery . . . resembled it very closely." He noted that such methods of classification ought to be remembered "some day at the polls." (See E. G. Hirsch to S. Wolf, August 7, 1903, *Thirtieth Annual Report of the Board of Delegates*, p. 5046.)

Cyrus Adler was of the opinion that even ethnically, the Jews no longer constituted a race so that from a practical standpoint such classification would result in errors. Converts to Christianity, though of Jewish stock, would not be listed as Jews; conversely, Jewish proselytes of other races would be listed as Jews. The result would then, to all extents and purposes become a matter of religious rather than racial classification. Though Dr. Adler reached this conclusion, he did not in this correspondence call Wolf's attention to any illegal consequences which might possibly have arisen from what would in reality become a religious, rather than a racial classification. (See C. Adler to S. Wolf, Aug. 6, 1903, *Thirtieth Annual Report of the Board of Delegates*, pp. 5045–5046.)

Gotthard Deutsch, another prominent Reform rabbi of the period, was equally as insistent as Wolf that the Jews were not a race in any scientific sense of the term. However, unlike Wolf, he saw no objection to the Government's classification of Jews coming from Russia, Roumania and Galicia as such. Deutsch observed that

> almost all of these people emigrate because they are Jews, and if the Government wishes to find out, for the sake of statistics, the reasons which bring immigrants to these shores, no reasonable man could object to it.

(See G. Deutsch to S. Wolf, August 9, 1903, *Thirtieth Annual Report of the Board of Delegates*, p. 5049.)

THE JEWISH QUESTION IN NEW YORK CITY

[1902–1903]

By Isaac Max Rubinow

Translated by Leo Shpall

TRANSLATOR'S PREFACE[1]

The opening of the present century was marked by the renewal of persecution of Jews in Russia and in other Eastern European countries. The pogroms in Kishineff and Homel aroused a cry of protest among world Jewry, and many a country including that of the United States raised its voice in protest against these measures of persecution. The Eastern European Jews, particularly those of Russia and of Roumania, again turned their eyes toward the United States and thousands upon thousands began to stream to these shores. The Jewish community in this country not only joined in this protest but stood ready to receive the newcomers and to help them adjust themselves. The United States had a very well organized Jewish community and educational, social, philanthropic and other communal institutions. In addition, the Russian Jews who began coming here in the 1880's had succeeded in striking root and in establishing their own communal institutions. These East European Jews began to make themselves felt in all fields of communal endeavor and their spokesmen assumed a prominent role not only in their own communities but also on the national scene.

Isaac Max Rubinow (1875–1936), physician, statistician and economist came to this country from Poland, in 1893. He received the degree of Doctor of Medicine from Yale University in 1898, but shortly after graduation, he left the medical profession and became interested in social work. In 1913, he published *Social Insurance*, an

---

[1] Dr. Oscar Handlin has just published a study, entitled *The Newcomer: Negroes and Puerto Ricans in a Changing Metropolis* (Cambridge, Mass., Harvard University Press, 1950), in which among other things he discusses the immigration problem in this country with special reference to various ethnic immigrant groups. In light of this, it would be interesting to compare the views set forth by Dr. Rubinow in his articles that were published in 1903, fifty-seven years ago, in the Russian-Jewish periodical, *Voskhod*, of St. Petersburg, an outstanding Russian-Jewish periodical, which are here translated into English for the first time.

authoritative reference work on the subject.[2] In 1914, he received the degree of Doctor of Philosophy from Columbia University and entered into government service in the Department of Statistics and Agriculture and in the Department of Commerce and Labor. From 1918 to 1922, he headed the Hadassah Medical Unit in Palestine. In 1923, he was made Director of the Jewish Welfare Society of Philadelphia. In 1928, he became Executive Director of the Zionist Organization of America and in 1929, Secretary of the Independent Order of B'nai B'rith.[3]

Doctor Rubinow contributed numerous articles to the Russian-Jewish monthly periodical, *Voskhod*, in which he dealt with Jewish life in this country in its many phases.[4] These articles were not only factual but analytical as well and Rubinow was able to evaluate Jewish life in the United States and give the reader a sociologico-historical description of the Jewish scene. The series of articles which are presented here in English translation with the present writer's annotations, relate to Jewish life in New York City at the beginning of the twentieth century.[5] In a sense they form a sequel to Doctor George M. Price's *The Russian Jew in America* which appeared in an English translation by the present translator in the *Publication of the American Jewish Historical Society.*[6]

I

It is about time that the Jews of Russia familiarize themselves with the life of the Jews in New York City. It is no joke! During the past twenty-five years New York has served as a haven of refuge for tens and hundreds of thousands of Russian and other Jews, and still this city continues to remain an enigma to them.

However, of late we must admit that Russian-Jewish periodicals have begun to take a more sober attitude toward Russian-Jewish immigration. There is greater interest in this theme and there is a

---

[2] *Social Insurance* was published in St. Louis.

[3] For his biography see the *B'nai B'rith Magazine*, vol. LI (Oct., 1936), pp. 5–6, by Edward Cruso. See also Marvin Lowenthal, *Henrietta Szold: Life and Letters* (New York, 1942), pp. 137–139, 149–151, 159–161 and 217–218.

[4] For a list of Rubinow's articles in the Russian-Jewish periodicals, see Leo Shpall, "A List of Selected Items of American Jewish Interest in the Russian-Jewish Press," in the *Publications of the American Jewish Historical Society* [=*PAJHS*], no. XXXIX, part 1 (Sept., 1949), pp. 87–113.

[5] They appeared in the *Voskhod*, 1903, vol. XXIII (May), pp. 94–104; (June), pp. 100–117; (July), pp. 123–127; (Aug.), pp. 105–113.

[6] See *PAJHS*, vol. XLVIII, no. 1 (Sept., 1958), pp. 28–62, and no. 2 (Dec., 1958) pp. 78–133.

greater desire to become more familiar with the American aspect of the immigration problem. We are beginning to comprehend that we are on the eve of an important historical moment.

In one of the New York Yiddish newspapers there recently appeared an attempt to ascertain the number of Jews residing in New York City.[7] When it appeared, I published the results and the statistical methods employed [in ascertaining the number]. This report stated that there were about 600,000 Jews in New York City.

Six hundred thousand Jews! This population which constitutes an appreciable percentage of the Jewish people makes the Jewish problem in New York City rather interesting. But New York is more than a place of abode for this large number of Jews. If New York has 600,000 Jews, it serves also as a place for which millions of Jews are longing and as a threshhold to the entire American Republic.

How does the immigrant Jew fare in this Promised Land? That immigration improved the economic status of the majority there is no doubt, otherwise, such an increase in immigration would have been impossible. But besides the economic reasons there are other reasons as well [for this increase in immigration]. In order to present the facts more clearly, it would be better to base these observations upon my personal experiences. Here I am in New York for more than ten years. These ten years were years of varied economic conditions, years of my university education, medical practice, literary efforts, and communal and political activity. They were good and bad years. These were years of longing for the land of my birth — a yearning which became dim as my interests in the new land increased and as my bond with it became stronger. I can safely and whole-heartedly assert that despite the fluctuations in my fortune, I did not suffer any setbacks because of my being a Jew. Not a day passed that I felt any discomfiture because of my Jewishness, that I was forced to ignore my brethren or to be ashamed of meeting them. I never held myself apart from the Jewish masses. For a time, I even lived in a Jewish neighborhood and the greatest part of the ten years I spent in Harlem.[8] At first, this area was exclusively Christian, but I witnessed its gradual settlement by Jews and how it became the uptown ghetto. I never was ashamed of the place of my residence and I had no reason to be. It is only natural that most of my friends

---

[7] The figures appeared in *Die Jüdische Welt*, Aug. 19, 1902, p. 2, as well as in the *New York Times*, Aug. 17, 1902, p. 5, col. 3. These figures were evaluated in *Niedielnaya Khronika Voskhoda*, vol. XXI, Sept. 12, 1902, pp. 26–28.

[8] The Harlem area at that time began at 125th Street and extended northward, encompassing the same area as it does today.

are members of the Russian-Jewish colony. However, there are also among them Germans, Hungarians, Frenchmen, et cetera. If there are just a few of them who are Americans, it is only because there are few native-born Americans in New York City. If I were to pen my autobiography, my Jewish origin would hardly reflect any sad experience. I say "hardly," because of one adverse incident. This, by the way, was the only one that I experienced. It was during my years in the medical school. Among my Jewish classmates there were, I must confess, three who were far from decent. At that time, the entrance requirements were low and among the students there were some who were totally unfit. The American students took a dislike to these three students and expressed it quite overtly. Several Russian students, in keeping with the old Russian tradition of solidarity and comradeship, came to the defense of the three students and protested in writing to the Dean. The Dean, in turn, sent a letter to the Student Council. This resulted in two or three meetings of the student body and a resolution was passed denying that there was any anti-Semitic feeling among the students. The resolution was far from sincere, but when the incident got into the press, it did create a bad impression, but left no aftereffect. Fortune played a joke on one of the instigators. He fell in love with a Jewish girl and because her parents were Orthodox Jews he had to embrace the Jewish faith [in order to marry her]. At present we are good friends. This is most probably the only incident of an anti-Semitic nature, that I encountered in the course of my ten-year sojourn in America.

But one swallow does not make a summer. My experience is by no means a general rule and I would not have mentioned it, had I not considered the experience typical. Let us consider the question from a broader point of view. How much do the Jewish masses suffer because of their Jewishness? Furthermore, is being a Jew the source of all their suffering, namely: physical, economic and moral.

A scientific study of the Jewish population of New York City still awaits its author, and perhaps it will never appear in a country where the authorities have intentionally omitted from their census questionnaires any reference to religious affiliation so as not to create a suspicion of the existence of religious intolerance in this country. Moreover, in addition to statistical data, ten years residence in the same environment can supply ample material to help one arrive at certain conclusions.

When we speak of Jewish masses, we do not mean to imply that they represent a homogeneous entity. They include Jews from Spain, Portugal, Germany, Russia, Hungary, Poland and Roumania, enlightened Jews, the uncouth, the ignorant, the wealthy, the bankers, the merchants, the members of the middle class and the huge working class. That is to say, they include all social subdivisions which one finds in any group of human society. Hence, we also encounter the same inner conflicts which arise because of such subdivisions.

As I have already indicated, the Jews who comprise one-fifth of the New York City population, have naturally dispersed themselves throughout its entire area. The famed East Side which has been described many times and which at one time included the preponderant majority of New York City's Jewish population is constantly growing in size, but the East Side still serves as the center of intellectual life for the Russian Jew. Its importance, however, is rapidly diminishing. While the new immigrants, without a knowledge of the language of the country, without relatives or friends, settle there because of necessity, the older settlers are moving to other parts of the city. I, personally, had an opportunity to watch how the street, on which our family was the first Jewish family, became the center of the uptown ghetto. Of course, by calling it a ghetto I am making use of poetic license, because side by side with the Jewish inhabitants there are Germans and Irish as well, and they would most probably take offense if I were to call this section a ghetto. Certain wealthy Jews at one time lived in the fashionable sections of New York City, but in recent years thousands of Jewish families have moved west of Fifth Avenue.

Economically, the Russian Jewish masses are not faring badly at all. The proportion of spontaneous mass immigration is the best indication of the rise or retrogradation of the well-being of America. If we want to discover the cause for the well-being of the Russian-Jewish masses, we must observe the economic progress of the country as a whole, because upon its progress depends the well-being of the Jew as well as that of the rest of the population. This is not the place to recount the economic and commercial advances made by the United States of America. Anyone interested in these subjects can read my studies which I have published in specialized periodicals.[9] What concerns us is the fact that we did not lag behind in this economic advance. Anyone who is interested in striking examples would be glad to know that Jews have in their midst an appreciable number of millionaires, although less than their proportionate share, if we take into account the years they have resided in this country. The wealthiest people in New York are non-Jews. We are dealing with America where the Jew who is

[9] *Russkaya Mysl*, Dec., 1901, pp. 55–68.

business-minded has to compete with the more capable American, Englishman, German and Irishman. There are Jewish bankers and factory owners in all branches of industry, but the unique Jewish branch is the garment industry, both retail and wholesale. In the manufacture of men's and ladies' garments and undergarments, the Jews of New York play an important role. Clothing in America has become much cheaper, and there is no doubt that the neatly dressed American public is indebted to the tattered, sometimes soiled Jewish masses.

In retail business, particularly in dry-goods, clothing and furniture, the Jews play a prominent part. The signs: Silberstein, Goldstein, and Cohen testify to that but it is difficult to judge by signs alone, since many Jews change their names, and one very often meets Jews with English or even Irish names. It is much easier to prove the above on Yom Kippur when one sees stores closed and notices on them stating that they are closed because of the holiday. Last year, for example, on Yom Kippur, I was in great need of a tie, and I had to pass at least twenty blocks until I found an open store. Non-Jews are well aware of this holiday and are not in any way hampered by it nor by Irish and Italian holidays as well. Cosmopolitan New York is accustomed to respect religious holidays since the general holidays are only of political significance.

By the way, on Yom Kippur, more than on any other holiday, one can get a true picture of the size of the Jewish population of New York City. The large majority of Jews who all year around do not come near a synagogue, on that day, seek out a house of worship. Scores and hundreds of Jewish houses of worship, temples and synagogues are not able to accommodate even half of those applying for admission. And in the course of these few days there is a demand for all sorts of halls. Dance halls are rented, theaters prefer to cancel their performances and are rented for purposes of worship, and even churches are rented as well.

Well, I have drifted from my subject and I will now come back to deal with the economic status of the Jews. Until lately, wealthy Jews and millionaires could be found only among the Portuguese and German Jews.. But the recent advance in commerce and industry has raised the status of the Russian Jews as well. Far be it from me to bow before Jewish or any other capital. As a man of liberal views, I am primarily concerned with the status of the workers who make up an appreciable majority of New York Jewry.

Speaking in terms of Russian currency (and the size of the budget of a working family), the average wage of a Jewish worker which is between twenty and thirty rubles a week (ten or fifteen dollars) may seem fantastic. The glazed photograph of miniature size [which the immigrant sends to his relatives in Europe] showing that fortunate person in a frock coat with a derby, cleanly shaven, with a short jacket and a gold chain, together with the glowing description of the carpets on the floor [of his home] ("I have on the floor a velvet carpet which is nicer than the table-cloth on your Naggid's [wealthy man's] table") reveals a picture of still brighter colors. Arrival in America is usually met by disappointment, but, after a while, there comes the time when enthusiastic letters are sent to Russia.

To measure the status of the Jewish masses we must use American standards. In comparison with the status of the Jews in Lithuania, the condition in New York is much superior, but this proves very little. The shortcomings of the economic status of the Jewish and the non-Jewish worker and the difference between the existing wage scale and the one which he deserves is well known and I could devote many pages to this subject.

But at the same time I must express my conviction (which will evoke protest among the intelligentsia of New York) that the Jewish masses are better off economically than the other immigrants, and extreme poverty in New York is not prevalent in the Jewish section. I think that I am familiar with the horrors of dire poverty. As a medical inspector of the New York Board of Health I had to spend several months in the poor sections of Brooklyn. When I beheld the privations of the Irish, the Italians, the Negroes and others, I had to admit that the condition of the Russian-Jewish masses is more or less satisfactory. The reason for it is their diligence and self-discipline which prevent the Jew from sinking to the lowest depths.

If we turn from industry to commerce or to to other spheres of human endeavor we do not come across any difficulties and obstacles which we can call specifically Jewish. We can definitely state that the Jew never violated the law. But even *de facto* the status of the Jew in many fields of endeavor is not any worse than it is *de jure*. In the legal and in the medical profession there are many Jews. Many of the best known legal firms are in Jewish hands and any meeting of the medical society will testify to the large percentage of Jewish physicians. I heard that of the five or six thousand physicians in New York City, fifty per cent were Jews and this is highly probable. Although the majority of these doctors practice among Jews, no discrimination exists, and, in the course of the many years of my practice, I have also taken care of Italians, Germans, Poles, Irish, French, Russians, Norwegians, Negroes and native Americans. The Jews are among the best physicians and surgeons in New York City.

Suffice it to mention the physiologist [Samuel] Meltzer[10] the stomach specialist [Max] Einhorn,[11] the surgeon [Charles] Gerster[12] and scores of others to prove the truth of the aforementioned statement. In the New York City public schools, thousands of Jewish teachers are employed. Many teach in the high schools and among them are a number of principals. In the free College of the City of New York over fifty per cent of the students are Jews. It is not difficult to find Jews among the professors of higher institutions of learning, in spite of the fact that most of these institutions are supported by private funds and are even sectarian in nature. I will mention some of them Professor of Economics [Edwin R. A.] Seligman; of French Literature [Frantz] Kohn; of Arabic and Semitic languages [Richard James Horatio] Gottheil; of Anthropology [Franz] Boaz — all of Columbia University, and scores of lecturers and instructors; Professor of German Literature [Abram] Isaacs, and Professor of Chemistry [Fritz] Leibe at New York University. In the recently established Rockefeller Institute of Medical Research [Abraham] Flexner, a Jew, was appointed its Director. I can cite such examples *ad infinitum*. The field of literature and belles-lettres is likewise open to Jews. Just to cite one or two examples: the well known *Jewish Encyclopedia* is published by a Christian firm[13] and many Christians work side by side with Jews; and among those engaged by the *International Encyclopedia*,[14] there are more than a dozen Jews.

In discussing the question of the status of the Jews, various people view it from a different standpoint. Some consider it their ideal to see that Jews are appointed professors in the colleges and universities. Others consider it their ideal to see the rise of a class of *shtadlanim*.[15] In New York City we do not have these *shtadlanim* but in political and civic life Jews play an important role. Although we have not had a Jewish Mayor, we did have a Jew serve as President of the

[10] Dr. Samuel James Meltzer (1851–1920) was a physiologist, associated with the Rockefeller Institute for Medical Research. See *American Jewish Year Book* [= *AJYB*], *5665 (1904–1905)*, p. 154.

[11] Dr. Max Einhorn was Professor of Medicine at the New York Post-Graduate Medical School. See *AJYB 5665, 1904–1905*, p. 84 and the *Jewish Encyclopedia*, vol. V (1903), p. 80.

[12] Dr. Arpad Geyza [Charles] Gerster (1848–1923) was Professor of Surgery at the New York Polyclinic, 1882–1894, and Professor of Clinical Surgery at Columbia University. See *Who Was Who in America*, vol. I (1897–1942), p. 449.

[13] The *Jewish Encyclopedia* was published by Funk and Wagnalls.

[14] The *International Encyclopedia* was published at the beginning of the twentieth century.

[15] *Shtadlanim* or Court Jews were affluent Jews who were influential at the courts of kings and princes. These Court Jews served as intermediaries between royalty and the Jewish communities. For details, see Selma Stern, *The Court Jew* (Philadelphia, 1950).

City Council who did perform the function of Acting Mayor.[16] In New York there are Jewish judges, Jewish members of the City Council, et cetera. Many Jews have city positions, such as doctors, engineers et cetera. Personally I do not attach any importance to the fact that Jews are holding high posts. But I am mentioning this because I know that it will give much pleasure to many simple souls in Russia. It is true that among the Jews who have attained prominence there are comparatively few Russian Jews, but it is their own fault (or it may be to their credit). The majority of the Russian-Jewish intelligentsia prefers to work among the radical working class and so far it has not taken an active part in the civic life of the land. However, the members of the Russian-Jewish intelligentsia are quite influential and popular among the workers. In these circles they work hand in hand with the Germans and Americans.[17]

Unintentionally we have passed from the economic aspect to the spiritual and social. From the members of the Russian-Jewish intelligentsia who reside outside of New York, I constantly hear that New York is the only place where the Russian Jew fares well. When I asked why, the answer was that in New York one can find an enlightened circle of friends, and social life is much better. You must remember that this statement is usually made by a person who has received his training in Russia and who still yearns for the mode of life that he led in Russia. Things are not so bad for the educated Jew [outside of New York City]. He can meet with the enlightened American and can find common interests with him. But what should the less educated Russian Jew do, the one who does not belong to the educated class or who has no profession? This man needs New York, Chicago and Philadelphia. Even the old Jew, who upon his arrival asks himself the question: "Well, What now? Who will bear a grudge against me now?" Even this Jew is eventually carried away by the impact of social life. True, his social activity is limited to a narrow circle, but it is still better than a mute life bereft of any responsibility to his fellow man. He tastes the first fruits of self-government, without being policed and without control from above. He goes to his synagogue and belongs to his society and to his burial or charitable organization. He is elected president or secretary, and, if not, he is able to criticize the president and his

[16] The City Council was then known as the Council of the Municipal Assembly and its President, between 1900 and 1903, was Randolph Guggenheimer.

[17] See the chapter on "Trade Unionism" in the *History of the Jewish Labor Movement in the United States* [Yiddish], ed. by Elias Tcherikower, vol. II (New York, 1945), pp. 346–395.

secretary. He delivers speeches before the audience, makes motions and corrections, casts his vote pro or con, and, thus, lives a full social life. But this is not all. Take a walk on the Bowery and look at the theatrical notices, which invite him to the theater or music hall. The Jewish East Side already has four theaters[18] and about a half a dozen music halls.[19] And what about the phenomenal growth of the Yiddish press and literature? There are about a half a dozen newspapers, monthlies, and weeklies,[20] many brochures and books of fiction, poetry, natural science and sociology. The normal diversions, the newspaper, the book and social life are not only inflating his ego, but are also capturing his interest — all these aspects constitute essential needs to the average resident, who, I am sure, will not make any startling discoveries, but he will be a useful citizen of society. These essential requirements are a part of the New York Jew, and he has the opportunity to satisfy them, and, if his financial status is satisfactory, then he is completely happy. That is why when the economy of the country is sound, when the majority of the population is employed and earns a living wage, the Jewish masses move forward with an expression of satisfaction on their faces. This does not mean that milk and honey flow on the streets of New York; nor that the Jew has nothing more to strive for. Regardless of how strong the protests and dissatisfaction with conditions may be, there is nothing specifically Jewish in this protest. There is nothing specifically Jewish in the causes for dissatisfaction, nor in the means of trying to remove these causes. In other words, the Jewish *Galut* [conditions of exile] has been done away with here. On the contrary, the elimination of the *Galut* has left the Jew with a great deal of energy and enables him to direct more attention to questions affecting humanity as a whole. But the existence of such [human] problems should not affect our [Jewish] way of life in this period of transition. As a result, we observe among New York Jews a cheerfulness and a manifestation of joy and elation which is so unusual among the Jews in Russia. This was noted by a Russian [non-Jew] who visited New York and was present at a Jewish ball. "And these are our Russian Jews?" he exclaimed, pointing at the

[18] The theaters were: The People's, Grand, Windsor and Thalia. For details, see Bernard Gorin, "The Yiddish Theater in New York," in *The Theater*, Jan., 1903, pp. 16–19. These theaters were then located on the Bowery.

[19] The Music Halls also were located on the Bowery and they presented vaudeville sketches.

[20] The Yiddish periodicals and newspapers were: *Jüdisches Tageblatt, Jüdische Gazetten, Die Jüdische Welt, Jüdische Zeitung, Die Neue Post, Der Morgenstern, Der Courier, Der Menschenfreund, Der Telegraph, Der Volksadvokat, Die Arbeiterzeitung* and *Die Freie Arbeiter Stimme.*

assemblage. "It is wonderful! What has become of their bent backs, of the fearful look on their faces! See how they walk in an upright manner. What a manifestation of courage, what a manifestation of independence in their manners, in their conversation!" But is New York responsible for this? Do we not see that these results were brought about by the elimination of the Jewish question and by the elimination of the *Galut*. But we have drifted far in our discussion and we are not prepared to concede that there is no Jewish problem in New York City.

II

"Answer me frankly: Do you regret that you were born a Jew?" This categorical question was posed to me by my interlocutor, one of the editors of the *International Encyclopedia*, a cultured person who is primarily interested in sociology and in human relations. We were discussing the question of racial conflicts. This direct question called for an explicit answer, and for a moment made me ponder.

"You see," I began slowly, "I want to give you a frank and honest answer. I could, of course, play the part of a theatrical hero and, beating my fist against my chest, I could declare that I am proud that I am a Jew, that I was born a Jew, that I belong to this great race, et cetera. But the insincerity of my answer would not have escaped your notice. I accept my Jewishness as an historical fact, which, in spite of myself, binds me together by means of hundreds of ties with my people. I must confess that in my childhood and youth in Russia my Jewishness seemed to me a source of suffering and unpleasantness, and I was then not mature enough to feel a sense of solidarity to my other fellow-sufferers. All my interests were of a Russian nature and my Jewishness was a hindrance to me. In those moments I regretted that I was born a Jew. Since then my outlook has changed. I do not know how I would have viewed this phenomenon were I now living in Russia, but here in New York the situation is quite different. I must frankly tell you that in the course of my ten-year sojourn in New York not a day has passed by on which I should have been sorry that I am a Jew. There has been no actual cause for me to regret it."

"It is really magnanimous of you to say that. But haven't you really lost anything here because of your Jewishness? You know how much they dislike and abuse the Jews in many places; you see how the press constantly discusses the Jewish question and is recommending ways and means of clearing the East Side."

"Where does magnanimity enter the picture? I am merely stating a fact. If anyone finds it convenient to discuss the Jewish question let him do so to his heart's content. That in cosmopolitan New York there is plenty of room for religious and racial prejudice, I do not doubt in the least. But why should the Jew feel it more than any other people? The Irishman dislikes the German, and the German despises the Irishman, while both deride the Italian, and all three are ready to attack the Negro, et cetera. This is sad indeed, but again this same cosmopolitan New York combats this national chauvinism. We, educated people, work harmoniously and peacefully in this editorial office, and there are among us Americans, Dutch, English, French, Scotch and Jews. And we are by no means an exception. To find examples of such co-operation between various ethnic groups in New York is by no means difficult. You meet these examples on every step. It would be ridiculous for the Jew to exclude himself from this setting and to consider himself a martyr. Of course, he can retaliate against this chauvinism towards him in the same manner, and he certainly does that [when the situation arises]. Take [the following] for instance! In Russia when the Jew was ridiculed on the stage and was pictured with long *pe'ot* [earlocks] with a long coat and with gesticulations similar to those of an ape, I was furious. Why? Because they derided us and we had no right to register our protest. But here, this type is presented from time to time on the vaudeville stage, and I laugh together with the rest of the audience because here it is done good-naturedly and without malice. Here on the Yiddish stage I can also see a comical characterization of the Irishman. Should then the Irishman cry out that there exists an Irish question? If you want to convince yourself of my assertion go to the Atlantic Garden.[21] You know that that is the music hall where, with a glass of beer for a nickel, you gain free admission to the performance. The owner is German, but this establishment is situated in the heart of the Jewish ghetto and the bearded Jews, their wives and the young people constitute three-quarters of the audience. And still, this shrewd businessman presents on the stage many such comical Jewish characters to the great amusement of the audience. True, the Jew is tolerant and he deserves a great deal of praise. But what is more important is the fact that he feels that there is no malicious desire to insult him. Let me cite another example. Next door to me there is a large but low-priced theater in which sensational plays are presented at a popular price. Two weeks ago a play written by an American playwright was presented in

[21] The Atlantic Garden was a popular place of amusement on the East Side which attracted both Jews and non-Jews alike.

which he ridiculed the Irishmen of New York. The main character was an Irish policeman with a green beard. Let me emphasize at this point that the owner of the theater was an Irishman. Our section of the city consists of Irishmen, Germans, and Jews and very few Italians. When the policeman with the green beard appeared on the stage, half of the audience rose to its feet like one man and threw rotten eggs and apples at the players. It was later discovered that this was planned beforehand by several Irish societies who decided to put a stop to this ridiculing of the Irishmen on the stage, and a president of one of the societies openly declared: 'Where did you ever hear that an Irish policeman should have a green beard?' Shall we then say that there exists an Irish question in New York? Of course, the Irish were absurd in making such a declaration."

"There is a great deal of truth in what you have said," retorted the editor. "But at the same time, there are facts which cannot be denied. For example, you will not be accepted in any of the exclusive clubs. People of a certain class will not invite you to their homes. You have to live an isolated mode of life. This social ostracism is perhaps not very important, but these minor barbs against one's self-esteem are sometimes hard to digest. I know that in the town where I was born there are several Jewish families there whose social life is very unattractive although they are well established."

"I cannot agree with you. What you say about your town may be true. But we are speaking now about the conditions in New York City. None of my friends nor I have experienced any social ostracism. I am not anxious to belong to clubs. But I know hundreds of Jews who do belong to many clubs, Masonic lodges and other organizations. True, there are a large number of Jews who do not belong to any clubs, but this is because they are not anxious to belong and prefer to be connected with their own societies. And there is no harm in this. A Jew lives among Jews as the Irish live among the Irish and the Italians live among the Italians. If the Irishman does not accept me as a member of his club, I have the satisfaction of not accepting him into mine. I repeat that the facts are exaggerated and that there is no social ostracism. What kind of social ostracism can there be when there are over 600,000 of us? Take a stroll through the streets of the ghetto and ask any Jew whether he even dreams about being in the company of members of other nationalities. He will answer: 'Let us hope that things should continue to fare well and that there should be no unemployment, and as far as societies are concerned, haven't we enough societies of our own?' The term ghetto which made the European Jew blush when it was mentioned does not embarrass the Jew here, because the ghetto is a voluntary one. Don't you know that the rent in the ghetto is fifty or seventy-five per cent higher than in any other section of the city? Hence, it might be assumed that an ostracism exists among Jews against the rest of the population? You are only partially right. There are clubs into which I will not be accepted. But why? Is it just because I am a Jew? Even if I were a native American, would the Knicker-bocker Club or the New York Athletic Club accept me? — me with my attire, with my social status, with my political views and, above all, with my means? And for that matter will they accept you? Will you then put ashes on your head or shed tears? You should know that I was a candidate for Congress in my district representing the Labor Party.[22] True, I received only 450 votes and my opponent received several thousand. Should I call this social ostracism? It is true that the [A, B, C and D's] and other Jewish millionnaires are trying in vain to get into the magic circle of New York aristocracy. Must I share their grief or make their grief mine? I am sure that if I would attempt to be accepted into the company of the aforementioned gentlemen I, too, would be just as unsuccessful as they are in trying to become a member of the Four Hundred. If the Jew in your town feels that he is socially ostracized I, indeed, sympathize with him and I will be the first to advise the Jews of New York not to move into the interior. Here we live together as one group and we need nothing else."

I cited this conversation because it captured my interest and I hope it will interest you. To my interlocutor I related only some of the facts that I had gathered in the course of these years. Now I will attempt to discuss the whole matter in a somewhat greater detail.

The question is no doubt an interesting one. The numerous facts which I have cited in the first chapter prove one thing: that in all branches of human enterprise the Jews stand on the same level with other ethnic groups, but we must not deduce from this that there are no exceptions. Let us take for example these Jewish million-naires. In social and political life they play an important part. Straus was an ambassador to Turkey. There is hardly a single important political meeting in New York to which [the B's and the C's] are not invited. But they are not successful in gaining admission into the parlors of the Christian millionnaires. The problem is one and the same, but its aspects are different and they are to be treated differently.

---

[22] There is no record of this assertion in any of his biographies, neither is it recorded in the newspaper files of that period.

I will again speak from personal observations and experience. I meet representatives of all nationalities, although most of my friends in New York are Russian Jews. In the houses of the latter, I likewise meet time and again members of different nationalities and their relationship is of the best. Naturally, these Russian Jews and their American friends have the same progressive views in common. These people are now in the minority in this country, but their number is growing and in their hands lies the future of America. To expect tolerance from the rest of the New York population for this group would be ridiculous. We must not forget that the alien segment of the New York population was born in Europe. In 1900, New York City's population numbered 3,437,207 souls. If we deduct the number of Negroes and the Chinese (67,304) there remain 3,369,898. Of this number of the white population, 1,270,072 or 37.7 per cent were born abroad. The first generation [born of immigrants] numbers 1,260,918, or 37.42 per cent. More than 75 per cent, therefore, are still steeped in the European tradition.[23] Even if the Jews should only constitute 15–18 per cent of the population, then out of the remaining 85–82 per cent, more than 60 per cent are still aware of anti-Semitism and are familiar with this product of European culture. If we take into account these conditions, then the change which has taken place in America is indeed remarkable. To come to definite conclusions on the basis of the relationship of one group to another is rather difficult. We are aware of the complexity of the problem. To solve it we must turn the pages of our history and study the attitude of the Jews during the past two centuries. Those to whom the *Jewish Encyclopedia*[24] is accessible will find valuable information in it on the subject [of the Jews in America] in the article entitled "America" and in the others pertaining to individual states. But even here there is data available only up to 1819 when the Jews of Maryland were granted the right to hold public office, and with this ended [the *Jewish Encyclopedia's*] description of the establishment of political equality [in the United States of America] which was initiated with the Declaration of Independence in 1776 by that remarkable document which Thomas Jefferson wrote under the influence of French and English philosophers, authors of the theory of natural rights of man. The later history of the relationship between Jews and Christians cannot be evaluated

[23] He compiled these figures from the 1900 census. Cf. Samuel Joseph, *Jewish Immigration to the United States* (New York, 1914), *passim*.

[24] Rubinow refers to the first volume of the *Jewish Encyclopedia* (New York, 1902), pp. 491–517. The Russian encyclopedia, *Yevreiskaya Entsyclopedia*, first appeared in 1906.

by any definite historical method, and I am not trying to write a history, but merely to shed light on the present state of affairs.

Everyone remembers the incident at the funeral of Rabbi Jacob Joseph which took place about a year ago.[25] In my articles about the incident which I then wrote I stated how there arose a tendency to describe this incident as a sort of a pogrom and how quickly this view was dropped. On the contrary, this incident raised the respect for Jews not only in New York but throughout America. To prove this assertion is very simple. The non-Jewish newspapers devote considerable space to Jewish life, and we do not refer to the [Rabbi Jacob Joseph] incident to which full pages were devoted. The non-Jewish newspapers direct a great deal of space to the dedication of a new building of a Jewish seminary,[26] to the death of a well-known rabbi, to the appointment of a rabbi, and even to his sermon, to a meeting of a philanthropic society and to a ball for the benefit of a Jewish hospital — to which at least two columns are usually devoted. But not only the newspapers, but even the periodicals are competing with one another with their articles on the life of the Jews in the New York ghetto. In American literature a demand arose for fiction on Jewish life which is supplied by a goodly number of writers, the most talented of whom is Abraham Cahan who is well known to the Russian public.[27] But even the works of lesser known writers find a market because the demand is so great. But this is not all. The American public is not only interested in Anglo-Jewish fiction. The Jews of Russia have spoken Yiddish for centuries, yet I have never read in any Russian [non-Jewish] periodical anything relating to a Yiddish novelist such as the article published in the *Atlantic Monthly*[28] about the Yiddish novelist, S. Libin [Israel Horowitz], author of Yiddish short stories. Try to find an intelligent Russian who should show an interest in the Yiddish theater. On the one

[25] See Rubinow's articles in *Niedielnaya Khronika Voskhoda*, 1903, vol. XXI (Aug. 8), pp. 23–26; (Aug., 15), pp. 25–28. See also Abraham J. Karp, "New York Chooses a Chief Rabbi," *PAJHS*, vol. XLIV, no. 3 (March, 1953), pp. 129–198.

[26] On the dedication of the Jewish Theological Seminary of America, see the *New York Times*, Nov. 21, 1902, p. 3, col. 3.

[27] See Abraham Cahan, *The Rise of David Levinsky* (New York, 1899). See also Moses Rischin, "Abraham Cahan and the *Commerical Advertiser*: A Study in Acculturation," *PAJHS*, vol. XLIII, no. 1 (Sept., 1953), pp. 10–36. Cf. Ephim Yeshurun, *Abraham Cahan Bibliography* (New York, 1948).

[28] *Atlantic Monthly*, vol. XCI (Feb., 1903), pp. 254–260. Examples of some of the novels dealing with Jewish life in the United States that were written by non-Jews are: C. Ogden, *The Jews* (New York, 1900); Horace Rollin, *Yetta Segal* (New York, 1898); Rose Perler, *Daughters of Israel* (New York, 1899); and James Walker Ludlow, *Deborah* (New York, 1901).

hand, there is hardly a New York newspaper or periodical which does not publish articles concerning the Yiddish theater and the plays by the playwright, Jacob Gordin, and others.[29] Many New York theater critics advise those who understand and speak German to go to the Yiddish theater to improve their literary taste.[30] The English newspapers took note of the extraordinary talent of Jacob Adler[31] and an American entrepreneur invited him to tour America with this troupe. Adler is to play the role of Shylock in Yiddish and the rest of the cast will play in English. I cite these facts because they serve as examples of the respect for the Jew, and not necessarily for the American-born assimilated Jew, but for the Russian-Jewish immigrant, whom the American, only several years ago, considered as being uncultured and semi-savage.

In order that these statements may sound plausible, I will quote a passage from American publications:

"They [the Russian Jews] are free of the stupid Philistinism of content and are not primarily interested in the dollar," writes Hutchins Hapgood about the Russian-Jewish intelligentsia. "Their poets sing pathetically of the sweatshops, of universal brotherhood of the abstract rights of man . . . In their restless and feverish eyes shines the intense idealism of the combined Jew and Russian — the moral earnestness of the Hebrew, united with the passionate, rebellious, mental activity of the modern Moscovite. The ideal, indeed, is alive within them. The defect of their intellectual ideas is that they are not founded on historical knowledge or on knowledge of the conditions with which they have to cope. In their excitement and extremeness they resemble the spirit of the French intellectuals of 1789."[32] This is what Charles Rice writes in the *Atlantic Monthly*:

> The Russian emigrants have been more or less fed this wholesome nourishment which refined their taste and sharpened their judgment. Nothing trashy, no printed matter below a certain literary level will permanently appeal to them. An American of culture, of fine discrimination, should he once gain an intimate familiarity with this class of Jews, would be astonished to find how superior their literary taste is than that of many a college-bred reader of magazines. These ignorant "foreigners," many of them grimy shop hands or peddlers, with the marks of culture long worn-off from their faces by years of fierce struggling for daily bread and a place in the world, will frequently display an unusual degree of literary, dramatic and general art appreciation.[33]

[29] *New York Times*, Jan. 15, 1901, p. 16, col. 6.
[30] *Ibid.*, May 26, 1901, p. 19, col. 3.
[31] *Ibid.*, Feb. 15, 1901, p. 10, col. 4.
[32] Hutchins Hapgood, *The Spirit of the Ghetto* (New York, 1909), pp. 47–48.
[33] *Atlantic Monthly.* vol. XCI (Feb., 1903), pp. 254–260.

I think that I have cited sufficient proof to substantiate my thesis that the American is learning to respect the Jew, and this respect makes social ostracism impossible. I could also cite here the opinion of the Secretary of State John Hay about the Jews, an opinion which he expressed in his statement on immigration from Roumania,[34] but since it is of a political nature I will speak of it later.[35] Different social groups judge people by different standards. We cannot, for example, expect members of the Four Hundred to respect the literary, artistic and scholarly achievements of the Jews. But the laboring masses, and particularly organized labor, respects the Jew highly for reasons which are self-evident. Having arrived from a land without a background in the field of organized labor, the Jews have grasped the idea of trade unionism very quickly and not only have they joined the ranks, but they have succeeded in occupying the *avant-garde*. I want you to know that I do not prostrate myself before great people, but it is rather interesting to note that the American Federation of Labor, an organization which lists about a million and a half workers (more than half of the organized workers of the United States), has been headed for the last few years by Samuel Gompers.[36]

[34] Philip Cowen, *Memoirs of an American Jew* (New York, 1922), pp. 263–264.

[35] *Voskhod*, 1904, vol. XXIV (June), pp. 111–126.

[36] [(*Rubinow's note*) The actual status of the Jews of New York is still an enigma to the foreigner. This is what Beckles Wilson says in his book, *The New America: A Study of the Imperial Republic* (London and New York, 1903), pp. 172–173:

> "It is estimated that within a radius of fifteen miles from New York City Hall there are more Jews than in the whole of Germany. Slowly but surely, the Jew is permeating the whole commercial life of New York and getting control of many trades within his fingers ... Gradually, too, the Gentile element, particularly the Irish and the Irish-Americans, are becoming aware of the pressure which industrial competition is putting upon them. The constant wholesale influx of poor Jews from Russia, Germany and Austria has led to a marked lowering of wages, and when this came home to the poor Irish, the persecution of the Hebrew commenced. The antagonism has recently evoked unseemly riots and as the increased cost of living and the ingenious method of the 'sweater' continue, serious trouble is to be feared."

We can tolerate a purely economic interpretation of this issue. But the author is unfamiliar with the existing economic conditions. He does not know that the Jew is an ardent supporter of the trade unions and fights more frequently than the Irish for an increase in wages. He grossly errs when he gives so much prominence to the disturbance which occurred near Hoe and Co. It is interesting to note that on the same page he opposes the restriction of the immigration of the Chinese since they are a hard working race. But when he speaks of the lowering of wages, to which other ethnic groups can the Chinese be compared?

> "The Jews [says Wilson] are about one-eighth of the population, yet they claim 115 out of the 4,000 millionnaires of the country, — about two and a half times as many as they are entitled to. Even leaving out the back woods and confining the inquiry

The best proof of the friendly relations which exist between Jews and non-Jews of the middle class and of the working class is provided by more or less frequent intermarriages. Unfortunately, there are no statistical figures to prove that. They would really be very instructive. But even without any statistical figures, there is no doubt that the number is considerable. I can mention over twenty of my friends who have intermarried with Irish, German and American native-born. These mixed marriages captured the fancy of the young novelist Herman Bernstein[37] and he devoted one of his short stories to this topic, which, if I am not mistaken, was published last year in the *Voskhod* in Russian translation.[38] We will not discuss the literary merits of this story here. But the moral which the author attempts to put forth in his exaggerated tale is penetrated with inexactitudes. Indifference to religion is the most characteristic trait of the people who intermarry. There is, therefore, rarely any conflict based upon religious differences. There are, however, many other conflicts which may arise in such a family, — conflicts which are peculiar to any family in this country. Our young writer grossly errs when he shows that the Jew who intermarries is completely estranged from his Jewish environment. This estrangement may be peculiar to the Jews of the older generation among whom inter-marriages were very rare, but in enlightened circles, where intermarriage is a more frequent occurrence, this estrangement has been eliminated.

III

If everything is in such a perfect condition then the reader may justly ask: "Why all the fuss?" But the fact is that not everything is as perfect as the reader might imagine. Glance through such periodicals as the *American Hebrew* and the *Hebrew Standard* for the past year and see the titles there of such articles as: "A Mass Meeting to Discuss the Jewish Question," or "The Jewish Question on the East Side," et cetera. You will suddenly become aware that there is a Jewish problem on the East Side among the poor and needy Jews, and this raises a question in one's mind: Is there really a specific Jewish problem? There is no smoke without fire and re-

---

to the town population, it is found that the number of Jewish millionnaires is still disproportionately large.]"

[37] [(*Rubinow's note*) See "The Awakening," in Herman Bernstein, *The Gates of Israel* (New York, 1902), pp. 69–87.]

[38] The story did not appear in the *Voskhod.*

luctantly you stop to ponder over this question. There is a great deal of commotion about it and this uneasiness is reflected in the American press.[39] Then what is the so-called Jewish question? There is no legal aspect to this problem. It is primarily of an economic nature. In the course of the past several years another aspect has come to the fore, namely, the moral one.

I have already stated above that the economic status of the Jewish masses has been more or less satisfactory, if we compare it with the status of the other elements of the working population. We are not to assume, however, that the economic status of the Jews is completely satisfactory. Go through the narrow streets of the Jewish section; look at the gigantic houses, each of which houses from twenty to twenty-four families in cages which do not deserve to be designated as rooms. Listen to the noise, the weeping and the shouting of the children who get in your way. Pay special attention to the density of the population and the crowded conditions, to the lack of fresh air and light and to the stench which you cannot avoid smelling, and you will undoubtedly exclaim: "It is impossible to live this way."

You would then feel a moral obligation to do something constructive for your suffering brethren. This attitude was taken by our German and other Jews — the old settlers of New York, when mass migration began years ago. But this sense of compassion then became mixed up with contempt and reflected itself in the manner in which charity was distributed. But aid was given; hospitals were founded; asylums were established, and these were subsidized by wealthy American Jews. Later the Educational Alliance was established, a large institution which renders some benefit, although it could render ten times as much as it does.

But the newcomer unfortunately was misunderstood both by the Americans and the American Jews alike. While it was perhaps ridiculous to expect the former to understand or even to attempt to understand the newcomer, the latter, by his attitude, committed a gross error, almost a crime. The American viewed the appearance of the peculiar newcomer with bewilderment and curiosity as he viewed all newcomers. This happened fifteen to twenty years ago, when a different element began to arrive and the place which was once occupied by the Germans, Irish and English then was occupied by the Italians, Hungarians and Jews. He did not see, however, why he should single out the Jew as the target for special antipathy.

---

[39] He refers to the articles which appeared in the *American Hebrew*. See notes 46 and 47, *infra*, pp. 119–120.

On the contrary, he sympathized with him because the Jew was a victim of religious persecution and appeared to be willing and anxious to work.

The German Jew, the old timer, however, was ashamed of his Russian cousin, and this shame created an iron barrier between the two groups. This brought about a great deal of misunderstanding. The German Jew forgot that when he first appeared on American soil, the Portuguese Jew who preceded him, regarded him with contempt. The characteristic indication of the state of affairs may be seen in the respectful attitude of the American [non-Jew] towards the members of the [Russian-Jewish] intelligentsia and in the hostility of the wealthy American Jew towards the intelligentsia.

Life in the Russian-Jewish colony in New York City has in the past ten or fifteen years made rapid progress without any help of the German Jew. The masses, who were downtrodden for many years, were content with the meager help which they had received and neither had the courage nor the audacity to register their protest against the persons from whom they had received aid. Thus, the wealthy Jew was aggressive and the poor Jew was humble and meek. He used to come quietly to the reading room of the Educational Alliance and eagerly grabbed hold of a book or newspaper in German, Russian or Yiddish and humbly endured the inquisitive looks at him. He answered meekly the inquiries which were directed to him out of sheer curiosity by the "Ladies and Gentlemen." And even if he felt offended, he suppressed this feeling with a sigh. I have a suspicion that the Russian Jews have for a time really looked upon themselves as inferior creatures.

But the Russian Jew grew in stature, not by days but by hours. More enlightened immigrants arrived and from the midst of these Russian masses the intelligentsia was outstanding, and, as time went on, the intellectual level of the Russian-Jewish masses was likewise raised. A Jewish university student has become a common occurrence. There came to the fore a Yiddish literature, a Yiddish theater, a Yiddish press — evidences of Jewish cultural life. All these efforts, all these achievements, were attained by the Jewish masses on the East Side, primarily by the Russian Jews among them, and they made these achievements without any help of the German or American-born Jews, who stood from afar during that period of cultural advancement. This is one of the phenomena which will help us understand the Jewish problem. All this advancement took place in the interval of ten or fifteen years before my own eyes, and I am basing my statements not upon rumors, but upon personal observations and actual facts. The wealthy German Jews, on the

other hand, not only made no attempt to help or to show any understanding, but did not even notice it. This is the severest accusation
which the Russian Jew can direct against the wealthy German Jew.
All this work was done by a small group of enlightened Russian
Jews, without money and without connections. How they attained
all this progress would have remained a mystery, had we not been
aware of another existing factor — the support given by the
Russian-Jewish masses.

All these years the Directors of the Educational Alliance closed
their eyes to the surrounding environment and followed the old
custom by directing their main attention towards Americanizing the
Jew. They thought that it was sufficient to teach the newcomer a
few patriotic songs. Of course, we should not blame the German
Jew either. He blindly adopted that American pedagogic method —
a method which calls for the intensive instruction of immigrants in
poetry of a patriotic nature. The German Jew accepted axiomatic-
ally the fact that the Russian Jew was incapable of transporting
his cultural treasures with him to his new environment. He held
this "Russian savage" in contempt — a contempt which was very
strong in Germany twenty-five years ago, but which has gradually
been disappearing, because in Germany, they have become more
familiar with Russian culture. The situation which I have described
above served as the basis for that antagonism. But many years
passed until this antagonism took on a definite shape. Besides the
United Hebrew Charities, with which the poor and the downtrodden
have come in contact, — that institution where he was unable to
express himself, protest or stand up for his rights, — the main center
where the uptown wealthy Jew came in contact with the poor
Russian and other Jews of the ghetto was the Hebrew Institute,
known later as the Educational Alliance. Here there was a library,
an auditorium, a reading room and clubs where the Russian Jew
was able to show his abilities, but even in that institution there
prevailed a feeling of haughtiness, of contempt and of animosity
towards the visitor. As we have said, the Educational Alliance was
the chief center of contact between the uptown and the downtown
Jew; hence it became the center of open conflict and disagreement,
which became particularly acute in the mid-nineties. The Director
of the institution was a sympathetic young man of Russian extraction, who was in full sympathy with the aspirations of the Russian
Jew. He was popular in the ghetto, and, among the intelligentsia,
he was progressive enough to speak calmly and without pathos about
philanthropy and, therefore, was able to smoothen out the rough
spots and to maintain peace and tranquility in this institution. But,

unfortunately, his influence was not effective enough, and the approaching conflict seemed inevitable. The majority of the new immigrants were workers and they joined the labor movement. The Russian-Jewish laborer won the esteem of his fellow-American worker, but this brought about a feeling of distrust on the part of the wealthy German Jews. That the bankers, men of means, who are at the head of the Educational Alliance, and even the professors dislike any organized labor movement is a self-evident fact. We have, therefore, been faced with a clash of views which was provoked by existing economic conditions. But why should this state of affairs have an effect on the relationship between the American Jew and the immigrant? The disciples of the theory of class struggle may contend that this conflict was bound to come. He may be right or he may err. One thing is evident. The affluent German Jews are definitely not in sympathy with the theory of class struggle. But at the same time in their attempt to express their opposition to it overtly, the Directors of the Educational Alliance caused dissension in Jewish public opinion. The auditorium of the Educational Alliance which was built to promote education and the free exchange of ideas became the scene of a campaign against any ideologies which dealt with the principles of unionism or co-operatives. Jewish and non-Jewish professors alike, as well as religious leaders, Jewish and Christian, preached from this platform about the detrimental influence of socialism. Even such an unimportant issue as the placing of the railroads under government control evoked a great deal of opposition. What prompted our cultured Americans to come forth with such propaganda? There could be no question about the influence of several thousand East Side Jewish workers in politics, or, perhaps, the esteemed leaders were somewhat embarrassed before their Christian neighbors when it became evident that the Jewish masses were becoming the vanguard in the struggle for these ideals. After all, we all feel ill-at-ease when our relative or even our namesake places us in an awkward position. Or perhaps there was an actual attempt to save the soul of the poor Jew, because side by side with the political propaganda they [the German Jews] began a religious propaganda as well. Sermons on the vanity of earthly goods, or the rewards in the life to come, on tolerance, et cetera were delivered from the pulpit. The enlightened people [of the East Side] became sick of that tendency which was so crudely stressed. But what did the wealthy uptown Jews accomplish by this propaganda? They did not become any more politically influential, but merely aggravated the situation and caused dissatisfaction, suspicion and lack of confidence on the part of the Russian Jew toward the philanthropic motives and communal leadership of the uptown

Jew. The Educational Alliance, thus, committed one blunder after another. A new Director, a member of the [Jewish] clergy was appointed, a man who, as is typical of the members of the American clergy, bows before wealth. In spite of all his attempts to win the confidence of the intelligentsia of the ghetto — the Russian Jewish intelligentsia, — the new Director failed in his attempts. A person who extols the philanthropists, who only emphasizes Americanization, cannot win the support of the intelligentsia. Contrary to the principles which guided Baron [Maurice] de Hirsch in the founding of the Educational Alliance, — who donated the money to make it an educational institution — the Educational Alliance has undertaken a rather unbecoming task of [attempting] to strengthen religion. Just imagine, the German and American Jews have all of a sudden decided to spread religion among the Polish, Lithuanian and Galician Jews. Doesn't it sound ridiculous? And what is more, large sums of money, which now have reached the amount of $18,000 a year, were set aside for this purpose. I cited these instances to show why there could be no common understanding between the uptown and downtown Jews, how they missed the opportunity to solve the East Side problem, if, by this rather inappropriate term, we mean the educational aspect — the co-operative attempt to help the Jewish population of the East Side. Even the educational aspect of the program is beginning to decline. The Board of Education is directing all its efforts.to provide educational facilities, to provide the immigrant with an elementary education. On the other hand, the question of earning a livelihood is not specifically Jewish. The question is solved very simply by procuring employment. And we must say that economically the Jewish masses have achieved their present status without any outside help.

In spite of the increase in the Jewish population the so-called specific Jewish problem ceased to be a problem. In its place, there came to the fore a number of common problems affecting the city population as a whole. There arose the problem of crowded conditions, of unsatisfactory dwellings in which the worker had to live, et cetera. The uptown Jew could not understand why this change is taking place. As the population of the ghetto increased the seven-story tenement building took the place of the former spacious private houses [to meet the crowded conditions]. But the uptown Jew called it a specific Jewish problem. And what was their answer to this so-called problem? The Jew must be Americanized. They refused to see that the conditions which exist in the Jewish section are no different than those existing in the Italian, Irish and German sections and that there is no need to make it specifically Jewish.

A striking example of this lack of understanding can be seen in the attempt of the German Jews to raise the moral standards of the Jewish East Side.

Two or three years ago a movement was set on foot, called by some in jest "the Renaissance of Morals." The basic cause for this movement was of a political nature — politics as we understand it in America, that is, it was essentially a political party struggle. The municipal government of New York was in the hands of the Democratic Party, known in New York as Tammany Hall. The Tammany organization established for itself a reputation for plundering the city's finances, upon which it looked as a source of personal revenue. One of the most popular methods of collecting that revenue was to impose a special levy on prostitution, so as to protect it from puritanical law, which strongly forbade it.[40] In 1901, before the municipal elections, it became evident that prostitution would become a vital issue and the opposing party would find it convenient to use this as a campaign issue. This abuse by Tammany would be easy to prove and it would be possible [for the opposing party] to gain a great number of votes. Tammany suspected it and it jumped ahead of the opposition. It started a war against prostitution and gave this campaign wide publicity. Since I am not writing a history of New York City, the reader might ask: "Why have you touched upon this question?" [I did it] to show that thanks to the extreme diligence of a few German Jews belonging to both Tammany and the Republican parties the question of immorality narrowed itself down to the Jewish neighborhood — [claiming] that it was concentrated in the Jewish section of the East Side, and the impression was created that the Jewish section was a nest of immorality. There is no doubt that these noble Jews were guided by the most noble intentions but their efforts were in vain. It reached the point where the Jews — the Russian Jews — whose standards of morality are praised even by the most ardent anti-Semites, were forced to endure false accusations of being immoral. We must admit that this provides a great deal of food for thought and reflection.

But what about this campaign? True enough, at the extreme end of the East Side, on Houston Street, and in nearby Allen Street above which tower the tracks of the elevated train and which is densely populated and has dark and stenchy houses, prostitution arose because the police permitted it. The situation was indeed to be deplored. A public school and a large synagogue were situated right

---

[40] *New York Times* (1901), March 10, p. 8; March 11, p. 22; March 13, p. 8; March 14, p. 6; April 17, p. 20 and a number of other items appeared in the *New York Times* during the course of the year 1901–1902.

next door to the house of prostitution and prostitutes resided in the same tenement house in which the poor workers lived. The encouragement of prostitution by the police was far from desirable or laudable. It was still more deplorable that prostitution penetrated into the Jewish section of the city, which is inhabited by thousands of honest Jewish families. This section, thus, became known as the Red Light District. It consequently served as the focal point of the neighborhood where not only Jews, but German, Irish and other [ethnic] groups resided — all recent immigrants, among whom there were a large number of single people, — all essential prerequisites for the flourishing of prostitution. We must confess that it likewise affected in a certain measure the Jewish members of the population, and the Jews contributed their share of prostitutes as well. May I point out that the vices affected mostly the so-called Americanized Jews, that is, those who have adopted the outward luster of so-called Americanization and who tried to shake off religious discipline and did not attempt to find an intellectual or moral substitute in its place. These vices developed among adherents of the Democratic Party among whom are many highly moral, uptown Jews, but among the supporters of the Labor Party with whom the Board of Directors of the Educational Alliance contended so bitterly there were very few [adherents].

It would be ridiculous to assume that there were no houses of prostitution in other streets, besides those populated by the foreigners on the East Side. In the heart of New York, in the district where theaters, restaurants and clubs are situated, licentiousness exists in its extremest form. It is, therefore, evident that in the so-called movement for temperance the aim was not really to do away with vice. No one wanted to see vice done away with more than the honest inhabitants of the East Side in whose face it stared so brazenly. They [the people of the East Side] constantly complained about the connivance of the police. If there was an honest desire to do away with it, the uptown and downtown Jews could have worked hand in hand. Instead, the campaign assumed the form of a crusade against immorality on the East Side. In the fashionable hotels there was constant talk about the moral infection emanating from the East Side, and about the need of propaganda which should come from the outside. The residents of the East Side did not deny that the existing conditions were detrimental to the young generation, but the East Side was infuriated when it was pointed at as being the source of this evil. It considered it an insult which it could not forget. "Just because the obscene Bowery on one side and Houston Street on the other constitute the natural boundary

of our section and the vice from these streets spreads throughout
our own streets, it does not follow that we have lower moral standards," the East Side protested loudly. "Unfortunately, in our section the workers must occupy the same dwellings as the prostitutes,
while in your sections decent people can have separate apartments."

IV

I do not want you to look upon the previous articles as an indict-
ment against a certain group of people, and to suspect that these
articles were written under the influence of party ardor. I only
wanted to emphasize the main causes which brought about these
misunderstandings and caused the people of New York to talk about
the existing conflict between the Russian and German Jews. One
of the main underlying causes was the [latter's] lack of understanding
of the [immigrant's] spiritual and intellectual aspirations and also
a total unfamiliarity with the existing economic conditions faced by
the poor immigrants when they arrive in this country. I do not
deny that there is a sincere attempt by the German Jew to help the
Russian immigrant. But the methods which the German used led
to an outcry, emanating from the East Side: "We do not want your
honey and free us of your compassion." The growing East Side
began to show signs of independence.

There was a time when a German Jewish hospital was the only
asylum for the ailing Russian. The Jew did not want to be confined
in a non-Jewish hospital. But thanks to the efforts of the inhabitants
of the ghetto, the sturdy building of the Beth Israel Hospital was
erected.[41] There was a time when the Educational Alliance was the
only place that had an adult education program. Gradually other
adult classes were established and other organizations were founded,
among which the Educational League stands out. It was founded
by Russian Jews.[42]

Concerning the founding of this school for workers, I have already
informed the reader in the *Voskhod*,[43] and there is, therefore, no need
for me to go into unnecessary details. I must, however, say that the
main topic of the day is a comparison between the work of the
Educational Alliance and that of the Educational League. In truth,
it is difficult to draw a definite line of demarcation because no comparison would do justice to either, because of the difference in their

[41] See the article by Boris Bogen in *Niedielnaya Khronika Voskhoda*, 1894, vol. XIII
(Jan. 23), p. 96.

[42] *Niedielnaya Khronika Voskhoda* (1902), vol. XXI (Feb. 24), pp. 24–29.

[43] *Ibid.* (1895), vol. XIV (July 9), pp. 780–782.

financial status. After a period of three years of hard work, of staging amateur performances to amuse the public, it [the Educational League] has in its treasury a pitiable $15,000, whereas the budget of the Educational Alliance is $50,000 a year. In this respect, the Educational Alliance has the upper hand. But the intellectual Russian-Jewish intelligentsia sides with the League and this the Alliance cannot ignore. At the meetings of the Educational Alliance their glowing progress reports have been time and again interrupted by excited members of the intelligentsia. At these meetings, however, the German Jews have never come face to face with an organized opposition. The Director of the Alliance, who resides on the East Side and has had an opportunity to come in contact with the Russian-Jewish intelligentsia, has come to the realization that in order to succeed the Educational Alliance must gain the confidence of the intelligentsia.

For a time it was thought that the German Jews would be willing to co-operate, grant concessions to the Russian Jews and yield to some of their demands. One fine morning ten to fifteen members of the Russian-Jewish intelligentsia received letters of invitation to attend a meeting of the Board of Directors [of the Educational Alliance] to discuss the matter of improving the work of this useful institution. Our members of the intelligentsia were elated at the thought that this would afford them an opportunity to point out to their benefactors some of the improvements which should be introduced so that the Alliance would command the respect [of the Russian Jews]. Speeches were prepared in advance [by the members of the intelligentsia] about the importance of showing respect and sympathy to their younger brother [the Russian Jew] et cetera. The results, however, did not justify the hopes [of the Russian-Jewish intelligentsia]. Those who were invited to the meeting were not given an opportunity to express themselves. They were merely requested to contribute to its [the Educational Alliance's] support. When one of the invited Jewish labor leaders politely made an attempt to speak about the need for some reforms he was not permitted to talk.

It is easy to understand what effect this incident and its outcome had when [news of] it spread the following day among the Jews of the ghetto. In the cafe, the main topic of conversation was the way the "millionaires" are trying to raise the morals of the working class and the blunders which the German Jews had committed in the course of the past ten years. Thus, the so-called attempt to restore amity and co-operation aggravated the situation and increased the animosity. The incident occurred a few weeks before the annual ball of the Educational League. It was natural, therefore, that this event should be used as an occasion for a demonstration against the so-called benevolence of the German Jews. "We do not need any one's pity and benevolence," read the announcement of the event. Only in our school, at the Educational League, the director, the teacher, the pupils — the members of the intelligentsia — are maintaining friendly relations [amongst themselves]. This relationship is not that of benefactors and recipients of charity. This protest meeting assumed even greater proportions than originally anticipated. The Educational League needed a play for this event and it turned to Jacob Gordin, the well known Yiddish playwright, who is an ardent supporter of the League. Jacob Gordin is well known for his bitter sarcasm. The play which he wrote (he wrote it in Russian and it was translated into Yiddish by his son) was entitled "The Benefactors of the East Side."

I have already made mention of this play in one of my previous articles[44] but because of the excitement which it engendered, I am taking the liberty to describe the incident in greater detail. When the play was read by the members of the board [of the Educational League] it evoked a great deal of Homeric laughter. From the literary point of view it was one of the weakest of Gordin's productions, mostly because it was written per order to illustrate a definite idea. It was a passionate, sarcastic and very clever pasquinade of the meeting to which the representative of the intelligentsia had been invited.

The scene of action takes place in the house of a Jewish millionnaire. Those assembled at this meeting are discussing ways and means to raise the economic, physical, intellectual and moral level of the Jewish East Side. Among those present at the meeting are the philanthropic ladies, a Christian, to whom the Jewish aristocrats are catering, the Reverend Dr. Knobel [garlic in Yiddish], and, for the sake of contrast, Goldberg, the Jewish labor leader from the East Side, whose attire evokes sarcastic smiles. The Reverend Dr. Knobel outlines to Goldberg the main points of his philosophy, namely, the importance of living in peace with their benefactors and of concealing their Russian extraction, because the German Jews despise the poor Russian Jews, et cetera. A series of rather humorous resolutions are adopted: 1. To open classes for cooking; 2. To cultivate music appreciation, whereby they will be enabled to improve their social status. The third points to the unsanitary conditions prevailing on the East Side and it recommends that model bathhouses be established where the immigrants would be taught how to take baths, et cetera. One of the lawyers present at the

[44] *Ibid.*

meeting stresses the need of introducing all sorts of sports such as boxing and wrestling, because the inhabitants of the East Side devote too much time to reading and thinking. Dr. Knobel, of course, stresses the significance of religion. All these proposals are interspersed with expressions of contempt for the Jews of the East Side whom the host designates as schnorrers and paupers. Finally, the Chairman calls upon the labor leader. Goldberg makes a heated speech which is interrupted from time to time by the Chairman's gavel, but the labor leader manages to tell the wealthy people what he thinks of them and of their attitude to the Jew of the East Side. The public applauded enthusiastically.

Two months have passed but the incident is still being discussed. In the Anglo-Jewish press, the *American Hebrew* was the only journal which reacted sympathetically to the protest of the Russian Jewish masses, and it stated that the 3,000 Jews who were present at the performance expressed their unanimous approval of Gordin's play, since it voiced their thoughts and feelings.[45] Of course, this incident caused quite a bit of consternation among the uptown Jews. "Why is your League so antagonistic to the Alliance"? they asked those representatives [of the League] whom they chanced to meet. The latter were forced to declare openly that the League does not seek out any conflict with the Alliance but it wants to achieve something which the Alliance does not or does not want to do. These facts cannot be concealed.

Professor Morris Loeb[45a] was right when, in a letter to the editor of the *American Hebrew*, he declared that the main issue under the discussion is: Who is to guide the destiny of the East Side Russian masses, the enlightened American Jews or the Russian-Jewish intelligentsia? But, after having made this statement, Professor Loeb then comes out with a whole series of rather surprising assertions, — surprising, because they come from a cultured person. "The struggle with which we are faced," says Professor Loeb, "is one between Eastern and Western civilization. Russian civilization is diametrically opposed to Western ideals." Then he briefly goes on to characterize the Russian form of government and he states: "Our culture and our humanitarian ideals are not in sympathy with the pessimism which has found expression in Russian literature."[46] The letter is entitled "Eastern and Western Civilization." Morris

[45] *American Hebrew*, Feb. 27, 1903, p. 499.

[45a] He was Professor of Chemistry at New York University and active in many Jewish communal endeavors. See *AJYB, 5665 (1904-1905)*, p. 145. For his necrology, see *PAJHS*, vol. XXII (1914), pp. 225-227, by Cyrus L. Sulzberger.

[46] *American Hebrew*, March 6, 1903, p. 592; and the editorial on p. 526 which defended the East European Jew.

94   AMERICAN JEWISH HISTORICAL SOCIETY

Loeb is one of the active members of the Board of the Educational
Alliance and his opinion represents that of the Educational Alliance
proper.

You may ask: Why have I entered into this lengthy discussion?
I assure you that I did it not to spread any gossip, but I feel that
this affair pictures realistically the existing sentiments and the
antagonism which prevails amid the Jewish social circles. This
can be best illustrated by the following excerpt from Loeb's letter:
"It is our duty to care for his [the Russian Jew's] speedy Americanization even more than for his physical welfare. Experience has shown
that the Jewish immigrant, once he was able to leave [Russia], [he]
could prosper without any outside help, particularly outside of the
ghetto; but the entry to the land will be forbidden, if it becomes
clear that they want to eat American bread, without acquiring
American ways. We have to fight with casuisticism which claims
that the antagonism between the Russian and the German Jews is
an attempt to cover up the antagonism between Eastern and
Western civilization."[47] A Jewish anecdote speaks of a poor speller
as a person who makes seven errors in spelling out the [Hebrew]
word Noaḥ. Professor Loeb reminds me of such a person.

Why do we need Americanization and what is its essence? This
question can be rightfully asked by the Russian Jewish masses of
Professor Loeb, and he can be required to give a clear-cut answer,
since the Americanization of the Russian Jew is one of the essential
aspects of the so-called Jewish question which deprives the American
philanthropist of his sleep. "The Russian Jew," says Professor
[David] Blaustein,[47a] "presents no problem upon his arrival in America." This statement he made in the course of his testimony before
the Industrial Commission.[48] Of course, the immigrant Jewish masses
need culture, although they are by far more cultured than the
Poles, Czechs, or Italian immigrants. But culture and education
is one thing and Americanization is something else. American liberty
would have more meaning if it were obligatory for all elements in the
population to accept the American way of life. Without doubt, the
process of assimilation is effective with the cosmopolitan population
of the United States. But why should one group try to outdo the
other in this process? Do we observe such a uniformity in the
American way of life? Do not the Irish and Germans preserve their
habits, customs, festivals, et cetera? In the final analysis, each

[47] Ibid.
[47a] He was Superintendent of the Educational Alliance. See his necrology in PAJHS,
vol. XXII (1914), pp. 206–211, by Jesse Isidor Straus.
[48] Report of the Industrial Trade Commission, vol. XIX (1901), p. 93.

group exerts a certain degree of influence upon American life. It would be ridiculous to assume that the American people is only a branch of the Anglo-Saxon race just because English is the spoken language of the country. The Irish and the Germans have contributed their share and now the Russian Jews have transplanted their ideals and traditions which have found expression in the field of literature, music, art, the theater and in the other fields of endeavor. At present, these Russian Jews are beginning to exert a certain degree of influence in many fields. Then why should they be subjected to that so-called Americanization process more than any other group? The wealthy Jew who suffers a great deal from social ostracism tries his best to erase his individuality and to compel the public to forget that he is a Jew. And when he imagines that he has succeeded, his Russian cousins shatter this idyll by the outward appearance of the latter. This prompts him to exclaim in despair "Let us Americanize him as quickly as possible." Gentlemen this is trifling and petty.[48a]

V

The bitter truth of the satire, "Benefactors of the East Side," is borne out by the fact that many of the expressions cited in it are now widely used. [To cite some of them:] "The Russians are beggars and schnorrers," says the Chairman of the memorable meeting, the wealthy Yoshke, who in English calls himself Jackie. "Jews eat American bread," says Professor Loeb. You should be ashamed of yourself, Professor Loeb. Just consult your colleagues the teachers of economics. It is true that the Russian Jew eats American bread, but it is also true that the American wears Jewish clothes. Doesn't

[48a] [(*Rubinow's note*) It is important to note that at least two American newspapers, the *New York Sun* and the *Boston Transcript*, who became interested in the conflict, openly expressed themselves in favor of the Russian Jewish masses. The Boston newspaper, containing the correspondence from New York, characterizes the difference in outlook of the two groups as follows: the diligence with which the German Jew attempts to prove that he is "not any worse than the others [the rest of the American population]" and the independence with which the Russian Jew acts, in the manner that he deems best; the fear of the German Jew that the Russian Jew will spoil the Jewish name, particularly because of the radicalism of the Russian Jew. The German Jew began to raise questions about the East Side ... The untidiness of the Russian Jew evoked in him a feeling of disgust. He despised their jargon ... The German Jew attacked [Israel] Zangwill and later [Abraham] Cahan because they depicted the Jew in an unattractive form. It became clear to him that the Russian Jew is the black sheep of the flock which one needs to cure "for the sake of the Jewish name" but in this he did not succeed and now "the German Jew does not know what to do."]

this even up the score? Professor Loeb thinks that there is a type of supply and demand where, in addition to paying the price, the purchaser is also compelled to add his thanks *gratis*. This is his conception of the exchange of products and human labor. *Da liegt der Hund begraben.*[49]

The tone of the benefactor, which Professor Loeb assumes, and he says that he speaks in the name of the American people, is one of the main reasons for the antagonism which I have described.[50] "We must care about this Americanization more than about his physical welfare." But the Jewish masses claim that the German Jews do not care for their physical welfare; they [the Russian Jews] are doing this by themselves and are endeavoring to solve their economic problems through their own efforts.

The uptown Jews insist upon their right to interfere and give advice. They call meetings to solve the East Side's problems. At these meetings we hear orations by rabbis and lawyers. They give advice: "Act so and so," "Don't do that and that." The German Jew puts the wagon before the horse, or the effect before the cause. The economic instability of the Jewish masses [it is alleged,] created the crowded conditions and brought about the housing problem. So far we as we know this problem is not specifically Jewish. But the uptown Jews decided that crowded conditions are the source of all material and spiritual evils. "If only they did not live in such crowded conditions!" exclaimed the proponent of reforms, and this took the form of organized propaganda. "Get out of the East Side," they kept on shouting from all sides. They even organized the Industrial Removal Office to help the Jews of the East Side. This movement was initiated by the Jewish Agricultural Society founded by the German Jews.[51] "If you will ask me what the inhabitants of the East Side need most," writes the President of the Society, the millionaire Sulzberger, — "I will answer, 'He needs a place to live. You cannot fight immorality so long as eight or ten people live in two rooms. Let all residents of the East Side move to other sections and make room for new arrivals. New immigrants have to settle there.' "

There is a great deal of truth in this statement. But the question immediately arises: Where should they move? [Should they] move

---

[49] The proverb, "Here is where the dog is buried" means "Herein lies the main issue under consideration," or "This is the crux of the matter."

[49a] [(Rubinow's note) *Report of the Industrial [Trade] Commission*, vol. XIX, p. 1072. Chapter Irrigation.]

[50] See *Niedielnaya Khronika Voskhoda*, 1903, vol. XXII (Sept. 4), pp. 4–6.

[51] See Samuel Joseph, *The History of the Baron de Hirsch Fund* (Philadelphia, 1935), pp. 116–149.

to other parts of the city? This is actually taking place without any widespread propaganda. As soon as the economic status of the immigrants is improved then Jewish families by hundreds, nay, by thousands, are moving to other parts of the city. And the residents of New York can see that. The ghetto, on the other hand, grows in size and is being filled by other newcomers. But even in the ghetto no two Jewish families occupy one apartment. The East Side will always remain crowded. Rent is the best indication of that. The Industrial Removal Office has begun to advocate removal into the interior, — into the agricultural states. But here we are facing many problems and we cannot dispose of them lightmindedly, when we begin to ponder upon the practical value of removal. It has been asserted that the concentration of the Jews in New York and other large cities constitutes an evil. This has found an echo in the Russian-Jewish press. I could fill pages upon pages with the articles which have appeared in the pages of the *Voskhod* dealing with the problem. At best, the Russian public has gathered the information from secondary sources. The editorial board will, therefore, forgive me, if I, after having spent ten years in New York and after having observed the situation, will share my observations with the reader.

"Go West, young man," advised the American for many years. To go West meant to become a pioneer. It meant to try one's good fortune and perhaps even to come back a millionnaire. English farmers, who sold their farms, figuring that they would buy land [out West] cheaply, business people and free lancers went West. They all had hopes of amassing a fortune. Later, even laborers went there in the hope of working for higher wages, because if the demand on labor was not great at least the supply was still smaller and the remuneration was higher. But this advantage was counterbalanced by the existing higher prices. The 1870's and 1880's witnessed a flow of Polish and German immigrants to the West. The strong and muscular German and Pole wanted to become farmers and they went out West with a great deal of confidence that they would succeed.

As time went on, the phrase remained but conditions have since changed. The population of the country has increased. The land which, so to speak, became fertile by merely scratching the surface, has risen in price and you cannot procure it any more for a song. The only land available is located in the sections of drought, where farming is only possible by means of irrigation, that is, with the help of capital and the aid of experienced farmers. Although a third of the land in the United States, excepting the Territory of Alaska and other possessions, belong to the Government, the Industrial Commission in its report to Congress stated that there is very little land left which an energetic farmer could cultivate because the water supply is insufficient.[52] Labor is compensated better out West than in the East, but the difference is becoming less and less. It has been proven by the science of economics that there is a tendency to equalize the scale in all parts of the country. Although the statistical figures dealing with the wage scale are not reliable, still, because of the absence of other data, the figures are rather informative. From 1890 to 1900, the average yearly earnings in the Middle States, New York, Pennsylvania and others, have decreased from $540 to $528; in the Pacific States from $670 to $597, — that is, the difference has decreased from eighty to forty-eight dollars. In the so-called Western States the wages increased from $565 to $597, but this is because these states are the ones that have made rapid economic advances. But in the Central States the wages are lower than in the East. "Why these details?" you may ask. I am giving these details to prove that in discussing the economic conditions we cannot be guided merely by sentimental feelings, but by actual figures and facts. Independent farming is almost impossible, and one must work only as a farm hand. If we compare farming with other types of work, declares the Industrial Commission,[52a] we see that the working day on the farm is much longer and that work is not steady and cannot serve as a permanent source of income. What economic incentive would then prompt the Jew to go West? You will agree with me that we cannot demand of the New York Jew to leave the city and thereby help solve the so-called Jewish question. And why is removal so essential, since no one has proven that such a problem exists.

There was a time when everyone looked to farming as a solution to the Jewish problem. I do not have to tell you about the trials and tribulations which the early agricultural attempts brought with them.[53] But will anyone stop to reflect that the main cause for this failure was the complete variance of the plan with the general tendencies of the civilized world. Humanity keeps on demanding more and more farm products but at the same time only a small percentage of the world population devotes its energy to agriculture and farming. Moreover, it is evident that technical devices employed in farming and the newly invented agricultural implements have decreased the

[52] [(Rubinow's note) See *Report of the Industrial [Trade] Commission*, vol. XIX (1901), pp. 93 ff.]

[52a] *Ibid.*

[53] See Leo Shpall, "Jewish Agricultural Colonies in the United States," *Agricultural History*, vol. XXIV, no. 3 (July, 1950), pp. 120–146.

demands for hands and for human energy. The tendency in the entire civilized world has been to move from village to city. This only proves that there must be an excess of population in the villages. Do you think then that these conditions are sufficiently conducive for city residents to move into the country and to become farmers? Here in the city the Jew lives by his own efforts and you are trying to transfer him to the village — be it even by philanthropic aid. On the other hand, let us say that we should confine ourselves to the removal of the Jew from New York to other cities. Then we would be faced with another difficulty. The immigrant who came to this country without means and who found friends here has no desire to move elsewhere where conditions are not only not any better, but where he virtually does not have any friends or acquaintances. Nevertheless, this removal is going on because of the utopian aim of the philanthropists, to rid New York of its surplus Jewish population. It is a luxury for poor Jews to guide themselves by such platonic ideas. "Let the new immigrants remain in New York and the earlier ones leave," so says the Removal Office. The latter must make room for the new ones. This indeed may be a laudatory objective, but far from practical. First of all, removal into the interior is going on anyway. Every American community with a population of several thousand, which I have visited (and I have visited many of them) has a number of Jewish families. Look at the articles in the *Jewish Encyclopedia* on the various states and cities [in the United States of America] and you will see that there is hardly a city or town without a Jewish community, synagogue, et cetera, and it is axiomatic that in almost all cases the majority [of these out-of-town Jews] came there via New York. True, the [Industrial Removal] Office plan can be made effective, but for whom? From my own personal observation and from the observations of others, I know that in the interior, — and by the interior I mean the entire country, — the Jewish population can be divided into three classes: persons of free professions, large and small businessmen, and peddlers, that is, persons who do business by carrying around their merchandise with them. We need not elaborate on the members of the first class, the intelligentsia; they are in the minority and they have no difficulty in adjusting themselves and present no special problem. There, therefore, remain the shopkeepers and the peddlers. For either of these the interior presents nothing advantageous. The important merchants are for the most part German Jews, who are "Americanized" and speak English fluently and who have the necessary poise and bearing, and are, thus, able to become members of the group in whose midst they are residing. If there are enough of them, they organize their own religious community, and thereby try to raise their own prestige. The important thing is that they have money. The small merchants are for the most part Russian Jews; they have less money and most of them speak a broken English. Although they earn a living, they are dissatisfied. They are isolated from the rest of the community, who look down upon them with contempt. They all live with the hope of returning to New York or to another large city. Finally, the peddlers are total outcasts. There was a time when the Jewish immigrants, unable to find employment, became peddlers. Their ignorance of the language, their pitiable look which bears the imprint of the history of trials, persecutions and tribulations, and their wandering around the country and the farms, which made the peddler's services a convenience for the farmer, helped in making the farmer's attitude towards him rather friendly. The peddler found it easy to save some money and the majority of them made a living. Many a wealthy Jew made a good beginning at peddling. But conditions have changed. Now you will hear that there is no money in peddling. Thousands of village stores have come into existence, and, thanks to the recently established free rural delivery, large stores have come into being that conduct a tremendous mail-order business. On the other hand, the number of peddlers has increased and competition has become keen. These new peddlers, with their unattractive appearance, have begun to annoy the people to such an extent that they have begun to chase them as they chase paupers and beggars. A considerable number of the country's population has begun to judge the Jew by the peddling population, and this has caused them to develop a contemptuous attitude towards him, and rightly so. If a man has the courage to appear on a platform before a crowd of Jews — that is, of Jewish immigrants — and recommend to them that they should move into the interior, even if he were to promise them material aid, the people of the East Side could rightfully ask him: "What group could I join upon my arrival [there]?" Of course, I do not speak of the members of the professions, big businessmen or capitalists. These people are not guided by the advice of a philanthropic society. Such advice is directed to the Jewish laboring masses. And what awaits them in their new abode? At the worst, they become peddlers and semi-beggars and, at the best, petty businessmen. They will live in a strange environment and become social outcasts. Does this prospect justify all this effort and propaganda? Is such a removal desirable from the standpoint of those who are moved, even if they assure some of the immigrants with financial success or even with the opportunity of becoming millionnaires (although this opportunity is as remote as that of any native-born Tom, Dick and Harry ever being elected President of the United States)? But the East Side's problems, such as rent, wages and the relation between work and pay still exist. Can these problems be designated as solved just because of the accidental success of several scores of people? As immigration increases, some of the new settlers will move into the interior anyway, but to achieve a large scale removal, we must establish favorable economic conditions. Only the members of the second generation which, undoubtedly, will be physically fit, will find employment in shops and factories, and will be able to adjust themselves to local conditions and merge with the local population,— that is, they will create the so-called melting pot. But if removal into the interior is hardly desirable, — and this also presents the question as to which people are to be removed, — there still remains a broader aspect to the problem: The removal from New York is essential for the entire Jewry of New York because, otherwise, the Jews threaten to take over New York and this danger is liable to evoke strong anti-Semitism. We saw that Professor Loeb fears this and that the Englishman [Beckles] Wilson anticipates it. Why should some Jews be afraid that New York will pass into Jewish hands? Is it because of the numerical superiority of the Jews? This is still not clear to me. In a democracy the form of government is a result of co-operative effort of all parties and of all segments of the population. In New York City, there are three distinct groups: the Irish, the Germans and the Jews. Neither the Irish nor the Germans are afraid of this phenomenon. Why then should some Jews fear it? The stronger they will become the more effective will their resistance be to any attack and they will be able to teach the other elements of the population to treat them with greater respect. Besides, how great is the danger of New York City becoming Jewish? Is this not a gross exaggeration? Fear makes mountains out of mole hills. To determine the future numerical status of New York's population will be the task of the future statistician, but he will have to be very careful when he evaluates his data. We know that forty or fifty thousand Jews arrive in New York annually, and, in the near future, the number and the ratio of the Jews to the rest of the population may even become greater. There may even come a time when the Jews will constitute not only a majority, but they will fill the city. If the Jews at first constituted five per cent, then ten per cent and now fifteen per cent of the population, it will in time constitute fifty-five or seventy-five per cent. What is more, a time may come when they will constitute eighty or even ninety per cent. This, of course, is undesirable. "The enemy has come and has conquered us." New York, the chief metropolis of North America, has suddenly become the property of the Russian Jew. Naturally, this will evoke strong opposition and will make anti-Semitism inevitable. This view may be taken seriously by some, and it may even be substantiated by all the laws of statistics. But a more striking error we cannot picture to ourselves. We assume a certain premise and we apply it in wrong instances.' Let us assume that the percentage of the Jews will increase. Does that mean that the increase will go beyond all bounds, — that is, beyond thirty or forty per cent? If you will recall the laws governing analytic geometry which also apply to statistics as well as the rules of elementary algebra, you will recall that although the quantity may increase, it will never go beyond certain limits. Thus, even though we have endeavored to state that the ratio will increase, we have not proven anything. The absolute number will increase, but the percentage ratio will remain moderate.

I tried to explain this fact to one of my friends in New York, who never thought in terms of statistics, and he considered me superficial. I am afraid that many of my readers will draw the same conclusions. But I am trying to explain a simple algebraic formula. If the increase in the number of Jews would depend solely upon Jewish immigration, then the danger which I have mentioned would indeed be a real one. But this percentage also depends upon other factors, most of which are in direct antithesis to Jewish immigration, and these factors are apt to decrease the percentage of the Jewish population. First, we must note that the fecundity of the Jewish population of New York is decreasing, and it only exceeds somewhat that of the German, Irish and even the Italian population. Besides, we must not forget that there is an Italian, Irish and German immigration, and the majority of these immigrants remain in New York City. Finally, many come to New York from the interior. To generalize, therefore, about the composition of the population is hardly possible. Of course, the increase of New York's Jewish population by five or six hundred thousand in a period of twenty years is a self-evident fact, but our fear should not be so great if we compare this increase with the general population growth of New York, — a population which increased during the same given period from 1,911,698 to 3,437,202, — that is by 1,525,504 or almost by eighty per cent. This fear that the cities will be filled up by Jews would lessen, if we would observe the phenomenal growth of the cities. The population of New York was 79,216 in 1800; 152,056 in 1830; 391,114 in 1840; 1,174,779 in 1860; 1,911,698 in 1880; and 3,437,202 in 1900. The population of Chicago was 4,470 in 1840; 109,260 in 1860; 503,185 in 1880; and 1,698,575 in 1900. The population of Philadelphia was 41,220 in 1800; 63,802 in 1830; 93,665 in 1840; 565,529 in 1860; 847,170 in 1880 and 1,293,697 in 1900. In the nineteenth century, the entire urban population increased from 210,873 to 24,992,199, and percentage-wise from 3.4 per cent to 33.1 per cent.[54]

When will the growth be checked? It is unthinkable that the entire population of this Republic will concentrate itself primarily in large cities and there will be no limit to its growth. Then what maximum can the city population attain? A hundred years ago a population of 3,500,000 would have seemed impossible. Now London alone has a population of 6,000,000. The area between Philadelphia and New York is filled with cities and the communication between these two gigantic cities is so rapid that New Yorkers are beginning in jest to call Philadelphia a suburb of New York.

So long as the cities will grow at the expense of the rest of the territory, the Jews will populate the cities, because history has made them an industrial and commercial people. This is, of course, the result of the existing economic conditions. The cities will no doubt react in some way to that growth, but when that will come about, we dare not predict. Urban life raises a great many pathological problems and these problems accumulate at a much greater pace than the growth of the cities. If the reaction must come, it will be accompanied by some radical changes in the economic condition which is bringing about this growth. The movement of people to the city is a drive for goods and labor on the market. When labor will cease being a commodity, then the difference between city and country will disappear. The city will then adopt the hygienic advantage of the village and the village will accept the cultural standards of the city. The difference between agricultural and industrial labor will then disappear as did the conflict between the Jews and the Hellenists.

VI

The Jews will not be allowed to enter this country, if it becomes evident that they do not wish to adopt the American way of life. So says Professor Loeb. And as matters stand now, there is every indication that the United States Government will restrict immigra-

---

[54] We do not know the basis for Rubinow's figures. For tables comparing the immigration of various years, see Isaac A. Hourwich, *Immigration and Labor* (New York, 1912), chapters 4 and 5, pp. 61–101.

tion to this country.[55] The question of the restriction of immigration
was taken up at the recent session of Congress. As a matter of fact,
the Department of Immigration has been accused of being too severe
with immigrants upon their arrival in this country. The Jews of
New York have expressed their protest against the Commissioner of
Immigration.[56] America is also expressing a certain degree of
pessimism with regard to immigration in general and with Jewish
immigration in particular, and thus, the open doors will soon be
closed to suffering Jewry. I came to the above conclusion after I
had made a survey of the situation, but I find it foreboding to make
any predictions because I do not want to emulate Professor Loeb
who speaks so convincingly about the inevitability of the measures
which will be undertaken. Instead of offering my conjectures permit
me to survey the entire problem historically.

If we will look back upon the brief but interesting history of the
United States, we will arrive at the following conclusions: The
struggle against immigration did not begin yesterday and it was not
caused by the opposition to the influx of Jews. Since the founding
of the Republic, and even prior to that time, during the colonial
period, this opposition did not cease.[57] From the bird's eye view which
I am here presenting, one should not conclude that the opposition to
immigration is lessening, despite the increase of immigration during
the course of the past several years, and by the change of the nature
of the immigrants. Years ago the Anglo-Saxons contributed the
largest proportion of immigrants, and now we are receiving ignorant
masses from Eastern Europe. Let us assume that this is true but
the fact remains that the opposition to immigration was just as
strong, if not stronger, during the years when the English and
Germans came to this country. This opposition was brought about
by a fear that the newcomers would outsmart the earlier settlers and
would supplant them — a sentiment which is far from laudable.
We must, however, state that the arguments advanced in those days
were not as blunt as those advanced now. I am not trying to discuss
the soundness of the arguments which were then and are now being

[55] See Cyrus Adler, *Jacob Schiff: His Life and Letters*, vol. II (New York, 1928), pp. 94–
114; and Mark Wischnitzer, *To Dwell in Safety* (Philadelphia, 1948), pp. 120–130.

[56] *Ibid.* The Commissioner of Immigration was Frank Sargent. For further information, see also Leo Shpall "The Galveston Experiment," *The Jewish Forum* (June, July and
August, 1945).

[57] Richmond Mayo-Smith, *The Influence of Immigration on the United States of America*
(New York, 1888); Prescott F. Hall, *Selection of Immigration* (Boston, 1884); Frederick
Krup, *European Immigration to the United States* (New York, 1869). For a detailed list
of pamphlets and books on the subject, see Barbara Miller Solomon, *Ancestors and Immigrants* (Cambridge, Mass., 1956), pp. 211 ff.

advanced. I am primarily interested in the attitude of the American public to the issue. I have before me several hundred pamphlets and books which discuss the issue, — material which was published in the nineteenth century.[58] I could easily prove that the Americans both invited and opposed immigration at one and the same time. But no one who has made a study of the immigration question will deny that immigration had a beneficial influence upon the economy of the country. As far back as 1700, a movement was on foot to limit the immigration of the Germans[59] and the arguments which were then advanced were hardly any different than those advanced now. There was the same fear of the spread of diseases, of pauperism et cetera. The great advocate of democracy, Thomas Jefferson, also feared immigration because the immigrants might bring with them monarchistic tendencies.[60] The well known Naturalization and Alien Acts of 1798 lengthened the required years of residence to be eligible for naturalization from five to fourteen years, and gave the President the power to deport any undesirable aliens. This was an immigration restriction which is unthinkable at present.[61] And opposition to the newcomer reached the climax in 1837, 1845 and 1856.[62] Suffice it to compare the American Party, whose slogan was America for Americans (which reminds us of the well-known anti-Semitic slogan in Russia, "Russia for the Russians"),[63] with the League for the Restriction of Immigration which exists at present in Boston, and which hardly has any funds to publish its pamphlets, to become convinced that I am stating the truth.[64] Moreover, the measures which were suggested in those days were much harsher than those suggested at present. Only those who had resided in this country twenty-one years were eligible for naturalization, declared a pamphlet published in 1837.[65] It further stated that this period of time

[58] *Ibid.*

[59] [(Rubinow's note) E. E. Proper, *Colonial Immigration Laws* in *Columbia University Studies in History, Economics and Public Law*, vol. XII, no. 2 (New York, 1901).]

[60] Article IV of the Articles of Confederation delegated to every state the right to control immigration to that state.

[61] The Alien and Sedition Act of 1798 enabled the President to order the departure from the United States of any alien whom he deemed dangerous in the country. This law must not be confused with the Alien Enemy Act of 1798.

[62] See Isaac A. Hourwich, *Immigration and Labor* (New York, 1912), pp. 61–81.

[63] The party was known as the Native American Party which in 1850 became the Know Nothing Party.

[64] For a bibliography on the League for Restriction of Immigration, see Barbara Miller Solomon, *op. cit.*, pp. 82–122.

[65] Barbara Solomon does not list any 1837 pamphlet and a copy of it could not be located by the present writer. Other contemporaneous literature listed in note 57, *supra*, p. 130 on the League substantiates Rubinow's assertion.

was essential for an immigrant to rid himself of his former outlook
upon things and to become accustomed to the American way of life.
And one of the speakers at the convention of the American Party in
1856 asserted that it is impossible for a person who has been brought
up under a definite form of government to adjust himself to another
form. That was the time when the foreigner was in the minority.
Now, however, the ratio has increased from one to forty to one to
seven. But unfortunately then and now the immigrants are looked
upon as unsuited to take part in the civic life of the country. They
were accused of being too conservative and now they are being
accused of extreme radicalism, which is a threat to this country.
Then and now statistical figures were used to prove that the immigrants fill the hospitals, prisons and insane asylums. All this may
serve as ample evidence that in the movement to restrict immigration there has been no specific anti-Jewish motive, and there is none
at present. In the 1840's and the 1850's when the agitation was at
the highest, and when rigid immigration restrictions were recommended, there was no Jewish immigration. Out of the 4,212,624
persons who migrated to this country between 1800 and 1855,
2,343,445 came from Great Britain and Ireland; 1,206,087 from
Germany; 7,185 from Italy, and only 938 from Russia.[66] If the
propaganda during the above-mentioned period brought no appreciable results, we must conclude that there were economic reasons
which made immigration necessary. One of the great authorities on
immigration, Professor Richmond Mayo-Smith stated:

> The control of immigration must be free from the base cry "America
> for Americans" and from any other spirit of trade-unionism of a selfish
> desire to monopolize the labor market.[67]

In other words, growing industry demanded the influx of cheap
labor and these demands always had the upper hand. That is why
not a single restriction or bill proposing restriction could become law.
In my opinion the restrictions existing now are reasonable and even
desirable.[67a] If America forbids entry to criminals, the insane, the
idiots and those afflicted with contagious diseases shall we consider
this attempt to keep them out a sign of prejudice? We also know
that in the past ten years the Government tried to introduce the

[66] He must have compiled these figures from the various census reports. These figures
are given without citation of any source and I do not know the exact basis for these figures.

[67] [(*Rubinow's note*) Richmond Mayo-Smith, *Emigration and Immigration* (New York,
1890), p. 68.]

[67a] [(*Rubinow's note*) It should be noted that towards the end of Cleveland's Presidency
the majority in Congress was Republican, i. e. of the opposing Party.]

so-called literacy test[68] but thus far this endeavor has been unsuccessful. Some of the sponsors of the bill demanded that the immigrant be required to know how to read and write, while others were only satisfied with the immigrant's ability to read. The bill passed both Houses, but was vetoed by [President] Grover Cleveland, and in his explanatory note [to his veto] he emphatically stated all of his reasons for opposing Congress.[69] In dealing with the issue, he pointed out that concentration in certain cities is undesirable but this is a temporary phenomenon. Unemployment, he indicated, was due to the prevailing crisis and not to immigration. In the course of his statement he declared:

> It was safer to admit a hundred thousand immigrants who, though unable to read and write, seek among us only a home and an opportunity to work than to admit one of those sturdy unruly agitators who cannot only read and write, but delights also in arousing through inflammatory speech the illiterate and peacefully inclined to become discontented.

Six years have passed and the bill was reintroduced again and again, and to this day it has not become law. This will give you a picture of the present trends opposing the restriction of immigration. Some accuse the immigrants of lowering the wage scale. This trend does exist, but there are other factors which prove that immigration is beneficial. Many employers, of course oppose restriction. On the other hand, many are of the opinion that the bill will benefit the laboring class and that is why this bill was introduced in Congress to prove to the laborers that Congress has its interests in mind. But the majority of the laborers are immigrants and they are not enthusiastic at all about the proposed fight against immigration. True, a large influx of immigrants does have an influence on the wage scale but American labor is aware of the fact that it is impossible to restrict immigration, and, instead, it struggles for higher wages and uses entirely different methods to combat low wages.

I must mention that the fight against immigration was not directed specifically against the Jews and no one raised his voice against them. It never became anti-Semitic in nature. It is true that among the Russian and Polish Jews, there were some undesirable elements but so also were they to be found among the Italians, Poles, Czechs, Hungarians, Syrians and Turks, all of whom had come from Eastern and other parts of Europe and Asia. In other words, the Anglo-Saxons wanted Anglo-Saxons and Germans ex-

[68] See Cyrus Adler, *Jacob Schiff: His Life and Letters*, vol. II, pp. 75–76.
[69] For the text of President Grover Cleveland's veto, see *Messages and Papers of Presidents*, vol. IX (New York, 1901), p. 757.

clusively, — that is the English, Scotch, Norwegians, Swedes, Dutch, and Danish. Of the Romance people only the French were considered desirable. The Yankess are displeased with the Irish and they are accusing them of using bribery in politics. We should, therefore, not feel offended if we are included among the undesirable elements. The Americans may be right. The above-mentioned elements are culturally inferior; their speech and attire are foreign to the Yankee. Why should he then be happy with a million or more Italians, Poles, Russians and Jews? When an American chances to visit Central Park and instead of a neatly dressed American sees a dirty crowd of Italian and Jewish women with their unclean-looking children who are trying to find shelter from the heat of their apartments, he is alarmed and this arouses in him a sense of antagonism towards these ignorant foreigners from which class his own parents most probably stemmed. We have, however, become accustomed to this phenomenon and this alleged annoyance with the foreigner has ceased to have any influence upon national politics. More substantial arguments have to be advanced to strengthen the opposition to immigration, and the arguments advanced apply least of all to the Jew. One cannot accuse the Jew that he has come here to amass wealth or not to spend his earnings here and to return to Europe as soon as he gets a chance, as is the case with the Italians, — or that American culture does not influence him, or that, as in the case of the Poles and Turks, the prisons and the hospitals are filled with them. There are very few Jewish prisoners. The Jews have hospitals of their own. On the contrary, the Jews fill the elementary schools and high schools. The Italians imported the Mafia and the vendetta; the Jews brought hungry mouths and a desire to work. I am not here to defend the Jewish immigrants. I am only posing these contrasts because they are being felt by American society. From my personal observations, I can say that the American Government will never pass any laws directed specifically against Jewish immigrants. The immigration restrictions will never go beyond the literacy test which was introduced during the Cleveland administration in 1897. Whether this bill will eventually pass I cannot predict. I merely want to remind the reader that the struggle has been going on for many years without any results. I do not even want to condemn the people who favor the bill. In spite of existing compulsory education, the literacy problem still remains unsolved in many states. The number of illiterates in the United States reaches several million. In 1890, it constituted 13.3 per cent, of the population, and 10.7 per cent in 1900. Illiteracy, therefore, is on the decrease but it still presents a

definite problem, and we cannot voice any protests, if the Americans
do not want to aggravate the situation and admit hundreds of
thousands of illiterates. It has been proven that illiteracy among the
children of immigrants is much smaller than among children of
American-born. The illiterates born in this country constitute 5.7
per cent, while the children born here of immigrants constitute only
1.7 per cent.[70] Whatever arguments one may advance for or against
immigration, the chances for the passage of the bill are very slim.
It depends a great deal upon the Jews themselves, not upon the
recent arrivals, but upon those Jews who have been living here for
several years and who can, therefore, exert a great deal of influence
upon the political life of the country. The following fact is very
significant. The League for the Restriction of Immigration which is
located in Boston and which defends the bill issued a statement that
German societies in all parts of the country had sent letters of protest
to Washington against the pending bill. The League, therefore,
issued a special pamphlet which was sent to these societies trying to
convince them that the bill would have no effect upon immigration
from Germany. The lesson for us is very clear. The more Jews we
will have in America, the more influence they will exert and the
greater will be the opposition to the bill. Let us suppose, for argument's sake, that the bill will eventually pass. The Russian Jew
should be the last to fear it. If the Jews constitute only 15 to 18
per cent of the illiterates, these illiterates come primarily from
Galicia and Roumania. Illiteracy there is much greater than in
Lithuania and Poland. My memory may not serve me well, but it
seems to me that an illiterate Jew from Russia is a rare occurrence.
The proposed bill requires of the immigrant the ability to read any
language, and Yiddish has been accepted as one of the recognized
languages in this country on par with any other language.[71]

It is possible that the immigration of women will suffer more than
that of men. The law, however, makes certain provisions in this
case as well. Thus, if a husband has established himself, he can send
for his wife although she may be illiterate, or an economically independent son can bring over his illiterate father and mother. The
passage of the bill will then force the head of the family to come
first and he then will be able to send for his family. It may also
prompt the women to strive for an education, and this would be far

[70] See Cyrus Adler, *Jacob Schiff: His Life and Letters*, vol. II, pp. 74–75; also Samuel
Joseph, *The History of the Baron de Hirsch Fund*, p. 242.

[71] See *Louis Marshall: Champion of Liberty*, edited by Charles Reznikoff (Philadelphia,
1950), vol. I, pp. 137–140.

from calamitous. We, thus, may be safely sure that the doors of
America will remain open to the Russian Jew, and the crocodile
tears which Professor Loeb is shedding are prompted by his making
mountains out of mole hills.

VII

Was ist der langen Rede kurzen Sinn?[72]

Contrary to my expectations my essay assumed much greater
proportions than I had originally anticipated. But I am compelled
to make certain conclusions. I do not want my essay to create an
impression that I am planning to wash dirty linen in public. I will,
therefore, summarize it in a few sentences. The concentration of the
Jews in New York City and the excitement which it has caused
furthered the belief that in New York there is a specific Jewish problem. Whatever patent remedy we may want to discover to aid the
Jew to find a way out of his precarious situation, we are still faced
with the fact that immigration to the United States in general, and,
to New York in particular, has proven most effective. The Russian
Jew has the right to know what the future has in store for him. The
Jew in Russia should not expect to find a land flowing with milk
and honey. The same social problems which exist in Europe exist
in America as well. But if he is ambitious and wants to work, he
will be able to earn a livelihood and not fare any worse than most of
the German, Italian or Irish immigrants.

Spiritually and socially the Russian-Jewish immigrant will undoubtedly undergo a metamorphosis. He will live a life of his own
and will not be dependent upon the whims of others. He will become
active in communal and civic life, and he will be able to devote to it
as much time as he desires or as time permits.

[72] Freely translated this means, "What is the sense of talking so much?"

Solomon Schechter
Comes to America

By ABRAHAM J. KARP

Three score years have passed since American Jewry's leaders in intellect and wealth joined forces to bring Professor Solomon Schechter to these shores. Philadelphia provided the intellectual leadership in the persons of Dr. Cyrus Adler, Judge Mayer Sulzberger and Dr. Solomon Solis-Cohen. New York's contribution was the philanthropic generosity of Jacob H. Schiff, the Lewisohns and Guggenheims. The former provided the persuasion and the latter the possibility of plucking from Cambridge University its Reader in Rabbinics and placing him at the head of a reorganized and endowed Jewish Theological Seminary of America.

The wooing and winning of Solomon Schechter has its fascination as a romance, and importance as a pivotal incident in the cultural and religious history of the Jew in America, for it brought into play a variety of forces and factors which coalesced to shape the American Jewish community. As the nineteenth century gave way to the twentieth, the men who felt responsibility for the future of Jew and Judaism in America recognized that the ever increasing immigration from Eastern Europe was rapidly, even violently, upsetting and reshaping the structure and pattern of American Jewish communal life. There were forces abroad which gave them great concern about the future of the Jew and the quality of his moral and spiritual life. These men and their co-workers were imbued with the optimistic philosophy current in America at that time, that any problem could be licked through the wielding of will and wealth. Danger provided a challenge; a problem would be turned into a project. What was now needed was a plan and the personnel to execute it. A Seminary for the training of English speaking rabbis who were traditionalist, promised salvation; Solomon Schechter was the man to give it direction and force.

Why was Schechter chosen? Why so ardently wooed? Why was he so eager to requite the affection? What did each of the contracting parties expect from this union?

A consideration of these questions would not only touch upon the interests, attitudes and visions of the participants, but would also throw light upon the historic forces which shaped American Jewish life in the decades which framed the turn of the century.

*　　*　　*

Cyrus Adler, in reminiscing about the coming of Solomon Schechter, remarked:

> I believe that eight cities claim the honor of being the birthplace of Homer. I cannot recall how many people claim the honor of having been instrumental in bringing Doctor Schechter to the United States.[1]

The wooing and winning of Solomon Schechter by the American Jewish community was a drama of twelve years' duration with a cast of major and minor players. Dr. Solomon Solis-Cohen reports that

> in the year 1890, I had the privilege of bearing a message from Sabato Morais and his colleagues of the Jewish Theological Seminary, then recently established in New York, asking Schechter to consider the possibility of joining the teaching staff of that institution.[2]

For a dozen years thereafter, intermittent but on-going negotiations continued, between Schechter and those anxious that he make the New World his arena for scholarly creativity and spiritual influence and leadership. Schechter himself was anxious that the matter remain current. Thus he writes to Alexander Kohut, rabbi, scholar and Professor of Talmud at the Seminary, in November, 1893:

> What is your College doing? America must be a place of Torah, because the future of Judaism is across the seas. You must make something great out of your institution if the Torah and wisdom are to remain among us. Everything is at a standstill in Germany; England has too few Jews to exercise any real influence. What will happen to Jewish learning if America remains indifferent?[3]

---

[1] Cyrus Adler, ed., *The Jewish Theological Seminary of America* (New York, 1939) , p. 10.

[2] *Students Annual, Jewish Theological Seminary of America, Schechter Memorial* (New York, 1916) , p. 61.

[3] Norman Bentwich, *Solomon Schechter* (Philadelphia, 1938) , p. 167.

Although the Seminary was located in New York, Philadelphia's Jewry felt it had at least an equal share in its founding and maintenance, and therefore, its direction. The founder and first president was the rabbi of Philadelphia's Mikveh Israel. It maintained a strong and active Seminary association. Among the most influential lay leaders were the aforementioned Dr. Solis-Cohen as well as Dr. Cyrus Adler and Judge Mayer Sulzberger. During the latter half of the nineteenth century Philadelphia was blessed with remarkable Jewish lay leadership—men of establshed and esteemed families, scholars in secular and Jewish studies, traditional in observance and conservative in religious outlook. They saw in Schechter a kindred soul, who would establish in America a sound base for Jewish scholarship and who would make traditional Judaism intellectually viable.

In the early 90's both Dr. Adler and Judge Sulzberger visited Schechter in England and came away impressed with the man and convinced that America must be his field of activity.

An opportunity for American Jewry to meet Schechter and for Schechter to see America soon presented itself. Congregation Mikveh Israel was the beneficiary of a trust estate created by Hyman Gratz "for the establishment and support of a College for the education of Jews residing in the city and county of Philadelphia."[4] Dr. Solis-Cohen was appointed chairman of a congregational committee to concern itself with this matter. The $6,000.00 per annum income from the trust was deemed insufficient to maintain a school of learning, so

> At a meeting of the committee held November 29, 1894, it was resolved that a series of lectures be given during the year 1894-95, and that Mr. S. Schechter, Reader in Rabbinics in the University of Cambridge, England, be invited to deliver a number of lectures of this series.[5]

The resolution was preceded by negotiations carried on by Dr. Solis-Cohen and Mr. Schechter. In reply to a letter of inquiry Schechter wrote on June 14, 1894:

> I think I could see my way to falling in with your convenient proposal: matters of this nature, as you say, are better discussed by word of mouth than by correspondence.[6]

4 Cyrus Adler, "Solomon Schechter," *American Jewish Year Book, 5677* (Philadelphia, 1916) p. 37.
5 *Publications of the Gratz College* (Philadelphia, 1897), p. 9.
6 *American Jewish Year Book, loc. cit.*

The word of mouth discussion was with Dr. Adler who visited England a few weeks later. At year's end, in a letter dated December 19, 1894, Schechter informs Adler of his acceptance of the invitation, thanks him for his kind efforts and exclaims: "What a joy in heaven it will be to see old friends again...."[7]

The Reader in Rabbinics who arrived in America for the first time in February 1895, was already a well known figure in Jewish scholarly circles. A product of Roumanian and Galician Yeshivot, he continued his studies in Vienna and Berlin. The West added scientific order and method to the knowledge he had amassed in the East. Added to scholarly acumen was a live and exciting personality. His was the happy combination of imagination and intellectual daring coupled with sound and solid scholarship.

The young Claude G. Montefiore met him in Berlin and persuaded him to continue his journey westward to England to act as the young man's tutor. After he was "inducted into the mysteries of the English language" Schechter became a leading figure in Anglo-Jewish intellectual life. Joseph Jacobs writes:

> It is impossible to convey any adequate idea of the genial radiance and *élan* of Schechter's personality at this period. At the height of his physical and mental vigor, appreciated for the first time at his true value, surrounded by an ever-increasing circle of admiring friends, he burst upon us as a blazing comet in the intellectual sky.[8]

A position was obtained in the University of Cambridge where he continued his scholarly output and developed a masterly style which won the admiration and envy of skilled writers for whom English was the native tongue. He put his knowledge and style to use in scholarly popularizations of various aspects of Jewish life and thought and gained ever wider popularity and fame. The University expressed its esteem by awarding him the degree of Master of Arts *honoris causa* in 1892.

This then was the man that was being brought to America to see and be seen. Schechter's coming was announced in Cincinnati's *American Israelite*,[9] and heralded in New York's *American Hebrew*.

7 *Ibid.*
8 *Students Annual*, p. 96.
9 *American Israelite*, Feb. 14, 1895, p. 5.

> The gentlemen who constitute the Trustees of the Gratz
> Fund . . . have manifested a wise and liberal-minded con-
> ception of their duty by prevailing upon Mr. Schechter . . .
> to visit this country and deliver a course of lectures . . .
> The Jews of America will certainly delight in according to
> Mr. Schechter a welcome that will well repay him for the
> trip; that will manifest to him that whatever may be at fault
> with Judaism as it is constituted in this country, we still have
> an ardent appreciation for ripe scholarship and warm sym-
> pathy with the studious temperament.[10]

Philip Cowen of *The American Hebrew* wanted Schechter to like
the American Jewish community and American Jewry to appreciate
Schechter.

> Mr. Schechter, indeed, deserves a great deal of credit. Now
> that the public has grown up to draw from the well of
> Hebrew learning transferred into the English tongue, he has
> given a wonderful impulse to the movement for creating this
> Anglo-Jewish literature, and he has indelibly impressed this
> movement with his scholarly character. It is to him that we
> owe in a great degree the fact that this Neo-Jewish literature
> shall be Jewish and scholarly.[11]

A plea is put forth that Schechter be invited to repeat his lectures
in New York, but the metropolis was apparently not yet ready for
him.

The lectures, six in number, which were delivered in the Academy
of the Fine Arts from February 11th through the 28th, were widely
quoted in the American Jewish press, and served to introduce
Schechter to an ever wider audience. His own reaction is typical
of him:

> I gave my first lecture yesterday. The hall was crowded, and
> I hope that at least a *minyan* understood my English, and
> that I shall be saved for the sake of the ten.[12]

This he wrote to Dr. Adler from the home of Judge Sulzberger.
His friendship with both men, who became life-long co-workers,
deepened and ripened during Schechter's sojourn here. Later they
were to be most instrumental in bringing him back to these shores.

Schechter returned to his scholarly work in Cambridge. His un-
earthing of the Cairo Genizah and his discovery of a Hebrew text

10 *The American Hebrew*, vol. LVI, no. 11 (Jan. 18, 1895) , p. 320.
11 *Ibid.*
12 *American Jewish Year Book*, p. 40.

of the Book of Ecclesiasticus, not only increased his scholarly stature, but gave him international popularity. To the popular mind here was a scholar-adventurer, combining all the best features of a questing mind and a courageous heart, braving the heat of Cairo and the dust of centuries in his search of truth. Small wonder then that when Sabato Morais, President of the Jewish Theological Seminary, breathed his last, the quest for a successor turned to a scholar sorting and deciphering manuscript leaves and fragments in Cambridge.

His name had been kept current and his fame celebrated by the two Jewish periodicals which represented the Conservative point of view, *The Jewish Exponent* of Philadelphia and *The American Hebrew,* thus preparing the ground for his acceptance as head of the conservative Seminary.

On May 9, 1897, Schechter wrote to his friend and confidant, Judge Sulzberger:

> I was lately approached from New York with the question whether I should care to come to New York to take charge of the Chancellorship of the Jewish Theological Seminary. I do not care to mention the name of my correspondent as the matter is confidential. Besides you know probably by now who it is. I have not answered him yet; but I am going to refer him to you. I hardly need to tell you that America has certain attractions for me. But I am anxious to be there quite independent as well as sure of doing there some good by founding there a school on a scientific basis. You probably know what I want or rather what I ought to want better than I myself. Hence the best thing is that you decide for me in this respect.[13]

Judge Sulzberger urged patience, as did Dr. Adler, as the latter attests:

> Some of his more impetuous friends urged him to join the Seminary at once, but I was very solicitous and in this Judge Sulzberger joined, that he should delay until we had a sufficient foundation to make him secure here.[14]

Schechter grew anxious. He yearned for America. He unburdened his soul in a number of interesting and instructive letters to Judge Sulzberger.

13 Letter, Schechter to Sulzberger, May 9, 1897, Library Jewish Theological Seminary of America [-LJTSA].
14 Cyrus Adler, ed., *The Jewish Theological Seminary,* p. 10.

New York offers nothing fresh as I see; but I gather from the *J[ewish] C[hronicle]* that the Gratz College was reorganized on a new basis, etc. I cannot deny that I hope better things from it, both for the College and perhaps for me. However, one disappointment more in the life of a Jewish student is not of much consequence and I am grown quite accustomed to it now.[15]

Sulzberger apparently urged Schechter to be content with his lot, for Schechter writes:

I have very little hope from anywhere but if I tell you that after years of killing work I have not the least hope that they will increase my salary with six pence, whilst on the other hand, education is very expensive here so that I have not the means to bring up my children in the way they ought to be brought up—you will perhaps see my reasons for not being quite content.[16]

What a poignant plaint of a scholar-father, who gives his life and health to the advancement of knowledge, but is not rewarded with the means to enable him to provide an education for his children! What makes the plaint all the more poignant is that it is made to a bachelor.

Matters take a turn for the better, for now Schechter discloses to the Judge:

The New York news are so far satisfactory and I thank you for all that you have said and you have done.[17]

Negotiations continue apace. The Seminary is again represented by Dr. Solis-Cohen. Schechter leans heavily on the advice of Judge Sulzberger. He asks his advice on certain expense stipulations and on the question of the proper title. As Schechter explains:

The question of title is also of some importance as I could undertake no reform in the place without the proper authority for doing so.[17a]

Schechter has obviously given considerable thought to his plans for the Seminary. No doubt he feels that matters are coming to a head.

While negotiations are going on, the name and stature of Schechter continues to grow in America. Thus when *The American*

---

[15] Letter, Jan. 14, 1898, LJTSA.
[16] Letter, March 8, 1898. LJTSA.
[17] Letter, June 26, 1898. LJTSA.
[17a] *Ibid.*

Hebrew conducts a symposium on, "A SYNOD:—Shall We Have a General Assembly," Schechter's is the only non-American whose opinion is solicited. His reply appears with those of Judge Sulzberger, Lewis N. Dembitz, Rev. Max Heller and Rev. Meldola De Sola of Montreal.[18]

An editorial note a month later states:

> The full text of Professor Schechter's introductory lecture at University College will be awaited with great interest . . . his intimation of the importance of the discovery of the original text of Ecclesiasticus in disproving certain assertations of Biblical critics are of the highest importance.[19]

In the spring of 1899, Henrietta Szold delivered an address before the New York Council of Jewish Women on "Catholic Israel." She quotes approvingly and at length from Dr. Schechter, attributing the phrase to him and expounding upon its meaning. Her address is published in *The American Hebrew*.[20]

Schechter hears of it and writes Sulzberger for a copy. "I should very much like to read it." In the same letter he writes:

> The *J[ewish] Chronicle* of today reproduces from *Jewish Exponent* a paragraph relating to my possible appointment in New York etc. Have you any fresh news from that place.[21]

The article Schechter refers to is the lead editorial in the October 6, 1899 issue which is titled:

A CALL FOR PROFESSOR SCHECHTER

> The Jewish Theological Seminary after fourteen years of existence, has arrived at a turning point in its career. . . . There is one man whom the friends of the institution have long and earnestly hoped could be induced to accept its leadership. Above all others available for the office Professor S. Schechter of Cambridge University, is superbly endowed with scholarship, with the force and convictions of a great personality, with a magnetism and a world-wide reputation admirably qualified to lift the Seminary to an eminence toward which the eyes of the Jewish people, scholars, students and laity, will be hopefully and enthusiastically directed. We believe that Professor Schechter's opportunities in this country

---

18 *The American Hebrew*, vol. LXIV, no. 11 (Jan. 13, 1899).
19 *Ibid.*, no. 17, Feb. 24, 1899.
20 *Ibid.*, vol. LXV, no. 1 (May 5, 1899), p. 9 and following issue.
21 Letter, Oct. 20, 1899, LJTSA.

would be practically unlimited and that his coming here would be productive of great results both in the Seminary itself and throughout the American Jewish Community. The efforts that [they] are now making to induce him to accept the call of the Seminary should be presented with unremitting fervor until they are crowned with success in the near future. The Jewish people can be depended upon to second and support every effort in this direction.[22]

A week later the *American Hebrew* echoed the *Exponent's* approval and appeal:

. . . the authorities of the Jewish Theological Seminary of New York are in want of funds to enable them to carry out their cherished project of placing their institution under the capable direction of the well-known Professor S. Schechter, now of Oxford [*sic!*] University, England. If a ripe scholar of such world-wide reputation as Professor Schechter, could be induced to settle and teach among us, who can doubt but that there would be a brisker and higher cult of Judaism as a resultant?

The Seminary, founded on tested lines, and aiming, *mutatis mutandis,* at reproducing in this land the tried and trusted methods of the Old World, has a distinct claim for support and encouragement. Every Jew who loves his race and religion, whatever be his "doxy" must recognize the value to American Judaism of the transference of the influence and labor of Professor Schechter to this land.[23]

While the journals were espousing the cause, negotiations continued on. By the end of October Schechter lists his rabbinic credentials for Sulzberger:

I have התרת הוראה [rabbinic ordination] from I. H. Weiss, . . . these last twenty years. It was given to me when I left the ביה״מ הגדול [*Beth ha-Midrash ha-Gadol*] in Vienna where Weiss was רב [rabbi] and lector . . . in the year תרל״ט [1879]. I have also one from the late Dr. Frankel, Rabbi in Berlin. I can give מורינו [*Morenu*-ordination] to anybody I like. I never referred to this fact in the J[ewish] C[hronicle] or any other paper as I hate advertising and despise such שטותים [foolishness].[24]

In November an official letter of invitation went from Mr. Blumenthal, President of the Jewish Theological Association.

[22] *The Jewish Exponent,* Oct. 6, 1899.
[23] *The American Hebrew,* vol. LXV, no. 24 (Oct. 13, 1899).
[24] Letter, Oct. 25, 1899, LJTSA.

Schechter "held out hopes to him of acceptance but did not commit myself positively."[25] Once again Schechter left everything to Judge Sulzberger's discretion.

The Judge is discreet and realistic. In a letter to Cyrus Adler he indicates the sacrifices which Schechter will be making, and he puts forth terms.

> If he is prepared to make the sacrifice of (1) scholarly implements, such as a library, and (2) social position, for which in this city a man without money cannot find even a proximity of an equivalent; if, further, he is prepared for a certain gratuitous hostility which could only be endured and not battled with, then I think that his usefulness here can be greater than anywhere else, and I have no objection to his accepting this offer. . . .[26]

Judge Sulzberger knows, however, the precarious financial situation of the Seminary. It had no endowment and its entire income was dependent on annual contributions. As a friend and representative of Schechter, he therefore insists

> provided that the sum alluded to is pledged, either by deposit or responsible subscription or absolute payment, to Schechter over four years, without the power of the Seminary for any reason whatever, to abridge this period.[27]

As the year 1899 came to a close, the whole matter was still unresolved. Schechter yearned to come and he encouraged Blumenthal to expect a favorable decision. What restrained him was the Judge's insistence that a proper contract be drawn up before Schechter should sever his ties in England. Sulzberger considered the time right psychologically for the advent of one who "has scholarship, talent, and enthusiasm." But. he is concerned with financial conditions in the country and positively unhappy with the composition of the Seminary's Board.

> I have intimated to Dr. Solis-Cohen that unless the Board of Trustees is reorganized on the basis of secularity, I shall advise your declination.[28]

At the time the Seminary was under the direction of a Rabbinical Board, which as Sulzberger put it

25 Letter, No. 16, 1899, LJTSA.
26 Norman Bentwich, op. cit., p. 168.
27 Ibid.
28 Ibid., p. 169.

may be properly orthodox in belief or expression, but they do not command the financial support of the only people to be relied upon to maintain the Institution in permanence.[28]

The Judge knows whom to turn to.

I have discussed the matter with Schiff, who is *the* Yehudi of New York, and we have agreed that to render the place assured, a friend of mine, Louis Marshall, should be president . . . with him at the head of us . . . things would be perfectly safe. Without him . . . I should feel equally unsafe.[28]

Schechter agrees and confesses:

I have always felt rather uneasy at seeing so many rabbis in the list of the trustees of the Seminary. . . .[29]

He tells of the visit of Mr. [Leonard] Lewisohn and reassures the Judge in a letter dated on the Ides of March:

I shall not accept any offer from America which does not come from you.[30]

Schechter had learned caution from the Judge to whom he writes at the end of 1900:

of New York I can only say כל הדברים יגעים [the whole matter is wearisome]. I had also some 12 days ago a letter from Mr. Lewisohn—the one I met in Germany . . . I have full confidence in him; but I have answered him that I should like to view first the situation in New York myself.[31]

The *Jewish Exponent* had been carrying on an enthusiastic campaign in furtherance of the cause. It invited an article by Israel Zangwill who was then in America. In the October 20, 1899 issue, Zangwill wrote of the competition going on between England and America for Schechter:

For Dr. Schechter is the greatest European scholar in Jewish Science . . . the ancient University of Cambridge, England rejoices in the possession of him. . . .
Dr. Schechter is the most wonderful combination of learning, wit and spiritual magnetism that it has ever been my good fortune to encounter . . . if America succeeds in obtaining Dr. Schechter . . . it will have done much to shift the center of gravity of Jewish thought to New York. . . .[32]

How could America not relish to gain the prize?

29 Letter, March 5, 1900, LJTSA.
30 Letter, March 15, 1900, LJTSA.
31 Letter, Dec. 9, 1900, LJTSA.
32 *The Jewish Exponent,* Oct. 20, 1899.

A week later an editorial plea is put forth:

> Here . . . he has original materials to work upon . . . a great
> living, throbbing community destined to play a leading part
> in the determination of catholic Israel. Dr. Schechter will
> come where the need is greatest, and that greatest need is here.
> Across the mighty waters the sound of the call is heard and
> like a parent's heart, the answer is unhesitatingly and unques-
> tionably I will come.[33]

The report in December of '99 that Dr. Schechter had accepted
the call brought forth warm response from all segments of American Israel. "An auspicious moment in the history of American
Israel," the *Jewish Messenger* proclaimed.[33a] Even the radical
reformer Emil G. Hirsch hailed his coming:

> The coming of this great scholar, facile princeps among
> modern students of rabbinical literature, will mark an epoch
> in the development of Jewish science in America. . . .[34]

The editor of *The Exponent,* Charles I. Hoffman, soon recognized that the necessary ingredient to assure the coming of Dr.
Schechter was adequate financial support. An editorial in early
1900 solicits generosity.

> The wealthy Jew or Jews who would signally associate them-
> selves with this would deserve and receive the immortality
> that comes to those who have aided in the establishment of a
> great and permanent undertaking.[35]

The wealthy Jew in this enterprise as in all major Jewish undertakings at the turn of the century had to be Jacob H. Schiff. In
1901, the death of Joseph Blumenthal made possible the reorganization of the Seminary.

How and why the reorganization of the Seminary took place is
worthy of a separate study. Sufficient for our purpose is the account
of Cyrus Adler who played a central role in this endeavor.

> In 1901, I . . . was invited to a man's party at the house of
> Mr. [Isidor] Straus. There was a small group standing to-
> gether and they were speaking of Jewish affairs in New York
> and particularly of Jewish education. I said . . . that the
> Jewish community of New York, which was destined to be
> the largest community in the world, was allowing its only

33 *Ibid.,* Oct. 27, 1899, p. 4.
33a As quoted *ibid.,* Dec. 27, 1899, p. 4.
34 *Ibid.*
35 *Ibid.,* Jan. 5, 1900, p. 4.

institution of higher Jewish learning to perish, and I told them something of the precarious situation of the Seminary. Mr. Schiff, who was a man of quick decisions, said to the men standing around, "Doctor Adler is right," and a few weeks later I received a letter from him, asking me when I was coming to New York next time, so that he might invite a few men to meet with us. Among the men, I remember, were Leonard Lewisohn and Mayer Sulzberger, joined the next day by Daniel and Simon Guggenheim. I shall not go into the steps that brought about the reorganization of the Seminary Board, with the powerful help of Louis Marshall, but suffice it to say, that within a few months an Endowment Fund of over one-half million dollars had been secured . . . which rendered it possible to invite Doctor Solomon Schechter . . . to come to America, as head of the Seminary.[36]

With an adequate endowment secured, Schechter's coming was now assured. Despite an increase in salary granted him by Cambridge University, Schechter was anxious to come to America. But even though both parties were eager that the on-going flirtation be crowned with consummation, the road of love had its hazards. Thus, Schechter in a moment of high indignation writes to Sulzberger in April 1901:

Please do not bother about the New York affair. I am quite sick of it. If they ever come to you and to me with anything fair we will consider it; but I have really too much to do to spend a thought on the humours of Mr. Schiff and his brother magnates. . . . If I ever go to America I mean to be treated like a gentleman and a scholar and also to be paid accordingly. If they cannot see that I might do something for America . . . then let them be d----d. . . .[37]

Sulzberger, who heretofore had been a reluctant intermediary, now becomes an eager proponent. For, in June, Schechter writes to him:

. . . what you tell me about New York is very satisfactory and I feel un-sicked. Everything is left to you, and when you will say the blessing, I will answer אמן [Amen].[38]

The blessing was said in the form of an invitation and contract and Schechter said, "Amen."

To his intimate friend Herbert Bentwich, he writes on December 24, 1901:

36 Cyrus Adler, *op. cit.,* pp. 9-10.
37 Letter, April 17, 1901, LJTSA.
38 Letter, June 14, 1901, LJTSA.

> I have to tell you that I have definitely accepted the New
> York offer. . . . It is with a heavy heart that I have to take
> this step, but it had to be done for the sake of my family, and
> perhaps also for the sake of American Judaism with which
> the future rests.[39]

It remains now for us to consider the questions which opened
this study. Why was Schechter chosen?

At the turn of the century Schechter was one of Jewry's leading
scholars. He had captured the popular imagination with his Genizah and Ben Sirah explorations and discoveries. He was a zealous
and observant Jew, but withal a man of the world, possessed of a
magnetic personality which won him adoring friends and disciples.
With all this he was possessed of a remarkable English prose style
which made his essays models of scholarly popularizations.

He was in training, experience and commitment the perfect man
to head an academic institution for the training of traditional
English-speaking rabbis.

There was also American "pioneer pride"—that pride which
caused other men of wealth to bring to America Europe's finest
art and rarest books—which moved Jewish men of substance to
choose Schechter. Jacob H. Schiff put it in his own direct manner:

> We in the United States, who are ever striving to secure the
> best, were not long in the discovery [of] Solomon Schech-
> ter. . . .[40]

Why did Schechter come to America?

Coming consists of departure and arrival. He was anxious to
leave England because he lived in a non-Jewish environment and
dreaded to raise his children without adequate Jewish associations.
He desired an education for his children, which his meager Reader's
salary would not provide.

He confides to Bentwich:

> I could not bear the idea of taking money from private
> individuals any longer.[41]

What rankled even more was that this money came largely from
Claude G. Montefiore who favored Sunday services[42] and who

39 Letter, Dec. 24, 1901, LJTSA.
40 *Students' Annual*, p. 161.
41 Letter, Dec. 24, 1901, LJTSA.
42 *The American Hebrew*, vol. LXV, no. 8, June 23, 1899, LJTSA.

declared that he felt more worshipful, more prayerful, more drawn Godwards when he heard English than when he heard Hebrew, although he understood the latter.[43]

As early as 1895, Schechter complained to Sulzberger about English Jewry.

> I cannot help saying that there is a little too much *Meshumadim* cult in England; which is probably due to the influences of the D'Israelis, Herschel and other illustrious successful *Meshumadim* [apostates]. I will protest against it.[44]

His protest appeared five years later in four letters to the *Jewish Chronicle* in which he is strongly critical of English Jewry's assimilationist tendencies, its "jingoism," its lack of spirituality and its indifference to Jewish learning.

As an East European Jew he is particularly sensitive to the discrimination practiced against the immigrant Jew in England. He bridles at Jewish communal life being under the benevolent despotism of "our stock exchange chaplains" who were destroying the Jewish consciousness. In justifying his first letter which Schechter confesses had a "horrifying effect," he writes to Sulzberger:

> It was . . . highly time to tell them (the stock exchange chaplains) that millions do not compensate us for their ignorance and that they hadn't any claim of intellectual or spiritual superiority over their brethren abroad—particularly the Russian Jews whom they are always bullying.[45]

Although the atmosphere in Cambridge was congenial to scholarship it was Jewishly unsatisfactory, and Schechter was above all a zealous, enthusiastic Jew. Life without Jews meant "spiritual death" to Schechter. True he has more manuscripts to edit that even a hundred years of life will exhaust but his ambitions are greater and higher. "In your country," he explains to Sulzberger, "I can hope to 'make school' and to leave תלמידים [students] which may prove useful to the cause of Judaism as well as that of Jewish scholarship."[46]

The "make school" which would provide scholarly, spiritual leadership for American Jewry, and which would foster Jewish

43 *The Jewish Exponent*, June 12, 1896.
44 Letter, Oct. 31, 1895, LJTSA.
45 Letter, Dec. 9, 1900, LJTSA.
46 Letter, June 26, 1898, LJTSA.

scholarship is what drew Schechter to America. In the letter just
quoted he proclaims, "My hope for the future of Judaism and its
literature is in America. . . ." The institution which would assure
this future is the Seminary, and Schechter is anxious to make it
his life's work. "It would lengthen my life" Schechter writes to
Sulzberger, "to be with you and [a] few other friends, together
all active to establish a school of תורה [Torah] in America where
the future of Judaism is."[47]

Freedom which Schechter craved and the frontier which his ad-
venturous soul yearned for drew him to the land, which he loved
from the days of his first visit. Lincoln was an early spiritual hero
and he was utterly fascinated by the Civil War. Even while in
England he badgered Sulzberger for more and more works on this
conflict.[48] Zangwill reports Schechter's reaction to America:

> "A great people," he cried to me enthusiastically on his re-
> turn, "great people."[49]

Schechter summed up his desire for America in a letter to Adler
on the first day of 1900.

> America has thus only *ideal* attractions for me, offering as it
> does a larger field of activity which may become a source of
> blessing to future generation. I also feel that I shall be more
> happy living among Jews. I want my synagogue and my
> proper Yomim Tobim among my people. There is also the
> question of the children being brought up among Jews, which
> is the only guarantee for the acquiring of a real heartfelt
> Judaism. . . . I am prepared to give the Seminary all my
> faculties, even my very life.[50]

Destiny marked Schechter for America and the forces of history
coalesced to fulfil this destiny.

Among the forces which "coalesced" were the Philadelphia group
which provided American Jewry its intellectual leadership, and
the New York millionaires whose concern and generosity gave
reality to the dreams and projects of the former.

What promise did Dr. Solomon Solis-Cohen, Judge Mayer Sulzberger and Dr. Cyrus Adler see in Schechter's coming to America?
The first saw in him the needed leader to give direction to American

[47] Letter, Dec. 21, 1899, LJTSA.
[48] See, for example, Letter to Sulzberger, Jan. 24, 1901, LJTSA.
[49] *The Jewish Exponent*, Oct. 20, 1899, p. 7.
[50] *American Jewish Year Book*, p. 52.

Jewry, "striving vaguely, not knowing what they want, but knowing that they want something. . . ." Sulzberger, ever the scholar, thought the time propitious for laying the foundations for a knowledgeable Jewry. "He who has scholarship, talent and enthusiasm may be more appreciated for the first time in our history than he who leads a party." Adler was anxious for the future of the Seminary, and saw in the enterprise of acquiring Schechter an opportunity to enlist in the Seminary's support the resources of Schiff and his friends. An observant Jew he was deeply disturbed by the inroad which reform had made and saw in Schechter the one possibility to establish an institution which would initially stay and eventually turn the tide.

The inroads of radical reform gave concern to a man like Schiff as well. What concerned him even more were religious indifference and political radicalism.

> Solomon Schechter . . . was the one man fitted to be placed at the head of the American Jewish Theological Seminary, . . . in which were to be reared a class of Jewish Rabbis who could be counted upon to maintain inviolate our faith in its ancient purity, and to assure through their ministrations and teaching adherence to Jewish forms and traditions amongst those, who both at the prsesent time and in coming generations need form the bulwark against the inroads of indifference and irreligiousness in the life of at least a large portion of American Jewry.[51]

Schiff, the Lewisohns, the Guggenheims and their group were much concerned about the children of the East European immigrant. The problem of the East Side agitated Uptown Jewry. The plight of the immigrant population moved many to Socialism and Anarchism. The social flux, the breakdown of the family unit, and the bewildering difference in social patterns often led to crime. There is no question that the Uptown Jews saw in the Seminary ordained rabbi and his teachings a force which would bring moderation, stability, order in the community and standards to personal life. Dr. Mordecai Kaplan, co-worker with Schechter, considers the chief motive of the newly constituted Board of Trustees under the chairmanship of Louis Marshall,

> to establish a training school for American trained rabbis who might stem the proliferation of gangsterism on the Jewish

[51] *Students' Annual,* p. 161.

East Side. Graduates of the then existing Hebrew Union College could not serve that purpose.[52]

Mrs. H. Pereira Mendes, wife of Shearith Israel's Minister and Chairman of the Committee on Religion of the National Council of Jewish Women reported in June, 1899:

> I have urged a plan for the religious betterment of our poorer brethren, by employing our English-speaking Seminary graduates, who are so eminently qualified for that work.[53]

The *American Hebrew* editorially applauds this suggestion pointing out that

> . . . the young men and young women, English speaking children of jargon-speaking immigrants are entirely "unchurched."[54]

Concern for those "unchurched" was a powerful motive in the reorganization and endowing of the Seminary which provided for Schechter's coming.

What the children of the immigrants needed was not only Judaization but also Americanization. Here, too, it was felt an English-speaking, Seminary trained rabbi could play an important role. In *The American Hebrew's* editorial obituary for Leonard Lewisohn, who gave "$50,000 toward the rehabilitation of the Theological Seminary," we find:

> most recent of all was his interest in the Jewish Theological Seminary, as affording the surest and safest means of handling the down-town problems of Americanizing the foreign element by sending among them trained and well-equipped Rabbinical teachers. . . .[55]

Even in the founding of a theological seminary, the strongest motive was the ongoing, inherent promise that "the uptown mansion never forgets the downtown tenement in its distress."

This attitude that the reorganization of the Seminary and the bringing of Schechter was primarily a philanthropic gesture must have crept into the negotiations with Schechter. He feels it 3,000 miles away. Ever the proud Jew he shares his chagrin with Sulzberger.

[52] Letter to author, April 12, 1963.
[53] *The American Hebrew*, vol. LXV, no. 8 (June 23, 1899), p. 231.
[54] *Ibid.*, p. 224.
[55] *Ibid.*, vol. LXX, March 8, 1902, p. 484.

I dearly hope that the magnates of New York do not believe that they have to deal with some *Maggid* who cannot possibly expect to be treated with the same liberality as the Rabbi-Preacher. . . . [56]

Schechter's coming, his leadership of the Seminary and the movement he founded did very much to bridge the gap between "uptown" and "downtown."

The arrival of Schechter on April 17, 1902, was widely hailed as the beginning of a new era in American Jewish religious life and scholarship. For once anticipations were not exaggerations. No single individual has contributed more to the furtherance of Jewish learning and perhaps no other has had greater influence on the course and direction of religious life.

The American Hebrew's welcoming editorial spoke prophetically:

He was born a Roumanian, was educated in Germany, has been studying and teaching in England, but it seems he will be especially at home in an American atmosphere, where he will be a leader in our development.[57]

While still in the euphoria of the honeymoon period, Schechter wrote to his friend Bentwich.

In brief the Seminary enthusiasm and the Schechter craze are at present very great. Let us pray that כן יהי לארך ימים [So may it be for the length of days].[58]

Schechter's prayer has been answered. The enthusiasm and the craze are with us six decades later.

[56] Letter, Nov. 5, 1901, LJTSA.
[57] *The American Hebrew*, vol. LXV, no. 22 (April 18, 1902), p. 656.
[58] Letter, June 1, 1902, LJTSA.

Henry Pereira Mendes:
Architect of the Union of Orthodox
Jewish Congregations of America

By Eugene Markovitz*

The mass of the East European Jewish immigrants coming to the United States at the turn of the century brought with them the traditional Orthodox Jewish mode of worship and observance. Here they found a society which was not hospitable to their ways. Not that religious freedom was abridged or in any way curtailed in this free land, but the social milieu acted strongly against transplanting the *shtetl*, their mode of living in their East European home towns and villages, to these shores. Observance of the Sabbath became extremely difficult. Observance of the dietary laws outside of New York City's East Side was burdensome and the religious education of their children was on the lowest level.

The deplorable condition of Judaism, specifically traditional Orthodox Judaism, is vividly portrayed in a contemporary description of the time, written in Hebrew by Morris Weinberger, entitled *Jews and Judaism in New York.*

> There are one hundred and thirty Orthodox congregations in New York City. Some claim their number to be two hundred and forty. They are both correct because the congregations are not well ordered and defined. Those who claim the larger figure probably include small *shtiblech* and *minyanim* as well as *klausen*. If one were to search for these in obscure courtyards and attics, their number might well exceed three hundred.[1]

* Dr. Markovitz is rabbi of the Clifton Jewish Center, Clifton, N. J., and Adjunct Professor of American History at Seton Hall University, Newark, N. J.

The author is indebted to Mr. A. Piza Mendes, son of Dr. Henry Pereira Mendes, who graciously made available to him the extensive collection of his father's private letters, newspaper clippings, pamphlets and articles, as well as other material relating to the period under consideration. This collection hereinafter is designated as the PM Collection.

[1] Morris Weinberger, *Ha-Yehudim veha-Yahadut be-New York* [*Jews and Judaism in New York*] (New York, 1887). The author was himself a devout Orthodox Jew and wrote with great passion rather than with detached historical objectivity. However, his general description and analysis are confirmed by other contempory writers. [See "Letter from Cincinnati — The Observer of Israel in America," *Ha-Meliz* (1889), no. 180, p. 1.] The author vividly portrays an Orthodoxy beset by inner conflicts between an

130

According to this observer, these congregations did not deviate in their physical arrangements from the Law, and some of them had a *Beth Hamidrash* attached to their house of worship where religious books were kept, and an occasional elderly worshipper would study in those books. After the daily service five or six men would remain to study the Talmud or the Pentateuch. Weinberger adds:

> These sessions, however, last no more than half an hour, and this, too, without depth or comprehension and in a rush because these men are poor and must toil to earn their livelihood.[2]

The real leaders of those congregations were *gabbayim* [lay religious functionaries], the presidents and the sextons, who truly controlled all affairs touching upon congregational life. As for the ordained Orthodox rabbis, there were no more than a few of them. They received neither the respect due them, nor the minimal emolument necessary to maintain themselves in dignity. The same author described how hundreds of preachers — *darshanim* — literally had to peddle their sermons and even those congregations who supported a preacher did so meagerly.

> These preachers are forced to supplement their incomes from a thousand other sources to merely keep their families alive.[3]

The only religious functionary held in esteem was the cantor, if he was blessed with a superior voice. As for the *shoḥet* [ritual slaughterer], he was completely under the rule of the crude owner of the chicken market, and his functioning according to the Law was undermined by the owner.

> At times the *shoḥet* is forced to slaughter two hundred chickens in one breath and woe unto him who is God fearing[4]

and took time out to sharpen the instruments of his calling. A large number of these were ill-prepared to function as *shoḥatim* and were religiously not attuned to this profession.

The state of Jewish education was most deplorable. The indifference of the Orthodox elements to their children's religious studies was graphically described by Weinberger. The level of instruction in the *ḥeder* did not go beyond elementary reading. Because of the over-abundance of small private schools and their untrained instructors, the competition for students was keen. Many advertised

---

ignorant laity and a weak rabbinate. Orthodoxy, he reports, is besmirched by its external enemies such as the Socialists and other anti-religious elements. "The enemies of our faith," he writes, "rejoice and are happy that they can ridicule and belittle us."

[2] M. Weinberger, *op. cit.*, p. 3.
[3] *Ibid.*, pp. 3–4.   [4] *Ibid.*, p. 2.

that they are willing to teach any Jewish child, whoever he may be, rich or poor, stupid or smart, for ten cents a week, or forty cents a month. The parents feel that the price may go lower and withhold their children from instruction in the belief that the price may go down to a penny an hour.[5]

On the entire East Side of New York there was only one Talmud Torah — at 83 East Broadway — which the author found of any merit. This was the Machzikei Talmud Torah. Some four hundred students studied there for four years under the best teachers available. They received free clothing and careful supervision for they came from the poorest of families. Yet even these children did not reach to the level of studying the *Mishnah*. Weinberger complained that many of the Orthodox leaders

> will think little of donating twenty dollars or more to support the cantor and the choir, and give not a cent to support the study of Torah.[6]

There were some congregational Hebrew schools uptown, notably that of Congregation Adath Israel on 57th Street. He mentioned, too, the Hebrew Free School, probably at 624 Fifth Street, where fifteen hundred students received an elementary education free. This school was supported "by the donations of wealthy Reform Jews and some German and Dutch Jews."[7] The most encouraging

---

[5] *Ibid.*, p. 18. While conditions in general in the field of Jewish education are truthfully portrayed by Weinberger, accuracy of detail is at times lacking. Among the most authoritative descriptions of the state of Jewish education at the time, the author has found the following: Alexander M. Dushkin, *Jewish Education in New York City* (New York, 1918), Bureau of Jewish Education; Nathan H. Winter, "The Role of Samson Benderly in Jewish Education in the United States" [unpublished doctoral thesis for the New York University School of Education, 1963]. See his chapter on "Jewish Education in the United States at the Turn of the Century." See also Henry Moskowitz, "A Study of the East Side Ḥeder," *University Settlement Association Studies* (New York, 1898), pp. 22–26; Jeremiah Berman, "Jewish Education in New York City, 1860–1900," *Yivo Annual of Jewish Social Science*, vol. IX (New York, 1954), pp. 247–275; *Fifty Years Work of the Hebrew Education Society of Philadelphia, 1848–1898*, published by the Hebrew Education Society, 1899; Julius Greenstone, "Jewish Education in the United States," *American Jewish Year Book*, vol. XVI (1914–1915), p. 94; Israel Friedlander, "The Problem of Jewish Education in America and the Bureau of Education of the Jewish Community of New York City," *Report of the Commissioner of Education for the Year Ending July 30, 1913* (Washington, D. C.: Department of Interior, Bureau of Education), ch. XVI, pp. 365–393; Bernard Drachman, "Jewish Education, Needs and Methods," *Menorah*, vol. VIII, no. 1 (Jan., 1890), pp. 15–18; and Lloyd P. Gartner, "The Jews of New York's East Side, 1890–1893," *American Jewish Historical Quarterly* [=*AJHQ*], vol. LIII, no. 3 (March, 1964), pp. 272–284.

[6] M. Weinberger, *op. cit.*, p. 22.

[7] *Ibid.*, p. 23. For a detailed description of the networks of schools operated by the

development in Orthodoxy was the establishment of the Yeshivat Etz Chaim — the mother of American Yeshivot.[8]

Orthodoxy in New York was in a chaotic condition, poor in resources and devoid of real leadership. Each congregation was an entity unto itself, and little or no co-operation was evident among them. Whereas the various liberal and Reform elements had eloquent spokesmen with mastery of the English language and various journals to expound their point of view, the Orthodox Jewish community had no articulate spokesman and certainly no leaders to give effective battle against its detractors. To be sure there were some native Orthodox Jews, notably the membership of Congregation Shearith Israel, but the contact between them and the mass of East European Jews on the East Side was minimal. The latter, in fact, did not really look upon them as real Orthodox Jews. Weinberger complained that they praised the Orthodox way of life, and strongly defended the traditional approach to Judaism, but simultaneously they showed a high degree of friendship and similarity to the Reformers and seemed to speak their language.[9] It was upon this discouraging scene that the Minister of Congregation Shearith Israel, Dr. Henry Pereira Mendes, entered.[10] He

Hebrew Free School Association, see Jeremiah J. Berman, "Jewish Education in New York City, 1860–1900," op. cit.

[8] For the history of Yeshivat Etz Chaim and its evolution to the present day Yeshiva University, see Gilbert Klaperman, "Yeshiva University: Seventy-five Years in Retrospect," AJHQ, vol. LIV, no. 1 (Sept., 1964), pp. 5–50, and no. 2 (Dec., 1964), pp. 198–201.

[9] M. Weinberger, op. cit., p. 34.

[10] Dr. Henry Pereira Mendes, son of the Reverend Abraham P. Mendes, was born in Birmingham, England, April 13, 1852. He received his Jewish education from his father who was the founder of Northwick College — a boarding school in London, where religious studies and secular education were combined, much on the style of the modern Day School. There is no evidence that he possessed Semichah — the traditional Orthodox Jewish ordination. He received his M.A. degree at the University College, London, and his Doctor of Medicine, at the University of the City of New York. He served as minister of the newly formed Sephardic Congregation of Manchester, England, 1874–1877, and was invited by Congregation Shearith Israel to succeed the Reverend Jacques Judah Lyons, serving the congregation up to 1923, as ḥazzan and minister.

During his long career as minister of this historic congregation, he engaged in many communal activities and many a present prominent Jewish organization owes its origin in part to him. Among those he helped found were: the Jewish Theological Seminary of America, 1886; the New York Board of Ministers, 1881; the Montefiore Home for Chronic Invalids, 1884; the Jewish Branch of the Guild for Crippled Children, 1896; the Union of Orthodox Jewish Congregations of America, 1897; the American Federation of Zionists, and the Young Women's Hebrew Association, 1902. He served all these groups and many others in an official capacity. Dr. Mendes was a prolific writer of literary criticism, novels, children's books and textbooks, as well as a stream of articles in the contemporary periodicals on various phases of Judaism and Jewish life.

recognized the weaknesses inherent in the situation and endeavored with some success to strengthen the structure of Orthodoxy in the United States of America. Somehow, in spite of the fact that his Orthodoxy was of the British variety and suspect to the East European Jews, he was successful in having himself identified with them and being considered by them as an Orthodox Jewish leader. At the same time, he gained recognition in the non-traditional camp and among non-Jews as an authentic Orthodox Jewish spokesman. He was one of the few modern Orthodox rabbis at the time, by no means the only one, who could defend Orthodoxy against its detractors and give it a voice in the world outside the East Side ghetto.[11]

In using the term "modern Orthodox" we have in mind a new trend that came into Orthodox thinking toward the end of the nineteenth century. It was an Orthodoxy that was uncompromising in its strict adherence to the Torah, both the written Bible and the Oral Law. It did not deviate from any of the traditions and laws. It differed from the Orthodoxy of most East European rabbis primarily in the mode of approach to secular education, to non-Orthodox groups, to external aesthetics, and to the degree of involvement in non-religious communal activities. In each one of these areas, Dr. Mendes, and others sharing his views — such as Dr. Bernard Drachman and Dr. Philip Klein — had definite views and philosophies in which they differed from what one might call the traditional East European Orthodox rabbi. Dr. Mendes possessed secular education and used it to defend Orthodoxy and to fight its detractors. He co-operated and worked with non-orthodox and secular Jewish groups, for the greater good of Judaism. He firmly believed that beauty and outward form and decorum were essential if Orthodoxy was to maintain itself, and retain the loyalties of its youth. Finally, Dr. Mendes held the view that everything relating to the moral welfare of the community, Jewish and general, must be the province of the rabbi. He did not confine his labors and activities to the synagogue alone. Thus, one may observe some areas of Jewish life in which he endeavored to utilize his talents on behalf of Orthodox Judaism. One of the prime areas in which he utilized his talents was his attempt to unify the Orthodox Jewish forces in America into a national Orthodox congregational organization.

The woeful situation of Orthodoxy in America, as described above, its lack of cohesion and absence of any authority led him to conclude

[11] See Eugene Markovitz, "Henry Pereira Mendes: Builder of Traditional Judaism in America" [unpublished doctoral thesis, Bernard Revel Graduate School of Yeshiva University, 1961].

that unity was the primary need of Orthodox Jewry. He, therefore, embraced and expounded various schemes for unity. At first he was one of those who advocated a Jewish synod — some unifying religious authority that would be recognized by all Jewish elements.[12] He had hoped that even Reform groups would be willingly bound by its decisions. Said he:

> Everyday a synod is deferred is a sin upon the shoulders of those who should hold it. All true men would respect the deliberate opinion of such a qualified and honorable body.[13]

This notion was favored by others, too. In an editorial, *The Jewish Messenger* asked for the establishment of a synod. It quoted at great length a speech by Dr. Sabato Morais, who also urged a conference for that purpose.[14] Dr. Mendes envisaged such a group to embrace all American Jewish congregations. The purpose would be "for the adjudication of ritualistic questions."[15] Two years prior to this, the Board of Delegates of American Israelites advocated the idea of a synod when it issued a statement saying that

> The expediency and propriety of convening a synod for the purpose of infusing into the conditions of modern Judaism the authorative exposition of Jewish ecclesiastical law.[16]

This was a most naïve and impractical idea. It should have been obvious that to expect Reform Judaism to submit to any kind of "ecclesiastical law" would negate the essence of Reform Judaism. Classical Reform and its American variety believed "that Jewish law must withstand the test of time and prove its worth in elevating the spiritual life of the Jew."[17] It was only when Dr. Mendes turned his attention to the more realistic goal of some kind of unity in Orthodox Jewish circles that a limited success was achieved. This came about through his founding and organizing of the Union of Orthodox Jewish Congregations of America in 1898.

Before this, many efforts had been made to unite the Orthodox

[12] In 1855, the Conference of American Rabbis [Reform] recommended at Cleveland the convening of a synod to give Reform some legal aspect by connecting it with the Talmud and other Jewish legal sources. In Orthodox Jewish ranks, the Reverend Isaac Leeser of Congregation Mikveh Israel and Congregation Beth El Emet of Philadelphia proposed a synod. See Maxwell Whiteman and Edwin Wolf 2nd, *The History of the Jews of Philadelphia from Colonial Times to the Age of Jackson* (Philadelphia, Pa., 1957), pp. 372–377.

[13] Sermon on the "Attractiveness of the Synagogue," newspaper clipping, exact date not given [PM Collection].

[14] *Jewish Messenger*, Aug. 20, 1888.   [15] *Ibid.*

[16] Statement made May, 1878, quoted in the *Jewish Messenger*, Sept. 3, 1886.

[17] Quoted by the *Jewish Advance*, Jan. 2, 1886 (PM Collection).

congregations of the East Side for common action on matters relating to observance. Judah David Eisenstein, a leader in those
movements, chronicles those attempts in his *Ozar Zikhronotai*, and
gives a detailed description of the most ambitious of those plans,
the organization of a Chief Rabbinate.[18] Before describing this
endeavor, it should be pointed out that as early as 1879 the Board
of Delegates of Orthodox Hebrew Congregations, a newly formed
group comprising twenty-six Orthodox congregations in New York,
had decided

> to bring over from Koenigsburg, Rabbi Meir Löb Malbim to head
> the religious interests of the movement.[19]

Congregation Shearith Israel appointed some of its trustees to
represent it in its endeavor to engage a Chief Rabbi.[20] These assured
the group of the financial support of Shearith Israel. However,
very soon thereafter Rabbi Malbim died, and with him the entire
plan died. It should be noted that Congregation Shearith Israel
favored the plan for unity. In a letter to the Board of Delegates of
Orthodox Hebrew Congregations, they stated that any scheme to
unite Orthodox Jewry upon a firmer basis would meet with their
approval.[21] They demanded, however, that the Chief Rabbi should
be a man "of experience in the peculiar aspect of Judaism in this
country." This was an important prerequisite to their support.[22]

The next most noteworthy attempt in this direction was the
election of Rabbi Jacob Joseph as Chief Rabbi in 1887. This was the
result of the union of a number of Orthodox congregations, among
them Beth Hamidrash Hagadol and the Kehal Adath Jeshurun, to
create a *Beth Din* and to regulate matters pertaining to divorce and
kashrut. Ir organized a form of a *kehillah* under the name of the
Association of the American Hebrew Congregations, and was to
finance its project from dues paid by the congregation and fees
paid by the butchers for supervision. After lengthy corresponuence
with the most outstanding rabbis in Europe, they elected Rabbi
Jacob Joseph to the post.[23] He arrived in August, 1888, and received a warm welcome from the Jews of the city, with thousands
of people following him wherever he appeared to speak. However,
no sooner did he begin to enforce some new regulations in the area

---

[18] Judah D. Eisenstein, *Ozar Zikhronotai* [Hebrew] (New York, 1929), pp. 258–262.

[19] David and Tamar de Sola Pool, *An Old Faith in the New World: Portrait of Shearith Israel, 1654–1954* (New York, 1955), p. 385.

[20] Minutes of Trustees, Congregation Shearith Israel, Aug. 18, 1879.

[21] *Ibid.*   [22] *Ibid.*

[23] Judah D. Eisenstein, *op. cit.*, pp. 258–262.

of *kashrut* when he found himself challenged from many directions. The failure of this attempt at unifying Orthodox Jewry under a Chief Rabbi may be ascribed to these factors: firstly, the "Modern Orthodox" element did not like him because he could not speak English in a polished manner.[24] He also seemed to lack the strength of leadership to hold the groups together and give them direction. In addition to this, the already existing rabbis opposed him and refused to recognize him as their superior. They opposed his new regulation on *shehitah*, and as a result, the butchers were encouraged to disregard him.[25]

Dr. Mendes, however, was friendly to the project and we find him and Dr. Drachman addressing representatives of the organization at a mass meeting.[26] He had, however, doubts of the possible effect upon the American scene of Rabbi Jacob Joseph who did not conform at all to the image of the rabbi he thought was needed upon the American scene. He was fearful that the emergence of the Chief Rabbi would spell the doom of the Jewish Theological Seminary of America he had helped found.[27] In the presence of the members of the Association of the American Hebrew Congregations, he wondered whether a Chief Rabbi would be able to effectively oppose the encroachment of Reform upon the American scene. He is quoted as cautioning them not to

> give way to false hopes. Those who come after you will be Americans — full-blooded Americans like your brethren farther uptown.[28]

Unlike Dr. Sabato Morais, his co-worker at the Jewish Theological Seminary of America, Dr. Mendes showed great respect for the Chief Rabbi and was helpful to him. He expressed publicly his approval of the idea and thought it might help unify Orthodox Jewry. Dr. Mendes joined Judge Philip J. Joachimsen, a well-known lay leader, in inviting the new Chief Rabbi to accompany them on an inspection tour of the Hebrew Orphan Asylum. Heretofore, the Russian Jew had been looked down upon and at best tolerated; now the rabbi was accorded respect and a fine status by the spiritual leaders of New York's best and most aristocratic congregation.[29] This new status was deemed of great importance in establishing the authority of the Chief Rabbi.

[24] *Ibid.*, p. 268.
[25] *Ibid.* See Abraham J. Karp., "New York Chooses A Chief Rabbi," *Publication of the American Jewish Historical Society* [=*PAJHS*], vol. XLIV (March, 1955), p. 174. Karp chronicles in detail the steps that led to the tragic neglect of the Chief Rabbi and to his untimely death in 1902.
[26] *Ibid.*, p. 145.
[27] *Ibid.*, pp. 153–154.
[28] *Ibid.*
[29] *Ibid.*, p. 160.

When Rabbi Jacob Joseph established his system of the inspection of *sheḥitah* to be financed by some form of modest tax on meat and poultry, it was Dr. Mendes who was one of his staunchest supporters. When the butchers and wholesalers showed defiance, Dr. Mendes and Dr. Drachman were asked by the Chief Rabbi to help bring those men in line. By lending their names to the project, they gave it importance and prestige.[30] It was with sadness, however, that Dr. Mendes analyzed at the very outset the almost impossible task facing the Chief Rabbi, who was ill prepared to face the challenge of the American scene. The *American Israelite* quotes him as describing this challenge to an audience of members of the Association. He posed the question:

> Has he the power and ability and education enough to enter the lists for Orthodoxy? Will he dare oppose the uptown ministers, some of whom maintain that God did not dictate the Torah word by word to Moses? Indeed, can he enter into a polemic with them in order thereby to lead the errant sheep back to the fold of our faith? Do you believe in the possibility that by virtue of the authority he possesses in the old country, he will be able to exert a salutary influence on the youth of America?[31]

Unfortunately, his prophecy was fulfilled. However, one of the desirable results of this venture was to encourage Dr. Mendes and a few others to organize a decade later the Union of Orthodox Jewish Congregations of America, and to guard properly against the pitfalls which destroyed the office of the Chief Rabbinate and the Association.

Immediately preceding the actual organization of the Union, Dr. Mendes was involved in an effort to organize a united orthodox rabbinate. In 1896, we find him to be one of the organizers of a group called the Orthodox Rabbinical Council of New York City. In a circular, the programs set forth by the group included the following:

1. Conversionist danger
2. Religious education
3. Social conditions
4. Free lectures and sermons
5. Congregations unable to maintain preachers of their own, and how to help them
6. Ritual matters, such as *milah* and divorce.[32]

---

[30] *Ibid.*, p. 169.

[31] *American Israelite*, March 30, 1888, quoted by Abraham J. Karp, *PAJHS*, vol. XLIV, no. 3 (March, 1955), p. 184.

[32] Circular in Yiddish and English, 1896 [PM Collection].

The fact that this circular was also written in the Yiddish language and contained among its signers rabbis from the East European school of Orthodoxy, indicates that this was to be a genuinely united Orthodox body. Some of the signers included were Rabbis Mendes, Bloch, Drachman, Marcus, Gur Yanowsky, Wechsler, Meisner, Tzinzler and Friedman.[32a] This, too, proved to be an abortive attempt, and the specific reasons for its failure can only be conjectured.

Concurrently with this plan of organizing the rabbinate, an effort was made to organize the Orthodox congregations. At a meeting held on March 17, 1896, at Adath Jeshurun Synagogue, a constitutional committee was formed and plans were discussed for an assembly of delegates and a board of directors, as well as the above mentioned council of rabbis.[33] The initiators of this plan knew the problems involved, and to insure themselves against certain failure they promised that this projected organization

> does not affect the autonomy of the congregations at all, but leaves them free and independent in internal matters — being only intended for matters of public and general action and there will be no expense to individual congregations.[34]

The founders knew very well that the strictly independent congregations dotting the East Side would not join unless their autonomy was assured. It was equally important that this scheme should not involve some of the literally pauperized congregations in any expense. It was two years later that the Union of Orthodox Jewish Congregations of America was launched on its career, with Dr. Mendes as one of its founders and its first President.

The constitution of the Union states that its function is

> to advance the interest of positive Biblical, rabbinical, traditional and historical Judaism, and we affirm our adherence to the authoritative interpretation of our rabbis as contained in the Talmud and the Codes.[35]

The Union, under the leadership of Dr. Mendes, embarked upon a series of activities designed to protect the Orthodox Jew in his right to observe his tenets. It also endeavored to protect Orthodoxy against doctrinal attacks from various quarters, and, assumed leader-

---

[32a] The writer was unable to complete the full names of some signatories.

[33] Letter addressed to Orthodox Jewish Congregations, Feb., 1896 [PM Collection].

[34] *Ibid.*

[35] *Constitution of the Union of Orthodox Jewish Congregations of America, Proceedings of the Sixth Convention — Union of Orthodox Jewish Congregations of America, New York, June 29th, 1913,* p. 34.

ship on behalf of Orthodoxy in areas where there was a minimum of differences in its own ranks. In describing some of these activities, its pioneering value to Orthodoxy is apparent, as also its weaknesses.

One of the first recorded actions involved the Jewish service men in the Spanish American War. Dr. Mendes asked the military authorities in 1898 to give official recognition to the Jewish holidays by granting furloughs to enlisted men and officers on those days. Actually, the first recognition given to Jewish service men and their religious needs occurred during the Civil War when Abraham Lincoln appointed the first official military Jewish Chaplain — after the Congress amended the law, a provision of which requiring an "ordained minister of some Christian denomination" had excluded Jews.[36] The United States Armed Forces were greatly reduced in number between the Civil War and the Spanish American War. This war, however, brought large numbers into the service, including a considerable number of Jews. To the surprise of all, the Army acquiesced in the demand of the Union.[37] Six years later, in response to a letter by Dr. Mendes, President Theodore Roosevelt himself instructed the War Department on September 8, 1904, that

> commanding officers be authorized to permit Jewish soldiers to be absent for attendance at services on the Jewish holydays.[38]

The War Department formally decreed that

> such enlisted men of the army of the Jewish faith as may desire to avail themselves of the privilege to be absent from their duties for such length of time as may be deemed necessary to enable them to attend Divine Services.[39]

should be given that permission.

We gain a close understanding of the functions, purposes and scope of activities of the Union from the presidential report given by Dr. Mendes at the annual convention of 1901. One must, of course, realize that such convention reports are intended, in addition to giving facts, also to enhance the role of the organization and its officers in the mind of the public. Seasoned participants and delegates to conventions will take such facts into consideration and make due allowances when they evaluate the work of an organization. Nevertheless, this report by Dr. Mendes and the other officers is an indication of the manifold activities and the ambitious program they envisaged for the Union. Dr. Mendes, in reviewing the first years of its existence, stated that

[36] Bertram W. Korn, *American Jewry and the Civil War* [paper back] (New York, 1961).
[37] David and Tamar de Sola Pool, *An Old Faith in the New World*, p. 335.
[38] *Ibid.*   [39] *Ibid.*

The Union of Orthodox Jewish Congregations of America was formed two and a half years ago to protest against declarations of reform rabbis not in accord with the teachings of our Torah, Nebiim and the accepted rulings of recognized sages of Israel. It stands for loyalty to Jewish law and custom. It stands for the establishment of a synod of certified rabbis, elders in official position — men of wisdom and understanding and known able men, God fearing men — men of truth, hating all self-advantage.[40]

Apparently, he had not given up his favorite project of a higher religious authority, the rulings of which would be accepted by most Jews, and hoped that the Union would become the instrument in creating this body.

The projection of his thinking on behalf of the Union indicates how the Union came to reflect his own point of view on this and other questions. He reported, for example, on Zionism in a manner reflecting his own private opinion.

I consider that the spiritual side of Zionism doesn't mean only the possession of a legalized home in the land of our Fathers. It means that, and much more. Our possession is already legalized by Him who gave it to us forever and who gives all lands to whom He pleases.[41]

He also emphasized views on a Torah-centered Zionism.[41a]

Among other areas of Jewish life where he reported activities by the Union are these: *kashrut*, transferring bar examinations from the Sabbath, help for victims of the Galveston Flood, and the promotion in Albany of a Sabbath law. A most interesting and little known incident is related by him in his report in regard to the then newly adapted Red Cross emblem. The Union demanded of the President of the United States

[40] *American Hebrew*, Jan. 4, 1901.

[41] *Ibid.* The Zionist views of Dr. Mendes were close to those of the subsequently organized Mizrachi, that of combining Torah [Jewish law] with *Avodah* [pioneer labor] to build the land. He attended many of the world Zionist Congresses and served on many of their important committees.

[41a] "Open Letter to Zionists," attending the Seventh Zionist Congress, by Dr. Mendes, which is attached to the copy of the *Proceedings of the Seventh Zionist Congress, held at Basel, July 27–August 2, 1905* (copy of these *Proceedings* at the Library of the Jewish Theological Seminary of America). In this "Open Letter," to the Zionists attending that Congress, Dr. Mendes appealed for a Zionism that would not limit its goal solely to a "legally assured home in Palestine, but will initiate a spiritual movement to turn Hebrews from transgressions" of the Divine Law. Zionism must strengthen the spiritual life of the Jews, he stated, both in Palestine and elsewhere. In 1936, one year before his death, in a letter to Dr. Pinkhos Churgin, an American Mizrachi leader, Dr. Mendes wrote that "I am a Mizrachi with all my heart," and restated his credo in religious Zionism which he preached during his entire ministry. See the *Mizrachi Jubilee Publications*, edited by Pinkhos Churgin and Leon Gellman (New York, 1936), p. 25.

the substitution of some other emblem than the Red Cross for Jewish physicians, nurses, and surgeons who had conscientious scruples against wearing what is an emblem associated with a religion whose doctrines are antagonistic to their own.[42]

Of course, he soon learned that many of the religious advantages he sought to gain for Jewish groups were actually spurned by them. Indeed, he complains of this fact in a letter to a newspaper in which he relates of his organization's success in obtaining Sabbath privileges for Jewish students at City College. He puts a challenge to them, "Will the Jewish students be sufficiently self-respecting to ask for rights which can be had for the asking?"[43]

Two years later at the Convention of 1903, Dr. Mendes was able to add many new areas in which the Union took an interest. The year before the suggestion of transferring the Sabbath to Sunday, which was seriously discussed by Reform rabbis, became a *cause célèbre* which agitated the minds of Orthodox leadership. The Union attacked the very notion of even giving it any thought. He asserted:

We contend that a Jewish conference should rule out of order any notion or suggestion to consider Sunday Sabbath, except to condemn it.[44]

He was also proud that the Union received leaves of absence for municipal employees on Jewish holidays. Among other activities, he reported that

We communicated with the city authorities in regard to the unseemly riots at the funeral of the late Rabbi Jacob Joseph. We communicated with Washington concerning the proposed immigration bill and its supposed exclusion of Hebrews able to speak only Yiddish, on the theory that Yiddish was not a recognized language.[45]

They also were active in making representation on behalf of the Kishineff Pogrom sufferers.

It is noteworthy that in spite of its varied interests and activities, the Union did not concern itself with some of the perennial issues plaguing Orthodoxy in the city. Such subjects as Jewish education, *kashrut*, unity in Orthodox ranks, and the authority of the Orthodox rabbinate seem to have been ignored because of the wide gulf separating the various Orthodox elements on those problems. This was a clear indication that actually the original purpose of organizing the Union was not fully achieved, and at most it could act effectively only in matters which would evoke no dissension in Orthodox ranks.

[42] *American Hebrew*, Jan. 4, 1901.   [43] *Ibid.*, May 17, 1901.
[44] *Ibid.*, June 27, 1903.   [45] *Ibid.*

As a matter of fact, the hundreds of small *shtiblech* and even many of the larger East Side congregations remained outside the Union. Prior to the 1903 Convention, the *American Hebrew*[46] in an editorial placed the problem in its proper prospective when it stated:

> The Orthodox congregations in this country, it must be said, lack entirely the sense of unity for which the Union of Orthodox Jewish Congregations of America has been striving ... They are content to exist as isolated congregations unwilling to meet in common sessions and it requires the greatest genius to point out to them the immense value of a united effort ... In the labors of its alert president and his secretaries it has used its influence to strengthen the traditional view of Judaism where it could.[47]

The Union of Orthodox Jewish Congregations of America has stood as a spokesman, the editorial continues, for the view that difficult as it is the traditional view of Jewish life is viable in the United States. It categorically states that the foreign-born rabbis are opposed to any and all forms of united effort.

Benjamin Koenigsberg, a well-known leader of the Union, reminiscing on the later period of Dr. Mendes' presidency of the Union and who served the organization in various capacities during that period, claims that actually the Union had aimed at functioning through lay leadership. As a leader on the East Side and as a prominent attorney, Mr. Koenigsberg was invited to join the Union in 1910.[48] The choice of Dr. Mendes, a rabbi, to serve as head of what was supposed to be a laymen group, was due to the fact that "he had the time and the ability" which few lay people could contribute. Mr. Koenigsberg asserted that the Union

> did not attract the synagogues and *shtiblech* of the East Side because those were mainly *landsmanschaften* and their interests were centered around their *minyan*, and the narrow personal, social and economic problems they found.[49]

He, furthermore, asserted that the Union leadership was fully aware of the lack of interest on its part and did not really make any strong effort to solicit their membership. He cited as evidence the fact that from the very outset the minutes of the Union were recorded in English and its business not transacted in the Yiddish language.[50]

---

[46] Editorial, *ibid.*, June 19, 1903.   [47] *Ibid.*

[48] Interview with Mr. Benjamin Koenigsberg, March 29, 1961.   [49] *Ibid.*

[50] *Ibid.* At its first convention, June 8, 1898, the Union elected secretaries for English as well as for Hebrew, but none for Yiddish. *American Jewish Yearbook*, vol. I (1899–1900), p. 99. At this first Convention the following officers were elected:

President: Dr. Henry Pereira Mendes, New York City;
First Vice-President: Lewis N. Dembitz, Esquire, Louisville, Ky.;

Those Orthodox Jewish congregations and laymen from the East Side who were active in the Union were apparently Americanized by then.

As a clear indication of the lack of co-operation on the part of the Orthodox rabbinate and of their attitude of indifference, and at times antagonism, one might cite the following exchange of letters between Dr. Mendes and the Agudat Harabbanim — the Union of Orthodox Rabbis of America. At the third convention of that rabbinical organization, its members received an urgent communication from Dr. Mendes enlisting their co-operation for some of the projects of the Union and bringing to their attention problems facing the Orthodox community.[51] A special committee was appointed by the rabbinical organization for the purpose of drafting a reply. The tone and the content of the reply clearly indicated that it did not consider the Union of Orthodox Jewish Congregations as truly representative of their conception of real Orthodoxy. Instead of promising to co-operate with the Union and possibly joining forces with the rabbis, they declared that

> our principal aim has always been directed to form and build up a Union of real Orthodox Congregations.[52]

Second Vice-President: Solomon Solis-Cohen, M.D., Philadelphia, Pa.;
Third Vice-President: Aaron Friedenwald, M.D., Baltimore, Md.;
Fourth Vice-President: Kasriel H. Sarasohn, New York City;
Treasurer: Jacob Hecht, New York City; and
Secretaries: Rev. Dr. Bernard Drachman and Max Cohen, New York City.

[51] *American Hebrew*, July 8, 1904, p. 204. In his letter, Dr. Mendes stated among other things:

> First, I am requested by Judge Newburger of the Court of General Sessions to bring to the notice of the rabbis the fact that certain marriages legal in Jewish law are illegal according to the laws of the State, for example, between an uncle and his niece.
> Second, the practice of Milah needs regulation. Cases are on record which point to fatal results due to the Mohelim not paying sufficient regard to surgical cleanliness. The State may pass a law forbidding all Mohelim who are not graduates in surgery to practice.
> Third, I hear that you are opposed to the seminary. The seminary was established to be a bulwark against reform Judaism as taught by the Cincinnati College.

In reporting this letter of Dr. Mendes which was read at the Third Convention of the Union of Orthodox Rabbis which took place at the Yeshibat Rabbi Isaac Elchanan, 156 Henry Street, New York City, the *American Hebrew* stated:

> He [Dr. Mendes] appealed to the rabbis to participate in the work of carrying on religious work among the young men, and took them to task for the lack of public spirit.

[52] The full text of the reply of the Union of Orthodox Rabbis to Dr. Mendes' letter appeared in the *American Hebrew*, July 30, 1904, p. 282, and reads as follows:

> Dear Sir:
> Your communication of 18 Tammuz to hand. In reply we desire to say as follows:
> First, regarding the request to you by Judge Newberger to bring to our notice the laws of the State that conflict with the Jewish law. You may assure the judge

In general they belittled the efforts of the Union in all the areas of its activity indicating that the Agudat Harabbanim worked more effectively in these areas.

Mr. Koenigsberg assigns much of the credit for the successful projects during the early days of the Union to Dr. Mendes personally. He was respected and beloved by all elements of Orthodoxy. He attributed his influence to such factors as being the minister of the oldest congregation in this country, his mastery of the English language, his friendly and thoughtful attitude to all people, and a soft-spoken and sincere manner. "I cannot picture him ever being angry," explained Mr. Koenigsberg.[53]

This failure to become the fully recognized spokesman for the Orthodox Jewish masses of the city did not discourage Dr. Mendes from maintaining unity as the true goal of the organization. At

---

that as American citizens we are loyal to the laws of the State, and it is hardly necessary to remind us of our duty.

Second, regarding the Mohelim, the Jewish law amply provides for the surgical cleanliness and carefulness, so much so that fatal results are very rare indeed. Nevertheless, we have taken measures to instruct the Mohelim to exercise extra caution at the operations.

Third, regarding the seminary. It was never our intention to proclaim a Cherem, but we do protest against the seminary calling itself orthodox since the professors of the seminary believe in the Higher Criticism. Besides, the professors, in our judgment, are not qualified as teachers in the Talmud and the Codes. We protest also against the students who graduate from the seminary as rabbis, inasmuch as they are not fit for the position of rabbi on account of lack of proper and sufficient learning. We are convinced that none of the graduates can pass an examination before a competent Jewish authority even for a Hatarath Horaah, much less a regular Semicha.

Fourth, regarding the Union of Orthodox Congregations in America, our principal aim has always been directed to form and build up a union of real orthodox congregations.

You say that you have been to Albany to fight for the Sabbath. This, we assure you, is highly appreciated by us. But you should have known the fact that almost every one of our rabbis in the State, directly or indirectly, worked in this matter, though, to our regret, without success.

With reference to the Jewish immigration and Kishineff, our efforts in the former and practical assistance in the latter are a matter of record though most of our work is done quietly without publicity.

Thanking you for your good wishes. . . .

It should be pointed out that Dr. Mendes was not entirely discouraged by this rebuff for he persisted in working toward some meeting of minds with the Agudat Harabbanim. Many years later, on June 15, 1914, a joint committee of the Union of Orthodox Jewish Congregations of America and the aforementioned rabbinical group adopted a resolution which indicates a spirit of harmony, albeit with reserve, that prevailed between them. It reads as follows:

RESOLVED: That it is the sense of this meeting that the religious principles and objects of the Union of Orthodox Rabbis and of the Union of Orthodox Jewish Congregations of America are identical and that in order to strengthen Orthodox Judaism in America, it is advisable to form a standing joint committee representing the two bodies. [*Report of the Seventh Convention of the Union of Orthodox Jewish Congregations of America, Arverne, Long Island, June 20–21, 1914*, p. 19.]

[53] Statement of Mr. Benjamin Koenigsberg, March 29, 1961.

the sixth convention of the Union of Orthodox Jewish Congregations of America, he disclosed

> the special sphere of duty and usefulness of the Union is to attempt to guide the hundreds of Orthodox congregations, *chebras* and societies throughout the country toward cultural Orthodox ideals, so that they can flourish in their American environment.[54]

He readily conceded that "some leaders of orthodoxy are not and can never be in harmony with us."[55]

In a sense one could hardly expect the older Orthodox rabbis to engage personally in some of the worldly and practical projects of the Union. The problem of working in harmony with non-traditional groups seemed no insurmountable problem to Dr. Mendes. As a founder and former President of the New York Board of Ministers, Dr. Mendes worked in close co-operation even with those ministers whose ideas he excoriated. At this particular convention he boasted of the fact that

> we organized a deputation to appear in Washington before the Foreign Relations Committee. It was participated in by the Honorable Simon Wolf representing the Union of American Hebrew Congregations.[56]

Its purpose was to get help to the Jewish victims of persecution in Russia and other countries.

One must credit the Union and Dr. Mendes, its perennial President in the early years of its existence, with many solid achievements in areas which still present a problem to Orthodoxy. He was able to report, for example, that

> The Union organized a Sabbath Committee some years ago with Dr. Drachman as Chairman. Its bureau of employment has found places for fifteen hundred Sabbath observers out of three thousand applicants.[57]

Of similar nature was the Union's alertness in the area of Anti-*Shehitah* legislation, a problem still very much with us. "I regret," he reports, "that the Massachusetts Society for Cruelty to Animals according to a pamphlet by its president proposes state legislation to secure stunning animals before Shehita. We shall watch this."[58]

---

[54] *Proceedings of the Sixth Convention of the Union of Orthodox Jewish Congregations of America, July 29th, 1913, New York City,* p. 24.

[55] *Ibid.,* p. 25.

[56] *Ibid.,* p. 10.

[57] *Ibid.,* p. 12.

[58] *Ibid*

Among the recurring problems in relation to the public schools which the Union attempted to solve, but without lasting success was the problem of Christmas in public schools. The Yiddish newspapers of the time describe the vigorous intervention of Dr. Mendes, Dr. Drachman and Mr. Albert Lucas, Secretary of the Union, with the New York City Board of Education. Jewish children, it seems, were coerced into participating in Christmas pageants and singing of carols and in general were subjected to a not too subtle course of indoctrination of Christmas and its observance. The complaint was

> that the principals in many public schools feign ignorance of United States laws regarding separation of church and state and introduce Christmas ceremonials into the school. The Union of Orthodox Jewish Congregations of America started a struggle in the United States and Canada against this *Shemad*, conversion campaign, in public schools.[59]

So closely was the Union identified with Dr. Mendes, and its ideals considered synonymous with his, that the organization refused to consider anyone else for leadership. At its seventh convention in 1915, he pleaded with the delegates to relieve him of office.

> I asked you last year and three years ago, in my illness, to accept my resignation. I have no longer the strength for leadership. I have always said that many years of preparatory work would be needed before the organization of American Orthodox Jewry would be possible.[60]

At last his resignation was accepted.

A tribute paid him by his contemporary and co-worker in the Union, Dr. Bernard Drachman, who also served as its head, indicates the unique role of Dr. Mendes in the history of the Union. He declared:

> His saintly character, his broad and spiritual concept of Judaism combined with scrupulous conscientiousness in the fulfillment of

---

[59] *Das Jüdisches Tageblatt*, Dec. 6, 1906.

[60] *Report of the Seventh Convention of the Union of Orthodox Jewish Congregations of America, Arverne, Long Island, June 20-21, 1914*, p. 29. In a similar vein, Dr. Mendes expressed the same reservation about his long tenure of office in an interview with *Young Israel* [no date], a volume containing biographical sketches of contemporary Jewish leaders, Dr. Mendes is quoted as saying:

> In my opinion the prospects of success [of the Union of Orthodox Jewish Congregations] would be assured if they had another president than myself, because I am an Englishman by birth and education and therefore perhaps not sufficiently in touch with the wants of the Russian section. I strongly objected to having this

ritual precepts, his absolute freedom, although a Sephardi, of purest lineage, from anything approaching narrowness of sectarian bias within the Jewish community, and his delicate responsiveness to the demands of the American environment, made him an ideal representative of Orthodox Judaism.[61]

---

honor thrust upon me, but as the Convention would hear of no refusal, I had to consent to it [clipping, PM Collection, p. 25].

[61] Bernard Drachman, "Forty Years of Loyal Service," *Orthodox Union*, vol. VII, no. 6 (June 9, 1940).

The author regrets that he was unable to locate the *Proceedings* of the earlier conventions and conferences of the Union of Orthodox Jewish Congregations of America prior to its Sixth Convention of June 29, 1913. [The American Jewish Historical Society is interested in locating any published or unpublished materials relating to the formative years of the Union of Orthodox Jewish Congregations of America and its various conventions, prior to the Sixth Convention of June 29, 1913 — I.S.M.]

THE REACTION OF REFORM JUDAISM IN AMERICA TO POLITICAL ZIONISM
(1897–1922)

By Naomi Wiener Cohen

INTRODUCTION

Any history of political Zionism during the first twenty-five years of its existence in the United States must take note of the opposition to the movement voiced by the religious groups within American Jewry. The Zionist movement, which can properly be regarded as an outgrowth of the traditional Jewish aspiration for a return to Palestine, meant, nevertheless, the secularization of this ideal with emphasis placed primarily on the national rather than the religious character of Judaism. It was this secular and areligious bent of the Zionists at the inception of their movement that aroused the opposition of various Orthodox and Conservative segments in American Jewry. The opposition voiced by the Reform group during this period, however, differed from that of its coreligionists qualitatively. Reform did not merely question the means employed by the Zionists to achieve their ideal, but rather discarded on theological grounds the very objective, Orthodox as well as Zionist, of a return to Zion.

According to Reform theology, Judaism was a religion with a universal message. The mission of the Jews, the bearers of this message, was to propagate the universal religion of the prophets throughout the world. Dispersion was, therefore, a vital condition in Reform thinking, and even the Messianic

149

era, which was envisioned as the realization of the prophetic ethics as taught by the Jews, precluded the traditional belief of a mass return to Palestine. Although theological differences alone would have been sufficient to make Reform Jewry anti-Zionist, other points of difference existed between the two movements. The reaction of the Reform group to the Zionist movement from the first Zionist Congress in 1897 until the establishment of the mandate over Palestine in 1922, which is the subject of this paper, was the product of multiple factors. The optimism of Reform theology — a theology which had been born in the wake of emancipation and the opening up of America — which minimized the significance of anti-Semitism, the almost "religious" love of Reform for America as the Promised Land, the consonance of Reform opinion with the prevailing American thought at the beginning of the twentieth century that all immigrants must become Americans in customs and ideals after the pattern of the older settlers, the fear of Reform Jews that Zionism would endanger their position as loyal Americans, the practical difficulties faced by the Zionist movement, must also be accounted for in the total setting from which Reform opposition to Zionism sprang.

Although there were some within the Reform camp who were Zionists from the outset, the large majority remained antagonistic to the Zionist movement throughout the first quarter-century of its history. Nevertheless, it would be inaccurate to assume that even the majority attitude underwent no change. As political Zionism evolved it was taken more seriously by Reform; ridicule was soon abandoned in favor of weightier counterarguments. Finally, with the promulgation of the Balfour Declaration and the San Remo decision on Palestine the shift in Reform opinion from anti-Zionism to non-Zionism, although not as yet repeated in official Reform resolutions, was clearly discernible.

Lack of space prevents an individual analysis of all the

above-mentioned factors, but they must be viewed as the matrix of the reaction of American Reform Judaism to political Zionism throughout the following discussion.[1]

I

Zionism as a practical movement to restore Palestine to the Jews was not unknown to American Jews even before the days of Herzl. As early as 1825 Mordecai M. Noah dedicated "Ararat," his island in the Niagara River, as the temporary homeland of the Jews until Palestine could be obtained.[2] After Noah, the idea of nationhood in Palestine was argued by Raphael J. De Cordova, lay preacher of Temple Emanu-El in New York.[3] In 1848, a Quaker of Philadelphia, Warder Cresson, who had served as consul to Jerusalem, converted to Judaism and advocated the restoration of Israel to Palestine.[4] Another isolated incident revealing political Zionist sentiment in the pre-Herzlian period occurred in 1891 when a petition was presented to President Benjamin Harrison asking him to negotiate with the European powers with the aim of acquiring Palestine for the Jews. Among the signers of this

[1] All manuscript material cited in this paper except for the Minutes of the Board of Governors of Hebrew Union College and other items especially designated were made available by Professor Jacob R. Marcus and the American Jewish Archives. I would like to express my thanks to Professor Salo W. Baron, Dr. Joshua Bloch, Professor Marcus, Professor Alexander Marx and Rabbi Isidore S. Meyer for their counsel and advice on various aspects of this study.

[2] Charles P. Daly, *The Settlement of the Jews in North America* (New York, 1893), pp. 104–138.

[3] Hyman B. Grinstein, *The Rise of the Jewish Community of New York* (Philadelphia, 1945), pp. 460–464.

[4] Anita L. Lebeson, *Jewish Pioneers in America* (New York, 1931), pp. 308–309. Even before Warder Cresson, the classic phrase that was to become the slogan for anti-Zionist sentiment after Herzl had been uttered. When the Reform Temple in Charleston was dedicated on March 19, 1841, Rabbi Gustavus Poznanski declared that "this synagogue is our *temple*, this city our *Jerusalem*, this happy land our *Palestine*." See Charles Reznikoff and Uriah Z. Engelman, *The Jews of Charleston* (Philadelphia, 1950), p. 140, and note 182 on pp. 296–297.

petition was Kaufmann Kohler, who later became one of the most outspoken anti-Zionists in the Reform camp.[5] Besides these incidents, American Jewry had contact with Palestine during the nineteenth century through the messengers who had come to collect funds for Palestinian relief. It is interesting to note here, too, that the Reform leader, Isaac M. Wise, endorsed the missions of the first messengers but that 1867 marked the beginning of his "progressive alienation from the Palestine ideal."[6] All these efforts, however, were not effective in arousing mass popular interest, either in the way of sympathy or opposition. It was not until 1896, with the publication of Herzl's *Judenstaat*, and 1897, with the calling of the first Zionist Congress, that American Jewry was awakened to the full implications of political Zionism.

Reform Jewry was quick to voice its opposition to the Zionist movement through the pulpit, the press, and various Reform institutions. One such institution was the Central Conference of American Rabbis, organized in 1889 through the efforts of Isaac M. Wise, and consisting after 1896 only of rabbis of the Reform group.[7] By 1890 the Central Conference was on record as doctrinally opposed to Zionism, for in that year, at its first annual conference at Cleveland, it incorporated the resolutions adopted at previous Reform conferences as its underlying principles. These included the resolution passed at the Frankfort Conference in 1845 by Samuel Hirsch, David Einhorn, Samuel Holdheim, and others which eliminated references to a return to Palestine and a Jewish state from prayers and ritual on the grounds that nationalism and statehood were not in consonance with Reform theology. Similar resolutions included were those from the Philadelphia

---

[5] *Palestine for the Jews*, A Copy of the Memorial Presented to President Harrison, March 5, 1891 (s. l., 1891).

[6] Salo W. and Jeannette M. Baron, "Palestinian Messengers in America, 1849–79," *Jewish Social Studies*, vol. V (April-July, 1943), pp. 115–162, 225–292.

[7] Max B. May, *Isaac Mayer Wise* (New York, 1916), pp. 337, 339, 343.

Conference of 1869 and the Pittsburgh Conference of 1885 which denied the restoration of the Jewish state under the Davidic dynasty a place in the creed of Reform Judaism.[8] The Central Conference reaffirmed these earlier positions in 1897, when, in response to a vigorous attack upon Zionism by Wise, it passed a resolution which stated:

> Resolved, That we totally disapprove of any attempt for the establishment of a Jewish state. Such attempts show a misunderstanding of Israel's mission which from the narrow political and national field has been expanded to the promotion among the whole human race of the broad and universalistic religion first proclaimed by the Jewish prophets. Such attempts do not benefit, but infinitely harm our Jewish brethren where they are still persecuted, by confirming the assertion of their enemies that the Jews are foreigners in the countries in which they are at home, and of which they are everywhere the most loyal and patriotic citizens.
>
> We reaffirm that the object of Judaism is not political nor national, but spiritual, and addresses itself to the continuous growth of peace, justice and love in the human race, to a messianic time when all men will recognize that they form "one great brotherhood" for the establishment of God's kingdom on earth.[9]

The same anti-nationalist spirit motivated resolutions adopted at Indianapolis in 1906 and at Baltimore in 1912 although Zionism was not specifically mentioned. The former read: "We herewith reaffirm that religion is the tie which unites the Jews, the synagog is the basic institution of Judaism and the congregation its unit of representation." The second one stated:

> Inasmuch as we are unqualifiedly committed to the total separation of Church and State, we discountenance any movement in Jewish communities on other than the religious basis which would violate

[8] Central Conference of American Rabbis, *Yearbook* (=*CCARY*), vol. I, pp. 80–125.

[9] *Ibid.*, vol. VII, p. xli. An interesting parallel can be found in the statement of the Board of Ministers in Germany. *Allgemeine Zeitung des Judenthums*, July 16, 1897.

this principle and tend to create the impression that the Jews are an *imperium in imperio*.[10]

In 1917, in a response to a request by the President of the Central Conference, Dr. William Rosenau, the Conference phrased a more vigorous resolution reasserting their anti-nationalist sentiments.

> We herewith reaffirm the fundamental principle of reform Judaism, that the essence of Israel as a priest people, consists in its religious consciousness, and in the sense of consecration to God and service in the world, and not in any political or racial national consciousness. And therefore, we look with disfavor upon the new doctrine of political Jewish nationalism, which finds the criterion of Jewish loyalty in anything other than loyalty to Israel's God and Israel's religious mission.[11]

Official Reform opinion did not deviate from the pattern laid down by all these resolutions even with the advent of the Balfour Declaration and the San Remo decision on the Palestinian mandate.[12] The Central Conference also manifested its anti-Zionism through the presidential messages as well as lectures and sermons delivered at the annual meetings by individual members.[13]

With the issuance of the Balfour Declaration several members of the Central Conference decided that more extreme measures must be employed to combat the growing challenge of political Zionism. On July 2, 1918, thirty rabbis met at Chicago to consider means of action, and a committee of seven, later expanded to thirteen, was appointed with Dr. David Philipson as chairman. The committee desired the

---

[10] *CCARY*, vol. XVI, pp. 180–183; vol. XXII, p. 108.

[11] *Ibid.*, vol. XXVII, p. 132.

[12] *Ibid.*, vol. XXVIII, pp. 133–134; vol. XXX, pp. 140–141.

[13] *Ibid.*, vol. II, p. 54; vol. VII, pp. x–xii; vol. VIII, pp. 167–173, 174–177; vol. XII, pp. 27, 89, 229–236; vol. XIII, pp. 370–372; vol. XVII, pp. 181–183; vol. XVIII, p. 146; vol. XXV, pp. 165–166; vol. XXVII, pp. 201–202; vol. XXVIII, pp. 173–175; vol. XXIX, p. 287; vol. XXX, pp. 182–185.

convocation of a special conference of prominent Jewish religious and lay leaders to discuss the subject of political Zionism and to formulate positive measures for combating it. The committee of rabbis also considered plans for an organization of American Jews on the platform of Americans in nationality and Jews in religion. The special conference was further discussed at a meeting on September 30th and October 2nd at which letters from prominent laymen, both favorable and unfavorable towards the project, were read. The net result of the affair was the decision by the committee to postpone the conference which had been scheduled to convene in October, 1918, "owing to a number of unlooked for occurrences which have taken place since steps towards issuing a call for such a conference were begun."[14]

II

The opposition of the Reform leaders in America to Zionism during this period must be viewed against the background of the thinking generally current in the United States at that time. It must be remembered that the end of the nineteenth century and early part of the twentieth century witnessed the strength of the extremist program of Americanization, which was an attempt to divest the immigrant of his former cultural habits and customs and make him adhere solely to the American way of life as set by the Anglo-Saxon stock.[15] This ideal, which emphasized complete political, economic, and cultural affiliation with America was held also by many Jewish leaders.

[14] *Correspondence on the Advisability of Calling a Conference for the Purpose of Combating Zionism* (New York, 1918), p. 3; *American Hebrew*, Oct. 11, 1918. The *Hebrew Standard* claimed that Philipson's desire for a special conference was motivated by the opposition of the League of British Jews to the Balfour Declaration. *Hebrew Standard*, Nov. 15, 1918.

[15] Edward G. Hartmann, *The Movement to Americanize the Immigrant* (New York, 1948), pp. 269-270; Isaac B. Berkson, *Theories of Americanization* (New York, 1920), pp. 55-56.

It was natural, therefore, that they should oppose any movement which entertained such aims as Zionism. This acceptance of the ideal of Americanization underlay the anti-Zionist attitudes of many Reform rabbis and was reflected in their attempts to discredit the spread of Zionism in the United States.

To the Reform Jews, Zionism was a philosophy of foreign origin which had nothing to recommend itself to Americans.[16] They associated Zionism in America with the newly-arrived Jewish immigrants from Eastern Europe. In 1897, Dr. Isaac M. Wise, in his presidential address to the Central Conference of American Rabbis, claimed that Zionism in America was the movement sponsored by those refugees who had been persecuted in Europe and who loudly voiced their home ideals in this country. The true American Jewish sentiment, however, excluding "the idiosyncrasies of those late immigrants," was opposed to the Zionist position.[17] The *American Israelite* echoed Wise's views when it claimed that the Zionist movement was limited to refugees from Eastern Europe, and that the general public should be aware that "the whole noise is made by some persons of recent immigration, with which we American Jews have absolutely nothing to do."[18] The *American Israelite* noted also that all Jewish newspapers edited or controlled by native Americans were strongly anti-Zionist.[19] In 1904 this Reform paper wrote:

> There is not one solitary prominent native Jewish-American who is an advocate of "Zionism." Aside from a very few young visionaries and impractical college professors, the Zionists in America are recruited entirely from the ranks of the newly arrived immigrants, and these know little of its political significance, and care less.[20]

---

[16] *American Israelite*, June 27, 1918.
[17] *CCARY*, vol. VII, pp. xi–xii.
[18] *American Israelite*, Jan. 13, 1898; Oct. 19, 1899.
[19] *Ibid.*, Jan. 10, 1918.
[20] *Ibid.*, July 7, 1904.

Similarly, when the questions of the American Jewish Congress and national rights for Jews were under discussion during the first World War, the Reform group maintained that the agitation in favor of these proposals was the work of the East European immigrants. On the advocates of the American Jewish Congress, the *American Israelite* stated:

> It may be safely stated that the large majority of American Jews, — using the term to describe the older settlers and their descendants, as distinct from the more recent immigrants — are opposed to the conference taking any action except along the lines set forth in the original call of the American Jewish Committee.[21]

In regard to Reform opposition to national rights, the *American Israelite* stated that nine-tenths of American Jewry wanted to be Americans and Jews only in religion, and desired English as their mother tongue. The other tenth "is worse than a detriment to us, it is a nuisance"; but since that tenth was more vociferous, the quiet protests of the "refined" American Jews against national rights were not heeded.[22] Dr. Morris S. Lazaron, speaking before the Central Conference in 1920, saw the advocacy of national rights by the East European immigrants as one manifestation of their influence upon Jewish separatism. He said in part:

> The influence of the immigrant Jew is most definitely in the scale of exclusiveness, clannishness. Such institutions as the Jewish Parochial Schools, or the tendency to inject into our American political system European conceptions of group rights and minority privileges, must be combated with all our influence and all our power. Because our persecuted brothers come from countries where national rights are recognized is no reason why we should encourage the importation of any such foreign conceptions here.[23]

The corollary to this reasoning was that Jews who had imbibed the spirit of American life were not in sympathy

---

[21] *Ibid.*, July 8, 1915.   [22] *Ibid.*, Aug. 17, 1916.
[23] *CCARY*, vol. XXX, p. 260.

with Zionism, and that as soon as these immigrants became Americanized they, too, would lose their interest in the Zionist movement.[24] The Reform group believed strongly that the Jew in America had to become American and assimilate;[25] hyphenated nationalism could not succeed in the United States.[26] In agreement with the view prevalent in the early part of the twentieth century that the immigrants in America must be cast into the American mould fixed by the older settlers, the Reform group felt obliged to aid in this process of Americanization of their coreligionists.[27] Isaac M. Wise, leader of Reform Jewry until his death in 1900, had fought for this extreme Americanization even before the rise of political Zionism. When the hordes of Russian Jews began streaming into the United States, Wise feared the Russification of the American Jew, and he renewed his fight for Americanism to counteract the influence of Yiddish and Jewish nationalism which had been brought by the immigrants.[28] Despite the fact that they found fault with some of the attitudes of the Jewish immigrants, it must be noted that the Reform leaders

[24] *American Israelite*, Aug. 10, 1905; Aug. 29, 1909.

[25] Leo M. Franklin, "A Danger and a Duty Suggested by the Zionistic Agitation," *Hebrew Union College Journal*, vol. II (March, 1898), p. 147.

[26] Samuel Schulman, "The Searching of the Jewish Heart," *Menorah Journal*, vol. IV (April, 1918), p. 91.

[27] Louis Lipsky, *Thirty Years of American Zionism* (vol. I of his *Selected Works* [in 3 vols.] New York, 1927), pp. 6-7; Horace M. Kallen, *Zionism and World Politics* (New York, 1921), p. 125; *CCARY*, vol. XXI, p. 113; Maurice J. Karpf, *Jewish Community Organization in the United States* (New York, 1938) p. 37. Rabbi Abram Hirschberg, speaking before the Central Conference in 1904, stated that the American Jews had to prove that the influx of immigrants involved no danger to American institutions. He said: "We must take them [the immigrants] by the hand and we dare not leave them until we have made them at home with our customs and institutions, our life and civilization, our ideals and the spirit of our progressive religion." *CCARY*, vol. XIV, p. 183.

[28] Isaac M. Wise, *Reminiscences*, translated from the German and edited with an introduction by David Philipson (Cincinnati, 1901), pp. 49, 85-86, 331; David Philipson, *Centenary Papers and Others* (Cincinnati, 1919), pp. 52-53. Wise's theme was: "We must be not only American citizens, but become Americans through and through outside of the synagogue." (Wise, *Reminiscences*, p. 331).

did much to preserve an open-door policy by the United States towards the refugees from Eastern Europe, and advocated an assured home for the Jewish immigrants in America rather than in Palestine.[29]

Political Zionism not only evoked counterattacks and denunciatory resolutions on the part of the religious leaders of the Reform group, but in several instances it had a more positive effect. Several of these Reform leaders saw the necessity of building up and strengthening the Reform movement which would concomitantly weaken the Zionists' position. David Philipson told the Reform rabbis that it was their duty to remain firm in and loyal to Reform principles when preaching from the pulpit, for in this way would others follow and stand strong against Zionism.[30] Dr. Rudolph Coffee advised that the Reform movement care for, what he called, the "Ghetto Jews," for as long as American rabbis did not preach other ideals, these "Ghetto Jews" would cling to Zionism.[31] In 1918, at the annual meeting of the Central Conference, President Louis Grossman urged the vitalization of Jewish life in Europe by American Reform Jewry. By the establishment of a Committee on Jews in Foreign Lands on the part of the Central Conference, and by exchange of workers, students, teachers, and leaders between the United States and Europe, Reform could be spread. Grossman was confident that the Conference

---

[29] *American Israelite*, July 9, 1903. For the statements of Reform leaders before the committees of Congress in behalf of unrestricted immigration see United States Congress, 61 Congress, Third Session, Senate Doc., no. 764, *Reports of the Immigration Commission: Statements and Recommendations Submitted by Societies and Organizations interested in the Subject of Immigration* (Washington, D. C., 1911), pp. 141–157, 182–227, 232–248, 265–286, and House of Representatives, 64 Congress, First Session, *Hearings before the Committee on Immigration and Naturalization* (Washington, D. C., 1916).

[30] Philipson, *Centenary Papers, supra*, pp. 245–246.

[31] Rudolph I. Coffee, "The Hebrew Union College and the Ghetto," *Hebrew Union College Journal*, vol. V (Dec., 1900), pp. 77–80.

can lead in the assimilation of the scattered remnants of the Jewish world and in the welding of them into a spiritual union such as will make the Zionist Utopia seem small and petty and a mere toy of the Chauvinists.[32]

III

Another institution through which the religious leaders of the Reform group in America expressed their opposition to political Zionism was the Hebrew Union College. Established in Cincinnati by Isaac M. Wise in 1875, the first permanent rabbinical school in America, it officially took an anti-Zionist stand when political Zionism appeared. When Wise, who was President of the college, opened the academic year in September, 1897, he said:

> Talmud Torah is the curriculum of this college. We want teachers of Judaism. Judaism, we say, and not nationalism, Judaism and not Zionism, Judaism and not Messiahism of any kind; that eternal Judaism which is not tied down to a certain piece of land here or there, or to a certain form of government and peculiar laws and institutions.[33]

Dr. Kaufmann Kohler, who was appointed Wise's successor in 1903, was similarly opposed to any Zionist tones in the school program. In his first address to the Board of Governors of the college he stated that he wished to make the school completely American and thus prove that the Jew in the United States was American. The American Judaism he advocated "stands for American thought and American spirit, and not for Zionistic neo-Hebraism or the language of the

[32] *CCARY*, vol. XXVIII, pp. 176–179. The Committee on the President's Message agreed to Grossman's idea but advised that conditions warranted its postponement (*ibid.*, p. 134).

[33] Philipson, *Centenary Papers, supra*, pp. 56–57. It should be noted, however, that despite Wise's anti-Zionist convictions, and his knowledge that Caspar Levias was an open and avowed Zionist, Levias remained on the faculty during Wise's presidency. Judah L. Magnes in *American Hebrew*, May 24, 1907; Max Heller to Joseph Stolz, April 5 and 22, 1907.

Jewish ghetto."[34] It was during Kohler's term as president of the Hebrew Union College that several incidents occurred involving members of the faculty imbued with Zionist sympathies. Judah L. Magnes, who was appointed to an instructorship in February, 1903, resigned his position in September, 1904, and the Zionist leader, Louis Lipsky, claimed that his resignation was forced upon him because he held Zionist views.[35] It was similarly charged from the Zionist side that Caspar Levias, instructor at the institution from 1895 to 1905, was obliged to leave because of his sympathy with Zionism.[36] A different account of Levias' dismissal has it that Max L. Margolis, when appointed to the faculty in 1905, demanded sole jurisdiction over the Bible department, thus ending the need for Levias' services.[37]

The incident which aroused the greatest furor, however, was in 1907 when Professors Henry Malter, Max L. Margolis, and Max Schloessinger resigned from their positions at the college. All three men were avowed sympathizers with the Zionist movement. Malter, a staunch Jewish nationalist, had presented his views several years before in a series of articles in which he criticized the content of Reform's theology and advocated a revival of the Jewish national ideal for the survival of Judaism.[38] These five articles had been published by the

[34] American Hebrew, Sept. 18, 1903.

[35] Lipsky, Thirty Years of American Zionism, supra, p. 35.

[36] E. R. Malachi, "Olam Hafukh," Hadoar, vol. XXIII (Feb. 26, 1943), p. 277. Malachi claims in the same article that Kohler disliked Russian Jews and favored those faculty members who were of German descent. Levias' presentation of his Zionist views may be found in CCARY, vol. VIII, pp. 179–191, and in his article "The Justification of Zionism," Hebrew Union College Journal, vol. III (April, 1899), pp. 165–175.

[37] In a conversation with Dr. Julian Morgenstern, Dec. 27, 1950.

[38] Henry Malter, "Backward, Then Forward," Hebrew Union College Journal, vol. VII (Oct., 1902–June, 1903), pp. 34–41, 75–82, 116–125, 176–186, 236–242. Malter's stay at Hebrew Union College was not a happy one ideologically, as revealed in his letters to Dr. David Neumark, published in Hatoren, vol. XI (July, 1925), pp. 61–74.

Hebrew Union College Journal, but the sixth, in which Malter was to present his own solution of the Jewish question was not allowed to appear.[39] Schloessinger, too, was a confirmed Zionist since his student days in Germany, at which time he was especially influenced by Ahad Ha'am. When he came to the United States he was active in Zionist groups, and a few months before his resignation he published an article which attempted to refute the thesis of the incompatibility of Reform Judaism with Zionism.[40] Margolis had a more checkered career as a Zionist. As a student at Columbia from 1889 to 1892 he sympathized with the Zionist cause. He later believed that Zionism was an unworthy ideal which implied a concession to the premises of anti-Semitism, since it seemed that the Zionists were trying to divert immigration directed to the United States, and because Zionism appeared as religious particularism thus justifying the attitude of Christian theologians towards Judaism. During this period Margolis wrote a theological creed for Reform Judaism in which the anti-Zionist attitude of Reform was reflected. Margolis returned to the Zionist fold soon after, however, and by 1905 he was ready to become a Zionist worker and not only a sympathizer.[41]

When these men resigned from the college the Zionists charged that they had been forced out because of their pro-Zionist views.[42] It is interesting that a month before the resignations of Margolis and Schloessinger were tendered a

---

[39] Alexander Marx, *Studies in Jewish History and Booklore* (New York, 1944), pp. 412–413.

[40] Personal communication from Mrs. Schloessinger, Nov. 22, 1948; Max Schloessinger, *Reform Judaism and Zionism* (Baltimore, 1907).

[41] Max L. Margolis to Dr. Harry Friedenwald, Jan. 11, 1907 (courtesy of the late Dr. Harry Friedenwald); *CCARY*, vol. XIII, pp. 294, 302–305.

[42] Magnes, secretary of the Federation of American Zionists, asked Friedenwald, president, what action the Federation should take on the matter. He added: "These men are after all giving up their positions because of Zionism." Judah L. Magnes to Dr. Harry Friedenwald, March 20, 1907 (courtesy of Dr. Harry Friedenwald). See also Max Raisin, *Dapim mi-pinkaso shel Rabbi* (New York, 1941), p. 218; Ahad Ha'am, "Siyman ha-she'elah," *Kol kitbe Ahad Ha'am* (Jerusalem, 1947), p. 399.

resolution was introduced at a meeting of the Board of Governors defining the stand of the college to Zionism. Asserting that the college combined the Jewish spirit with American ideals, the resolution went on to state that the college recognized no political creed other than fealty to American institutions. The phrase "America is our Zion" was reiterated as still expressive of the college's position.[43]

To what extent the three professors were allied with one another and their resignations part of a united gesture is not revealed in the documents examined. Malter's motives for resigning, on the surface at least, bear no relationship to those of his colleagues. In a letter written to the Board of Governors on December 14, 1906, he submitted his resignation, to become effective at the end of the scholastic year, on the grounds of "unjust treatment" at the hands of the college. His complaints, however, concerned matters of tenure and salary.[44] It was therefore primarily on the incidents preceding the resignations of Schloessinger and Margolis that the Zionist charges could be based.

In February, 1907, Schloessinger had asked Kohler's permission to attend a banquet in New York given for the Zionist leader, Shmariah Levin. The request was refused, but Schloessinger took his leave of absence, nonetheless, and participated in the Levin affair. He returned to the college several days later and Kohler preferred charges of insubordination against him. Schloessinger's answer to the Board of Governors was that Kohler, when consulted, had expressly stated that he was not concerned about the loss of teaching hours and that he would have granted the request had the purpose been different. Schloessinger felt that Kohler, in attempting to prevent his participation in the Zionist meeting, had acted in contravention

[43] Hebrew Union College, Minutes of the Board of Governors, Feb. 26, 1907.

[44] Henry Malter to the Board of Governors of the Hebrew Union College, Dec. 14, 1906.

of the regulations of the faculty which guaranteed freedom of personal opinion on all subjects.[45]

The incident immediately preceding the resignation of Margolis concerned a Zionist sermon which Margolis had delivered in the chapel of the Hebrew Union College.[46] Margolis outlined the conflict which ensued with Kohler in a letter addressed to Rabbi Charles S. Levi, President of the alumni of the Hebrew Union College. According to Margolis, Kohler violated the rules of the college and his own personal pledge when a public scene ensued in the college chapel after Margolis had delivered his sermon. Two years earlier, Kohler had assured Margolis that he would not be interfered with in his expression of theological opinions. Moreover, under the rules for the governing of the faculty, *Lehrfreiheit* was guaranteed; a faculty member could not be criticized before students, nor could he be questioned as to his personal opinions (provided those that conflicted with the purposes of the college were not introduced into the classroom). Margolis maintained that he had never introduced the subject of Zionism into his classroom,[47] and that Kohler had also used the pulpit to express his own partisan

[45] Kaufmann Kohler's report to the Board of Governors of the Hebrew Union College for the meeting of [Feb. 28, 1907]; Board of Governors to Max Schloessinger, Feb. 27, 1907; Max Schloessinger to the Board of Governors, no date. The report of Schloessinger's insubordination is also found in a letter from Judah L. Magnes to Dr. Harry Friedenwald, March 22, 1907 (courtesy of the late Dr. Harry Friedenwald).

[46] Max L. Margolis, "The Message of Moses," *The Maccabaean*, vol. XII (Feb., 1907), pp. 41–46.

[47] This statement was corroborated by students of Dr. Margolis in a letter of twenty-five students to the Board of Governors of the Hebrew Union College, March 19, 1907. This letter was written on the stationery of the college, the caption of which reads: שלום רב לאהבי תורתך /Hebrew Union College/ Dr. K. Kohler, President. The following is the text of the letter:

Cincinnati, O. March 19, 1907

To the Board of Governors of the Hebrew Union College; —

Dear sirs,

In view of the report current that Dr. Max Margolis has discussed Zionism while teaching at the Hebrew Union College, we, the undersigned, who have had the good fortune to study under him, deem

views. He further claimed that Kohler denied him freedom in his teaching because he was a Zionist. In an interview which he had with the President of the college after the sermon episode, Margolis quoted Kohler as saying:

> "the College was not an academic institution where mooted questions might be freely discussed and the students trained to think for themselves and arrive at their own conclusions." He made reference to my controversial articles which had appeared in the Jewish press; he declared that, had I informed him of the nature of my sermon, he would not have allowed me to preach it.

Margolis added: "Dr. Kohler further stated that as a Zionist I could not be entrusted with the teaching of Biblical Exegesis at the College."[48] Margolis repeated the statements made by Kohler during the interview in his letter of resignation to the Board of Governors, and he claimed his own inability to teach Bible in line with any one partisan viewpoint.[49]

Kohler answered Margolis' charges in two of his own communications to the Board of Governors.[50] He claimed that Margolis had misrepresented the facts of the interview and distorted Kohler's words. He, Kohler, was always in favor of

it our duty to state that Dr. Margolis has never, in any way, discussed Zionism in class, but, on the contrary, has always sought to avoid any such discussion.

(Signed): Joseph I. Gorfinkle	J. Blau	
Samuel Thurman	H. Rosenwasser	
Horace J. Wolf	J. Singer	B. Laas
Felix A. Levy	George Fox	
William Reisz	Leo B. Hexter	
Sam. Schwartz	Elkan C. Voorsanger	
Aaron L. Weinstein	Morris S. Lazaron	
Jacob Pollak	Emanuel Jacubowitz	
Arthur B. Bonnheim	L. D. Gross	
I. Isaacson	M. Hoffman	
H. Buchofski	Charles B. Latz	
David Rosenbaum	Benno Leon	

[48] Max L. Margolis to Charles S. Levi, April 8, 1907.

[49] Max L. Margolis to the Board of Governors of the Hebrew Union College, March 10, 1907.

[50] Kaufmann Kohler to Bernhard Bettmann, President of the Board of Governors of the Hebrew Union College, March 14, 1907; Kaufmann Kohler to the Board of Governors in Hebrew Union College, Minutes of the Board of Governors, April 30, 1907.

free scientific investigation, but it was Margolis who approached the Bible with "a preconceived partisan opinion detrimental to the principles of American Reform Judaism, inducing him, as I told him, to falsify facts and wilfully misrepresent the position of Reform theology." Since any rabbinical school must hold fast to its fundamental principles, Kohler informed Margolis that he could no longer be entrusted with teaching the Bible. Never, at any time in the college's history, was complete *Lehrfreiheit* guaranteed, and in his teaching as well as his articles Margolis was infusing ideas "subversive" of Reform principles. Since Margolis' appointment to the college his opinions on Zionism underwent a change, "and the character of his scholarship and his scientific views have consequently been changed materially." Kohler revealed to the Board that a week before the interview had taken place, he learned that Margolis was considering resigning when a letter arrived from Harvard University stating that Margolis was about to sever connections with the Hebrew Union College and inquiring about Margolis' character and ability.[51] Margolis' resignation, therefore, could not have been totally influenced by his interview with Kohler.

Kohler also implied in his letters to the Board of Governors that Margolis' statements reflected a personal attack upon him. In answer to Margolis' charge that Kohler had used the college chapel to air his own personal views, Kohler claimed this practice as the right of the president of a theological school to direct the students to an appreciation of religious principles. His custom of daily chapel talks to the students had been curtailed after Margolis' arrival at the college when Margolis had assailed them as "unacademic." Kohler further claimed that

> with the cessation of my brief exhortatory addresses in the chapel, my influence on the moral and religious conduct of the students

[51] C. H. Toy to Kaufmann Kohler, March 5, 1907.

is no longer the same and the discipline of the College has greatly suffered owing to a certain disrespect and disloyalty shown to me as President and by the attitude of those antagonizing my views.

It should be noted at this point that Kohler had complained about the insubordination of Malter, Schloessinger, and Margolis prior to the aforementioned incidents of 1907. In 1906 complaints addressed by several students against certain attitudes of the faculty were taken to the Board of Governors by these three men without the consent of Kohler and the faculty. Kohler, in his report to the Board of Governors on the incident, criticized the professors for their "spirit of rancor and insubordination," singling out Margolis for causing disharmony among the faculty as well as students.[52] In February, 1907, Kohler also reported that one of Margolis' articles reflected a personal challenge to Kohler as well as a denunciation of Reform principles.[53] The existence of a personal conflict between Margolis and Kohler is further attested to orally. Dr. Julian Morgenstern, a graduate of the Hebrew Union College who was appointed to the faculty in 1907, has stated that the differences between Margolis and Kohler can be best explained in the light of Margolis' secretly cherished ambition to become president of the college in Kohler's stead.[54] Nonetheless, in Kohler's answer to Margolis' charges, he asked that the Board of Governors take no cognizance of personal differences between him and Margolis but discuss Margolis' resignation on the basis of principle, that is, Margolis' antithetical views towards Reform Judaism.[55]

On the basis of this desire to ignore personal differences it

[52] Kaufmann Kohler to the Board of Governors of the Hebrew Union College, May 31, 1906; Henry Malter, Max L. Margolis, and Max Schloessinger to the Board of Governors of the Hebrew Union College, May 9, 1906.

[53] Kohler's report to the Board of Governors of the Hebrew Union College for the meeting of [Feb. 26, 1907].

[54] In a conversation with Dr. Julian Morgenstern, Dec. 27, 1950.

[55] Hebrew Union College, Minutes of the Board of Governors, April 30, 1907.

is understandable why the issue appeared to the public as
merely one of *Lehrfreiheit* and bigoted prejudice against Zionism. Even in the student body of the Hebrew Union College
the question seemed clear-cut. Despite the meeting of a member of the Board of Governors with the students at which he
denied that Zionism was the cause of Margolis' resignation,
two students resigned from the college because Margolis'
Zionist views were discriminated against by the administration.[56] The press, too, expressed various opinions on the incident, but all from the point of view of *Lehrfreiheit*.[57] Kohler
himself discussed the issue publicly as concerning the dangers
of Zionism at the Hebrew Union College. Since the aim of the
college, according to Kohler, was to inculcate the specific religious views of Reform, it was necessary to prevent

> a Zionist professor from twisting and distorting the grand universal
> teachings of the prophets and sages of Israel or of the Pentateuch
> with the view of turning them into crude and nationalistic utter-
> ances.[58]

The alumni of the college manifested different reactions to the
issue. Although a circular letter sent out by the President,
Rabbi Levi, concentrated on the question of *Lehrfreiheit*, opinions of the Reform rabbis varied. Attacks were made by
some on the college for its discriminatory action; others suspected Margolis' motives and sincerity in his Zionist views and
condemned him for defying Kohler; still others criticized
Kohler for his ineptitude in maintaining peace at the college.[59]

[56] Gotthard Deutsch to Joseph Stolz, May 4, 1907; *American Hebrew*, May 17, 1907.

[57] *Hebrew Standard*, Jan. 25, 1907; *American Hebrew*, May 17, 1907; *Reform Advocate*, April 6, 1907. *The Maccabaean*, despite its Zionist views, conceded the possibility of a personal element in the fight at the college. *The Maccabaean*, vol. XII (April, 1907), pp. 155–156.

[58] *Jewish Exponent*, April 5, 1907; *Reform Advocate*, April 6, 1907.

[59] *American Hebrew*, March 22, 1907, May 24, 1907; *The Maccabaean*, vol. XII (April, 1907), pp. 160–161; circular letter of Charles S. Levi to the alumni of the Hebrew Union College, April 19, 1907; Joseph Silverman to Joseph Stolz, April 24, 1907; Moses J. Gries to Charles S. Levi, April 26, 1907; Moses J. Gries to Bernhard

Only David Philipson, a member of the Board of Governors at that time, whose account of the affair appeared years later, attempted to prove that the issue had been disloyalty and insubordination on the part of the professors rather than Zionism. He said in part:

> In the interest of truth it must be stated that had there been nothing involved except the Zionistic issue the professor [Margolis] and his colleagues could have remained despite the fact that the president of the institution and the Board of Governors were almost to a man strongly non-Zionistic.[60]

Two members of the alumni, Rabbis Charles S. Levi and Joseph Stolz, who were also members of the Board of Governors attempted to restrain the Board from accepting Margolis' resignation and aimed at a reconciliation between Kohler and Margolis. Their efforts, as well as the petitions submitted by the students to the Board, were in vain, and Margolis' resignation was finally accepted.[61]

An echo of the 1907 affair in which Zionism may have been a contributing cause was heard in the Hebrew Union College in 1915. On February 15th of that year a special conference of the Board of Governors was held in order to afford an opportunity to Rabbis Max Heller and Stephen S. Wise to

Bettmann, April 26, 1907; Max Heller to Joseph Stolz, April 5 and 22, 1907; Samuel Deinard to Bernhard Felsenthal, March 5, 1907, Felsenthal Collection, American Jewish Historical Society.

[60] David Philipson, "History of the Hebrew Union College, 1875–1925," *Hebrew Union College Jubilee Volume* (Cincinnati, 1925), p. 44; *idem, My Life as an American Jew* (Cincinnati, 1941), pp. 156–157.

[61] Joseph Stolz to Bernhard Bettmann, April 29, 1907; Charles S. Levi to Joseph Stolz, May 7, 1907; *American Israelite*, May 2, 1907; Hebrew Union College, Minutes of the Board of Governors, April 30, 1907. The vote on Margolis' resignation was 13 to 2, Jacob Ottenheimer and Levi in the minority. Schloessinger's resignation had been accepted unanimously by the Board on April 9th (Hebrew Union College, Minutes of the Board of Governors, April 9, 1907). In his account of the affair, David Philipson stated that the professors did not expect their resignations to be accepted, and Margolis had tried to withdraw his. Philipson, *My Life as an American Jew, supra*, pp. 156–157.

lay certain grievances before the Board. What the nature of these grievances was may be gleaned from the resolutions passed at that session to the effect that the President (Kohler) had no objection to Zionist addresses delivered at the college outside the chapel, and that students might even preach on Zionism or refer to it if the sermon were religious in tone.[62] The results seemed to have been satisfactory to Rabbi Heller,[63] and on this basis he protested to Kohler in March, 1915, that his son had been refused permission by Kohler to preach on Zionism. Heller maintained that it had been the suggestion of Dr. Emil G. Hirsch at the meeting of February 15th that Heller's son preach a sermon on Zionism, religious in tone. Kohler replied that he had no recollection of Hirsch's suggestion, and that he had rejected the sermon since the text was not chosen to fit the *haftorah* of the week in question.[64] Heller withdrew the charges since the case was not clear, but made it evident that he did not doubt his son's veracity.[65]

In 1920, the statement of the Hebrew Union College on the San Remo Declaration on Palestine proved that the college had not deviated from its early anti-Zionist position which had been formulated by its founder, Isaac M. Wise. The remarks stated in part:

> We declare that no one land, Palestine or any other, can be called "the national home for the Jews," as has been done by the Supreme Council. Each land, whereof Jews are loyal citizens, is the national home for those Jews. Palestine is not our national home, since we are not now and never expect to be citizens of that land.[66]

---

[62] Hebrew Union College, Minutes of the Board of Governors, Feb. 15, 1915.

[63] Isaac Bloom (secretary of the Board of Governors) to Max Heller, March 9, 1915.

[64] Max Heller to Kaufmann Kohler, March 12, 1915; Kaufmann Kohler to Max Heller, March 16, 1915. These letters were included in the Minutes of the Board of Governors, March 23, 1915.

[65] Max Heller to Isaac Bloom, April 12 and May 6, 1915.

[66] Hebrew Union College, Minutes of the Board of Governors, May 25, 1920.

IV

Reform Jewry in America voiced its opposition to political Zionism through its lay leaders and institutions as well as through its religious organization. The Union of American Hebrew Congregations, representing the Reform congregations of the country, was the most important of these institutions. Founded by Isaac M. Wise in 1873, it became, what may be called the guardian of the Hebrew Union College and the lay arm of the Central Conference of American Rabbis. It, too, quickly voiced its opposition to Zionism in a resolution adopted in December, 1898, which stated:

> We are unalterably opposed to political Zionism. The Jews are not a nation, but a religious community. Zion was a precious possession of the past, the early home of our faith, where our prophets uttered their world-subduing thoughts, and our psalmists sang their world-enchanting hymns. As such it is a holy memory, but it is not our hope of the future. America is our Zion. Here, in the home of religious liberty, we have aided in founding this new Zion, the fruition of the beginning laid in the old. The mission of Judaism is spiritual, not political. Its aim is not to establish a state, but to spread the truths of religion and humanity throughout the world.[67]

Twenty-one years later, despite the progress made by the Zionist movement, the Union's attitude was still unchanged. In 1919, it reaffirmed its 1898 resolution and added:

> In accordance with the spirit of our whole history we declare that it is imperative for the welfare of Jews everywhere as a great religious community with a universal message for humanity that Israel dedicate itself not to any aspiration for the revival of a Jewish nationality or the foundation of a Jewish state, but to the faithful and consistent fulfillment of its religious mission in the world. We, therefore, do not seek for Israel any national homeland, it being

[67] Union of American Hebrew Congregations, *Proceedings*, vol. V. p. 4002.

our conviction that Israel is at home in every free country and should be at home in all lands.[68]

Among the members of the Union of American Hebrew Congregations who were opposed to political Zionism was Isaac W. Bernheim of Louisville, Kentucky. Motivated by this opposition and by the desire to make the differences between Zionists and Reform Jews distinct and clear-cut, Bernheim advocated the formation of what he called the Reform Church of American Israelites. Bernheim explained the outlines of his project in a letter sent to the annual meeting of the Central Conference of American Rabbis in 1918 and in an address delivered before the council of the Union of American Hebrew Congregations in 1921. In both presentations of his views Bernheim denounced the Zionists and their nationalistic aims, and protested the loyalty of Reform Jewry for America. He stated:

> Zionism, political and otherwise, of the imported or domestic brand, was not . . . a thing to our liking, nor can it ever receive our support. Here is our Palestine, and we know no other.

To prove the patriotism of the Reform Jews and to disassociate them from acts of the Zionists which might imply a divided loyalty, Bernheim proposed that the Church be made up of "100 per cent Americans." This was necessary according to him in order that "the voice of the real American Israel may be heard" and not the voice of the Zionists speaking in the name of all American Jewry. Since Zionists employed the term "Jewry" in attempts to signify a separate entity, Bernheim proposed that the use of the terms "Jew" and "Jewry" be given exclusively to the Zionists. This concept of "Jewry" ought not to exist in the United States since no religious body should raise a barrier between itself and other citizens. In

[68] *Ibid.*, vol. IX. pp. 8520–8521.

addition, Bernheim claimed that the word "Jew" as well as the words "temple" and "synagogue" had bad connotations and were the bases for accusations that the Jews were a foreign entity. Therefore, he urged that the name "Israel" be substituted for "Jews" and that houses of worship be renamed "Reform Churches of American Israelites." In this way, according to Bernheim, could Reform Jews demonstrate that

> we are Americans by nationality, that our longings are not for an Oriental Palestinian homeland, that our hearts are here, our homes are here — here in America.[69]

Bernheim himself admitted that his proposals met with great opposition from the pulpit and press, and the entire project was short-lived.[70]

The program for a separatist movement very similar to that of Bernheim's was published in the *American Hebrew* of March 28, 1919. Here, too, it was proposed to substitute a different name for "Jewish" and form a new religious association. Opposed to all acts which made Jews appear apart from Americans and which cast doubts upon their loyalty to America, the anonymous proponents of this program refused to be allied even as coworshippers with the Zionists and thus suffer the consequences of Zionist actions. They claimed that they could worship God and retain the ethical tenets of Judaism without the label "Jew," and that this change of name would constitute the crowning point of the Reform movement.[71]

[69] *CCARY*, vol. XXVIII, pp. 141–144; Isaac W. Bernheim, *The Reform Church of American Israelites* (Buffalo, 1921).

[70] Isaac W. Bernheim, *An Open Letter to Rabbi Stephen S. Wise* (Louisville, 1922), p. 1. He later claimed, however, that thousands of laymen had endorsed his program and that he was just about to organize them into an effective group when the death of his wife made him unfit for the task. *Idem, The Closing Chapters of a Busy Life* (Denver, 1929), p. 100.

[71] *American Hebrew*, March 28, 1919.

V

The opposition of Reform Judaism to political Zionism was voiced through its religious and lay institutions and leaders. Still another channel through which public sentiment against the Zionist movement was aroused was the press.[72] In its appeal to the public the Reform press did not emphasize the serious arguments against Zionism which were heard in the more learned circles, but for the most part it indulged in a defamatory campaign to discredit and ridicule the Zionist movement. Among the most important of the Reform papers in the period from 1897 to 1922 were the *American Israelite*, founded by Isaac M. Wise, and the *Reform Advocate*, edited by Dr. Emil G. Hirsch. Favorite targets of the newspapers were the leaders and members of the Zionist movement. The leaders were accused of being mere politicians, self-seekers who exploited their followers for money and for power, and men who hid under the cloak of an ideal in which they themselves did not believe. Members of the movement were charged with having turned to Zionism because of personal disappointments, with advocating it for selfish reasons, and with using idealism for material advantage. It was also claimed that every professional beggar became a Zionist in order to be sent to Jerusalem and supported at someone else's expense.[73] When Solomon Schechter publicly joined the Zionists, the *American Israelite* commented:

> It seems that Zionism is a sort of 'Salon des Refuses' in Judaism, giving to all those who believe that the Jewish world has not completely done them justice an opportunity of enlightening public opinion.[74]

[72] Through the newspapers the Reform leaders called directly upon the public to express active opposition to Zionism. For example, see *Reform Advocate*, May 29, 1897; *American Hebrew*, July 2, 1915.

[73] *American Israelite*, Aug. 26, 1897, Sept. 2, 1897, Sept. 16, 1897, Jan. 8, 1903, March 16, 1916, May 30, 1918, June 27, 1918; *Reform Advocate*, June 19, 1897, Sept. 25, 1897; Isaac M. Wise, "Zionism," *Hebrew Union College Journal*, vol. IV (Dec., 1899), p. 47.

[74] *American Israelite*, April 4, 1907.

The attitude of the *American Israelite* towards the Zionist membership was summed up in the following statement:

> The whole Zionistic movement in this country is a farce which is played by ignorant people largely to show their contempt for those who try to advise them. That a few educated men should be found among them is only another proof that education is not always productive of good judgment.[75]

Another point of criticism which the Reform press frequently made was the lack of unity among the Zionists. They commented on the fact that various factions existed within Zionism, that there were quarrels among the leaders, and they inferred from the splits in the Zionist ranks reported in their own columns that a Jewish state would be run on the shaky foundations then common among Spanish-American republics.[76] Other charges raised against the internal organization of the Zionists were that their expenses were high, they wasted both time and energy, they were procrastinators, and they had more leaders and talkers than actual workers.[77] Ironically enough, the Zionists were also accused by the *American Israelite* of being intolerant with those who disagreed with them and of resorting to slander in attacks upon their Reform opponents.[78]

In all fairness to the *American Israelite*, however, its favorable comments on Zionism and Zionist leaders should be noted. Herzl's qualities were praised after his death, and the collection

[75] *Ibid.*, March 10, 1898. By the name-calling device in which the Reform press did not hesitate to indulge, terms like "irresponsible" and "visionaries" used to depict the leaders were among the most mild. Herzl was known as "Moses," "Don Quixote," "chief of the clan"; Nordau became "Sancho Panza"; Henrietta Szold was the "Joan of Arc" of Zionism; Louis Lipsky was the "St. George" who tried futilely to slay the dragon of anti-Semitism, and Zionists as a group were termed "Ziomaniacs." *Ibid.*, Sept. 16, 1897, Nov. 17, 1898, Dec. 8, 1898, July 6, 1899, Jan. 17, 1918; *Reform Advocate*, Sept. 4, 1897.

[76] *American Israelite*, April 7, 1898, June 23, 1898, July 16, 1903; Gotthard Deutsch, "Zionism," *Hebrew Union College Journal*, vol. IV (Dec., 1899), p. 68; *American Hebrew*, April 29, 1921.

[77] *American Israelite*, Nov. 1, 1906, June 24, 1909, May 5, 1910, Jan. 11, 1912, March 18, 1915, June 13, 1918, July 28, 1921.

[78] *Ibid.*, May 2, 1907, Dec. 28, 1916, Sept. 28, 1922.

of money for Herzl's children was supported. Zionism was also approved of insofar as it developed a spirit of self-reliance among its adherents and attracted those intellectual persons who hitherto had found no place for themselves in the Jewish fold.[79]

It is interesting to note how the Reform press tried to minimize the activities and strength of the Zionists throughout the twenty-five year period. In 1897 Zionism was regarded only as a mid-summer sensation, and even before the first Congress was held both the *American Israelite* and *Reform Advocate* reported that political Zionism had collapsed.[80] When the first Congress did convene the papers called it a novelty, a farce, and at best a charity convention.[81] From then on, Congresses were sneered at and were said to mark the beginning of the end of Zionism; Zionism in general was regarded as a passing fad which was continually dying out.[82] According to the Reform press, political Zionism collapsed in 1897, it had ceased to exist in 1898, it was waning in 1903, it was hopeless in 1904, it languished with the death of Herzl, it died with Nordau, it was abandoned in 1909 and 1912, and it was given up in 1919, 1920, and 1922.[83] At the same time that the press was burying Zionism, it was wont to show changes in the Zionist position that differed from the original nationalistic ideal. In 1907 it claimed that Zionism was no longer working for a home for the Jewish people but rather establishing "a nursery farm for the rearing of model Jews"; in 1911, that Zionism was limited to temporary colonization; in 1913, that it was only a philanthropic movement; and in

[79] *Ibid.*, July 21, 1904, Dec. 8, 1904, May 28, 1908, Nov. 11, 1915.

[80] *Ibid.*, Aug. 5, 1897, Sept. 9, 1897; *Reform Advocate*, Aug. 21, 1897.

[81] *American Israelite*, Sept. 9, 1897, Sept. 16, 1897, Sept. 23, 1897.

[82] *Ibid.*, Oct. 6, 1898, Sept. 7, 1899, Aug. 30, 1900, Sept. 3, 1903, Feb. 3, 1910, July 15, 1920.

[83] *Ibid.*, Aug. 5, 1897, June 23, 1898, Sept. 3, 1903, June 9, 1904, Dec. 10, 1908, Aug. 5, 1909, July 14, 1910, Sept. 26, 1912, April 29, 1920, Feb. 9, 1922; *Reform Advocate*, Aug. 21, 1897; *American Hebrew*, Aug. 8, 1919.

1919, that it dwindled again to a mere colonization project.[84] In these ways as well as by criticizing the leaders, members, and activities of the Zionists did the Reform group continually seek to disparage political Zionism through the press.

VI

The opposition of the Reform group to Zionism throughout the years under discussion was culminated and summarized in testimony presented by two Reform Rabbis, Dr. David Philipson and Dr. Isaac Landman, before the Committee on Foreign Affairs of the House of Representatives in 1922. In the Sixty-seventh Congress, Representative Hamilton Fish introduced the following resolution expressing United States approval of the principles outlined for the mandate over Palestine:

> Whereas the Jewish people have for many centuries believed in and yearned for the rebuilding of their ancient homeland; and
> Whereas owing to the outcome of the World War and their part therein the Jewish people, under definite and adequate international guaranties are to be enabled, with due regard to the rights of all elements of the population of Palestine and to the sanctity of its holy places, to re-create and reorganize a national home in the land of their fathers: Therefore be it
> *Resolved by the House of Representatives (the Senate concurring),* That the Congress of the United States hereby expresses its profound satisfaction in that outcome of the victorious war which promises the building up of a new and beneficent life in Palestine, rejoices in this act of historic justice about to be consummated, and on behalf of the American people commends an undertaking which will do honor to Christendom and give to the House of Israel its long-denied opportunity to reestablish a fruitful Jewish life and culture in the ancient Jewish land.

Hearings were held on the bill, and Rabbis David Philipson and Isaac Landman testified before the House Committee.

[84] *American Israelite*, March 7, 1907, Sept. 7, 1911, July 10, 1913, June 26, 1919.

In his testimony, Philipson quoted various resolutions passed by the Central Conference of American Rabbis and the Union of American Hebrew Congregations against Zionism, and he outlined Reform theology which, to him, could never be reconciled with the concept of the Jews as a national group. He further stated that Zionism made the Jews appear alien in the eyes of others, and no reflection ought to be cast on the patriotism of the Jews in America. He objected in particular to the Balfour Declaration which accentuated the alienism of the Jews, and he stated: "I object to any country being called the national home of the Jewish people. America is my national home." He added that Zionism not only did not solve the Jewish problem but rather increased the troubles of the Jews by adding an impetus to anti-Semitism. The only solution to the Jewish question, according to Dr. Philipson, would be the granting of full freedom for the Jews everywhere. Moreover, Dr. Philipson stated that he was opposed to the bill because the United States government had no authority to interfere in the internal matters of a religious group, because America should not become entangled in European politics, and because the bill seemed to appeal to the "Jewish vote." Dr. Landman similarly denied the existence of a Jewish vote, and he echoed Philipson's sentiments on the Balfour Declaration. He went on to say that no Jew in America was opposed to the rebuilding of Palestine, but that a majority were against a Jewish nation in the political sense. Although Dr. Landman's views on the agreement of all Jews for the rebuilding of Palestine was not a sentiment current among the Reform group from the outset of political Zionism, both men gave an exposition of the typical Reform arguments against Zionism from the first Zionist Congress in 1897 to the issuance of the mandate over Palestine in 1922.[85]

---

[85] United States Congress, House of Representatives, 67 Congress, Second Session, *Hearings before the Committee on Foreign Affairs on H. Con. Res. 52* (Washington, D. C., 1922), pp. 1, 65–67, 99–116.

VII

Figures are not available as to the number of Reform Jews who were Zionists, either by affiliation or by sentiment, during the first quarter-century of political Zionism, but it may be safely stated that the overwhelming majority were anti or non-Zionists.[86] There were notable exceptions, however, in the small minority segment; men like Dr. Gustav Gottheil, Professor Richard Gottheil, Dr. Bernhard Felsenthal, Dr. Stephen S. Wise, and Dr. Max Heller were among the outstanding Reform Jews who advocated Zionism. The Gottheils, Wise, and Felsenthal were charter members of the Federation of American Zionists, organized in 1897, and these men presented their pro-Zionist views to the public through conventions, pulpit, and press.[87] They as well as other religious leaders in the Reform group who advocated Zionism tried to prove that Zionism and Reform Judaism were not incompatible and that, therefore, the advocacy of one did not necessarily mean disloyalty to the other.[88] This minority had its voice heard even in the Central Conference of American Rabbis when discussions on Zionism were held. They introduced resolutions

[86] Dr. Edward N. Calisch, Reform rabbi of Richmond, Va., wrote in 1905 that 145 of the 150 liberal Reform congregations were anti-Zionist "both in pulpit and pew." *American Hebrew*, March 31, 1905. In 1931 the survey of Reform Judaism in the cities reported that Zionists were present in one out of every five Reform families. *Reform Judaism in the Large Cities* (New York, 1931), p. 48.

[87] Richard Gottheil, *The Life of Gustav Gottheil* (Williamsport, 1936), pp. 190–195; Emma Felsenthal, *Bernhard Felsenthal, Teacher in Israel* (New York, 1924), pp. 74–84; Gustav Gottheil, "Zionism," *Hebrew Union College Journal*, vol. IV (Dec., 1899), pp. 54–55; Bernhard Felsenthal, "Some Remarks Concerning Zionism," *Hebrew Union College Journal*, vol. IV (Dec., 1899), pp. 48–53; *American Hebrew*, Dec. 10, 1897, Jan. 13, 1899, Sept. 29, 1899, June 15, 1900; *American Israelite*, Sept. 13, 1900, Oct. 6, 1904. Louis Lipsky, commenting on pioneer Zionists like Gottheil and Felsenthal, said in retrospect that American Jewry was adjusted too well to enable these men to take their congregations with them in the advocacy of Zionism. Lipsky, *Thirty Years of American Zionism, supra*, p. 245.

[88] E. Felsenthal, *Bernhard Felsenthal, supra*, pp. 76–77; M. Schloessinger, *Reform Judaism and Zionism, supra; American Israelite*, Oct. 28, 1897, Dec. 6, 1906; *American Hebrew*, Dec. 10, 1909; C. Levias, "The Justification of Zionism," *supra*, p. 172.

favoring phases of Zionist activities or achievements, and they submitted minority reports opposing the anti-Zionist proposals of various committees.[89] It was not until 1935, however, that the pro-Zionist group, by then a majority, succeeded in reversing the anti-Zionist stand of Reform Judaism.[90]

Reform Jewry as a body did not remain indifferent to the task of the physical rebuilding of Palestine even before the reversal of its anti-Zionist stand. When the Balfour Declaration and the mandate proved that political Zionism was no longer a utopian dream, offers were forthcoming from the Central Conference of American Rabbis to aid in the reconstruction of Palestine on a non-nationalistic basis.[91] In 1919, Rabbi Louis Grossman, then President of the Central Conference, said that American Jewry would respond to the call for rehabilitating Palestine since rehabilitation would "sustain the love of home in Palestine in the same degree and the same spirit as in all other countries where Jews have free and un-hampered opportunity to exercise privileges and enjoy rights to commerce and labor."[92] A year later, President Leo M. Franklin announced that although he had declined an invitation

[89] *CCARY*, vol. XVII, pp. 31, 81; vol. XXVI, pp. 132, 135–136, 138–139; vol. XXVIII, p. 135; vol. XXIX, pp. 299–300; vol. XXX, pp. 107, 142–143, 151–152; vol. XXXI, pp. 85–86.

[90] *CCARY*, vol. XLV, pp. 103, 112.

[91] Isolated proposals from the Reform group for working with Zionism on a non-nationalistic basis were made before 1919. As early as 1911 the *American Israelite* proposed that if Zionism gave up the Basle program and Herzl's *Judenstaat*, the enterprises for the advancement of Palestine would be encouraged by the paper (*American Israelite*, Nov. 16, 1911).

In 1913, Rabbi Joseph Krauskopf stated in an address before the council of the Union of American Hebrew Congregations that he was ready to aid Zionism if it would change its name to Agriculturalism and aim only to establish settlements for Jews who were denied rights elsewhere (Union of American Hebrew Congregations, *Proceedings*, vol. VIII, p. 7103).

In 1918, Rabbi Isaac Landman suggested a union of Zionists, non-Zionists and anti-Zionists to work for the rehabilitation of Palestine if Zionists would discard their idea of a political state. His proposal was accepted by Rabbis Samuel Schulman and David Philipson, two of the staunchest opponents of Zionism in the Reform camp (*American Hebrew*, Oct. 25, 1918, Nov. 1, 1918).

[92] *CCARY*, vol. XXIX, p. 133.

of the Zionists, in the name of the Central Conference, to participate in an extraordinary convention to celebrate the San Remo mandate decision, the Central Conference would co-operate to make Palestine a refuge and a place for fuller expression of the "spiritual genius of the Jew." The resolution adopted by the Central Conference of that year stated that they believed that the homeland of the Jews was the world and that co-operation in the reconstruction of Palestine might imply tacit acceptance of Zionism, but that they were ready to offer their services. They also suggested the formation of a non-partisan union of Jews for the purpose of sending aid to Palestinian Jews.[93] Franklin wrote to the Zionist Organization of America offering the aid of the Central Conference, but the Zionists merely acknowledged the letter and did not avail themselves of the offer.[94] The willingness of the Central Conference to help in Palestinian work on non-nationalistic lines was concretized in their agreement with the Palestine Development Council to take part in the economic reconstruction of Palestine.[95]

Agitation for the union of Zionists and non-Zionists for the rehabilitation of Palestine came from the *American Hebrew*, under the editorship of Dr. Isaac Landman, from the beginning of 1919. Since the *American Hebrew* had adopted the Reform position under Landman's leadership, it naturally favored a non-nationalistic union. The paper maintained that as long as the Zionist Organization tenaciously held to its nationalist aspirations non-Zionists would not co-operate in the rehabilitation task and that in this way Palestine would suffer. It claimed that Palestine would not be a Jewish homeland for the next century and that the Balfour Declaration and the mandate were not political victories for Zionism. Therefore, according to the *American Hebrew*, Zionism for all practical purposes

[93] *Ibid.*, vol. XXX, pp. 141–142, 182–185.
[94] *Ibid.*, vol. XXXI, pp. 86–87; *American Hebrew*, June 2, 1922.
[95] *American Hebrew*, June 23, 1922.

was eliminated, and as soon as the Zionist Organization ceased misleading its followers by false nationalistic propaganda, non-Zionists could co-operate in rebuilding Palestine. The paper wrote that "as long as . . . the American Zionists persist in befuddling and bamboozling their followers and the rest of American Jews, there can never be a union of the Jews of this country to hasten the new economic era that must now dawn on the Holy Land." The slogan of the *American Hebrew* was "Scrap Zionism and build Palestine!" When Churchill's White Paper appeared and interpreted the Balfour Declaration as meaning a Jewish home in Palestine and not Palestine as a Jewish home, the paper was pleased. It felt that political Zionism had been crushed, that now Palestine could be rebuilt, and that the "new era for Palestine has begun."[96]

* * *

The twenty-five years following 1922 saw major changes in the Reform attitude towards Zionism. The non-Zionist, rather than anti-Zionist, trend which became manifest after the Balfour Declaration continued in the twenties with Reform co-operation in the rehabilitation of Palestine and the work of the Jewish Agency. The next two decades marked the beginning of the active pro-Zionist policy which meant the advocacy, for the first time, of the political aims of Zionism by the preponderant majority of Reform leadership. Echoes of the traditional aggressive anti-Zionism were still heard, however, from the small minority who organized the American Council for Judaism in 1943 and whose policies were largely reformulations of the sentiments voiced by Isaac M. Wise in his address before the Central Conference in 1897. Thus, within a period of fifty years, did Reform Judaism run the entire gamut of opinion with respect to political Zionism.

[96] *Ibid.*, Jan. 31, 1919, Feb. 14, 1919, July 18, 1919, Oct. 3, 1919, April 29, 1921, Dec. 23, 1921, July 28, 1922, Aug. 11, 1922.

A PORTRAIT OF ETHNIC POLITICS

The Socialists and the 1908 and 1910 Congressional
Elections on the East Side[1]

By ARTHUR GOREN

INTRODUCTION

In the course of the first two decades of the twentieth century the
Socialist Party gained relatively important footholds in two metropolitan areas, German-populated Milwaukee and the Jewish lower
East Side of New York. Both districts sent Socialists to Congress
in the latter half of this period and in Milwaukee notable victories
were registered in municipal elections.

By 1900, the Ninth Congressional District of New York, carved
out of the heart of the lower East Side, had become the most
densely populated area of Russian-Jewish immigration.[2] It had also
acquired its reputation as the habitat of a vigorous, young radical
movement. The year 1904 saw the District's Socialist candidate
poll 21 per cent of the vote.[3] Two years later Morris Hillquit raised
the Socialist share of the vote to 26 per cent.[4] Eventually, Hillquit's

---

[1] The present writer is greatly indebted to Professor William E. Leuchtenburg of
Columbia University for his thorough reading of this paper and the resulting criticism and
suggestions. He also benefited from a number of discussions with Dr. Lloyd P. Gartner
of the American Jewish History Center.

[2] The smallest geographic division for which the United States Census of 1900 has
published statistics on country of birth of foreign-born population, and foreign-born
parents of native population, is the city, hence the difficulty in arriving at an accurate
picture of the population composition of the East Side for 1900. The United States Census
for 1910 supplies these statistics for Assembly Districts in New York allowing a fairly
precise view of the East Side's population make-up. See Appendix, Tables I and II,
infra, pp. 227–228. *The Jewish Encyclopedia*, (New York: Funk and Wegnalls Co., 1905),
vol. IX, p. 284, mentions a census taken by David Blaustein in May, 1904, who arrived
at a figure of 320,000 Jewish inhabitants of the East Side. In *University Settlement Studies*,
October, 1905 — June, 1906, p. 106, the figure of 450,000 Jews living on the East Side is
suggested.

[3] *The Worker*, (New York), Nov. 10, 1906, p. 1: *Zukunft*, vol. XIII (Dec., 1908), p. 768.

[4] *Infra*, p., 207 note 25.

successor as candidate, Meyer London, was elected to Congress from the East Side.[5]

The political campaigns in the lower East Side attracted considerable attention. Progressives saw the Socialist "David" pitted against the Tammany "Goliath." Others, disquieted by the frenzied agitation of the East European radicals, found support for their immigrant restriction stand. Americanized coreligionists of the Jewish immigrant populace feared anti-Semitic repercussions that would ultimately endanger their hard won position.

Of all the parties in the ghetto, the Socialist Party was least responsive to the ethnic interests of the residents of the ghetto. Cosmopolitan in outlook and faithful to its class allegiance, the Party was hostile to what it considered to be the conflicting loyalties invoked by "nationality." Furthermore, despite the ethnic locale, in its political ambition to embrace the American working-class it sought to avoid the suspicion of domination by "foreign groups."

The central theme of this investigation of the 1908 and 1910 political campaigns on the Jewish East Side is the impact on an ethnic-centered, new immigrant community of a political ideology posing imperatives transcending the ghetto parochialism. The unexpected dimensions of Morris Hillquit's defeat in 1908 and his replacement in 1910 by Meyer London indicate the conflict and the compromise the Socialist politician was compelled to make in his encounter with the immigrant community. The two campaigns also form part of a transition period in the history of the Socialist Party. By 1910, the East Side radicals were elevated to the status of a "serious threat." As this study will indicate the new show of strength was possible only when due recognition was given to the local interests of the ghetto.

[5] Lawrence H. Fuchs' study, *The Political Behavior of American Jews*, (Glencoe, Ill.: The Free Press, 1956), is a helpful survey of the subject. On pp. 47–55 and 121–129, Fuchs covers in more general terms aspects of the subject of this study. Several inaccuracies deserve to be corrected. Henry Mayer Goldfogle served in Congress sixteen years, but not beginning in 1910. He was elected for the first time to the 57th Congress in 1900, served continually through the 63rd and again in the 66th Congress (March 4, 1919 to March 3, 1921) [page 48]. In 1910, Meyer London and not Morris Hillquit ran for Congress from the Ninth Congressional District [page 127]. Hillquit could not always count on "about 40 per cent of the total vote in Jewish congressional districts," [page 127]. In his first two campaigns running from the Ninth Congressional District, he received 26 per cent in 1906 and 21 per cent in 1908. For his three later campaigns running from the 20th Congressional District in 1916, 1918 and 1920 Fuchs is correct. Goldfogle, not London, was elected from the Ninth, and not the Twelfth Congressional District in 1910 [page 128]. London was not defeated by Goldfogle in 1914 but was elected to Congress for his first term [page 128].

I

THE 1908 CAMPAIGN: PROFILE OF VICTORY

On October 31, 1908, the Socialist *New York Evening Call* carried on its front page in large type and framed in a black border Eugene Debs' "A final word to you on the eve of battle."[6] Debs did not address his order of the day to all the socialist forces. He singled out the voters of the Ninth Congressional District of New York for these special words of encouragement.

> The East Side [he wrote] is destined to be a historic battleground. It is here that capitalism has wrought its desolation, here that it has spread its blighting curse, like a pestilence, to destroy manhood, debauch womanhood and grind the blood and flesh and bones of childhood into food for mammon.
>
> It is here on the East Side where the victims of capitalism struggle and suffer, that the hosts of freedom must spring from the soil, fertilized by the misery of their class.
>
> Hillquit, the working class candidate for Congressman can and should be elected so that the working class may have its first representative in the national Congress.[7]

There were other indications besides Debs' unparalleled appeal to the voters of a particular district that the Socialist Party had mounted a major offensive on the East Side. In the two Assembly Districts, the Sixth and Eighth, which made up much of the lower East Side, Hillquit's running mates were Robert Hunter and James Graham Phelps Stokes. The three were drawn from the first echelon of the national leadership.

"The Ninth" offered the best chances for a breakthrough. In the logic of the socialist analysis it possessed the basic elements needed for victory: the "desolation capitalism has wrought" was nowhere more evident; its Socialists were alert, militant and numerically significant; and they were appealing to a public consisting by and large of impoverished wage earners.

To this socialist dialectic, Hillquit, in an interview granted to a *New York Times*' reporter, appended an analysis of the political balance of power in the district which he predicted would spell-out his election.[8] The Democratic vote for Congressman would be reduced by these factors: the stringent new election law decreasing

[6] Reported also in *New York Times*, Nov. 1, 1908, p. 5.

[7] This was the only direct appeal made by Debs to a particular district that appeared in the *New York Evening Call* during the entire 1908 campaign.

[8] *New York Times*, Oct. 19, 1908, p. 2.

the number of enrolled voters in the District would eliminate Tammany floaters and repeaters;[9] the Presidential campaign would preclude the Republican machine "voting openly" for the Democratic candidate for Congress as in 1906; and finally, the Hearst candidate would remain in the field at Tammany's expense.[10] Thus, four candidates were vying for 11,000 votes. The one receiving 4,000 votes, Hillquit reasoned, was assured of election. In the light of this campaign arithmetic, Hillquit needed to improve his 1906 showing by three hundred votes to win. The reporter compared the "lukewarmness" of the other campaigns to the "enthusiasm, buoyant and bubbling over, among the Socialists of the lower East Side." . . . "Republican and Democratic leaders," he concluded, "see much truth in Morris Hillquit's prediction."

The stir created by the Debs' campaign and the support of a stronger local ticket were additional sources of Hillquit's optimism. However, aside from such political variables he undoubtedly postulated the uncompromising support of the growing Socialist movement in the Jewish quarter. The Jewish trade union movement provided functionaries and rank-and-filers who were gaining political experience in each succeeding campaign.[11] The socialist *Forward*, surmounting earlier vicissitudes to become a leading Yiddish daily by 1908, possessed organizational resources of consequence,[12] and particularly striking was the growth of the *Arbeiter Ring*, a fraternal order of Jewish workingmen sympathetic to the Socialist Party. Its New York City membership increased from 5,103 in 1906 to

[9] The new law required the signature of the voter on registration and election days. If the voter claimed he could not write he was required to answer identifying questions. *New York Times*, Oct. 4, 1908, p. 5; Oct. 13, 1908, pp. 1–2.

[10] *New York Times*, Oct. 19, 1908, p. 2; *New York Evening Call*, Oct. 13, 1908, p. 6; *infra*, p. 207, note 25.

[11] Morris Hillquit, Meyer London, Max Pine, Jacob Panken were some of the more prominent Socialist candidates for office with trade union experience; *infra*, note 12; Melech Epstein, *Jewish Labor in U. S. A.* (New York, 1950) vol. I, p. 344, suggested that the depression of 1907–1908 weakened labor union activity and stimulated efforts on the political front.

[12] N. W. Ayer and Sons' *American Newspaper Annual*, (Philadelphia: N. W. Ayer and Sons, 1907), p. 1129 estimates the *Forward*'s circulation for 1906 at 52,190. Ayer's *Annual*, 1909 edition, p. 1143, gives the *Forward*'s circulation for 1908 as 53,539. The *Forward* which had begun stating its circulation daily over the masthead gave its circulation on September 1, 1908 as 72,353. Abraham Cahan discusses the progress of the *Forward* in *Bleter fun Mein Leben*, vol. IV (New York: *Forward*, 1908), pp. 536–538. From 1907 on, its financial situation improved and its circulation rose. On the role of the *Forward* in the trade union and Socialist movement on the East Side during the period, see, Cahan, *op. cit.*, pp. 542–543, 547 and 549; M. Osherowitch, "*Di Geschichte fun Forverts*: 1897–1947" [typescript, New York Public Library], pp. 136–140.

10,233 in 1908.[13] Meanwhile, the booming Russian immigration brought reinforcements of highly literate, "ready-made" socialists.[14] The Socialists conducted their most vocal and best organized campaign to date.[15] Outside help augmented the Party's district organization. Hillquit, in his autobiography, tells of the "hordes of young intellectuals" who "came down daily to speak at street corners."[16] William Dean Howells endorsed the Socialist ticket.[17] Lincoln Steffens remembered his days on the East Side as a police reporter and backed Hillquit and his comrades as the only way of breaking the evil machine.[18] Charles Edward Russell chose the week before election to join publicly the Socialist Party and endorse Hillquit.[19] In the final weeks of the campaign the Socialist Party was averaging twenty-five meetings a night with audiences aggregating 25,000, the *New York Times* estimated.[20] The *New York Evening Call* found confirmation of the effectiveness of the East Side campaign in the dissension and panic reportedly rampant in Timothy ("Big Tim") Sullivan's down-town Tammany domain.[21] "Tammany Hall on East Side Panicky," one story ran ten days before election.[22] A week later a page one headline read, "Tammany

---

[13] The figures were computed from the branch membership totals in the *Sixth Annual Report for the Year 1906 and Proceedings of the Seventh Annual Convention of the Workmen's Circle*, General Executive Committee, (New York: Workmen's Circle, 1907), pp. 43–44, and *Eighth Annual Report of the Workmen's Circle* for the year 1908, General Executive Committee, (New York: Workmen's Circle, 1909,) pp. 77–81.

[14] Hillquit explained the growth of Socialism on the East Side and the large number of first-time voters who registered as Socialists as resulting from "ready made Socialists who came from Russia.", *New York Times*, Oct. 19, 1906, p. 2; see also A. Cahan, vol. IV, p. 547; see also A. Menes, *The Jewish People: Past and Present*, vol. IV, (New York: *Jewish Encyclopedia Handbooks*, 1955), pp. 360–363.

[15] *New York Times*, Oct. 19, 1908, p. 2; *Zukunft* [Yiddish], Nov. 1908, p. 714. A. Cahan, vol. IV, p. 548; On the organization of the campaign see *New York Evening Call*, Sept. 18, 1908, p. 1; Oct. 17, p. 1; Oct. 24, p. 1.

[16] Morris Hillquit, *Loose Leaves from a Busy Life*, (New York: Macmillan, 1934), p. 115; Harry Rogoff, *An East Side Epic*, (New York: Vanguard, 1930), p. 57.

[17] Hillquit, *op. cit.*, p. 115.

[18] *New York Evening Call*, Oct. 28, 1908, p. 1.

[19] *Ibid.*, Oct. 28, 1908.

[20] *New York Times*, Oct. 26, 1908, p. 3.

[21] *New York Evening Call* (1908), Oct. 8, p. 1; Oct. 13, p. 1; Oct. 17, p. 1; Oct. 21, p. 1; Oct. 22, p. 2; Oct. 23, p. 1; Oct. 26, p. 1; Oct. 30, p. 1. Sullivan was described as losing his grip on the party machine for the following reasons: the loss in Democratic registration; his candiate was defeated for a Tammany nomination; inability to protect his alleged gambling and narcotics activities from police action. See also *New York Times*, Oct. 27, 1908, p. 4, for further indication of dissension within the Democratic Party and the demands of insurgent leaders for new tactics in party campaigning on the lower East Side.

[22] *New York Evening Call*, Oct. 23, 1908, p. 6.

Heelers are Desperate."[23] A sense of confidence unusual for Socialist leaders led them to expect the votes of sympathizers reluctant in the past to waste their ballots on a Socialist candidate with no chance of winning.[24] Impressed by their own showing in 1906, convinced they were cheated out of victory then by an eleventh hour deal, the East Side Socialists anticipated sending the first Socialist congressman to Washington.[25] A week before election Hillquit felt certain enough of victory to declare that were the opposition to combine behind a single candidate he would still be able to win.[26] The *New York Times* in a survey of the congressional election campaign saw no likelihood of change in New York with the exception of the "Ninth."[27]

Yet, when the returns were counted, Hillquit ran a distant second behind Tammany's Henry Mayer Goldfogle. His total vote was nearly a third less than his 1906 showing and one had to look back to the lean election years of the first part of the decade to find a comparably bad showing.[28] The post-mortems offered by the Socialist commentators were quick to explain the defeat: a deal between the Democrats and the Republicans to defeat the Socialist at all costs:[29] Tammany terror;[30] the continual movement of Socialists out of the East Side to Brownsville and the Bronx leaving a mounting

---

[23] *Ibid.*, Oct. 30, p. 1.

[24] *New York Times*, Oct. 19, 1908, p. 2; *New York Evening Call*, Oct. 13, 1908, p. 6.

[25] The results of the 1906 election for Congressman of the Ninth Congressional District of New York were:

> Henry M. Goldfogle [Democrat and Independence League]......7265
> Charles Adler [Republican]................................2733
> Morris Hillquit [Socialist]..............................3616

New York Times, Nov. 8, 1906, p. 3; *The Worker*, Nov. 10, 1906, p. 1. The campaign attracted wide attention, see *New York Times*, Nov. 7, 1906, p. 6. Goldfogle succeeded in running on Hearst's Independence League ticket despite court action by the Socialists to remove his name. *New York Times*, Oct. 21, 1906, p. 2. Hillquit claimed that in a four-cornered race the Hearst candidate would have pulled enough votes from the Democrat's Goldfogle to give the Socialists the victory. Hillquit, *op. cit.*, pp. 109–115. See also Charles Edward Russell, *Bare Hands and Stone Walls* (New York: Scribner, 1933), p. 200; A. Cahan, *op. cit.*, vol. IV, p. 548; *Forward*, Oct. 29, 1908, p. 4.

[26] *New York Times*, Oct. 26, 1908, p. 3.

[27] *Ibid.*, Nov. 1, 1908, p. 3.

[28] *Zukunft*, Dec. 1908, p. 768.

[29] The *Forward's* headline, Nov. 4, 1908, was, "Tammany Does Business with Republicans and Wins over Hillquit." This was based on a *New York Times* report, Nov. 3, 1908, p. 1, of a deal between the Democrats and Republicans whereby Republican regulars would vote for Goldfogle to insure Hillquit's defeat. See also *Forward*, Nov. 4, 1908, p. 8; *New York Evening Call*, Nov. 4, 1908, p. 1; *Zukunft*, Dec. 1908, p. 768.

[30] *New York Evening Call*, Nov. 5, 1908, p. 5.

residue of Tammany-dependent shop-keepers and peddlers.[31] One *Forward* commentator appended a psychological explanation: The Old World antipathy of the Russian Jew for all bureaucratic activity explained his indifference to becoming naturalized, registering and finally voting.[32] However, in their analysis of the defeat, the Socialist commentators chose to ignore those issues which revolved around the ethnic interests of the population of "the Ninth."[33]

II

THE ALLEGED SPECIAL INTERESTS

"The Ninth" was not merely the district of tenement houses, sweatshops and immigrant radicals. The heart of the Jewish ghetto and the point of concentration of Yiddish-speaking Russian Jews served as the unofficial reception center of the newly arrived immigrants during the decade of their highest influx into this country.[34] An uninhibited, self-contained social and, in certain respects, economic life, eased the ordeals of its inhabitants. Four Yiddish daily newspapers and a score of periodicals published on the East Side, offered the comfort of the familiar word and the full range of political and literary tastes.[35] "Here a man was . . . safe among his own kind."[36] This sentiment found expression in the pre-eminence of the *Lands-*

[31] *Forward*, Nov. 5, 1908, p. 1; the *Zukunft*, Dec. 1908, p. 768, remarked that "as the ships bring the greenhorns the moving vans move out the radicals."

[32] *Forward*. Nov. 9. 1908, p. 4.

[33] Nachman Syrkin's analysis of the election in the Ninth Congressional District emphasized the immigration issue as the cause of Hillquit's defeat. *Zukunft*, Dec. 1908, p. 748. Syrkin, ideological mentor of the Socialist-Zionists, was not fully accepted in Socialist circles. The closest a Socialist came to admitting publicly the primacy of the immigration issue in the defeat of Hillquit was when M. Baranof wrote:

> Such questions should not be raised at a time when the proletariat must unite to fight the always united enemy. The immigration question must be discussed in quieter times. Let the comrades . . . have an effective answer ready for the time when they will again appeal to the members [of the Socialist Party] in a referendum . . . The Socialist Party, if it erred, will not be afraid to admit it [*Forward*, November 12, 1908, p. 4].

[34] See *infra*, pp. 227–228, Tables I and II.

[35] N. W. Ayer and Sons' *Annual*, 1909 edition, p. 1143 lists the following Yiddish dailies with their circulations: *Tageblatt* (68,442), *Jewish Morning Journal* (67,664), *Forward* (53,539), and *Warheit* (59,522). The *American Jewish Year Book, 1909–1910*, (Philadelphia: Jewish Publications Society, 1909), p. 219, lists the following weeklies or monthlies which were published in New York in December, 1908: *Arbeiter, Freie Arbeiter Stimme, Der Kibetzer, Dos Naye Leben, Der Yiddisher Kempfer, Die Zukunft.* I have not included the weekly editions of the daily newspapers which appeared under separate titles.

[36] Oscar Handlin, *Adventure in Freedom*, (New York: McGraw-Hill, 1954), p. 103.

mannschaft in the ferment of East Side institutional life.[37] However, the ascendancy of the *Landsmannschaft* in Jewish life represented not merely nostalgia for the warmth of the "old home." It also indicated an overwhelming concern for the kinsmen left behind in the *shtetl* [small East European town]. Consequently, not only the synagogue and the mutual aid society were established on the *Landsmannschaft* principle but the great majority of the socialist-oriented *Arbeiter-Ring* branches, as well, despite the Socialist injunction calling for the unity of the working class.[38] Just as the Yiddish press coverage revealed the apprehension of the newly-arrived immigrant for the well-being of his family and townsmen on the "other side," so the functions of the *Landsmannschaft* were attuned to their transportation, reception and initial settlement.[39] We must bear in mind that the four years prior to the 1908 campaign witnessed a new wave of pogroms in Russia and the extinction of all radical and progressive hopes for a more liberal Russian policy. The tempo of relief work rose sharply.[40] Prominent individuals, including radical intellectuals heretofore passive in Jewish communal life, now accepted a more active role.[41] Immigration figures continued to climb. The prevalent feeling was stronger than ever that the Jews of Russia had no alternative but emigration.

[37] Lamed Shapiro, "Immigration and the Landsmannschaft," *The Jewish Landsmannschaften in New York* [Yiddish], (prepared by the Yiddish Writers Group of the Federal Writers Project, Works Progress Administration), (New York: I. L. Peretz Yiddish Writers Union, 1938), pp. 27–30. According to Shapiro's statistics 255 societies were established in New York City on the *Landsmannschaft* principle between 1906 and 1910. For the organization of federations of *Landsmannschaften* at this time, see Samuel Margoshes, "The *Verband* Movement in New York City," *Jewish Communal Register.* (New York: The Jewish Community of New York, 1917/1918), p. 1286, also Samuel Schwartz, "Landsmannschaft Federations," *Jewish Landsmannschaften in New York*, pp. 52 ff.

[38] Between 1906 and 1910, 85 *Landsmannschaft* branches of the *Arbeiter-Ring* were founded according to Lamed Shapiro, *Jewish Landsmannschaften*, p. 32; see also Melech Epstein, *op. cit.*, p. 307.

[39] Samuel Schwartz, in *Jewish Landsmannschaften*, pp. 52, 53; Lamed Shapiro, in *Jewish Landsmannschaften*, p. 27.

[40] During this period the "National Committee for the Relief of Sufferers of Russian Massacres," the "American Jewish Relief Committee," "The Jewish Self Defense Fund" were organized, not to mention collection of funds through the fraternal orders and *Landsmannschaft* groups.

[41] On the effect of the Kishineff pogrom in 1903 and the Russian Revolution and pogroms in 1905 on Jewish radical intellectuals, see Samuel Niger's succinct summary, "Yiddish Culture," *The Jewish People*, vol. IV, pp. 362–363. The organization of the American Jewish Committee in 1906 should be seen as part of a heightened sense of responsibility on the part of the leaders of the settled Jewish community. Nathan Schachner, *The Price of Liberty: A History of the American Jewish Committee* (New York, 1948), pp. 7 f.

This atmosphere of crisis coincided with the public discussion on immigration: the renewed attempt to enact a literacy test, the establishment of the Dillingham Commission, the negotiations on Japanese immigration, Russia and the American passport debate.[42] Jewish organizations, ambitious to play a role in Jewish communal life, joined in the fight against the "restrictionists."[43] Thus, on the individual and institutional plane the note of anxiety and fear lest the doors of asylum close dominated the new immigrant ghetto. This anxiety expressed itself in a high pitched sensitivity to the immigration restriction issue. One can appreciate, then, the shrillness of the debate when this very issue was injected into the campaign in the Ninth Congressional District and the accusation of supporting the restrictionist stand was hurled at the Down-town Socialists.

Not unrelated to the immigration issue was a second theme which ruffled the pride of the Jewish quarter. For the social reformer, immigration restrictionist, socialist and up-town co-religionist, the ghetto of the Lower East Side epitomized a host of evils — crime, prostitution, disease, machine politics at its worst, and cultural backwardness. Though much of this picture of the degrading conditions of the ghetto was drawn by those wishing its inhabitants well, the Jewish quarter rebelled against this image. Characteristic of this sensitivity was the reaction on the East Side to an article by the Commissioner of Police, General Theodore Bingham which appeared in the September, 1908 issue of the *North American Review*. By implication the Commissioner attributed fifty per cent of all crimes committed in New York City to Jews.[44] While Louis Marshall

[42] John Higham, *Strangers in the Land* (New Brunswick: Rutgers University Press, 1955), pp. 128–129, 162–163; *American Jewish Year Book, 1909–1910*, pp. 29–41. Twenty-five bills to restrict immigration were introduced into the House of Representatives alone from July, 1907 to August, 1908. *American Jewish Year Book, 1908–1909*, pp. 74–76.

[43] Among the organizations dealing with the question were: Jewish Immigration Committee of New York, American Jewish Committee, Board of Delegates of the Union of American Hebrew Congregations, Union of Jewish Orthodox Congregations, National Council of Jewish Women, the Independent Order Brith Abraham, the *Arbeiter-Ring*, the Federation of Galician and Bucovinian Jews, Federation of Roumanian Jews, Federation of Russian-Polish Hebrews of America, Federation of Jewish Organizations, Hebrew Sheltering and Immigrant Aid Society.

[44] In part, Bingham wrote:

... It is not astonishing that with a million Hebrews, mostly Russian, in the city (one quarter of the population), perhaps half of the criminals should be of that race, when we consider that ignorance of the language, more particularly among men not physically fit for hard labor, is conducive to crime... The crimes committed by the Russian Hebrews [are those of]... burglars, firebugs, pickpockets and highway robbers — when they have the courage... The juvenile Hebrew emulates the adult in the matter of crime percentage [*North American Review*, vol. CLXXXVIII, Sept. 1908, pp. 383–384].

and other respected Jewish citizens from "up-town" cautioned restraint and sought to deal with the incident away from the public's eye, protest meetings were held on the East Side.[45] The *Tageblatt* called for mass demonstrations demanding Bingham's resignation for besmirching the name of the Jews of the East Side.[46] The good intentions of Lincoln Steffens' muckraking letter or Deb's rhetoric on behalf of Hillquit emphasizing the need to "clean up" the abominations of the East Side were equated by many with Bingham's accusation.[47]

At the first Hillquit rally in the 1908 campaign, which Abraham Cahan, editor of the *Forward*, chaired, the candidate for Congress said:

> The issues thus defined by the Socialist Party in its National platform are also the issues in this Congressional District of New York . . .
>
> It is true that our district is inhabited largely by a foreign-born population . . . [That] the naturalized citizen of Russian-Jewish origin is as much a citizen as the native American of Dutch or Puritan origin is fact as well as theory.
>
> The interests of the workingmen of the Ninth Congressional District are therefore entirely identical with those of the workingmen of the rest of the country, and if elected to Congress, I will not consider myself the special representative of the alleged special interests of this district, but the representative of the Socialist Party and the interests of the working class of the country so understood and interpreted by my party . . ."[48]

The irony of two Russian Jews, Morris Hillquit and Abe Cahan, solemnly declaring they recognized "no special interests" in the lower East Side may have been lost to the socialist audience of Russian Jews. The rhetoric delivered by known citizens of the ghetto in the language of the ghetto obscured the anomaly. Nevertheless, in the maze of ghetto organizations dedicated in one fashion

---

[45] On the series of meetings on the East Side which culminated in the "Clinton Hall Conference for the Organization of the Jewish Community of New York," Oct. 11 and 12, 1908 (*American Hebrew*, vol. LXXXIII, Oct. 16, 1908, p. 583), see *American Hebrew*, Sept. 11, 1908, p. 449; *Warheit*, Sept. 14, 1908, p. 1; *Tageblatt*, Sept. 14, 1908, p. 1. On the position of the "Uptown Jews" see the editorial "Jewish Sensitiveness" in the *American Hebrew*, Sept. 11, 1908, p. 444, and the rejoinder in the *Tageblatt*, Sept. 14, 1908, p. 4. For Marshall's reply see *American Hebrew*, Sept. 25, 1908, p. 502.

[46] *Tageblatt*, Sept. 16, 1908, p. 4.

[47] A *Tageblatt* editorial entitled "The Socialist Bingham's Calumnies against the East Side" saw Lincoln Steffens', Robert Hunter's and Morris Hillquit's "preachings on the immorality of the East Side" as giving credence to Bingham's accusations [Oct. 30, 1908, p. 4].

[48] *New York Evening Call*. Sept. 12, 1908, p. 3.

or another to ethnic continuity, socialism was unique in preaching an involvement in American life and concern for issues transcending the ethnic group.

III

THE ARRAIGNMENT

On the day before election Louis Miller, Abe Cahan's old comrade and now archtraitor of the down-town Socialists, wrote in his *Warheit*:

> The American people has one position of high honor, the office of the President. For this highest office it seeks out its finest, most famous, most devoted and loyal son. We Jews in the quarter possess only the office of Congressman. It is not much, perhaps, but it is all we have. To whom shall we give this office, to a person who has always been with us, or to a person who never cared to know us and has no desire to know us now, who when he comes among strangers denies that he is a Jew, who was, is and will always remain a renegade. Morris Hillquit's coming to us Jews when he wants our vote should by itself be sufficient reason for not voting for him.[49]

With the refrain, "Where was Morris Hillquit when . . .," the *Warheit* itemized its charges of indifference to the interests of the Jewish quarter: the strike of tenants over the raising of rents in January, 1908;[50] the organized boycott of the Kosher meat whole-

[49] *Warheit*, Nov. 3, 1908, p. 4. Mordecai Soltes, *The Yiddish Press: An Americanizing Agency* (New York, 1925), pp. 22–23, gives the political complexion of the *Warheit* as Democratic. A. Cahan, vol. IV, p. 502, records that Louis Miller, editor of the *Warheit*, began to fight the Socialist Party and her candidate and then went on to become "Tammany's energetic defender . . . among the Yiddish-speaking public." Founded in 1905 in opposition to the *Forward* by Louis Miller, the *Warheit* tried to capture part of the Socialist following of the *Forward*. In its opposition to the *Forward*, it developed Jewish nationalist sympathies. Ber Borochov, Chaim Zhitlowsky, Nachman Syrkin contributed to its columns. See D. Kaplan's article, "The Warheit" in *75 Years Yiddish Press in the United States of America, 1870–1945* [Yiddish], ed. Jacob Gladstone, Samuel Niger, Hillel Rogoff, pp. 62–83. In the 1908 campaign, the *Warheit* fought the *Forward* accusations of having been bought by the Democratic Party [*Warheit*, Sept. 10, 1908, p. 1, Sept. 13, 1908, p. 4, Sept. 18, 1908, p. 4, Nov. 1, 1908, p. 4, Oct. 25, 1908, p. 4]. Whatever the truth there is in the *Forward's* claim that Miller's support of the Socialist Labor Party candidate was a manoeuver to confuse and split the socialist vote in Tammany's interests, the *Warheit's* editorials attacked Hillquit as a betrayer of Socialism and the "Jewish people," appealing to the public as a Socialist newspaper in 1908. *See Forward*, Oct. 28, 1908, p. 4 and *Warheit*, Nov. 2, 1908, p. 4.

[50] *Ibid.*, p. 4. On the rent strike see *New York Times*, Jan. 1, 1908, p. 3; Jan. 2, 1908, p. 8; Jan. 3, 1908, p. 2; Jan. 5, 1908, p. 9; Jan. 6, 1908, p. 7; Jan. 8, 1908, p. 16; Jan. 9, 1908, p. 16; Jan. 11, 1908, p. 8. A Socialist "Committee of Ten" attempted to direct the

salers who raised prices in 1907;[51] Julia Richman's campaign urging deportation of immigrants guilty of violating the push-cart ordinance;[52] the bankrupcy of fraternal and benevolent funds during the 1907–1908 crisis;[53] Commissioner of Police Bingham's accusation of criminality among the Jews.[54]

The catalogue of indifference concluded with this accusation:

> Where was Morris Hillquit in the days of the pogroms when old, infirm people marched and women threw their jewels into the collection plates to help? When the entire Jewish people, radicals and conservatives, young and old, united in brotherhood in the great day of tragedy.[55]

The reference was to the burst of mass meetings and appeals for funds triggered by the Kishineff pogrom in 1903. Months of agitated activity had reached a climax on December 4, 1905 when 125,000 Jews dressed in mourning garb marched to Union Square from the lower East Side.[56] A young, American-born Reform rabbi, Judah L. Magnes, headed the sponsoring organization, "The Jewish Defense Association." Serving on the Executive Committee was the Reverend Zevi Hirsch Masliansky, renowned Orthodox Jewish preacher. A Jewish labor leader and former Socialist candidate for Congress from the Ninth Congressional District, Joseph Barondess, acted as Grand Marshal of the procession.[57] Jacob H. Schiff, philanthropist banker, personification of propriety and Americanism, made his contribution to a fund avowedly buying arms for clandestine Jewish defense units in Russian towns.[58] For the moment it appeared that

---

strike to reduce rents in the tenement houses. Jacob Panken, Mr. and Mrs. J. G. Phelps Stokes are the prominent Socialists mentioned in connection with the Committee.

[51] *American Hebrew*, Sept. 25, 1908, p. 493.

[52] *Ibid.*, April 3, 1908, p. 552. A District School Superintendent on the East Side, her appeal to Police Commissioner Bingham evoked a furor in the Yiddish press and a petition was circulated for her removal. *Louis Marshall, Champion of Liberty*, 2 vols., ed. Charles Reznikoff, (Philadelphia: Jewish Publication Society, 1957), p. 1125–1126; *Warheit*, Sept. 12, 1908, p. 4.

[53] *The Hebrew Standard*, vol. LII, April 3, 1908, p. 6. *American Hebrew*, Aug. 28, 1908, p. 395; Sept. 25, 1908, p. 493; *Fifty Years of Social Service: The History of the United Hebrew Charities of New York City* (New York, 1926), pp. 70–72.

[54] *Supra*, p. 211, n. 47.

[55] *Warheit*, Nov. 3, 1908, p. 4.

[56] *New York Times*, Dec. 5, 1905, p. 6; *American Hebrew*, vol. LXXVIII, Dec. 8, 1905, p. 73.

[57] On Magnes, see, Norman Bentwich, *For Zion's Sake: A Biography of Judah L. Magnes* (Philadelphia: Jewish Publication Society, 1954), p. 38. On Barondess and Masliansky see, L. Shpizman (ed.), *History of the Labor Zionist Movement of North America* [Yiddish] (New York: Yiddisher Kempfer, 1954), p. 103.

[58] Bernard G. Richards, "Amul iz Geven a Kehillah," *Zukunft*, vol. L, Feb. 1945, p. 83.

fraternal factionalism and strife had been forgotten in the name of "brotherhood in the great day of tragedy." Three years later the *Warheit* reminded the voters of Morris Hillquit's abstention.[59]

The crime of indifference became one of outright treason in the conservative *Tageblatt*'s arraignment.

> Morris Hillquit belongs to those who hide their Jewish nationality . . . who crawl after the Gentiles on all four. It was not enough for him to change his name . . . not only did he run away from his people, he . . . backed closing the door of the land of freedom to those who like himself wished to find a home in America.[60]

"The assimilationist, alienated from his people, ashamed of his nationality" Morris Hillquit could not represent the million Jews of New York!

> Every right-thinking Jew will recognize that the Jews of New York should have as their representative in Congress a Jew who bears in mind Jewish interest. If Morris Hillquit were to be elected it would mean that New York Jewry would have no representative in the Congress of the United States.[61]

In the broader campaign the Jew had the same interest as any other citizen.[62] The campaign within "the Ninth," however, was unabashedly a Jewish campaign.[63] It became so the moment Morris Hillquit declared it was not.

With muckraking zeal, Hillquit and his supporters exposed the ignorance, crime and moral depravity of the East Side, depicting it as the ultimate proof of decadent capitalism.[64] The picture of the ghetto the Socialist campaign presented to the American public appeared so slanderous in the eyes of the *Tageblatt* that it rose to defend not only the good name of the East Side's Jewish quarter but of American Jewry at large. From this ethno-centered outlook, alone, the paper criticized the campaign tactics of the Socialists.

[59] *Supra*, p. 212, n. 50. In 1903, following the Kishineff and other pogroms, the Executive Committee of the Socialist Party of New York warned Jewish Socialists not to desert Sosialism and be swept along by the stream of Jewish nationalism (*The Worker*, July 12, 1903, p. 1).

[60] *Tageblatt*, Oct. 26, 1908, p. 4. Hillquit had changed his name from Hilkowitz. The *Tageblatt* as a rule supported the Republican Party and its candidates. Soltes, *op. cit.*, pp. 22–23. In the 1908 campaign, while overtly for the national and State Republican ticket, the paper passed silently over the Party's candidate for Congressman from the Ninth Congressional District and concentrated its entire attack on Hillquit.

[61] *Ibid.*, Nov. 2, 1908, p. 4.

[62] *Ibid.*, p. 4.

[63] *Ibid.*, p. 4. See also editorial, "The Jewish Vote," *ibid.*, Oct. 23, 1908, p. 4.

[64] *New York Evening Call*, Oct. 28, 1908, p. 1; *Tageblatt*, Oct. 30, 1908, p. 4.

"We are greenhorns. We must guard our honor and the fate of those who must yet come."[65] Such propaganda, the *Tageblatt* declared, was ammunition in the hands of the enemies of the Jews:

> They [the Socialists] must show how low society has fallen under the present system. They tell the whole world that they come to rehabilitate the filthy, backward Jews ... No wonder the anti-Semite hurls his lies at the East Side. No wonder the public considers the East Side a center of crime. It is enough for a Gentile to hear Morris Hillquit's speech to label the East Side the hell of America and the Jews who live there the worst of all nationalities in America.[66]

In this manner, "the Socialist Bingham," as the *Tageblatt* dubbed Hillquit, would speak to Congress endangering the Jews of America.[67]

> We are as well off as others ... It is the lowest lie that the East Side is immoral or is as poor as the "comrades" say ... We must not allow the East Side to be so portrayed ... We are citizens, as upright and as honest as others ...[68] He who says the East Side is filled with corruption, neglect and filth must not represent the East Side.[69]

Morris Hillquit was certainly the commanding figure of the Socialist Party in the East. A person of consequence at Party conventions, delegate to International Congresses, leading theorist, his interests and ambitions lay on a national plane. As Debs himself had put it, his election would give Congress a representative of the working class.[70] He had long outgrown the confining parochialism of local politics. The opposition, however, campaigned on no other level.

Sensational appeals to ethnic sentiments could in part be met by Morris Hillquit's national reputation and his fame as a lawyer, a socialist version of the American success story: Russian immigrant, formative years amidst the poverty of the East Side, early struggles to improve conditions there, on to law school to become a fighter for the oppressed of the world. Running mates Max Pine, in the Fourth Assembly District, veteran organizer of the United Hebrew Trades, and Jacob Panken, popular orator in the Eleventh Senatorial District, together with Abe Cahan and his *Forward*, spoke the language of

[65] *Tageblatt*, Oct. 30, 1908, p. 4.
[66] *Ibid.*, Nov. 1, 1908, p. 4; see also, Oct. 30, 1908, p. 4.
[67] *Ibid.*, Nov. 1, 1908, p. 4.
[68] *Ibid.*, Oct. 30, 1908, p. 4.
[69] *Ibid.*, Nov. 1, 1908, p. 4.
[70] *New York Evening Call*, Oct. 31, 1908, p. 1. At his ratification rally, Hillquit said: "If elected [I will consider myself] ... the representative of the Socialist Party and the interests of the working class of the country ... " *New York Evening Call*, Sept. 12, 1908, p. 2.

the ghetto.[71] The Socialists did take up the cudgel of race pride
sufficiently to be rebuked by the *Tageblatt* for their brazenness in
appealing for Morris Hillquit as a Russian Jew.[72]

But interlaced through the diatribes appeared the dominant strand
of the immigration issue. A leader of American Socialism, he was now
held accountable for all actions of his Party. An exponent of a
moderate position in the Party, he was now roundly rebuked for
his own ambivalence on immigration and tagged a restrictionist and
enemy of the immigrant workingman.

IV

REBUFF AND POST MORTEM

David Shannon has aptly summarized the Socialist Party's official
policy on immigration as a straddling of two opposing principles.[73]
On the one hand, the socialist scripture called for the international
solidarity of the working class. On the other hand, co-operating with
the trade unions and wooing the American laborer required a stand
favoring immigration restriction.

In 1904, Morris Hillquit, representing the American Socialists
at the International Socialist Congress in Amsterdam, supported
the minority resolution of restriction of immigration from "backward races." Hillquit went to the 1907 Socialist Congress in Stuttgart, instructed by the National Executive of the American party to
"combat importation of cheap labor calculated to destroy labor
organization, lower the standard of living of the working class and
retard ultimate realization of socialism."[74] When Hillquit wrote
that he opposed the immigration of workers from industrially backward countries "who are incapable of assimilation with the workingmen of the the country of their adoption," he was referring to Asiatic
immigration.[75] Its applicability to Russian immigration was not

[71] Hillquit's native tongues were Russian and German. He learned to write Yiddish
on the East Side but did not use it on the speaker's platform. *Loose Leaves from a Busy
Life* (New York, 1934), pp. 32–34; A. Cahan, vol. IV, p. 549.

[72] *Tageblatt*, Oct. 26, 1908, p. 4. Several years later Louis Boudin criticized Socialist
tactics in the East Side campaign denouncing "the pestilential atmosphere generated by
the appeal to national and race feelings." *New York Evening Call*, Dec. 15, 1910, p. 6.

[73] David Shannon, *The Socialist Party in America*, (New York: Macmillan, 1955),
pp. 47–48; see also Ira Kipnis, *The American Socialist Movement 1897–1912* (New York:
Columbus Press, 1952), pp. 276–288.

[74] *Ibid.*, pp. 277–278; L. Shpizman, *op. cit.*, pp. 206–207. In *The Worker*, Nov. 9, 1907,
p. 3, Hillquit in an article, "The Stuttgart Resolution on Labor Immigration," wrote that
the resolution of the National Executive of the American Socialist Party was a compromise.

[75] Kipnis, *op. cit.*, p. 277.

overlooked on the East Side. Just five months before the 1908 campaign, the Chicago Socialist Convention had avoided acting on a Resolutions Committee draft of an anti-immigration plank by voting to appoint an investigating committee to report to the next convention. The delaying action did not conceal the vigorous restrictionist sentiment at the Convention.[76]

At the opening rally of the campaign, Hillquit deftly sought to identify the socialist restrictionist sentiment with the problem of Asiatic immigration.

> As for the question of Asiatic exclusion, it may be an issue for the workingmen of the Pacific slope . . . but the workingmen of this congressional district have but a remote abstract interest.

By referring to a basic tenet of International Socialism, the demand "that the doors of all civilized countries be left open to the unfortunate working men . . . especially the victims of political oppression," he sought to deflect the attack.[77]

In Daniel De Leon, the Socialist Labor Party's candidate, Hillquit had a shrewd and knowledgeable opponent who waged his campaign with single-minded purpose: to embarrass and abuse his old adversary, Morris Hillquit. Fully aware of Hillquit's vulnerability on the question of the Socialist Party's position on immigration, De Leon adopted a double line of attack. The Socialist Party had violated socialist canon and Hillquit had inspired that policy.[78] Louis Miller's widely-read *Warheit* trumpeted the De Leon exposés throughout the ghetto. Hillquitian proposals made to convention committees were exhumed from protocols. *Bund* [Jewish Social Democratic Party in Russia] representatives were quoted as saying that Hillquit's resolution at Stuttgart "was like a knife plunged into live flesh."[79]

In the closing weeks of the campaign immigration had become the pivotal issue. The rebuttal Hillquit delivered on October 23rd revealed a master debater arguing the more difficult side of the proposition.[80] Referring to the 1907–1908 depression with the re-

---

[76] *Ibid.*, pp. 206 and 279; Shannon, *op. cit.*, p. 49.

[77] *New York Evening Call*, Sept. 12, 1908, p. 3.

[78] *Warheit*, Sept. 10, 1908, p. 1. "The 'agitation' against immigration is directed mainly against the Jews and this is a crime. It is also a crime against Socialism. There are no 'progressive' races and 'backward' races. There is only a capitalist class and a workers class. To divide the workers into races is the doing of capitalists. . . . " From DeLeon's speech, *Warheit*, Oct. 22, 1908, p. 1.

[79] *Ibid.*, Oct. 29, 1908, p. 4. See also, *ibid.*, Sept. 13, 1908, p. 4.

[80] Indication of the importance of the speech may be found in the *New York Evening Call* announcing that a Yiddish translation would be distributed to all the voters of the

sulting decrease in immigration and sharp increase in departing immigrants Hillquit declared:

> Immigration is not an issue in this campaign . . . The Problem . . . is how to stop emigration.[81]

He offered the following syllogism: "The capitalist system forces the worker to emigrate from land to land in search of bread; this cannot be stopped as long as capitalism exists"; hence the Socialists by destroying capitalism will solve the immigration issue. As in his earlier speech, he invoked socialist humanitarianism as assurance that the Party stood for an open door "especially for the sufferers of economic exploitation, race and political attacks, refugees like the Russian Jews."[82] The Socialist Party, however, was against "the abuse of immigration." Capitalist shipping companies artificially stimulated emigration of European workers. Socialists and union men had been called upon at Stuttgart to prevent the importation of strike-breakers and contract labor thus recognizing that immigration was not always desirable.[83]

Establishment of a category of "undesirable immigration," however, was not likely to allay the fears of the Jewish quarter. A single desperate logic ruled the immigrant community: an open door for immigration; restriction in any form would eventually affect Russian immigration.[84] In such a situation, however brilliantly Hillquit couched his reservations, the Jewish quarter insisted on an unqualified stand for unrestricted immigration. As a spokesman of American Socialism, Hillquit could not meet this sectional demand. He spoke with the circumspection of a presidential nominee and not with the regional partiality expected of a Congressional candidate.

In the course of the acrimonious campaign, the incumbent, Congressman Henry M. Goldfogle, received slight attention in the pages of the Republican inclined *Tageblatt*, the Hillquit-flaying *Warheit*, and the Socialist *Forward*. The radical, Hillel Rogoff, a keen observer of the East Side, has provided us with a partial explanation:

> Campaigning was done almost exclusively by the Socialists, Tammany relying upon the effective work of their henchmen on Election Day.[85]

District (Oct. 24, 1908, p. 1). The *Warheit's* longest and most vitriolic attack against Hillquit appeared in answer to this speech. Oct. 24, 1908, p. 4.

[81] *Forward*, Oct. 23, 1908, p. 4. See also *New York Evening Call*, same date.

[82] *Forward*, Oct. 23, 1908, p. 4.

[83] *New York Evening Call*, Oct. 22, 1908, p. 2.

[84] See John Higham, *op. cit.*, pp. 128–129, 160–165, C. Reznikoff, *Louis Marshall*, pp. 109–115.

[85] Hillel Rogoff, *op. cit.*, p. 57.

Goldfogle may not have found it necessary to conduct an active campaign and hence the opposition's denunciation of Tammany as the villain and Goldfogle as a mere tool. The disregard for the latter, however, may have reflected other considerations than disdain or lack of newsworthiness. Goldfogle, as representative of the East Side, was not particularly vulnerable. In the tradition of American political life, the Congressman championed the special interests of his District. As a freshman in Congress, he introduced the "Goldfogle Resolution" which called on the President to use his good offices for equal treatment of all American passport holders.[86] The representative of the lower East Side in Congress thereafter became the advocate of naturalized Jewish citizens of Russian birth discriminated against while travelling in Russia. He, thus, became chief protagonist of the honor of the American passport, placing principle above material gain, America's egalitarianism above Czarist prejudice. Vicariously he struck a blow for the downtrodden.[87] On the other hand, Socialist ire was not likely to be aroused by a fight to abrogate an 1832 Treaty of Commerce and Navigation with Russia. The issue, nevertheless, touched the sense of dignity and belonging of the new American of the East Side. Similarly, the day in December, 1905 when the Jews mourned the victims of Russian pogroms, Goldfogle offered a resolution to the effect that the House of Representatives express its profound sorrow and horror at the massacres and that the President use his good offices to prevent such outrages.[88] When Police Commissioner Bingham's article incensed New York Jewry in September, 1908, Congressman Goldfogle addressed an emergency conference of communal leaders.[89] Goldfogle's vulnerability to attack lay not in his record but in his connection with the machine. Tammany, therefore, became the more likely villain. [90]

Observers miscalculated the Socialist strength by employing the faulty index of campaign ardor. "Whenever we had a Socialist procession march through the streets the enthusiasm was tremendous

[86] *Journal of the House of Representatives*, First Session of the Fifty-Seventh Congress, p. 541. A pamphlet entitled, "Russian Persecution and American Jews," a translation of Goldfogle's speech into Yiddish was distributed throughout the East Side.

[87] *The American Jewish Year Book, 1909–1910*, summarizes the Congressional activity on the passport issue in which Goldfogle's legislative work is particularly clear (pp. 29–64). See also C. Reznikoff, *Louis Marshall*, pp. 49–108. On Goldfogle's role in Congress as spokesman of the "Jewish interests," see Jacob Magidoff, *The Mirrors of the East Side* [Yiddish] (New York: Published by the author, 1923), pp. 117–131.

[88] *New York Times*, Dec. 6, 1905, p. 6.

[89] *American Hebrew*, Sept. 11, 1908, p. 449; *Warheit*, Sept. 14, 1908, p. 1.

[90] J. Magidoff, *op. cit.*, pp. 122–125.

and spontaneous," Charles Edward Russell wrote in retrospect. "When election day came around . . . we had the cheering and the old parties had the votes."[91] In the aftermath of the 1908 election when the campaign processions no longer marched, M. Baranof, a Socialist journalist of the East Side, explained the phenomenon of loud cheers and few votes. He wrote:

> It would be a good thing if the comrades of down-town would establish a committee whose task would be helping Jewish workers become citizens. It now seems that we Jews make the most noise before the elections and make fools of ourselves when we can't vote on election day.[92]

The Census of 1910 bore out what East Siders knew so well. Only 18.6 per cent of the foreign-born males of voting age in the Second, Fourth and Eighth Assembly Districts were naturalized.[93] The new wave of Russian Jewish immigrants, containing many influenced by the Jewish Socialist movement in Russia and seared by the Russian Revolution of 1905, was bringing ready-made Socialists to America.[94] These Socialists were in all likelihood attending the campaign meetings but they would not be going to the polls in significant numbers until after 1910.

Yet despite the debacle, Hillquit nevertheless ran well ahead of his party's standard bearer, Eugene Debs. The East Side voter was splitting his ballot. Hillquit claimed that the Republican machine, seeing no hope for its candidate and fearing a Socialist upset, connived with Tammany, instructing its followers to "split for Goldfogle."[95] An examination of the election returns for offices in the Ninth Congressional District other than that of Congressman discloses an amazing pattern of party irregularity. The Republican presidential nominee, William Howard Taft, ran 5 per cent ahead

[91] Charles Edward Russell, *op. cit.*, p. 206.

[92] M. Baranof, *Forward*, Nov. 12, 1908, p. 4. Rogoff in his biography of London writes:

> During the campaign weeks the East Side districts rocked with socialist agitation. The Socialist candidates were hailed as Messiahs. The open air meetings were monster demonstrations of public confidence and affection. The whole city knew it. . . The marvels of the Socialist strength would grow until the day of election. Then during the twelve hours between the opening of the polls and their closing the strength would melt away [Rogoff, *op. cit.*, p. 16].

[93] See *infra*, p. 228, Appendix, Table II. Percentages have been computed on the basis of the U. S. Bureau of the Census, *Thirteenth Census of the United States: 1910 Abstract with Supplement for New York*, pp. 635–636.

[94] *Supra*, p. 206, note 14. See also Jacob S. Hertz, *The Jewish Socialist Movement in the United States of America* [Yiddish], (New York: Der Wecker, 1954), pp. 123–128.

[95] M. Hillquit, *op. cit.*, p. 116; *supra*, p. 207, note 29.

of his running mate for governor, Charles Evans Hughes. Undoubtedly, Taft's favorable statement on the passport issue, made from an East Side platform late in the campaign, together with the good-will harbored for Theodore Roosevelt, contributed to Taft's stronger showing in the Jewish quarter.[96] More difficult to explain was the 7 per cent difference in the Socialist vote and the 11.5 per cent difference in the Republican vote for assemblymen in neighboring districts.[97] Obviously, personalities weighed heavily with the East Side voter. As the Jewish immigrant boy who made good and as the advocate of the laboring man, Morris Hillquit carried an appeal beyond the Socialist ranks. Thus, we can understand his 21.23 per cent of the vote compared to Debs' 13.56 per cent in the Ninth Congressional District.[98] On the other hand, Morris Hillquit appeared in too controversial and equivocal a light to command the broad support of the population of the Jewish quarter. The hard political facts pointed to his 1,133 loss in votes compared with his 1906 total rather than to his 897 lead over running-mate Debs.[99]

That the Socialist Party was in the process of learning the lessons of the campaign was borne out by the new candidate it offered to the electorate of the Jewish quarter in 1910. With Meyer London, the Socialists strove to avoid a conflict of interests. The Party began to recognize grudgingly what an increasing number of Jewish Socialists were agitating for: that socialism operating in the ghetto must acknowledge the legitimacy of the ethnic loyalties of its inhabitants. The Jewish Socialists coming in the new wave of immigration were making their presence felt within the Jewish labor movement and in the periodical press. The lines of ideological conflict were evident. Newer immigrants, radical but committed to the Jewish group, opposed the older, cosmopolitan leadership anxious to merge with their American radical comrades.

[96] See *infra*, pp. 229–231, Appendix, Table III. For Taft's speech at the Thalia Theater, Oct. 28, 1908, see *New York Times*, Oct. 29, 1908, p. 1.

[97] Robert Hunter and J. G. Phelps Stokes were the Socialists running for Assembly in neighboring districts while David Robsen and Joseph Segal were the Republicans. Socialist Robert Hunter despite charges of allegedly harboring anti-Semitic sentiments, *Warheit*, Oct. 30, 1908, pp. 1 and 4; Nov. 3, 1908, p. 4, ran slightly ahead of Max Pine, veteran organizer for the United Hebrew Trades and a fellow Socialist candidate for Assembly in an East Side district.

[98] Louis Boudin in his criticism of the local Socialist campaign strategy mentioned that during the Hillquit campaign circulars were distributed with instructions of how to vote Democrat, Independent and Republican and "split for Hillquit" [*New York Evening Call*, Dec. 15, 1910, p. 6]. Boudin implied that this tactic emanated from Hillquit's campaign headquarters. If it did, it ran counter to the type of campaign Hillquit waged. See also Appendix, *infra*, pp. 229–231, Table III.

[99] *Ibid.* and *supra*, p. 207, notes 25 and 29.

V

THE 1910 CAMPAIGN: NEW TACTICS

At the Socialist Congress held in May, 1910, Meyer London was one of two delegates representing the Jewish Agitation Bureau which was organized in 1907 for the purpose of recruiting Jewish workers for the Socialist Party and Trade Unions. It was suspected of Jewish "nationalistic" tendencies by the "old guard."[100] When London raised the question at the Congress of the voting rights of the Bureau's delegates, Morris Hillquit, the Chairman, ruled that representatives of foreign language organizations were not delegates. They had only advisory status, and were unable to vote or serve on committees.[101] Weeks later, Meyer London received the Socialist nomination in the Ninth Congressional District. Hillquit, high in the inner councils of the Party was replaced by London who never rose above leader of the East Side. Hillquit was enmeshed in the compromises of national politics while London, single-mindedly, served the interests of his constituency. His biographer, possibly with Hillquit in mind, said this of London:

> The older labor and socialist leaders on the East Side considered his presence among them as temporary. It was expected that he would gradually attach himself to the general American movement and go into the non-Jewish sections to live. But he did not. London was drawn more and more into the East Side Socialist and Trade Union activities. He remained on the East Side because his services were needed there, because his heart was there.[102]

It was London who served as legal counsel of the *Arbeiter Ring*, the radical fraternal order, thereby earning its undeviating loyalty.[103] And it was London who was invited to attend the conference of the Joint Board of Cloakmakers Unions in August, 1908, to consider the

---

[100] From the Bureau's inception, the leadership of the Socialist Party organization in New York City was antagonistic to it. Hertz, *op. cit.*, pp. 91–107. In December, 1908, the National Executive hired an organizer for Yiddish-speaking elements. In January, 1909, Hillquit moved to have the organizer recalled. Hertz, *op. cit.*, p. 112. At the 1910 convention, when concessions were made to foreign language groups, the Jewish Agitation Bureau, influenced by the cosmopolitan outlook of the older Jewish Socialists, was the only foreign language body which did not take advantage of the resolution. Hertz, *op. cit.*, p. 118. For a contemporary view of the conflict between "nationalists" and "cosmopolitans" and the Jewish Agitation Bureau, see *Zukunft*, vol. XIV, March, 1909, p. 187 and Zivyon (Ben Zion Hofman), "The Jewish Agitation Bureau," *Zukunft*, May 1909, pp. 274 ff.

[101] Hertz, *op. cit.*, p. 117.

[102] Rogoff, *op. cit.*, p. 18.   [103] *Ibid.*, p. 52.

calling of a general strike. In the throes of Union disorganization and financial distress, the Union leaders convened in an air of utter despondency. London's role in encouraging them became legendary.[104] In the summer of 1910, as counsel for the cloakmakers he stood at the helm of the "revolt of the 70,000."[105] London emerged in the fall of 1910 as a popular hero of the Jewish labor movement and his Party's leading candidate for public office. The *Forward* boasted that the Socialist Party

> has proven it is a "workers party" . . . with brilliant possibilities of winning the campaign . . . because this year [the Party] established close ties of co-operation with the broad laboring masses . . . .[106]

At the Socialist convention in Chicago, the immigration issue sent to committee two years before for further study was again discussed. The majority report submitted called for "unconditional exclusion" of all Mongolian races. Refusal to exclude certain races and nationalities

> would place the Socialist Party in opposition to the most militant and intelligent portion of the organized workers of the United States, whose assistance is indispensable to the purpose of elevating the Socialist Party to political power.[107]

From the floor of the convention, Hillquit offered a substitute resolution which placed the Party on record favoring legislative measures to "prevent the immigration of strike-breakers . . . and the mass importation of workers . . . for the purpose of weakening the organization of American labor . . ." The resolution, at the same time, opposed the "exclusion of any immigrants on account of their race or nationality" and demanded that the United States be "maintained as a free asylum" for the persecuted.[108] The resolution was accepted 55 to 50. David Shannon in his history of the Socialist Party wrote pointedly that

> the first paragraph . . . was one that might have been written by an American Federation of Labor convention; the second paragraph might have been written by an International Congress of Marxists.[109]

Meyer London opposed any form of immigration restriction. He supported the Hillquit compromise because it rejected race as a basis for exclusion.[110] The Socialist-Zionists who opposed Hillquit in

---

[104] *Ibid.*, p. 19; Melech Epstein, *op. cit.*, p. 398.

[105] Rogoff, *op. cit.*, p. 29; Cahan, *op. cit.*, vol. IV, p. 544.

[106] *Forward*, Oct. 3, 1910, p. 1.   [107] Kipnis, *op. cit.*, pp. 282–288.

[108] Shannon, *op. cit.*, pp. 49–50.   [109] *Ibid.*

[110] Kipnis, *op. cit.*, p. 285. For London's report of the Convention, see *Zukunft*, vol. XV, July, 1910, p. 401 ff.

1908 in protest of the Socialist Party's position on immigration still found the Convention's immigration resolution unsatisfactory. It would, however, campaign for London who openly favored free immigration.[111] No longer was the local candidate being identified with the entire Party.

A colleague of Cahan and Hillquit in the early days of Socialist activity, the pragmatic, undogmatic London had allied himself with the vital movements on the East Side. He could make his bid for the support of the undoctrinated, the down-trodden as well as the literate Socialists. During the campaign, the *Forward* carried the following interview of a storekeeper:

> As a businessman I will work and vote for Meyer London. Our interests demand this ... The politicians sap the blood of us businessmen ... The honest businessman must have someone who will take his part, [someone] the politicians will fear ... When Meyer London will be elected he will be under no obligation to anyone. As a citizen of the East Side he will be in a position to accomplish a great deal. He will liberate us from graft ...
>
> The East Side has no father or mother, no spokesman ... When Meyer London is elected to Congress he will be the spokesman of the Jewish Quarter both in Washington and in New York.[112]

We have no way of verifying that such an interview did take place. This would not alter the fact that in 1908 the *Forward* had not appealed to "storekeepers and businessmen." It had conceived of Hillquit as representing the "working class" in Congress and not the Jewish quarter. The *Forward*'s interview was indicative of a change in campaign tactics as different from 1908 as the candidates were different.

Following the 1910 election, a series of letters to the editor of the *New York Evening Call* in response to Louis Boudin's article, "Milwaukee and New York" corroborated the change in tactics. In Milwaukee, there had been less than a 10 per cent difference between the highest and lowest vote polled on the Socialist ticket. In the Ninth Congressional District, London had run more than two to one ahead of the Party's candidate for governor. According to Boudin,

> In the London campaign, racial and subracial prejudices of voters were appealed to. The Russian-Jews were appealed to because Comrade London was also a Russian Jew.[113]

[111] Shpizman, *op. cit.*, p. 208. For the position of the Socialist-Zionists in the 1908 campaign see *Warheit*, Sept. 2, 1908, p. 2.

[112] *Forward*, Oct. 20, 1910, p. 1.

[113] *New York Evening Call*, Nov. 25, 1910, p. 6.

A member of London's campaign committee replied that London had been selected to run because of his "tremendous popularity with the workers of the East Side." As for the accusation of appealing to "racial prejudices," the campaign worker wrote,

> We have not made any stronger use of it not withstanding the temptations which came from the enemy.[114]

Other letters indicated that an effort had been made to appeal to non-socialists. A Professional League had been organized. The *Arbeiter-Ring* and the Cloakmakers Union established campaign committees. The propaganda published by these committees, one letter explained, did not present Socialism as the issue. The campaign highlighted Meyer London's character, and Goldfogle's infamy. As one writer put it,

> The keynote of the campaign was "split for London" and with this race prejudice was appealed to, nationality was appealed to, and, in fact, everything except the class consciousness of these workers.[115]

It was freely admitted that the vote of the small businessman and professional had been energetically pursued.[116]

London's 33.09 per cent of the vote was 11.86 per cent better than Hillquit's 1908 showing.[117] In 1908, except for Congressman, the Socialist vote in the Ninth Congressional District for other city and state offices ranged from a high of 17.87 per cent to a low of 12.88 per cent. In 1910, again excluding the vote for Congressman, the Socialist vote carried from 15.78 per cent to 15.12 per cent.[118] A consolidation and a moderate gain in the straight-ticket Party vote had taken place. The growth in Socialist strength did not preclude London receiving two votes for every one the remainder of his ticket received. The London campaign and London's appeal had reached well beyond the regular Socialist following.

What the Boudins and Hillquits regarded as a "pestilential atmosphere generated by the appeal to national or race feelings . . . [and] unsocialistic practice . . ." denoted, rather, recognition by the local Party that "special interests" indeed existed.[119] The impas-

[114] *Ibid.*, Nov. 29, 1910, p. 6.
[115] *Ibid.*, Dec. 3, 1910, p. 6; Dec. 6, 1910, p. 6; Dec. 7, 1910, p. 6.
[116] *Ibid.*, Dec. 6, 1910, p. 6.
[117] In 1910, Hillquit was the Socialist candidate for Associate Justice of the Court of Appeals and received 1,581 votes in the Ninth Congressional District, 15.78 per cent of the votes cast for that office. *Official Canvass of the Vote Cast, The City Record, City of New York*, Dec. 31, 1910, p. 41. See *infra*, pp. 235-236, Appendix, Table V.
[118] See Appendix, *infra*, pp. 229-238, Tables III, IV, V, VI.
[119] *New York Evening Call*, Dec. 15, 1910, p. 6.

sioned debate two years before had revealed the depths of these "national and race feelings." Anguish for the fate of brethren left behind and dedication to the task of their removal to America transcended other loyalties. These emotions together with the continued efforts at restricting immigration heightened group allegiances. Rather than expose conditions on the East Side, the representative of the Ninth Congressional District was expected to defend the good name of his District and its citizens. The Socialist, London, rooted in the East Side, responded to these demands. Finally elected to Congress in 1914, Meyer London told his victory rally:

> When I take my seat in Congress I do not expect to accomplish wonders. What I expect to do is take to Washington the message of the people ... I want to show them what the east side of New York is and what the east side Jew is.[120]

Re-elected in 1916 and elected for a third term in 1920, Meyer London dominated the political scene on the Jewish East Side for most of the decade. This period witnessed the crystallization of the "Jewish Socialist Federation," the last of the Socialist language federations to be organized. The Federation's organization, so long prevented by the "old guard," indicated the ascendancy of the newer immigrants committed to ethnic continuity. Beginning with 1910, the energetic Jewish labor movement entered its period of gigantic growth. London had been associated with both. The "old guard" Socialists became inactive in the Jewish quarter or underwent a change of heart and accepted the ethnic factor as a legitimate one. The 1908 and 1910 campaigns on the lower East Side illustrate the most striking development in this process.

---

[120] *New York Times*, Nov. 9, 1914, p. 14. The boundaries of the Ninth Congressional District were slightly redrawn prior to the 1912 elections to include parts of the 2nd, 4th, 6th, and 8th Assembly Districts and renumbered the Twelfth Congressional District. The results of the 1912 election for Congressman of the Twelfth Congressional District were:

Henry Goldfogle [Democrat]	4,592	[39.42% of the whole vote]
Alex Wolf [Republican]	839	[7.18% of the whole vote]
Meyer London [Socialist]	3,646	[31.22% of the whole vote]
Henry Moskowitz [Progressive]	2,602	[22.18% of the whole vote].

See *Official Canvass of the Vote Cast in the County of New York, The City Record*, Board of the City Record, City of New York, Dec. 31, 1912, p. 177.

The results of the 1914 election for Congressman of the Twelfth Congressional District were:

Henry Goldfogle [Democrat]	4,947	[37.98% of the whole vote]
Benjamin Borowsky [Republican]	1,133	[8.67% of the whole vote]
Meyer London [Socialist]	5,969	[47.98% of the whole vote].

See *ibid.*, Dec. 31, 1914, p. 59.

JEWISH-AMERICAN UNIONISM, ITS BIRTH PANGS AND CONTRIBUTION TO THE GENERAL AMERICAN LABOR MOVEMENT

By Selig Perlman

I

AMERICA'S SOCIAL SETTING AND THE IDEOLOGICAL EVOLUTION OF ITS LABOR MOVEMENTS, GENERAL AND JEWISH

This paper assumes a knowledge of the main facts of the two distinctive streams of labor history with which it deals, the Jewish-American and the general American. The paper has two objectives: first, a comparison of how each found out what goals it could set for itself with adequate chances for success; and second, how it happened that the Jewish unions, so pathetic even in the eyes of well-wishers in their earlier phases, later turned into the teachers of the larger movement of how to carry labor's influence into wider and wider spheres of American life.

The program of the larger labor movement did not come out of the book of any thinker-seer like Marx, but was a "trial and error" outgrowth of the labors by a great variety of agitators, organizers, and union builders, only a few of whom have attained lasting and wide fame. American labor history is thus, in the main, a record of such variegated experimentation, an experimentation which has extended, despite breaks in the continuity in organization, over more than a century. The Jewish labor movement, although with an ideational origin and drive, likewise underwent the experimental text. In either instance the experiment was not with a mere segment of America's society, its industrial segment alone, but ultimately with the whole expanse of American life, notably its ideals and values.

There were altogether three decisive phases of this experimenting by labor with the "whole of America," each with unique "laboratory findings" of basic significance. The first was the Gompers-Strasser experiment in the 1870's and 1880's, which came up with a knowledge of the "lay of the American land" so far as a labor movement was concerned — that private enterprise was unassailable, and that the road to salvation lay not through government and political action but through collective economic action; and that the mass of American workmen of heterogeneous ethnic origins and cultures could be held together, and tenuously at that, only by a job-conscious program which eschewed the "farther-looking" but in actuality divisive objectives.

The second chapter in labor's experiment with America was the New Unionism of the garment industries after 1910, an experiment begun in a special corner of America, on the East Side of New York and its equivalents elsewhere, but, like the bigger Gompers-Strasser one, soon extending to wider areas. This experiment was by Jewish labor — an "only one-generation proletariat," in the words of Will Herberg, as subsequently revealed — but inspired and held together by the ideal of international socialism brought over from Russia. In the long run this specifically Jewish "age of discovery" yielded lessons not very different from those learned a generation earlier by the Gompers-led group; but it emerged, as we shall see, with an "open-end" program free of the strict inhibitions of its older brother.

The third chapter in this experimenting by labor with the "whole of America" was under the warm sun of the New Deal, meaning President Roosevelt and his reformer intimates, which extended high patronage to some of the boldest "findings" of the New Unionism while also validating the Gompers-

Strasser findings as regards the entrenchment in America of the capitalist order and the futility of third parties. There is, thus, a distinct unity in the *ensemble* of the American labor development, despite its "unordered" beginnings and lack of control by clear-cut ideologies as in the labor movements of the other continents. In this unity of development, Jewish unionism holds a place second to none.

From Individualistic "Anti-Monopoly" to "Groupist Job-Consciousness"

In Western Europe and Britain with their heritage of domination over labor by the landlords, capitalists and officials of the monarchical states, the wheel of history was permanently turned when, prodded by agitators from within or without its ranks, labor awoke to a realization of the economic and social exploitation it lived under and to an urge to make itself heard in protest. Thereafter, whatever the vicissitudes of that protest in the society whose foundations it challenged, labor's awareness of its wrongs as a class hardly ever dimmed again. For, where the labor movement starts while the workingman is still without the franchise, there is in the last analysis no need of a theory of "surplus value" to convince him that he and his like are in a class apart and should therefore be "class conscious." Not so where the line of division is merely an economic one. Such a line becomes distinctly blurred by the constant "osmosis" between one economic class and another, by fluctuations in relative economic bargaining power of employer and employee with changes in the business cycle, and by other ever changing circumstances.

By and large, America has scarcely ever had a "settled" wage earning class in the European sense. For this the "frontier" and the characteristic American "class mobility" are largely accountable. As a result, employers have found it not at all difficult to perpetuate in the mind of labor their own psychology of individualistic competitiveness and of the perfect legitimacy, almost the duty, of self-advancement. And to the extent to which they succeeded in keeping labor individualistic, and until our own time no one could really doubt it, the birth of a permanent and effective labor groupism was held back. To be sure, there were other factors in addition to this purely psychological one, such as economic or physical intimidation. Nevertheless, without the worker's spontaneous individualism stemming from his optimistic appraisal of his own or in any event his children's prospects for rising in the economy and society, no economic autocracy, however buttressed by the sort of industrial militarism revealed in the latter thirties by the LaFollette sub-committee, could have sufficed to keep the basic American industries non-union as they were kept.

Yet, even where American labor manifested itself as a movement, and that we date back to 1828, to the rise of the Workingmen's parties of New York, Philadelphia and elsewhere, individualism continued for long to rule labor's mind, albeit in the guise of a program calling for collective action, the program of the anti-monopoly movements. In these movements, whether as the leading element or a mere camp follower — from the above-mentioned beginnings in the twenties, through the "free homesteadism" in the forties and fifties, the "greenbackism" of the sixties and seventies, the populism of the eighties and nineties, and the Bryanism and LaFollettism of the more recent periods — labor in effect acknowledged its mental dependence on the middle class, the farmers, small merchants and manufacturers, and in actuality espoused the latter's key objective of "making economic *individualism* safe for the small fellow." For, in this extraordinarily long period in American labor history, down to the rise in the eighties of the American Federation of Labor and its victory over the Knights of Labor, labor acted collectively, frequently through "third" political parties, only in order to regain the opportunity to "atomise" itself economically by an escape into self-employment, either as individuals or co-operatively, through the self-governing workshop.

The latter, its name and ideological externals notwithstanding, was at bottom an individualistic device, since it aspired to have self-determining small groups exchange their products on a market restored to freedom by a vigilant anti-monopoly government either "busting" trusts or opening to the small fellow, as an individual or in small groups, the heretofore inaccessible credit opportunity, land opportunity, etc., whichever "panacea" the particular "anti-monopoly" program deemed central. As brought out in the *History of Labor in the United States* (vol. II, S. Perlman, New York, 1908, pp. 205–235, 269–332) and later corroborated in Gompers' autobiography, it took the espousal by American labor of the Marx-formulated conviction that wage labor could never attain emancipation except through organizing separately from the other classes, however loud the latter's protests against the *status quo*, to plant the seed of permanent unionism on American soil.

Previously, the trade unions, which since the eighteen-thirties arose during stretches of prosperity under the spur of the rising cost of living, were wont to rush into a common third-partyism with those insurgent middle classes as economic depression took over, only to find themselves virtually wiped out at the end of the political whirl by the internal dissensions thus engendered as well as by the deflation of the aroused fantastic hopes. Gompers, a trainee of this school of *trade union* socialism, taught labor to stick to the humdrum job interest instead of chasing the will-o'-the-wisp of social panaceas and third-partyism and to muster enough self-restraint to refrain from plunging into politics when business depression rendered a job-centered program temporarily sterile.

Thus the Gompers unionism replaced in labor, at least in organized labor, both the conventional individualism of the

businessman as well as the more idealistic variety of individualism, the anti-monopoly variety. There are still some who
regard Gompers' victory over Powderly of the Knights of
Labor as the stamping out of the tender shoots of a modern
and vision-rich labor movement by something crass and
grossly opportunistic. In our view, the Knights, far from
adumbrating the latter-day class conscious labor programs,
were in effect the last cry of middle class reformism, individualistic in itself and having perpetuated the same in its spiritual
vassal, the pre-Gompers labor movement.

"COLUMBUS' TAILORS" AND THEIR EPHEMERAL UNIONS

Just as the general American labor movement needed to be
lifted out of the thinking pattern of "Individualism made safe
for the small fellow" to the qualitatively opposite one of union
job control, so the first Jewish immigrants from Eastern
Europe needed a similar metamorphosis in values before
becoming suitable human material for a non-ephemeral unionism. These two labor mentalities, the Jewish and the general
American, fated (in a later period) so surprisingly to converge,
indeed had sprung in as unlike environments as the human
mind can imagine. The individualism of the American workingman, whether of the orthodox conservative or of militantly
anti-monopoly variety, sprang from a consciousness of opportunity abundance.[1]

By contrast, the *Luftmenschen*, who composed the greater
share of the immigrants from that quarter prior to the turn
of the century,[2] brought with them the sort of individualism

---

[1] S. Perlman, *A Theory of the Labor Movement* (New York, 1928, 1949) pp. 249–253.

[2] I. Lifshitz, in *History of the Jewish Labor Movement in the U. S.* [in Yiddish],
(New York, 1943), vol. I, p. 70, says, in regard to the immigrants of the period:

   We know from other sources that among the Russian-Jewish immigrants there
   were few artisans trained in the homeland (as contrasted with the immigrants
   from Austria) and that they first became wage earners on American soil.

which accepted a scramble for whatever could be seized of the scant economic opportunity as the only chance of bare survival. The dweller in the small town in the Pale of Settlement in Russia, only able to scrape together enough to keep himself and family alive during the week, with some cheer for *Shabbes* (Sabbath) on the market day when the peasant came to town to trade, was in no condition to develop either the individual self-restraint or the confidence in his fellow workers needed for the sort of united front shown by the medieval gildsman or by the mature modern trade unionist. And recent historical scholarship has established the fact that the bulk of the earlier pre-Kishinev (1903) immigration was of this economically light-weight sort and with barely any roots in any economic soil — the very same element which after the sixties had been streaming to Warsaw, Lodz, Ekaterinoslav, Bialystok and Odessa.[3]

Arrived in New York and the other metropolitan centers, this first wave of immigration from the Russian Empire underwent the same "productivization" or "laborization" as in the new centers of industry in the old land.[4] In each instance, there was thus engendered a Jewish working class, but a working class with "groupist" habits yet to be developed. The eagerness to rise to the position of employer, even if it was only the humble one of the sweat-shop boss, was an overpowering passion and, on a lower level of aspiration, namely wage earning, an equal economic individualism prevailed. As yet the more solid group of hereditary Jewish artisans, who while never officially recognized as were the medieval gilds in the West, yet were in a measure "groupist by custom," had not begun a mass movement to these shores. Professor John R. Commons, who studied this new Jewish proletariat for the

---

[3] Jacob Lestschinsky, "The Economic Development of the Jews in the United States," in *The Jewish People: Past and Present* (New York, 1946), vol. I, pp. 391–405.
[4] *Ibid.*

McKinley Industrial Commission, described its socio-economic mentality in the following words:

The Jew's conception of a labor organization is that of a tradesman rather than that of a workman. In the manufacture of clothing, whenever any real abuse arises among the Jewish workmen, they all come together and form a giant union and at once engage in a strike. They bring in ninety-five per cent of the trade. They are energetic and determined. They demand the entire and complete elimination of the abuse. The demand is almost unanimous and is made with enthusiasm and bitterness. They stay out a long time, even under the greatest of suffering. During a strike, large numbers of them are to be found with almost nothing to live upon and their families suffering, still insisting, on the streets and in their halls, that their great cause must be won.

But when once the strike is settled, either in favor of or against the cause, they are contented, and that usually ends the union, since they do not see any practical use for a union when there is no cause to fight for. Consequently, the membership of a Jewish union is wholly uncertain. The secretary's books will show 60,000 members in one month and not 5,000 within three months later. If, perchance, a local branch has a steady thousand members from year to year, and if they are indeed paying members, it is likely that they are not the same members as during the year before. A German union, on the contrary, will have the same members year after year, well or ill, with little change. The Jew joins the union when it offers a bargain and drops it when he gets, or fails to get, the bargain.

The Jew is also exceedingly abstract and metaphysical and greatly interested in general principles. His union is always, therefore, except in time of a strike, a forum for the discussion of socialism and the philosophy of the labor movement. The socialist element acquires control when the workingmen stay away from the union, and they urge an organization devoted mainly to propaganda on the principles of the solidarity of all labor, without much attention to trade differences. The Jewish labor press, pamphlets, and speakers, nearly all recruited from the socialists, have continually engaged in these discussions, neglecting the formation and strengthening of their unions. These statements are substantiated again and again in the history of the trade in

New York. It is a saying on the East Side that there is always a strike going on somewhere.[5]

In September, 1938, when I had the privilege of being the guest of the Webbs in Passfield Corner, Mrs. Beatrice Webb, who had begun her career as a social investigator by taking a job in a London garment shop, remarked to me about the extreme individualism of the Jewish immigrants from Eastern Europe and their eagerness to "get out of their class," traits for which she had a scornful reaction.[6]

THE CIRCUITOUS AID TO STABLE JEWISH UNIONISM FROM THE FIRST RUSSIAN REVOLUTION

While the earlier Jewish immigration from Russia, 1880 to 1900, was, as was seen, of virtually "superfluous people" with the flimsiest sort of economic roots, the mass agitation since

---

[5] *Trade Unionism and Labor Problems* (Ginn & Co., 1905), "Sweating System in the Clothing Trade," pp. 316–335. Originally from *Report of the U. S. Industrial Commission*, vol. XV (1901), pp. 319–352.

[6] Beatrice Webb said the following in her study on the "Jews of East London" for Charles Booth's *Life and Labour of the People* (reproduced in S. and B. Webb, *Problems of Modern Industry*, London, 1902), pp. 44–45:

> And it is by competition, and by competition alone, that the Jew seeks success. But in the case of the foreign Jews, it is a competition unrestricted by the personal dignity of a definite standard of life, and unchecked by the social feelings of class loyalty and trade integrity. The small manufacturer injures the trade through which he rises to the rank of a capitalist by bad and dishonest production. The petty dealer or small money-lender, imbued with the economic precept of buying in the cheapest and selling in the dearest market, suits his wares and his terms to the weakness, the ignorance, and the vice of his customers; the mechanic, indifferent to the interests of the class to which he temporarily belongs, and intent only on becoming a small master, acknowledges no limit to the process of underbidding fellow-workers, except the exhaustion of his own strength. In short, the foreign Jew totally ignores all social obligations other than keeping the law of the land, the maintenance of his own family, and the charitable relief of co-religionists.
>
> Thus the immigrant Jew, fresh from the sorrowful experiences typical of the history of his race, seems to justify by his existence those strange assumptions which figured for *man* in the political economy of Ricardo — an Always Enlightened Selfishness, seeking employment or profit with an absolute mobility of body and mind, without pride, without preference, without interests outside the struggle for the existence and welfare of the individual and the family. We see these assumptions verified in the Jewish inhabitants of Whitechapel; and in

1897 under the leadership of the revolutionary *Bund* eventually set off to the United States, as a by-product of the struggle in that remote country, a stream of more solid elements. These "second-wave immigrants" were the skilled Jewish artisans who for generations had ministered to the wants of the peasants, officials and nobles of Poland, Lithuania, White Russia and the Ukraine, and who had lived as compact occupational groups, a pattern which manifested itself even in their devotional life — in prayer houses, for instance, frequently bearing the names of specific handicrafts. To these, the propaganda of the *Bund* brought a fresh messianic hope, this time of a new world under the beneficent rule of the international proletariat, a world stranger to either exploitation or racial inequality. The *Bund* was both a political and an economic organization, and in each field it shone by its practicality and thoroughness. True, the new gospel came to master the lives only of a minority, but tens of thousands were stirred to hope and to act.

Next came the Czar's government's ripost. As the Jewish workers and intellectuals were admittedly in the front ranks of the struggle against the Autocracy, as manifested in mass strikes and in open demonstrations, and because the opportunity to employ the Jew as a lightning-rod for popular wrath has always been a temptation which governments ruling solely in the interests of an upper class seldom resisted, a wave of officially inspired and even officially carried-through "pogroms" broke out. The Kishinev pogrom in 1903 heralded the new official policy and after the temporarily successful revolutionary movement of October, 1905, pogroms became a mass phenomenon. Immigration to America then became almost a mass flight.

Unlike the earlier immigrants from Russia, these newer ones

---

the Jewish East End trades we may watch the prophetic deduction of the Hebrew economist actually fulfilled — in a perpetually recurring bare subsistence wage for the great majority of manual workers.

needed much less purging of excessive economic individualism to render them fit for unionism. The Bund's socialism, building upon their habitual groupism, had already produced much of the required cementing substance. In fact, the delay of some years which occurred in the mutual discovery of the two labor streams, the general American and the Jewish, was not because the newcomers lacked the feel for labor solidarity but because the established American type of unionism with its limited objective at first chilled the Bundists to the bone. On the other hand, the latter saw in the sweat-shop system which greeted them as their exclusive job opportunity a conclusive validation of the Marxian teachings. The intellectual Bundists, who came with this immigration, knew how to turn the horrors of the sweatshop to good propagandist use.

These "second-wave immigrants" also found on the East Side a struggling socialist movement under earlier-arrived intellectuals, such as the ever-devoted Abraham Cahan and his co-workers on the *Forverts*, men destined to play a leading rôle in integrating the East European Jew into American life, but who at that time, hard as they worked at the sisyphus-like task of helping garment trade unionism to take root, were convinced that not the union but the Socialist Party branch would be the mobilization point of Jewish labor. Thus, virtually all the influences that played upon this all-important "second immigration" — the recent Russian experience, the nature of the contact with their American present, and the incessant urging by the already-Americanized leaders — have moved them to continue pursuing in America the same goal which the Czar's triumph had just removed from their reach in the land of their birth and to continue to do it under the flag of their own political party.

Not until the shirtwaist makers' strike of 1909 and the cloakmakers' in 1910 had shown how combative unionism could be even in the American setting, where the broader labor movement remained distressingly lethargic as regards labor's "wider scope," did unionism as such shine forth in their eyes as a true instrumentality on a par with the Socialist Party. Subsequently, the misfortunes as well as the missteps of that Party — the alienation of the Western militants by the anti-sabotage resolution of 1912, the pro-labor attitude of the Wilson Administration, the Socialists' anti-war stand in 1917, and the October Revolution — dethroned it as the hope of Jewish labor. Thereupon the garment unions, which had never regarded themselves as in any way the Party's rival, came to assume primacy in the minds of the active workers and in the general arena — virtually by default and to fill in a painful void. The day of the New Unionism was at hand!

The first beneficent contact of the Jewish unions with the larger America was with the Social Settlement workers. These cultural colonizers from the older and better situated American stocks soon discovered that beneath the alien and chaotic exterior of Ghetto life there was imbedded, in at least an appreciable minority of the dwellers, a passionate commitment to the same high humane ideals by which they themselves had originally been moved to "go into the people." This friendship never cooled and culminated in the New Deal era when native American idealism sat in the highest place in the nation. In the meantime, the struggling Jewish unions had been getting comfort, advice, and a chance for an adequate hearing in the court of public opinion through the concern in their welfare of such persons as Jane Addams, Florence Kelley, Lillian Wald, Phelps Stokes and others. During the "Uprising of the 20,000," the shirtwaist makers' strike in 1909, this warm "introduction" to public opinion sent society women to keep vigil in night police courts so that the arrested girl pickets might get something closer to justice. The garment employers, particularly the larger ones, feeling more assailable than their non-Jewish *confreres*, who generally could count, in their labor disputes, on an almost automatic support by the big press, became quickly aware that there was in the larger America, in which they, too, were of course striving to find recognition, an influential though wholly unofficial group of moral censors observing their conduct and voicing authoritative judgment. Subsequently, when out of the dramatic struggles by the Jewish unions there emerged significant new institutions such as the "Protocol of Peace" in the New York cloak trade in 1910 or the Hart Schaffner and Marx agreement in 1911, these same moral censors of employer behavior turned into doting foster parents of their own discoveries, the union leader prodigies, an attitude which in the case of Sidney Hillman, almost turned into a veritable personal cult.

In the Roosevelt train the leaders of the Jewish unions were accepted both as trusted members of the service personnel as well as favored passengers. We are still too close to the event of the Roosevelt Revolution fully to appreciate the changes which it has wrought in America's socio-political atmosphere, in the structure and functioning of government, and lastly, in the redistribution of social power among the several economic groups — big business, farmers, labor, and small business. Here was a man of political genius, who knew intuitively how to get the balky horses of his political team to pull in harness. He began by banishing the paralyzing fear of the depression, and himself lead off by showing no fear at violating time-hallowed taboos in government finance and elsewhere whenever he felt that the country's recovery and the moral and physical salvaging of humans were at stake. Until he lost control of Congress in the election of 1938, he was master of both the country's internal and foreign policy, thereafter only of the latter, by a superb charisma as well as by his knowledge of how the numerous lines of personal and group self-interest ran and intertwined. In the Rooseveltized America, as is well known, the labor movement was given a key rôle in enhancing mass purchasing power, the *sine qua non*, the Rooseveltians believed, of enduring prosperity.

To the Jewish union leaders the Roosevelt leadership of the country meant the ascendancy to power of the very humanitarian group which they had found so responsive since their first contact with the social settlement workers. One important result was discernible at once. In the eyes of the Jewish-American leadership as a whole and, above all, in the eyes of the Jewish employers in the garment industries, the stature of these union leaders with their free access to the White House to plead if necessary not alone their own cause but also that of their industries as a whole, had suddenly attained gigantic size. For instance, when in wartime, the old established garment centers felt they needed protection from the favoritism the purchasing divisions of the armed services were allegedly showing to seekers after government contracts from non-metropolitan areas, the garment industries in New York, capable of turning out army equipment, were restored to their opportunity just because they were the wards of their own influential labor leaders. Hillman's rôle as chief labor administrator in the successive agencies dealing with war production was especially imposing. At a later date, Hillman's part in Roosevelt's fourth Presidential campaign, was even more so. The alleged order issued by Roosevelt to his managers in that campaign to "clear it with Sidney," so thoroughly exploited by the Republican campaigners, merely capped the climax of the rise of the Jewish labor leadership to the highest position of influence ever held by any Jewish group in America, looking away from such personages as Oscar S. Straus, Theodore Roosevelt's Secretary of Commerce and Labor, Justices Brandeis, Cardozo and Felix Frankfurter, Bernard Baruch, Governor Lehman, and very few others, if any.

II

THE JEWISH UNIONS AND A NEW APPROACH TO THE
PROBLEMS OF PRODUCTIVITY

By 1910 the Gompersian labor movement had had practically three decades of solid experience behind it. The third decade was one of struggle for existence no less than the first two. Anti-unionism had entered on a permanent offensive in Big Industry: U. S. Steel had taken its Cato's oath in 1901 and was fully living up to it. Medium-sized industry, such as machinery production, swelled the cohorts of the National Association of Manufacturers as well as of the militant employers' associations in specific industries. All of these were more than "containing" unionism after its surge in the early years of the present century. Meantime, the flood of unlimited immigration from Austria-Hungary, Italy, Russian Poland, and the Balkans kept the anti-union employer supplied with an effective alternative to the embattled native Americans and the earlier comers from Europe's North. Simultaneously, on the vital public opinion front, President Eliot's glorification of the strikebreaker as the contemporary American hero, to refer to this moral intervention by a well-meaning outsider, was an Amen to the court anti-strike injunction. Evidently, labor had made its bid during the McKinley-Roosevelt era of prosperity, but got thrown back to the smaller industries in the larger cities, to the railroads and to the coal regions.

As if that were not enough, triumphant management was now about to be acclaimed "scientific" in a science-worshipping age as the usherer-in of the so-called "second industrial revolution." As for that revolution itself, whereas the earlier technical revolution revolutionized just the tool, this one aimed to alter the workers' bodily behavior while at work on the basis of "time and motion studies," coupled with wage inducements to conform to the new way of industrial life.

It was indeed none other than the champion of labor's rights, Louis D. Brandeis, who made the nation aware of these experiments by F. W. Taylor, Gantt, Emerson, and Gilbreth. When, as attorney for the shippers before the Interstate Commerce Commission in a freight-rate case, he charged the railroads with having neglected a possible saving of one million dollars a day through the practices of "scientific management," it was like a shot heard round America. The way in which this name took and the acclaim given to this new public favorite has made unionism feel more than ever its loneliness in its own country.

Labor spokesmen seemed to go along with President Brown of the New York Central who was more than skeptical. Said John Mitchell:

> I do not believe that anything can be safely saved on them (the railroads); if there is waste of $300,000,000 a year, it is outside the sphere of costs occupied by the workman. And I am against the premium or bonus system and against too much specializing.[7]

Gompers, several months later, expressed agreement with Mitchell. Scientific Management had defended the bonus system as differing from piece work, but he was unconvinced.[8]

Professor John R. Commons, fresh from his study of the period of the 1840's for the *Documentary History of American Industrial Society,* in which the Fourierites were the "efficiency" protagonists of that day, sided with the labor leaders. He maintained that economic distribution did not lend itself to a scientific determination and that unionism had to pursue its concentration on distribution:

> As a matter of fact, modern trade unionism is a survival of all kinds of experiments in organization, including cooperation, politics,

---

[7] Alpheus T. Mason, *Brandeis, A Free Man's Life* (New York, 1946), p. 331.
[8] *Ibid.*

and joint membership of employers and workmen; and it has
survived only to the extent that it has chosen to enforce policies
that restrict the employers.[9]

Fifteen years later a synthesis of the unionists' revolt and
an objective analysis was expressed as follows:

> In scientific management unionism saw an enemy with a technique
> designed to undermine its bastions and to destroy solidarity in
> the ranks of labor. In addition, two of the basic implications
> of scientific management excited the workers' rebellion. One such
> assumption, that the workers' stored up fund of technical knowledge
> may be of questionable value and must be subjected to a critical
> "time and motion" study, offended the worker's pride of craftsman-
> ship. The other assumption, that his claim to his job must be a
> constantly renewable claim by conforming to the "scientifically"
> set standard of performance and with "seniority" left out of consider-
> ation, rendered hopeless his dream of attaining citizenship in
> industry. For, unionism has developed its own conception of
> industrial morality, in which the workers' relationship to industry
> and to the employer is as a group rather than as separate individuals.
> Under this conception the waning efficiency of the older worker,
> if such should be the case, is compensated by the extra efficiency
> of the younger worker. The union thus "collects" from the individual
> in his youth and "disburses" it back to him when he is past the
> height of his vigor, a species of old age insurance expressed in
> a continued right to a job, with the employer's and industry's
> interests presumably unaffected.

Unionism also felt, although it perhaps failed to emphasize it,
that the first scientific managers, who blandly relegated collective
bargaining to the garret of history as arbitrary and unscientific,
actually reared their own wage structures, whether in the form
of differential piece rates or of bonus percentages, on the clearly
unscientific "going" or "market" rates, and that the height of the
bonus or "reward wage" superstructures was likewise determined
arbitrarily, by considering the unscientific but thoroughly human
factor of the relative bargaining power of employer and employee.
Moreover, with the "scientific" task set by time and motion study

9 "Unions and Efficiency," *American Economic Review*, September, 1911, pp.
463–464.

and with the worker's rate of pay determined by the former as a yardstick, the worker became automatically classifiable as to efficiency and "cooperation," through the very computation of the amount owed him in wages. Hence, employers were enabled to differentiate at a glance between employees as to their relative claims to being kept on the job. Hence, too, each employee was set to compete for the job, against every other employee in his group, engendering in each a psychology that was the very opposite of the solidarity of unionism. Add to these the deep suspicion of time and motion study as a mere subterfuge for speeding-up; the fear that through such studies the employer is enabled to penetrate into the skilled workers' trade secrets and to multiply his competitors at will; the dread of heavier unemployment as a result of a more speedy using up of the ever-limited job opportunities — and the deadly opposition of unionism to scientific management becomes intelligible.[10]

As seen above, American unionism's abandonment of the panacea of producers' co-operation in the nineties made it turn its back on production in order to center on distribution. Changes in production came to be considered as dangers in themselves and therefore to be blocked as long as possible. Nor did they as a rule[11] feel any shame at "running away" from trying a union-wise domestication of the wild animals of technological change.

Labor's sentiments and value judgments being what they were, its action was guided by a passionate écrasez l'infâme. Therefore, the riders to appropriation bills under the pressure of the labor lobby prohibiting the introduction of scientific management methods in government arsenals.[12] In a country with the highest industrial dynamic, labor emulated, albeit on a more sophisticated plane, the machinery-breaking by the Luddites in England a century earlier!

[10] S. Perlman and P. Taft, *History of Labor in the United States* (Macmillan, 1935), vol. IV, pp. 158–160.
[11] The Typographical Union, which accepted the linotype on condition of the employment of skilled printers to operate it, was an exception.
[12] Perlman and Taft, *supra*, p. 158.

Yet what was needed to get labor and the country out of this *impasse* was to work out a pattern of reconciliation between unionism and the "second industrial revolution" and to give unionism an acknowledged rôle within the process of continuous and technological change.

At the time, the prospects of such a reconciliation were far from bright. Among the engineers a slight left wing was forming as when Robert G. Valentine spoke before the Taylor Society of New York, in 1915, of the necessity to secure labor's "consent," without, however, altering labor's attitude in the least.

As regards the revolutionary-minded Jewish garment unions, there was at first scarcely any likelihood that countenancing the boss's sharpest anti-union tools would appeal to them in the least. Yet they alone among American unions were qualified by their positions in their own industry as well as by their previous ideological conditioning to "take a stab" at the new model. What was needed was, first of all, an absence of "awe before the boss," as a creature of superior endowment and unmatchable social prowess. The garment unions' leaders indeed felt themselves at least the equals of the employers with whom they dealt as regards technical proficiency; in fact, many of them believed that the successful employer was where he was because they, the union leaders, had preferred a rôle to them far more significant than that of mere money-maker. Added to this self-confidence was their proven ability to establish a friendly *rapport* with a vital element of the extra-Jewish American world, the "settlement workers" and their like, who aided and admired them as the better voice of American labor. Consequently, the general American unionist's fear of thoughtlessly unpegging what his union had pegged down against the will of his powerful employer, was not shared by the Jewish union leader when he contrasted his own progress at "belonging" in this new land with that of the employer in his trade.

But not alone the absence of fear made the Jewish unionists "naturals" for this path-breaking job. As socialists nurtured on the *Communist Manifesto*, they were convinced that a social class (and that category, of course, found its crowning glory in the proletariat) could prove its fitness to rule through a demonstrated proficiency in handling the ever-dynamic "productive forces" of society. Consequently, had they contented themselves with a display of the orthodox unionists' allergy to technical change, to use Hoxie's concept if not precise words, they would have, in their own eyes, but "issued to themselves a certificate of mental poverty." Thus, both their objective to build a socialist order, later to be sure, relegated to the non-urgent category, and also the immediate consideration of a more effective job bargaining, impelled these Jewish unionists to demonstrate by their actions that scientific management "did not bite." Thus it came about that the early divorce of American unionism from the problems of production, which had occurred when it turned from the self-governing workshop to job consciousness, stood a good chance of being revoked by these new practitioners of unionism who had for long been widely held incapable of practicing any unionism whatsoever!

Space prevents going into the details of the pathbreaking experiment in the Cleveland women's garment industry in 1921,[13] in which a social-minded employer, Morris A. Black, who in turn convinced the other leading employers, and a devoted and far-sighted union leader, Meyer Perlstein, after a mutual conversion to the legitimacy of the other's objectives, came forth with the plan of lifting the union's obstruction to scientific management. The price exacted was the employer's guarantee to his regular employees of forty weeks employment for the year and a recognized place to the union

---

[13] See Louis Levine, *The Women's Garment Workers* (New York, 1924), pp. 360–381.

in supervising the "second industrial revolution." This supervision extended over the selection of a fair human sample for setting standards by the process of time and motion study as well as in the conduct of that process itself, and was "sealed" by the employers' recognition that there can be no objectively scientific method of wage setting, rendering collective bargaining superfluous.

The Cleveland experiment earned for its authors a just fame and became widely known in industrial and labor circles. This experiment, though later abandoned, was the germ of today's management engineering department of the International Ladies' Garment Workers' Union under Dr. William Gomberg, the author of the pioneer study, *A Trade Union Analysis of Time Study*[14] and recently a leading consultant, in conjunction with the European Cooperation Administration, of the British and Continental Trade Union movements on productivity questions.

Social movements, which serve their membership on a day-to-day basis, notably labor movements, are prone to "routinize" their actions as did the ancient craft gilds, unless someone makes a "fresh eye approach" to the whole situation. We know from the history of science how many centuries it took to overcome the Aristotelian conception of the static as being the "normal," or the flogiston fallacy in chemistry. That social movements should show a similar mental inertia, is not surprising. Their leaders are compelled to make decisions, frequently critical ones, amidst a medley of forces, inseparable and unpredictable, and therefore develop a reluctance to shift the angle of vision for fear of reaping mental confusion or, worse, jeopardizing the very survival of their charge. The classical example of the boon of a "fresh eye approach" was Walter Bagehot's in regard to Britain's system

[14] Chicago, 1948.

of government. The accepted view had been Burke's formula of "King, Lords and Commons," a fragmentized entity. Bagehot, by shifting his viewpoint, saw that the government of England was in reality an integrated entity, under the Cabinet. Similarly, about the time of World War I, American unionism needed a fresh eye approach, not indeed to re-assay its earlier fundamental discoveries as to which objectives were attainable in the American environment and would not unite the community against it as a subversive menace, but to counteract ossification in the area of action not "outlawed" by public distrust, namely job action.

The Jewish unionists who broke the taboo against scientific management were at first merely solving "tactical," day-to-day problems. The supreme solution, they still thought, would come from a "working-class strategy" determined by the "immanent forces of history." As yet they would have rejected with indignation a suggestion that in their "fresh eye" approach to the production problem they were, in a manner, merely bringing up to date that which Strasser and Gompers had learned a generation earlier. In fact, they believed that their very objective of a society freed of the private ownership of the means of production and governed by the working class has dictated their concern with the problems of *their* industry as a whole, which included, of course, methods for higher productivity. However, as socialism in America "seemed unavoidably delayed," the new viewpoint opened the door to a better give and take with private management, since by showing how snugly unionism could be made to fit in with scientific management, there came the double result, first of humanizing the latter and, second, of pointing a new way to orthodox A. F. of L. unionists, if they would only consent to discard their fear of scientific management and demand an equal share with their employers in the working of it.

III

THE EXPANSION OF THE INDUSTRIAL GOVERNMENT PATTERN

The Voluntary Umpire System

Another of the mental "fixities" in the general labor movement was the fear of admitting any outsider within the trade-agreement sphere. In "technical" language, the issue was between "negotiation" and "arbitration." According to the orthodox tenet, the outsider might mediate but must never be allowed to arbitrate. This was a heritage from the British trade unionism of the sixties and seventies, which the founders of the A. F. of L. deeply revered and sought to emulate. The idea was deeply rooted in the social past of the British laboring class. As a subject class with a traditional inferiority of status, now that it had won "recognition" from some employers, it was fearful of losing the substance of it to the allegedly impartial outsider. Students of the problem generally agreed with this view and gave it a "social efficiency" underpinning by virtually repeating the verdict of the inadequacy of the outsider. So Louis D. Brandeis, the unquestioned authority on industrial relations since the Protocol of Peace in 1910, and chairman of the Board of Arbitration under that settlement, deliberately curtailed the functioning of this tri-partite board by convening it as rarely as possible. If thrown on their own, he felt certain, the "newlyweds" will learn how to live together peacefully without having to call in the neighbors to make peace.

But such orthodoxy or fixity scarcely fitted the Protocol situation. The industry's structure was forever shaking from basic internal disturbances — "inside" shops trying to hold their own against the contractor or sub-manufacturing system;

while on the psychological side, one could scarcely speak of a common ground or even of a mutual acceptance. To the larger manufacturers, the union was an aggregation of semi-barbarians under dangerous leaders, and a sizable minority of the union membership heatedly articulated in the terms of the Marxian class struggle. To these militants fresh from the Russian Revolution, the mere signing of the Protocol of *Peace* was a serious compromising of their basic ideology; and now Brandeis was pushing them into a "compromise within a compromise." His reluctance to use the Board of Arbitration as a tribunal in the unadjusted grievance cases looked, in the eyes of this group, like forcing the wage earner into the detested school of opportunism if not to a return to the old subservience to capitalism.

Furthermore, to these same revolutionaries any tradition coming from conservative British unionism carried only slightly more weight than the babbling of an infant. How much attention had those people, suddenly so authoritative, paid to Marx when he lived among them? No, labor must not permit itself to be lulled into a willingness to "sit at the seashore and wait for the weather to clear." The class struggle can be made to proceed even under the Protocol, albeit without bloody barricades. The deadlocked issues, status and power issues everyone of them, must be resolved by a Committee for Immediate Action under an "impartial chairman." The New York Cloakmakers won their demand, even though the chief protagonist, Dr. Isaac Hourwich, the Chief Clerk of the union, was eliminated by the combined pressure of those, including the members of the United States Commission on Industrial Relations, who thought they were rallying for constructive ideas in collective bargaining and unionism and against an influence aiming to undermine both. The new institution lasted as long as the Protocol.

The same impartial chairman system had been getting undramatically on its feet in the Hart Schaffner and Marx agreement concluded in 1911. Professor Leo Wolman has put it succinctly in his authoritative article on the Garment Trades in the *Encyclopaedia of the Social Sciences* (vol. VI, p. 583):

> From the slender beginnings in 1911 the practice of arbitration as a continuous function has become general in the organized sections of the industry. Under this system, which had its most complete development in the men's clothing industry, there has been set up a detailed code of industrial law and judicial decisions, constituting in substance the rules and regulations for the conduct of labor relations in the industry.

This conclusion in regard to the rôle of the garment trades in the matter of the use of the industrial umpire needs to be qualified in the interest of accuracy, as well as to escape the charge of ethnic chauvinism on the writer's part. In anthracite coal the Board of Arbitration which issued the Award that settled the long 1902 strike, an award repeatedly renewed for three-year periods, provided for appeals to itself to resolve disputes of application of the points in the Award in particular cases, a procedure similar to the one under the General Motors agreement today, and thus has a clear historical priority in adjudication by umpire in grievances cases. Still earlier, for a goodly stretch after 1901, the National Civic Federation, a non-governmental organization with a tri-partite Board of Directors, on which Samuel Gompers, Mark Hanna, and Oscar S. Straus respectively represented labor, capital, and the public, engaged in promoting trade agreements. These, however, were not "judicial" acts but just of "advance mediation."

In the garment trades the "impartial chairman" soon turned into more than a disputes umpire set in motion by means of a grievance procedure. He was instead a day-to-day functionary to supervise the joint "rate" and "production standards" committees and, if need be, to resolve their deadlocks. In this fashion these unions, as well as the umpires, have gained an entry into a sphere which in other industries still remains management's "sacred preserve" — perhaps the image of a new day of "welfarized capitalism" and "dynamicized trade unionism," in industry in general. This species of pioneering is, of course, inextricably connected with the above-described garment trades solution of the "scientific management" problem.

Thus a realized demand by a still revolutionary-minded group in the New York cloakmakers' union, essentially distrustful of any management-labor agreement, and a parallel development in Chicago with no thunder and lightning and enjoying the benefit of the "light hand" of Sidney Hillman, have between them made a vital contribution to the American conception of "industrial government," a contribution, although, as said above, which may still be something of the "music of the future," but which, be it noted, of itself has no quarrel with private capitalism.

THE "COMMON LAW OF THE JOB"

The garment unions have employed the Voluntary Umpire System to stimulate a most comprehensive "common law of the job," by a steady accretion and case by case. While with the older unions the pressure for a greater and greater job control by the union coupled with a fuller and fuller recognition of what amounts to the worker's property right in his job was on the whole an intermittent act and occurred only at agreement renegotiations, it became with the garment unions a continuous and systematized drive. The litigation brought to the "impartial chairman" for adjudication tended to center on the sort of cases through which these rights, both of the union and of the individual member, would be assured a luxurious growth. About a dozen years ago, speaking before the Silver Jubilee Convention of the Institute of Labour Management of Great Britain on the subject of "Some Problems of Industrial Government in America," the writer had the following to say as regards the job control by American unions as a whole and by the garment trades unions in particular.

Another consequence of the same basic psychological phenomenon is the greater insistence by American unionists as compared with your own upon "job control," namely, the taking over as far as the employers will let them the function of job administrators. Since American labour finds it difficult to organise and stay organised, the organisers naturally reach out for the domination of the jobs in order to strengthen their union organisations. This is best illustrated in the unionised print shops, where the employers must deal with the employees exclusively through the foremen, but the foremen must belong to the union, and should an employee be discharged it is the union that sits in judgment between the foreman and the discharged employee. One might say that the American printers have thus realised something resembling a job dictatorship. However, they are perfectly willing to negotiate with the employers on matters of wages, hours and other working conditions.

Yet I do not want to give the impression that unionism in America is tyrannical and oblivious of the common interest of employers and employed. The unions in the garment trades, such as the International Ladies' Garment Workers' Union and the Amalgamated Men's Clothing Workers, have arrived at the most advanced form of union-management cooperation precisely by travelling the route of job control. In these industries the unions have, in fact, attained for their members what amounts to a property right in their jobs. But precisely because these unions have made such a thoroughgoing conquest in their respective fields, have they come to feel a heartfelt interest in the prosperity of their respective industries. For these unionists as practical men have no desire to be "job poor" as some folks are "land-poor." Property in the job is meaningless if the job is dormant owing to chronic trade depression, and they therefore take the strongest interest in promoting the efficiency and prosperity of their industry. But such union-management cooperation could

never have come to pass had not the union felt complete confidence
of its acceptance as an institution in the industry. It is only under
such conditions that a union will consent to forego many of its
restrictive policies and develop a positive efficiency-promoting
programme.[15]

ANTICIPATING THE WELFARE STATE

The Protocol of Peace and the Hart Schaffner and Marx
agreements, of 1910 and 1911 respectively, virtually confronted
a void in the area filled in the advanced European communities by protective labor legislation and social insurance. In
the garment trades with their sweatshops the biggest lack was
shop sanitation. Accordingly, it is cheering to be able to state
that the most successful new institution under the new dispensation of the Protocol was the Joint Board of Sanitary
Control under the devoted ministration of Dr. George M.
Price.

Another substitution of "agreement law" for statute law
was in the domain of what we now designate social security.
Unemployment, the greatest menace for all wage earners, old
and young, was given priority. In the America of the 1920's,
still confident that its free enterprise system yielded the perfect society, the rise of industrial unemployment funds by
agreement between employers and unions, as in the Chicago
men's clothing industry and other garment trades, was exotic
to the point of the sensational. A national leader in one of
those unions observed with satisfaction that an employer's
consent to contribute two or three per cent of his payroll
towards an unemployment or pension fund meant more in
making the country aware of that union's prowess and significance than the winning of a raise in wages several times
the size.

[15] *Labour Management*, January, 1939, p. 15.

All in all, this sort of pioneering by the garment unions made two distinct contributions — one on the substantive side, in paving the way for the compulsory system under the Social Security law under Roosevelt, and another one on the instrumental side, in foreshadowing the resort to "social security by agreement" in the post-war period when labor, having found Congress reluctant even to carry out the provisions of the original Act as regards the stepping up of the contributions scale, turned to relying on its bargaining power in securing the old age pensions which have suddenly assumed such a high place in labor's hierarchy of wishes.

A Union Guardianship of an Industry

The New Unionists began with the Kautskian conception, so authoritative in the days of the Russian Revolution of 1905, of the part the Proletariat was to play. The economy was controlled by its own laws of growth and evolution and the proletariat, although the first to feel the discomfort of a leaking roof and broken window-panes while the structure was still under capitalist ownership and management, was under a sworn duty not to take on any mending jobs but to await the "Day After" the "Revolution" to step into its great rôle of architect and builder of a brand new structure, the structure of the socialist economy. Capitalism's own evolution, spurred by the capitalists' profit motive, will have prepared the required building material in the shape of concentrated productive units. That the "proletariat" might have deliberately to substitute itself for the immanent forces of history and to control the shape of the economy even this side of the "Revolution" was a totally unexpected "poser." Yet such was the task confronting the "proletariat" of the American garment trades, notably in women's wear. In that industry fate had decreed that the "proletariat" assume a guardianship

over the industry and a hegemony long before any such transfer of "title" — to safeguard the elementary interests of the
wage earners.

The main trouble was that the law of the concentration of
capital was not working as it should. Towards the end of the
century production in factory units seemed on the way to
becoming the standard way, but then the "wheel of history"
turned backward with the factory yielding to the sweatshop.
Whereas, in "normal" industries labor was getting a free ride
from the economic spontaneity, here labor was to become a
mere draft horse for day-to-day tasks before it could even
dream of performing as history's race horse.

Space forbids going into detail. Suffice it to point out the
International Ladies' Garment Workers Union's "new industrial program" in the twenties, whereby the union through
its control over the labor supply would forcibly concentrate
the industry; the heart-break-house task in apprehending
and bringing back "runaway" shops; the protection of the
metropolitan centers of production from having their and
the union's foundation sapped by the rise of new centers;
the union's concern over the industry "pricing itself out of
the market" and initiative in lowering costs as Hillman's
X-Plan in Hart Schaffner and Marx in the middle twenties;
and, finally, the union being obliged to throw lifesaving belts
to foundering employers in the shape of financial aid. Con-
trasting their own manifold and extra tasks with that of
other unions, it is a wonder that garment trades unionism has
not developed something analagous to a "minority group"
consciousness. Here one might be tempted to employ the
Russian proverb about "poor Makar" on whom "all the pine-
cones are falling," if one did not know how buoyant a group
these garment labor leaders really are and also that mental
depression is only the lot of those who feel crushed by their
task.

IV

NEW SERVICES TO THE MEMBERSHIP

As this paper aims to show, primarily in terms of social theory, how these Jewish-officered and Jewish-manned unions became integrated into the wider American movement and what "dowry" they brought into the common household, it seems unnecessary to go into a description of the numerous activities and services to the membership whereby they have almost reproduced the comprehensive manner in which the medieval gilds enveloped the lives of their members. Who has not heard of the pioneering by Fannia Cohn, the secretary of the Workers' Education Department of the International Ladies' Garment Workers' Union, in workers' education, and of what the same union has done to provide recreational facility, such as the Unity House? Or of the achievements of the Amalgamated Men's Clothing Workers in co-operative housing and in operating banks not indeed to pursue an objective, such as "workers' control of industry," by the route of investment, the star to which labor was invited to hitch its wagon in the same twenties, but to render services to members which other banks were not in a position to render or would not render, such as guaranteeing cash transfers to relatives in the still war-torn countries, or extending to members small personal loans at no higher rates of interest than banks charged to businessmen.

V

EXPERIMENTS IN POLITICS

Perhaps the most spectacular "repeat experiment" by the Jewish unions of what had been carried out by the Gompers-led unions in earlier times has been with political action.

Gompers had rejected a labor party or any third partyism, having observed the lightmindedness with which the Lassalleans, Singletaxers, Populists, and other ideological politicians have toyed with the inner solidarity of the trade unions which they had in tow, in utter disregard of the latters' fragility from the religious, cultural, and ethnic diversity of their membership. Also, Gompers had had a good lesson in American constitutional law from the misspent effort to lift the conditions of cigarmaking by statutory enactment as well as a lesson in politicians' mores in this effort and in others. To him, after this enlightenment, the game of politics was scarcely worth the candles, to put it most mildly. For limited though urgent objectives, anti-injunction laws heading the list, "collective bargaining" with the established parties seemed to be the road of the least risk to the stability of the organization as well as holding the promise of possible *immediate* gain. Hence, with "great expectations" scarcely cherished, he was ready to acclaim the Clayton Act of 1914 with its procedural modifications of the injunction as Labor's Magna Charta.

By contrast, the New Unionists' fealty to the socio-political conception of the labor program, originally Gompers' source of inspiration as well, proved with them far too deeply rooted to be easily discarded. Their longer sojourn inside the socialist chrysalis has impressed upon them the belief that when, at long last, American labor will seize its history-determined rôle and take America's destiny into its own hands, that miraculous non-miracle will transpire under a Socialist Party or at least a Labor Party formation. Consequently, it was not until the Socialist Party was completely derailed by the World War and the October Revolution that the New Unionism took to political action under its own colors and its direct leadership. In the 1924 LaFollette presidential campaign, the old Socialist Party tutelage appeared over for good. But it was the New Deal that really brought out new configurations undreamed of in the earlier and simpler age — configurations kept open at either end, towards an eventual labor party or towards a stable partnership with the Roosevelt forces in the Democratic party. The advance by the American Labor Party in 1936 beyond Gompers' "limited scope political bargaining in politics" was more in the larger size of the political investment, in the ingenuity of the device of the same names on both tickets, the Democratic and the American Labor, and in the surrender to the charisma of the Leader of the New Deal than in an espousal of a radically different political method.

The American Labor Party was obviously designed in part to abate the repugnance of those to whom the Democratic label spelled Tammany, especially to mobilize for Roosevelt (and Lehman) the socialist and independent vote. Third Partyites, notably the old-line Socialists who still cherished the dream of beholding with their own eyes an American *replica* of the socialistic British Labour Party, could go on dreaming their dream, while "collective bargainers in politics" could watch with relish the mounting prospects of great objectives to be attained immediately. As is frequently the case with subtly conceived plans and compromises, what finally came about was quite the unforeseen — the Party's eventual capture by the Communists and the rise of the Dubinsky-led Liberal Party as a successful salvaging operation. Once more the Gompers diagnosis was validated by the failure of either Labor party to spread beyond New York.

The partnership of the New Unionists and the Roosevelt forces became a national by-word in the 1944 "Clear it with Sidney" campaign. Again, as in the arena of industrial government, the New Unionists, now half in the A. F. of L. and half in the C. I. O. and heading the Political Action Committee of the latter, showed how that which was in essence among Gompers' original findings in his experiment with the "whole of

America," admitted of a more far-reaching and more flexible use than practiced by his titular successors, when hands, at once skilled and bold, such as Hillman's, were at the right moment at the helm of things.

In view of the close intertwining between political action and ideology, the following should carry great weight.

The recently deceased Abraham Cahan was indisputably the pathfinder for the laborized Jewish immigration. For the greater length of his extraordinary activity as mass educator through his newspaper and as counsellor to leaders, he was a devoted socialist. It, therefore, speaks worlds for the fundamental affinity between the native American liberalism in the tradition of Jefferson, Lincoln, Wilson, and Roosevelt and the soul of the immigration which has been in great measure conditioned by the pre-Soviet revolutionary ideals of Russia, to have William E. Bohn, the distinguished editor of the *New Leader*, bring out the following in his "Abraham Cahan, A Great American":

> I cannot think of Abe Cahan without recalling one great scene, some months after Roosevelt had started on his New Deal. The Socialists, believing in a set of inherited stereotypes, thought that nothing good could come out of a "capitalist" party. Before a great gathering of Socialists at Madison Square Garden, Abe Cahan, just returned from Europe, bluntly told all of the assembled theorists that they ought to give up their slogans and support Roosevelt in his concrete proposals. I can picture him standing there, the little man of the wide platform, saying plainly, in simple words, what he had to say. No one thinking back to that time can realize what a shock he sent through that crowd.[16]

As regards the ideological "forest change" in the mass mind of Jewish-American labor, to use Frederick Jackson Turner's phrase, although the use of this term in this connection

[16] In the issue for September 17, 1951.

should be unexpected, to say the least, the following is of significance:

> A matter of especial interest to the student of industrial relations is the re-emphasis that this highly developed collective bargaining system places upon the difference in function and interest existing between the entrepreneur and his workers. In the coat and suit industry, while the union, of course, steps in to curb the exercise of managerial power at many points (that is, regarding discipline, the contractor relationship, and working conditions) generally it displays not the slightest interest in, because it has not the slightest motive for, disturbing the traditional business functions of investment, risk-bearing, product differentiation, and individual marketing. The union is interested in questions of efficiency and of technological innovation because these are factors closely connected with the industry's capacity to pay wages and because some employers appear to show insufficient concern for such matters. It is interested in the general price level indirectly, because of the close connection with wages. Nevertheless, the disparity between functions of management and those of labor are so fully accepted by the union that any likelihood of union usurpation of the characteristic managerial responsibilities, whether by evolution or revolution, is remote indeed. For one thing, sharing the relatively low profits of management is scarcely of interest to the union, since by raising the level of wages by a moderate percentage it stands to increase the workers' earnings by an amount exceeding total profits. Advocates of worker participation in management will be well advised to make some important exceptions in the apparel trades. Labor's interests are certain to bear more closely on the state of the industry as a whole rather than upon the direction of the individual firm. Through its effects upon labor costs, the union surely exerts a powerful influence on the price structure of the industry and in that manner may be said to share responsibility for the effects of the latter upon output. But this in no way implies that the union wants to go into business. Its interest in market control, important as it may be, arises directly from its interest in higher wages.[17]

[17] D. E. Robinson, *Collective Bargaining and Market Control in the New York Coat and Suit Industry* (New York: Columbia University Press, 1950), pp. 217-218.

VI

THE GARMENT TRADES UNIONS IN THE GREATEST CONSTITUTIONAL CRISIS OF THE AMERICAN LABOR MOVEMENT

The garment trades unions have pioneered for the other unions of the land in open-handedness to the cause of aiding the unorganized and the grievously exploited to get on their own feet. When the Amalgamated Men's Clothing Workers' Union, then only five years old and of "illegitimate origin" so far as the book of the A. F. of L. was concerned, gave in 1919 to William Z. Foster a check for $100,000 in aid to the steel strike he was leading as Gompers' man, it set a precedent for itself and the other needle trade unions. In a way, it was in pursuit of two traditions, the old Jewish one of free giving for the "ransoming of captives" and the younger socialist one of the solidarity of all workers. Yet the main theme in this section of this paper is not a test of the heart but of the head. How much grasp have these unions shown of how the American labor movement was being held together and of the existing dichotomy in it, or at least the juxtaposition of stability and expansion? This calls for an analysis of the "government" in the wider movement as it affected the above dichotomy when the New Deal made expansion into the mass production industries at long last possible.

Thirteen years ago, in the same year when the C. I. O. became the Congress of Industrial Organization instead of the Committee for Industrial Organization, but four months before that decisive event, the author wrote the following in the *Saturday Review of Literature*,[18] and will now quote from it at length in order to make plain his criterion in passing judgment on the statesmanship shown by those who were

[18] April 23, 1938, pp. 12–13.

leading the unions of our special interest in that, the greatest
crisis of American Labor history:

The current crisis in the American labor movement has already
inspired a not inconsiderable literature. It is only to be expected
that the dominant note in most of the recent output, both books
and magazine articles, should be that at long last American unionism
has reacted "normally" to its capitalist environment, in repeating
the behavior of British unionism fifty years earlier. But the problem
is why British labor was able to absorb its "new unionism" without
an internal catastrophe, whereas here we have an ever sharpening
civil war threatening the effectiveness if not the existence of both
the "old" and the "new" unionism. It will not do to lay the blame
on reactionary or adventurist leadership (depending on factional
viewpoint), or to fall back upon the oft-asserted predilection of
the English for "constitutional" procedure.

To people on the outside, the labor movement is either a
potential instrument to enact a new social order along the lines
of their own particular blueprint, or a truculent unionism of the
"more now" variety. Neither view is conscious of the labor
movement as a "going government," its dominant problem being
how much or how little to govern its constituent organizations.
On the whole the degree to which a labor movement in a given
country operates as such a "government" is determined by the
degree of class consciousness which, as a psychologically cementing
influence, acts as an effective substitute for the mechanical process
of governing. It is here that the difference in the governments of
the labor movements of Britain and America lies. British labor
can afford to permit competing unions in the same craft as well
as competition for members between craft unions and an industrial
union, since there is a common class consciousness among British
workers which acts to avert disastrous internecine war and above
all treasonable alliances with the employers by one union against
a rival union. Accordingly, British unionism has never made its
central organization, the Trades Union Congress, into an agency
to keep order by allotting definite jurisdictions to each union. Not
internal government but external policy — pressure on Parliament —
has been the *raison d'être* of the Trades Union Congress.

*   *   *   *

The governmental evolution of American labor was different. At the time when new unionism began to grip England, the labor movement here took shape as the American Federation of Labor. This organization arose on the ruins of the Knights of Labor, a centralized body constantly given to interfering in the affairs of the trades. The founding fathers of the A. F. of L., especially Samuel Gompers, naturally emphasized the right of the affiliated unions to unhindered self-government. But as a matter of fact it was the menace of "dualism," namely the menace of organizations under the Knights of Labor engaging in cut-throat competition with the craft unions, that had caused the latter to form a defensive alliance in the American Federation of Labor and above all made them endow that organization with the all-overshadowing function of protecting jurisdictions. Thus while Gompers and his associates kept speaking of the Federation as if it were a perfect anarchist commune which any union was free to join or quit at will, from the beginning the Federation has really functioned as a government, the sole source of all jurisdictional grants and their supreme defender. Instead of being, like the British federation, merely an arena for ideological disputes and for formulating labor's demands on the country, the American Federation has acted as a governing entity.

It stands to reason that, in an organization thus constituted, a demand for structural changes in the union movement necessarily involves the basic governmental function of the Federation and is therefore likely to evoke a constitutional crisis. For here issues of strategy and personalities, explosive materials in themselves, are fatally commingled with the problems of maintaining orderly government. To the open-eyed observer the most startling element in the A. F. of L.-C. I. O. war has not been the *élan* of the newer organization but the solidification of the ranks in the older organization, and the spirit of resistance to the bitter end among the very groups in the A. F. of L. ideologically sympathetic to industrial unionism. This did not happen at once, but only as the issue became the defense of the established governmental procedure of the Federation. Progressives and socialists began to prefer conservative government to disruption and anarchy.

*   *   *   *

If the A. F. of L. is a "lost cause," where does its resistance power come from? Are its defenders not doomed to failure in this age of machine technology and mass production demanding a class-conscious labor movement and unionism by industry? Is not there anything in the theory of the survival of the fittest? The answer is that one must not become overwhelmed by the sole importance of the technological factor in determining the fitness or unfitness of a labor movement. Labor is hardly headed for a metamorphosis into an unskilled factory proletariat. The idea that it is so is a survival from early Marxism. Whether the real, deep-seated aspirations of those who joined the new C. I. O. unions differ from those of craft unionists is more than open to question. Both movements can well be explained on the basis of a job consciousness without assuming any revolutionary class consciousness. Both are thinking above all in terms of job control and of normal agreements with the employers. Moreover, in the heat of the battle the banners are becoming strangely interchanged as are the arguments advanced before labor boards. Federation representatives are found organizing industrial unions, and C. I. O. lawyers are found arguing against elections by entire plants.

On the issue of labor in politics and reliance on labor legislation, the differences are likewise exaggerated by the exigencies of factional maneuvering. It is noteworthy that the Federation's attack on the National Labor Relations Board was not followed up by a demand for a congressional investigation.[19] Obviously, the Federation aims to influence the Board rather than destroy it, and with it the very valuable governmental promotion of unionism. Also a return to the Federation's policy of the twenties, with its almost exclusive reliance on economic action and its shyness of politics, is out of the question under a "reconstructed" Supreme Court and a contracting capitalist economy which forces the government to take up the slack.

Nor is there any appreciable difference in their respective fighting effectiveness. Where the C. I. O. has the advantage of a more flexible and more inventive strategy, the older organization derives strength from its more ready acceptance by the middle classes, which so far as labor is concerned will more easily forgive violence that does not advertise itself as revolutionary than they will overlook a revolutionary label even if pasted on by an enemy. The plea for unity raised by President Dubinsky and others is well supported

---

[19] In this regard the author admits failure as a forecaster of events. However, the content of the next sentence has fared better.

by searching analysis. A labor movement which for over fifty years has lived as a unified government will never again see peace if it continues as two rival labor sovereignties. What is in store in the absence of peace is an endless succession of drawn battles rather than an Appomattox.

On this test, assuming that the "teacher" is justified in "grading" on the basis of a criterion elaborated in an old "lecture," which the "students" in question have *not* attended, David Dubinsky, Max Zaritzky and their co-workers score one hundred per cent. It goes without saying that these leaders need to offer no additional proof of their devotion to the cause of organizing the unorganized. All the more reason why their decision not to follow John L. Lewis in smashing the unity of the American labor movement even for the sacred cause of more unionization was a conclusive demonstration of responsible intelligence sitting in the driver's seat.

The leading rôle of these unions in saving the remnants of the European labor movements smashed by the fascists, in re-building those same movements after the war, and in promoting the new International of democratic unions is too well known to claim any space in this already over-long exposition.

VII

PROSPECTS

We have dealt with a complex and evolving phenomenon resulting from a merger of two unique labor culture streams, each with its long antecedents and with its own ideational drives. To the Jewish labor movement the general American movement was simultaneously a parallel labor movement continually adapting itself to succeed in the perennial task of surviving in the rather inclement American climate and also in itself a major contact area of that American environment. What grew out of that contact was no "inter-penetration of opposites" of the Hegel-Marx book, but a "cross fertilization of cultures," to use a famous sociologist's phrase. So much for the near-miracle of the New Unionism which so thoroughly confuted the pessimism of both John R. Commons and Beatrice Webb about the Jew's ability to be a good unionist. But what about this near-miracle enduring? The Jewish leadership seems to have realized that the Jewish parents' passion to lift their children to a higher status than their own is in a fair way of validating a part of Mrs. Webb's psychological diagnosis, even if the undercurrent of disgust in her verdict has been exposed as a piece of probably unintended callousness.

It appears as though the still Jewish leadership is watching the draining away of the original Jewish membership as the Jews are getting out of the labor ranks in the industry to be replaced by those of Italian and the Slavic nationalities as well as by Negroes, Mexicans, and Puerto Ricans, and large numbers of old-stock Americans in the provinces, with an ambivalent reaction. As members of the ethnic group with the longest record of persecution and adverse discrimination, they cannot but feel great pride in their own clear record on the minorities issue as when judged by the test of deed. It is doubtful that there is another union milieu where a Negro feels as much at home. Yet it raises the question of whether leaders from these newer groups will possess the capacity — not the so-called innate capacity which remains an insoluble mystery, but the one engendered by historical experience and by long cultural self-determination as a social group — to step into the places of Hillman, Dubinsky and their like. Yet it may even be harmful to speculate on this matter. Here our faith in the human spirit with its potentialities enhanced by democratic opportunity should be adequate to keep our hope afloat.

Jewish Immigrants in Business: A Sociological Study

BY MOSES KLIGSBERG

INTRODUCTION

1. Methodological Note

We propose to investigate the influence of *Iddishkeit* [Jewishness] on the attitudes and behavior of Jews in business. Let us however, first clarify the question itself. Obviously, *Iddishkeit* does not affect the Jew in the sense that, prior to entering into a commercial exchange or venture, he consults the Bible, Talmud or *Shulḥan Arukh* for the appropriate pattern of behavior in the given case. The Jew, in buying and selling carries no handy little Biblical reference to guide him around the pitfalls of business enterprise. *Iddishkeit* may influence the behavior of a Jewish businessman, but it would be idle to seek any such influence in the direct, conscious utilization of canonized texts. We must, instead, focus on his living ethnic heritage: the folkways and mores, the pattern of living which, transmitted from generation to generation, manifest themselves in a spontaneous, unconscious, "natural," so to speak, manner. It is indeed the case that one's *Iddishkeit* may be the immediate and direct cause of a specific situation. Thus, for example, a Jewish businessman is confronted with the problem of whether or not to keep his business open on the Sabbath. This conflict of interests between economics and beliefs, important and characteristic as it is, does not, however, constitute the crux of our problem.

Our investigation will be limited to eastern European Jewish immigrants. Arriving in America as adults, their "Jewish personality" had already been molded. It is, therefore, necessary for us briefly to consider some important aspects of the general character of *Iddishkeit* as it was lived in the old country. This will provide us with a frame of reference within which the findings of our study can be placed.

The ideal procedure would be to observe a number of Jewish businessmen over a substantial time period, attempting to discover the existence of characteristics specific to this group. We might then be able to trace logically any such patterns to their Jewish heritage. This is well nigh impossible. Fortunately, there is available a body of data the use of which is a highly satisfactory substitute procedure. The Yivo Institute for Jewish Research of New York has in its possession a large collection of autobiographies of Jewish immigrants.[1] These were composed for purposes other than those of the present study. Hence we can avoid a chief danger such material generally presents, namely, that the writer, aware of the theme of the study and of its implications, may unconsciously tend to succumb to the temptations of self-congratulation, or at another extreme, of apologetics. Though one may entertain reservations about the utility of autobiographies for this type of research in general,[2] there

---

[1] In 1942, the Yiddish Scientific Institute — YIVO (now the Yivo Institute for Jewish Research) of New York, sponsored a contest for Jewish immigrants in America and Canada. The theme of the paper to be submitted was: "Why I Left the Old Country, and What I Have Achieved in America." In the announcement of the contest, the Institute made it clear to the prospective participants, that in order to give a clear and detailed account of this subject, it was necessary for them to compose a complete autobiography. Details of the contest were published in the Yiddish and Anglo-Jewish press. The nearly 250 contestants, almost without exception, complied with the request to submit an autobiographical account, the entries averaging 100 pages. In subsequent years, YIVO collected similar essays, and the total number of autobiographies now are over 300. In 1952, YIVO sponsored a supplementary contest, limited to those who had already submitted essays. The purpose of this was to have the writers bring their entries up to date, accounting for the war and post-war years, 1942–1952. There were some sixty supplementary essays submitted. The great majority of the contestants belonged to the secular sector of the Jewish immigrant population and were predominantly workingmen and artisans. There were, however, a sizable number of people from the traditionally religious environment and also a number of businessmen.

[2] For the use of autobiography in social science research, see John Dollard, *Criteria for the Life-History* (New Haven: Yale University Press, 1935); Gordon W. Allport, *The Use of Personal Documents in Psychological Science* (New York: Social Science Research Council, 1942); Louis Gottschalk, Clyde Kluckhohn and Robert Angell, *The Use of Personal Documents in History, Anthropology and Sociology* (New York: Social Science Research Council, 1945); Moses Kligsberg, "Socio-psychological Problems Reflected in the Yivo Autobiography Contest," *Yivo Annual for Jewish Social Research*, vol. I (New York, 1946); Moses Kligsberg, "The Golden Land: the Jewish Immigrant in America: Self-Portrait," *Commentary*, vol. V, no. 5 (May, 1948), pp. 467–471; Moses Kligsberg, *Child and Adolescent Behavior Under Stress: An Analytical Topical Guide to Collection of Autobiographies of Jewish Young Men and Women in Poland (1932–1939) in the Possession of the Yivo Institute for Jewish Research* [prepared under a grant from the United States Department of Health, Education and Welfare, Public Health Service, National Institutes of Health] (Yivo Institute for Jewish Research, 1965); Max Weinreich, *Der Veg tsu Undzer Yugnt* [The Approach to Our Youth] (Vilna: Yivo, 1935).

is little doubt that the authors' self-consciousness with regard to commercial behavior patterns was minimal. It seems safe to assume that the material relating to this area is not particularly subject to distortion.

Adult Jewish immigrants, much as all other immigrants, arrived on our shores, their personalities having been formed by a particular social and ethnic environment. Thrust into the often diametrically opposite conditions of American life, the old patterns came under the impact of intense disintegrative pressures. Some of the more superficial and external ones were shed rapidly; others underwent modification; still others were maintained well-nigh intact. The pace and scope of the process of adaptation was wholly individual, and took different forms. In order to comprehend the metamorphosis of a particular individual, it is necessary to review briefly the relevant aspects of the former style of life, establishing a base line from which change can be measured and evaluated.

The ethnic heritage of which we have spoken hitherto was the *passive* part of the spiritual baggage of the immigrant. In addition, he brought with him an active set of goals and aspirations: the Jewish immigrant came to America not merely to live with greater ease. He arrived with a powerful urge to achieve a goal, and with the dynamism appropriate to such an urge. It is immaterial whether he was aware of this, or whether he rationalized his emigration by assigning other motives for leaving his home.

For general background on East European Jewish history, see Salo W. Baron, *The Russian Jew under Tsars and Soviets* (New York: Macmillan Co., 1964).

For general background on Jewish emigration to the United States, see Oscar and Mary Handlin, "A Century of Jewish Immigration to the United States," *American Jewish Year Book*, vol. L (Philadelphia, 1949), pp. 1–84; Liebmann Hersch, "Jewish Emigration during the Last 100 Years," *Algemayne Entsiklopedye* [Yiddish], *Volume Yidn I* (Paris, 1939), pp. 441–482; Samuel Joseph, *Jewish Immigration to the United States From 1881–1910* (New York: Columbia University Press, 1914), and Mark Wischnitzer, *To Dwell in Safety: The Story of Jewish Migration since 1800* (Philadelphia: Jewish Publication Society of America, 1948).

For social and cultural patterns, see Louis Finkelstein, ed., *The Jews, Their History, Culture and Religion*, 2 vols., third edition (New York: Harpers, 1960), pp. 376–426, 1234–1253, 1536–1596 and 1694–1735; Nathan Glazer, "What Sociology Knows about American Jews," *Commentary*, vol. IX, no. 3 (March, 1950), pp. 275–284; Nathan Glazer and Daniel P. Moynihan, *Beyond the Melting Pot* (Cambridge, Mass.: Massachusetts Institute of Technology and Harvard University Press, 1963); Oscar Handlin, *Adventure in Freedom: Three Hundred Years of Jewish Life in America* (New York: McGraw-Hill, 1954), Oscar I. Janowsky, ed., *The American Jew: A Reappraisal* (Philadelphia: Jewish Publication Society of America, 1964), pp. 27–52, 53–74, 339–359 and 385–399; and Marshall Sklare, ed., *The Jews: Social Patterns of an American Group* (Glencoe, Ill.: The Free Press, 1958), pp. 4–22, 138–146, 451–474, 493–502, 520–534 and 560–594.

2. The Goal of the Immigrants

Let us first consider this last point. Our thesis regarding the centrality of an active set of goals in emigration stands in direct contradiction to the generally accepted, "classic" explanation of Jewish emigration. According to the latter, eastern European Jews were motivated to emigrate en masse to America, at least as of the eighties of the last century, primarily by poverty and persecution. This explanation rests on the superficially compelling evidence that the first great wave of emigration came in the wake of the pogroms of 1881 in Russia; the second wave followed the pogroms of 1903 and the upheaval resulting from the Russo-Japanese war in 1904. It does not account for the emigration upsurge during the subsequent years which were years relatively pacific, including also the "quiet" years between the catastrophes.[3]

The notion that people flee starvation and pogroms is, on the surface, a most logical one. However, under careful scrutiny, it fails to stand up as an explanation of emigration, becoming less and less adequate as further research brings new facts to light. In the first place, the large numbers emigrating from Galicia (in Austria-Hungary) during the same period were proportionately as great a part of the Jewish population as those who left the Czarist Empire. Though the poverty in Galicia was as oppressive as in Russia, this backward province was free of pogroms and oppressive decrees. Secondly, the number of emigrants in the wake of a catastrophe such as that of 1881 or 1903 was but a small percentage of those who were affected by it. The victims of hunger and persecution were far greater in number, at all times, than those who emigrated.

[3] This is evidenced clearly by the statistics of Jewish emigration to the United States. In the year 1882, the first complete year after the wave of Russian pogroms, 13,202 persons entered; in 1883 — 8,731; in 1884 — 11,445; in 1885 — 16,862. If the pogroms were the principal cause for the emigration from Russia, then logically the wave of emigration should have receded and not continued to rise as we see from the aforementioned figures. In the subsequent years, the number of emigrants were as follows: from 1886 to 1890 — 137,089 persons (an annual average of 27,400); from 1891 to 1895 — 218,463 persons (an annual average of 43,700), etc. After the Kishinev pogrom of 1903 and the Russo-Japanese War in 1904, the emigration wave jumped from 76,203 in 1903 to 106,236 in 1904. But this rise continued up to 1908 with an annual average of 128,770. It declined in 1909, but, thereafter, it continued to rise from 1910 up to World War I in 1914. We observe here a fluctuation that shows no parallelism between the waves of emigration and the especially high incidence of anti-Jewish outbreaks in Russia. More readily one may state that it was the economic conditions in the United States that motivated such emigration, for it should be noted from general immigration data that the rise of Jewish emigration to this country paralleled the general trend of emigration to the United States of other ethnic groups.

The "catastrophe" theory, moreover, distorts the rôle played by persecution in Jewish life. Persecution, discrimination and disfranchisement were an integral part, so to speak, of Jewish life in Europe in the course of nearly a millenium. The theological conception of the Exile aided the Jew in bearing the bitterness of his lot: the Jews were exiled from the Holy Land as a just punishment for the transgressions of Israel against the laws and commandments of the Lord. The Gentiles who persecute the Jews are not to be held personally accountable; they are but the divine instruments of His will, the means whereby He as a Father chastises His Chosen People. Salvation must await the coming of the Messiah; this is the case irrespective of the geographic location of Jews. The profound inner acceptance of this metaphysical-theological conception of Exile, in which the sufferings of Israel are seen as part of the divinely-ordained world order, lightened the burden of persecution *subjectively* experienced by the devout Jew. Being the will of God, anguish was borne with great fortitude.

It is, furthermore, an historical fact that in the course of centuries, the disfranchisement of the Jews was increasingly, albeit slowly, diminished. Their lot notably improved following the period of emancipation, particularly in the second half of the nineteenth century. It is important to bear in mind that the sense of deprivation and injustice is fundamentally subjective; in large part, it is measured not by objective, absolute standards, but by subjective comparisons. One will feel good or bad today relative to one's feelings yesterday. Jewish disfranchisement was indeed great in the last quarter of the nineteenth century; there is, however, no doubt that the lot of the Jews had markedly improved in comparison with the situation of a generation or two prior thereto, not to speak of earlier times.

It does not, therefore, stand to reason that, precisely at a time when the fate of the Jews took a decided turn for the better, *de jure* and *de facto*, Jews suddenly began to feel the pressure of discrimination and disfranchisement more than ever before, and turned to seek greater freedom by emigrating to a distant, unknown world and sever their bonds with the *Kehillah* [Jewish community] and one's folks. The theory that persecution was the primary motivation — there is no doubt that it played a considerable part as a catalyst — for the mass emigration of the end of the nineteenth century must be rejected.

Nor does the factor of poverty and hunger account for emigration any more adequately. It has already been mentioned that the number of those who suffered from poverty and hunger was vastly greater than the number of emigrants. Secondly, those who emigrated were by no means the most poverty-stricken. The costs of the long journey were, in those days, prohibitive for many. There is sufficient evidence to contend unhesitatingly that it was not the poorest, but the somewhat better off, who emigrated. Though poverty, too, provided a stimulus, it was not the major factor in the mass migration.

What, then, were the dominant motives which account for this vast population movement? In order to answer this question, we must turn to a consideration of several outstanding motifs of the Jewish way of life and of the mentality of the members of the Jewish community of eastern Europe. (These characteristics are, perhaps, true of Jews in general.)

3. "Takhlis" in the Life of the Jew and in the Old Country Environment

From the very earliest childhood days, there was one word with which the Jew in eastern Europe was constantly confronted. It inevitably came to be a guiding principle throughout his life. This was the concept of תכלית [takhlis]. The word comes from the Hebrew root meaning to "complete, finish, end, accomplish, fulfill, consume." As it was used by eastern European Jewry, takhlis refers to an orientation toward a final outcome, i. e., towards an end-goal. The word was heard most frequently with reference to a question of major importance, to the making of a fateful decision. It was with the aid of this concept that final decisions were made in matters central to a person's future. וואס וועט זיין דער תכלית ["Vos vet zayn der takhlis?" ("What will the takhlis be?")] — this was invariably the crucial question which led to the fateful conclusion. Immediate benefits or hedonistic satisfaction of the moment were always secondary considerations. The important question was: to what will this step lead, what will be achieved thereby in terms of an end-goal, what will the takhlis be? Faced with the question of the future of one's child, for example, the principle of takhlis was the basis of the decision taken. A comfortable, easy and relatively well paid opening might easily be rejected in the event that one did not foresee it leading to a takhlis. On the other hand, one did not hesitate choosing long years of deprivation, hunger, and loneliness, far from home, in a yeshiva or apprenticeship, were one convinced that it led to a takhlis. Satisfaction and utility in the here and now would always defer to the end-goal and to the road thereto — as difficult as it might not be — to the way which would lead to a final achievement in life, to a takhlis.

Many individual phenomena of Jewish life can be more adequately comprehended by considering the rôle and function of the *takhlis* principle. Let us take, for example, the phenomenon of sobriety. Drunkenness, as is well known, never took root among Jews. It would be utterly naïve and nonsensical to attribute this to a moral superiority of Jews over Gentiles. It should even be noted that alcoholic consumption was by no means unknown even among orthodox Jews. No little was drunk on Purim, *Simhat Torah* and other festive occasions; among *Hassidim*, a glass of brandy was always welcome. Alcoholism as a social problem, however, was not to be found. How can this be explained? Drinking is among other things, a matter of enjoying the satisfaction of the moment, a pastime of the here and now, in and for itself, in which the Jew took little interest. He was far more concerned with the final result, in that to which the activity would lead: in other words, in the *takhlis*. Since drunkenness ultimately leads nowheres, since nought is achieved thereby, since it has no *takhlis* — the Jew seeks neither consolation nor resolution in Bacchus. Many people, caught in a difficult situation from which they see no way out, will turn to drink as a means of forgetting, of gaining momentary relief. A Jew, confronted by a painful, unhappy dilemma, were it even to occur to him to drown his sorrows in drink, would immediately ask himself: what will the *takhlis* of it be? Since it could lead to no positive resolution of the situation, but ruin the efforts to attain a *takhlis*, he would not turn in this direction. We can see no other explanation of this striking phenomenon among Jews, other than that of the predominant *takhlis*-principle, the maxim that all of one's activities must be goal-directed and lead to some positive final result, and every distraction, as luring and as attractive as it might momentarily appear, would be rejected. This was the most powerful barrier against the spread of alcoholism among Jews.

Another significant factor, — rather a psychological one — which causes Jews to avoid drunkenness, is the great respect and honor that they ascribe to the *kopf* [head], the seat of all mental faculties, the organ for learning, which is so highly regarded by Jews, and considered the most important guide towards a *takhlis*. The greatest compliment that Jews can give a child is to say that he has "a good head" [א גוטן קאפ] or that he has a "keen head for learning" [א שארפן קאפ צום לערנען]. This also applies to an adult. A person who has "a good head" is highly regarded; one has more confidence in him, and one places greater trust in him. Concerning such a gifted person, one ordinarily will declare that he will attain his *takhlis* [ער וועט שוין זיינס דערגרייכן]. For this reason, there exists among

Jews such a dislike for an individual who does not respect his head
[*kopf*] (meaning thereby his disregard for the mental faculties that
reside in the head), and which demonstrates openly his degradation
and corruption. This, in fact, happens to a drunkard who loses
control of his mental faculties and emotions, who babbles foolishly,
prattles meaninglessly and uses profane language, etc. The sight
of a drunkard stirs in a Jew a feeling of nausea. He will, therefore,
avoid any act which he deplores in others. Thus, a Jew may drink,
but he will not permit himself to lower himself to a state of ine-
briety, — that is to say, to a degradation of respected intellectual
and mental faculties and the control thereof.

The principle of *takhlis* is also one of the major factors in the
notable solidarity, strength and stability of the Jewish family. The
family is kept united by the concern for the *takhlis* of the children,
a process which goes on for years, sometimes as much as two decades.
Even in those cases where the match is not a particularly fortunate
one, the mutual concern for the children's *takhlis* is often a decisive
factor in preventing the dissolution of the family. (Quarrels and
conflicts are by no means rare between Jewish spouses, but they
seldom lead, at least in traditionally-oriented families, to a final
break because of the concern of parents for their children's *takhlis*.)

In the traditional world of eastern European Jewry, the heights
of achievement — of *takhlis* — were reached in the spheres of learning, status, and financial security. A rabbinic position was the
ultimate in achieving all three. Thus, the highest ideal of parents was
to see their son become a rabbi. תורה איז די בעסטע סחורה ["*Toireh
is di beste skhoireh*" ("Learning is the best of goods")], as the
old saying has it. Second place in the status hierarchy was taken
by the substantial merchant-scholar.[4] For that matter, the ranking

---

[4] One of the oldest and most widely-sung lullabies in eastern Europe follows:

אונטער [דעם קינדס נאמען] וויגעלע	*Unter [child's name] vigele*	Behind little [child's name] cradle
שטייט א גאלדן* ציגעלע	*Shtayt a goldn* tsigele*	Stands a little golden* goat
דאס ציגעלע איז געפארן האנדלען	*Dos tsigele is geforn handlen*	The goat has gone to trade
ראזשינקעס מיט מאנדלען	*Rozhinkes un mandlen*	In raisins and almonds
דאס איז די בעסטע סחורה	*Dos is di beste skhoireh*	This is the best trade
[דעם קינדס נאמען] וועט לערנען תורה	*[Child's name] vet lernen toireh*	Little [child's name] will study Torah.

* Another variant for גאלדן [*goldn* = golden] is וויסע [*vayse* = white]. See Judah Loeb
Cahan, *Yiddish Folksongs with Melodies* [Yiddish] (New York: Yivo Institute for Jewish
Research, 1957), items no. 328 and no. 337, pp. 305 and 313.

of any occupation was heightened considerably were its occupant
a learned man. Thus, even the *ba'al-agoleh* (teamster), the lowest of
the lowly occupations, was accorded due respect were he a true
scholar. (It will be recalled that the legend of the *Lamed-Vavniks*,
the thirty-six saintly men, invariably describes them as being of
very low rank in the occupational scale.)

This conception of *takhlis* is perhaps the most striking expression
of a unique philosophy of life. A man realizes his full significance
only in having achieved something, in having improved on something, in having advanced in his environment, or, at least in having
maintained a high standard already achieved by his milieu. There
can be neither meaning nor satisfaction in simply living one's life:
one must achieve something, get somewheres. This, it can be said,
is the core of the Jewish outlook for the individual, and underlies
the fundamental rôle of the conception of *takhlis* in the past, and
even in the present, of Jewish existence.[5]

As long as the Jewish community constituted a socially isolated
entity, i. e., as long as there existed the so-called eastern European
"ghetto,"[6] as long as all authority which mattered was an integral
part of one's own community, the limitations and restrictions upon

---

The music to the lullaby above is:

[5] The problem whether the *takhlis* maxim is rooted somewhere deeper in Jewish tradition, or has its source in the Jewish faith, i. e., in the principle of personal responsibility
[מצוות] (*miẓvot*) and מעשים טובים (*ma'asim tovim*) [fulfilling God's commandments and
the performance of good deeds] is not dealt with in this study. It deserves special treatment and further elaboration.

[6] It should be noted that this is a misleading term. Jews did not live in a ghetto in
eastern Europe (after the abolition of the legally enforced geographic concentration in
one section of a city) any more than did the Flemish in Belgium, or the Italian-speaking
inhabitants of Switzerland. They were rather a closed, historico-cultural entity, who
were also more or less territorially concentrated.

Jews had little psychological impact upon the development of the individual, and proved to be no obstacle to the realization of a *takhlis*. They were, rather, regarded as limiting natural phenomena, fixed and external, in the same category as winter, cold, storm, or natural catastrophes. One adjusted to these facts of nature; they bore no significance for the development of the individual, for his self-respect and self-evaluation.

With the gradual disintegration of the homogeneous, isolated social structure which the Jewish community had constituted, and the rise of modern, secular movements, beginning with the *Haskalah* [Enlightenment], Jewish disfranchisement took on new meaning in Jewish society, and began to play an increasingly disturbing rôle in the life of the individual. Thus, for example, as long as university studies had no value for Jews, the limitations on general education were not felt to be any hardship. At the moment, however, that large numbers of Jews began to subscribe to an increasing desirability for a secular education, the discriminations in this area were felt as insufferable burdens. Hence, the second half of the nineteenth century which, objectively, marked a decided improvement in the legal position of eastern European Jewry, was subjectively experienced as a more and more difficult period. The discriminations which had, for the daily life of the traditional Jew, been of little importance for generations on end, began to be felt as more and more painful.[7]

The barriers to achievement by Jews in the outside world were felt most acutely by those who sought a *takhlis* there. The Jew who aspired to be a rabbi or wished the status of a scholar, though aware of the existence of wicked Gentiles who harm Jews and refuse them equal rights, found this to be no hindrance to his striving for his end-goal, his *takhlis*. In contrast to such a one, he who had rejected the old *takhlis*-values, and adopted new ones, who wanted to become a doctor or a lawyer, experienced the full impact of discrimination, almost as if they had come into being just then, and had been created precisely in order to ruin his life. It was, of course, not only the young who felt this way; their parents and closer relatives, — given the intense family unity of the Jews — identi-

---

[7] With reference to education, Sholom Aleichem [Shalom Rabinowitz] has immortalized this modern situation in his literary works. See for example, his short stories "A Doctor," and "Gymnasia," and his play "It's Difficult To Be a Jew," in his *Alle Verk fun Sholom Aleikhem* (New York: Folksfond Oysgabe, 1925), vol. V, pp. 99–115, vol. XXVI, pp. 173–195, and vol. XX, pp. 9–164.

fying themselves with the aspirant, suffered as bitterly as he himself did.[8]

The goal of economic mobility belongs to the same order of phenomena. As long as wealth without learning had little worth, Jews made little attempt to seek wealth where there was no possibility for learning. Once the authority of traditional scholarship had been weakened in the eyes of many Jews, there remained little reason to adhere to the limited material potentialities of the small town and to occupations which in and of themselves promised little for their occupants and — and what was of even greater importance — which had no *takhlis* for the younger generation.

These were the motives which led to the rise of large numbers of Jews who left for another country, for a land in which disfranchisement (of long standing, but which only now had begun to be felt) did not exist. This was a land in which one could achieve a *takhlis*, and which held even greater promise for one's children.

In sum, neither poverty nor hunger nor discrimination was the *principal* motive for Jewish emigration; it was, rather, the search for *takhlis*. A Jew came to America in order to have the perspective of working himself up, of his children being able to be socially and occupationally mobile, to achieve something, to carve out an individual niche marked by positive achievements.

As for evidence of this hypothesis, there is the fact that, at first, orthodox Jews did not leave eastern Europe for America. In the early days, America was regarded as profane. Even later, when they did begin to go, at no time did they constitute a large part of the emigration. Those orthodox Jews who emigrated, moreover, were, in large measure, what may be termed *passive* emigrants, i. e., parents who went over or were brought over by their children. Had poverty been a major motivation for emigration, this would not have been the case. There is not the slightest basis for assuming that poverty was more concentrated among irreligious or semireligious Jews than among the strictly orthodox. If anything, the opposite was certainly true.

[8] The same applies in the area of social relationships. The traditional Jew makes no attempt to enter into social relationships with Gentiles, if only because of the barrier of *kashrut* [the observance of dietary laws]. He is not troubled in the least by the fact that the Gentile world may exclude him from clubs or personal relations. If anything, the contrary was true. It was precisely this type of Jew for whom this thought was furthest from his mind. It was the secular Jews, who had begun to perceive social intercourse with Gentiles as a symbol of equality of rights, who intensely felt the pressure of this type of "bigotry." In fact, this type of "discrimination" is, together with discrimination in professional education and the like, a source of some of the most intensely bitter feelings on the part of American Jews.

In other words, once the hegemony of the religious-traditional conception of *takhlis* had been displaced, and large numbers of Jews transferred their search for *takhlis* to the outside world, the old, latent restrictions began to be felt in all their intensity. Masses of Jews reacted by migrating to a new land, where these hindrances to finding a *takhlis* would not be met. They left not because of the simple desire for a bit of more bread, but for the opportunity of individual self-realization (which often meant at the cost of a lower standard of living, deprivation and bitter toil during the many years of being a "greenhorn").

It was with this spiritual baggage, that is, with the aspiration to seek a *takhlis* for oneself and, it must be stressed, even more so for one's children, that Jewish immigrant masses from eastern Europe came to America.

This fundamental concept will allow us, we believe, to comprehend more easily certain typical behavior patterns of Jewish immigrants in the United States. By referring to the experience of liberation from hunger and persecution alone, we could not possibly explain the immense dynamism and zeal which the greatest number of Jewish immigrants manifested in America. We could not thereby comprehend the patience with which they bore the immensely difficult conditions of life — the sweatshops and tenements — and the fact that so small a number returned to the old country (for which they yearned with moving nostalgia) after hunger had been stilled and the sharp pain of persecution dulled. Little can be understood by postulating only negative motives, by considering only that from which the immigrants fled. By taking into account the positive motivations — the desire to achieve real, concrete things — the conduct of the Jewish immigrants becomes far more comprehensible.

It was this impetus to achieve something concrete, to realize a *takhlis*, which brought many immigrants to business. At this point we are confronted with a further problem: Did the masses of Jews who sought their destiny in business plunge into the chase after wealth with neither moral, communal nor traditional inhibitions of any sort? Were there any internalized factors which checked, modified or channelized their behavior? We will attempt to answer this question by analyzing some of the immigrant autobiographies in the possession of the Yivo Institute for Jewish Research.

I

THREE CASE HISTORIES

1. One Man, Two Roads

We will proceed by sketching in the background in each case, of the person whose autobiography we are about to consider.

Samuel Slobod[9] [Autobiography No. 1] was born in Slutsk, White Russia in the sixties of the last century. His father, a baker by trade, was a learned man. Owning his own shop, he provided his family with a fair standard of living. Samuel attended the government-sponsored elementary school for Jews in Slutsk. After his graduation, in 1881, he was enrolled in the famous Vilna Jewish Teachers' Seminary, which turned out teachers for the government-sponsored Jewish Schools. Returning to Slutsk on vacation during the summer of 1883, Samuel was drawn into a conspiratorial group of revolutionary student youth. Before long, however, the police were on his trail. Thus forewarned, he fled to his brother's home in Riga, Latvia. Living under an assumed name, he earned his keep as a tutor, not doing badly at all. Shortly thereafter, a letter arrived from Aunt Rachel, who had emigrated to America some years before, and had found her way to Boston. It was then, Slobod writes, that

> the idea of emigrating first came into my mind . . . I couldn't sleep a wink that night. I lay and thought: To be sure, what I earn covers all my expenses and even allows me to put aside a few rubles each week. *But what will be the takhlis? Can I depend on giving lessons for an entire lifetime?*[10]

It was thus that he decided to emigrate to America. Our hero arrived in Boston, met by his Aunt Rachel, at the end of 1884.

Let us digress for a moment, and consider this Aunt Rachel, for this bears a relationship to our theme. Slobod describes his protectress as follows:

> Aunt Rachel was an Amazon of a women. An excellent *balebuste* [housekeeper], she had also been a real business-woman from her girlhood days on . . . Upon their [that is, she and her family] arrival in America . . . she loaded up with a pack of dry-goods and set out to peddle, mostly in the Irish parts of town. Before long, she was in command of English, picking it up from her customers and rolling

[9] This is a pseudonym.

[10] Chapter I, p. 26 of the autobiography. Italics by M.K.

it off her tongue with a true Irish brogue. By the time I came to America, the primitive days of peddling with a pack were over and done with. She had an established route, and supplied her customers with every item under the sun, from a pin to sets of furniture . . . After each Sabbath day had drawn to a close, and long into the night, the house looked like a tax collectors' office: men, women and children would arrive to make their weekly payments . . .

I found Uncle Yankl [Rachel's husband] contributing his bit to the family upkeep by making suspender straps . . . He used to get this work, to be done at home, from a suspender factory . . . He had never been of much use in business . . . He earned no more than a pittance. It was Aunt Rachel who was the breadwinner in this home, and upon whom the family depended.[11]

We have referred to this description because it conveys a concrete case characteristic of the traditional Jewish mode of life in eastern Europe, immortalized in literature, such as Peretz's classic tale "Mendl Braynes" ["Mendl, the husband of Brayne," i. e., a man who is identified not by his own name, but by that of his wife].[11a] It is the woman who makes a living, while the man spends his time studying sacred Scripture, engaged in the far more important task of earning his right — and on behalf of his wife as well — to an עולם הבא [olam haba (an eternal place in the heavenly realm)]. In this case, suspender making — a meaningless occupation at which he was incompetent — had replaced the Torah for Uncle Yankl, but he was undoubtedly the type who, in the old country, had spent his days and nights in study, and was unable to develop a new active, effective pattern of living.

Now to return to our hero and relate, as far as possible in his own words, the story of his early days in America. Though received with the utmost warmth by Aunt Rachel and the other members of her family, he "didn't have the patience to take it easy for a while." Learning by chance from a newspaper advertisement that longshoremen were needed in Charlestown (in Boston harbor), a few days after his arrival saw him unloading cargo. Try as they might, the family could not dissuade him from undertaking such heavy work. But several days on the docks turned the trick. Unwillingly, he followed the advice of his relatives, and became a capmaker in the shop of a distant relation. Within a few weeks, however, he had stalked off the job, ostensibly because the foreman had unjustly criticized him. (It does not take much to see that

---

[11] *Ibid.*, chapter II, pp. 3–4.

[11a] Isaac Loeb Peretz, "Mendel Braynes," *Collected Works* [Yiddish] (New York: CYCO, 1947), vol. II, pp. 87–94.

what underlay his quitting was his unwillingness to stay in the shop, which held forth little promise for the exercise of initiative and for advancement.) After a brief consultation with Aunt Rachel, it was decided that Samuel become a peddler. And if it was to be peddling, then let it be in the "country" immediately, for "out in the country I will be among Americans, and will be forced to stumble along in English . . . and, in due time, I will become fluent." Preparations for the venture were begun.

> My preparations consisted of riding downtown, where I purchased an English-Russian dictionary. I intended to use it Sundays and evenings, to aid me in reading an English book or newspaper. But then the idea grew more and more grandiose: *If I was already playing around with a dictionary, then why not dig up an English book which would interest the Russian public and try to translate it into Russian?* . . . With this notion in mind, I visited the Boston Public Library. I went through the catalogue, searching for a book which would interest the Russian reader.[12]

Slobod finally found a book entitled *In the Lena Delta,* written by George W. Melville, the former Chief Engineer of the United States Navy. The book related the dramatic story of the good ship *Janet* and its 1879 voyage with an expedition headed for the North Pole, which had met a tragic ending in Siberia. The story itself was well-known throughout Russia, as Slobod knew, and thus he thought the book a most appropriate one to be made available in Russian. On his way back from the library, he purchased a copy of Melville's book. Aunt Rachel, in the meantime, had arranged for him to obtain goods on credit at a firm with which she dealt, and calling on her own experience, had fixed him up with a peddler's pack. Finally, she gave him whatever instruction she deemed valuable and necessary. Slobod chose to start out peddling in the town and surrounding countryside of Belfast, Maine. He describes the beginning of his venture as follows:

> There I was, on a crossroads in Belfast, Maine, dressed in full peddler's regalia: a large pack on my back, a basket hanging down in front of me. I stood looking at a large road sign, which gave the mileages to places of which I had, of course, never heard. Let it be this road; what difference does it make? And I set forth. The load felt like a ton of bricks. Noting that the sweat had started dripping from my brow, I carefully covered the goods in the basket with oilcloth, gritted my teeth and continued on. About a mile out

---

[12] Chapter II, p. 12. Italics M.K.

of town, I started knocking on doors. I was turned down at the first 15 homes, but the attempts were not wholly unprofitable; I had picked up two English words: "not today." I rang up my first few sales in the course of the next 15 houses. . . . Before the day was out, I had had an encounter with a dog, leaving a piece of my pants behind. . . .[13]

At five or so, it being winter, Slobod began to look for a lodging, but all he heard was "We cannot accommodate you . . . we have no accommodation." "It was already a quarter to six" he writes, "and still no place to stay. But I had acquired a few more English words — accommodate, accommodation." Finally he found a place. This is how he describes the end of his first day of peddling:

Right after supper I went up to my room and sat down to work. Each time I had made a sale, I had recorded it in my notebook. I now checked these sales against the list of wholesale prices which Friedman Brothers had given me, and calculated that I had made a profit of $2.73. Then I took out my dictionary and the copy of Melville, and began to translate. It was a hell of a tedious job. [The autobiography was written in Yiddish; this last phrase, however, was set down in English by Slobod — M.K.] I almost went blind, having to look up every single word in the dictionary. Every bone in my body ached; my eyes kept on closing. Finally, after I'd finished half a page, I went to bed.[14]

Let us pause to review what we already know about our hero. Clearly, his is a dynamic personality, exuding self-confidence, a man undeterred by difficulties. He makes no complaints about having a bitter lot. He knows full well that to achieve something, no mean price has to be paid, and he is, it seems, quite willing to do so. He has little desire to spare himself. All this, however, is hardly extraordinary. There were undoubtedly, energetic people of this sort among every ethnic group. What is unique about this Jewish peddler is that, among the wares loaded in his pack, he took along a book, which he proposed to translate for Russian readers. After the first long day of peddling, in a totally strange environment, finally having found a place to stay overnight, weary and undoubtedly under a good deal of nervous tension, he doesn't sit back to relax and rest. Instead, he sits down to translate a book from English into Russian. The utter naïveté of thinking oneself capable of effectively translating a book, with the aid of a dictionary, from a wholly foreign language,

---

[13] *Ibid.*, chapter II, p. 15.
[14] *Ibid.*, chapter II, p. 16.

is beside the point. The social-psychological aspect of this phenomenon is what interests us: the ambition of a man to achieve something materially, to improve his lot economically, and *at the same time*, to stay alive intellectually, and the fantastic energy required by this dual drive.

Would it not be perfectly understandable for a person starting to make his way in a new and strange land to put aside his intellectual ambitions for the time being? Here, however, we see quite the contrary occurring. The notion of translating a book right at the outset is undoubtedly a result of a powerful drive to maintain intellectual vitality, even under the most inappropriate of conditions. In other words, the choice is made to work doubly hard rather than to give up one's spiritual life even temporarily. The image of the peddler who takes, along with all his merchandise, a book to translate, quite naturally brings to mind the Jewish country peddler in eastern Europe, journeying from village to village with a heavy load of pitifully poor goods, but never without his prayer-book or even a *seferl* [a rabbinic book] to look through in his spare moments.

The story of the translation, incidentally, had a tragi-comic ending. Having completed his work, Slobod wrote to a Russian publisher in St. Petersburg, only to be informed that the book had, in the interim, been translated and published by someone else. He consoled himself with the thought that he at least had had an intensive "training" in English.

Success in business came rapidly. In no time at all, Slobod purchased a horse and wagon, and established a permanent route out of Oldtown, Maine. Before the year was out, he had managed to save several hundred dollars. He brought over his older brother Hershl and his family [four persons] from Riga, and paid back the money Aunt Rachel had advanced for his own ship ticket. He tried to take Hershl into the peddling business, but to no avail, so he set him up in his old trade, bookbinding.

His own affairs constantly improved.

> My new stock of winter goods ... sold like hotcakes. The colder it got, the more business I had ... I used to arrive at my lodging for the night completely frozen, but with a bank balance growing steadily, neither rain nor snowstorm frighten one away. *Yet from time to time the old question would come to mind: What is the takhlis? Am I going to be a peddler all my life? No, I cannot spend my lifetime this way, I thought.*[15]

[15] *Ibid.*, chapter II, p. 40. Italics M.K.

Two factors are noteworthy here. Firstly, the notion of *takhlis* is a permanent element in his mentality (i. e., the reference to the *"old* question"). Secondly, it is rather unusual for a person to think of giving up a business just when everything is going very smoothly. This occurs only with one in whom the drive toward an end-goal (a *takhlis*) is deeply rooted, with one who evaluates what he has, not in terms of what it is in itself, but in terms of its relation to his goal.

In any case, he was forced to relinquish his peddler's route out of Oldtown. There had been systematic theft from his stock, and some highly unpleasant quarrels between Slobod and his customers erupted. Returning to Boston, he got a job as manager in a newly-established capmaking firm at a most satisfactory salary. Before long, a different trend of thought began to occupy him:

> Here I was, two years in America, constantly preoccupied with the American materialist spirit, with business, with enterprise, with making my way up in the world. But now that I had found a firmly established position, paying good wages, the long dormant Russian spirit which I had infused from the Russian literature of the day, the spirit of . . . "going to the people" emerged. More and more, I felt the desire to start a radical movement among the Jews of Boston.[16]

Slobod became one of the founders of a Jewish Educational Society, which affiliated with the Knights of Labor and later emerged as an anarchist group. He was one of its most active members. During this period, a socialist co-operative colony, "Topolobampo," modelled on the ideas of Robert Owen, had been established on the California-Mexico border. Slobod was overcome with enthusiasm for this venture. On the spur of the moment, he decided to join the colony. Withdrawing the $900 he had saved up, he left for California. In San Diego, however, he accidentally met someone who had just returned from the colony. He told Slobod about various disturbances that had taken place there, and the latter's enthusiasm was considerably dampened by this information. At this point in the autobiography, he writes that he began to be aware that

> the two conflicting ideologies which have taken possession of me are making life impossible for me. On the one hand, there is the American ideology, which stresses that "Charity begins at home." Take care of yourself, of your family, before all else . . . But, on the other hand, the Russian ideology howls in loud criticism: only by enlightening mankind, showing that it must rid itself of the capitalist sys-

---

[16] *Ibid.*, chapter III, p. 4. The key phrase "going to the people" of the Russian revolutionary movement of the 1870's and 1880's was Идти в народ [*idti v'narod*].

tem ... only when there shall be no poverty in the world ... only in this way can you help yourself. ...[17]

In any case, he decided not to join the colony. Instead, he purchased a piece of real estate on the shores of the Pacific while at an auction in San Diego. Noticing a curiosity shop which seemed to be doing a land-office business, it occurred to him to go into the same line somewheres in the east. He chose to make the attempt in Newport, R. I., then one of the wealthiest resort towns in the country. Purchasing a stock of "curiosity" goods from a wholesale house, he managed, in the course of his first summer, to make a neat profit of several hundred dollars. Whatever was left of his goods, he disposed of at the New England country fairs.

Slobod's next stop was New York, where he looked around for a new line of business. "The Russian ideology, however," he writes, "pushed the American ideology into the background. Instead of going into business, I became active in radical circles."[18] He joined the anarchist group "Pioneers of Liberty," and was sent to Baltimore to organize a branch there. The trip was not an altogether altruistic one, for he also proposed to start a new business, as well as organize a branch of the Pioneers. He set up three novelty stands at three major squares in the city, and prospered.

> When I was convinced that my business had been firmly established, I began to think of my second task, namely, founding a branch of the "Pioneers of Liberty."[19]

Slobod was no less successful in this than he had been in business. Within a period of eight months, the branch had 200 members. Several months later, he was sent as delegate to the convention in New York at which, he writes, the *Arbeter Tsaytung* was founded, and at which the left wing split off to set up *Di Varhayt*. He went along with the latter.[20]

---

[17] *Ibid.*, chapter III, pp. 17–19.

[18] *Ibid.*, chapter III, p. 24.

[19] *Ibid.*, chapter III, p. 26.

[20] Our autobiographer's memory is slightly faulty at this point. The convention was, in fact, initiated by the anarchists, who proposed to sponsor a joint, bipartisan radical newspaper with the socialists. The convention broke up, largely due to the unwillingness of the latter to co-operate. Just who was in the majority is disputed to this very day, though most recent evidence seems to point to the anarchists. In any case, it was shortly thereafter that the socialists began to publish the *Arbeter Tsaytung* and the anarchists followed suit with the *Fraye Arbeter Stimme*. The *Varhayt* had been a short-lived anarchist paper in 1889. The conference took place in 1890, and marked the definitive split in the Jewish radical movement between the anarchists and the socialists.

In the meantime, our hero's younger brother Meyer had emigrated to America. Things were not going too well with him, he wrote from Boston to Samuel in Baltimore. "Charity begins at home" once more began to ring in his ears. He returned to New York, seeking a business in which he could set up his newly-arrived brother. Making a deal with a delicatessen firm in New York, he opened up a delicatessen store in Boston, putting Meyer in charge. At the same time, he saw to it that Meyer's family was brought over from the old country. The first store having succeeded, he opened a second for his brother Hersh — by this time, Harry — who was plugging along, not very happily, at making suspenders. (The bookbinding venture had failed, and Uncle Yankl had brought him into this.) The second store went over even more than had the first, and Slobod began thinking in terms of another. He also thought about bringing over the rest of the family. It was then that he received a letter from the "Pioneers of Freedom," to the effect that he had been selected as manager of their organ, which at that time and in subsequent years, was a leading radical Yiddish journal in New York. "Duty calls" (Служба не дружба [*sluzhba nye druzhba*]), he remarks. Leaving his brothers with detailed instructions on how to run the businesses, he departed for New York, agreeing to take the post, though he insisted that it would be only temporary.

He remained as manager for eight months, constantly in touch with his brothers and directing the business from afar. During the same period, he brought his sister and another younger brother to the States, and made arrangements for his father, now a widower, to follow. The journal having found a new manager, "the American ideology rose from the dead"[21] and back he went into business.

While in New York, he learned of a firm which sold ship tickets and arranged for the transmission of money abroad. He recalled that wishing to do so for a Boston resident was a cumbersome and unpleasant matter; it meant "climbing up three flights of decrepit steps to Mr. Reinharz's stifling, tiny apartment."[22] It struck Slobod that he could set up a division of these purposes in each of his two large delicatessen stores. No sooner said than done. He inquired into all the necessary formalities and details, and then took off for Boston. Within a few days, each of the stores had been partitioned. In one part, delicatessen was sold; in the other, customers could arrange to purchase ship tickets and send money to relatives abroad.

---

[21] *Ibid.*, chapter IV, p. 1.
[22] *Ibid.*, chapter IV, pp. 1–2.

Success was rapid. Slobod soon hit upon an idea for expansion of his enterprise. He had noted that his customers — who were culturally and socially very close to him, who felt *haymish* [at home] with him — tended to mistrust the imposing, formal banks of *di fremde* [the strangers] with their savings. Whereupon he arranged to be licensed as a private banker, liquidated the delicatessen stores, and turned both places into offices for deposits, insurance, currency exchange and transmission, and ship tickets. Evidently his was the touch of Midas.

Nevertheless, within a few years, there having been constant conflicts among the sisters-in-law, Slobod withdrew his share of the capital, left his brothers, and moved to Pittsburgh, there returning to the delicatessen business. This, too, was not to be a permanent residence. His wife's sister had had to move to Denver for reasons of health, and the Slobods followed her there. Upon the advice of Dr. Chaim Spivak (a well-known figure in the radical movement of the time) he opened a boarding-house, specifically suited for those waiting for admission to the noted Denver sanitarium. Once things were running smoothly in the house, he went into the cattle business with a partner. Both ventures prospered. Several years later, his sister-in-law having died, he liquidated his interests, and returned to New York with a capital of $30,000.

At this point, the narrative was cut short. The years that followed, Slobod explained, were typical ones in the life of any businessman, and probably held no particular interest for anyone. YIVO requested him to add to his autobiography by telling about his children and those of his siblings. He responded with a detailed account of some hundred members of his more immediate family, going into the third generation. (Slobod was close to eighty when he wrote his autobiography.) It is noteworthy that all the members of the family had invariably gone into business enterprise of one sort or another, large or small scale trade, manufacturing, and the like. The two professionals had married into the family.

* * *

Analyzing the history of this individual, it is evident that we are dealing with a Jew engaged in business enterprise neither at the top nor the bottom of the commercial ladder. He manifests:

1) a powerful drive to make his way up economically, accompanied by immense energy, initiative and sound judgement;

2) a tendency to pioneer. Most frequently, he sought to realize his goal not by following the beaten path of business enterprise,

through successful competition, but rather by seeking out new ways, by being one of the first in any field.

3) At the same time, the drive to advance economically was markedly and frequently checked by two factors of a social-moral nature: (a) powerful ties to his family, going even beyond brothers and sisters; and (b) a sense of responsibility vis-à-vis a social ideology, despite the fact that he was rather one of its more peripheral adherents.

As for the first restraining factor, it will be recalled that no sooner had he accumulated a few hundred dollars, in little more than a year after his arrival in America, than he used it to bring his brother's family from Riga, rather than re-invest it in his business. His brother having arrived, and evidently a type ill-suited to the dynamism of American life, he was concerned about setting him up in business, helping him till he was able to stand on his own feet. He behaved similarly with regard to his other brothers.

As regards the second restraining factor, we have seen that simultaneously with a powerful drive toward success in business, Slobod had a strongly developed sense of duty toward an ideology in which he believed. More than once (managing the radical periodical, organizing anarchist groups in Boston and Baltimore, and other instances which we have omitted) he gave up or neglected his business affairs in order to meet the demands placed upon him by his ideology.

A third characteristic element which emerges from a study of the autobiography is the constant, life-long interest in intellectual matters, despite his not being a professional intellectual, but rather, a man intensely involved in business. His translation of a book into Russian at the outset of his peddling career will be recalled. A second expression is worth citing. In the sequel to the autobiography, he writes the following about his son:

> I suffered much sorrow in the matter of my son's education. I have no idea whom he takes after, but he simply refused to learn ... I would send him to Sunday school, but instead of going to school, he would go off to play hookey. I would bring books home for him to read which I thought to be appropriate for his age, but ... I found the book on the floor, and my son buried in a "Yesi-Jimmy" [Jesse James? — M.K.], a cheap detective story.[23]

---

[23] *Ibid.*, chapter V, p. 14.

At his wit's end, he enrolled the boy in a private high school for children of wealthy parents, paying an annual tuition of $700–$800 — quite a sum at the time — but he writes, "I paid this, however, with *great joy* . . . The boy left the school having acquired a sound education [p. 15]." We can here see the typically Jewish immense respect for education. The son was far from being a delinquent. In all probability, he was simply a typical American youngster, primarily interested in sports, detective stories, etc. For the father, however, this was a tragedy, and he strained himself to the limit of his material ability, so as to assure the son of a superior education. The son, incidentally, later became a successful business-man and the head of a respectable family.

In summary, we have considered the case of a Jewish middle class businessman whose attitudes and behavior in business were continuously influenced by social and moral factors, namely, by: strong ties and a sense of responsibility toward an ideology in which he believed, and a belief in the duty to sacrifice on its behalf; an extremely high evaluation of education, intellectual endeavor and attainment, and the desire to maintain an active intellectual exist-ence. The writer of the autobiography himself has put it in terms of a struggle between two ideologies: the one which stresses self-enrichment, the other, the acceptance of duties toward other men and toward ideas as the primary value. He himself is aware of the frequency with which the second tore him away from pursuing the first. In other words, he felt it to be a dynamic, living force, perpetually influencing his way of life.

2. *Struggling for Integrity*

Leyb [Leon] Berman[24] [Autobiography No. 144] was born in 1896 in a small town in the neighborhood of Minsk, White Russia. Both his parents had come from respectable homes, his father being some-what of a scholar. They eked out a meagre living from their horse-drawn mill. Though there was enough to eat, clothing was another matter. Leon never had anything but hand-me-downs from his older brother until he himself began to work. His father had high hopes for his younger son: after he had completed *ḥeder* [elementary school], he was sent to the *yeshiva* at Bobroisk, to become a rabbi.

[24] This is a pseudonym.

The youth, however, was scarcely attracted by a rabbinical career; he preferred business. Made miserable at having to "eat days" [students at the *yeshiva*, away from home, generally ate their meals as guests with a different family each day of the week] and sleeping on the cold, hard benches of the *yeshiva*, he returned home. "Early in life I began to think of great cities, and of seeking a *takhlis* for myself. My parents suffered quite a bit because of this, but there was nothing they could do about it," he writes [p. 21].

Leon helped his father around the mill. By the time of his *bar miẓvah*, he was a *melammed* [elementary school teacher] of village children. At fifteen he ventured out on his own, beginning to deal in grain. Later, an uncle of his, a partner in a large mill in a city, gave him a good post. He was instructed to keep an eye on the partner, lest he steal from the business. It was not long, however, before he became aware that it was the uncle who had to be watched. Badgered once too often by his uncle about keeping his eyes open, Leon burst forth with: "It's not the partner, but you yourself, who has to be watched." Immediately realizing what his outburst would lead to, he stormed out, slamming the door, and quit his job.

Having managed to save up a fair sum, he returned home, once again going into grain dealings, but this time on a somewhat larger scale. He travelled about, visiting large cities and staying in hotels. Seeing the great wide world, he was drawn to it more and more. It was then that he began thinking of emigration to America. The Beilis blood-accusation trial[25] led him to fear that a terrible catastrophe for Jews was in the offing. Moreover, he was certain that a war was imminent. Despite the fact that everyone laughed at him, he left for America, though he was an independent merchant and in good circumstances at the time. He arrived in the United States in March, 1914.

He went to stay at a cousin's home in Baltimore. The latter, a saloon-keeper, was very harsh with him, demanding payment for the slightest service. Berman left his cousin to work in a junk shop. He was not particularly happy in this work, for he dreamed of being on his own, and of studying law. He soon left for Philadelphia to stay with other relatives. Here too he met with a rather cool reception; these were well-to-do people, and ashamed of the "greenhorn." He left them, and rented a small room in a poor section of town. The next period was rather rough: he worked at various manual jobs, barely managing to earn his keep. Finally, he obtained

---

[25] See Maurice Samuel, *Blood Accusation: The Strange History of the Beilis Case* (Philadelphia: Jewish Publication Society of America, 1966).

a position in a store at a weekly salary of nine dollars. He was, however, not to last at this job very long. On leaving the store one day, he wrapped up his jacket, carrying it under his arm. The manager, suspicious of his having stolen something, called him back and asked to see the package. Berman complied with the request, and then angrily threw the jacket into the manager's face. Needless to say, he found himself out of a job.

Again he spent his days looking for work, starving, sleeping in parks (once almost freezing), until finally he managed to look up some distant relatives. These were poor, but kindly folk. Through them he made the acquaintance of a fellow in a small New England town, whom he joined, and with whom he became good friends. His new friend was not only very poor, but ran a very inefficient household into the bargain. Berman went to work for a junk shop that had recently been opened. He gained the confidence of the owners, and was soon appointed foreman of the shop. Working harder than the others, and loyal to his employers, he was taken on as a semi-partner, and promised that, in due time, he would become a full partner. Despite the fact that he was cramped and uncomfortable in his dwelling, he remained on, out of loyalty to his friend and knowledge that the family badly needed his help. In March, 1917, he had a bad accident at work: a heavy metal case fell on him, almost crushing his chest. The doctors practically gave him up for lost, but he recovered, although his health was impaired. On his return to work, his employers informed him that not only had they changed their minds about taking him into partnership, but that they had decided to fire him as well.[26]

He decided to enter the junk business on his own, and succeeded in making a go of it. Things did not go badly. At one time or another, he was in different lines of business, turning a profit here, taking a loss there, once again coming out on top. About 1918, he moved to New York. Under the influence of Dr. Chaim Zhitlovsky, Berman decided to become "productive." Leaving all other things behind, he left for Pennsylvania to work in a coal mine. While there, he lived with a Lithuanian family. Both men and women were constantly getting drunk. Somehow getting involved

[26] In connection with this incident, he later relates:

For a long time thereafter, I simply burned with the desire for revenge . . . Years later I ran into one of the partners . . . He had lost all his money, and was impoverished. I gave him $300. to start a new business. He never returned this loan, though he is quite well to do now . . . From the moment that I gave him the money I felt an inner peace; the idea of revenge evaporated forever [Berman's Autobiography, p. 100].

in one of the brawls, our hero suffered a severe beating. He decided
to quit mining while the quitting was good.

He went back into business, this time in Baltimore, at first in the
junk business, and later in a grocery store. He lost money in the
latter, thanks to his partner. Then he became manager of a section
in junk business owned by two brothers. He rose rapidly, and was
instrumental in the tremendous growth of the enterprise. He became
head salesman, travelling on behalf of the firm to Japan and Europe.
After several years, however, he quit the company as a result of
failing to get a bonus which he believed due him. Despite the plead-
ings of the owners, he refused to return. He went into business on
his own, with one partner. Following the death of the latter (whose
heirs managed to get away with some things unjustly), he remained
in business for himself. Though there were ups and downs, he was,
by and large, successful, and became a moderately well-to-do man,
whose wealth amounted to about $40,000 to $50,000. After the
business had become solidly established, he branched out into
government contracts. This involved him, however, in a labyrinth
of "red tape," and he suffered substantial losses. On one occasion,
he reports, he was threatened by an immense loss as a result of
this "red tape." He tried to straighten things out, but was only
sent from one place to another, from one official to another, and
things got more and more involved. Finally, he went to the Head
of Purchasing, in Washington, of the government department with
which he was involved. He could get nothing out of him. One word
led to another, and then, Berman writes:

> I took out the key to my office, and put it on the fellow's desk ...
> I'm giving him my key, let him take over the business. He can be
> proud of himself that he used the entire American army to kill a
> fly ... I stalked off into a corner of the office and sat down. I sat
> there from nine to four, Monday to Friday. I had decided that I
> would sit there until I managed to set things straight ... Friday
> morning, he called me over to his desk and asked me what I
> wanted....[27]

The end of the matter was that Berman won his point. The
Gordian knot of red tape was cut at one stroke, and he was able to
go ahead with the contracted merchandise. He managed to get
away with only a slight loss. By and large, however, his affairs went
smoothly, and his financial position was solidly established.

The following is how he sums up the economic aspects of his
life in America:

[27] *Ibid.*, pp. 146–147.

> The period between 1936 and 1942 was the most successful,
> financially, of my life. It's true that I work very hard in my business,
> a bit too hard, and one's strength is running out, but the work pays
> off [p. 155].

Throughout his entire life in America, the cultural side of Berman's
life was never neglected. From the very moment of his arrival, he
read Russian books, borrowed from the public libraries. He was
secretive about this, for a number of his relatives mocked the
"greenhorn" for wasting his time at such stupidities. In the course
of time, he shifted to Yiddish literature, of which he became a fervent
partisan, reading everything that was published in Yiddish. As his
financial position was secured, he took to buying everything that
was produced in American Yiddish literature, and became one of
its leading material supporters. Politically, he joined the Poale
Zion movement, becoming very active, particularly in its Yiddish
school system, in which he was involved from its earliest days in
the 1920's. In the city in which he finally settled, he became one
of the leaders of the Jewish Community Council and of the Zionist
movement.

He sums up his communal life in the following words:

> Throughout all the years of struggle, I always took part in public
> affairs. I contributed to various funds and institutions. Yet I never,
> turned down an individual who approached me for assistance. I
> believe that the forest consists of individual trees, and the trees
> must not be neglected because of the forest [p. 152].

On one occasion, this attitude cost him some $13,000, in doing a
favor for a distant relative of his wife. He took over this fellow's
entire debt, rather than suffer him to go under, and this despite the
fact that his beneficiary persistently added to the debt sub rosa.

Berman later submitted, in response to YIVO's request, a supplement to his autobiography, covering 1942–1952, the war and post-
war years. By the beginning of the war, he had become one of the
leaders in his branch of the industry, whose product is of some
importance in the conduct of war. He was elected head of the
manufacturers' association in his branch. In his acceptance speech,
he stressed that he regarded it as his major function not to permit
a black market to develop in the industry during the war. During
a conference between representatives of the government and of the
industry, a Navy officer came out with an anti-Semitic remark.
("A certain group," he said, "is committing sabotage, and not
delivering the goods on schedule.") Berman sprang up to protest
the remark, ripping the officer wide open, and pointed out that

this very officer was himself the responsible party in the affair, for he had awarded a contract involving millions of pounds of merchandise to a stranger outside of the industry, one who had no notion of how to go about things. When things had quieted down, he volunteered to take responsibility for overcoming the critical shortage. Within a few days, he was able to provide the government with half a million pounds of merchandise, a sufficient amount to meet the crisis.

At a second occasion, the mayor of the city in which the industry convention was taking place was the guest speaker. He spoke at great length about the Nazi destruction of Lidice, but never mentioned a single word about the Nazis' extermination of the Jews. Berman, who was chairman of the meeting, immediately expressed a sharp protest. (This specific branch of the junk industry, and the convention itself, consisted of 95 per cent Jews.)

In Berman's city, a dealer was arrested on a black market charge. This led Berman and several other men in the industry to form a voluntary commission to fight the formation of a black market from within. They disclosed their plan to the local government administrator, who approved. They were successful in their efforts, and a black market in the industry did not materialize. (Berman notes that the same effort was made in other branches.)

In 1948, Berman became seriously ill, and was confined to bed for a long time. No sooner had he recovered, than he had a relapse, and spent another long period as an invalid. After his convalescence, he returned to business. No longer having the strength to conduct its affairs alone, he took in a partner. He comments thereon:

> My wife, children and I could live on the money I have managed to save. But what would then happen to the contributions of $10,000 annually which I make to various causes? There are only two alternatives open to me: to turn down everyone who approaches me — this would require a heart of stone, which I do not possess; the second way would be to leave the city, settle down in a small town in Florida, and cut myself off from all Jewish affairs. This, too, I had no desire to do. I must, therefore, remain in business, earn as much as I can, in order that I shall be able to make my contributions.[28]

* * *

Here we have a person with a clearly distinct personality. His maxims in life, followed with rigid consistency, were: integrity as regards others; preserving his own self-respect and personal values

---

[28] *Ibid.*, part II, p. 68.

even at a high price; responsibility toward individuals and toward society. Thus, he confronted his own uncle with the just accusation that it was he himself who had best be watched for thievery, knowing full well that it would cost him his job; he threw his jacket into the manager's face for suspecting him of being a thief, though he had gotten the job after weeks of starving and knew that this would put him back on the streets (which actually happened). In business dealings, he always aspired to be honest, and strenuously insisted on maintaining his dignity and prestige. He often preferred to take a loss rather than compromise with his sense of personal worth. Thus, he did not shrink from speaking up sharply and directly even to high government officials, when he felt that they were in the wrong. During the war, he not only refrained from seeking easy profits by circumventing the law, but took the lead in maintaining the honor of the entire industry. Throughout his life he also was active in the Jewish community. Personally, his cultural and intellectual life was on a high level, and his four children received both a sound Jewish as well as a college education.

This is an example of an upper middle class Jewish businessman, who has worked hard to achieve the substantial economic position he has reached.[29] Yet with this drive to become wealthy, he invariably exercised self-control and maintained his principles of decency, morality and self-esteem. He preferred to reject a profit — or, for that matter, even his daily bread, in his days of poverty — rather than betray the principles in which he believed. Though deeply involved in working his way up the economic ladder, he never deserted the service of a cause (the Jewish community in general, Zionism in particular), to which he contributed heavily. The principle of *zedakah* [philanthropy] is so deeply rooted in his very being, that he would rather, ill as he is, continue to work hard, than relinquish his potential as a philanthropist.

---

[29] At one point, in connection with his experiences in 1919–1920 shortly before he was married, he writes: "We wished to have our own home, servants and a car. I thought to myself that if in only two years ... I have managed to accumulate $30,000, in not many more years I will have $50,000 or perhaps even $75,000 [p. 108].

3. In Pursuit of Culture and Education

Ezriel Pressman [Autobiography No. 189][30] was born into a poor family in the White Russian city of Minsk in 1881. His father was a carpenter. A few years after his birth, the family moved to a hamlet near the town of Smolevich, his father going to work in a newly-established match factory. The men worked twelve hours daily. Their very low wages scarcely sufficed to support their families, and things were particularly difficult in Ezriel's family of twelve souls (three of the ten children were boys). He describes his mother's endless toil: cooking, baking bread, cleaning, washing, mending, darning, and so on, into the late hours. Thus, his entire childhood and youth were spent in surroundings of hard work and poverty. At first he studied under a *melammed*, whom the few Jewish families had brought to the village. He then was sent to live with an older brother in Minsk, where he studied at the Talmud Torah and "ate days." "I was an exceedingly conscientious student," he writes, "and in this lay my only joy.... And though my food was invariably poor, things went well with my studies."[31] In the older classes, Russian was taught. Our impatient young scholar hired an older lad to teach him Russian, paying nine kopecks[32] a week, which left him twenty-five kopecks to sustain himself when he had no "days." He managed to learn to read and write enough Russian to get himself into the Russian elementary school.

> Though I had to go hungry because of the 9 kopecks my wish was realized . . . I could have gone ahead much further in studying, for I had the opportunity to enter a preparatory school . . . But my father said: "My dear son, I can help you but little . . . and I keep on thinking — what will be the *takhlis?*"[33]

It was decided that Ezriel would be apprenticed to a tailor. The boy of eleven was sent to his brother-in-law, a journeyman tailor. He later returned to Minsk to work in a shop there. He was drawn into the newly-organized and illegal *Bund* (the General Jewish Workers Union) and became a very active member. Finally, in 1900, he was arrested and sentenced to three years exile in Siberia. After an arduous, slow journey, he arrived at the destined place of Siberian exile, the village of Boyskoye, near Minusinsk. He managed

---

[30] After Ezriel Pressman had written his autobiography for the YIVO contest, he had it published as *Der Durkhgegangener Veg* [Yiddish] (The Traversed Road).

[31] *Ibid.*, pp. 20 and 22.

[32] Roughly the equivalent of one kopeck is one cent.

[33] *Ibid.*, pp. 22–23.

to develop good relations with his neighbors, manifested a great deal of energy and vitality, and thus did not get along too badly. In 1903, while in Siberia, he was drafted for military service. As an exile, he was placed in a battalion, under rigid and severe discipline, in the sufficiently harsh Czarist army. Being blessed with a capacity for getting along with people and making friends, Ezriel came through his army experience soundly. Then, after almost four years in Siberia, he was released, and returned home toward the end of 1906.

Settling in Minsk, he once again became active in the labor movement. He became secretary of the semi-legal tailors' union. At this same time he fell in love and, in the summer of 1907, he married. In the aftermath of a strike in a garment factory, he was once again arrested and imprisoned. After half a year in jail, he was transferred to Orsha, near Vitebsk, and then to Vilna. During this difficult period, his wife had given birth to a boy. "It became more and more clear," he writes, "that this was no way to live. And I began to consider how to improve things."[34] He decided to emigrate to America. Thinking to go alone, and later to send for his family, he tried to slip over the border illegally, but was once again arrested. He was, however, detained only a month this time. His second attempt to cross the border proved successful. In July, 1908, he arrived in the United States.

He travelled to Pittsburgh, joining his wife's sister's family. The husband, a carpenter, took him along to the shop where he was employed. One of Pressman's first impressions of America is quite characteristic:

> My first *Shabbes* in America made a most painful impression on me. My brother-in-law arrived home from work Friday ... He made *kiddush*, my sister-in-law had prepared a good, Sabbath, homelike meal ... Everything was fine and pleasurable that evening. On the morrow — on the morning of *Shabbes* seeing my brother-in-law dress in his overalls, take his saw, and leave for work, the entire Sabbath eve of America turned sour for me.[35]

This reaction — the response of a person himself irreligious, one whose spiritual education was in a strongly anti-clerical and free-thinking political party — is most characteristic. His intellectualized break with religion had not overcome the deeply rooted involvement in tradition and religious ways of life. The sympathetic predisposition for the old patterns, even when they had been abandoned on

[34] *Ibid.*, p. 101.
[35] *Ibid.*, p. 114.

rational grounds, it may be noted, played an important rôle in molding the spiritual physiognomy of the American Jewish community.

Pressman moved to Youngstown, Ohio, where he went to work in a tailor shop. He sent for his wife and child. The family settled down, grew. He became very active in the Workmen's Circle. Later, they returned to Pittsburgh, where he worked in a shop. Though by now a foreman, he remained very active in the clothing workers' union. It was at this time that he contracted a severe case of tuberculosis, and was confined to a sanitarium for a long time. When finally discharged, he returned to Youngstown. He borrowed some money from friends and opened a grocery store. Somehow or other, he managed to make a living.

With America's entry into the war in 1917, prices rose, and Pressman prospered. He sold the grocery and bought a shoe store in Ashtabula, not far from Cleveland. His luck had turned. In short order, he became the most solidly established, financially speaking, Jew in town. As such, he was compelled, as it were, to assume the post of president of the congregation, though he protested to the handful of congregants that he was not religious. (Here we see a clear example of the compelling strength of social status over conflicting personal inclinations.) The town, however, was very small, limited in its opportunities for cultural and social expression and stimulus. "Thus," he writes, "I derived little enjoyment from living there, for is it not written: 'For man shall not live by bread alone' — one needs something spiritual as well."[36] In the postwar crisis, Pressman was hit hard. He was forced to close his business, and was once again a poor man.

Back he went to Youngstown, where he became a salesman for the Ohio Notion Company. Somehow or other, he managed to get back on his feet. He once again became active in the Workmen's Circle, and was particularly interested in its Yiddish school, attended by all three of his sons. He took great pride in the fact that his children were among the leaders in the youth activities — the children's paper, and the like — read Yiddish literature, etc. He summarizes this chapter of his autobiography which, characteristically enough, he calls "My Spiritually Golden Epoch," as follows:

My son Gershon would take a volume of Sholom Aleichem along with him to high school. . . . My second son Zalman used to try his hand at writing Yiddish poetry . . . My third son, named after I. L. Peretz, was already old enough to be enrolled in the Workmen's

[36] *Ibid.*, pp. 139–140.

Circle school. I felt exalted ... "Children I have reared, brought up ..." This was indeed a truly golden epoch in my spiritual life.[37]

With business conditions bad, Pressman's employers cut his wages. Once again he returned to the grocery business. His wife being an efficient businesswoman, they got along adequately, and Pressman gave the major part of his attention to the Workmen's Circle school. He also supplemented the family income by working as a truck driver.

Upon their oldest son's graduation from high school, the Pressmans decided to move to New York, allowing the boy to attend City College evenings, while he worked in the day. Due to some unforeseen technicality, the son was not able to enter City College. Learning that he would be accepted in a college in South Carolina,

my son left for the South. His trip had to be made on foot. Prior to his departure, my younger son Zalman took off his new sweater and a good pair of shoes, which he had bought for himself, and said to Gershon: "Take these with you. You're leaving, going amongst a lot of strange fellows, so you'd better have some better clothing." [Pressman comments on this episode:] This shows how close my sons were to each other, and how great their readiness to sacrifice, even under the most difficult of circumstances, for the sake of learning.[38]

The family bought a cleaning store in Hoboken, half an hour's ride from New York. Pressman once more became extremely active in the Workmen's Circle, serving on the District Committee. He was particularly involved in cultural activities: a choir, organizing lectures and cultural evenings, and the like. After describing the deep satisfaction derived from these affairs at some length, he closes this section of his account by saying:

It was this spirit that kept my wife and myself from despair, at a time when things had indeed become difficult.[39]

The 1929 depression forced him to close the cleaning shop. He returned to New York to seek work as a tailor. At the same time, he remained preoccupied with his earlier labor of love: the Workmen's Circle schools. In due time, his older son married, became a dentist, and set up a private practice. The two younger boys went into business. With this, the peak of Pressman's life was past. Later, things became worse, as he got older and suffered from poor health.

* * *

[37] *Ibid.*, pp. 148–149.
[38] *Ibid.*, p. 158.
[39] *Ibid.*, p. 162.

In the life history of Ezriel Pressman, we have a clear case of the consequences of an intense concern with culture and education for a small-scale businessman. These drives, beyond doubt, prevented him from concentrating the immense energies which he had manifested during his early years of exile in Siberia on his business career. We have seen that at one time he had even become well-to-do as the owner of a shoe store in Ashtabula. The crisis following the first World War was by no means overwhelming; many prosperous businessmen were easily able to weather the storm. The fact, however, that Pressman was frustrated and unhappy in the town, unable to find his spiritual satisfaction, most probably played a rôle in the total collapse of his business. And again, having re-established himself in Youngstown, with things going smoothly, he undertook to start from scratch once more, moving to New York in order to allow his son to attend City College. (He could not afford the luxury of having him attend a paid college.) The stirring episode of the son's departure for school in the distant South is then unfolded. (The younger son, incidentally, who had gone to work in a store, continued to send money to his brother at college.)

Presumably the frustrating and painful fact that Pressman's own education had been cut short at an early age (at eleven, it will be recalled, his family's poverty prevented him from taking advantage of the opportunity to continue his studies in a Gymnasia, and he was forced to work) had kindled a powerful attachment to education and cultural expression — a drive which was to be manifest throughout his life. This sense of the centrality of culture and education was transmitted to his children: the family, unable to afford a professional education for all three sons, united their efforts in having one of them, at least, symbolize its craving for a high educational status.

In brief: this case history has allowed us to view the life of a small-scale Jewish businessman who explicitly and consciously placed a higher value on spiritual than on economic achievements, a pattern which necessitated willingly-borne sacrifices of economic opportunities for the sake of spiritual contentment.

II

CONCLUSIONS

What conclusions do these case histories allow us to draw? We would like to stress that final, definitive statements cannot be reached on the basis of this material,[40] and would prefer to regard

[40] As indicated *supra*, p. 284, note 1, the over 300 autobiographies in the collection

it rather as a fruitful source of tentative hypotheses. These hypotheses would, of course, require further study for elaboration and scientific confirmation. We can formulate our conclusions, thus qualified, in the following manner:

1. The principle of *takhlis*, which played a central rôle in Jewish life in the old country, did not disappear in the course of the ocean voyage. It continued to be a force of major, compelling potency in the United States as well. Actually, the *takhlis*-principle was the chief motive force leading those who had broken with the authority of traditional life in the *shtetl* [the small town] to emigrate; penury and persecution were catalytic agents, hastening and making easier, but not determining, the process of uprooting oneself from one's home. The major motivation was the search for social and material advance, to improve living conditions in the search for a *takhlis*.

2. Among those immigrants to whom an economic *takhlis* was central, and who entered business with an intense desire to work their way up materially as rapidly as possible, there nevertheless were manifested specific restraining, modifying, factors of a social-moral character.

3. Chief among these were the factors of *education* and *knowledge*. The drive to become wealthy, as powerful as it might have been, gave way and became secondary to matters of education. Thus one of our cases relinquished a solidly established material position in order to allow his son to have a higher education; a second extended himself far beyond his financial limits to foster his child's education, where the boy — an average youngster — had not been sufficiently stimulated by public school.

4. Another factor which exercised a restraining influence was the tie to a social ideal. Once such an attachment had been formed, it was never easily abandoned, even when economic interests impelled one towards an opposite direction. The ideal led to sacrifices on its behalf in the event of conflict with the drive for greater material betterment. It should be explicitly noted that there is no doubt that ties to a traditional, religious way of life, may be as important an influence as a social ideology. Our case material, however, con-

which have been used as source material in this study are, for the most part, those of manual and white collar workers, as well as a few professionals. There were few businessmen among the writers. For lack of space, we have limited ourselves to a presentation of only three case histories, which we believe to be interesting and highly suggestive examples. Even had all the cases of businessmen been presented, however, it would still have been necessary to be cautious in drawing final conclusions.

tains no evidence in support of this hypothesis, for the participants in the autobiography contest were almost exclusively people from the secular sectors of the Jewish immigrant community.

5. A further factor of a similar order was that of deep family ties. It was one's unquestioned duty to aid members of one's family — which concept often included distant relatives — and to regard their needs as one's own. Arranging for the immigration from the old country of one's siblings, not to speak of one's parents, was as important as bringing over one's wife and children. Assisting them to establish themselves in a new environment was regarded as an elementary duty.

It would require an extremely extensive study, using a larger number of cases, to ascertain whether these characteristics are fundamental to the Jewish group. It would, moreover, be desirable to conduct similar investigations among those ethnic groups who migrated to America en masse during the same period (Poles, Italians, etc.). Only then would it be possible to determine with any degree of certainty whether these were ethnic characteristics of the Jews. We have here only attempted to formulate a number of tentative conclusions. Further investigation and testing of these conclusions will allow us to clarify a major problem in the social psychology of a large, significant segment of American society.

AN EARLY 20th CENTURY HEDER
Hester Street, New York.

The Maccabæan

·A MONTHLY MAGAZINE OF JEWISH LIFE AND LITERATURE

Vol. 1   October, 1901   No. 1

Announcement

AT the convention of the Zionist Societies of the United States, held at Philadelphia June 19th, it was unanimously resolved to establish a monthly journal. The journal was to be a means of inter-communication between the Zionist societies composing the Federation, and at the same time it was meant to furnish the means for a more complete and thorough discussion of our platform than is possible in journals which have other and more general objects in view. From these journals we have received many courtesies in the past ; some of them have been most friendly and sympathetic to our cause. To all of them we owe a certain debt of gratitude. In making our bow to the public we gladly acknowledge this debt and add our thanks to the acknowledgement. We have not come to antagonize any one or any party in Judaism ; but rather by preaching the truth as we see it, to focus towards one objective point the diverging forces in Jewry.

This objective point is the end and aim of Zionism. To reconstruct the Jewish people, to lead them to an organized national existence, to make Jewish religious life possible, to foster the study of Jewish literature and history, to provide a stable home for the oppressed and downtrodden of our race—these are the objects which our organization has in view, and for these objects THE MACCABÆAN will stand. As the Zionist organization includes Jews of all kinds and qualities, so will THE MACCABÆAN turn an attentive eye to every form and phase of Jewish life ; not so much for the purpose of criticizing and fault-finding, but in order to discover the ideas and forces which bind us together. In the fear of God and without fear of man we shall search for the truth, confident in the aid of Him who has ever guided Israel.

RICHARD GOTTHEIL.

Notes

THE " Jewish Chronicle " still harps on the theory that Zionism is stagnating. The blind spot in the " Chronicle's " eye is abnormally large. Our organizations, despite many difficulties, are becoming more cohesive, our views are being stated even more definitely and from every side encouraging reports of new recruits come to hand And in addition, moneys are being sent with confidence to the central organization. And yet, ignoring these evidences of substantial preliminary work, our good contemporary blandly announces that in its opinion the record of the movement " resolves itself into a tale of stagnation tempered by correspondence."

AN amendment will be offered at the coming International Congress of Zionist societies granting national Federations absolute jurisdiction within their respective territory. This is a step leading to the complete effective federation of Zionist organizations throughout the world. It is an unquestionably necessary step in the progress of the movement. Unless the societies are bound to one another with clearly defined rights and duties, the propaganda must prove ineffective. The English-speaking delegates to the International Congresses have at all times insisted on representation by federation as the basic principle of organization. To the Zionist environed by democratic institutions—as in the United States, which is a federation of states—it seems to be a fatal error not to recognize the right of each effective federation to the control of the societies within its territorial jurisdiction.

This method will not eliminate the right of appeal, in case of a grievance, to the Actions Comité, and in certain specified cases further appeal to the general Congress. Nor will the federation rule apply where no federation is possible or existent. But where, as in the United States, Canada, England, and elsewhere, a complete and effective federation has been established with much hard labor the International Congress should, in justice to these Federations, recognize their authority in their district. It is our sincere hope that this amendment to be offered to the Constitution will meet the Congress's approval. The most difficult obstacle in the way is the opposition of the Continental delegates, who seem to be unable to comprehend the principle of federal representation.

NEW YORK, May 8th, 1903.

DEAR SIR :—

Great distress prevails at Kischineff, Russia, by reason of the Anti-Semitic riots last week, wherein we are informed that more than one hundred persons of the Jewish faith were killed, from five to six hundred were injured, and many others were made homeless and suffered the destruction of their property. The *Alliance Israélite Universelle* has cabled requesting our co-operation in securing financial relief, stating that several million francs are needed for this purpose. After a discussion of the situation, we believe that this community should co-operate liberally with the *Alliance Israélite* in providing relief; and your subscription is therefore solicited. In view of the necessities of the case, you are urged to send promptly whatever contribution you may desire to make, to MR. DANIEL GUGGENHEIM, Treasurer of the Relief Fund, 71 Broadway, New York City.

Yours truly,

EMANUEL LEHMAN, CHAIRMAN,	LOUIS MARSHALL,
NATHAN BIJUR,	HENRY RICE,
JOSEPH B. BLOOMINGDALE,	JACOB H. SCHIFF,
SIMON BORG,	ISAAC N. SELIGMAN,
DANIEL GUGGENHEIM,	LOUIS STERN,
CHARLES L. HALLGARTEN,	ISIDOR STRAUS,
MYER S. ISAACS,	CYRUS L. SULZBERGER,
MORRIS LOEB,	ISAAC WALLACH.

LETTER OF SOLICITATION
For victims of Kischineff pogrom
New York, May 8, 1903

תלמוד ינקאי

מכיל בקרבו ש״ם מסכתות הלא הנה:

מסכת הדיוטות, מסכת חנוכה, מסכת נכסים, מסכת מסוה

מסכת כזבים, מסכת עמיקה.

ונלוה בסופו

מדרש אסתר והגדה לסיפרים

מאת

גרשון ראזענצווייג.

הוצאת בית מסחר הספרים של ש. דרוקערמאן

50 קאנאל סטריט נויארק.

1907.

פ ס א. ח. ראזיענבערג, 11 ראבינגערס סטריט נויארק.

TALMUD YANKAI
by Gershon Rosenzweig
Satire on America in Talmudic form and language
New York, 1907

תלמוד בבלי

ומסכתות קטנות ירושלמיות

עם

פירוש רש"י (והמיוחס לרש"י). רשב"ם (למסכת פסחים ולב"ב).
ר"ן (למסכת נדרים). תקלין חדתין (למסכת שקלים). מפרש (פי'
מספיק לאבות דר' נתן ולמסכתות קטנות) ע"פ הבנין יהושע להגאון
ר' יהושע פאלק מליסא והנחלת יעקב להרב ר' יעקב (יאקב)
נוימבורג, ועוד הרבה מפרשים.

ועם

מסורת הש"ס ותורה אור להג"מ יהושע בועז ז"ל עם הוספת רבות מהגאון ר'
ישעיהו (פיק) ברלין ז"ל ותאונים אחרים שבאו אחריו. חלופי גרסאות והגהות
הב"ח והגר"א ועוד גאונים הרבה. גם לקוטים שונים מגדולי המפרשים על מקומות
הרבה קשי ההבנה בתלמוד ובפירוש רש"י. והמבאר ביאור מלות הלועזיות שנזכרו
במפרשי התלמוד שבהוצאה זו.

ראה זה חדש הוא

הוספנו בסופי השמטות הש"ס בגמרא ורש"י ההסרות בהש"ס שנדפסו בארצות הגוצרים
הונה כ"ט"ס ישן נושן הגדפס בלי הסרון מכי"ק הז"ל תיבה על תיבה ואות על אות ממש.
ועוד הוספנו מפתחות הפרקים עפ"י א"ב בכל ששה סדרי משנה.

———

ניו יארק

הוצאת מ"ע "דער מארגען זשורנאל"

תרע"ג

THE BABYLONIAN TALMUD
One-volume edition published as subscription bonus by
Yiddish daily *Der Morgen Journal*, 1913

א בילד פון ניו יאָרקער ייִדישע צייטונגען און זשורנאלן, אין פארשידענע שפּראכן,
אין 1917-1918

THE JEWISH PRESS IN AMERICA IN 1917–1918

AIDING WORLD WAR I SUFFERERS THEME IN JEWISH FOLK SONGS

JEWS AND THE WAR

September 1, 1914.

STATEMENT OF Mr. LOUIS MARSHALL,
PRESIDENT OF THE AMERICAN JEWISH COMMITTEE.

A meeting of the Executive Committee of the American Jewish Committee was held yesterday at which communications were received from various parts of the world concerning the condition of the Jews in consequence of the late Balkan war and of the present general war raging in Europe.

It was decided to appropriate $2,500 for the benefit of the Jewish orphans at Sofia, Bulgaria, who had lost their parents during the late war.

Cablegrams were received from Hon. Henry Morgenthau, the American Ambassador at Constantinople, and from other reliable sources, indicating that the Palestinian Jews were confronting a serious crisis in consequence of the discontinuance of contributions which have hitherto been received by them from their brethren in the several European lands which are now at war with each other. It was reported that the destruction of a number of flourishing colonies was threatened, unless financial assistance was at once forthcoming. The sum of $50,000 was stated to be immediately required to relieve the situation, and that a responsible committee had been formed, of which Dr. Arthur Ruppin, of Jaffa, was the Chairman, for the purpose of administering the funds that might be forwarded, for the establishment of a free loan society and for the support of families which, because of the fact that their bread-winners had been called into the army, were in a destitute condition. The Committee appropriated the sum of $25,000 for this purpose, Mr. Jacob H. Schiff adding $12,500 to this sum, and it being understood that the Zionist organizations would undertake to secure the remaining $12,500 needed to carry on this relief work.

The Committee then considered the effect of the war upon the Jews of Russia, Germany, Austria, the Balkan States, and other parts of the world, the assistance of whom it was believed would inevitably demand serious consideration from their co-religionists, especially in the United States. In order to cope with the serious problems which in all probability must soon be dealt with, a sub-committee was appointed to gather authentic information with regard to the situation of the Jews who might be affected by the existing calamity, and to make recommendations as to ways and means by which necessary and adequate assistance might at the proper time be rendered to all sufferers, without discrimination. The Committee proposes to call upon other organizations to co-operate with it to aid in the formulation and carrying out of plans for the accomplishment of results commensurate with the immensity of the problem.

THE EARLIEST EFFORT TO ORGANIZE AMERICAN JEWISH RELIEF FOR JEWS ABROAD DURING WORLD WAR I

By the President of the United States of America.

A Proclamation.

WHEREAS, I have received from the Senate of the United States a Resolution, passed January 6, 1916, reading as follows:

"Whereas in the various countries now engaged in war there are nine millions of Jews, the great majority of whom are destitute of food, shelter, and clothing; and

Whereas millions of them have been driven from their homes without warning, deprived of an opportunity to make provision for their most elementary wants, causing starvation, disease and untold suffering; and

Whereas the people of the United States of America have learned with sorrow of this terrible plight of millions of human beings and have most generously responded to the cry for help whenever such an appeal has reached them; Therefore be it

RESOLVED, That; in view of the misery, wretchedness, and hardships which these nine millions of Jews are suffering, the President of the United States be respectfully asked to designate a day on which the citizens of this country may give expression to their sympathy by contributing to the funds now being raised for the relief of the Jews in the war zones."

AND WHEREAS, I feel confident that the people of the United States will be moved to aid the war-stricken people of a race which has given to the United States so many worthy citizens;

Now, therefore, I, WOODROW WILSON, President of the United States, in compliance with the suggestion of the Senate thereof, do appoint and proclaim January 27, 1916, as a day upon which the people of the United States may make such contributions as they feel disposed for the aid of the stricken Jewish people.

Contributions may be addressed to the American Red Cross, Washington, D. C., which will care for their proper distribution.

In Witness Whereof, I have hereunto set my hand and caused the seal of the United States to be affixed.

DONE at the City of Washington this eleventh day of January, in the year of our Lord one thousand nine hundred and sixteen, and of the Independence of the United States the one hundred and fortieth.

[SEAL.]

WOODROW WILSON

By the President:
ROBERT LANSING
Secretary of State.

[No. 1320.]

PROCLAMATION by PRESIDENT WOODROW WILSON
"Contribution Day for Aid of Stricken Jewish People"
in World War I

229 EAST BROADWAY, NEW YORK

Dear Sir:—

Enclosed please find a letter from Europe received by our Society which is intended for you. According to arrangements made with the German and Austrian authorities in the war zones by our special representative, Mr. Isidore Hershfield, the sending of letters by people in the occupied territory to their friends in America was authorized, provided such letters are addressed to our Society and are written in a certain form. These letters come to us open and we are forwarding them to the addressees at our expense in conformity with the promise made by our Mr. Hershfield to the authorities above mentioned, regardless of the race or creed of the persons involved.

If you wish to send a message to your relative in response to his letter we suggest the following:

1. Fill out the enclosed application form.
2. In the space opposite the word "Remarks" write a message in condensed form such as "We are well, we have sent money, or we will send money."

This message will be compiled by us and transmitted to your relatives by our European correspondent through whom only communication is possible for the present.

Very truly yours,

LEON SANDERS, President

Szanowny Panie:

Załączamy Państwu list z Europy, który otrzymało nasze Towarzystwo.

Według umowy zawartej z rządami Niemieckim i Austryackim a naszym wysłannikiem Panem Isidore Hershfield w sprawie wysyłania listów z zajętych ziem wojną, do swych przyjaciół w Ameryce, zezwolono, aby listy adresowano do naszego stowarzyszenia i by pisano w pewnej formie. Te listy przychodzą do nas otwarte, a my je odsyłamy według adresów znadujących się wewnątrz, naszym kosztem, według obietnicy uczynionej przez Pana Hershfield władzom wyżej wymienionym, bez różnicy narodowości lub wiary osób interesowanych.

Jeżeli Pan życzy sobie przesłać jaką wiadomość lub list do krewnych, radzimy co następuje:

1. Wypełnić załączony kwestjonarjusz.
2. W miejscu, naprzeciwko słowa „Uwagi," napisać treść w skróconej formie, jako to: Jesteśmy zdrowi; przesłaliśmy pieniądze, lub prześlemy pieniądze

Powyższa wiadomość będzie dopełniona przez nas i przesłana do Pańskich krewnych przez naszego korespondenta w Europie, przez którego obecnie można się tylko porozumiewać z osobami, zamieszkałemi w miejscowościach objętych wojną.

Z poważaniem,

LEON SANDERS

President

ווערטהער הערר:—

מיר שיקען אייך א בריעף וואס איז אנגעקומען פאר אייך פון יורעפ צו אונזער סאסייעטי. לויט ארראנדזשמענטס וואס אונזער ספעציעלער שליח מר. איזידאר הערשפילד האט געמאכט מיט די דייטשע און עסטרייכישע בעאמטע אין די מלחמה-געגענדען איז ערלויבט די איינוואוינער פון די איינגענומענע פראווינצען צו שיקען בריעף צו זייערע קרובים אין אמעריקא אויב נאר די בריעף זיינען אדרעסירט צו אונזער סאסייעטי און זיינען געשריבען אין א געוויסער פארמע. די בריעף קומען צו אונז אן אויפגעפעטנטע, און מיר שיקען זיי איבער צו די פערזאנען פאר וועמען זיי זיינען בעשטימט, אויף אונזערע עקספענסעס. מיר טהוען עס אהן צו מאכען אונטערשייד צווישען ראססען און סעקטען, לויט דעם פערשפרעכען וואס איז געגעבען געווארען פון מר. הערשפילד צו די בעאמטע.

אויב איהר ווילט ענטפערען אייערע פריינד אויף די בריעף ראטהען מיר אייך פאלגענדעס:

1. פילט אויס די אפליקיישאן-פארם וואס מיר האבען אייך צוגעשיקט.
2. אין דעם לעדיגען פלאץ אנטקעגען די ווערטער „אנ-[illegible]" שרייבט א גרוס קורץ אזוי ווי מעגליך, לויט [illegible] פארם: „מיר זיינען געזונד. מיר האבען אייך [illegible] געלד אדער מיר וועלען אייך שיקען געלד".

דיזער גרוס וועט איבערגעשריבען ווערען פון אונז און מיר וועלען דאס איבערשיקען צו אייער קרוב דורך אונזער [illegible] אין אייראפא, וועלכע זיינען די איינציגע דורך [illegible] קען פערלויפיג שיקען בריעף פון דאנען.

ערגעבענסט אייערער

לעאן סאנדערס, פרעזידענט

Instructions in English, Polish and Yiddish for arranging correspondence between America and German and Austrian occupied war zones in Eastern Europe during World War I.

JEWISH
BLOODSHEDS
IN POLISH UNIVERSITIES

COME & PROTEST
AT CITY COLLEGE CAMPUS
(Lincoln Statue)

RALLY: THURSDAY, Dec. 15th
AT 12 O'CLOCK

- MARCH -
To Polish Consulate
Halting at Columbia University

STOP THE JEWISH MASSACRE
And The National Insult

Jewish Student Defence Executive

PROTEST MEETING
New York, 1932.

AMERICAN
JEWISH·CONGRESS·COURIER

Vol. I, No. 1   *Official Bulletin of American Jewish Congress*   April 21, 1933

NEW PROTEST MEASURES ADOPTED

Joint Conference of 600 Organizations Held in New York Wednesday, April 19, Takes Strong Action

A call to more vigorous action against the Nazi program to exterminate Jewish life in Germany was sounded at the conference convened by the American Jewish Congress at the Pennsylvania Hotel, Wednesday evening, April 19. Two thousand delegates, representing six hundred organizations and societies, concurred unanimously in the adoption of three resolutions moving for a renewal of protest; for a "Protest March" through the streets of New York on May 10, the day on which books of Jewish authorship are to be publicly burned in Germany, and for the obtaining of signatures to a petition to be presented to the United States Government and the League of Nations, urging their co-operation in the effort to secure justice for the German Jew.

The keynote of the meeting was struck in the opening address by Bernard S. Deutsch, President of the American Jewish Congress, who said:

"In the face of this grave situation confronting the Jews of Germany, we meet here tonight in the determination that the struggle against Hitlerism shall go on. We shall continue with all means at our disposal to stir the conscience of the civilized world to the end that full justice shall be done to the Jew in Germany."

Dr. Stephen S. Wise, Honorary President of the American Jewish Congress, urged the adoption of all the resolutions, but in doing so he asked the delegates for their material support to make it possible for the Congress to carry through the program adopted by the conference. He asked also for faith in the leadership of the American Jewish Congress.

"Generals," he said, "cannot make announcement of plans in advance of action. You must have faith in the leaders you have democratically chosen. Whenever you lose confidence in us who lead, we are ready to yield the direction of your affairs to other leaders. But while we lead, you must have full trust in us and in our powers. And you must give generously, even to your last dollar, to enable the work of the Congress to move forward."

Dr. Wise then listed a number of acts upon the part of the Nazis that he termed as brutal as murder itself:

"If it be said that the Executive Committee in charge of the boycott in Berlin declared that this united battle against the Jew 'shall be completed in perfect quiet and with greatest discipline,' and if it be said that the Nazi government laid down the law 'Do not touch the hair of a single Jew throughout this campaign,' I call attention to the unspeakable brutality of the last word of the Nazi regulations: 'We shall finish with the Jews through the relentless power of our regulations'.

"The regulations of the boycott declared that those in charge of the boycott will be responsible that in Jewish businesses there shall be no discharge of any Christian person but those of the Jewish race shall be summarily dismissed, irrespective of the religion adopted by such members of the Jewish race. Two months' advance payment on the day of the boycott to all non-Jewish workers and personnel, but summary dismissal of all Jewish workers—without one word about pay. The English word for that is brutality. Stronger words could be used. Let brutality suffice!

"I call it brutality added to brutality to declare that the victims of the Hitlerite decree shall not be permitted to leave Germany. At one and the same time their regulations provide that Jews shall not live in Germany while decrees virtually deny Jews the right to leave the country with such possessions as they have.

"I say nothing of the brutality and worse of arranging for an Alexandrine demonstration at which all Jewish books shall be burned and in this matter Hitlerism perhaps is right. Germany must destroy the poems of Heine for Heine at moments believed that Germany was a land of freedom, and Hitlerism has given the lie to Heine and proven that Germany is a land of tyranny."

Others who spoke at the conference were Samuel Margoshes, editor of the Day, who presented the resolution for the "March"; Alexander Kahn, who offered the resolution for renewal of protest; S. Z. Tygel, who presented the resolution for the petition; and Joseph T. Tennenbaum, Abraham Goldberg, Meyer Brown, Abraham Tulin, Samuel D. Levy, Isidore Apfel, Charles Cowen, Joseph Weinberg, Nathan D. Perlman, Louis Siegal and Elias Ginsberg.

OFFICIAL BULLETIN of
THE AMERICAN JEWISH CONGRESS
Vol. I, No. 1, April 21, 1933

REMEMBER?

In Flanders fields the poppies blow
Between the crosses row on row,
*   That mark our place; and in the sky*
* . The larks, still bravely singing, fly*
Scarce heard amid the guns below.

DO THESE CROSSES MEAN ANYTHING TO YOU?

The German lust for power is again disturbing the world. Millions of Nazis are now goose-stepping to war. Our millions died, happy in the belief that they were sacrificing themselves to save the world for democracy, to guarantee eternal peace. The Nazi Reich, under a crazed lance-corporal who ran away from Flanders fields, now menaces the world just as the Kaiser threatened it in 1914. The enemy is here again.

We are the Dead. Short days ago
We lived, felt dawn, saw sunset glow,
*   Loved and were loved, and now we lie*
*   In Flanders fields.*

WAS THEIR DEATH IN VAIN?

Today millions are being persecuted for their belief in democracy. Thousands are being tortured in concentration camps because they speak for human rights and liberties. Other thousands are being starved and driven penniless from the homes of their forefathers. The beast is abroad in the land.

Take up our quarrel with the foe:
To you from failing hands we throw
*   The torch; be yours to hold it high.*
*   If ye break faith with us who die*
*   We shall not sleep, though poppies grow*
*   In Flanders fields.*

ARE YOU KEEPING THE FAITH?

Here in America Nazi agents and self-seeking agitators are spreading the disease which is destroying Europe. Here ignorant men and women are now accepting the stupid prejudices and inhuman doctrines of Nazi Germany.

On whose side are you fighting? Are you carrying the torch of American ideals or the bloody sword of hatred and persecution and war?

Non~Sectarian Anti~Nazi League

TO CHAMPION HUMAN RIGHTS, *Inc.*

20 WEST 47ᵀᴴ STREET, NEW YORK · MEdallion~3~2720

is dedicated to the task of combating the Nazi menace both here and abroad. It is composed of members from every race and creed, all bound together in the determination to safeguard fundamental human rights and liberties and to preserve American principles and ideals. The LEAGUE serves to inform the American people regarding German-paid propaganda and subversive Nazi activities in the United States which violate our noblest traditions and threaten the existence of our basic institutions. It advocates the boycott of German goods and services as the only peaceful weapon capable of stopping the spread of Nazism throughout the world and of liberating the people of Germany from their tyrants.

JOIN US IN OUR FIGHT!

"*In Flanders Fields,*" by John McCrae.

OBJECTIVES OF THE NON-SECTARIAN ANTI-NAZI LEAGUE
TO CHAMPION HUMAN RIGHTS

ANTI-NAZI BOYCOTT COMMITTEE
JEWISH WAR VETERANS
OF THE UNITED STATES

National Headquarters
276 FIFTH AVENUE
NEW YORK CITY

Telephone
MUrray Hill 4-1380

I. GEORGE FREDMAN,
Commander-in-Chief

Dear Friend:

If you believe in the doctrine of "Life, Liberty and the pursuit of Happiness", you will help our cause.

600,000 Jewish souls - helpless men, women and children - are at the mercy of the Nazi terror in Germany. Your help is needed to save them from starvation, torture and annihilation. Thousands of non-Jews have also been deprived of their rights.

The Jewish War Veterans of the United States comprising men who fought in all wars of our Republic, are conducting a national campaign of protest and enlightenment.

The distribution of the enclosed seals is a part of our campaign. Please use them. If you believe our effort should be continued, a contribution from you will be appreciated. An addressed envelope is enclosed for your convenience. Of the funds received, part will be used to relieve needy Jewish refugees.

This is your battle as well as ours! With best wishes for your own health, safety and happiness, I am

Sincerely yours,

JEWISH WAR VETERANS OF THE UNITED STATES

Morris Mendelsohn

Past Commander-in-Chief,
Chairman

Make checks payable to Jewish War Veterans of the U. S. or insert money in enclosed envelope.
COL. MAURICE SIMMONS
Treasurer

(Please use these stamps on the back of mail only.)

(See Other Side)

LETTER SOLICITING SUPPORT
of the anti-Nazi boycott by
the Jewish War Veterans of the
United States

TITLE PAGE OF YIDDISH TRANSLATION OF BIBLE
by YEHOASH (S. Bloomgarden), American Jewish Poet
New York, 1941

IMPORTANT

ABOUT MANNER OF DRESS

A REQUEST TO ALL JEWISH DAUGHTERS

▼▼▼▼▼▼▼▼▼▼▼▼▼▼▼▼▼▼▼▼▼▼▼

Remember your responsibility to Yiddishkeit and please dress as is befitting a Jewish daughter, (such as wearing longer sleeves and higher necklines) for so does G-d demand of us.

As human beings, we were given dignity which makes man different from animal. This dignity is preserved with "Tznius."

In it says "Kol Kvudah Bas Melech Pnimoh" which means, — The honor of a king's daughter lies in her modesty. Since every Jewish daughter is a Bas Melech, she should dress herself with modesty befitting a princess.

We must never forget the "Chesed" with which the Almi-ghty has always guided us, and that we must always be deserving of this chesed. We were redeemed from Egypt in the "Zchus" of the "Righteous Women" of Klal Yisroel and before G-d gave us the Torah he commanded Moshe Rabbeinu to speak to the Jewish Women first, for she upholds the Jewish home.

Today, as well, the responsibility to uphold the dignity of the Jewish home lies with the Jewish daughters. Please fulfill your responsibility and dress accordingly.

TO JEWISH YOUNG LADIES: CALL FOR MODESTY IN DRESS
Brooklyn, New York

The Cleveland Bureau of Jewish Education: A Case Study (1924-1953)

By OSCAR I. JANOWSKY

INTRODUCTION

Bureaus of Jewish Education have played an important role in the educational efforts and achievements of American Jewry. They have been central agencies organized in local communities to provide co-ordination and guidance for the independent and often ideologically discordant individual schools of a city or, in a few instances, of a larger territorial unit. The best of the Bureaus have pioneered in the promotion of standards, the provision of facilities for teacher education and licensing, the encouragement of research and experimentation, the preparation of resource materials, the evaluation of pupil achievement, the utilization of camping as a means of education, and other aspects of teaching and learning. The central aim of the Bureaus has been to advance Jewish education on all levels (including the child, youth and the adult) on a co-ordinated community-wide basis. They have sought to interpret to the local community the values of Jewish education of whatever ideological orientation, and they have pressed the local leaders to recognize Jewish education as a community responsibility, especially in the financing of educational efforts.

Beginning with the first enduring Bureau of Jewish Education in New York City in 1910, such agencies have been established in various parts of the country, so that to-day some thirty-five or more are functioning. They are variously denominated (Jewish Education Committee, Jewish Education Association, etc.), but the majority have retained the title "Bureau."

The standard work on the Bureaus is *Central Community Agencies for Jewish Education* by Abraham P. Gannes (Philadelphia: The Dropsie College for Hebrew and Cognate Learning, 1954). What follows is a case study in depth of one Bureau of Jewish Education, that of Cleveland, Ohio. The writer has studied the entire accumulation of the Minutes of the Board of Trustees of the Cleveland Bureau, and of its numerous committees, from 1924 to the summer of 1953. In addition, every important survey or study which could be located was read and analyzed — the records of the Joint Education Committee of 1928–1929, the Jewish Education Survey of 1936, the Memorandum on the Jewish Educational Situation of 1940, the Survey of 1946, and others.

The occasion for this study was The National Study of Jewish Education, sponsored by the American Association for Jewish Education and organized and for a number of years directed by this writer jointly with Uriah Z. Engelman. The research and writing of this part of the Cleveland Study was done entirely by this writer, and the paper is published with the approval of Dr. Engelman, the former and present presidents of the American Association for Jewish Education as well as the former and present executive directors of the organization, the Executive Committee of the Cleveland Bureau, and the Jewish Community Federation of that City.

In the following historical survey, it will be helpful to distinguish four periods in the Bureau's history, namely:

1. The Formative period — 1924–1931;

2. Depression and Despair — 1931–1940;

3. Recovery and Dynamic Activity — 1940–1945; and

4. The Quest for Co-ordination and Unity — 1946–1953.

*   *   *

The Bureau of Jewish Education was organized in 1924, as a result of a Survey Report on Jewish Education which was submitted early in that year. The Report revealed that 14,611 Jewish children of elementary school age, or 69 per cent of the Jewish child population, were receiving no Jewish education, and that "the vast majority" of the 8,300 Jewish youth of the community (15–20 years of age) were "unaffiliated with any Jewish activity." It was also clear that the existing communal schools — the Talmud Torahs and the Sabbath Schools — were receiving inadequate financial support for the proper performance of their educational functions.

The Report recommended that a Bureau of Jewish Education be established to concern itself with the problems of Jewish education "for the entire community." This was to entail "adequate support and development of present communal educational institutions, primarily the Talmud Torahs"; a study of the whole problem of Jewish education in Cleveland for the purpose of "making propaganda and enlisting support in the interest of the unschooled children and youth"; and "advice and general assistance to promote educational activities under congregational and institutional control." Specifically, four tasks were envisaged for the Bureau, namely:

1. The establishment of "a form of extension education to reach, en masse," many of the unschooled children of elementary school age, and equally suitable methods of extension education for youth between the ages of 15 and 20;

2. The organization of a Hebrew high school, with a regular division for graduates of the elementary schools and an extension division for students of high school age without previous training;

3. The establishment of a teachers training school for Hebrew teachers, Sunday School teachers and club leaders. The Report added that "a school of observation and practice should be conducted in conjunction with this training school"; and

4. The creation of a "financial agency for the purpose of increasing and stabilizing the source of income for recognized schools under communal direction." This was underscored as the "immediate task" of the Bureau.

To these major tasks, the Report added the warning that the "autonomy of co-operating institutions" should be safeguarded.[1]

The Survey Report thus outlined the goals of the projected Bureau. In fact, however, the recommendations of the Report may be reduced to the following two major objectives:

1. The stimulation and co-ordination of educational efforts, involving schooling and extension activities for the unschooled, the training of teachers, and general guidance for the congregational institutions; and

2. The stabilization of the finances of the existing communal schools, which implied increased revenues and subsidies as well as businesslike direction to eschew deficits.

With these primary purposes, the Bureau struggled for thirty years and, while uneven progress was made from time to time in both directions, the aims remained unrealized.

Periodizing history is frequently arbitrary and always hazardous. However, if presumed to be approximate, the identification of chronological units in the functioning of an institution serves a useful purpose in focussing attention upon major trends and achievements. With this in mind, we shall venture to indicate four well-marked periods in the life of the Bureau.

[1] "Major Recommendations from the Survey Report on Jewish Education," in Minutes of Board of Jewish Education [= MBJE] July 28, 1924, Exhibit A. All Minutes of various Committees and Boards cited in this study are located at the Bureau of Jewish Education, Cleveland, Ohio.

I

THE FORMATIVE PERIOD — 1924–1931

The seven-years from the inception of the Bureau until the assumption of financial responsibility by the Jewish Community Federation[2] proved the most eventful period in the history of the institution. Policies, programs, relationships, even conflicts, were then fashioned and modified or adjusted in accord with the working possibilities of a divided Jewish Community. It was then that the idea of maintaining a financial instrument for Jewish education independent of or parallel with the Federation was tested and found wanting. During those years, too, the principle of central communal responsibility for Jewish education through the Federation was advanced with cautious persistence until opposition yielded to acquiescence.

The leading figure in the organization of the Bureau and during its formative period was Rabbi Abba Hillel Silver, who served as President or Chairman of the Board of Trustees (the title varied in the early period) from 1924 to 1932. He chaired numerous meetings of the Board and its committees, secured the co-operation of recognized and able community leaders, clarified the aims and functions of the new agency, encouraged extension activities, teacher training and other means of expanding the range and effectiveness of Jewish education, and worked assiduously in the organization of fund-raising campaigns. Even more notable were his services in balancing the opposing forces on the Bureau Board, in promoting united efforts on the part of the proponents and opponents of intensive Hebraic education, and in retaining the good-will and co-operation of the Federation. His leadership contributed markedly to give the Bureau status as a community rather than a factional institution.

During the first two or three years of its existence, the Bureau launched or projected a variety of significant activities which, if properly sustained by community funds, might have achieved, in large measure, the first major objective of the Bureau, namely, the stimulation and co-ordination of Jewish Education. Surveys of existing communal schools not only yielded significant information on enrollment, withdrawals, teacher's salaries, financing, and various aspects of administration, but they also provided the occasion and

---

[2] The proper title was then the Federation of Jewish Charities, and subsequently, the Jewish Welfare Federation, but to avoid confusion we shall employ the name which has since become current.

the precedent for external analysis, at least of educational procedures. The Sabbath Schools then seriously in need of supervision,
received professional attention: in one year withdrawals declined
from 56 per cent to 46.5 per cent; it was anticipated that stabilization would be achieved within an additional two year period;
monthly meetings of the principals and occasional staff meetings
were held; and the study of the curriculum was foreshadowed. A
Director of Extension Education was engaged in 1926, and the
Bureau sponsored neighborhood holiday celebrations, each of which
attracted 5,000 children (about half of them unaffiliated and unschooled), and summer story-hour centers with an attendance of
about 400. One effective enrollment campaign, conducted in October, 1926, with the co-operation of the Council of Jewish Women,
Hadassah, the Temple Sisterhoods and others, brought 1,300 or
1,400 additional children into Bureau Schools. A monthly Jewish
Educational Bulletin for adults and adolescents was inaugurated to
interpret Jewish education to the community. A Jewish Teachers
Institute was organized, and plans were formulated to combine it
with the Hebrew Teachers Institute into a College of Jewish Studies,
which was to include a high school department, classes for club
leaders and social workers, and even adult Jewish education was
projected. At the same time, the Bureau began to study the trouble-
some problem of tuition fees and grappled with the educational
needs created by the shifting of the Jewish population to new areas.

The Bureau co-operated with the Camp Wise Association in a
sustained effort to "judaize" the camp, with the Council Educational
Alliance, and with the newly-formed (apparently with Bureau help)
Jewish Education Committee of the Federation's Recreation Conference in "intensifying Jewish Cultural activities" in existing clubs
and in the training of club leaders, for whom educational materials
were prepared. Aid was extended to the Young Judea Clubs. The
effective Extension Education Committee of the Bureau prepared
plans for weekly extension activities (for unaffiliated children), em-
bracing illustrated lectures, Bible "movies" and slides, Jewish
music and dramatics and religious services. It talked about programs for Jewish college students and about the organization of
Jewish clubs in the Senior and Junior High schools of Cleveland
which were to be federated in a League. It projected a conference
— a permanent conference — of the group-work agencies, orphan
homes, synagogues and temples, B'nai B'rith, Council of Jewish
Women and other groups to co-ordinate the work of extension
education. Parent-teachers meetings were held, and projects were

outlined for an ambitious Speaker's Bureau and for a Library of Jewish Information.[3]

The high-water mark of this exuberant period of communal planning for Jewish education was reached in 1926. A[braham] H. Friedland, Educational Director of the Bureau, Superintendent of the Cleveland Hebrew School and admired leader of the Hebraic forces of the community declared proudly that the Bureau had gone "over the top" in educational work during that year.[4] Three new Religious Schools were opened, when only two had been planned; although no new Hebrew schools had been projected, two were actually opened; the original goal of 500 new pupils was exceeded by more than 800 in the enrollment campaign; the Jewish Teachers Institute was reorganized on a two-day-a-week basis; and the Hebrew Teachers Institute achieved an enrollment of 100. All elements had reason to be pleased with the educational accomplishments. Fund-raising, however, lagged far behind the requirements of an effective Bureau, and it was on this unyielding obstacle that the promising effort of the Bureau foundered.

The fund-raising campaigns of the Bureau were planned well and prosecuted with vigor and intelligence. A handful of lay people under the leadership of the President succeeded in involving the Federation group, including its president, representative leaders of the congregations, the Jewish Women's societies, which functioned through a Jewish Women's Committee, some of the Orthodox elements, and a Young Men's Group. A Jewish Education Club was organized. In the Spring of 1927, the campaign apparatus of the Federation, with Division Chairman, was employed. But all these

---

[3] On these activities and plans, see MBJE, Dec. 15, 1924; March 24, and Exhibit 4, July 21, August 18, Nov. 23, 1925; April 19, July 6, Sept. 1, Oct. 26, 1926; Jan. 16, 1927; Minutes, Executive Committee, Sept. 15, 1925; Minutes (Joint) of Executive Committee and Finance and Budget Committee, June 2, 1925 and Exhibit 6; Minutes, Educational Executive Committee, June 8, June 18, Sept. 20, 1926; Minutes, Extension Education Committee, Aug. 14, Aug. 18, Sept. 18, 1925; Feb. 12, Feb. 18, March 10, April 23, May 28, Aug. 19, 1926; Feb. 11, Feb. 28, 1927; Minutes, Joint Meeting of Extension Education Committee and Committee on School Locations, Aug. 10, 1927; Minutes, Publicity Committee, Aug. 12, Aug. 26, 1925; Minutes, Sabbath School Committee, Aug. 26, 1926; Minutes, Joint Meeting of Sabbath School Committee and Council of Jewish Women, Aug. 10, 1925; Minutes, Conferences on Sabbath Schools, June 16, Sept. 7, 1925; Minutes, Committees on Co-operation of Council Educational Alliance and Bureau, May 28, 1926; Minutes, Conference on Co-operation of Bureau and Camp Wise Association, n. d. (c. Feb. 1927); Minutes, Conferences of Representatives of Council Educational Alliance, Cleveland Hebrew School and Board of Jewish Education, April 29, May 6, 1925.

[4] MBJE, Feb. 17, 1927.

efforts were unequal to the task of raising about $100,000 annually which the Bureau required for proper functioning. In 1925, about $39,000 was raised and in 1926, over $53,000. These campaigns were far from failures, for it was recognized that the "process of educating the community to the cause of Jewish education was very slow." However, when redoubled efforts in 1927 yielded $62,583.99, discouragement became marked. Viewed in perspective, the raising of more than $62,000 for Jewish education in 1927 was a remarkable achievement. At the time, however, it resulted in serious curtailment of Bureau activities and impelled the hard-pressed leadership to look to Federation for financial deliverance.[5]

The Bureau struggled through three more years of discouraging efforts to raise the necessary funds, with the burden falling increasingly upon the President. The income fell consistently to less than $56,000 in 1928, some $52,000 in 1929, and a little over $45,000 in 1930. Repeated efforts were made to induce the Federation to assume responsibility for the budget. In June, 1928, a Joint Study Committee of the Federation and the Bureau began a searching analysis of the situation of Jewish Education in Cleveland. Some fifteen sessions were held and on July 3, 1929, it recommended that the Bureau be reorganized and that "the Federation include the general field of Jewish Education as one of its activities."

The President negotiated repeatedly with the Federation during 1930, but it was not until December of that year that he was able to report definitely that the Bureau would be included in the Federation's united Jewish Campaign of 1931. The following month he informed the Board that the Bureau had been admitted into the Jewish Welfare Fund for 1931, with an anticipated allotment of $50,000. The commitment was for 1931 only, but, once the decisive step had been taken, the association proved permanent.[6]

[5] MBJE, Dec. 15, Dec. 24, 1924; Jan. 6, 1925; Feb. 10, April 19, Dec. 1, 1926; Feb. 17, May 18, 1927; Minutes, Finance and Budget Committee, Oct. 27, 1925; Feb. 12, 1926; Sept. 22, Oct. 12, Nov. 2, 1927; Minutes, Campaign Committee, Sept. 24, Oct. 1, Dec. 7, 1925; March 9, 1926; Minutes, Conference . . . Representing Congregations and Profession, Jan. 6, 1925; Minutes, Joint Conference of Boards of Trustees (of Temples) and Board of Jewish Education, Nov. 6, 1925; Minutes, Joint Meeting of Boards (of Temple Sisterhood), Council of Jewish Women, and Co-operative League of Jewish Ladies Societies, Nov. 18, 1925; Minutes, Pre-Campaign Conference, Sept. 27, 1926; Minutes, Jewish Education Club, April 13, 1926.

[6] MBJE, Jan. 19, Feb. 16, May 17, June 25, Sept, 27, Dec. 26, 1928; Jan. 28, April 29, Oct. 7, 1929; Jan. 5, Sept. 11, Dec. 4, 1930; Jan. 15, 1931; Minutes, Executive Committee, Nov. 1, 1927; Minutes, Finance and Budget Committee, Jan. 8, May 22, 1929; April 17, 1930; Minutes, Joint Jewish Education Committee, June 1, 1928 to July 3, 1929.

By 1931, when the Federation finally came to the rescue, the Bureau had been reduced to a shell. Lack of funds had compelled first economies, then curtailment of activities, with a consequent flagging of interest, until little remained beyond the determination of a handful to carry on. Schools were closed, enrollment fell off, the Cleveland Hebrew School staggered under deficits, the offices first of Extension Education Director and then of Executive Director were abolished, the progress of the Sabbath Schools was arrested, the Extension Education Committee "was totally without funds," necessitating the abandonment of the summer story-hour centers and the reduction of the holiday celebrations to a minimum.

The Bureau, however, survived. The President and the hard core of the Board held the group together, supervising the office, raising funds and planning activities. The Educational Director and several volunteers continued to work with the group-work agencies. The unschooled children received some attention through holiday celebrations. Above all, the Jewish Teachers Institute and the Hebrew Teachers Institute continued to function.[7]

The idea of the Bureau had taken root and the principle of community responsibility for Jewish education through the Federation had finally been recognized. Structurally, even the shell of a Bureau was an asset. If adequate funds were to become available through the Federation, the devotees of Jewish education could be counted on to revive the activities which had perforce been allowed to languish, and to plan further for the stimulation and co-ordination of Jewish education.

II

DEPRESSION AND DESPAIR — 1931–1940

The second period in the history of the Bureau was characterized by extreme depression, when income was reduced to a minimum, services were curtailed beyond the margin of safety, some of the most important leaders withdrew and, for a time at least, the Bureau was little more than a name and an ideal. That it did not disappear entirely was due primarily to two men — Rabbi Barnett Brickner, the President from 1932–1940, and A. H. Friedland, who continued to serve as Educational Director until his untimely death in the fall of 1939.

[7] MBJE, Oct. 21, 1927; March 22, Oct. 24, Nov. 15, Dec. 26, 1928; April 29, Sept. 24, Nov. 21, 1929; Jan. 16, April 3, 1930; Jan. 15, 1931; Minutes, Finance and Budget Committee, Nov. 13, 1928; Minutes, Board of Trustees of Jewish Teachers Institute, Oct. 31, 1927; Minutes, Conference of Council Educational Alliance and Bureau, Oct. 9, Oct. 16, 1928.

Rabbi Brickner rallied the remaining lay forces of the Bureau and even succeeded in attracting some new volunteers, whom he led in a sustained "holding action" for Jewish Education. Himself a leading local and national figure, he preserved the status of the Bureau as a community agency, emphasizing intensive, Hebraic schooling as well as extension education. He pressed his colleagues repeatedly to re-examine and formulate the aims and functions of the Bureau. When he relinquished the Presidency, recovery was well in sight with rising budgets and a new and energetic Executive Director at the helm. The Bureau had been a "protective agency for Jewish education" since its inception. During his administration, this function proved the primary and lasting contribution.

A. H. Friedland was the leading protagonist of intensive Hebraic education, but as Educational Director he served the Bureau with zeal and dedication in all its undertakings. When the Bureau was organized in 1924, he was Superintendent of the Cleveland Hebrew School, and that institution remained the center of his professional interest. However, his status and influence in the community were determined not by this limited function, but by his ideal which was the extension of Hebraic Culture. The architects of the Bureau recognized at its very inception that Friedland was "eminently capable of directing the development of Jewish Education," and he was soon entrusted with "all the educational planning of the Bureau, including the work of extension education and the other projects contemplated by the Board, in addition to the field of the existing Hebrew Schools and Religious Schools." In this capacity he directed the preparation of materials for, and dealt with the educational needs of, the Council Religious Schools and extension education; he co-operated in the work of neighborhood holiday celebrations, planned courses for club leaders, headed the Jewish Teachers Institute and, in general, acted as the professional educational spokesman of the Board.

During the difficult period of the 1930's, Friedland pressed the Board to recognize the needs of the Cleveland Hebrew School as the first claim upon the meager funds. However, when the Bureau staff and office disappeared and he remained the sole professional worker, he readily assumed the numerous tasks entailed in Bureau activities. He concerned himself with the curriculum and hours of instruction of the Council Religious Schools, prepared for its teachers a handbook in the teaching of Jewish history, and guided the schools in the introduction of text books and libraries. He served as adviser to the League of Jewish Youth and worked with the Young Judea Clubs, prepared holiday booklets, planned radio broadcasts, co-operated with the Council Educational Alliance in club leader work, held conferences on adult education with the Council of Jewish Women, Hadassah, and other Jewish organizations, addressed numerous meetings and conferences, presented to the Board statistics on the Jewish child population of Cleveland (1935) and on teachers' salaries in various cities (1934). He even found the energy to experiment with standardized tests and with home reading for pupils. The children's literature, especially *Sippurim Yofim*, which he produced and which sold many thousands of copies, was an achievement of the first order. He introduced the *Oneg Shabbat* in the Hebrew schools. When he became seriously ill in 1935, we are told that he directed the educational work from the hospital. In a word, Friedland's intense and varied activities and his personality established him as an educational force in the community. And he possessed the magnetism to attract not alone followers but devoted disciples.[8]

The Bureau required dedicated workers to survive, because the Great Depression blasted the hopes even for minimal budgets which affiliation with the Federation had encouraged. The necessary funds simply could not be raised even by the Federation. The anticipated allotment of $50,000 for 1931 (the first year of affiliation) was reduced to less than $39,000. In 1932, the Federation found it possible to appropriate only $20,892 to the Cleveland Hebrew School and $2,785 for all other Bureau needs. And in 1933, when no guarantee at all for the "immediate future" could be held out, the Bureau received a little over $18,000. It was not until 1938 that the Federation allotment exceeded $40,000.

The Cleveland Hebrew Schools, and the Council Religious Schools were allowed the first claim on these meager funds, and they proved insufficient. Budgets were slashed, teachers' salaries cut, staff reduced, hours of instruction in the Hebrew Schools shortened 20 per cent. In 1932, the latter were closed entirely during the three summer months, while in 1933 the school year of the Council Religious Schools was reduced to six months. A miracle kept the Hebrew Schools open at all — a latter-day miracle in the shape of teachers, who continued their work even when salaries were over $22,000 in arrears in 1938. The situation was well summarized at the close of

---

[8] MBJE, Oct. 9, 1924; Feb. 10, March 1, 1926; Oct. 31, 1927; Feb. 16, Nov. 15, 1928; Jan. 30, March 2, Dec. 26, 1933; Feb. 8, May 22, 1934; Feb. 25, Sept. 16, Dec. 3, 1935; March 18, Oct. 21, 1936; June 22, 1937; Feb. 27, 1939; Minutes, Finance and Budget Committee, Feb. 12, Feb. 19, 1926; Minutes, Executive Education Committee, June 8, Sept. 20, 1926; Minutes, Extension Education Committee, Feb. 12, 1926; Jan. 10, 1933; April 30, 1935; Minutes, General Membership Meeting of Bureau, Jan. 24, 1935.

1935 in a letter to the President. For over three years, it read, the Hebrew Schools

> have managed to lead a wretched existence on a budget which brought about the impairment of standards and the victimization of the entire staff.[9]

Needless to say, the budgets of the Bureau (as distinct from school subsidies) and its extension activities reached the vanishing point. As early as 1932, the office expenses of the Bureau had, according to the Board minutes, fallen from $12,500 in former years to less than $3,000, and in the following year, the Bureau office was abandoned entirely, and the secretary's desk was moved to the office of the Hebrew School. The House Committee found some comfort in the thought that the closer association of the secretary with the Educational Director was "much more satsifactory than heretofore." The stipend for extension education was reduced so thoroughly that in 1933, when a Sukkot radio program was planned, the sum of $15.00 was authorized "to be spent for the talent."[10]

Homeless (so far as an independent office was concerned), without professional staff, other than the Educational Director, and virtually without funds for extension education, the Bureau nevertheless continued to function. A minimum of extension education was provided with the aid of volunteers, among whom Nathan Brilliant figured prominently. Mass holiday celebrations were held intermittently, occasional holiday radio programs were given, some 20 young Judea Clubs with about 200 members (1935) were assisted. A League of Jewish Youth claiming 65 organizations and 4,000 members (1936) received much attention from the Educational Director who served as its adviser. From time to time, efforts were made to increase the enrollment, especially of the Council Religious Schools. Contact was maintained with the Council Educational Alliance and assistance rendered with Jewish content in club work. The most significant achievement during this period was the Jewish Teachers Institute, or Institute of Jewish Studies, as it was often called. With a negligible budget, it was reorganized in 1934, and grew rapidly from a register of 25 to a school of 200 to 300 students. It met each year in a different Temple or Synagogue; distinguished Rabbis, even those distant from the Bureau, volunteered their services in unit courses; and the Educational Director planned the

---

[9] Klein to Brickner, in MBJE, Dec. 3, 1935.

[10] MBJE, Oct. 13, 1931; Jan. 14, March 3, Aug. 15, 1932; Jan. 30, March 2, April 24, May 25, Oct. 2, 1933; April 24, Oct. 31, 1934; Dec. 3, 1935; March 31, 1938; Minutes, Extension Education Committee, Sept. 18, 1933.

curriculum and lectured as well. However, in 1938, the enrollment dropped disastrously almost to the level of the early 1930's, and in the fall of the following year, the Board decided to defer the re-opening of the Teachers Institute until a new Bureau Director had been appointed.[11]

Community-wide problems involving Jewish education likewise received the attention of the Bureau. During the first decade of its existence, only the Cleveland Hebrew School and the Council Religious Schools received support from the funds they were able to marshall, although the rigorously Orthodox *Yeshivath Adath B'nai Israel* and one of the Yiddish schools made efforts to achieve affiliation.[12] In the 1930's, however, the pressure from these sources increased and compelled the Bureau to give some consideration to the problem.

In 1931, the *Sholem Aleichem Folk Shul* applied for affiliation. A committee investigated the school and agreed that it represented "a fine spontaneous type of self-expression in Jewish life," and was, therefore, "entitled to the full co-operation of the Bureau." It recommended affiliation with a small subsidy. Affiliation was approved and a representative of the school joined the Bureau Board in 1932.[13] The latter, however, decided that no new financial responsibilities could be assumed, when the Bureau was unable to meet the needs of the "present agencies."

The *Yeshivath Adath B'nai Israel* pressed for a subsidy in 1936, but the Board decided to await clarification through the Berkson-Rosen Survey which had been launched. In 1937, the Federation voted to allot $3,000 to the *Yeshivath Adath B'nai Israel* and lesser sums to the Workman's Circle Schools and the *Yiddish Folk Shule*. However, the Bureau Board felt that this action had been premature, and it was decided to leave the determination of the relationship of these bodies to the Bureau to the Implementation Committee which was expected to consider the Berkson-Rosen recommendations.[14]

[11] MBJE, Jan. 15, June 3, Oct. 13, 1931; March 3, May 26, Nov. 10, Dec. 21, 1932; Jan. 30, 1933; Feb. 8, April 24, Sept. 26, Oct. 31, 1934; Feb. 25, May 29, Sept. 16, Dec. 3, 1935; Feb. 26, Oct. 21, Dec. 22, 1936; June 22, Dec. 2, 1937; Jan. 13, June 2, Sept. 29, Dec. 27, 1938; Feb. 27, March 30, June 2, Nov. 16, 1939; Minutes, Extension Education Committee, May 12, Oct. 29, 1931; Nov. 4, 1932; Jan. 10, 1933; April 30, 1935; Minutes, 12th Annual Meeting, Bureau of Jewish Education, April 16, 1936.

[12] MBJE, May 21, 1926, May 18, 1927.

[13] The school was discontinued in 1942 and affiliation was then terminated. See "Report of Nominating Committee," in Minutes, Board of Trustees of Bureau, March 16, 1942.

[14] MBJE, Nov. 30, 1931; March 3, May 26, 1932; Sept. 26, 1934; March 18, 1936; April 7, Oct. 14, 1937; March 31, 1938; Jan. 18, 1940.

The question of introducing the study of Hebrew in the public high schools likewise commanded the attention of the Bureau. Hebrew had been successfully introduced as a foreign language in public high schools of New York City, and a majority of the Bureau Board believed that the experiment should be repeated in the high schools of Cleveland with large Jewish student enrollments. Vigorous leadership in this cause was provided by Ezra Shapiro. A product of the Cleveland Hebrew School (he was in turn student, teacher and member of the Hebrew School Board), he was intensely devoted to Jewish education and Hebraic culture, and at the same time he was thoroughly at home in the American environment. He was elected to the Bureau Board in July 1930, and rose rapidly to leadership both in the Bureau and as its representative in the Federation. In 1939, he was elected President of the Cleveland Hebrew School.

The matter was first broached by the President of the Bureau, in 1936, but it came to a head two years later when a committee headed by Ezra Shapiro unanimously reported in favor of the project. An entire meeting was devoted to a discussion which often sparkled and, in the end, the motion to approve and to urge the Jewish Community Council to take action was carried 19 to 5. The Executive Committee of the Community Council, however, decided that the time was inopportune, although it agreed that Hebrew was intrinsically worthy of study in the public high schools.[15]

Throughout this period, too, the Board tried repeatedly to reappraise and redefine the functions of the Bureau. Rabbi Silver had raised the question immediately on the assumption of financial responsibility by the Federation. Rabbi Brickner outlined his views soon after he assumed office. Committees were appointed and reports were heard. The Berkson-Rosen Survey made a searching analysis and outlined a significant program. But no decisive action was taken by the Board. After fifteen years of effort, the Bureau remained an agency for the channelling of subsidies and an instrument for a variety of desultory educational activities. A co-ordinated community-wide program remained to be developed.[16]

[15] MBJE, Jan. 9, 1936; Nov. 7, Dec. 27, 1938.
[16] MBJE, Jan. 15, 1931; Nov. 10, 1932; Dec. 26, 1933; May 22, 1934; May 29, 1935; Minutes, Special Study Committee of Bureau, April 13, 1931; Minutes, Extension Education Committee, Feb. 3, Nov. 4, 1932; Isaac B. Berkson and Ben Rosen, 1936 Jewish Education Survey of Cleveland, Part III — the Bureau of Jewish Education, Functions, Organization and Finances.

III

RECOVERY AND DYNAMIC ACTIVITY — 1940–1945

By 1940, the ravages of the Great Depression had been forgotten, economic recovery had restored confidence, and the Federation had begun to allocate larger sums to the Bureau. After nearly fifteen years of frustration, the Bureau was in a position to assume effective educational leadership in the community. At the same time, the irritations which had since its inception disturbed the relations of the Bureau with the Cleveland Hebrew School abated. In 1940, George J. Klein, Chairman of the Administrative Committee of the Cleveland Hebrew School, was elected President of the Bureau, and the element represented by him became truly "the backbone of the Bureau." In that year, too, Azriel L. Eisenberg was named Director of the Bureau. Young, energetic, and resourceful, with executive ability and a full awareness of new developments in Jewish education throughout the country, he was able to provide five years of effective leadership. He regarded the Bureau as an agency for the entire community, and, although the communal schools claimed his first attention, he won the confidence of and rendered service to the congregational schools as well. His impact upon the community was felt so quickly that hardly six months after his arrival, Rabbi Rudolf Rosenthal was able to state that the Bureau had already been "of great service" to congregational schools and was making its influence felt "very definitely" in every congregation.[17]

The Director made numerous supervisory class visits, especially but not exclusively in the Cleveland Hebrew School and the Council Religious Schools, submitting reports to the directors of the schools with comments and suggestions, and he was regularly on call for consultation and guidance. He met with school directors and discussed with them matters affecting curricula, teachers, texts, enrollment, etc. He held district conferences (Kinsman, for example) of all elements concerned with Jewish education for the consideration of common problems. He administered uniform tests to graduates of congregational Hebrew departments and experimented with a co-operative high school class for such students.

Special attention was devoted to the Jewish teaching profession, teacher training and teaching aids. A survey was made of the Jewish religious teachers of Cleveland and the Board apprised of the unsound state of the profession. The Jewish Teachers Institute

---

[17] Minutes, Study Committee of the Bureau, Feb. 10, 1941.

was reopened and in-service training rendered through conferences, seminars, especially during the summer, work-shops, clinics and demonstration lessons. Teaching-aids were provided in the form of holiday workbooks and "Observations," a bulletin for the improvement of teaching. A Jewish Teachers Council was organized and its co-operation secured in planning uniform salary scales. A Board of License was established and a retirement and pension plan adopted.

Considerable activity developed in extension education and youth work. Holiday celebrations and occasional radio programs were continued. The Hebrew Readers Group (*Hakoreh Hazair*) reached a membership of some 300, and far larger numbers read *World Over* and pictorial stories from the Bible. Efforts to co-ordinate Jewish Education with the work of the Council Educational Alliance and other recreational agencies continued. Adult classes were organized. The League of Jewish Youth was merged with the Young Adult Bureau in the hope that a unified program would result. The Young Judea Clubs were reorganized and new units established. The Zionist Youth Council was aided. And a person was added to the staff to assist the Director with youth activities.

The Bureau made its technical facilities available and provided services to all schools and youth groups which desired aid. The publication department furnished educational materials to all schools. The Joint Purchasing Agency and Book Store sold thousands of books and units of educational materials to a dozen schools of all types.

Camp Galil, too, should be mentioned. The Director established and maintained this summer camp on a self-sustaining basis. Although "indirectly and unofficially" connected with the Bureau, the Board heard reports of its progress and lent it its enthusiastic encouragement.[18]

Parallel with the extensive activities and services of the Bureau, this period saw the admission of new educational elements, a clarification of the meaning of affiliation, a reorganization of the structure of the Board and some very significant attempts at community-wide co-ordination of Jewish education.

[18] On these varied activities, see MBJE, Sept. 30, Nov. 4, 1940; Feb. 17, March 17, April 21, June 10, Sept. 15, Oct. 20, 1941; Jan. 26, Feb. 16, Sept. 22, Oct. 27, Nov. 16, Dec. 21, 1942; Jan. 25, Feb. 15, June 28, Nov. 15, 1943; Jan. 17, Feb. 22, March 20, April 17, June 12, Sept. 25, Oct. 23, Nov. 20, 1944; Jan. 22, May 28, Oct. 22, 1945; 17th, 18th and 20th Annual Meetings, Bureau of Jewish Education, May 28, 1941; April 22, 1942; April 26, 1944; Minutes, of Meeting, Representatives of Kinsman Schools, Nov. 28, 1940; Minutes, Faculty Committee, Jewish Teachers Institute, Oct. 15, 1941; Minutes, Bureau-Council Educational Alliance Committee, Dec. 2, 1942; Minutes, Meeting of Representatives of Congregational and Communal Schools, July 26, Aug. 7, 1944.

Mention has been made of the efforts of the *Yeshivath Adath B'nai Israel* and the Yiddish schools to affiliate with the Bureau.[19] In 1940, negotiations began in earnest, and despite difficulties, especially with the *Yeshivath Adath B'nai Israel*, an accord was finally reached and affiliation was approved by the Board in 1941. Recognizing the prevalent diversity in the philosophy and practice of Jewish life, full autonomy was assured in matters affecting courses of study, orientation and methodology. However, the new affiliates agreed to conform to a code of hygienic, sanitary and safety requirements and to "certain minimum standards of record keeping." The Bureau gave assurances that it would "extend its maximum facilities to all institutions affiliated with it." One stipulation aroused misgivings. The Board insisted that the reasonable budgetary needs of the older affiliates, namely the Cleveland Hebrew School, the Council Religious Schools and the Institute of Jewish Studies, should be the "first fiscal obligation" of the Bureau and that only additional funds should be "fairly and equitably" allocated. The *Yeshivath Adath B'nai Israel* feared that the funds which it had reason to expect might in the future be diverted toward the support of the above institutions. A clarification that the stipulation would not apply to *additional* allocations by the Federation removed the apprehensions, and the new affiliates joined the Bureau in mutual confidence and good faith.[20]

At all times, the burden of work of the Board of Trustees of the Bureau, not unlike other similar bodies, was borne by a small number of persons. In times of discouragement, when activities languished, and even attendance at meetings shrank, reorganization was attempted in the hope of attracting new and active elements. Thus, early in 1935, provision was made for a Board of 51 with a rotating membership, involving a three-year term of service and the retirement of one-third each year. In 1941, however, when the influence of the Bureau began to be felt in the congregational schools and in the community as a whole, the desire to achieve a "representative" Board led to an extensive reorganization.

Under the leadership of Rabbi Armond E. Cohen, a Study Committee devised a plan whereby the principle of rotation was retained and representation allotted in definite proportions to the affiliated agencies and to the community at large. Moreover, two

[19] See *supra*, p. 334.

[20] Minutes, Board of Trustees of Bureau, April 21, May 20, June 10, June 23, 1941; Minutes, Study Committee of Board, Oct. 28, 1940; Memorandum, Committee on *Yeshivath Adath B'nai Israel*, June 19, 1941; Memorandum, Committee on Workman's Circle Schools, Dec. 12, 1941.

categories of affiliates were distinguished, namely, the communally-supported agencies and the congregations which maintained schools. Finally, the number of representatives of each of the first category of affiliates — the Cleveland Hebrew School, the *Yeshivath Adath B'nai Israel*, etc. — was determined by the size of the school and the number of sessions per week (number of children multiplied by number of sessions). The congregational affiliates were allotted from one to four representatives, depending upon the size of the adult membership of each. The new Board which took office in May, 1941, consisted of 60 members distributed in the following proportions: 24 (40 per cent) represented the communally-subsidized schools; 24 (40 per cent) were named by the congregations; and 12 (20 per cent) were co-opted to represent the community at large. One further important step was taken in 1944, when a representative of the Hebrew Teachers Association was invited to join the Board as a non-voting member.[21]

The vitality of the Bureau during this period was reflected not only in the changed structure of the Board, but in the character of its meetings as well. Discussions of fundamental questions in Jewish education were held more frequently, and in 1944, it was decided to devote part of the business meetings of the Board to a consideration of important developments in the field. Thereafter, for five consecutive monthly sessions, the Director led in discussions of the status of Jewish education in Cleveland, the all-day school, Hebrew in the high schools, the camp as a Jewish educational agency, and the aims, program and achievements of the *Beth Hayeled*.[22]

The most important achievements of the Bureau during the early 1940's were in the area of co-ordination. The efforts to extend the services and guidance of the Bureau to all Jewish educational agencies of the community were, of course, laudable, but the cumulative effects of such endeavors could result in the enhancement of Jewish education only if the congregational as well as the communally-subsidized schools shared in the determination of objectives and willingly co-operated in their implementation. The Board and the Director were well advised in fashioning and utilizing the Committee on Co-ordination, which proved its worth during this period.

The Committee on Co-ordination resulted from a discussion

[21] On the Board reorganization, see Minutes, Board of Trustees of Bureau, April 24, Dec. 18, 1934; Jan. 20, March 17, 1941; June 12, Sept. 25, 1944; Minutes, Study Committee of Board, Jan. 15, 1941; Minutes, 17th Annual Meeting of Bureau, May 28, 1941.

[22] See Minutes, Board of Trustees of Bureau, Sept. 15, 1941; Nov. 15, 1943; Sept. 25, Oct. 23, Nov. 20, Dec. 18, 1944; Jan. 22, Feb. 19, 1945; Minutes, Executive Committee of Board, Sept. 15, 1944.

respecting duplication and lack of co-operation among the schools which the Director precipitated at a Board meeting in November, 1941. Some members saw the need for a unified Jewish public education system for the entire city. Others would allow for autonomy, but urged united efforts in matters affecting teachers, hours of instruction, curricula and the like. Since practically all favored co-ordination of some sort, the Board decided to set up the Committee.

Under the chairmanship first of Ezra Shapiro and subsequently of Myron Guren the Committee defined rather broadly the range of co-ordination. The school calendar, hours of instruction, qualifications of teachers, supervision, the curriculum, even the consolidation and amalgamation of schools were to be considered; and all schools, even the congregational, were to be included. To be sure, the complex questions of curriculum, supervision and consolidation defied easy solution, but the Committee did formulate a very significant program of action, which the Bureau Board approved on June 17, 1942.

The program included three sets of recommendations. The one-day-a-week schools were urged to adopt a uniform school calendar with a fixed minimum number of sessions per week, and at least two-and-a-half hours of instruction per week. Qualifications for Confirmation were recommended, among them the ability to read Hebrew and attendance at Sabbath and Holiday Services. In principle, the consolidation of the Council Religious Schools with the Congregational schools was approved, but obvious difficulties led to the recommendation that for the time being only the high school units be merged.

For the two and three-day-a-week congregational schools, a uniform calendar was likewise recommended, and a minimum of 125 hours of Hebrew instruction per year, in addition to the other subjects. The "intensive" schools (meeting four to six times a week) were advised to set up a committee for the study of enrollment and turn-over, curriculum, methods, teachers' qualifications, achievement tests, etc., and the attention of the schools was directed especially to a consideration of the possibilities of consolidation. Finally, a *Bar Mitzvah* certificate was recommended and requirements indicated.

It is most significant that when the committee met in February, 1944, to review what had been achieved, real progress was noted, except in the case of the Council Religious Schools which lacked "facilities and teachers." The school year had been extended, a uniform school calendar adopted, hours of attendance increased, and confirmation requirements broadened. It is equally significant that the least progress was made in the "intensive" schools which clung to their respective individualities.

In 1944, the Committee on Co-ordination and the Board concerned themselves with the establishment of a Board of License for teachers (already mentioned above), sick leave, group insurance, etc.; with the establishment of a College of Jewish Studies; and with various plans for the extension of "intensive" education and the improvement of the teaching of Hebrew.[23]

One other achievement remains to be noted. The Bureau had never had an adequate home, and many felt that this deficiency resulted in a loss of identity as well as prestige. In 1941, the Director reported that the Bureau and Cleveland Hebrew School offices were inadequate and undignified, that the Jewish Teachers Institute was without permanent quarters, and that the Hebrew Teachers Institute was housed in a broken down "fire trap." He recommended (and others had urged this before) that a building be secured for the central activities of the Bureau. The Board approved unanimously and Samuel Rosenthal assumed the leadership in raising the necessary funds. A building was purchased on East Boulevard and named the "Friedland Educational Center of the Bureau of Jewish Education." The Bureau moved into its own quarters in 1943.[24]

The achievements of the Bureau during the period 1940–1945 were truly far-reaching, but a word of caution must be injected. No comprehensive program was achieved for the kind of service which might permeate the Jewish educational endeavors of the community, and this lack touched the very core of Jewish Education.

The Director did propose in 1941 an extensive plan for Bureau activities which included trained supervision with adequate staff, an experimental model school, studies of curricula, textbooks, and methods of teaching, periodic testing of pupils, provision for secondary Jewish education and for teacher training, and other significant services. These functions had indeed been recommended for the Bureau by the Berkson-Rosen Survey of 1936, but had been disregarded. During this period, progress was made in administrative devices, formal requirements relating to confirmation, teaching-aids, teacher training and teacher-welfare. Through his personal

[23] See Minutes, Board of Trustees of Bureau, Nov. 17, Dec. 15, 1941; Jan. 26, May 25, June 17, 1942; Nov. 15, 1943; Feb. 21, March 20, June 12, 1944; June 20, 1945; Minutes, Committee on Co-ordination, Jan. 15, April 13, June 9, 1942; Feb. 14, 1944.

[24] Minutes, Board of Trustees of the Bureau, Jan. 20, Feb. 17, 1941; Dec. 21, 1942; April 21, May 19, Sept. 20, Oct. 18, 1943; Jan. 17, 1944; Minutes, Building Committee, Nov. 24, 1942; Sept. 15, 1943.

influence, the Director also succeeded in providing educational guidance and stimulation. But the basic problems of educational standards, supervision and achievement could not be dealt with effectively. And the aims and objectives of Jewish education were rarely on the Bureau agenda. The question had barely been raised.[25]

IV

THE QUEST FOR CO-ORDINATION AND UNITY: 1946–1953

In the fall of 1945, Azriel L. Eisenberg was invited to direct the newly-organized Bureau of Jewish Education in Philadelphia. He was released by the Board, but the feeling was widespread that his leadership would be missed. For the better part of a year, an acting-director was in charge of the Bureau, and in September, 1946, Nathan Brilliant, who had for many years served the Bureau faithfully and well in a volunteer capacity, became its Director.

This period witnessed a great deal of activity on the part of the Director and the Board. In the main, however, it may be characterized by the following efforts or accomplishments: the completion and consolidation of some of the gains of the preceding half-dozen years, the extension of the Bureau's influence in the community through the Adult School of Jewish Studies and through the admission of new affiliates; the erection of a new Bureau building; and sustained efforts at co-ordination and especially efforts at mergers, which proved in large measure unsuccessful.

The traditional extension activities of the Bureau, especially in youth work, were continued under a director of youth activities, whose services and salary were shared by the Bureau, the Zionist Youth Commission and Camp Galil. The camp, incidentally, continued to thrive until the site was sold early in 1953. In 1952, a TV Sunday School was inaugurated. With the co-operation of the larger synagogues and temples, Sunday School programs were presented for one-half hour on six successive Sundays during the year. The Bureau library which contained books and periodicals in three languages was expanded to include film strips, slides, records and other audio-visual aides. The latter especially were in demand by schools, youth groups, the community centers, and others. The Bureau assisted the Council Educational Alliance with Jewish content materials and co-operated with the Jewish Community Cen-

[25] See Minutes, Study Committee, Feb. 10, 1941; Minutes, Board of Trustees of Bureau, April 21, 1941; June 28, Nov. 15, 1943.

ters, for whom a "Great Jewish Books" course was elaborated by the Director. The Bureau also shared in the formulation of plans by the Federation's Social Agency Committee for the integration of Jewish education and group work services.[26]

The Board of License, previously established, proceeded with the work of rating and classifying teachers into categories, according to which permanent and temporary licenses and teaching permits were awarded. On February 25, 1946, the Bureau held a reception in honor of the first recipients of teaching licenses.

In the early 1940's, Rabbi Armond E. Cohen, the Director and others had urged that uniform salary scales for teachers be set up in co-operation with the Hebrew Teachers Association. During this period, the latter co-operated with the Bureau and its Educational Directors Council in elaborating "A Code of Practice and Rating Scale" which dealt with the duties and responsibilities of Hebrew teachers, appointments and dismissals, hours of service, salaries, provisions for settling controversies, and similar matters. This applied only to teachers in afternoon "Hebrew" schools, but in November, 1952, the Educational Director's Council decided to draft a similar "Code" for Sunday School teachers.[27]

The question whether Hebrew should be introduced into the public high schools, a subject of controversy in the 1930's, again occupied the attention of the Board. This time the proposal related only to the Cleveland Heights High School, and the non-Jewish school authorities were co-operative. Unlike the 1930's, the Bureau Board unanimously pressed the issue. The Executive Committee of the Jewish Community Council, to whom the matter was referred in 1949, hesitated, first urging the Bureau to desist and then reversing itself. When, however, the General Assembly of the Jewish Community Council gave its sanction, the Bureau proceeded with the negotiations. In the end (in 1951) the requirement of the school authorities that a minimum of 50 students be assured was not met, and the plan miscarried.[28]

[26] Minutes, Board of Trustees of Bureau, June 30, Oct. 27, 1947; Jan. 19, Feb. 16, 1948; Oct. 17, Nov. 21, 1949; Jan. 21, Sept. 15, 1952; March 16, 1953; "Summary of Report of Group Work Study Committee as Approved by Social Agency Committee of Jewish Welfare Federation" in Minutes, Board of Trustees of Bureau, Nov. 24, 1947.

[27] On the Board of License and Teachers Codes, see Minutes, Board of Trustees of Bureau, June 12, Nov. 20, 1944; Dec. 17, 1945; Jan. 21, Feb. 25, April 19, Nov. 19, 1946; Nov. 24, 1947; July 28, 1948; Nov. 27, 1951 (includes final draft of Code); Sept. 15, Dec. 15, 1952.

[28] See Minutes, Board of Trustees of Bureau, July 26, Nov. 10, 1948; Jan. 30, March 28, June 20, Sept. 19, Nov. 21, 1949; Feb. 27, May 21, 1951; Minutes, Committee on Hebrew in High Schools, Nov. 3, 1948; Jan. 25, 1949; Jan. 22, April 18, 1951.

This period witnessed the reorganization of the Teachers Institute and the development of an Adult School of Jewish Studies. With the shortage of teachers acute, and many of substandard competence functioning in the schools, it became imperative to provide training for immediate local needs. The Director, therefore, devoted his energies to the organization of the Cleveland Institute of Jewish Studies, which made provision for the training of Hebrew and Sunday School teachers, in-service courses, and classes for adults. The Institute was placed under an autonomous Board of Governors and admitted to the Bureau as an affiliate. The registration rose again to significant numbers, and, under Rabbi Jacob Kabakoff as full-time Dean, the first graduation of teachers since 1939 was held early in 1953. Plans were also formulated for "cadet teachers" in the various schools, and Mrs. Barnett R. Brickner took the initiative in securing scholarship funds to help defray the costs of college education for students preparing for the career of Hebrew Teaching.[29]

The Council Religious Schools likewise underwent reorganization. The schools had been established and maintained by the Council of Jewish Women long before the Bureau came into existence. Soon after the establishment of the Bureau, both the budgets and the direction of the schools became its responsibility. Officially, however, the Religious Schools remained a Council project. Between 1944–1947, negotiations between the Bureau and the Council of Jewish Women culminated in the establishment of an independent Board representing the community at large. Early in 1947, the Council of Jewish Women relinquished sponsorship of the schools, and in June of the same year, the name was changed to the United Jewish Religious Schools.[30]

The greatest efforts of the Bureau, and in the long run the most important, were concerned with co-ordination. Two committees devoted themselves to this problem, namely, the Committee on Co-ordination (also active in the early 1940's) under Myron Guren

[29] Minutes, Board of Trustees of Bureau, March 18, Nov. 19, 1946; Jan. 20, May 19, 1947; Jan. 19, March 15, June 21, July 26, Sept. 20, Nov. 10, 1948; March 28, June 20, Sept. 19, 1949; Feb. 6, 1950; Sept. 19, Oct. 20, Dec. 15, 1952; Jan. 19, March 16, 1953; Minutes, Board of Governors, Cleveland Institute of Jewish Studies, Nov. 8, 1948; N. Brilliant, "Memorandum to Social Agency Committee On Need of an Adult School of Jewish Studies . . . Under the Auspices of the Bureau of Jewish Education, May 28, 1947," in Minutes, Board of Trustees of Bureau, May 19, 1947.

[30] Minutes, Board of Jewish Education and Board of Trustees of Bureau, Oct. 26, 1926; June 16, 1927; June 12, 1944; May 28, 1945; Jan. 21, Feb. 25, 1946; Feb. 17, Oct. 27, 1947; March 28, 1949; Minutes, Conference on Sabbath Schools, June 16, 1925; Minutes, Joint Meeting of Sabbath School Committee of Board and Council of Jewish Women, Aug. 10, 1925; Minutes, Extension Education Committee, Oct. 31, 1927.

and the Educational Directors Council headed by the Director. In a sense, too, the work of the New Applications or Admissions Committee was closely related to Co-ordination.

The most important educational agency admitted during this period was the Hebrew Academy, an all-day school. An application was first received in June, 1944, and resubmitted at intervals thereafter. The Bureau Board several times voted disapproval of constituent membership which would entail a subsidy for the Hebrew Academy. Some members were uncertain of the "desirability and feasibility" for the Bureau "to sponsor and help in the financing of all-day Jewish schools" in Cleveland. However, the chief stumbling block was the relationship of the Hebrew Academy to the Rabbinical College of Telshe (*Telshe Yeshivah*), which had organized the day-school and apparently controlled its policies. The Board felt that a school without local autonomy should not be subsidized. After protracted negotiations, the Hebrew Academy applied in April, 1947, for membership as an affiliate "without subsidy," and the Board approved during the following October. However, in January, 1948, a request for a subsidy was again submitted, with the assurance that the constitution had been changed and that there was "no tie up" with the *Telshe Yeshivah*, except for the six Rabbis who served as appointees of the *Telshe Yeshivah* on the Board of Education of the Hebrew Academy. The Bureau Board voted approval of a subsidy for the "day school" of the Hebrew Academy.[31]

In considering other applications for admission, the Bureau Board attempted to apply principles which would discourage fragmentation and irresponsibility. A Yiddish school of the Jewish Peoples Fraternal Order was denied affiliation and a subsidy because facilities for the Yiddish type of education were available in the same neighborhood. Affiliation even without a subsidy was refused a school whose ideology paralleled that of the *Yeshivath Adath B'nai Israel*, and the applicant was advised to merge with the latter.[32]

The Educational Directors Council, consisting of the professional heads, assistants or associates of the congregational as well as communal schools, began to meet under the chairmanship of the Bureau Director in 1940. Evidently feeling its way and uncertain of its purpose, it convened intermittently for a number of years on call of

[31] Minutes, Board of Trustees of Bureau, Sept. 25, 1944; Oct. 22, 1945; Feb. 25, March 18, 1946; Jan. 20, March 17, April 21, Oct. 27, 1947; Jan. 19, Feb. 16, 1948; Minutes, New Applications Committee, July 22, 1947; Minutes, Admissions Committee, Feb. 5, 1948.

[32] Minutes, Board of Trustees of Bureau, Nov. 19, 1946; Oct. 27, 1947; May 17, 1948; Oct. 17, Nov. 21, 1949; Minutes, New Applications Committee, July 22, 1947.

the Bureau Director and did not assert itself. By 1949, however, it was meeting regularly and discussing projects for teacher-training, teacher salaries and codes, teaching-aids, and especially a uniform school calendar. During the first half of 1953, it was quite active: the Sunday School directors and those of weekday and the all-day schools discussed each other's programs "with understanding and helpfulness"; a series of tests was proposed for Sunday School classes; a Code of Practice for Sunday School Teachers was discussed; a uniform school calendar was approved. However, the potentialities of this body far exceed its achievements.[33]

The admission into the Bureau of the Hebrew Academy in 1948 extended communal responsibility and financial support to three systems of intensive Hebrew education, namely, the Cleveland Hebrew School, the *Yeshivath Adath B'nai Israel* and the all-day school of the Hebrew Academy. Moreover, the latter operated also an afternoon school which received no Federation subsidy. The question, therefore, arose whether the Cleveland Jewish Community required three separate systems of afternoon schools.

The Federation was pressing for consolidation, certainly as early as 1946. The Survey of Jewish Communal Schools conducted by Bernard Levitin early in 1946 (then Acting-Director of the Bureau) revealed that the enrollment of the *Yeshivath Adath B'nai Israel* had declined 45 per cent since 1936, while that of the Cleveland Hebrew School had decreased only nine per cent. Moreover, in 1946, *eight* branches of the Cleveland Hebrew Schools provided Jewish education for 655 pupils, whereas the 186 students of the *Yeshivath Adath B'nai Israel* required as many as *five* branches. At the close of 1946, the Director of the Bureau reported that he had found the teachers of the *Yeshivath Adath B'nai Israel* inadequate, pedagogic methods antiquated, facilities extremely bad, at least in two of the branches, and enrollment and attendance records faulty. The inadequacies, although not denied by the spokesman of the *Yeshivath Adath B'nai Israel*, were atributed to the loss of their principals several years previously, and especially to lack of funds. He said that better teachers would be engaged if more money were made available. However, the Bureau Board decided to address itself to the more fundamental problem of duplication, with its consequent waste and inefficiency.[34]

[33] Minutes, Board of Trustees of Bureau, Dec. 16, 1940; Feb. 15, 1943; Jan. 17, 1944; May 17, 1948; Dec. 19, 1949; Sept. 19, 1950; Dec. 15, 1952; April 20, 1953; Minutes, Educational Directors Council, Nov. 23, 1948; Jan. 13, Feb. 10, Oct. 13, Nov. 30, 1949; March 8, 1950; Jan. 24, April 30, Nov. 20, 1951; May 6, May 13, June 4, 1953.

[34] See Minutes, Board of Trustees of Bureau, Jan. 21, Dec. 18, 1946; Oct. 27, 1947; Bernard Levitin, "1946 Jewish Education Survey...." in Minutes, Co-ordinating Committee, April 2, 1947.

The initiative was taken in December, 1946, by the Committee on Co-ordination, headed by Myron Guren. After thorough discussion, the Committee presented to the Bureau Board in May, 1947, a recommendation that steps be taken immediately to effect a merger of the Cleveland Hebrew School and the *Yeshivath Adath B'nai Israel* into one communal Hebrew School system under a new name. The Bureau Board approved, and a special merger committee, representing equally the two school systems, was named and instructed to prepare a definitive plan of merger which, it was hoped, would be implemented in September, 1947. The Merger Committee worked "long and arduously," but since the *Yeshivath Adath B'nai Israel* refused to accept the proposal, a substitute plan was presented to the Board.

The substitute plan suggested that the *Yeshivath Adath B'nai Israel* schools accept the supervision of the Bureau for an experimental period of one year. This meant that the supervisor of the *Yeshivath Adath B'nai Israel* schools would be selected with the approval of the Bureau Director to whom he would be responsible; that teachers would be required to meet the standards of the Board of License: that the school offices and records would be housed in the Bureau; and that the plan would be evaluated at the close of the experimental year. The *Yeshivath Adath B'nai Israel* rejected the substitute plan and countered with its own proposal. It would accept Bureau supervision provided its "autonomy and Orthodox ideology" were preserved. The school records would be open to inspection by the Bureau Director during the experimental year, but neither the records nor the school offices would be moved to the Bureau. The Director of the Bureau would be consulted in the selection of a principal or supervisor, and the latter would be responsible to the Bureau "in administrative matters." Finally, the teacher standards set by the Board of License would be followed "as much as possible." Thus, after a full year of fruitless negotiations, the deadlock remained.

In 1948, the Bureau tried again. The Committee on Co-ordination resubmitted the merger resolution, which the Board had adopted in May, 1947. The Executive Committee took a vigorous stand, and the President exclaimed, "We cannot condone the present wasteful process. An equitable merger can and must be worked out." Letters were addressed to the boards of directors of the two school systems and, in July, 1948, the replies were received: the Cleveland Hebrew School accepted the merger plan, but the *Yeshivath Adath B'nai Israel* again declined. Finally, in September, 1948, the professional heads of the Bureau, the Cleveland Hebrew School, the *Yeshivath Adath B'nai Israel* and the afternoon school of the Hebrew

Academy met and agreed unanimously to advise "the ultimate creation of a common administration" for the three groups of afternoon schools "in order to centralize the control of all administrative matters," and to eliminate duplication. The realization of this "ultimate" objective, however, was postponed to an unidentified future. The report of the meeting went on to say, "The Committee recognized the fact that there are today sufficient differences in method and approach which may warrant the existence, for the present, of two separate school systems," that is, the Cleveland Hebrew School on the one hand, and the *Yeshivath Adath B'nai Israel*, and the Hebrew Academy afternoon school on the other. The Bureau Board acquiesced and the far-reaching merger plan was thus shelved.

The word "shelved" is used advisedly, because the objective of merging or consolidating the communal afternoon schools was not abandoned — postponed indefinitely, yes, but not repudiated entirely. In fact, the consolidation of schools as such remained not only an ultimate ideal but an immediate desideratum. Both the *Yeshivath Adath B'nai Israel* and the Cleveland Hebrew School bid for the absorption of the Hebrew Academy afternoon school, with the *Yeshivath Adath B'nai Israel* carrying off the prize. In fact, the *Yeshivath Adath B'nai Israel*, which prevented the fashioning of a unified communal system of afternoon schools, reached out avidly to merge independent orthodox schools with its own system. The school of the Oheb Zedek Congregation was absorbed with a minimum of consultation. An attempt was even made to operate a Sunday School at the N'vai Zedek Congregation. And when, in the midst of these efforts, the fundamental question of consolidation with the Cleveland Hebrew School was raised, the Bureau Board was informed that the *Yeshivath Adath B'nai Israel* was "moving step by step." It would absorb first the Oheb Zedek and Hebrew Academy afternoon schools and later "perhaps" further negotiations with the Cleveland Hebrew School would prove more timely.[35]

One practical aspect of co-ordination was accomplished to the mutual satisfaction of all concerned. The dispersal of the Jewish population necessitated transportation which each school attempted

[35] Minutes, Board of Trustees of Bureau, May 19, June 30, Oct. 27, Dec. 15, 1947; March 15, May 17, June 21, July 26, Sept. 20, 1948; Jan. 30, Feb. 21, Dec. 19, 1949; Minutes, Committee on Co-ordination, Dec. 18, 1946; April 2, Dec. 9, 1947; July 7, 1948; Feb. 10, 1949; Memorandum, Meeting Executive Committee, May 12, 1948; Minutes, Special Merger Committee, June 10, 1948; Memorandum Concerning a Possible Merger . . . . (meeting of Bureau and School Directors.) Sept. 30, 1948.

to provide. The Bureau Board named a Committee on Transportation to inquire into the possibilities of providing more economical and more efficient service. Under the leadership of Joe Zell, this Committee attacked the problem in the fall of 1949 with energy and consummate skill.

The Transportation Committee canvassed the situation and found that early in 1950, some 400 children made use of communal transportation, involving a combined cost to the schools of about $22,000 annually. Practices in other cities were canvassed with the aid of the American Association for Jewish Education, and an expert of the Cleveland Transit System was engaged as a consultant. By October 8, 1950, an effective plan had been introduced, whereby a uniform pass, purchased by the children, was employed by all co-operating schools, and the proceeds were used to purchase and keep in repair the necessary vehicles. The plan proved immediately successful and, on the suggestion of the Bureau Director, the Committee on Transportation was established as a standing committee to manage the funds and administer the operation.

This success encouraged the Bureau Board to attempt an extension of the powers of the popular Transportation Committee, by designating it the Transportation, Tuition and Enrollment Committee. But difficulties arose immediately. The business-like Committee, seeking to ascertain first the basic facts in the situation, requested all subsidized schools to submit their rosters of pupils, including the exact tuition of each child and the period of delinquency. The Cleveland Hebrew School and the United Jewish Religious Schools sent in the necessary lists, but the *Yeshivath Adath B'nai Israel* and the Hebrew Academy "were reluctant to release the names of their children." They regarded this information as so confidential that even their own Boards of Directors did not receive such lists. They were ready, however, to provide summaries without names. After lengthy discussion, the Bureau Board decided in March, 1951, that the lists should again be requested, but that they be available only to the Committee. The Bureau Minutes record no further action in the matter. Apparently, this effort at co-operative action was thus stalled at its inception.[36]

[36] Minutes, Board of Trustees of Bureau, June 20, Sept. 19, Oct. 17, 1949; Feb. 6, June 19, Sept. 19, Nov. 20, Dec. 26, 1950; Jan. 15, March 26, Sept. 17, Nov. 27, 1951; Dec. 15, 1952; Jan. 19, 1953; Minutes, Executive Committee, June 19, 1949; Minutes, Transportation Committee, July 14, Dec. 26, 1950; Minutes, Transportation, Tuition and Enrollment Committee, Jan. 9, March 20, July 16, Sept. 24, 1951; March 20, Dec. 3, 1952.

Closely related to co-ordination was the question of representation on the Bureau Board of Trustees. Reference has been made to the two types of affiliates of the Bureau and to the formula of representation[37] which determined the composition of the Board. During this period, opposition developed to the inflexible formula favoring "the intensity of Jewish education," and two other unmet needs became evident. Many favored an increase in the number of members-at-large, so as to involve in the work of the Bureau more community leaders not directly associated with Jewish education. Similarly, it appeared desirable to allow representation on the Board to agencies concerned with non-formal Jewish education. For example, the Young Israel Institute of Jewish Studies and Camp Galil applied for affiliation without subsidy, but the Board was obliged to reply that neither could be admitted under the Constitution.

The matter of representation was under consideration for some time, but it came to a head in February, 1952, when it was proposed that the Board be increased to a maximum of 90 members with one-third allotted to each of the two categories of affiliates, namely, the communally-subsidized schools and the congregations which maintained schools, and one-third to the Jewish Community-at-large. This was passed unanimously, and the 28th Annual Meeting of the Bureau on April 20, 1952 approved the change in Article IV of the Constitution, and authorized the new Board of Trustees to elect 15 members-at-large in addition to the 12 already serving on the Board.

At the same time, the phrase "and the intensity of the education" was deleted, thereby withdrawing constitutional support from the rigid formula of enrollment multiplied by number of sessions per week. The new formula embodied in the Constitution was more flexible. It read: "The number of representatives ... shall be in relation to the number of students by them enrolled, due recognition to be given to the number of days per week of instruction offered by such agencies." Equally significant was the fact that the revised Article IV employed the term "affiliated [communally supported] schools and educational agencies," and this provision appeared to authorize the affiliation of agencies occupied with non-formal education. The Board serving for 1953–1954 was composed as follows:

[37] See *supra*, pp. 338–339.

Representatives of Communal Schools 28

> Cleveland Hebrew School 9
> Hebrew Academy 6
> United Jewish Religious Schools 4
> *Yeshivath Adath B'nai Israel* 6
> Institute of Jewish Studies 1
> Hebrew Teachers Federation 2
>
> ――
> 28

Representatives of Congregations Maintaining Schools 27

> Community Temple 1
> Euclid Avenue Temple 5
> Gates of Hope 1
> N'vai Zedek 1
> Park Synagogue 5
> Taylor Road Synagogue 2
> Temple Emanu El 2
> Temple On the Heights 5
> The Temple 5
>
> ――
> 27

Representatives-At-Large[38] 22

TOTAL 77

A very significant achievement of this period was the revolutionary change in the educational character of at least some of the Board meetings. It had been the practice to hear reports on the communally subsidized schools. But these had been, as a rule, perfunctory, noting enrollments and some of the public functions, and the congregational schools had been virtually beyond the ken of the Board.

The Director of the Bureau introduced a novel form of reporting, which provided for panel discussions. He served as moderator,

[38] The Minutes of April 20, 1953 list only 10 at-large members, but the Minutes are obviously incomplete, as is indicated by the Minutes of June 25, 1952. See also, Minutes, Board of Trustees of Bureau, May 17, 1948; Sept. 19, 1950; May 21, 1951; Jan. 21, Feb. 25, June, 1952; April 20, 1953; Minutes, Constitution Committee, Jan. 27, 1952; Minutes, Study and Planning Committee, May 21, 1951; 28th Annual Meeting of the Bureau, April 20, 1952.

posing questions and problems to which the educational directors of the school or schools under discussion addressed themselves, and the Board members eagerly asked questions and offered comments. Especially noteworthy were the efforts to probe into aims, objectives and achievements, and to include the congregational schools in the panels. Thus an experimental panel was held at the Board meeting of March 26, 1951 on all communally-supported schools, and a fairly clear comparative picture presented of enrollments, school buildings and branches, hours of instruction and the like. It was agreed to discuss "curriculum" at the following meeting, but it apparently proved too ambitious an enterprise, for it was not done at that time. In December, 1952, the project was revived with a panel on the afternoon schools of the Temple on the Heights and Park Synagogue. In January, 1953, the educational directors of the Temple and the Euclid Avenue Temple discussed the afternoon Hebrew Schools of the Reform Congregations. The following April, the curricula and aims of the Cleveland Hebrew School and the *Yeshivath Adath B'nai Israel* were compared and in June, 1953, the Hebrew Academy was the subject of consideration.[39]

The final achievement of this period was a permanent home for the Bureau. We have noted that a building had been purchased and occupied in 1943,[40] but within a few years, it proved inadequate for the growing needs of the Bureau. An auditorium was lacking and the room space was insufficient to accommodate nearly 2,000 persons (end of 1947) who attended meetings or classes each month. The addition of a wing to the building was considered and rejected. The building was finally sold and a new site purchased on Taylor Road. During 1949–1950, there were negotiations with the Jewish Community Centers for the erection of a joint building to house recreational as well as Bureau and educational activities, but in the following year, it was agreed that the Bureau proceed on its own. A limited campaign was launched, construction was begun early in 1952, and by November of the same year, the Board held its first meeting in the new home. On May 17, 1953, the building was officially dedicated as the "Beth Friedland."[41]

[39] See Minutes, Board of Trustees of Bureau, March 26, 1951; Dec. 15, 1952; Jan. 19, April 20, June 22, 1953.

[40] See *supra*, p. 341.

[41] Minutes, Board of Trustees of Bureau, April 21, Nov. 24, 1947; Jan. 19, Sept. 20, 1948; Feb. 21, Sept. 19, 1949; June 19, Sept. 19, 1950; Sept. 17, Nov. 27, Dec. 27, 1951; Feb. 25, March 31, June 25, Oct. 20, Nov. 17, Dec. 15, 1952; March 16, 1953; Minutes Executive Committee, July 5, Aug. 1, 1950; Aug. 1, Sept. 16, Nov. 25, 1951; Minutes, Meeting of Representatives of Jewish Community Centers, Cleveland Hebrew School and Bureau, Feb. 2, 1949; Minutes, Site Committee, March 18, May 13, 1951; Dedication of Beth Friedland, May 17, 1953.

CONCLUSION

This survey of the Cleveland Bureau of Jewish Education served as the basis for an "Agenda of Recommendations" presented by this writer and Uriah Z. Engelman as directors of the Cleveland study. The recommendations had relevance to the situation in that city. However, some conclusions drawn from the history of the Cleveland Bureau should shed light on the efforts and achievements of Bureaus elsewhere in the country.

The Cleveland Bureau of Jewish Education attracted leadership of the highest order: Rabbis of national eminence — Abba Hillel Silver, Barnett R. Brickner, Armond E. Cohen; laymen of true stature — Ezra Shapiro, Myron Guren and others; professional educators of high rank — A. H. Friedland, a leading figure in the Hebrew movement, Azriel Eisenberg, now the professional head of the Jewish Education Committee of New York, Nathan Brilliant, Jacob Kabakoff and others. The dedication of these men was exemplary, their vision of the needs of Jewish education far-reaching, their goals realistic, their mood characterized by patience, tolerance of opposition and a readiness to compromise in order to achieve the attainable. Yet, the reward of their efforts was often frustration, and their achievements (during the period under review) hardly commensurate with the time and energy devoted to the cause.

1. *Achievements of the Cleveland Bureau*

The achievements of the Bureau were of considerable significance. It became a symbol of community responsibility and a facility for communal unity in Jewish education. Its propaganda and public relations induced community leadership to recognize that schooling as well as welfare merited community support, and its unrelenting pressure resulted in an increase of subsidies and allocations.[42] As the central agency for Jewish education, the Bureau likewise served as the common meeting-ground for educators and laymen of various and differing orientations and organizational loyalties.

The Cleveland Bureau grappled with the problem of teacher training and tried to alleviate the acute shortage of teachers. It established a Board of License for the certification of teachers and concerned itself with codes of practice, salary scales and pension

[42] The figures (compiled from a variety of unpublished sources, including tables of the Jewish Community Federation of Cleveland, the Survey of the Joint Jewish Education Committee, 1928–1929, the Berkson-Rosen 1936 Jewish Education Survey of Cleveland, the audited annual financial reports of the Bureau) are given in the unpublished Partial Draft of Study of Jewish Education in Cleveland, 1953, by Oscar I. Janowsky and Uriah Z. Engelman, pp. F11–14.

schemes. It evolved minimum requirements for the affiliation of schools, especially in matters of health, safety and financial stability, and otherwise attempted to perform the functions of a qualifying agency. It frowned on the expansion of schools without proper facilities, on the establishment of uneconomical or inefficient units and on efforts which duplicated available services. Schools were pressed to devote attention to business-like methods of administration, and central auditing provided a minimum of external supervision in financial recording. Surveys of schools were made at intervals, calling attention to deficiencies and trends.[43]

The Bureau strove to promote co-ordination and to provide services for the improvement of Jewish education. It maintained a central library of books and educational materials and furnished some instructional aids and child literature. Common planning resulted in a co-operative and effective solution of the transportation problem which had baffled the individual schools.

The Bureau took the initiative in educational matters of concern to the entire community. It was the center of discussion and agitation for the introduction of Hebrew into the public high schools. It sought to provide extension education for the unschooled, attempted to promote educational camping and adult education, and sought to influence recreational agencies to emphasize Jewish content in their activities. Finally, the Bureau was for many years the only central agency which recognized the educational implications of the shifting of the Jewish population of Cleveland. It sought to steady the process of disruption of old centers and to create educational facilities in new neighborhoods.

2. Deficiencies of the Cleveland Bureau

Despite the eminence and dedication of its leadership, the Cleveland Bureau did not succeed, during the period surveyed, in becoming the all-embracing central agency for Jewish education in the community. It failed to enlist the full confidence and co-operation even of some of its affiliates, the ultra-orthodox for example. And the congregational schools, especially of the large and influential synagogues and temples, remained on the periphery of the Bureau's functioning; there were contacts and occasional services but no intimate and sustained functional relationships.

[43] See Minutes, Board of Jewish Education and Board of Trustees of Bureau, March 16, 1927, Feb. 16, 1928, Dec. 26, 1933, March 15, 1943, Dec. 18, 1944, Sept. 24, 1945, April 21, Oct. 27, 1947, May 17, June 21, 1948, Nov. 21, Dec. 19, 1949, Jan. 16, Sept. 19, Oct. 16, Dec. 26, 1950, Dec. 15, 1952; Minutes of Executive Committee, June 2, 1925; Minutes, First Meeting of Board of Trustees of Jewish Teachers Institute, Oct. 31, 1927.

The most fundamental objectives of educational leadership eluded the Cleveland Bureau. No thorough study of curriculum could be undertaken. Far too little attention was devoted to the consideration of basic aims in Jewish education, even of the intensive variety. No sustained effort was made to identify goals, measure achievement or appraise the efficacy of the various types of Jewish schools. Constructive supervision — classroom observation, model lessons, individual and group conferences on a continuing basis for the discussion of aims, methods and achievements — was beyond the range of Bureau activities, except for a brief period during the early 1940's.

The Bureau could do little to improve the status of the Jewish teacher. Salaries remained low and, until the 1940's, often in arrears. This was, of course, a community responsibility, but the lay leaders of the Bureau did not attack this evil with sufficient vigor.[44]

The Bureau served for many years as the fiscal arm of the community Federation for the channeling of subsidies to affiliated schools. But it never succeeded or attempted to formulate a clear-cut policy to govern subventions or to relate them to standards of achievement.[45]

The Bureau concentrated its best energies on formal Jewish schooling, while extension, youth and adult education, as well as the educational potentialities of the recreational agencies, received only what energies and funds could be spared after the primary interest had been served. This implies no criticism of the Bureau, for it made repeated attempts to cope with these deficiencies. It is recorded as a condition inherent in the situation.

Finally, Bureau activities and services, valuable as they were, lacked the force of sustained effort. In large measure, they were desultory, individual projects rather than ongoing units of a clearly formulated and comprehensive plan. The Bureau was obliged at intervals to revive activities and reactivate projects, and the cumulative effects of continuity and planned activity toward a desired goal were lost.

3. Reasons for Inadequacies of the Bureau

There were special difficulties in Cleveland which hampered the work of the Bureau, but these were of secondary importance. The fundamental problems were common to all American local Jewish

---

[44] See, Minutes, Joint Jewish Education Committee, June 1, 1928 and "Financial Reports" following Minutes of Oct. 12, 1928; Minutes, Board of Jewish Education or Board of Trustees of Bureau, Sept. 27, 1928, Oct. 13, 1931, March 18, 1936, May 18, 1937, March 31, 1938, Sept. 15, 1941, Feb. 15, 1943, Sept. 15, 1952; Minutes, Finance and Budget Committee, Feb. 19, 1926. See also, Study of Jewish Education in Cleveland, cited, pp. F6-7.

[45] See for example, Minutes, Board of Trustees of Bureau, Jan. 16, 1950.

communities, and they affected virtually all Bureaus. These were: (1) inadequate financial support; and (2) the divided Jewish community with its deep ideological and organizational cleavages.

(1) During the period surveyed, the Cleveland Bureau never secured a viable budget for proper functioning. The indispensable need was recognition of the Bureau as the central agency for Jewish education with community-wide financial support. The proper source of such support was the Jewish Community Federation, the symbol and financial instrument of united Jewish efforts for communal purposes. But during the 1920's, the Federation was not ready to assume direct responsibility for Jewish education. Some individuals active in Federation participated in fashioning the Bureau, and the Federation rendered assistance to Bureau leaders in organizing fund-raising campaigns. But the Bureau was not included as an integral part of Federation during the 1920's; Rabbi Silver and his co-workers were expected to maintain and finance the Bureau as an independent communal agency, apart from the Federation.[46] As a result, the energies of able leaders were diverted from constructive educational work to fund-raising which proved inadequate and resulted in frustration and discouragement.

In 1931, the Federation was obliged to assume responsibility for the Bureau budget, but by that time the Great Depression had reduced community resources to a minimum. By that time, too, circumstances had compelled the Bureau to resort to deficit financing of existing schools, a tendency which the depression years hardened into a policy that endured throughout the period studied.

During and after the 1940's, as Federation fund-raising increased, allocations for Jewish education rose, but the bulk of the funds was channeled to support the affiliated schools. The Bureau remained without sufficient funds for constructive supervision, for educational experimentation, for research, and for other educational functions which an effective Bureau should perform.[47]

(2) To a considerable degree, lack of funds was itself the consequence of a more fundamental difficulty, namely, deep cleavages in the Jewish community with respect to the nature and purpose of Jewish education. Some elements looked upon education as an adjunct of the synagogue and therefore outside the area of unified communal financing; the latter, they thought, should devote itself to philanthropy and the defense of Jewish rights. Others were content with the minimum of education provided by the Sunday School.

[46] See MBJE, April 16, July 28, 1924; Minutes of Conference of Jewish men and Women of Cleveland Representing All the Congregations and the Professions, Jan. 6, 1925; J. Slawson, "Jewish Education Situation in Cleveland....," in Minutes of Joint Jewish Education Committee, July 20, 1928, Exhibit A.
[47] See *supra*, p. 353, note 42.

Even among the proponents of intensive Jewish education, there were sharp differences between the rigidly orthodox and those who placed emphasis upon cultural Hebraic studies. Overtones of "nationalism *versus* religion" in Jewish education were likewise heard, as were the claims of Yiddish groups and discordant views on the responsibility of the community for "all-day" or Yeshivah education.[48]

From the very first years, the Bureau recognized the legitimacy of differing types of schools and the ideological diversity which they represented.[49] This was regarded by individual schools as the right to "autonomy," an ill-defined term which was invoked to thwart efforts of the Bureau to concern itself even with administrative supervision or tuition fees. Co-ordination and co-operation for the improvement of standards, evaluation of achievement and educational supervision were, of course, out of the question.[50] A truly effective Bureau could not be fashioned in a divided community.

A final and very important factor remains to be noted. An effective Bureau would be expected to exert influence throughout the community, including the congregational schools. The latter, however, were not only autonomous but quite independent, regardless of their representation on the Board of the Bureau. Their independent financing and functioning removed an important segment of Jewish education from community responsibility, as represented by the Bureau.

The effects of congregational schools upon the development and functioning of a Bureau were evident not only in Cleveland but elsewhere in the country as well. And the problem has become more complex since this study was made. Congregational schools have grown in numbers, so that today they account for over ninety per cent of Jewish school enrollments. Morevoer, the denominational and ideological commissions on Jewish education (Conservative, Orthodox, Reform, Yiddishist) have grown in influence and effectiveness, paralleling in many instances the work of the Bureaus in the local communities. The student of current developments in Jewish education, especially as they relate to Bureaus, will do well to explore the relationship between community Bureaus and national denominational bodies, for the parallel efforts have not as yet been coordinated in most communities. This remains one of the unresolved problems in Jewish education.

[48] See for example, MBJE, Oct. 24, 1924, Dec. 27, 1927, April 29, June 24, 1929; Minutes, Board of Trustees of Bureau, Dec. 26, 1933; Minutes, Joint Jewish Education Committee, June 22, Oct. 19, 1928; Minutes, Finance and Budget Committee, Nov. 25, Dec. 22, 1927; Minutes, Campaign Committee, Sept. 24, 1925.

[49] MBJE, Sept. 27, 1926. See also, 12th Annual Meeting of Bureau, April 16, 1936.

[50] See Minutes, Committee On Constitution, Dec. 12, 1924; MBJE, March 10, 1925; Minutes, Joint Education Committee, Dec. 19, Dec. 31, 1928.

AMERICAN JEWRY, THE REFUGEES AND IMMIGRATION RESTRICTION (1932–1942)*

By David Brody

INTRODUCTION

The Jews of America had benefitted greatly from the American tradition as "the asylum of the oppressed of all nations." The larger part — or their parents — had migrated from Eastern Europe after 1880. Like others of recent origin, they had resented and strongly objected to efforts to restrict immigration. In vain they had opposed the literacy clause of the Act of 1917 and the national origins system of the Act of 1924.[1] Immigrants had built the United States. To limit the inflow, particularly on the basis of false racist doctrine, ran counter to fundamental American principles.

By 1932, objection had shifted imperceptibly to general, although silent, approval. For most immigrant groups, the question of immigration policy was a dead issue. Until the advent of Hitler it was so for Jews as well. The change in attitude is significant, but so long as immigration problems remained in the background, no more could be grasped than the prevailing sense of vague, undefined acceptance. The position of American Jews after 1933 provides the sole exception to this situation. Nazi persecution forced attention to the restrictive laws, and crystallized the thinking of Jewish groups.

This study will attempt to define the Jewish attitudes and efforts concerned with American restrictive policy from 1932 to 1942, when refugee problems provided a constant stimulus. It will try, secondly, to uncover the causes behind the positions taken. Some of the

---

* This study received the first prize of the Historical Essay Award of the American Jewish Historical Society in observance of the American Jewish Tercentenary (1954–1955), sponsored by the Louis M. Rabinowitz Foundation. The author would like to express his thanks to Professor Oscar Handlin for his counsel and criticism on various aspects of this study.

[1] The Johnson Law of 1921 made available to every nationality an immigration quota of three per cent of the foreign-born of that nationality in the United States in 1910. The Immigration Act of 1924, superceding this provisional measure, dropped the quota to two per cent based on the 1890 population. This Act also outlined the permanent policy, which was to go into effect in 1929. A statistical study of the population in 1920 was made. 150,000 were to be admitted each year, every nation outside of Asia having a quota based on the percentage of people derived from it by birth or descent in the total American stock in 1920.

proximate causes refer exclusively to Jewish groups; but the underlying force, relating to the process of cultural adjustment, applies to
some extent, to all recent immigrants.[2]

I

American immigration policy during the thirties was bound up
with the economic consequences of the depression. By the end of
1932 an estimated fifteen million people were unemployed and
economic distress was widespread. President Hoover had issued an
order in 1930 instructing American consulates to enforce restrictions
as severely as possible, in particular, the clauses excluding persons
likely to become public charges.[3] Immigration had dropped from
241,700 in 1930 to 35,576 in 1932, of which 2,755 were Jews.[4] The
theory was that immigrants would aggravate conditions by creating
more unemployment, cheap competition for American workers, and
a heavier drain on public relief. This view was almost universally
accepted. *The New York Times*, for example, estimated that by
December, 1932, 500,000 persons had been refused visas. "Had they
come," the editorial concluded, "they would only have swollen the
number of unemployed. No one can question the wisdom of this
policy in general."[5] In the presidential campaign both Roosevelt
and Hoover endorsed the Executive Order of 1930.[6]

American Jewish groups agreed. "Everybody, even those elements most vitally affected by the unfortunately necessary limitations, understands that the economic situation warrants restrictions,"
wrote a Jewish editor.[7] He was not exaggerating; no significant
portion of American Jewry dissented. Jewish statements differ from
non-Jewish ones only in the regretful tone in which some of them were
cast.[8] Whatever immigration activity there was related to efforts

[2] Because of the nature of the American Jewish community, this study will rely on the
statements and the publications of the various Jewish organizations as a primary source of
information. Unlike the Catholics, the Jewish community lacks a hierarchical unity and
is, in fact, almost anarchical in structure. At the same time it is very highly organized;
the large number of organizations reflect every major group difference within the total
community. Thus, organizational statements may be legitimately accepted as speaking
for definite groups within the Jewish community. (See Maurice J. Karpf, "Jewish Community Organization in the United States," *American Jewish Year Book* [=*ÀJYB*],
1937–1938, vol. XXXIX, pp. 62–126.)

[3] *The New York Times* [=*Times*], March 22, 1933, p. 8.

[4] *AJYB, 1945–1946*, vol. XLVII, p. 653.

[5] *Times*, Dec. 24, 1932, p. 12.

[6] *Public Papers and Addresses of Franklin D. Roosevelt* (New York, 1938), vol. I, p. 854.

[7] *Times*, Oct. 24, 1933, p. 9. The editor was Joseph Brainin.

[8] *B'nai B'rith Magazine*, vol. XLVII (Oct., 1932), p. 3.

by Jewish welfare agencies to reunite families, parts of which remained in Europe.[9]

Early in 1933 the National Socialist Party assumed control of the German government. A wave of violent terrorism broke out against the Jewish population, followed by their expulsion from professional positions and a general boycott of all Jewish business. The news had an electric effect on the American Jewish population. Rabbi Stephen S. Wise, Honorary President of the American Jewish Congress, stated, "I cannot remember Jewry being so wrought up against anything happening to American Jews as the sudden reversion on the part of a great and cultured and liberty-loving people to practices which may be mildly characterized as medieval."[10] Although the expressions of protest were made with the disunity characteristic of American Jewry, there was unity in the indignation at the German outrages.

The crisis in Germany immediately affected Jewish views on American immigration policy. It was soon clear that for many German Jews emigration was the only escape. In response, almost all the larger Jewish organizations urged that the administration of the laws be liberalized to allow German refugees to come to America. There were no demands that the quotas be enlarged.[11]

The House Committee on Immigration held a hearing on a proposed amendment allowing review of consular refusals of visas. Max J. Kohler testified on behalf of B'nai B'rith and the American Jewish Committee. An acknowledged immigration expert, his testimony may be taken as representative of the greater part of the Jewish community, particularly since the American Jewish Congress sent a letter expressing substantially the same views.[12] At the outset he stated explicitly that he did not challenge the Executive Order of 1930. "I think that is a salutary thing," he said, "but our plea is in behalf of non-laborers and some exceptional persons." Kohler noted that consuls were unable to take account of an applicant's relatives and friends in America, nor could they judge his economic ability or whether he would compete with Americans. Moreover, the

[9] See statements of B'rith Abraham and the Hebrew Immigrant Aid Society, *Committee of Immigration and Naturalization* (House of Representatives), March 16, 1932, p. 2 and June 18, 1932, p. 100. Also Nathan Perlman of the American Jewish Congress, *Times*, April 25, 1932, p. 32.

[10] *Times*, March 22, 1933, p. 1. On conditions of the Jews in Germany see the *AJYB, 1933-1934*, vol. XXXV, pp. 21-40.

[11] *AJYB, 1932-1933*, vol. XXXIV, p. 38 and the *Times*, March 24, 1933, p. 2 and May 8, 1933, p. 7.

[12] *Committee on Immigration and Naturalization*, May 18, 1933, p. 8.

United States had always been a refuge for people fleeing political persecution.

That should have an important bearing on this case, though if it is likely that the person is to become a public charge, taking into account all the agencies that are at his disposal to prevent that, or if it is likely that his admission is going to be harmful in competing with the laboring class in this country, it is different.

And to make certain there was no misunderstanding, he reiterated, "I oppose special legislation for their [German refugees] benefit."[13]

The most extreme statement came from Judge Nathan Perlman, who urged that special quotas be set up for the refugees, but he too emphasized that the immigration laws were to remain unchanged.[14]

The agitation to enable some Jewish refugees to enter the country proved reasonably effective. Under-Secretary of State William Phillips informed the Joint Consultative Committee, a coalition set up by the three major Jewish organizations to cope with the crisis, that "the attention of the consular offices has been called to the importance of showing to each applicant the utmost consideration consistent with the reasonable, faithful and just application of the law."[15] In December, 1933, Attorney General Homer S. Cummings ruled that consulates were obliged to give visas when the Secretary of Labor had accepted a bond from a responsible person in the United States.[16] Partly as a result of these changes, Jewish immigration rose from 2,372 in 1933 to 4,137 in 1934 and 4,837 in 1935.[17] This accomplishment satisfied the Jewish organizations; for the next four years there was little discernible agitation for increased immigration.

During the spring of 1934, six bills were pending in Congress to decrease or stop the inflow entirely. The American Jewish Committee opposed these bills chiefly because of the "recognized unwisdom of enacting permanent legislation in times of emergency, when the aims sought can be achieved as they had been in the matter of immigration, by the stricter interpretation of existing law."[18] This was the usual basis of objection to such legislation:

[13] *Ibid.*, pp. 2–6.

[14] *Times*, Nov. 30, 1933, p. 24.

[15] *American Jewish Committee Annual Report, 1934* (New York, 1934), p. 58.

[16] *B'nai B'rith Magazine*, vol. L (Dec., 1935), p. 84.

[17] *AJYB*, vol. XLVII, p. 653. On the Ellis Island Committee of 1934 set up by President Roosevelt to investigate and make recommendations on American immigration policy, see the *Times*, April 29, 1934, p. 28.

[18] *American Jewish Committee Annual Report, 1935* (New York, 1935), p. 62. See also the testimony of Mrs. Cecilia Davidson of the National Council of Jewish Women on the Starnes-Reynolds Bill, providing for a ninety per cent reduction in the quotas. *Committee on Immigration* (Senate), 1937, p. 87.

expediency, not principle. During the decade of the depression, American Jewry was on the defensive; it felt satisfied if no alterations were made, for clearly any change would be in the direction of reduced immigration.[19]

The German quota, moreover, was never filled before 1938; the need for a reasonable increase could be met through more liberal interpretation. When the Nuremberg laws in the summer of 1935 forced an increased exodus, the Joint Consultative Committee succeeded in its "efforts for the removal of administrative hindrances to immigration to the United States, which, in the light of the present emergency, were unnecessarily burdensome."[20] The number of Jewish immigrants consequently jumped to 11,352 in 1937.

The proximate cause of the lack of enthusiasm in advocating a more liberal policy prior to 1938 lay in the prevailing economic conditions, and particularly in their effect on the Jewish population. Certain consequences of the depression applied only to the Jews. By necessity — and later by tradition — Jewish communities had always cared for their own unfortunates, and the practice was transmitted to America. As an editorial proudly put it, American Jewry had always been faithful to its obligation, accepted when the first Jews arrived in New Amsterdam, that no Jew would ever be permitted to fall on the charity of the general community.[21] The Jewish population had been hard hit by the depression. The welfare agencies coped with the situation as best they could, and, indeed, much was accomplished to supplement government relief. But certainly they would not be able to handle an influx of immigrants. This opinion was particularly current among wealthier Jews who, through the community federation welfare funds, contributed the larger portion of charity. According to one critical writer, the "classic dictum of many of our leading Jews" was: "We . . . Americans are greatly and increasingly overburdened by our responsibilities toward those of our brethren among us who are in distress and we decidedly do not want any more immigrants who are likely to become public charges."[22] The sense of responsibility of Jews for their less fortunate brethren thus acted to discourage the impulse to bring larger numbers of refugees to America.

[19] "No one who knows the situation can have much hope that the immigration policy of the United States will become less restrictive than it is now. On the contrary, the tendency is for more restriction, and it is likely that the next few years will see further restrictive legislation." (*AJYB, 1937–1938*, vol. XXXIX, p. 67.)

[20] *American Jewish Committee Annual Report, 1936* (New York, 1936), p. 59.

[21] *B'nai B'rith Magazine*, vol. XLVII (April, 1933), p. 217; and *ibid.* (Nov., 1932), p. 129. Rufus Learsi, *The Jews in America* (New York, 1954), p. 28.

[22] *Ibid.*, vol. XLIX (March, 1935), p. 135.

Another economic condition had a more pervasive influence. As the depression deepened, economic discrimination became common. George Sokolsky concluded that American Jewry faced the danger of becoming an economically "submerged class." Not only were employers not hiring Jews; there were reports that they were being fired when non-Jews became available. By 1938, the American Jewish Congress reported that its survey indicated economic discrimination had reached a record high mark.[23] To make matters worse, there were evidences that Jewish employers were discriminating against Jewish applicants. The *Yiddishe Welt* of Cleveland stated that "fifty per cent of the Jewish employers refuse to employ Jews. A plan is being worked out to remedy this disgraceful discrimination."[24] Inevitably, the argument that immigrants compete with Americans for existing jobs was of much greater force to Jews whose employment opportunities were already severely limited. The burden of a new mass of Jewish jobseekers would fall on them.

Treatment of the refugees in this country verifies the conclusion that a large part of the Jewish population feared the economic effect of immigration. The refugee was handled shabbily in a large number of cases. Jewish employers exploited many of the newcomers, working them excessively long hours for very low wages.[25] The "psychological fear of a refugee invasion," stated one Jewish journalist, caused some relief agencies to

> speak of refugee absorption in terms of its causing the best possible reaction on the rest of the Jewish population. Put bluntly, this means keep the refugee down, don't let him take a good job even if he gets it himself, because somebody might be annoyed with him.[26]

Other evidence supports the conclusion that refugees were regarded as a grievous burden. In 1935, the National Federation of Temple Brotherhoods urged that refugees be taken out of New York City, where most of them tended to congregate.[27] The *B'nai B'rith Magazine* ran an editorial in 1937 along the same lines:

> Many (too many) of them remain in New York ... The struggle for work becomes more difficult as their numbers increase; their increasing numbers may become a social irritation as they seek places in the life of a community already overcrowded.

[23] George Sokolsky, *We Jews* (New York, 1935), p. 185; *Times*, Dec. 28, 1938, p. 5.
[24] *Yiddishe Welt* (Cleveland), March 12, 1937, p. 206. (*Foreign Language Newspaper Digest*, Cleveland, 1937, vol. III.)
[25] *Congress Bulletin*, vol. VIII, no. 6 (1941), p. 10.
[26] *Ibid.*, p. 10 and no. 13, p. 10.
[27] *Times*, March 23, 1935, p. 12.

When the first proposal was made in March, 1935, the number of refugees in the entire United States was not much more than 8,000, and by the summer of 1937 could not have been above 25,000; and nearly half of these refugees were outside New York.[28] Nevertheless, it was feared that a community of over two million Jews could not absorb all the refugees and that friction and higher unemployment were likely to occur. Clearly, during these years of economic distress, there was a good deal of anxiety among Jews that refugee immigration would be detrimental to their economic interests.

American Jewry was not indifferent to the fate of German Jewry or the refugees. Throughout these years an effective anti-German boycott was carried on. Mass demonstrations, protests, and representations to the American government took place periodically. Jewish magazines and newspapers always included articles on the conditions of the German Jews. The general belief was that the Jews would have to leave Germany. The *Yiddishe Welt* stated in 1937: "The only solution for the Jew is to immigrate! Where to?"[29] Various solutions were presented in this paper during the course of the year, immigration to Palestine being the most popular. But in all the issues for 1937, there was only one unfavorable direct reference to American immigration policy.

> To tell the truth, I'm growing indifferent to the announcement, that one can cross the ocean in two days. Will they let the Jews come in by this method? The newspapers say that aviation is bringing distant countries together. Why, there never was a greater distance between countries than at present.[30]

Beyond this solitary, and rather resigned, statement, the relation between the necessity for German Jewry to emigrate and a more liberal American immigration policy was passed over in silence.

Jewish organizations before 1938 found themselves in a peculiarly difficult position. On the one hand, there was an emotional and moral attachment to the ideal of an America open to all who wished to enter. On the other, public opinion was clearly hostile to increased immigration, and the Jewish organizations themselves felt little desire to advocate publicly a more liberal system. This conflict manifested itself in curiously contradictory statements.

In March, 1935, B'nai B'rith wrote a letter to the Senate Immigration Committee endorsing the Kerr-Coolidge Bill, which proposed to legalize the status of non-criminal aliens who had

---

[28] *B'nai B'rith Magazine*, vol. LI (May, 1937), p. 249; *AJYB*, vol. XLVII, p. 495.

[29] *Yiddishe Welt*, Sept. 8, 1937, p. 495.

[30] *Ibid.*, July 24, 1937, pp. 401–402.

no proof of legal entry. B'nai B'rith believed it was "meritorious because . . . those who are permitted to remain are subtracted from the quota, and therefore there is no enlargement of the quota numbers."[31] The very next month the organizational magazine published an editorial on the arrival of a boatload of refugees. "One remembered that such numbers of Jews formerly were brought to America on almost every ship. This was in the time when America proudly called itself the haven of the oppressed."[32] The dilemma faced all American Jews who were sincerely concerned with the fate of overseas Jewry. B'nai B'rith had tried to resolve it, but more often, the question of immigration policy was simply ignored and solutions were sought in other directions.

Prior to 1938, the common belief that immigration increased unemployment and generally worsened economic distress was unquestioned. But increasingly, economists discredited this idea. Early in 1939, new economic arguments were presented at a Congressional hearing of a proposed bill to reduce immigration "to protect American labor." A witness pointed out that a large percentage of immigrants were non-producers, and that others had started businesses which employed many Americans. More important, he stated that economists did not agree that immigration hurt the economy; the depression came after immigration had been cut off.[33] In 1940, Columbia University published *Refugees at Work*, which indicated conclusively that the refugees since 1933 had not displaced American workers; on the contrary, they had actually increased employment through their "transplanted skills."

These new views, of course, penetrated rapidly to Jewish circles. The American Jewish Committee's *Annual Report* in 1939 approvingly noted the information. An article by Felix S. Cohen in the *Contemporary Jewish Record* demolished the economic arguments against immigration. He proved statistically that the states with the highest standard of living had the highest percentage of foreign-born. As to unemployment, "laws restricting immigration have the same economic consequences as pneumonia or birth control; that is to say, the removal of the potential producers and consumers from our society."[34] Similar articles of lesser quality appeared in other periodicals.

[31] *Committee on Immigration*, March 3, 1936, p. 217.

[32] *B'nai B'rith Magazine*, vol. L (April, 1936), p. 217. Compare also the statements made *ibid.*, vol. L (April, 1936 and Aug., 1936), *passim.*

[33] *Committee on Immigration*, March 21, 23 and 27, 1939, pp. 155–156 and 167. Note reference to Stuart Chase's statement that "continued prosperity in America depends upon the continued expansion of our population."

[34] *Contemporary Jewish Record*, vol. III (March, 1940), pp. 141–148.

How far this new economic information seeped down below the articulate groups is difficult to ascertain, undoubtedly not to any great extent. But if many Jews still feared the economic effects of immigration, the articulate groups which wielded weight did not. Moreover, economic conditions were gradually improving, particularly after 1939. Although economic fear may have continued to have some influence, it was no longer a moving force.

II

The position of European Jewry deteriorated rapidly in 1938. The Austrian *Anschluss* signalled a new wave of terror in Germany. Mass arrests and widespread destruction followed the bloody November riots. Through Nazi influence anti-Semitism was meanwhile spreading to other European countries. General war broke out in September, 1939, and with each successive German conquest, thousands more were added to the already swollen refugee population. By November, 200,000 war victims were wandering aimlessly in Europe.[35]

The attitude of American Jews toward the immigration laws in 1938 and afterward must be viewed against this grim European background. For the first time the quotas for the continental European countries were being completely filled. The State Department unbent enough to combine the Austrian and German quotas, and gave those refugees in America on visitor's visas extensions on the ground that "it would be cruel and inhuman" to send them to German concentration camps. But much more than this was needed.

In September, 1938, the German Jewish newspaper *Juedische Rundschau* appealed to the United States to increase the German quota, even if it meant decreases in the future. The newspaper reported that the quota was filled until 1940, even for those fortunate enough to have papers.[36] American Jewry could no longer say that all those who desired — and had sufficient means — were able to immigrate to the United States. Events demanded a clear-cut stand on American immigration policy.

Two congressmen, Emanuel Celler and Samuel Dickstein, actually launched abortive attempts to enable more refugees to enter the country. Both were Jewish and represented predominantly Jewish districts in New York City. Celler introduced a bill to lift the quotas. He advocated a temporary change to meet the emergency, rather than

---

[35] *National Jewish Monthly*, Nov., 1939, p. 60; *AJYB, 1939–1940*, vol. XLI, p. 379.
[36] *Times*, Sept. 17, 1938, p. 2; *ibid.*, Sept. 13, 1938, p. 3.

an actual revision.[37] Dickstein, the chairman of the House Committee on Immigration, was even more explicit in his efforts to offer asylum to more refugees while maintaining the principles of the immigration law. Meeting with Mayor La Guardia of New York City, he suggested an "emergency quota," admitting refugees under the unused quotas amounting to 120,000 a year.

> The existing law would not be substantially altered, and each immigrant would have to meet present standards of entry and produce proof that he would not become a public charge.[38]

This was no radical proposal, but it was as far as Jewish spokesmen went at the time. The fate of the two bills was clear all too soon.

The following February, Representative Celler announced that the two measures were being tabled for the present. He said that because of public opinion in the South and West it would be dangerous to press for passage. If he tried to bring his bills out of committee, other bills to reduce or halt immigration would be introduced and probably passed.[39] Celler did not exaggerate. A *Fortune* survey of opinion the next month disclosed that eighty-three per cent of the American people opposed increasing the immigration schedules.[40] Celler concluded rather lamely that the organizations represented at the Conference of the American Committee for the Protection of the Foreign-Born, where he was speaking, should organize in favor of bills like his and conduct a wide radio and publicity campaign to educate the public "in your direction." This unhappy experience indicated without the slightest doubt that all efforts to increase immigration beyond the quota limits were doomed to failure.

The hopelessness of the cause cannot, however, be taken as the sole reason for the silence of the Jewish organizations. Uniformly, they ignored the attempts of the two congressmen to increase refugee immigration. Even the *American Jewish Year Book*, published by the American Jewish Committee, did not mention the bills in its "Review of the Year." *B'nai B'rith Magazine* had included an editorial in August, 1935, praising a bill of Representative Vito Marcantonio similar to Samuel Dickstein's as "good old Americanism"; in 1938, it had nothing whatever to say about these more urgently needed measures.

Jewish groups may have been engrossed in the Evian Conference, which took place at this time. Indeed, the refugee problem was of

[37] *Ibid.*, March 25, 1938, p. 1; and *The Jewish Forum*, July, 1938, p. 100.

[38] *Times*, Nov. 20, 1938, p. 3.

[39] *Contemporary Jewish Record*, vol. II (March, 1939), p. 93.

[40] *Ibid.*, p. 93; and Feb., 1939, p. 4.

such proportions by the middle of 1938 that only international action could have solved it. The State Department plan called for a conference of twenty-nine nations to meet at Evian, France, in July, 1938. The object was to set up "a special committee for the purpose of facilitating the emigration from Austria and Germany of political refugees." The proposal, it was emphasized, was not to interfere with refugee rescue work already being done. "Furthermore, it should be understood that no country would be expected to receive a greater number of immigrants than is permitted by its existing legislation."[41] This last stipulation had particular importance, since it meant in effect that the United States had no intention of altering its own laws.

The Evian Conference turned out to be "preliminary and exploratory." Its meager results were the creation of an intergovernmental committee at London, the recommendation that consulates should not insist on formal passports, and the request that participating governments inform the committee on "details regarding such immigrants as each government may be prepared to receive."[42] The *American Hebrew* wrote at the conclusion of the conference, "the hopes of hundreds of thousands of actual and potential refugees are rapidly sinking."[43] A few American Jews "placed their faith in the good will and sincerity of the United States."[44] But most, even when acknowledging that preliminary groundwork had been laid, were gravely disappointed.[45]

The reaction of American Jewry to the Evian Conference throws a good deal of light on their attitude on immigration and the refugee problem. Despite intense interest in the fate of the victims, there was no apparent desire that the United States liberalize her immigration laws. It was indeed felt that the main obstacle was the unwillingness to lower barriers; but as the *American Jewish Year Book* blithely commented on the Conference, "the disinclination of *other* countries to accept more than a limited number of refugees was observed."[46] There were even occasional statements praising America's generosity concerning the refugees. Until American entrance

---

[41] *AJYB, 1938–1939*, vol. XL, p. 98.

[42] *Contemporary Jewish Record*, vol. I (Sept., 1938), p. 22.

[43] *Ibid.*, July, 1938, p. 22.

[44] *The Jewish Morning Journal* (New York City) in the *Contemporary Jewish Record*, vol. I (Sept., 1938), p. 22; see also statement of P. Wise, observer at the conference for the American Jewish Committee in the *AJYB*, vol. XL, p. 98.

[45] The *Contemporary Jewish Record* published a "Digest of Editorial Opinion" on the Evian question in its Sept., 1938 issue. See also the *Jewish Forum*, Aug., 1938, p. 121.

[46] *AJYB*, vol. XLI, p. 194 (my italics).

into the war, the prevailing Jewish attitude was that, if the quotas were held open, the United States was doing its share.

Jewish approval of the existing laws was silent, as it were, by default. For this reason, the supporting testimony of Rabbi Stephen Wise at a Joint Committee hearing in April, 1939, has particular importance. The hearing was on the Wagner-Rogers Bill, which proposed to admit 20,000 refugee children in two years, the number to be deducted from future quotas. The Bill was popularly supported throughout the country, being openly opposed only by Senator Robert R. Reynolds of North Carolina and by patriotic organizations.[47] Rabbi Wise was a very influential leader on the Jewish scene; certainly he was the most popular and widely-known. At the outset he stated:

> I want to make it plain that, so far as I am concerned there is no intention whatsoever to depart from the immigration laws which at present obtain. I have heard no sane person propose any departure or deviation from the existing law now in force.

This was about as authoritative a statement as could be obtained from the American Jewish community. Wise based his appeal solely on humanitarian grounds. But if there was a conflict between the interests of the country and the children, "speaking for myself as a citizen, I should say, of course, that our country comes first." This was a peculiarly difficult point for a man of his position to make; and it is highly significant that he should have mentioned it, since the committee had not requested a statement on such a possible conflict. Apparently, Rabbi Wise had prepared himself for the painful question. That it weighed on his mind is shown by a misunderstanding which occurred directly after the last quoted statement. Asked if he favored increasing the area from which the children might be taken, Rabbi Wise replied:

> Hard as it may be to answer your question, Mr. Congressman, I feel that the country and the Congress should not be asked to do more than take care of a limited number of children. The bill provides for 10,000 each year for a period of two years. After all, we cannot take care of all of them. Germany has a population of five or six hundred thousand Jews.[48]

Rabbi Wise had forced himself to this rather unhappy resolution, but clearly he did not rest comfortably with it. Most Jewish leaders and organizations did not have to fear an unsympathetic cross-

[47] *Ibid.*, p. 195.
[48] *Joint Hearings before Senate and House Committees on Immigration*, April 20–24, 1939, pp. 155–159.

examination, and they avoided the embarrassing conflict by simply ignoring it.

Almost nothing is to be found in the Jewish literature between 1938 and 1942 expressing significant dissatisfaction with the immigration laws. *B'nai B'rith Magazine* had run periodically editorials on "the Old America," when the door was open to all who wished to enter; this might be construed as an implicit criticism of the quota restrictions. After 1938, such editorials no longer appeared. The *Annual Reports* of the American Jewish Committee made no adverse mention from 1938 to 1942 of the immigration laws. The American Jewish Congress also maintained silence. The issues of its organ, the *Congress Bulletin*, for the year 1941, when conditions in Europe were considerably worse than in 1939, criticized American policy only in one exceptional case when a ruling was issued that, for fear of spies, no refugees with relatives in Nazi-occupied territory were to be admitted.[49] The basic immigration laws were nowhere open to question; but any tightening of the stipulated limits immediately drew protests.

The significant exception to this position was the non-Zionist labor organizations belonging to the Jewish Labor Committee.[50] It was the one Jewish national protective organization during this period which did not regard the immigration laws as manifestations of traditional American generosity. One of its original aims was "to fight for the right of free immigration in all countries" — including the United States. This was obviously more of a final goal than an immediate expectation. Somewhat more realistically, the Committee in September, 1940, urged that "America must not lock her doors in the face of these helpless, these suffering men and women."[51] This policy statement, made when the quotas were being completely used, meant in effect that radical changes should be made in the laws, although the Committee was less interested in the technicalities if only more refugees were admitted.

[49] *Congress Bulletin*, vol. VIII, no. 13 (1941), pp. 3–4.

[50] The Jewish Labor Committee was organized in 1934 under the chairmanship of B. Charney Vladeck to represent the organized labor segment of the Jewish population. Its member organizations included the International Ladies Garment Workers Union, Amalgamated Clothing Workers of America, United Hebrew Trades, Workmen's Circle and numerous other unions and labor organizations. Some of these were not exclusively Jewish. The member organizations agreed not to be represented in any other national protective organization, so that the Labor Committee may be taken as the authoritative voice of this part of the Jewish population. There is some overlapping of organizations represented in the American Jewish Committee and the American Jewish Congress. B'nai B'rith, which acts through its Anti-Defamation League in the same capacity, is not represented in either of these groups.

[51] *Workmen's Circle Call*, vol. VIII (June, 1940), p. 15; *ibid.*, Sept., 1940, p. 4.

The differences in attitude reflected the kind of people with which the organizations were concerned. The American Jewish Committee spoke for the wealthy segment of the Jewish community; B'nai B'rith and the American Jewish Congress, for the middle and professional classes. The Jewish Labor Committee represented the Jewish working class.[52] Each group naturally looked to the safety of refugees of its own class, although all expressed concern for refugees of all classes. When the Nazis were engulfing the continent, labor leaders and other liberal leaders faced death if they remained in Europe. The Jewish Labor Committee did then exactly what the other organizations had done earlier for the scholars, professionals and business people; it raised money and brought them to America.[53] The fact was that until 1939, Nazi persecution had hit the Jewish upper and middle classes hardest. After the defeat of Poland in September, 1939, the Jewish masses found themselves in an increasingly difficult position; and the efforts of the Jewish Labor Committee mirrored the change.[54]

The position of the *Landsmannschaften* rounds out the picture of American Jewry's views on the immigration laws during this period. These groups were organized on the basis of old country ties. More than any other kind of Jewish organization, they were concerned with the fate of their brethren who had not emigrated. They represented those who had not yet lost their old country identification. Except for more intense concern with overseas developments, the *Landsmannschaften* turn out to hold essentially the same views as the other Jewish non-labor organizations. The 1941 issue of *Polish Jews*, the yearbook of the American Federation for Polish Jews, revealed the deep concern of Polish-American Jews for the fate of Polish Jewry. The yearbook spent much space and many articles discussing solutions to the post-war problems of the Polish Jews. Poland in 1940 contained over three million Jews, and all of them could not possibly have come to America. But none of the writers believed that any one solution would do; all felt that a combination of solutions was needed to resettle Polish Jews successfully after the war. Yet the possibility of migrating to America was never mentioned.[55]

[52] *AJYB*, vol. XXXIX, pp. 76–78.

[53] *Call*, vol. VIII (Oct., 1940), p. 93. The Labor Committee, moreover, did not limit ts efforts to rescuing only liberal leaders who were Jews.

[54] Antagonism between Eastern European and German Jews might have been an added factor. The Jewish Labor Committee represented the segment of the Jewish population which maintained ties with Eastern Europe, and the traditional dislike possibly affected their attitude toward the difficulties of the German Jews. However, there is no clear evidence of this in the current Jewish literature.

[55] *Polish Jews*, 1941, *passim*.

The difficulties of the Polish Jew had in fact existed long before the German conquest. Poland had been hit hard by the economic depression, and the Jews, making up the petty middle-man class, suffered most of all. Reports coming from Poland had indicated that almost the entire Jewish population was reduced to pauperism. Until 1939 "the forgotten Jews of Poland" were often overlooked for the more dramatic difficulties of the German Jews.

From its inception in 1934, the Jewish Labor Committee had been aware of this problem. It stated then that "the Jewish question must be solved in the countries in which the Jews lived . . . ."[56] The Committee held this as a cardinal principle throughout the thirties. After the war broke out and Jewish thinking turned to the post-war world, the Committee reaffirmed that it "categorically rejects all theories of 'superfluous' Jews and all attempts to force Jews to migrate."[57]

Non-labor groups leaned toward colonization as the way of solving European Jewry's ills. B'nai B'rith had been considering Biro-Bidjan as a site for Polish Jews as early as 1935.[57a] After 1938, a veritable flood of similar proposals appeared, including the Phillipines, Alaska, Lower California and Australia.[58] The plan that made the most headway was that proposed by Rabbi Wise for a colony in the Dominican Republic. Five hundred families were settled on the land, but further investigation revealed that at best, 5,000 white people might be able to exist on the area offered by President Rafael L. Trujillo.[59] The other programs got no further than the enthusiastic planning stages.

The colonization proposals reveal the thinking of a large part of American Jewry during the dark days of 1939 and 1940. They expressed the widespread concern over the plight of overseas Jewry and served as psychological compensation for the inhospitality of the United States — and perhaps of some American Jews. Although the proposals were undoubtedly sincere, the thinking behind them was unrealistic. They were usually made by middle-class groups such as B'nai B'rith and the American Jewish Congress.

The Workmen's Circle and the Jewish Labor Committee did not favor colonization. They recognized the difficulties such plans

[56] *Times*, April 5, 1934, p. 10.

[57] *Call*, vol. IX (Dec., 1941), p. 14.

[57a] *B'nai B'rith Magazine*, Feb., 1935, p. 159, and Nov., 1936, p. 43.

[58] In 1941, Representative Dickstein offered a bill for refugees to colonize Alaska, the number settling there being deducted from unused quotas for the past six years. *Times*, Jan. 30, 1941, p. 4.

[59] *Times*, March 27, 1940, p. 8.

involved. Moreover, their views on the rights of Jews to remain in their native lands or to immigrate freely anywhere in the world — including America — did not create the necessity for colonization measures.

Palestine presented an entirely different picture. The colonization plans were desperation efforts; settlement in Palestine was a good in itself. The Cleveland *Yiddishe Welt* wrote, "There are many plans proposed for Jewish settlement. All they amount to is a finger pointed to a spot on the map. When, however, we say Palestine, that has a meaning and a certainty."[60] The idea of a Jewish National Home in Palestine was exceedingly attractive to the mass of American Jewry. Disagreement centered only on its political nature. The Zionists, led by Rabbi Wise, believed it should be a state. The non-Zionists argued that it should not have political power, but should be a protectorate. The Jews, they insisted, did not have a national identity. But all felt that Jews should be allowed to immigrate freely to Palestine.

The desire for a Jewish National Home has an important bearing on Jewish attitudes toward immigration policy, particularly in the case of ardent Zionists. To them Palestine was not merely a place of refuge, but the site for a future Jewish state. Jewish settlement there was a positive goal rather than a forced necessity, as was colonization elsewhere. Zionists preferred to see Jewish refugees go to Palestine not particularly because they did not want them in America, but because they did want them in Palestine.[61] Before 1938, this may have been an important motive, but after the *Anschluss* there were more than enough Jewish refugees to go around, and even Zionists backed other colonization projects. The Zionist aspirations of American Jews could not have been a primary force in determining Jewish views on American immigration policy in the grim period from 1938 to 1943.

During these five years of great refugee distress in Europe, American Jewry generally asked only that the restrictive laws be applied liberally within the legal limits. The question here is why the demands were so very limited. Partly the answer related to the recognition that public opinion opposed any changes. But this does not explain why Rabbi Wise stated explicitly at a congressional hearing, "I have heard no sane person propose any departure or

---

[60] *Yiddishe Welt*, Feb. 3, 1937, p. 434.

[61] Toward the end of 1945, President Harry S. Truman issued a directive to facilitate the admission of 39,000 refugees to America. Rabbi Wise commented that he was "happy" about the President's announcement, but that he would have preferred to see them in Palestine. *Times*, Dec. 24, 1945, p. 9.

deviation from existing laws now in force."[62] Nor does it explain the general acquiescence in, and even approval of, the immigration laws. There was, on the other hand, great and continued agitation against the English White Paper, stopping immigration to Palestine, which seemed entrenched with equal permanence. The proximate cause of this attitude of acceptance lay in the social conditions which prevailed during the years before the American entry into the War.

By the end of the decade, anti-Jewish sentiment had reached a danger point in the United States. In the earlier years anti-Semitism appeared in petty social distinction and, as the depression deepened, in economic discrimination.[63] Neither of these forms constituted an open attack on American Jewry.

The situation changed radically in 1939. Father Charles E. Coughlin's radio speeches became increasingly more virulent, Nazi and nativist groups openly held demonstrations and broadcast "Buy Christian" slogans and anti-Jewish leaflets. These efforts had their effect. By May, 1939, there was a considerable amount of discussion in the press and radio on "the Jewish problem," and among Jews a "growing apprehensiveness."[64]

Organized anti-Jewish agitation diminished somewhat during 1940, largely because of the growing unpopularity of the Nazis. But it was replaced by an indigenous form which frightened Jews even more than the blatant type, for this campaign had a much wider base of support. Jewish writers generally — and probably correctly — identified this new anti-Semitic form with the appearance of strong isolationist sentiment. The *America First Bulletin* spoke of "numerous groups which fight for America's entry into the war — foreign and racial groups which have special and just grievances against Hitler."[65] This identification of American Jewry with "internationalist" groups resulted in a growing popular anti-Jewish sentiment. The *Congress Bulletin* stated:

> At no time in American history has anti-Semitism been as strong as it is today. At no time has that particularly smug mealy-mouthed, "some-of-my-best-friends-are-Jews" type of anti-Semitism received such widespread public utterance on political platform, in the houses of Congress and in the news.[66]

[62] *Joint Hearings*, April 20, 1939, p. 155.
[63] *B'nai B'rith Magazine*, vol. XLIX (Feb., 1939), p. 155.
[64] *Contemporary Jewish Record*, vol. II (May, 1939).
[65] *AJYB, 1941–1942*, vol. XLIII, p. 109. See the sections on " Anti-Jewish Movements" in the *AJYB*, vols. XLI–XLIII, for a complete discussion of the anti-Semitic problem.
[66] *Congress Bulletin*, vol. VIII, no. 7, p. 7.

Against this unhappy background of anti-Jewish sentiment — both radical and respectable — American Jewish views on the immigration laws must be seen and interpreted.

American anti-Semitism must have had a discouraging effect on Jewish efforts to liberalize the immigration laws. But once beyond this assumption, almost no direct evidence exists in the relevant literature to indicate that there was such a relationship.

Jewish organization recognized early that attempts to increase immigration would antagonize unfriendly groups. In 1935, David MacCormack, Commissioner-General of Immigration, warned advocates of more liberal immigration policy:

> One of the best ways to promote [latent racial and religious] antagonisms is to advocate increased immigration, particularly during a period of depression and unemployment.[67]

Undoubtedly, most Jewish spokesmen accepted this statement; there is no evidence that any did not. The pertinent question is to what extent this recognition influenced their stand when anti-Jewish agitation was at a peak in the years before 1942.

The evidence indicates that a good deal of anxiety existed among many Jews at this time not to provide justification, or a source, for anti-Semitism. For this reason they wanted to make themselves as inconspicuous as possible in American political life. A *B'nai B'rith Magazine* editorial in November, 1936, stated:

> During the election campaign just over we heard a great deal to this effect: that the Jew efface himself as much as possible from public life lest he appear too prominent and make himself a shining mark for enemies.[68]

The editorial repudiated such thinking, and asserted that Jews should not fear to do their part for the country. The important fact is that this magazine felt that such thinking was widespread enough to warrant comment.

A young Jewish writer accused B'nai B'rith in "painful instances" of having "actually tried to bring pressure to prevent Jews from assuming leadership in liberal movements . . . for the explicit reason that the causes were unpopular and such leadership might result in local outbursts of group discrimination." This statement came from a collection of essays, mostly by younger Jews, on *How To Combat Anti-Semitism in America*. They urged rejection of the "sha-sha philosophy of Jewish polemics, which sought to turn away wrath with

---

[67] *Times*, March 4, 1935, p. 4.

[68] *B'nai B'rith Magazine*, vol. LI (Nov., 1936), p. 43. See also Rabbi Wise's bitter statement on this subject in his *As I See It* (New York, 1944), p. 261.

gentle words, to obscure the Jew from public gaze."[69] For at least
a significant number, then, the reaction to anti-Semitic threats must
have been of the "sha-sha" variety.

Jewish sensitivity appears in subtler ways. *B'nai B'rith Magazine*
ceased to include editorials on the American tradition of free immigration. There were occasional references to the United States'
"generous" treatment of the refugees, which was in fact quite ungen-
erous. Through the Jewish periodical and related literature of the
period when a statement favoring a more liberal immigration policy
does appear, it turns out to be a quotation from a non-Jewish source.
In fact, statements of this sort in Jewish periodicals and organizational literature form the miserly bulk of those advocating more
liberal immigration.

This desire to avoid aggravating what was believed to be an
already dangerous situation caused silence or passive approval of
immigration restriction, at this time a highly combustible topic,
particularly to those patriots and isolationists most sensitive to the
"Jewish problem." These Jews feared to make easy targets by
advocating proposals like the Celler and Dickstein Bills, or openly
backing unpopular liberal organizations like the American Civil
Liberties Union, which did favor increased immigration.

The Jewish Labor Committee spoke a good deal more forthrightly
than the non-labor groups. It manifestly showed its dissatisfaction
with American hospitality. Significantly, it differed sharply from
non-labor organizations in its reaction to anti-Semitism.

> The Jewish Labor Committee believes that anti-Semitism is a smoke
> screen for reaction and has thus allied itself with liberalism. [It] urges
> Jewish progressives to identify their fight against anti-Semitism with the
> struggle for democracy and freedom.[70]

Considering anti-Semitism as part of the detested system of "reaction" rather than as an isolated attack on themselves, the labor
groups were not affected by threats in the same way as non-labor
groups, who did not think in these terms. The attitude of Jewish
labor groups toward anti-Semitism thus correlated positively with
their stand on immigration policy.

As a complete explanation of their silence on immigration policy,
however, the possible desire to avoid arousing anti-Jewish sentiment
leaves much to be desired. Some non-labor groups did not hesitate
to speak out on other matters where they with equal effectiveness

[69] *How to Combat Anti-Semitism in America* (New York, 1937), p. 33. This volume was
sponsored by the American Jewish Congress.

[70] *Call*, March, 1941, p. 3.

stirred up anti-Semitism. Mass protest meetings and an anti-German boycott probably did more during 1940 and 1941 to arouse isolationists than advocacy of greater immigration could have done. Rabbi Wise, who was so eager to show that he favored the existing immigration laws at the Congressional hearing, turned out to be extremely outspoken on other issues which served equally well to increase anti-Semitic sentiment. On the other hand, the American Jewish Committee and B'nai B'rith did not sanction the boycott and mass meetings. The most that can be concluded here is that fear of anti-Jewish agitation was a factor in discouraging some Jewish groups from advocating increased immigration.

The connection between large scale Jewish immigration to America and the creation of anti-Semitism had another side. Besides the advocacy of increased immigration, the very presence of large numbers of recent Jewish immigrants in the United States would be a constant source of anti-Jewish feeling. Konrad Heiden stated that Jews widely recognized Jewish immigrants as the source of anti-Semitism. He noted that Theodor Herzl, the founder of Zionism, had said that migrating Jews carried anti-Semitism with them to America. The vast amount of philanthropy to aid the Jewish refugees, Heiden charged, was given "to prevent the Jewish masses from becoming floating centers of anti-Semitic infection."[71]

The significant fact was that Heiden, while vigorously proclaiming the right of Jews to immigrate freely, believed that such immigration would cause anti-Jewish feeling. "The immigration of fresh Jewish masses, it is said, would only stir up anti-Semitism. Then let there be anti-Semitism!"[72] Clearly, this view hurt his main contention that Jews had an undeniable right of free immigration. He obviously assumed that American Jews generally recognized this as a fact. Stated in terms of the effect on anti-Jewish sentiment, the presence of many Jewish immigrants differs very little from advocacy of increased immigration. Both are in fact open to the same qualifications; but there is also an important difference.

The thought of having large groups of alien Jews in America framed the immigration question in a most decisive way. The consequences went much deeper than the creation of anti-Jewish sentiment. The presence of many Jewish immigrants meant inevitably to American Jews that they would be identified with groups which they, as well as non-Jews, considered alien; Jewish immigration was directly related to their own position in American life. The

[71] *Voice of the Unconquered*, vol. III (April, 1945), p. 3.
[72] *Ibid.*, p. 3.

connection between the presence of refugees and the insecurity of American Jews underlay Jewish views on restrictive immigration policy.

III

The discussion thus far has attempted to explain the lack of Jewish enthusiasm to liberalize our immigration policy by proximate causes which arose out of conditions peculiar to the time: economic distress, anti-Semitism, popular opposition and Zionism. These offer partial explanations, but even taken together, they do not provide a satisfactory answer to the puzzle of the general Jewish acceptance of the quota system. The question was not peculiarly Jewish; no immigrant groups of recent origin showed a real desire to change the immigration laws. Since the change in attitude after 1924 was uniform, there must have been a fundamental force which worked on all of them. The question will be probed here only in terms of the Jewish groups, but the general conclusions would apply to some extent to all immigrant groups.

The quota system in effect discriminated against Jewish immigrants from Eastern Europe. Of the 153,000 persons legally permitted to immigrate annually to the United States under the Law of 1924, the English quota was 65,700 and the German quota 27,000. The Jewish populations of these countries respectively were 300,000 and 600,000. The pre-war Jewish population of Eastern Europe, excluding Russia, exceeded four million. But the annual immigration quota from this area was not above 10,000.[73] Thus the immigration law put Eastern European Jews at a great disadvantage. Yet the Jewish periodical literature of the period, aside from periodicals connected with the Jewish Labor Committee, indicated no great dissatisfaction with the inequitable arrangement.

The Jewish communities of Eastern Europe differed basically from those in the rest of the western world. In Eastern Europe the Jews were culturally, as well as religiously, distinct from the non-Jewish community. During the centuries of isolation in the ghettos, Eastern European Jewry had developed a Yiddish culture which diverged totally from the culture (or cultures) of the country in which it lived. Religious orthodoxy permeated their isolated existences and prescribed to an amazing degree the proper performance of the normal functions of life. Self-dependent, these Yiddish-speaking enclaves in Eastern Europe had developed their own distinctive way of life.

---

[73] *Immigration Laws and Regulations* (Washington, 1944), pp. 257–258; *AJYB, 1942–1943*, vol. XLIV, p. 428.

The great Jewish migration occurred between 1880 and 1914, when over a million and a half Jews immigrated to the United States. The great mass of these came from Eastern Europe, and they carried with them the Jewish culture of the Polish and Russian ghetto. Primarily, they settled in large cities, particularly New York, where they could be among *landsleute* and could carry on the old way of life. These first generation Americans spoke Yiddish mainly, and English haltingly if at all. The Yiddish theater, press and literature became thriving cultural forms in the United States. For these people, in effect, the long migration westward had not cut off their Old World existences. The East Side in New York with its religious and charitable activities became a sort of New World replica of the European ghetto.

By the beginning of the thirties, it was clear that the Yiddish culture was declining. The fact was commonly recognized and widely discussed by Jewish periodicals and press throughout the period. Writing of the dim future of the Yiddish press, Abraham Cahan, editor of the *Jewish Daily Forward* [Yiddish], concluded, "The children are becoming Americanized, and it is only natural; they live in this country and it treats them as its own children."[74] The American-born children of the Jewish immigrants normally grew up ignorant of their Yiddish background. The newer generation was educated in the public schools, spoke English as its native language, and moved out of the restricted world of its parents into the non-Yiddish American community. Chaim Zhitlowsky, speaking before the Yiddish Culture Society, pictured the second generation Jews in this way:

> They have absorbed a certain national pride, not a Jewish nationalism, however, but an American .... They were proud of the fact that they are children of the American people, of its language and of its culture. English is their national language; the English culture their national culture.[75]

Two terms were used, often interchangeably, to signify this adjustment: assimilation and Americanization.[76] Uniformly, Jewish writers

[74] *B'nai B'rith Magazine*, vol. LI (June, 1937), p. 211; see also M. Baker and Paul Masserman, *The Jews Come to America* (New York, 1932), p. 6. "The future of the Yiddish tongue, of Yiddish literature, of the Yiddish press is dark. The older generation, the Yiddish-speaking generation, is dying out. Yiddish, itself, is spoken by a constantly diminishing portion of unassimilated Jewry, and is eschewed almost entirely by the younger generation."

[75] Chaim Zhitlowsky, *The Future of Our Youth in this Country and Assimilation* (Pittsburgh, 1935), p. 90.

[76] The term "assimilation" usually had a slightly different connotation than "Americanization." An editorial in *B'nai B'rith Magazine* referred to two kinds of assimilation. To

looked on American culture (or any other term to designate the Anglo-Saxon features of American life) as something fixed, completed, and unchanging. In order to become more American, one had to become less Jewish (i. e., Yiddish). To make the distinction one author referred to "American Jews" and "Jewish Jews." When a Jew went from the latter to the former group, he was "assimilated."

The significant fact was not that they were losing the distinguishing characteristics of the Yiddish-speaking generation, but that many looked on the process as inherently good and tried to hurry it along. They were eager to be accepted as full-fledged Americans, to be indistinguishable from other Americans except for religious affiliation.[77]

The reverse of the urge to become American was a desire to obliterate the Yiddish culture. "The new Jew is disturbed, troubled, burdened with a heritage which he has renounced as alien yet which will not free him." The "Old" and "New" Jew were in basic conflict.[78]

The desire to be "American" was the source of deep-rooted insecurity, for, as one writer put it, "the new Jew [felt] assimilated but undigested in the non-Jewish world."[79] While he had successfully assumed the outward features, he was, in his own mind, still set apart as somehow non-American.

The urge to be an integral part of the American community manifested itself in the statements of Jewish leaders. Speaking to the American Jewish Congress, Rabbi Stephen Wise asserted: "We are Americans, first, last, and all the time. Nothing else that we are, whether by faith or race or fate, qualifies our Americanism."[80] It was not the truth of the quotation that was significant, but the fact that he felt impelled to verbalize it at all. Rabbi Wise's statement was not isolated; a remarkable number of statements of similar

lose one's Jewish identity was wrong. "The other form of assimilation began when the ghetto walls fell ... This process has been seen at its best in the United States. Here the Jew has been assimilated as a citizen and has preserved his identity as a Jew ... This is the right kind of assimilation." (vol. XLVII, p. 2.) This latter type was synonymous with Americanization.

[77] According to Sokolsky's *We Jews*, *supra*, significant numbers had converted or "passed," that is, concealed their Jewish identities.

[78] M. Baker and P. Masserman, *The Jews Come to America*, *supra*, pp. 6–7. There is the amusing instance in the notices of the marriage brokers' columns of the Yiddish press of "ladies and gentlemen" "emphasizing the fact that they are 'American,' that is to say, that their Jewishness has been reduced to an unobtrusive level." Ludwig Lewisohn, *The American Jew* (New York, 1950), p. 74.

[79] M. Baker and P. Masserman, *The Jews Come to America*, *supra*, p. 6.

[80] Stephen S. Wise, *As I See It* (New York, 1944), p. 67.

import exist in the literature of the period, often as arguments against Zionism. (Wise, of course, was a Zionist leader.)[81]

B'nai B'rith Magazine ran a series of editorials extending throughout the decade on the "Jewish vote." They asserted uniformly and emphatically that there was no such thing, and called on Jews "to repudiate any political enterprise that had to do with Jewish votes." Rabbi Wise bitterly accused a small group of Jews of having "conjured up the spectre of a Jewish vote."[82] The significant point was not that there was not a Jewish vote, but that spokesmen were so violent in claiming that there was none. They protested — perhaps too much — that Jews voted as Americans — like other Americans.

The urgent desire to convince others that Jews were, above all, patriotic Americans provides a possible explanation for the testimony of Rabbi Wise at the hearing in 1939 on the proposed bill to admit 20,000 refugee children. The other Jewish spokesman who appeared before the Committee exhibited the same defensive attitude. This was Sidney Hollander, President of the National Council of Jewish Federations. He had just returned from Europe (April, 1939) and had found refugee conditions there grim. Unless the refugees escaped, he said, "nothing lay ahead but extermination." He put his statements on a humanitarian basis; children were being left homeless, and the United States ought to save some of them.

Hollander emphasized that the children were both Jewish and Gentile. "Statements have been made ... that if this bill is passed it will benefit primarily Jewish children. I have no reason to believe that this is true. If it were, I doubt if I would as strongly urge the passage of this bill." He concluded with this extraordinary remark:

> If I thought for a moment that this would involve a lessening of support for those in this country, or even a straining of the funds needed here, I would hesitate to sponsor this bill.[83]

In partial explanation of the two men's statements, it ought to be noted that at the time anti-alien sentiment related to the rising popularity of isolationism was sweeping the country. The flood of anti-alien bills presented during 1939 and 1940 in the Seventy-Sixth Congress clearly revealed the public mind. Senator Louis B.

---

[81] See a statement by Maurice Wertheim, President of the American Jewish Committee and a non-Zionist, which is representative of this variety of patriotic argument against Zionism in the *American Jewish Committee Annual Report, 1942* (New York, 1942), p. 42.

[82] S. S. Wise, *As I See It, supra,* p. 261.

[83] *Joint Committee Hearing,* April, 1939, pp. 90–95.

Schwellenbach noted that "to condemn aliens . . . is perhaps the best vote-getting argument in present day politics."[84] The "assimilated but indigested" Jew must have been peculiarly pained by the temper of the times.

The underlying reluctance of American Jews to see a large influx of Jewish immigrants had its source in the vital desire to be completely "American" in their own minds and in the minds of others. Jewish writers clearly recognized that immigration restriction caused the decline of the Yiddish culture. B'nai B'rith Magazine, referring to "the Closed Gate," asked, "Whence is refreshment for Jewish life in America to come in the future? What substitutes for the flame of these multitudes who came here and kept alive the tradition of the Torah?"[85] The converse was that restriction would aid in the process of Americanization.[86]

The gap between the facts so far ascertained and the conclusion that they resulted in a desire to continue the quota law is not easily closed. No Jewish leader or periodical stated that immigration ought to be restricted so that American Jews could be successfully assimilated in the American community. Moreover, the plight of the German Jews during the thirties obscured the basic issue of the Yiddish-speaking immigrants. The German Jews, unlike the Polish and Russian Jews, were non-Yiddish in background; they considered themselves Jews only by religious tie. Their coming to America had no stimulating effect on the Yiddish culture. But even in their case, American Jews were reluctant. Although they were not Yiddish, German refugees were nevertheless alien. This must have been one of the considerations behind B'nai B'rith's suggestion in 1937 that many refugees be moved out of New York City. American Jews were loath to be identified with any groups which they considered foreign to American society.

The intervening years of little immigration before the advent of Hitler had hardened the attitude toward alien Jewry — Yiddish or otherwise. One Jewish writer stated that the American Jews in 1933 were "economically and psychologically unprepared" for "the refugee influx." "We had forgotten what immigrants looked like. Almost literally, they were men from Mars, a vicious, bloody Mars." She

[84] Contemporary Jewish Record, vol. III (May, 1940), p. 245.

[85] B'nai B'rith Magazine, vol. XLVII (Nov., 1932), p. 3; see also M. Baker and P. Masserman, The Jews Come to America, supra, p. 366.

[86] In 1933, Harold Fields, executive director of the National League for American Citizenship, stated that the reduction in immigration had speeded up the process of assimilation of the foreign-born. Times, Aug. 6, 1933, section II, p. 4.

continued, "Had the stream of immigration been continuous before 1933, no immigrant phobias would have been built up."[87]

Because Jewish representatives rarely verbalized their thoughts on the relation between immigration and assimilation, the testimony of Mrs. Cecilia R. Davidson, representing the National Council of Jewish Women, at several Congressional hearings is particularly revealing. In identifying the Council, she stated that "its members are all American citizens, and many of them can boast of ancestors who came before the Civil War." This was a telling point, for it established the Council as unusually "American" for a Jewish organization. One of its major functions was "to assist foreign-born women, girls, and children in becoming part of the American community." Mrs. Davidson favored the Kerr-Coolidge Bill, legalizing the status of certain classes of aliens, "so that we can really devote ourselves to the work of assimilation."[88] At an earlier hearing, she had said, "Now, when the restrictive immigration law went into effect, one of the most important arguments . . . was that we were then having an opportunity to catch up with the people already in the country, to try assimilate them, to try to incorporate them into our American civilization and American life . . . I think we were getting along very nicely."[89] Taken in conjunction with the general Jewish attitude toward adjustment to American life (as they conceived it), Mrs. Davidson's isolated statements indicate somewhat more clearly that for those who desired to be accepted without qualification, immigration restriction would be considered a wise measure.[90]

But the interrelated facts thus far uncovered do not provide conclusive proof of the effect of assimilation desires. The position of the Jewish Labor Committee takes on added significance in this context. This organization, as we have seen, spoke out forthrightly against the quota system as discriminating against Jews. Its program included a statement that after the War

[87] Libby Benedict, "A Case of 'Philanthropitis'," *Congress Bulletin*, vol. VIII, no. 6 (1941), pp. 9–10.

[88] *Senate Commiteee on Immigration*, March 3, 1936, pp. 171–174.

[89] *House Committee on Immigration*, 1932, p. 12.

[90] It is difficult to tell whether Jews whose American antecedents went back before the Yiddish-speaking immigration influx in 1880 had the same sense of insecurity or the same degree of it. Probably, the deeper American roots made the insecurity somewhat less, but their identification with the rest of American Jewry (if only by religious tie) must have had some effect. To some extent, these Jews were represented in the American Jewish Committee and the National Council of Jewish Women, and the positions of these groups on immigration may be taken, with reservations, to reflect the views of older American Jews.

Jews are to be guaranteed the right of free immigration and emigration. All laws and practices, designed to curtail the rights of Jews to free emigration or immigration or the choice of a profession or trade are to be revoked and banned.[91]

No other Jewish organization made such a statement at any time.

It is extremely important, then, to note another statement adopted at the Workmen's Circle Convention in 1942 and incorporated in the Jewish Labor Committee's "Post-War Peace Demands."

The basic law of such countries [where Jews lived in large numbers and in compact masses] must acknowledge the Jews to be a national group with a language, a culture, and a national life of its own.[92]

This statement too was peculiar to the Jewish Labor Committee and its affiliated organizations. Unlike the non-labor groups, these did not want to see the Yiddish culture decline. "Yiddish is the secular bond that holds together the majority of Jews — the simple people, the workers, the small shopkeepers."[93] They looked on Jews in all lands as a distinct national group held together by the Yiddish culture. "The Yiddish press speaks today as the voice and heart of this new consciousness to act as a national unity." This concept was completely at odds with the views of the non-labor groups.

The Workmen's Circle made energetic efforts to keep alive Yiddish culture in America by establishing schools and sponsoring cultural activities. Non-labor organizations did not engage in such efforts to maintain Yiddish life. B'nai B'rith, recognizing that the Yiddish press and theater were losing their audiences, expressed its sympathies, and suggested that an Anglo-Jewish press and theater be established to fill the void. A striking difference thus existed between labor and non-labor groups in their views on the continued existence of the Yiddish culture.

The difference extended into their thinking on their place in American life. The labor groups had not the sensitivity and insecurity of non-labor groups, although they were aware of these feelings in others. Reviewing *The American Jew* by Oscar Janowsky, a labor writer stated:

It bears witness to the alarming deterioration of the vigor and the courage which characterizes the immigrants from Eastern Europe two generations ago ... The book betrays a labored attempt, on the one

[91] *Call*, Vol. XI (Sept., 1943), p. 11.

[92] *Ibid.*, July, 1943, p. 28.

[93] *Ibid.*, vol. IX (Dec., 1941), p. 4.

hand, to prove how very much a part of America the Jews are; on the other hand, to assure the Jews that there is every reason in the world to feel optimistic about the development of Jewish life in this country.

Jewish labor displayed no such conflict; it accepted the Yiddish heritage wholeheartedly and expressed no doubts about its position in American life.[94]

It is extremely significant that labor and non-labor organizations, differing in their views on the Yiddish culture and their place in American society, should differ along the same lines in their positions on Jewish immigration. The inevitable conclusion must be that rejection of the Yiddish heritage and a frustrated desire to be considered completely American — in their terms — underlay the general reluctance to see masses of Jewish immigrants come to America. The labor groups, accepting the Yiddish culture and having no anxieties concerning their place in the American community, did speak out vigorously against the quota system. In addition to the proximate causes, this process of cultural adjustment was a fundamental force which directly influenced the views of American Jews on the restrictive immigration laws.

POSTSCRIPT

Tragic events conspired to solve the refugee problem for American Jewry. The entrance of the United States into the War effectively dried up further immigration. Jews understood that the best way to help European Jewry was to win the war, and throughout 1942 they said nothing about bringing refugees to America. During the summer months of 1942, reports were received that the Nazis were in the first stages of exterminating the Jews of German-occupied Europe. American Jews reacted strongly with moral protests and fasting. As more appalling data arrived, the extent of the tragedy began to be comprehended; two million Jews had been slaughtered by January, 1943. Outrage was now channelled into specific demands, including opening America's doors to whoever could manage to get out of Europe. Spokesmen bitterly accused government officials of laxity in trying to save refugees. For a short time Jewish frustration focused on restrictionist policy.

The turning point came in the early Fall of 1943 when the American Jewish Conference met. For the first time, every important organization consented, however reluctantly, to meet in an assembly

[94] *Ibid.*, vol. XI (April 1943), p. 18.

truly representative of American Jewry. The purpose was "to establish a common program in connection with post-war problems." As it turned out, the Zionists had the backing of the great majority at the Conference. In the rising enthusiasm, other proposals were subordinated or absorbed by the dominant interest in Palestine. A resolution by the Jewish Labor Committee for the right of free immigration was overwhelmed. Nothing was said about American immigration policy, a rather startling development in view of the agitation on this matter preceding the meeting. The main achievement of the Conference was that it registered authoritatively American Jewry's desire that the survivors of the Nazi concentration camps create a Jewish commonwealth.

Zionism resolved the dilemma of American Jewry; it provided a home for the remnants of European Jewry without incurring an immigrant exodus to the United States.

SOCIAL DISCRIMINATION AGAINST JEWS IN AMERICA, 1830–1930*

By John Higham

INTRODUCTION

A hallmark of the intellectual culture of our day is an almost superstitious awe and distrust of ideologies. Defined as rigid systems of ideas which interpret life in terms functional to someone's bid for power, ideologies purport to explain what they seek to coerce. Disseminated by the agitator, the propagandist, or the intellectual, they distort reality, attack the foundations of belief, and threaten the independence and integrity of the human mind.[1] Obviously part of our anxiety about them stems from the demonstrated power of the totalitarian brain-washer. Less obviously but perhaps more basically, the fear of ideologies derives from an irrationalist strain in modern thought, which assumes that dark forces within most men make them easy victims of the expert myth-maker.

Modern social research has felt especially the fascination with ideologies, and many social scientists have labored to expose their political and psychological dynamics. There is a consequent tendency to fix upon ideology as the critical factor in many a social

---

* This study was initiated at the request of the American Jewish Committee and carried out with its generous support. In the hope that disinterested historical research might help it to understand the problem of social discrimination better, the Committee submitted to me several questions, including the following: When and why has discrimination against Jews increased and diminished in America? In what respects has discrimination against other minority groups been comparable to or different from the situation of the Jews? If some places have had a tradition of significantly less discrimination against Jews than has the rest of the United States, what factors are peculiar to the Jews and to the general social life in those places? Have intellectual and political doctrines played any part in causing or in lessening social discrimination? I am especially indebted to Mr. Milton Himmelfarb for helping to define these challenging lines of inquiry. The Committee, however, made no other effort to guide my research and has no responsibility whatever for the conclusions I reached. The chronological limits of the study were chosen largely for convenience; they mark off the period which previous research enabled me to re-examine with some confidence in the time that was available to me.

At many points I am also indebted to the able research assistance of Sondra Herman.

[1] See Karl Mannheim, *Ideology and Utopia: an Introduction to the Sociology of Knowledge* (London, 1936), and Arthur Edward Murphy, "Ideals and Ideologies, 1917–1947," *Philosophical Review*, vol. LVI (July, 1947), pp. 374–389.

problem, in the perhaps tenuous hope that the problem will yield to a reasonable solution once the ideological magic is exorcised.

Much of the study of anti-Semitism in recent years has taken this direction. Ideological anti-Semitism lends itself readily to analysis, for it is melodramatic, easily documented, and scary. This kind of anti-Semitism blames the major ills of society on the Jews; it concerns and addresses the whole body politic. When successful, it becomes a mass movement, and Nazi Germany, to say nothing of the Ku Klux Klan in America, proved how successful it could be.

We recognize fairly commonly a theoretical distinction between the gigantic unrealities of the ideologist and the more ordinary antipathies embedded in the mores of a community. The former arise primarily from subjective sources within the aggressor, the latter from actual contact between groups.[1a] Often, however, the distinction becomes lost, especially when it is blurred and enveloped by the scapegoat theory of prejudice. Irrational myths are held responsible for everyday problems of social adjustment; and if the myths do not appear in any clearly organized form, at least there are always stereotypes. The stereotype, too, artificially structures reality; it is the myth cut down to size. It, too, is supposed to call forth aggressions against a presumably innocent scapegoat.

Thus, most studies of anti-Semitism made in the last twenty-five years reflect an Orwellian anxiety over the power of irrational beliefs. Prejudices of every magnitude are attributed much more largely to the hidden frustrations of an aggressor than to any objective situation. The essay that follows tries to show the inadequacy of this view for interpreting a century of American-Jewish relations. Social discrimination, the kind of anti-Semitism that affected American Jewry most closely, owed very little to ideological sources. Ideological anti-Semitism had a more or less separate existence. It never became powerful enough to narrow significantly the horizons of individual opportunity. Nor did stereotypic thinking, that other bogey of modern scholarship, play a decisive role. Stereotypes, by generalizing antagonisms, made discrimination possible; but they did not create it. An actual conflict situation produced the patterns

[1a] Shlomo Bergman, "Some Methodological Errors in the Study of Anti-Semitism," *Jewish Social Studies*, vol. V (1943), pp. 57–58; Eva Reichmann, *Hostages to Civilization: The Social Sources of National Socialist Anti-Semitism* (Boston, 1951), pp. 30 ff. A related distinction between prejudices and antipathies is suggestively developed in Louis Wirth, "Research in Racial and Cultural Relations," *Proceedings of the American Philosophical Society*, vol. XCII (1948), p. 384. See also Bohdan Zawadzki, "Limitations of the Scapegoat Theory of Prejudice," *Journal of Abnormal and Social Psychology*, vol. XLIII (1948), pp. 127–141.

of exclusion that gradually delimited the opportunities of American Jews, and the degree of exclusion depended upon the sharpness of the conflict. Discrimination issued not from primarily irrational, subjective impulses but rather from a very real competition for status and prestige.

THE PREWAR ERA, 1830–1860

On the eve of the German immigration that began in the late 1830's, there were probably less than 15,000 Jews in a total American population of 15,000,000.[2] This tiny minority, descended largely from colonial settlers, dwelled in a few large trading centers. Engaged particularly as foreign traders and as stock and money brokers, the Jews formed on the whole a well-to-do and well established part of the merchant class. By all accounts they occupied a secure, stable, and untrammeled place in American society.[3]

Throughout the antebellum period, Jews continued to enjoy almost complete social acceptance and freedom. There was no pattern of discrimination in the sense of exclusion from social and economic opportunities which qualified Jews sought. A distinction should be drawn, however, between actual social relations and stereotypes or ideas; the prevalence of good relations does not mean that American attitudes toward Jews were ever wholly favorable. Behavior and belief do not necessarily coincide in any area of life. Unfavorable attitudes about a whole ethnic group do not necessarily compromise our practical response to individuals. If the situation encourages a harmonious adjustment, the attitudes remain mild or impersonal. Thus, the image of Scotchmen as a stiff-necked, penurious people and the image of Englishmen as snobs has not handicapped members of either of these groups in America. Similarly, the Jews in early nineteenth century America got along very well with their non-Jewish neighbors although American conceptions of Jews in the abstract at no time lacked the unfavorable elements embedded in European tradition.

Ethnic stereotypes are seldom simple, black-or-white responses, and American impressions of Jews have been especially many-sided and ambivalent. They played two entirely different roles in the nineteenth century imagination, one religious and the other economic.

---

[2] One observer estimated the American Jewish population at 6,000 in 1826, another at 15,000 in 1840. *American Jewish Year Book, 1899–1900*, p. 283.

[3] Morris U. Schappes, ed., *Documentary History of the Jews in the United States, 1654–1875* (New York, 1950), pp. 142, 158, 226.

They were the instruments and unwilling witnesses of a divine purpose; and they represented the virtues and vices of modern business. Some students have emphasized the religious image as the characteristic one in early America and have pointed out the awe-struck sympathy and self-identification that an Old Testament, Puritan culture felt with the archetypal people of God.[4] Indeed, until the 1840's at least, the average American seemed to think of Jews primarily as ancient patriarchs in flowing robes, smelling of frankincense and myrrh. Yet Christian orthodoxy also presented the Jews as rebels against God's purpose. The justice of their ruination supplied the text for many a sermon.[5] The ideological potentialities of this atmosphere were such that the great New York *Herald* once blazoned forth a breathless exposé of ritual murder in the Near East. Jewish fanatics, the paper reported, had bled to death a Christian missionary, ground up his bones, and mixed his blood with unleavened bread.[6]

The economic stereotype of the Jew as a businessman is more relevant to modern anti-Semitism, since Christian stereotypes faded into the background with the increasing secularization of society and the multiplication of personal contacts with real live Jews. Discrimination, when it came, exploited secular rather than religious attitudes. It is worth noting, therefore, that the impression of Jews as aggressive businessmen had always been widespread in

[4] Edmund Wilson, *A Piece of My Mind* (New York, 1956), pp. 90–102.

[5] Clarence H. Faust and Thomas H. Johnson, eds., *Jonathan Edwards: Representative Selections* (New York, 1935), p. 155; Ethan Smith, *View of the Hebrews* (2nd ed., Poultney, Vt., 1825), p. 14; "The Present State of the Jews," *Western Monthly Review*, vol. II (1829), p. 437; Osborn W. Trenery Heighway, *Leila Ada, the Jewish Convert* (Philadelphia, 1853), pp. 111–117, 226; John Marsh, *An Epitome of General Ecclesiastical History* (7th ed., New York, 1843), pp. 163–165, 449.

[6] New York *Herald*, April 6, 1850, p. 1. The story cropped up again several years later in James O. Noyes, "The Jews," *The Knickerbocker*, vol. LIII (1859), pp. 50–51. And in some places vague superstitions of this kind lived on for many decades. At the opening of the twentieth century Missouri country folk were still singing "The Jew's Daughter," a ballad concerning the sad fate of a little boy enticed into a Jew's house, though he has heard that those who enter such a place never come out:

> She pinned a napkin round his neck,
> She pinned it with a pin,
> And then she called for a tin basin
> To catch his life-blood in.

> "Go place my prayer-book at my head,
> My bible at my feet,
> And if any of my playmates ask for me
> Just tell them that I am asleep."

Journal of American Folklore, vol. XIX (1906), pp. 293–294.

America, even in an age of biblical piety when most people had never seen a Jew. The same writers who emphasized the religious significance of God's ancient people often depicted the modern Jew as sunk in the love of gain.[7]

Like the Christian stereotype, the economic stereotype had both positive and negative, both friendly and unfriendly, connotations. On the favorable side, the Jew commonly symbolized an admirable keenness and resourcefulness in trade. In this sense, his economic energy seemed very American. In another mood, however, keenness might mean cunning; enterprise might shade into avarice.[8] Along with encomiums on the Jew as a progressive economic force — a model of commercial energy and integrity — went frequent references to conniving Shylocks. The earliest published plays containing Jewish characters (1794, 1823) portrayed Shylock types, and by the 1840's the verb "to Jew," meaning to cheat by sharp practice, was becoming a more or less common ingredient of American slang.[9] Apparently the praise of Jewish enterprise considerably outweighed the jibes at Jewish avarice in the early nineteenth century. But the widespread and traditional presence of the negative judgment, and the ease with which the positive judgment could pass over into it, suggest that anti-Semitism did not lie dormant because of a lack of appropriate attitudes.

What, then, kept the Shylock idea sufficiently mild and impersonal before the Civil War so that no pattern of social discrimination issued from it? Partly, of course, we must credit the countervailing strength of democratic and humanitarian ideas in a period when the United States welcomed European immigrants of every sort and condition. But a contrast between the early and the late nineteenth century indicates that certain objective conditions affected the reception of the Jews more directly and immediately than did the general state of public opinion. From a comparative point of view, we must look to the character of the Jewish community and to the structure of the society in which it lived.

---

[7] Hannah Adams, *The History of the Jews* (London, 1818), pp. 544–545; *A Course of Lectures on the Jews* (Philadelphia, 1840), p. 193; American Sunday-School Union, *The Jew, at Home and Abroad* (Philadelphia, 1845), p. 12; Sarah S. Baker, *The Jewish Twins* (New York, 1860), p. 33 and *passim*.

[8] Rudolf Glanz, "Jew and Yankee: A Historic Comparison," *Jewish Social Studies*, vol. VI (1944), pp. 3–30.

[9] Stephen Bloore, "The Jew in American Dramatic Literature (1794–1930)," *Publication of the American Jewish Historical Society* (=*PAJHS*), vol. XL (1951), pp. 345–360; Mitford M. Mathews, ed., *A Dictionary of Americanisms on Historical Principles* (Chicago, 1951), vol. I, p. 905; "Present State of the Jewish People in Learning and Culture," *North American Review*, vol. LXXXIII (1856), p. 368.

As for the Jews themselves, they comprised in the early nine-teenth century too small, too insignificant, and too well assimilated a group to seem a problem. Though often successful, they had occupied a relatively comfortable middle-class station for a long time. They offered no target for envy either because of numbers or because of any rapid group advancement.[10]

With the arrival of a sizeable German-Jewish immigration in the 1840's, this stable situation began to change. The newcomers spread rapidly throughout the country, making their way usually as peddlers. Concurrently, the incidence of disparaging comment seems to have increased somewhat. According to Rudolf Glanz, caricatures of Jewish peddlers in popular plays, songs and stories tended more to display dirtiness and dishonesty from the late 1850's on;[11] and two decades later a distinguished rabbi, in the earliest thoughtful study of the problem, traced the beginnings of anti-Jewish feeling in America to the coming of the German Jews in the 1840's.[12] Many of the peddler-pioneers met warm and gracious receptions on their rural circuits. Also, many Americans had not yet learned to distinguish Jews from other German immigrants.[13] Yet gradually the growth of the Jewish population brought it more and more to public attention, and not all of the attention was favorable.

While the relative invisibility of the early American Jewish community protected it from discrimination, the general fluidity of American society also militated against restrictive barriers. The

[10] As late as 1860 an editorial in the New York *Journal of Commerce* summed up the situation succinctly:

> In this city, and generally throughout this country, where their rights are never invaded, they live so quietly that unless one goes into their quarters, he seldom meets with them. Few of our citizens know them socially, and all are too willing to believe Shylock their true type.

In other words, a widely prevalent stereotype remained abstract and inoperative. M. U. Schappes, *Documentary History*, p. 402.

[11] Rudolf Glanz, "Notes on Early Jewish Peddling in America," *Jewish Social Studies*, vol. VII (1945), pp. 131-133.

[12] Gustav Gottheil, "The Position of the Jews in America," *North American Review*, vol. CXXVI (1878), pp. 305-306. There is some confirmation for this view in the Jewish press, which in the 1850's reported anti-Jewish diatribes that were harsher than one would expect a couple of decades earlier. See e. g., *The Asmonean*, vol. V (1852), p. 195, and *The Occident and American Jewish Advocate*, vol. XIII (1855), pp. 123-132.

[13] Joshua Trachtenberg, *Consider the Years: The Story of the Jewish Community of Easton, 1752-1942* (Easton, 1944), pp. 118-119; M. U. Schappes, *Documentary History*, pp. 310-311; on peddlers see Oscar S. Straus, *Under Four Administrations* (New York, 1917), p. 6, and Adolph Kraus, *Reminiscences and Comments* (Chicago, 1925), pp. 13, 21.

United States in the early nineteenth century afforded white men a rough equality of opportunity that few countries have ever equaled. There were, of course, aristocratic groups that maintained social distinctions based on pride of family; but their pre-eminence was slight and ill-defined. A general simplicity and informality of manners, a lack of luxury, the total absence of a hopelessly impoverished populace, the prevailing modesty of social aspiration, and confidence in one's own advancement all contributed to the plastic nature of community life. Men rose and fell individually without straining the underlying structure of group relationships.[14]

The only instance so far reported of anti-Semitic discrimination in the ante-bellum period is the kind of exception that helps to prove the rule. In contrast to the generally democratic and fluid character of American life, the United States Navy was a stratified society in which habits of snobbery and even of cruelty strengthened the principle of hierarchy. Uriah P. Levy, a fourth- or fifth-generation American, enlisted in the Navy in 1812 after serving in the merchant marine. During a long and stormy career, he rose from the ranks to become the commanding officer of a squadron. Imperious and headstrong, resented by regularly commissioned officers for his swift ascent from the ranks, he was repeatedly court-martialled for his scrappiness. Often his Jewishness added to his troubles; many fellow officers snubbed him at mess and deeply resented serving with a "damned Jew."[15] Levy's personal difficulties in the stratified world of the Navy foreshadowed the later Jewish problem that developed when America as a whole became more status-conscious.

THE GILDED AGE, 1870–1900

The Civil War inspired a flurry of ideological anti-Semitism, bringing upon the Jews temporarily the accusation of disloyalty. This ferment, however, subsided when hostilities ended, without having affected the habitual intercourse of Jews with their neighbors.[16] A pattern of discrimination began to take root only in the 1870's, as the pre-war situation decisively changed. Now a new

---

[14] These statements are necessarily impressionistic, due to the lack of sharply defined historical studies of the American social structure. When we do have such studies, the history not only of the Jews but of all such special groups will become much clearer. Alexis de Tocqueville, *Democracy in America* (New York, 1840), vol. II, remains the best general account.

[15] Abram Kanof, "Uriah Phillips Levy: The Story of a Pugnacious Commodore," *PAJHS*, vol. XXXIX (1949–1950), pp. 8, 24–30, 51–52.

[16] Bertram Wallace Korn, *American Jewry and the Civil War* (Philadelphia, 1951), pp. 121–188; M. U. Schappes, *Documentary History*, p. 466.

status-consciousness was altering the simplicities of the early republic; and American Jewry was becoming a very different community
from what it had been in the 1830's. The changes within Jewish life
and in the society around it acted together to generate anti-Semitic
restrictions.

By 1877, German and some Polish immigration had swelled the
Jewish population of the United States to a quarter of a million.
The immigrants and their families by that time vastly outnumbered
the descendants of the older Jewish population. The newcomers had
settled and adopted mercantile roles in every state, so that Jews
became visible almost everywhere. They had also swarmed into
New York City, where about one-fifth of American Jewry was now
concentrated.[17] (The fact is important because the first restricted
resorts catered largely to a New York clientele.)

Moreover, by the 1870's a remarkable proportion of the Jewish
immigrants who had arrived in the forties and fifties was prospering
mightily. It seems highly unlikely, proportionately speaking, that
in any other immigrant group so many men have ever risen so
rapidly from rags to riches. The first-generation millionaires included the manufacturer Philip Heidelbach, the bankers Joseph
Seligman, Lewis Seasongood, and Solomon Loeb, the railroad magnates Emanuel and Mayer Lehman, and a good many more.[18]
The general body of American Jews participated in the same upward
thrust; a survey of 10,000 Jewish families in 1890 showed that
7,000 of them had servants.[19]

These immigrants derived largely from poor villages and humble,
uneducated families.[20] In America they acquired money much more
rapidly than culture. The intellectual drive and distinction so
prominent in American Jewish life today apparently did not arise
until after the coming of the East Europeans. In the middle of the
nineteenth century there was no American Jewish literature, and
the only Jewish periodical with intellectual pretensions, *Israels
Herold*, expired in three months from public indifference.[21] As late

---

[17] An 1880 estimate puts the Jewish population of New York City at 60,000. *American
Jewish Year Book, 1918–1919*, p. 32. For other statistics see *ibid., 1945–1946*, p. 644,
and Nathan Glazer, "Social Characteristics of American Jews, 1654–1954," *American
Jewish Year Book, 1955*, p. 9.

[18] Isaac Markens, *The Hebrews in America* (New York, 1888), pp. 139–173.

[19] N. Glazer, "Social Characteristics," *loc. cit.*, p. 10.

[20] The best study of social origins is Bernard D. Weinryb, "The German Jewish Immigrants to America (A Critical Evaluation)," in Eric Hirshler, ed., *Jews from Germany in
the United States* (New York, 1955), pp. 116–118.

[21] Bertram Wallace Korn, *Eventful Years and Experiences: Studies in Nineteenth Century
American Jewish History* (Cincinnati, 1954), pp. 31–34, 45. See also E. Hirshler, *Jews
from Germany*, pp. 142–143.

as 1881 a Jewish newspaper, discussing card-playing, complained that American Jewry "reads very little and plays very much."[22]

Not only were most Jews more or less uncultivated, but also there is considerable evidence that many were loud, ostentatious, and pushing. Both Jews and friendly non-Jewish observers confessed something of the kind. The San Francisco *Hebrew* affirmed that the Jews' offensiveness of manner would disappear before long. Other Jews grieved that the conduct of some of their people brought obloquy upon all. One admitted that the body of rich Jews had mounted too rapidly to the top of the commercial ladder.[23] Anna Laurens Dawes' generally warm and sympathetic book attributed to "the German Jew"

> the half education and the little breeding of the small trader. He adds to this the shrewdness of his nation and the self-assertion which has grown out of the long certainty that he is despised. When such a man becomes very rich in a country where riches are made into a golden calf and worshipped as in America . . . he naturally assumes the manners of the peacock, and receives the usual dislike of that bird among his fellows.[24]

One of the best contemporary studies noted that European manners in general were less restrained than those of English and American society: while Americans increasingly emulated the cold reserve practised in England, a German (whether Jew or Christian) did not think he was intruding when he attempted to open a conversation with strangers.[25]

Thus a new stereotype, superimposed on the Shylock image, took form after the Civil War. In cartoons and in a good deal of middle class opinion, the Jew became identified as the quintessential parvenu — glittering with conspicuous and vulgar jewelry, lacking table manners, attracting attention by clamorous behavior, and always forcing his way into society that is above him.[26] To treat this stereotype entirely as a scapegoat for somebody else's psycho-

[22] Rudolf Glanz, *Jews in Relation to the Cultural Milieu of the Germans in America up to the Eighteen Eighties* (New York, 1947), p. 44.

[23] San Francisco *Hebrew*, March 30, 1894, p. 1; *American Hebrew*, Aug. 19, 1887, p. 19; *Jewish Messenger*, May 10, 1889, p. 5; Nina Morais, "Jewish Ostracism in America," *North American Review*, vol. CXXXIII (1881), p. 270; Edwin J. Kuh, "The Social Disability of the Jew," *Atlantic Monthly*, vol. CI (1908), p. 438.

[24] Anna Laurens Dawes, *The Modern Jew: His Present and Future* (Boston, 1884), pp. 29–30.

[25] Alice Hyneman Rhine, "Race Prejudice at Summer Resorts," *Forum*, vol. III (1887), p. 527.

[26] *Ibid.*, p. 525. See also cartoon reprinted in John Higham, *Strangers in the Land* (New Brunswick, 1955), plate I.

logical frustrations is to over-emphasize the irrational sources of "prejudice" and to clothe the Jews in defensive innocence.[27] The parvenu stereotype held up a distorted mirror to the immigrants' foreignness and cultural limitations and above all to their strong competitive drive and remarkable social mobility.

Still, the American tradition of treating people as individuals posed a substantial obstacle to group ostracism. If American society had kept its old openness, group discriminations might not have accompanied the new stereotype, at least as quickly as they did. But during the Gilded Age a general struggle for place and privilege upset the pattern of urban life. A large part of the American middle class was becoming rich. From small town women's clubs to Fifth Avenue drawing rooms, pomp and splendor enhanced the significance of money as a mark of distinction. At every level so many successful people clamored for admission to more prestigious circles that social climbing ceased to be a simple and modest expectation; it became a genuine social problem. The problem had two aspects. While material acquisitions stimulated vast numbers to swift social advancement and the money standard seemed to qualify them for it, the new urban, industrial economy also widened enormously the gap between rich and poor. Thus, the pace of social climbing increased at the same time that the distance to be traveled lengthened. A hectic social competition resulted from the greater penalties of being left behind and the greater opportunities for getting ahead.[28] In order to protect recently acquired gains from later comers, social climbers had to strive constantly to sharpen the loose, indistinct lines of status. With a defensiveness born of insecurity, they grasped at distinctions that were more than pecuniary, through an elaborate formalization of etiquette, the compilation of social registers, the acquisition of aristocratic European culture, and the cult of genealogy. These were all criteria that could not be met by money alone.

---

[27] Until twenty-five years ago sober and humane observers repeatedly took note of the core of reality behind the stereotype. See Bruno Lasker, *Jewish Experiences in America* (New York, 1930), pp. 71, 97–98, on the Jews as "an aggressive minority"; Louis Golding, "Anti-Semitism," *Outlook*, vol. CXLVIII (1928), pp. 248–249; Ralph Philip Boas, "The Problem of American Judaism," *Atlantic Monthly*, vol. CXIX (1917), pp. 150.

In 1930's, however, staggered by the outburst of ideological unreason occurring in Europe, scholars and publicists closed their eyes to the objective content of prejudices. The study of anti-Semitism thenceforth developed almost entirely among social psychologists, whose primary interest inevitably lay in the subjective levels of experience.

[28] On these changes there are helpful perspectives in such studies as Arthur M. Schlesinger, *Learning How to Behave* (New York, 1947), Dixon Wecter, *The Saga of American Society* (New York, 1937), and Mrs. John King Van Rensselaer, *The Social Ladder* (New York, 1924).

The Jews symbolized the pecuniary vices and entered more prominently than any other ethnic group into the struggle for status. Practically, anti-Semitic discriminations offered another means of stabilizing the social ladder, while, psychologically, a society vexed by its own assertiveness gave a general problem an ethnic focus.

There is no need to assume, nor any clear evidence to show, that the pattern of discrimination began at the top of American society and spread downward.[29] Instead, the evidence suggests that insecure social climbers rather than relatively more secure patricians first resorted to this means of reducing competition. Several years before the Seligman incident at Saratoga captured headlines, a New York National Guard regiment put in operation a policy of excluding Jews.[30] In 1876, a hotel on the Jersey shore advertised in the New York *Tribune* that "Jews are not admitted." And by that time Jews were also beginning to have trouble at the Saratoga resorts.[31]

The highly publicized exclusion of Joseph Seligman, one of the leading American bankers, from the Grand Union Hotel in Saratoga in 1877 brought into the open a trend already under way. Yet even this event lacked the patrician overtones usually attributed to it. No longer the unrivalled summer capital of the United States, Saratoga in the seventies was steadily losing ground to Newport, Nahant and Long Branch. Instead of a fortress of the best society, Saratoga was becoming a flashy resort of the *nouveaux riches*, where wealthy sportsmen mingled with prominent politicians, Wall Street tycoons, Western copper kings, ladies of easy virtue, as well as a good many Jews. Moreover, the Grand Union was not quite the most

[29] This standard view is held by historians as different as Oscar Handlin and Carey McWilliams; cf. Handlin, "The Acquisition of Political and Social Rights by the Jews of the United States," *American Jewish Year Book, 1955*, pp. 72, 74, and McWilliams, *A Mask for Privilege* (Boston, 1948), pp. 17–21. Both seem to assume that discrimination grows as reactionary opinion-makers impose undemocratic values on the innocent masses. Such an assumption not only appeals to our democratic instincts but serves to complete the circuit between ideology and mass behavior. If, however, my structural view is correct, discrimination can arise more or less simultaneously at every social level where a crush of applicants poses an acute problem of admission. Discrimination is probably much less a game of follow-the-leader than one of limiting the followers.

In this connection a comparison with England is illuminating. There anti-Jewish discrimination is not presently a problem in aristocratic institutions, where other principles of selection are well established and secure. A pronounced problem does exist, however, in the suburban golf and tennis clubs which serve a rising middle class. Howard Brotz, "A Survey of the Position of the Jews in England" (unpublished paper, Library of Jewish Information, American Jewish Committee, 1957), p. 39.

[30] M. U. Schappes, *Documentary History*, pp. 559–560.

[31] New York *Tribune*, June 1, 1876, p. 4; Hugh Bradley, *Such Was Saratoga* (New York, 1940), p. 188.

fashionable establishment there, though it had made headway by entertaining President Grant in 1869.[32] The ban which the Hotel imposed on Jews in 1877, in an obvious attempt to improve its social rating, reflected the exigencies of the parvenu spirit faced by uninhibited competition and uncertain rewards.

Saratoga soon became a battleground. Rather than knuckle-under, Jews retaliated by buying several of the leading hotels. In a decade half the summer population was Jewish. Against this influx, non-Jewish establishments blatantly publicized a restrictive policy, even (it is said) setting up placards: "No Jews or Dogs Admitted Here." But the real battle was lost; Saratoga's decline as a center of social prestige continued.[33]

During the 1880's anti-Semitic discriminations spread like wildfire through the vacation grounds of New York State and the Jersey shore. The problem was more acute at resorts than elsewhere, for no other institution combined such indiscriminate social mingling with such ardent social aspirations. Ten years after the Seligman incident, an acute reporter asserted that in the Catskills a nearly equal division had developed between resorts with an all-Jewish clientele and those that accepted only Christians. Significantly, she added that prejudice was most pronounced among patrons of cheap boarding houses, where the charges ranged from $5.00 to $10.00 per week.[34]

A dramatic but quite ineffective blow fell in 1879 near the center of American Jewish life. Austin Corbin, the developer of Manhattan Beach, issued a public statement of his fervent wish that the Jews would go elsewhere. A new and booming resort, Manhattan Beach drew daily great throngs of New Yorkers of all sorts, races and conditions. Corbin's huge Manhattan Beach Hotel had facilities for hundreds of daily commuters who munched their sandwiches and puffed happily on cheap cigars in the Grand Pavilion. Corbin hoped that his regular patrons, a "somewhat exclusive" type, would make Coney Island "the most fashionable and magnificent watering place in the world," but these fled before the swarm of transients. "We cannot," he declared bitterly, "bring the highest social element

[32] The details of the Seligman incident are in Lee M. Friedman, *Jewish Pioneers and Patriots* (New York, 1943), 269–278, which exaggerates the eminence of Saratoga and of the Grand Union. H. Bradley, *Such Was Saratoga*, pp. 135–159, 187–188, sketches a fuller and more reliable background. See especially Bradley's comments on the United States Hotel and the Clarendon Hotel (pp. 158–159).

[33] *Ibid.*, 188; *Public Opinion* vol. III (1887), p. 441.

[34] A. H. Rhine, "Race Prejudice," *Forum*, vol. III, p. 524.

to Manhattan Beach if the Jews persist in coming."[35] Again discrimination was an instrument of social ambition; and again, as at Saratoga, the interdict failed to hold.

Aside from resorts, two other institutions showed discriminatory tendencies in the eighties. Certain eastern private schools, chiefly those for girls, began as a matter of policy to reject applications from Jewish children.[36] Meanwhile, social clubs in some of the big cities were blackballing proposed Jewish members. Mentioned as a common practice by a writer in 1881, this interdict often met considerable resistance as it spread during the nineties. A liberal minority kept a loophole open in the Columbia Club of New York by giving a place on the Board of Governors to a Jew. The University Club of Cincinnati broke up about 1896 when the lone Jewish member proposed admitting another.[37] New York's august Union League Club was rocked in 1893 by the majority's refusal to add Theodore Seligman to the few Jewish members of long standing, though he was the son of one of the Club's founders. Although a number of socially prominent members supported Seligman, an opposition led by "hustling young chaps" carried the day.[38] However the whole pattern started, it is evident that by the end of the century Jewish penetration into the most elite circles in the East had become almost impossibly difficult. In fact, in the seventies and eighties Jews in New York, Rochester, Baltimore, Detroit and other cities formed their own fashionable clubs.

THE RISE OF THE EASTERN EUROPEANS, 1900–1917

If the exuberance of the Gilded Age diminished somewhat in the early twentieth century, wealth none the less remained conspicuous, social climbing continued apace, and the pattern of discrimination steadily expanded. The break-through had been made, and now no

[35] *Coney Island and the Jews* (New York, 1879); *Jewish Messenger*, Aug. 1, 1879, p. 2.

[36] *Ha-Maggid*, vol. XXIX (1884), p. 36; *American Hebrew*, April 4, 1890, p. 165. A good many instances of this kind of exclusion in the 1890's are indexed in Jacob R. Marcus, "Index to Americana in European Jewish Periodicals" (American Jewish Historical Society), pp. 20, 24, 28.

[37] N. Morais, "Jewish Ostracism," *North American Review*, vol. CXXXIII, p. 270; *Selected Letters of George Edward Woodberry* (Cambridge, Mass., 1933), pp. 27–28; Claris Edwin Silcox and Galen M. Fisher, *Catholics, Jews and Protestants* (New York, 1934), p. 78.

[38] *Jewish Messenger*, April 21, 1893, p. 4. This affair caused much public comment not only because Seligman was evidently a cultivated gentleman but also because of the close historical association between the Union League and the Republican party.

one tried very hard to stem the widening consequences. Indeed, one important circumstance of the early twentieth century put the Jews at a greater disadvantage than before. This was the rise of the East European Jews. They had been pouring in great waves into the urban slums for some time, of course; but before 1900 the first generation had remained there, almost as isolated from the German Jews as from the older American population. Socially and economically, the East Europeans could not push upward as rapidly as the Germans had done; but by 1907 a few of the new immigrants were becoming rich as clothing manufactuers and real estate speculators, while many of the second generation were beginning to enter middle class life.[39] Together with other factors, this process helped to reduce the sharp cleavage between the two Jewish communities in America.[40] But the partial integration of East Europeans into the Jewish middle class strengthened the surrounding walls of discrimination.

Because immigration became a general problem toward the end of the nineteenth century and because the East European Jews looked as bizarre and unkempt as any of the other immigrants, they aroused distaste among native Americans from the moment they landed. At first, public comment (abetted by assimilation-minded German Jews) often distinguished between the new and the older Jewish population to the latter's clear advantage.[41] But after 1900 the differentiation lessened in actuality and almost vanished in popular thought. Consequently, the nativistic feelings excited by the still growing immigration from eastern Europe applied to American Jewry as a whole. Furthermore, the behavior of many of the newcomers who got ahead in the world confirmed the parvenu stereotype.[42] The descendants of their German predecessors were acquiring a more subdued gentility, but the very size of the East European influx overshadowed this evolution.

Accordingly, discrimination in summer resorts, clubs and private schools increased during the years before the First World War. The Century Club in New York rejected the distinguished scientist

---

[39] This process is best portrayed in Abraham Cahan, *The Rise of David Levinsky* (New York, 1917), but see also Burton J. Hendrick, "The Great Jewish Invasion," *McClure's Magazine*, vol. XXVIII (1907), pp. 310–320.

[40] See the perceptive comments in N. Glazer, "Social Characteristics," *loc. cit.*, p. 19.

[41] New York *Tribune*, June 28, 1882, p. 4; *Allgemeine Zeitung des Judenthums*, Oct., 9, 1891, appendix, p. 4; *Reports of the Industrial Commission* (Washington, 1901), vol. XV, pp. 194–195 and *passim*.

[42] On this point see the realistic but not unkindly picture of a Catskill resort in Cahan's *Rise of David Levinsky*.

Jacques Loeb because he was a Jew. At least in the higher degrees of Masonry, most lodges now kept out Jews, compelling them to form their own segregated chapters.[43] Some of the very best preparatory schools (such as Andover, Exeter, and Hotchkiss) are said to have put no artificial obstacles in the way of Jewish applicants, but apparently most schools established very small Jewish quotas. One well-known private school which resolutely refused to discriminate lost practically all its Christian clientele because it attracted too many Jews. Then Jewish parents would no longer send their children there because the school had become too Jewish. So it was ruined and had to be shut up.[44]

A similar trend affected summer resorts with equal or greater severity. Thrown into resorts of their own, the Jews converted Far Rockaway and Arverne, as well as parts of the Catskills, into almost exclusively Jewish settlements in the summertime. Long Branch, New Jersey, lost its former grandeur and became largely Jewish.[45] The classic example was nearby Lakewood, a new and luxurious winter resort. In the 1890's the leading hotel had turned away Nathan Straus, whereupon he promptly built next to it a hotel, *twice as large*, for Jews only. In a few years other Lakewood hotels sold out to Jewish operators, and kosher establishments multiplied on all sides.[46]

Also, we now find the first evidence of segregation at work in the summering places of the Midwest and Far West. The Chicago *Tribune* published its first resort advertisements specifying "Christian" or "Gentile" clientele in 1913, and the frequency of such notices increased steadily thereafter. About the same time, a Minnesota hotel-keeper told B'nai B'rith that he cared little whether he entertained Jews or non-Jews, but the latter would abandon a place when the Jews appeared in any number. "This," he stated, "was an equally desirable condition, except for the fact that Jewish people were much more likely to desert a summer resort en masse and go to another, whither the finger of fashion pointed, than was

[43] *American Jewish Year Book, 1914–1915*, p. 141; Sydney Reid, " 'Because You're a Jew,' " *Independent*, vol. LXV (1908), p. 1212.

[44] Professor Richard J. H. Gottheil writing for the London *Jewish Chronicle* and reprinted in *American Citizen*, vol. I (1912), pp. 146–147. See also Norman Hapgood, "Jews and College Life" and "Schools, Colleges and Jews," *Harper's Weekly*, vol. LXII (1916), pp. 53, 77.

[45] R. J. H. Gottheil in *American Citizen*, vol. I, p. 146.

[46] William Nelson, *The New Jersey Coast in Three Centuries* (New York, 1902), vol. II, p. 32; Konrad Bercovici, "The Greatest Jewish City in the World," *Nation*, vol. CXVII (1923), p. 261.

the case with non-Jews, and that he would then have an empty hotel on his hands."[47] The problem was circular. The more desperately the Jews sought to escape from confinement and move up the social ladder, the more panic-stricken others became at the possibility of being "invaded." And the irony was this: the difficulties arose from an acceleration of one of the oldest and commonest processes in American society.

The resort problem became so acute that some Jews at last sought the protection of public law. The American Jewish Committee put pressure on the New York legislature to enact a civil rights bill forbidding places of public accommodation from advertising their unwillingness to admit anyone because of race, creed, or color. Violations were to be punished as misdemeanors. Governor William Sulzer signed the bill into law in 1913. In the next few years, with the aid of the Anti-Defamation League of B'nai B'rith, similar measures were enacted in several other states.[48] These long forgotten laws form one of the small beginnings of the twentieth century movement to outlaw discrimination.

Two further types of discrimination appeared in the prewar years. The social life of many eastern private colleges fell in line, as the sons and daughters of East European Jews enrolled in large numbers and quickly demonstrated their intellectual prowess.[49] They arrived at a bad time. An all-absorbing, extra-curricular life of sport and snobbery was overrunning the campuses at the turn of the century, making hard study and good grades unfashionable and creating an intricate status system dominated by the Ivy League.[50] After 1900, extremely few Jews were elected to the Princeton clubs or to the fraternities at Yale and elsewhere. The literary and gymnastic societies at Columbia kept Jews entirely out, and at Harvard one of the best college dormitories suffered a serious decline in reputation because a good number of Jews lived there.[51] As a result, Jewish students gradually formed their own fraternities, the first appearing

[47] B'nai B'rith News, Nov., 1914, p. 1; A. L. Severson, "Nationality and Religious Preferences as Reflected in Newspaper Advertisements," American Journal of Sociology (= AJS), vol. XLIV (1939), p. 545.

[48] American Jewish Committee, "Seventh Annual Report, 1914," pp. 30–31 (Louis Marshall Papers, Box B, in Archives of the American Jewish Committee); A. Kraus, Reminiscences, p. 228.

[49] As early as 1901, C. C. N. Y. was "practically filled" with Jewish students, and in 1908, they comprised 8.5 per cent of the male students in 77 collegiate institutions. Industrial Commission, Reports, vol. XV, p. 478; N. Glazer, "Social Characteristics," loc. cit., p. 15; Alexander Francis, Americans: An Impression (New York, 1909), p. 187.

[50] Ernest Earnest, Academic Procession (Indianapolis, 1953), pp. 204–236.

[51] Ibid., 216; N. Hapgood, "Jews and College Life," Harper's Weekly, vol. LXII, pp. 53–55; American Citizen, vol. I, p. 147.

at Columbia in 1898.[52] Some of the same feeling infected college faculties. By 1910, there were complaints that few Jews could gain entry or advancement in academic circles.[53] In the years just before the war, a few colleges began to limit Jewish enrollment, but on the whole restrictions operated only in the unofficial areas of social intercourse. And in all respects the western state universities preserved a freer atmosphere than eastern institutions, while southern schools showed very little anti-Semitism at all.[54]

A second advance in the pattern of discrimination during the period from 1900 to the First World War affected American Jewish life far more generally and profoundly than could any campus snobbery. While the second generation of East European Jews was heading toward college, their parents were moving out of the original enclaves of immigrant settlement. Before 1900, residential segregation in concentrated ghetto areas had been the natural and accepted situation of East European Jews. Thereafter, pulled by the hunger for social status and pushed by the pressure of new arrivals crowding in from overseas, the more ambitious moved out to better neighborhoods, where ethnic concentration might be less and a more Americanized culture might prevail.[55] Similar residential changes

[52] In 1887, Jewish students at the University of Rochester allegedly felt no social separation from others; in 1911, they established their own fraternity. Stuart E. Rosenberg, *The Jewish Community in Rochester, 1843–1925* (New York, 1954), pp. 117, 207. In general, see Alvin E. Duer, ed., *Baird's Manual: American College Fraternities* (Menasha, 1940).

[53] Charles S. Bernheimer, "Prejudice Against Jews in the United States," *Independent*, vol. LXV (1908), p. 110; A. Francis, *Americans*, pp. 84–85. In the nineteenth century the church connection of most private colleges had stood in the way of hiring Jewish teachers, but I am not aware that they faced obstacles in the secular university until the twentieth century. See W. Stull Holt, ed., *Historical Scholarship in the United States, 1876–1901, As Revealed in the Correspondence of Herbert Baxter Adams* (Baltimore, 1938), p. 70.

In 1910, four Jewish professors were dismissed from the Medical Department of Washington University under conditions that suggested prejudice. *American Hebrew*, Aug. 6, 1910, p. 350.

[54] *American Citizen*, vol. I, p. 147; N. Hapgood, "Jews and College Life," *Harper's Weekly*, vol. LXII, pp. 54–55.

A rabbi who had studied the question said in 1908 that collegiate discrimination came entirely from students; he had never heard of faculties or administrations discriminating against Jewish students. Eight years later, Hapgood declared that some colleges had begun to limit Jewish enrollment. Evidently, the upward spread of discrimination from private schools to colleges was related to a similar elevation in the educational level of second generation youth. Cf. S. Reid, " 'Because You're a Jew,' " *Independent*, vol. LXV, p. 1212, and N. Hapgood, "Schools," *Harper's Weekly*, vol. LXII, p. 77.

[55] The general process is described in Paul Frederick Cressey, "Population Succession in Chicago: 1898–1930," *AJS*, vol. XLIV (1938), pp. 60–64.

Apart from a few specialized articles, however, there is not a single scholarly study that deals primarily and intensively with the history of the eastern European Jews in America. In order to understand discrimination in a realistic context, I have had to extemporize a

had occurred among the German Jews in the larger American cities in the nineteenth century; but apparently German Jewish communities had not been so large and compact that their eruption provoked strong resistance.[56] Between 1897 and 1917, however, the Jewish population of the United States rose from less than one to more than three and a third million.[57] Accordingly, the East European masses poured out of constricted slum districts with a force that set off conflict and attempts at restriction all along the urban frontier.

Already at the turn of the century a great stream of humanity was crossing from the Lower East Side of New York into Williamsburg, Greenpoint, and Brownsville. The older Brooklyn settlers took so unkindly to the newcomers that the latter established a Jewish Protective Association in 1899 to spur civil action against Jew-beating rowdies.[58] Another sizable colony formed in Harlem. As it expanded, many a landlord in the area hung out a "to-let" sign bearing the warning, "No Jews."[59]

During the 1900's, also, Boston Jewry broke out of the tenement districts around the harbor and pressed southward, with consequences much the same. As the migration descended upon the middle-class suburbs of Dorchester and Roxbury, home-owners either fled or resorted to restrictive covenants. In Roxbury a mass meeting of Jews demanded more adequate police protection against hooligans. Real estate agents in both areas refused to rent apartments to Jews; and often their neighbors' unpleasant behavior forced Jews to vacate newly acquired homes.[60]

Meanwhile, the East European Jewish settlement in Minneapolis expanded from its primary base into the adjacent Oak Lake district, which had been snobbish and substantial. The thought of living

---

good deal of that history by piecing together bits of data from a wide range of sources, particularly from sociological studies and community histories written during the last twenty-five years. Inevitably, the result is only a provisional sketch.

[56] On the residential mobility of German-American Jews before 1900, see Isidor Blum, *The Jews of Baltimore* (Baltimore, 1919), pp. 27-28; Maurice H. Krout, "A Community in Flux: The Chicago Ghetto Re-Surveyed," *Social Forces*, vol. V (1926), pp. 277 ff.; Rosenberg, *Rochester*, 105-106.

[57] *American Jewish Year Book, 1945-1946*, p. 644.

[58] Samuel Abelow, *History of Brooklyn Jewry* (Brooklyn, 1927), pp. 11-13; New York *Tribune*, June 29, 1899, p. 11.

[59] Industrial Commission, *Reports*, vol. XV, p. xlvi; K. Bercovici, "Greatest Jewish City," *Nation*, vol. CXVII, p. 261.

[60] Francis Russell, "The Coming of the Jews," *Antioch Review*, vol. XV (1955), pp. 21-22; *American Hebrew*, Aug. 12, 1910, p. 374; *American Jewish Year Book, 1913-1914*, p. 244.

near rag peddlers and junk dealers evoked bitter opposition. But after the first Jewish pioneers had passed the outer fringes, the whole district was rapidly taken over.[61] With local variations, the same process started in many other booming cities during the prewar years.[62]

THE TWENTIES

Virtually the whole system of anti-Semitic discriminations was worked out by 1917. The most important new barriers to come into existence after that time applied to relationships that were primarily economic (business activity, employment) rather than social and that lie therefore outside the range of the present study. On the whole, the decade of the 1920's witnessed a consolidation of existing exclusionist practices, although some notable additions occurred, and a decline began in one or two fields toward the end of the decade.

In the early twenties discriminations of all kinds gained an extra incentive from the aggressively conformist nationalism that came out of the First World War. For the first time an ideological note sounded in the rhetoric of discrimination. Popular writers criticized the Jews for maintaining a seclusive solidarity instead of becoming "American first"; restricted communities advertised themselves as composed of "fine upstanding American Families";[63] and in the Midwest the Ku Klux Klan widened the cleavage in many places.[64] Yet this agitation, insofar as it affected segregation, did little more than accentuate established patterns.

Against every obstacle, the Jews continued to prove themselves the most mobile of American ethnic groups. The main force now

---

[61] Albert I. Gordon, *Jews in Transition* (Minneapolis, 1949), pp. 27–28, 30, 46.

[62] An English traveler reported that in St. Louis and many other American cities anyone who bought property in the best residential districts must come under legal obligation not to sell or lease "to boarding-house keepers or Jews." A. Francis, *Americans*, p. 85. On Jewish residential mobility during this period see also P. F. Cressey, "Population Succession," *AJS*, vol. XLIV, pp. 67–68, and Charles Reznikoff, "New Haven: The Jewish Community," *Commentary*, vol. IV (1947), pp. 470–471.

[63] Don C. Seitz, "Jews, Catholics, and Protestants," *Outlook*, vol. CXLI (1925), pp. 478–479; Herbert Adams Gibbons, "The Jewish Problem," *Century Magazine*, vol. CII (1921), p. 792; John Jay Chapman to Louis Marshall, December 13, 1920, and clipping from Bronxville *Press*, March, 1925, in Marshall Papers, Box B (American Jewish Committee Archives).

[64] Robert S. Lynd and Helen Merrell Lynd, *Middletown* (New York, 1929), pp. 479, 481–484; Leonard Bloom, "The Jews of Buna," in *Jews in a Gentile World*, ed. Isaac Graeber and Stuart H. Brett (New York, 1942), pp. 198–199. The Klan was almost everywhere more anti-Catholic than anti-Semitic, and its anti-Semitism was much stronger in the North than in the South.

beating against the walls of discrimination consisted of a second, and even a third, generation. Many of them, determined to prove they *were* "American first," were fleeing more or less consciously from their Jewish heritage and identity.[65] Some, of course, gained at least a conditional acceptance; but the rebuffs that others met were all the more painful because of the social distance they had put between themselves and their immigrant fathers.

A general urban expansion into suburbs took place during the twenties, with the result that ethnic groups were scattered more widely and more mixed neighborhoods came into being.[66] Accordingly, one gets the impression that residential discrimination became more intricate, often less absolute, but also more widely diffused. Particularly in smaller cities, such as Newburyport, Jews found their way into all sections of town in spite of a great variety of obstacles.[67]

In New York the lines of separation held more firmly. Second generation Jews poured out of the tenements of Manhattan into the apartment houses of the Bronx and Brooklyn. In Brooklyn the tide rolled south, engulfing Borough Park, Bensonhurst, and Coney Island — Corbin's old domain which now was more solidly Jewish than the Lower East Side of Manhattan had ever been.[68] At nearby Sea Gate, gentile exclusiveness made its last stand on the New York beaches, but one restrictive device after another failed to stem the Jewish influx.[69] A parallel migration of non-Jews during the 1920's pre-empted most of the booming suburbs of Queens, although not without challenge; by the end of the decade Jews were con-

---

[65] Leo Srole, "Impact of Antisemitism," *Jewish Social Studies*, vol. XVII (1955), p. 276; Samuel Koenig, "The Jews of Easterntown," *Jewish Review*, vol. V (1948), pp. 26, 29.

[66] President's Research Committee on Social Trends, *Recent Social Trends in the United States* (Washington, 1933), p. 564.

[67] W. L. Warner and Leo Srole, *The Social Systems of American Ethnic Groups* (New Haven, 1945), pp. 44–45, 307–309.

[68] An elaborate survey of Jewish population movements in New York City between 1916 and 1925, made by the Bureau of Jewish Social Research, is reported in the New York *Times*, March 18, 1928, sec. X, p. 12. The survey estimates that the Lower East Side was 23.5 per cent Jewish in 1916 and had a similar proportion of the city's total Jewish population. By 1925, when only 15 per cent of New York Jews lived there, Coney Island, Tremont, and Brownsville had become more than 95 per cent Jewish. Thus the main movement was from Manhattan to segregated neighborhoods in other boroughs. Nevertheless, there was evidence of some dispersion. In 1925, seventeen sections of the city contained 82 per cent of its Jews, whereas the same percentage had lived in thirteen sections in 1916.

[69] W. Schack, "Conquest of Sea Gate," *Menorah Journal*, vol. XVIII (1930), p. 54.

testing rental restrictions in Jackson Heights.[70] Other battlegrounds lay in Manhattan itself, where upper class Jews flocked to Riverside Drive. As the Drive became "too Jewish," some of them, through real estate coups, scaled the dizzy social heights of Park Avenue.[71]

Suburbanization brought with it the country club. There the barriers held quite rigidly, though an occasional "pet Jew" might be accepted. Reluctantly, Jewish suburbanites organized their own country clubs; whereupon one of the leading associations of such clubs ruled that Jewish clubs would be admitted to associate membership only.[72]

Social discrimination reached a climax in the quota systems adopted by colleges and medical schools. Following precedents earlier established in the private schools and in campus social life, many college administrations set limits on Jewish admissions. This, the only major extension in the pattern of discrimination during the twenties, came with a rush soon after the war; and the critical factor was the clamorous pressure of postwar youth on the facilities of higher education. General college enrollments spurted so rapidly that the whole prestige system built up in earlier years seemed threatened by democratization; and second-generation Jews (who, unlike the Catholics, had no colleges of their own) stood out more and more as the most numerous and successful ethnic minority invading the campuses.

The first big interdict descended at Columbia University and the University Heights branch of New York University. On these little cultural islands in the urban sea, the proportion of Jewish students had risen to forty percent or more. Fearful of losing entirely their Ivy League atmosphere, the administrations cut Jewish registration sharply by instituting "psychological" and "character" tests.[73] At Harvard College, where Jewish enrollment had reached about twenty per cent, President Lowell in 1922 made the *faux pas* of openly recommending what other institutions were doing covertly. In a series of stormy meetings, the faculty first approved and later

[70] New York *Times*, Feb., 2, 1927, p. 4; Heywood Broun and George Britt, *Christians Only: A Study in Prejudice* (New York, 1931), p. 256.

[71] K. Bercovici, "Greatest Jewish City," *Nation*, vol. CXVII, pp. 260–261; H. Broun and G. Britt, *Christians Only*, pp. 258–263.

[72] C. E. Silcox and G. M. Fisher, *Catholics, Jews and Protestants*, p. 78; Leo M. Franklin, "Jews in Michigan," *Michigan History Magazine*, vol. XXIII (1939), p. 89.

[73] "May Jews Go to College?" *Nation*, vol. CXIV (1922), p. 708; H. Broun and G. Britt, *Christians Only*, pp. 74–75, 106–110; Ralph Philip Boas, "Who Shall Go to College?" *Atlantic Monthly*, vol. CXXX (1922), pp. 444–448.

rescinded Lowell's graceless proposal. But a quiet and discreet application of differential standards on the entrance examinations partially accomplished the administration's objective.[74] Smaller colleges, perhaps more rigidly than some of the large ones, elaborated their application questionnaires, required a photograph of the candidate, and enforced a geographical distribution. On the other hand, some of the big private institutions in urban centers, such as Pennsylvania, Chicago, and Fordham, held out against the discriminatory trend. That the situation was far from desperate is indicated by the fact that in the twenties there was no flight of Northern Jews to the unrestricted state universities of the lower South and the trans-Mississippi West; Jewish enrollments there remained very slight.[75]

Much more formidable were the barriers thrown up around the medical schools. Quotas spread throughout the country and became increasingly severe as the decade advanced. Hundreds of Jews applied to foreign medical schools; and thousands more, defeated, turned to dentistry or pharmacy. The best comparative statistics are for graduates of the College of the City of New York (= C.C.N.Y.). Among non-Jewish graduates who applied to medical schools, the proportion accepted varied between seventy and eighty per cent during the period from 1927 through 1930. Among the Jewish applicants from C. C. N. Y., the number accepted some place or other declined steadily from 50 per cent to 20 per cent.[76]

The acuteness of the problem derived from economic — not just social — competition in a difficult supply-demand situation. As a result of the reforms that transformed American medical schools after 1910, medical education was severely limited by costs greatly in excess of student fees.[77] By contrast, the law schools did not discriminate, for they operated at a profit and could expand with enrollment demands. Yet the traffic jam was also a function of a

---

[74] Harris Berlock, "Curtain on the Harvard Question," *Zeta Beta Tau Quarterly*, vol. VII (May, 1923), pp. 3–5; F. Russell, "Coming of the Jews," *Antioch Review*, vol. XV, p. 23 footnote. See also "The Jews and the Colleges," *World's Work*, vol. XLIV (1922), pp. 351–352.

[75] The fullest data are in H. Broun and G. Britt, *Christians Only*, 72–123.

[76] *Ibid.*, 145.

[77] The total number of medical students in the United States actually declined from over 28,000 in 1904 to less than 20,000 in 1927. In pointing to this factor O. Handlin, "Acquisition of Political and Social Rights," *loc. cit.*, p. 76, says that discriminatory admission policies date back to about 1910. The earliest discussion of the problem I have found is Louis I. Newman, *A Jewish University in America?* (New York, 1923), p. 11.

rush of second-generation Jews toward a profession where they could escape stereotypic identification as businessmen, operate as individuals, and exercise fully their keen intellectual capacities. Even in the face of heavy restrictions, Jews constituted about eighteen per cent of American medical students at the end of the decade.[78]

While these new areas of discrimination developed, an older interdict showed some signs of weakening. Segregation at resort hotels began to diminish in the 1920's. Whether the new civil rights laws played a real part is hard to say. In the states without them resort owners still flaunted such slogans as, "Altitude 1,860 ft. Too high for Jews." Where the laws applied, they at least compelled subtlety.[79] But a forceful deterrent to discrimination did materialize in the form of the automobile. Many of the settled, all-season guests of yesteryear took to the road. Now vacation areas teemed with hotels and cabins catering to tourists who stopped for a short time only. These establishments could not afford to be as arbitrary, and did not need to be as socially conscious, as the older type.[80] They accepted the passing throng. Here was mobility with a vengeance.

Wherever the summer resort still seemed to confer prestige upon those who frequented it, a problem still existed. But for many, that institution now had a more purely recreational value, and access to it correspondingly widened. In other areas of American life, the struggle for status continued unabated. And discrimination reflected, as it had for fifty years, a conjunction of two factors: the great *but insecure* inequalities of a middle class society in which men striving for distinction feared inundation; and the urgent pressure which the Jews, as an exceptionally ambitious immigrant people, put upon some of the more crowded rungs of the social ladder.

REGIONAL AND LOCAL VARIATIONS

No part of the country seems to have escaped entirely the status panic that caused discrimination. Even the South, historically the section least inclined to ostracize Jews, was not completely unaffected. In the nineteenth century Jews belonged to the most fashionable city club in Richmond; by the 1940's it and other leading Richmond clubs excluded them. In New Orleans, one of the very

[78] H. Broun and G. Britt, *Christians Only*, pp. 150, 162.
[79] *American Hebrew*, March 30, 1923, pp. 645, 670.
[80] H. Broun and G. Britt, *Christians Only*, p. 266.

best cities for Jews, they no longer received invitations to the Mardi Gras balls, though a Jew had been the first King of the Mardi Gras in 1872.[81]

Within such broad chronological uniformities, however, anti-Semitic discrimination has varied greatly from place to place. All the evidence for the period under review agrees that it generally affected small towns less than cities of perhaps 10,000 population or more; that it influenced the trans-Mississippi West less than the East or older Middle West; and that it touched the South least of all. A closer look at some of the sharpest contrasts between localities should help to test the causal pattern evident on the national level. Although we may not know enough about the total social structure of various cities and sections to see the whole picture, at least the more obvious differences in Jewish-gentile relations should be illuminating.

Certainly the striking Southern situation offers one key; contrasts between Northern cities provide another. Three medium-sized cities that took form at about the same time present especially salient differences: Minneapolis, St. Paul, and San Francisco. By 1920, the Jews of Minneapolis lay under a singularly complete ostracism. It was perhaps the only city in the land that shut out Jews from the service clubs (Rotary, Kiwanis, and Lions), to say nothing of the local realty board and the numerous civic welfare boards.[82] Across the River, the twin city of St. Paul behaved somewhat more decently. Jews could at least belong to the local service clubs and the Automobile Club. San Francisco presented the other extreme. There, acceptance of Jews extended very widely in elite social organizations, civic activities and even residential patterns.[83] Thus discrimination has been strong in Minneapolis, moderate in St. Paul, and weak in San Francisco, as in the whole South. Yet all three cities had concentrated Jewish districts produced by recent immigration, and the ratio of Jews to the total population in 1930 was highest in

[81] David and Adele Bernstein, "Slow Revolution in Richmond, Va.," *Commentary*, vol. VIII (1949), p. 542; Julian B. Feibelman, *A Social and Economic Study of the New Orleans Jewish Community* (Philadelphia, 1941), pp. 133–135.

[82] Charles I. Cooper, "The Jews of Minneapolis and Their Christian Neighbors," *Jewish Social Studies*, vol. VIII (1946), pp. 32–33; Seldon Menefee, *Assignment: U. S. A.* (New York, 1943), pp. 101–102. Menefee found outspoken anti-Semitism almost entirely lacking in the Middle West except for Minneapolis.

[83] Carey McWilliams, "Minneapolis: The Curious Twin," *Common Ground*, vol. VII (1946), pp. 61–64; Earl Raab, " 'There's No City Like San Francisco,' " *Commentary*, vol. X (1950), pp. 369–371.

San Francisco (6.5 per cent) and lowest in Minneapolis (3.5 per cent).[84]

What differentiated these cities from one another? What, on the other hand, did such obviously unlike places as San Francisco and the South have in common? Separate studies have advanced a good many reasons for the peculiar situation in each of these localities, but only a few of the alleged explanations withstand comparative analysis. For example, in the case of Minneapolis attention is sometimes given to the anti-Semitic influence of religious fundamentalism emanating from the Baptists' Northwestern Bible Institute. Yet in the South, where Baptist fundamentalism was stronger than anywhere else, it is said to have nourished a persistent respect for the people of the Book.[85] Obviously, religious ideology still cut in one direction or another depending upon circumstances.

If we examine the areas of low discrimination, two circumstances stand out. Both the South and San Francisco fought for decades to uphold white supremacy in the face of a colored race, the Negro in one, the Oriental in the other. For a long time this overriding preoccupation bound all white men together as partners and equals. By the time other ethnic issues intruded, the Jews had become more fully integrated in the local culture than anywhere else.[86] As late as 1916, the leading anti-Japanese organization in San Francisco, the Native Sons of the Golden West, held a mass meeting to raise funds for persecuted European Jews; and the Grand President of the Native Sons, forgetting for the moment the Oriental issue, asked San Francisco to "say to all mankind that there exists in this world one spot at least where every one worthy is entitled to citizenship, and where every citizen is within the pale."[87]

---

[84] Sophia M. Robison, ed., *Jewish Population Studies* (New York, 1943), pp. 152–182. On St. Paul see also Calvin Schmidt, *Social Saga of Two Cities* (Minneapolis, 1937), and *Universal Jewish Encyclopedia*, vol. IX, p. 315.

[85] C. I. Cooper, "Jews of Minneapolis," *Jewish Social Studies*, vol. VIII, pp. 34–36; Harry L. Golden, *Jewish Roots in the Carolinas* (Greensboro, N. C., 1955), p. 56. Even in the South itself the "Biblical Judaism" which Golden extols had contrary implications; it was the ideological mainspring of the Ku Klux Klan.

[86] On the South see C. Bezalel Sherman, "Charleston, S. C., 1750–1950," *Jewish Frontier*, vol. XVIII (1951), pp. 14–16, and H. L. Golden, *Jewish Roots*, pp. 47–48.

[87] *Grizzly Bear*, March, 1916, p. 3. The same spirit of white solidarity seems to have operated in frontier communities exposed to Indian attack. In 1851, a Jewish weekly approvingly quoted the following editorial comments from the *Minnesota Democrat* (St. Paul):

> In vain have nations and sects hurled anathemas against ... the Jew .... He belonged to a superior race .... He was a WHITE man — he was of the God-appointed,

A second, and undoubtedly more important, factor in the two areas was the relatively stable character of the local Jewish communities. Outstanding Jews achieved a notable and highly respected place in both public and private life before the status rivalries of the late nineteenth century crystallized. In early San Francisco Jewish mayors, judges, financiers, and merchants helped to construct the basic institutions of the city. In the ante-bellum South widely scattered Jewish merchants partly made up for the lack of a native merchant class. In both areas assimilation proceeded even to the point of extensive intermarriage. Later immigrations did not come with disruptive force. An old line, patrician leadership maintained rapport with the non-Jewish elite while gradually absorbing the newcomers. The proportion of Jews to the total population did not vary much from decade to decade.[88] Consequently, the social climbing of Jews never stood out sharply or took on any special significance.

A dramatically different situation obtained in Minneapolis. There the early German Jews did not lay an adequate foundation for the integration of later immigration. The first Jewish settlers arrived fifteen or twenty years after Minneapolis took shape in the 1850's, and they never acquired a position of any importance in civic life. Then Russian and Rumanian Jewish ghettos materialized swiftly in a section abutting directly on an upper middle class neighborhood. A head-on collision ensued.[89] In neighboring St. Paul, where relations have been better, the Jews established themselves earlier in the history of the city, developed a wealthier and more influential Jewish community before 1900, and presumably experienced a more even rate of growth.[90]

In summary, each of our test cases shows a direct correlation between discrimination and the degree to which the growth of the local Jewish community disturbed the existing social structure. But one must beware of an explanation so elastic that it embraces an endless range of ethnic conflicts. Did not other European minorities

---

ruling, progressive race of humanity, for such all nature, all experience, all the philosophy of facts, and the attestations of religion, prove the white race to be. Therefore, it was, that the Jew, in accordance with the Eternal Will, so wonderfully preserved his civilization, and survived every catastrophe." [*Asmonean*, vol. IV (1851), p. 36.]

[88] Raab, " 'There's No City Like San Francisco,' " *loc. cit.*, pp. 370–372, 376. On the South, in addition to references already cited, see Charles Reznikoff and U. Z. Engelman. *The Jews of Charleston* (Philadelphia, 1950), pp. 186–188, 193–197, 235–237.

[89] See *supra*, pp. 18–19, and the accounts of Minneapolis and St. Paul in *Jewish Encyclopedia* (1904), vol. VIII, pp. 599–600.

[90] *Ibid.*; C. McWilliams, "Minneapolis," *loc. cit.*, pp. 63–64.

who flooded into the cities of America along with the Jews disturb
the social structure also? Was their fate any different?

THE CONTRAST WITH OTHER MINORITIES FROM EUROPE

No one who has looked beneath the surface of the American scene
will doubt that discrimination of some kind and degree has affected
other European groups in America aside from Jews. The Italians
and Irish, especially, come to mind. But if we may judge from the
existing historical and sociological literature, social discrimination
against these groups has never seemed much of a problem. In contrast to the voluminous evidence that has long been available on
anti-Semitic discriminations, no one has bothered to investigate the
comparable difficulties of other groups. Apparently there is no
study in immigration history or in American social history that
contains more than passing allusion to the rebuffs of non-Jewish
Europeans seeking acceptance in native American society.

We know well enough what general attitudes native Americans
have had toward the larger immigrant groups; we can define the
various ethnic stereotypes. But stereotypes, we must remember,
may not have any significant behavioral consequences. Unfavorable
attitudes need not produce discriminatory acts. Consequently, we
can only hypothesize the extent to which opinions became actual
barriers raised against individuals personally qualified for some
opportunity or achievement. Nevertheless, a study of attitudes has
at least a suggestive value for the present theme. Insofar as attitudes
reflect reality, they may help us to understand how the Jewish
situation differed from that of other immigrant groups.

Ordinarily — except, that is, during periods of political or economic crisis — Americans have rated immigrant groups according
to their approximation to the cultural and racial norms of American
society. Orientals, being more conspicuously remote in culture and
race than any European group, have fared worse than any. At the
opposite end of the spectrum, the British and Anglo-Canadian
peoples have hardly seemed foreigners at all; a sense of cultural
identity even exempted them from the Anglophobia that was widespread in nineteenth century America. The image of southern and
eastern Europeans, on the other hand, excited strong dislike long
before a mass migration from those regions began.[91]

[91] J. Higham, *Strangers in the Land*, pp. 24–25, 65–66. Note, in the case of the British,
the same disjunction between ideology and social reality that we observed in early
American-Jewish relations. Anglophobia, a political ideology, was as harmless to English
immigrants as ideological anti-Semitism was to Jews.

In the case of nearly every immigrant group, unfavorable judgments have softened as the forces of assimilation have reduced the cultural gap. Thus, American opinions of the Germans rose steadily from a low point in the 1850's to a high point in 1913, plunged disastrously during the political crisis of the War, and then quickly rebounded. The Irish too, at one time so unpopular that they constituted a separate caste in American society, have gradually risen in reputation during the last eighty years in spite of recurrent waves of nativism. This improvement has derived not only from a growing tolerance of Catholicism but also from increasing social differentiation among the Irish and their integration into an over-all American culture. Indeed, the social assimilation of the Irish has undoubtedly been a large factor in the decline of anti-Catholic feelings. Similarly, antipathy toward southern and eastern Europeans has greatly diminished since the 1920's.

What about the Jews? Their experience, during the period under review, was different. Whereas other European groups generally gained respect as assimilation improved their status, the Jews reaped more and more dislike as they bettered themselves. The more avidly they reached out for acceptance and participation in American life, the more their reputation seemed to suffer. Moreover, this contrast in the trend of sentiment corresponded to a basic difference in ethnic stereotypes. Ordinarily, old-stock Americans have felt at least equal and usually superior to the ethnic minorities in their midst. Only during periods of crisis, when beset by a sharp sense of danger, have Americans imagined such groups as the Germans or the Irish to be qualitatively more vigorous and potent than themselves. Normally, unfavorable stereotypes have stressed the ethnic's inferiority — his incapacities which are thought to drag down or hold back American society. Jews, however, have commonly left the opposite impression of equal or superior capacity. Unfavorable stereotypes have pictured an overbearing Jewish ability to gain advantage in American life. Only one other important immigrant group — the Japanese — has normally been disliked for its strength rather than its weakness.[92]

The stereotype of Jewish power becomes, of course, grossly unreal, particularly in the context of ideological anti-Semitism. But in a relative sense, the difference between the Jewish stereotype and the

---

[92] Chester Rowell, "Chinese and Japanese Immigrants — A Comparison," *Annals of the American Academy of Political and Social Science*, vol. XXXIV (1909), pp. 223–230; Carey McWilliams, *Prejudice: Japanese-Americans* (Boston, 1944), *passim*.

stereotypes of other European immigrant groups probably reflects very roughly a real cultural contrast. The other groups with backgrounds markedly different from the American have progressed relatively slowly in the United States. The social expectations of the first and even the second generations have characteristically been modest; often a peasant's fatalism and a peasant's habit of deference to superiors have curbed their desires, so that critics have thought of them as inert, backward, etc. But the relative slowness of assimilative mobility has protected many immigrant peoples from painful rebuffs. Probably only a limited proportion of nineteenth century Irishmen wanted to belong to native American groups, just as the Italians in Burlington, Vermont, in the 1930's did not want to move into a neighborhood where the people were "too classy to sit out on their porches."[93] The aspirations of these nationalities have been economic (and sometimes political) long before they sought an equivalent social status. Consequently, the barrier they felt and struggled against was economic discrimination. It is significant that the bulk of the available evidence on discrimination against non-Jewish European immigrants concerns occupational restrictions. The nineteenth-century newspaper advertisements warning "No Irish Need Apply" referred to jobs, not to membership in clubs.[94]

The Jews, on the other hand, met little economic discrimination before 1910 or so, for they did not enter labor markets crowded with other applicants. They encountered social discrimination much earlier, however. And the reason seems clear. Compared to other groups with a background markedly different from the American, they progressed rapidly in the United States, and their social aspirations kept pace with their economic advance. They wanted the full privileges and opportunities of the middle-class society into which, unlike the other major immigrant groups, they moved en masse. Perhaps we are now in a position to understand why social discrimination against Jews but not against other European peoples has long seemed a problem worth writing about: our sense of injustice is most easily stirred when people are denied something they passionately want.

[93] Elin Anderson, *We Americans: A Study of Cleavage in an American City* (Cambridge, 1937), p. 43.

[94] Oscar Handlin, *Boston's Immigrants* (Cambridge, 1941), p. 67. See also Severson, "Nationality and Religious Preferences," *AJS*, vol. XLIV, pp. 540–550, and references to discrimination in J. Higham, *Strangers in the Land*. On the difficulties of a rising Irish middle class in the 1890's, however, see Thomas Beer, *The Mauve Decade* (New York, 1926), pp. 156–165.

THE ROLE OF IDEOLOGY

If the discussion so far has been persuasive, it should suggest that virtually the entire story of social discrimination can be explained and understood without reference to ideological factors. This does not mean, of course, that ideologies have never played an important role in Jewish-gentile relationships. In Europe the myths of anti-Semitism have done so time and again. Nor should we conclude that these myths have no importance at all if they do not affect the daily lives of the people whom they slander. Ideological anti-Semitism may serve the ulterior purposes of its exponents without materially damaging its victims. It may supply the rationale for an agitator seeking power; it may give a certain stimulus to general policies such as immigration restriction or isolationism; or it may simply provide an inconsequential outlet for general social frustrations and aggressions. Similarly, ideological campaigns may have serious psychological effects on Jews without destroying their status in the community; many Jews may come to depend upon the cries of the ideologist in order to maintain a defensive posture and to nourish a sense of separateness. In America, anti-Semitic ideologies have worked in all of these ways, but they have not determined the range of social opportunity.

Among the ideologies commonly held guilty of fomenting anti-Jewish discriminations, the oldest is Christianity. Whatever the role of early Christianity, in the nineteenth and twentieth centuries it has functioned more to elicit sympathy for the Jews than hostility toward them. In both respects — and they tend to cancel one another — the influence of Christianity has been blunted by the secular nature of most of the involvements between Christians and Jews. Discrimination has been aimed at the social and economic Jew, not at Judaism. The one significant Christian attack on the Jew came from the Ku Klux Klan in the 1920's. Based as it was on an aggressive rural Fundamentalism, the Klan activated old folk myths of the Jews as Christ-killers and carnal sinners. Temporarily, some Jewish merchants suffered boycotts, and a certain amount of social cleavage may have lingered in former Klan areas. But in many such areas, particularly in the South, the Jews have remained freer from discrimination than they are in Northern urban centers where the Klan was very weak. Even at the time, most of the Klan's anti-Semitism was discharged against the shadowy, imaginary Jew who lived far away in the big cities. Klansmen felt a little guilty and ashamed at picking on the Jews whom they had known as good neighbors all their lives.[95]

More commonly, students of anti-Semitism locate the heart of the modern Jewish problem in a second ideology; racism. Here too, differences between America and Europe have not been clearly enough appreciated. At least before 1930 American racists never singled out the Jew as the exclusive, and rarely as the major, object of attack. Even in the period 1910–1925, when racism became a powerful stimulus to immigration restriction, its doctrines were fashioned to outlaw indiscriminately all the peoples of the new immigration from southern and eastern Europe. Typically, American racists elaborated a Nordic myth against the Alpines and Mediterraneans in preference to Gobineau's Aryan myth that applied more clearly to the Jews. Thus racism does not help us much in understanding the latter's special difficulties. And when Negroes, Orientals, or Indians were in question, race-thinkers often accepted the Jew as a white ally.

The most significant ideological attack on American Jewry has focussed not on religion or on race but rather on political subversion. The International Jew, half banker and half Bolshevik, is seen as conspiring to seize control of the nation. This belief, foreshadowed during the Civil War and partially emergent in the 1890's, really crystallized around the time of the First World War. It should perhaps be called anti-Semitic nationalism, for it immolated the Jew on the altar of national loyalty. If any pattern of ideas activated discrimination, surely the nationalist theme must have done so.

Yet an examination of the life history of anti-Semitic nationalism shows no close correlation with the incidence of social discrimination. Both the ideological attack and discrimination obviously received an initial impulse from the rise of Jewish immigration in the latter decades of the nineteenth century. Also, when most intense, as in the early 1920's, the ideological agitation undoubtedly sharpened the edge of discrimination.[96] Otherwise, however, the two forms of hostility took separate and even divergent courses. Whereas discrimination steadily increased from the 1870's to the 1920's, anti-Semitic nationalism rose and fell cyclically. It reached a minor peak in the 1890's, dropped out of sight for about a decade, climbed again

---

[95] Which is why the boycotts of Jewish merchants usually failed abysmally. Information from former Klan leader. See also Samuel Taylor Moore, "Consequences of the Klan," *Independent*, vol. CXIII (1924), 534.

[96] See above, p. 19.

during the period of the First World War to a new climax in the
early twenties, and then faded away for a second time.[97] Also, the
two hostilities had their strongest impact in different places. The
nationalist ferment, as manifested by the Populists, Tom Watson,
the Dearborn *Independent*, and the Ku Klux Klan, was most widespread and in many ways most intense in the small town culture of
the South and West, where the local Jews were usually not regarded
as foreigners or outsiders.[98] A product of status rivalries in an urban
middle class, discrimination rested on foundations much more
tangible than the spectres that sometimes haunted the rural
imagination.

If the myths of anti-Semitism have contributed so little toward
discriminatory patterns of behavior, can we expect democratic
ideas, deliberately propagated, to work effectively against these
massive realities? For this question the period under review offers
an uncertain and inadequate ground for judgment. Democratic
ideas failed to stop the discriminatory trend, but one should not
conclude therefore that they had no effect at all. Undoubtedly they
retarded the developments in point. The best ideological weapons
were available to the Jews. Their defenders could — and did —
openly seek public sympathy by appealing to the traditions of
American democracy; whereas discrimination advanced more or less
covertly, without the active support of major organs of public
opinion and without explicit articulation of ideological premises.
Yet democratic beliefs did not play a measurably positive role, for
they lost a good deal of their meaning and vitality in ethnic relations
during the whole period under review. Even the Progressives usually
thought of equality only in political and economic terms, and no one
mounted a vigorous ideological offensive against the barriers of race
and nationality. To appraise the capabilities of an ideological assault
on discrimination, scholars must some day turn to the years since
World War II, when the Jewish defense agencies and the propa-
gandists for "cultural democracy" have carried out a massive

---

[97] For an explanation of this cyclical movement see John Higham, "Anti-Semitism in
the Gilded Age: A Re-interpretation," *Mississippi Valley Historical Review*, vol. XLIII
(1957), pp. 570–578.

[98] For the same phenomenon — strong nativism and little discrimination — in a
small town in New England see Toby Shafter, "Fleshpots of Maine," *Commentary*,
vol. VII (1949), pp. 63–64. A study of Colorado contains evidence that anti-Jewish
stereotypes too may be stronger in small towns, where the few local Jews have good
relations with the rest of the community, than in large cities, where discrimination obtains.
Omer C. Stewart, "Rural Anti-Semitism," *Frontier*, vol. II (Aug , 1951), pp. 14–16.

campaign, and when all indices show a dramatic decline in discrimination.

Quite possibly democratic ideologists, armed with civil rights legislation, have contributed far more to the recent widening of social opportunity than their anti-Semitic counterparts ever did to narrow it. On the other hand, our own age may prove in a more fundamental sense to be a happy consummation of the theme of this paper. We may be moving away from discrimination primarily because the "status revolution" of the last century is coming full circle. The great class differences that arose in the late nineteenth century have vastly diminished in recent years. Competition for place and privilege have eased, and opportunity has become more general.[99] Concurrently, American Jewry, relieved of the pressure of mass immigration, is changing too. With the maturing of a third and fourth generation, it is becoming more stable and more securely established in the American social order.

[99] Frederick Lewis Allen, *The Big Change: America Transforms Itself, 1900–1950* (New York, 1952).

EMERGING CULTURE PATTERNS IN AMERICAN JEWISH LIFE

The Psycho-Cultural Approach to the Study of Jewish Life in America[1]

By ABRAHAM G. DUKER

"The Cultural Approach to History" was the topic of discussion at a number of sessions at the 1939 meeting of the American Historical Association.[2] Culture contacts have been the subject of intensive study by anthropologists, originally in application to primitive cultures. This field, in turn, gradually developed into "historical" anthropology, "functional" anthropology and finally into the "new" anthropology of today, termed by some spokesmen as "socio-psychology" or the

[1] This essay is an extension of a paper read at the forty-seventh Annual Meeting of the American Jewish Historical Society in a symposium on the study of American Jewish history [see the *Publications of the American Jewish Historical Society* (=*PAJHS*), no. XXXIX, part 3 (March, 1950), pp. 207–317] under the title, "The Psycho-Cultural Approach to the Study of Jewish Life in America." Much of the material on which this essay is based has been accumulated by the author in connection with the preparation of a syllabus on culture patterns, in the course on "Socio-Psychological Aspects of American Jewish Life," at the Training Bureau for Jewish Communal Service. Some of the material appeared in mimeographed form in September, 1948, as part of a larger mimeographed syllabus on *Intellectual Aspects* [of the American Jewish community], which was separated from it in the following year and appeared as a mimeographed syllabus on *Culture Patterns*. The author hereby acknowledges his debt to the faculty-staff, lecturers, fellows and students at the Training Bureau for Jewish Communal Service for the benefits of stimulation and discussion in the process of preparing the material and teaching the subject, and to Miss Helen Frankel for technical assistance. Some aspects of the subject were discussed by the author in a paper read before the Annual Meeting of the Yiddish Scientific Institute (Yivo) in January, 1949. This material is also largely incorporated in the present paper.

[2] Cf. *The Cultural Approach to History*, edited for the American Historical Association by Caroline F. Ware (New York, 1940). See in particular the essays in "Part Two: Cultural Groups," pp. 61–89.

"psycho-cultural approach," an attempt to integrate the concepts of psychology, psychiatry and anthropology as a tool in the study of individual and group behavior. Of late, emphasis has increasingly been placed on the study of the cultural characteristics of different national groups.[3]

Without embarking into a discussion of the techniques involved in this methodological approach, and after stressing due caution as to the danger of oversimplified generalizations based on psychiatric interpretations, we suggest that applications of these approaches to the study of Jewish culture patterns in America would help to extend our knowledge of history.[4] We view culture trends as a legitimate branch of the

[3] A good introductory summary on the methodology of the anthropological approaches is contained in Raphael Patai, *On Culture Contact and its Working in Modern Palestine*, no. 67 of the titles in the *Memoir Series of the Anthropological Association*, reprinted from the *American Anthropologist*, vol. XLIX, no. 4, part 2 (Oct., 1947).

A propagandistic popular application of the "new" anthropology not without anti-Semitic aspects is Geoffrey Gorer's *The American People: A Study in National Character* (New York, 1948). See particularly the parts dealing with American Jewry, pp. 202 ff. Cf. book reviews by Abraham G. Duker on the English Page of *The Day*, April 18, 1948, and by Professor Horace M. Kallen in *The American Journal of Sociology*, vol. LIV, no. 5 (March, 1949), pp. 474–476. For a critical review of publications dealing with this approach, see Robert Endelman, "The New Anthropology and Its Ambitions," in *Commentary*, vol. VIII, no. 3 (Sept., 1949), pp. 284–291, which, however, fails to mention Gorer's view of the American Jew.

A most important publication dealing with the adjustment of the Jews in Minneapolis is Rabbi Albert I. Gordon's *Jews in Transition* (Minneapolis, 1949), where the reader will find many parallels to developments indicated in this paper. Since we had well-nigh completed this paper before the appearance of Gordon's volume, we did not document all the parallels..

[4] Unfortunately, little attention has been paid to these aspects by the American Jewish historians, whose interests ought to include also the way of living of the people with the history of which they are concerned. American Jewish history has been devoted almost exclusively to the study of events, incidents and famous personalities, often treated from the point of view of Jewish contributions to American life, and, except for communal history, rarely paying attention to its contents and culture patterns and mores. It is significant that the *PAJHS* contain practically no material dealing with mores, practices and adjustment. The only article of direct relevance of this subject is Jeremiah J. Berman's "The Trend in Jewish Religious Observance in Mid-Nineteenth-Century America," *PAJHS*, no. 37 (1947), pp. 31–53. Sociological studies deal largely with the adjustment of Jewish immigrants and their children. Of late, greater emphasis has been placed on research about the religious beliefs and

history of mores and religious belief, — in themselves branches
of history. We also feel that the consideration of the historical
background introduces an element of solidity into the approach,
particularly so when it comes to evaluating group cultural
developments and characteristics. It is necessary to concentrate on the study of the process of transculturation, acculturation and deculturation, all too readily lumped together as
"Americanization," as they have affected and affect the immigrant generation and the native born Jew and his children.[5]

practices as well as on views on Judaism and Jewish adjustment with the use of the
questionnaire and the intensive interview methods. See, for example, Abraham G.
Duker, "On Religious Trends in American Jewish Life," *Yivo Annual of Jewish Social
Science*, vol. IV (New York, 1949), pp. 51–63, which contain some references; Abraham
N. Franzblau, *Religious Belief and Character among Jewish Adolescents* (New York,
Teachers College, Columbia University, 1934); Henry Loeblowitz Lennard, "Jewish
Youth Appraising Jews and Jewishness," *Yivo Annual of Jewish Social Science*,
vol. II–III (New York, Yiddish Scientific Institute-Yivo, 1947–1948); Leibush
Lehrer, "National Character," *Yivo Bleter*, vol. XXXI–XXXII (New York, Yiddish
Scientific Institute, 1948), pp. 293–351 (see also, Moshe Kligsberg, "Amerikaner
Yiddishe Zelner vegn zich un vegn Yidn," [American Jewish Soldiers about Them-
selves and about Jews], *ibid.*, pp. 233–243; J. Steinbaum, "Yiddishkeit bei Tsvantsik
Yiddishe Mishpoches in New York," [Jewishness among Twenty Jewish Families in
New York], *ibid.*, pp. 208–232); Philip Morton Kitay, *Radicalism and Conservatism
toward Conventional Religion* (New York, Teachers College, Columbia University,
1947); Joseph Zeitlin, *Disciples of the Wise* (New York, Teachers College, Columbia
University, 1945). Of the many works in the field, a basic one is *Jews in a Gentile
World*, edited by Isacque Graeber and Steuart Henderson Britt (New York, 1942),
which contains many studies. The volume generally reflects the theory that Jewish
"self-segregation" is the chief cause of anti-Semitism.

In a different category is the community study approach developed by W. Lloyd
Warner and his associates in the study of Yankee City and other communities. This
method has served to bring out significant data on the acculturation and deculturation
of ethnic groups, including the Jews, in a small New England industrial community.
Cf. W. Lloyd Warner and Leo Srole, *The Social Systems of American Ethnic Groups*
[vol. III of the *Yankee City Series*] (New Haven, Yale University Press, 1945). This
method of inquiry could be employed advantageously in studies of Jewish life in different localities, should the Jewish community in this country acquire a more positive
attitude towards research in contemporary history, sociology and adjustment problems. Cf. Symposium on social research in the *Yivo Annual of Jewish Social Science*,
vol. IV (1949).

[5] The use of these terms is suggested in the Introduction by Bronislaw Malinowski
to Fernando Ortiz, *Cuban Counterpoint: Tobacco and Sugar* (New York, 1947); and in
Phyllis M. Kaberry's Introduction to Bronislaw Malinowski, *The Dynamics of Culture*

The sources and materials for studies of this kind in the Jewish field range from labels on packages and cans to phonograph records and newspaper advertisements. Naturally, the task of gathering information on the constantly evolving culture patterns of a community of about five million is beyond the ken of an individual scholar. In the present paper, we shall attempt to apply some of our researches to certain manifestations of culture patterns without at all pretending to enumerate in detail all of the problems or topics of research or, for that matter, to exhaust the data on any one of them. Our aim is primarily to call attention to research needs in this field.

In studying the emerging culture patterns of the American Jew, cognizance must be taken of the profound effects of the period of closed immigration. It is unlikely that this country will see a new influx of Jewish immigrants, sufficiently large in size and rooted in Jewish tradition to appreciably influence the trends of American and Christian acculturation and Jewish

Change: An Inquiry into Race Relations in Africa (New Haven, 1945). We wish to thank Dr. Sidney Axelrad of the Training Bureau for Jewish Communal Service for help in clarifying these concepts.

As we have already indicated elsewhere in our paper, "Psycho-Social Trends" in the symposium on the "Impact of Current Trends on Jewish Center Membership," *The Jewish Center Worker*, vol. X, no. 3 (Oct., 1949), p. 19:

> The process of transculturation, or the give and take of mores and cultural values that goes on between the immigrant and the native or between different component groups living together eventually results in attaining a synthesis in culture, accepted by all. This is taking place in American civilization. American culture has been stabilized predominantly along Anglo-Saxon and Christian Protestant patterns. Therefore, the immigrant or other ethnic and religious minorities, while contributing to the transculturation process, are at the same time also passing through both the processes of American acculturation and ethnic deculturation. The first, American acculturation, implies the adaptation of the prevailing patterns. The second, ethnic deculturation, implies the conscious or unconscious shedding of a group's own patterns, often leading to complete assimilation of individuals within the predominant culture. In the case of the Jews, this type of final absorption is unattainable because of the unwillingness of the non-Jewish majority to assimilate large numbers of Jews. It is nevertheless important to examine on the basis of Jewish experiences and the democratic pattern how far this process of acculturation can go without leading to a predisposition stage of final assimilation.

This was also reprinted under the title *Cultural Adjustment and the Goals of the Jewish Center* (New York, 1949).

deculturation.[6]   The overwhelming majority of the Jews in
this country were born here, and have received their education
in this country.   Hence it can be assumed that the Jewish
community's emerging culture patterns are, to a large extent,
the same as those of the general American community in terms
of language, leisure time activities, demographic developments,[7]
and, as we shall see, even of stereotypes in thinking, — including religious concepts as well.   At the same time the Jewish
culture patterns will continue to contain sizeable though
varying residues of Jewish mores and ways of expression, —
some inherited from the European immigrants, others having
originated, developed or considerably altered here.

Some mores, developed in this country, failed to survive

[6] Cf., Mark Wischnitzer, *To Dwell in Safety: The Story of Jewish Migration since
1800* (Philadelphia, The Jewish Publication Society of America, 1948), pp. 267–273;
and Abraham G. Duker, *Jewish Public Relations and the DP Admission Act* (reprinted
from *The Reconstructionist* (Oct. 1, 1948), where it appeared under the title: "Admitting
Pogromists and Excluding Their Victims."

[7] Following are some important publications on various aspects of Jewish adjustment: Nathan Goldberg, *Population Trends Among American Jews, Jewish Affairs*,
series no. 5 (April 15, 1948), his "Occupational Patterns of American Jews," *The
Jewish Review* (published by The Jewish Teachers Seminary and People's University,
New York), vol. III, no. 1 (April, 1945), pp. 3–24; vol. III, no. 3 (Oct.–Dec., 1945),
pp. 161–186; vol. III, no. 4 (Jan.-March, 1946), pp. 262–290; also his *Economic Trends
among American Jews, Jewish Affairs* series, vol. I, no. 9 (Oct. 1, 1946) and *Patterns
of Jewish Occupational Distribution in the United States and Canada* (New York,
Jewish Occupational Council, 1940).   In addition other surveys and local studies
have been made, among them in particular, Leonard Bloom, "The Jews of Buna,"
in *Jews in a Gentile World, op. cit.*, pp. 180–199; Uriah Z. Engelman, "Medurbia,"
Contemporary Jewish Record, vol. IV, no. 4 (Aug., 1941), pp. 339–348; (Oct., 1941),
pp. 511–521; Samuel Koenig, "The Jews of Easterntown," *The Jewish Review*, vol. V,
nos. 1–4 (Jan.-Dec., 1948), pp. 1–29, and his "The Socio-Economic Structure of an
American Jewish Community," in *Jews in a Gentile World, op. cit.*, pp. 200–242; and
Charles Reznikoff, "Chronicles of the Lost; American Series," *Commentary*, vol. I,
no. 6 (April, 1946), pp. 20–29, and Albert I. Gordon, *op. cit.* On status level, see
Wesley and Beverly Allinsmith, "Religious Affiliation and Politic-Economic Attitude:
A Study of Eight Major United States Religious Groups," *The Public Opinion Quarterly*,
vol. XII, no. 3 (Fall, 1948), pp. 376–389; Edward C. McDonagh, "Status Levels of
American Jews," *Sociology and Social Research*, vol. XXXII, no. 6 (July-Aug., 1948),
pp. 944–953; Julian L. Greifer, *Neighborhood Centre: A Study of the Adjustment of a
Culture Group in America*, New York, 1948 (abstract of a Ph.D. thesis at New York
University).

beyond the immigrant generation. The story of such a development may be gathered from the title of a newspaper article, namely, " 'Jewish' and 'Non-Jewish' Cigars and Cigarettes,"[8] dealing with differences in smoking tastes brought from abroad and adjusted here under the influence of prevailing conditions. The roomer or boarder system, maintained during the immigration period by most immigrant families, primarily for economic reasons, and secondarily as a continuation of the Old World pattern of hospitality, has similarly undergone a great transformation in consequence of American acculturation.[9] The changes in the standards of home hospitality to both stranger and friend in an industrial and urban society are indeed worthy of investigation as are other trends indicated here.

Study is also needed on the parallels and differences in development among Jews and other ethnic groups in this country. Too often, Jewish scholars and observers tend to forget that other ethnic groups also face similar problems of adjustment and group definition. Of course, there are basic

---

[8] Jay Grayson, "Yiddishe un 'Nit-Yiddishe' Cigars un Cigarettn," [Jewish and 'Non-Jewish' Cigars and Cigarettes], *Forward* (New York), May 13, 1949, p. 2.

[9] Cf. S. Heller, "Haintige Borders Zainen Andersh fun di Amolige" [Today's Boarders Are Different from the Former Ones], *Forward*, Sept. 16, 1949, p. 5. With ecological changes, other social or psychological "types," too, have disappeared or are on their way out, as for instance the *shlepper* (puller), a person employed to "pull" customers into the store. Cf. Louis Wirth, *The Ghetto* (Chicago, 1928), pp. 233–34. Wirth's *Schacherjude* (*ibid.*), p. 248, seems to be a non-Yiddish expression, evidently used by Jews in Germany and Austria. The changes in the type of the *allrightnick* (*ibid.*), p. 249, and, as we believe also, the changed attitude towards the nouveau riche are worthy of investigation. The distinctions between Wirth's *Deutschland* and the "ghetto" Jews (*ibid.*), pp. 248 ff., already drawn too sharply at the time of the book's publication, are indeed much paler today in consequence of acculturation and the internal Jewish melting pot to which we referred above.

Changes in "types" are also evident from a study on differences in gestures of "assimilated" Eastern [European] Jews and those of immigrants. See David Efron, *Gesture and Environment: A tentative study of some of the spacio-temporal and "linguistic" aspects of the gestural behavior of Eastern Jews and Southern Italians in New York City, living under similar as well as different environmental conditions* (New York, Kings Crown Press, 1941).

distinctions between Jews and other ethnic groups. These stem not only from the varying yet to some extent common courses of adjustment in this country, but even more so from their differing historical backgrounds as well as the social conditions in the countries of origin at the time of the emigration.

Though Jewish settlement on this continent dates back to the sixteenth century and while Jewish communities in what is now the United States originated in the middle of the seventeenth century, most of the Jews of America stem from Eastern Europe and thus constitute part of what is commonly called the "newer" immigration.[10] Outstanding differences in the European background of the Jewish and the other ethnic immigrant groups in this country have influenced differing courses of development. In the case of the Jewish immigrants, the old home ties have been maintained more in terms of the local European community town or city rather than country or state of origin. This is the result of the more tenuous political ties and cultural identification with the former homelands because of the traditions of persecution and alienation.[11]

---

[10] "These distinctions are viewed by the more liberal scholars as historical myths conveniently concocted for the purpose of retaining the country's American Anglo-Saxon and Protestant character," we wrote in *The Jew in American Society, Syllabus,* Training Bureau for Jewish Communal Service (New York, 1948) [mimeographed]. The historical origins of this classification are covered in Edward N. Saveth, *American Historians and European Immigrants, 1875–1925* (New York, 1948); cf. its review by Morris U. Schappes in *Jewish Life,* (Feb., 1949), p. 30. See also Edward N. Saveth "The Study of Man — The Immigrant in American History," *Commentary,* vol. II, no. 2 (Aug., 1946), pp. 180–185. Judging by current DP legislation, the onus of the inferiority of the "newer" immigration is on its way out so far as Christian East European immigrants are concerned, but not in the case of the Jews. Cf. A. G. Duker, *Jewish Public Relations and the DP Admission Act, op. cit.*

[11] With the exception of Charles B. Sherman, *Yidn un Andere Etnishe Grupes in die Fareinikte Shtatn* [Jews and Other Ethnic Groups in the United States] (New York, 1948), it can be said that the comparisons and contrasts between Jews and other groups have not been seriously dealt with in the literature in the field. We have attempted to draw some general conclusions in *The Jews in American Society, Syllabus,* Training Bureau for Jewish Communal Service (1948) [mimeographed], which appeared

This distinction constitutes the main factor in *Landsmann-schaft* organization based on city and town rather than on region and country.[12] It is still too early to evaluate the connection with the newly established state of Israel in the scale of attachments. Perhaps, the closest parallels to the Jewish group to be found in American society are the religio-ethnic groups identified with a national church, as, for instance, the followers of the Syrian rites, the Greek and Ukrainian Greek Orthodox, the Carpatho-Russian and Hungarian Greek Catholics (Uniates).[13] Unlike Roman Catholics and Protestants, these religio-ethnic groups did not find here established English language churches, into which their children could assimilate. Studies of common processes and differences in the adjustment of these groups, as well as of the Jews, are most desirable. It is always, however, necessary to call attention to the major distinguishing fact that these minorities, small as they may be, are still part of the large Christian majority in this country.

before the publication of Sherman's valuable study, whose conclusions we are glad to note are similar to mine.

Interesting examples of Polish attempts to work out ideologies for the status of an ethnic group are, Joseph Swastek, "What is a Polish American?" *Polish American Studies*, vol. I (New York, 1944); also his "What is a Polish American?" *Polish Institute of Art and Science Bulletin*, vol. III, no. 1 (Oct., 1944), pp. 73–83; and Thaddeus Slesinski, "Development of Cultural Activities in Polish American Communities," *Polish American Studies*, vol. V, no. 3–4 (July-Dec., 1948).

For a comparison of Jews with Negroes in the educational sphere, see Louis Wirth, "Education for Survival: The Jews," *American Journal of Sociology*, vol. XLVIII, no. 6 (May, 1943), pp. 682–691, where the point is not made that the Negroes are also members of the Christian majority.

[12] On *Landsmannschaften*, see Works Progress Administration in the City of New York, Yiddish Writers' Project, *Die Yiddishe Landsmanshaftn fun New York* [Jewish Landsmannschaften of New York] (New York, The J. L. Peretz Writers Club, 1938). A summary of the book by I. E. Rontsch, with many errors and mistranslations appeared as "The Present State of Landsmannschaften," *Jewish Social Service Quarterly*, vol. XV, no. 4 (June, 1939), pp. 360–378.

[13] Cf., for instance, Afif I. Tannous, "Acculturation of an Arab-Syrian Community in the Deep South," *American Sociological Review*, vol. VIII, no. 3 (June, 1943), pp. 264–271. No comparative data are brought out directly in the article, but parallels with Jews can be easily noted.

The Jewish ethnic also displayed a greater degree of religious liberalism and free thinking because of the influences of enlightenment and secularism.[14] An important element in this connection is the sudden contact of the Jewish immigrants from the Orthodox milieu and its rigid communal control and influences with the relatively free urban society in the United States. Other contributing factors are the higher educational level and urban background as well as a swift process of adoption of the mores of the general society. Religious and national group loyalty (with Zionism as a major expression) and the tradition of an historical community of fate, coupled with increasing anti-Semitism and social ostracism have helped to check the process of Jewish deculturation. The sheer weight of numbers has also played an important role in this resistance.

Not only is the Jewish community greatly influenced by the American cultural melting pot, it is also going through the process of a miniature melting pot fusion of its own, with its sub-ethnic ingredients rapidly combining to produce the pattern of the native American Jew. The overwhelming majority of the American Jews is East European in origin. It is this group and its descendants that is in the process of

[14] For the impact of the Haskalah (enlightenment) and secularization, see Salo W. Baron, *A Social and Religious History of the Jewish People* (New York, 1937), vol. II, pp. 190 ff., and his *Modern Nationalism and Religion* (New York, 1947), pp. 213–249. The ideological trends in East European Jewry and to some extent their transformation in this country are to be found in Oscar I. Janowsky's *Jews and Minority Rights* (New York, 1934), and on a more popular level in Max Gottschalk and Abraham G. Duker, *Jews in the Post War World* (New York, 1945). There is also a sizeable literature of memoirs and books particularly on the labor movement. For a brief summary of labor trends see Bernard D. Weinryb, "The Adaptation of Jewish Labor Groups to American Life," *Jewish Social Studies*, vol. VIII, no. 4 (Oct., 1946), pp. 219–244. A somewhat idealized approach on the spiritual life of Polish Jewry is contained in the introductory essay by Abraham Joshua Heschel to Roman Vishniac's *Polish Jews* (New York, 1947). An interesting approach with emphasis on secularization and including some illustrations from literature is Solomon A. Birnbaum's all too brief "The Cultural Structure of East Ashkenazic Jewry," *The Slavonic and East European Review* (London), vol. XXV, no. 64 (Nov., 1946), pp. 73–92.

absorbing all others in a miniature internal Jewish "melting pot" with a resultant culture pattern, where the Jewish residues are distinctly of East European origin, but not without some contributions of the other groups. The distinctions between the sub-ethnic Jewish groups such as Litvaks (Lithuanians, including the White Russians), Rumanians, Ukrainians, Poles, and Galicians do not seem to outlive the first generation in this country. This is in contrast to the longer lasting differences between the descendants of the German culture periphery and the East European Jews[15] not to speak of the antagonism between the Sephardim and Ashkenazim. In this connection, it is also important to note that the cultural contacts between immigrant Jews and other immigrants, hailing from the same country, do not seem to outlive the immigrant generation. The study of dual cultural ethnicism also presents some important problems to the researcher.[16]

[15] We prefer to use the term "German culture periphery" rather than "German Jews" because until about the third quarter of the nineteenth century the *maskil* (the enlightened Jew) presented almost the same type, culturally speaking, whether his residence was in Berlin, Prague, Budapest or Warsaw. His European cultural language was German rather than that of the local population. In Yiddish terminology he was identified as *der Daitch*. Non-German individuals of this type usually found no difficulty in assimilating with the German Jewish immigrants in this country. Cf. Abraham G. Duker, *American Society Today, Syllabus*, Training Bureau for Jewish Communal Service (July, 1949), p. 18 [mimeographed]; and *ibid., Jewish Migrations Syllabus*, Training Bureau for Jewish Communal Service (June, 1949), p. 4 [mimeographed].

[16] See Rudolf Glanz, *Jews in Relation to the Cultural Milieu of the Germans in America up to the Eighteen-Eighties* (New York, Marstin Press, 1947), a translation of the Yiddish article which appeared originally in the *Yivo Bleter*, vol. XXV, no. 1 (Jan.-Feb., 1945), pp. 70–95; no. 2 (March-April, 1945), pp. 203–234 and in his "The Immigration of German Jews up to 1880," in the *Yivo Annual of Jewish Social Science* vol. II–III (New York, 1947–48), pp. 81–89. Dr. Glanz has called attention to the dual cultural relations of the German Jews in this country, most of whom, in addition to their Americanization, in the sense of acquiring the knowledge of the English language and American mores, have also retained cultural and organizational contacts within the German immigrant community, as well as their specifically Jewish religious-cultural affiliation with the Jewish community. The politically radical German Jewish immigrants of the Hitler period have tended to retain their German group contacts, possibly in contrast to the more conservative and the more consciously religious or

EMERGING CULTURE PATTERNS

Examples of the influence of the sub-ethnic Jewish groups can be found in a number of areas. For instance, the most prevalently accepted Hebrew pronunciation in synagogue worship is that of the Lithuanian Jews. The German Jews contributed the pronunciation of the *holem* (e. g. the Litvak *oi* in *olam* was abandoned in favor of the German *ou*). The

nationalist Jewish elements. For similar developments among Hungarians and Czech Jews, see Emil Lengyel *Americans from Hungary* (Philadelphia, J. B. Lippincott Co., 1948), and Guido Kisch *In Search of Freedom: A History of American Jews from Czechoslovakia* (London, Edward Goldston, 1949). Similar multiple ethnic culture contacts also exist among Jewish immigrants from other "emancipated" countries as well as from a certain periphery of the linguistically or otherwise assimilated elements from the "unemancipated" countries. The duality among Russian speaking Jews is a less striking one. It commenced with the emigration of the Socialists and radicals in the 1880's and it would seem that at times the Russianized Jewish intellectuals constituted the major spokesmen of the progressive Russian cultural expression in this country as differentiated from the Greek Orthodox native Russians. The Union of Russian Jews conducted public forums on Jewish subjects in the Russian language as late as 1949. Dr. Mark Wischnitzer informs us that eight issues of *Zarya*, a Russian-Jewish weekly were published in New York in 1943, while one issue of *Yevreiskaia Zhizn* appeared in the same year. Russian Jews are active in the Russian press and relief activities of both the center and Socialist groups, a relationship established since their revolutionary contacts were made under the Tsar and strengthened by their common flight from Soviet Russia.

The latest Jewish immigration from Poland shows a similar tendency of living in both cultural milieus, the Polish and the Jewish. The conscious assimilationists, of course, avoid as much as possible Jewish identification. On the other hand, the more Jewishly conscious elements have retained their own organizations and press, functioning in the Polish language, in contrast with the Yiddish speaking *Landsmannschaften* of the earlier arrivals now in the process of linguistic Anglicization and with considerable overlapping with recently established organizations of former Displaced Persons, who arrived here following World War II. This difference is due to the great progress of Polonization among the Jews in Poland since that country's attainment of independence in 1918, as well as to the character of the émigrés who managed to arrive here either immediately before the outbreak of World War II or during the War. Many of those were recruited from the more affluent individuals, who were either visiting this country in connection with the World's Fair of 1939 or managed to flee from Poland during the early stages of the war, thanks to financial or political connections. The desire for a local Jewish center on the part of the most recent Polish immigrants is expressed by Dr. Philip Turk, "Danger Signals in the House of Polish Jewry," *Our Tribune, English Supplement of Nasza Trybuna*, vol. X, no. 1 (Jan.-Feb., 1949), and by Roman Mogilanski, "Potrzeba Rodzimego Ogniska" [The Need for a Native Hearth], *Nasza Trybuna* (New York), vol. X, no. 2 (March-April, 1949), pp. 1–2, which represent some of the many opinions on this subject.

American environment can be credited with the pronunciation of the letter r.[17] On the Yiddish stage, the predominant pronunciation of Yiddish is the Galician and Ukrainian, with the Lithuanian pronunciation usually· employed as comedy relief to typify the comical "Litvak." The American Jewish dietary patterns are predominantly East European, as evidenced by *blintzes, borsht,* and other dishes. The latest loan words and word forms borrowed by the English language from the Jewish group also stem mainly from the East European Yiddish milieu.[18] This emerging residual East European

---

[17] An interesting variation is the tendency among *hazzanim* to retain vestiges of the Polish pronunciation, such as *oo* for *o* in *yisroel, ai* for *e* in *melekh*. We leave further investigation in this field to specialists in music and linguistics. It would also be interesting to begin to note the influences in liturgical expression of the Israeli Sephardic pronunciation now that it is on the way of being introduced into synagogue worship in this country.

[18] Cf. H. L. Mencken, *The American Language* (New York, 1937), pp. 216–18, 633–636, who also refers to articles by C. K. Thomas, *American Speech* (June, 1932; Oct., 1933) and by Robert Sonkin, *ibid.,* (Feb., 1933). Cf. also Mencken, *The American Language, Supplement II* (New York, 1948), pp. 151 ff., *passim,* and references in footnotes to pp. 259–262. Other pertinent articles are J. H. Neuman, "Notes on American Yiddish," *Journal of English and German Philology,* vol. XXXVII, no. 3 (July, 1938), pp. 403–421; A. A. Roback, "You Speak Yiddish, Too!" *Better English* (Feb., 1938), pp. 49–58; and Julius Rothenberg, "Some American Idioms from the Yiddish," *American Speech* (Feb., 1943).

Distinctions should be drawn between Hebrew and Yiddish terms introduced into English and utilized only by Jews: *grager* (Purim noise-maker), *nahit* (chicken-peas), *kittel* (white robe) and other words or expressions of Jewish origin which have made their way into the general American vocabulary through the comic strip, radio or vaudeville. Thus Al Capp has introduced through his *Li'l Abner* comic strip the word "nogoodnik" (*Sunday Mirror,* New York, June 5, 1949 and following — possibly earlier). Capp also uses the very common prefix "shm–" as coined in the phrase "technicality-schmecnicality" (same strip, *Daily Mirror,* New York, June 14, 1949). A parallel is the use of "Atom-schmatom" in the column "In the Wind," *The Nation* (Aug., 20, 1949), p. 176. Similarly, Carl Gruber has one of his characters exclaim: "Soup! Schmoop! Who cares" in "The Berrys" (*The Star,* New York, June 19, 1949). The *shmoe,* a substitute with possible Freudian connotations belongs in the same category. Al Capp's creation "The Shmoo" whose Yiddish origin is without doubt, has been republished in a book *The Life and Times of the Shmoo* (New York, 1948). Its character, "the Shmoo," has become an American institution. The name of a horse in Lariar-Spranger's comic strip *Ben Friday* is "Nellie Nudnick" (*New York Herald Tribune,* Dec. 1, 1949). These are mentioned in order to point to the comic strip as a source for the study of Yiddish loan words and expressions in English. In

majority slowly but surely manages to absorb, by marriage and influence in other ways, groups that are less related culturally such as the Sephardic and even Yemenite.[19]

The problems of acculturation and deculturation are often viewed among Jewish ideologues as peculiar to American Jewry. Such developments, however, are products of the

turn the acceptance of these expressions by the general public affects to a large extent also their retention among Jews. Radio scripts constitute an additional source with which we hope to deal on another occasion. It is an assumption of general familiarity with some Yiddish words that prompt one "Joe Suburban" to say in a letter to the editor, "O, tempora! O, tsores!" (*Daily Compass*, New York, May 23, 1949). Maurice Schwartz is portrayed as a delightful "shlimozzle" in his role in "Hershel, the Jester" in a review by J. P. S. in the *New York Times*, December 14, 1948. We wish to record an interesting description of the Italian "Grocchi" as a "Macaroni schlamozzle" as tendered by Stanley Frank in *Collier's* and reported in the *New York Post Home News*, December 20, 1948. Dr. Joshua Bloch informed us of the word "Beitzimer" for Irish (derived from the Hebrew "*beitzim*" which in Yiddish is "Eier") and "Makkes" (the Hebrew word *makkoth*) for beatings. For an illustration of material found in trade argot, see David Geller, "Lingo of the Shoe Salesman," *American Speech*, vol. IX, no. 4 (Dec., 1934), pp. 283–286, and the "Addenda" by J. S. Fox, *ibid.*, p. 286. For vulgarisms, see an Editor's Note to a letter to the editor, editorial page of the *New York Post-Home News*, Oct. 31, 1948; and Jeffrey Freece in *American Speech*, vol. XXII, no. 3 (Oct., 1947), pp. 234–5.

In a different category is the *ritualarium*, used in lieu of *mikveh* (ritual bath). We believe that this is the first appearance in print of the term *Gillies*, an opprobrious word for Galicians, which we heard in New York in 1948. To Dr. Jacob Shatzky, we owe the following: "to shiver" (to sit *Shiva*) and "all of a sudden" for *alav ha-shalom*.

Relatively little is known of the burlesque poetry, some of it strongly self-depre-catory if not mildly anti-Semitic, such as "Levy at the Bat," an incomplete transcript of which we secured two years ago from a Brooklyn boy. It contains many Yiddishisms. The vaudeville field will undoubtedly yield many more similar items. This area of culture transfer reflects much of the psychological impact and changes in status. In a different category are attempts to create folk motives in a mixture of Yiddish, Hebrew and English, in imitation of similar songs in Eastern Europe, and of Italian and German dialect songs, such as Philip Ney's "Folks Motivn," among which "O'Brien, Yidn shreien, Just Now," seems to be the most popular one. Cf. *Yiddish America*, *Zamlbuch* [Yiddish America, Collective Volume], edited by Noah Steinberg (New York, 1929), pp. 271–279.

[19] The Syrian Jewish Congregation in Brooklyn was served by Ashkenazic rabbis. Cf. "The Magen David Syrian Jewish Community" by Rabbi Morris J. Rothman, Assistant Rabbi and Youth Director of Magen David Center, *The Orthodox Union*, vol. X, no. 5 (June, 1943), pp. 6–7. Rabbi David Hecht, an Ashkenazi, was spiritual head of the Congregation in 1948 and 1949. There are no data on intermarriage between these sub-ethnic groups and the Ashkenazic majority.

adjustment of Jews to conditions of living in the emancipated Western communities and are not indigenous to American Jews alone. With regards to economic structure, urban concentration, demographic developments, linguistic assimilation, intermarriage and religious observances, the American Jew shows a pattern that in our opinion differs from trends in other emancipated, immigrant-receiving countries only in the effects of the varying numbers and times of entry of the immigration waves.[20]

Basic to the understanding of the emerging culture pattern is also an appreciation of the influence of Christian religious practices and beliefs upon American Jews and particularly the adaptation of some of their stereotypes. Without entering into the problem of whether or not the United States can properly be spoken as legally being a Christian nation, American civilization is to a large extent influenced by Christian customs and practices, and, in consequence, there is much unconscious permeation of those customs and even stereotypes among Jews. A most obvious example is the observance of Christmas and its derivatives. We note the assertion by a Jewish writer of the notion of the Jewish God as being the vindictive Deity of the Old Testament in contrast to the kind, loving God of the New Testament and his acceptance of the Christian usage of such a term as "Pharisees."[21] Of course,

[20] The comparative study of culture patterns of Jews in different western communities still needs to be undertaken. We have called attention to this problem in "Religious Trends in American Jewish Life," *Yivo Annual of Jewish Social Science*, vol. IV (1949), p. 51, note 2.

[21] Cf. Abraham G. Duker, "Religious Trends in American Jewish Life," *op. cit.*, where some examples are cited. An example of a cliché is the following reference by columnist Albert Deutsch, "Like a great Jewish rabbi before him, Stephen Wise scorned the Pharisees and spoke to and for the despised multitudes ... Wise, many years ago, literally drove the money-changers from his own Temple." The same column contains the following: "He was of the stuff of Ezekiel and Jeremiah, of Amos, Micah and Hosea. He preached up with passionate zeal the teachings handed down by these 'latter prophets,' teachings later summed up in the most concise and inspiring set of ethical principles ever enunciated — the Sermon on the Mount." (*New York*

in the final analysis, this reveals this particular Jewish writer's ignorance of Jewish theology. It would, however, be worthwhile to investigate whether or not there are sufficient instances of similar Jewish-Christian religious syncretism among Jews to justify their characterization as a trend.[22]

The influence of the American environment is also seen in the areas of religious practices by Jews. It is not merely a question of relaxation in observances. Here account must also be taken of the initial predisposition to secularism among the immigrants which they had brought with them from those places in Europe where *Haskalah* and modernization had made serious inroads in the Jewish community. The free and largely urban American environment has hastened the process. In addition, the American environment has served to change and modify religious customs and mores that have been retained. Specifically American in influence is the emphasis on the importance of Hanukkah, due to its seasonal incidence with Christmas, a festival that exercises an overwhelming impact upon all, particularly the children. This rather popular festival in the Jewish scheme of holidays has become a most significant one.[23] Among the recent innovations testifying to the increasing in its celebration are the appearance in 1949 of Hanukkah gift wrapping paper and ribbon, of Aleph Beth (Hebrew alphabet) chocolate bars and of the Hanukkah chocolate boxes. An innovation but a few years old is the appearance of

Post Home News, April 20, 1949). This was also reprinted without comments in the *Congress Weekly* (May 2, 1949), p. 7.

[22] We have heard of a case in a Midwestern city where a girl born on Rosh Hashanah was named Gloria Beth. Her mother explained to the rabbi the reason for this choice, — Gloria in memory of her grandmother Goldie, and Beth in honor of Bethlehem, a sacred city, in order to signify the daughter's birth on a sacred day. While Bethlehem is obviously a place much revered in Jewish tradition, the person who told us of this incident assured us that the mother, a member of his congregation, had no awareness of this fact. It is the familiar Christian association which recommended itself in this instance..

[23] More on Christmas observances among Jews will be found in my "Religious Trends . . .," *op. cit.*, pp. 52–53.

signs in stationery stores advertising "Hanukkah Greeting Cards with Jewish and English."[24] We have mentioned elsewhere the presentation of Elijah the Prophet bearing gifts for children as a figure very much akin to Santa Claus. A recent innovation in a Southern community was that of "Uncle Max, the Hanukkah Man."[25] Conversations with rabbis as well as general observation reveal that Shabuot would have enjoyed less popularity except for the introduction of confirmation ceremonies.[26] In addition to Rosh Hashanah, there is greater attendance at the synagogue on the days on which *Yizkor* or the prayer for the dead is recited.[27] Perhaps the new American custom of consecration will help to restore the children's celebration of Simḥat Torah. The popular children's festival of Lag ba-'Omer seems to be restricted only to those attending all-day Jewish schools, while *Tu Bishevat* (Jewish Arbor Day) is in the same category, except for its limited revival under the influence of Zionism. How far such effects extend cannot be determined without further research.

Passover is in a different category because of its dietary requirements, which are independent of synagogue attendance.[28] A noticeable decline in the observance of such important fasts as the Seventeenth of Tammuz and the Ninth

[24] The record of the development of the custom of using Jewish greeting cards in this country is virtually a closed book. The Rosh Hashanah (New Year) greeting card was among the earliest that became widespread. There are also greeting cards with Jewish content and Yiddish text for Mother's Day, possibly also for Father's Day. For a popular survey of the New York greeting card and its derivatives, not all of them American (the check on the Bank of Heaven for 120 years of good life; heavenly lottery winnings; coupons for possessions in Palestine), cf. Daniel Persky "Tashi," *Hadoar* (Sept. 23, 1949), pp. 988–990.

[25] Cf. Abraham G. Duker, "Religious Trends . . .," *op. cit.*, p. 53, note 10. Mr. Isaac Rivkind called our attention to a letter by Mrs. Ida R. Schwartz of Charleston, S. C., in the *Jewish Morning Journal*, Jan. 3, 1950, p. 6, containing a description of "Uncle Max, the Hanukkah man." Uncle Max is described as being a person groomed to represent an elderly man of patriarchal appearance, wearing "traditional clothes and a nice yarmulke, coming from Eretz Israel on a good will mission." He distributed the Hanukkah gifts to the children and explained to them the meaning of the festival. Cf. also Dr. Klorman's column, *ibid.*, Dec. 18, 1949.

[26] Gordon, *op. cit.*, p. 110.

[27] *Ibid.*, p. 113.   [28] See *infra*, note 68.

of Ab is to be recorded. Daily services are in the same category on an even weaker level, with some efforts to maintain a precarious hold on Sunday mornings, an interesting American innovation. A number of home and semi-public observances connected with holidays also seem to be on the decrease, such as the use of the *ethrog* (citron) and *lulav* (palm branch) on Sukkot, the sale of *ḥameẓ* and the observance as a fast day by the first-born males of the day preceding the Passover, the *kapparot* custom before Yom Kippur, and the purchase of the spring wardrobe before Passover. The *tashlik* custom seems to be still fairly popular in the cities among the Orthodox.[29] The extent of the observance of the Sabbath as a day of rest, as judged by questionnaire studies, conversations with rabbis, sermons and articles in the press is declining continuously,[30] — this again, in contrast to Hanukkah. Other Christian influences, also found outside the United States, are the use of the rabbinical and cantorial robe, the custom of prayers uttered by the rabbi in English that are not found in the traditional prayer book, as well as some postures during prayer.[31]

Another area of influence is based on the prestige values of general concepts, which range higher than the traditional Jewish ones. For instance, preference is given to the use of the term Reverend Doctor or Doctor to that of Rabbi. Often they are applied to men who do not bear these titles.[32] While

[29] Jacob Z. Lauterbach "Tashlik, A Study in Jewish Ceremonies," *Hebrew Union College Annual*, vol. XI (Cincinnati, 1936), pp. 207–340, states that "in the last few years the popularity of the ceremony has suffered a great setback due to the fact that the Jews are mostly city dwellers and concentrate in large cities ... (p. 339)." He predicts that "the Halakah, the arch enemy of superstition will ultimately be the cause of the complete abolition of the *Tashlik* ceremony (p. 340)."

[30] Gordon, *op. cit., passim.*

[31] A monograph on these changes is a desideratum.

[32] This, of course, is not an exclusive American custom, traced as it is to emancipation. For an adverse reaction to this practice see William B. Silverman "An Article About a Title," *Hebrew Union College Monthly* (Feb., 1945), p. 9. In a different category is the increasing usage of the Roman Catholic term "retreat" for religious sessions of rabbis and even laymen which, of course, do not resemble the original institution. A publicity release tells of "religious retreats" for Jewish chaplains (*JWB Circle*, Feb. 1950, p. 3).

Yiddish traces its origin to the modification of the German language by the loan of words from Hebrew in areas dealing with religious observances, morality and affection, American Jews generally substitute in these areas Hebrew terms by English ones, as seen in the use of the terms "sexton" for *shamash,* "cantor" for *hazzan,* "cemetery" for *bet olam.*[33] We have already mentioned that the borrowings of Yiddish expressions by the English language are of low prestige value.[34]

A comparison with the wide range of home and family customs practiced in the daily life of the traditional Jewish milieu shows that a great many have disappeared following a generation or two of life in this country. We are not considering here the area of religious changes due to the Reform position.[35] Let us observe, for instance, the variety of customs associated with birth.[36] The custom of displaying in the maternity room the *shir ha ma'alot,* a written or printed sheet of paper containing the text of Psalm 121 together with some cabbalistic inscriptions, is on its way out, largely in consequence of the abandonment of the home encouchement.[37] The maternity hospital also served to make obsolete the

[33] Typical is the sign at the entrance to the Jewish cemetery in Haverhill, Mass., where the inscription *Haverhill Jewish Cemetery* is duplicated by a Yiddish version in Hebrew letters, *Haverhill Yiddisher Cemetery.*

[34] See note 18.

[35] Developments in Reform Judaism seem to be pointing back to the tradition, as exemplified in the readaptation of the *atarah* on the *tallit,* restoration of the Shofar blowing, with the American innovation of the addition of a trumpet mouthpiece with a shallow bowl to the ram's horn; cf. the Reports in the Central Conference of American Rabbis, *Yearbook,* particularly those of the Joint Committee on Ceremonies, *passim.*

[36] A good summary of home and public observances is contained in W. M. Feldman, *The Jewish Child* (London, 1918). For contrasts, cf. Gordon, "From the Cradle to the Grave," *op. cit.,* pp. 121–147.

[37] The *Shir ha-Ma'alot,* printed sheets bound in tablets, are still sold in New York's Jewish religious book stores on the East Side, retailing at five cents. We have not had the opportunity to investigate the extent of their sales. For a description, cf. E. A. Wallis Budge, *Amulets and Superstitions* (London, 1930), pp. 224 ff. Incidentally, Hassidic rabbis still sell amulets in New York City and probably in other places as well. Not all the purchasers, to our knowledge, can be classified as Orthodox or even observant Jews.

custom of the *shema* recitation by school boys at the bedside.[38]
The practice of *ben zakhar* or *shalom zakhar*, a convivial
gathering held on the Friday evening after the birth of a male
child at the home of the parents, has well-nigh disappeared
in this country, so much so that rabbis from medium sized
communities had to resort to listing of rare individual cases
to prove that it still exists. As a matter of fact signs of its
disappearance were also visible in Europe many years ago,
since references to it in prayer-books were omitted. The
ceremonials at the circumcision rites, even when performed
by *mohalim* and not by physicians have been considerably
changed.[39] The *pidyon ha-ben*, the redemption of the first-born
male child on the thirtieth day after his birth seems to be
holding its own to a wider extent.[40]

[38] Together with this also disappeared the *Wachnacht* (watch night), preceding the
day of circumcision. For its description, see Judah D. Eisenstein in *Jewish Encyclopedia*, vol. XII, pp. 454–455. It would be interesting to find out whether the *Holle
Kreish* practiced in Germany in connection with the naming of girls is still retained
in this country either among descendants of the earlier German immigrants or among
the contemporary refugee immigrants. For its description, see article by Kaufmann
Kohler in *Jewish Encyclopedia*, vol. VI, p. 443. For attitudes on childbirth and ceremonials connected with it in the East Side immigrant milieu, see Jean Jaffe's interview
with Dr. Abraham I. Rongy in *The Day* (March 6, 1949).

[39] The custom of performing the circumcision ceremony in the synagogue has
disappeared. Similarly, the sermon has practically disappeared from the circumcision
ceremony. Interestingly, *Brit Itzḥak, A Manual Comprising the Rite of Marriage,
Circumcision, Redemption of the First Born, and Confirmation: and the Usual Prayers
for These Ceremonies; also Speeches Designed for Such Occasions*, by Rev. I. L. Kadushin
(New York, 1897), contains Hebrew texts of three speeches for the occasion (pp. 41–47),
perhaps testifying to the prevalence of the custom at the time of the book's publication.
The circumcision certificate appears to be an American innovation. A text of it in
English and Hebrew (For Good Remembrance at a Happy Hour) is published in
Kadushin's *Brit Itzḥak*, p. 87. It would be interesting to study the extent of the
distribution of these certificates. The substitution by the word *godfather* for *sandek*
also seems to be popular. The American invented surgical circumcision apparatus has
been the subject of much consideration in the responsa literature. The circumcision
feast has been substituted by the serving of refreshments in the hospital hall, and
special quarters for the performance of the circumcision ceremony are available in
Jewish hospitals.

[40] To our knowledge this ceremony is still celebrated mostly in the home rather
than in public halls like other family customs. We hope to investigate this further.
Cf. Gordon, *op. cit.*, p. 123.

We have not heard of the practice of the first birthday visit to the synagogue by boys. Insistence on the *sha'atnez* prohibition continues to be urged by Orthodox rabbis.[41] Despite these and the advertisements of *sha'atnez* laboratories in the press,[42] it is doubtful whether this prohibition is widely observed. It can be presumed that the custom of wearing a small *tallit* (*arba kanfot*) is practiced only among the strictly Orthodox.[43] Similarly, it can be surmised that the week-day morning custom of laying on phylacteries is practiced only among the very Orthodox. In this connection, a new custom may be pointed out, that of the Breakfast Prayer Clubs on Sunday mornings in Orthodox and Conservative synagogues, probably an American innovation. We wish that we could give more information on the retention of the *kapparot* custom. We believe that salutations such as *gut Shabbos*, or *gut Yomtov*, have managed to survive to a larger extent than *shalom alekhem*. We have no data on the uses of the *mizrah* in the home though it is sold in Jewish bookstores. It would be interesting to survey the proportion of homes which still attach the *mezuzah* to their doorposts. We have rarely heard of the ceremony of the dedication of a new home (*hanukkat ha-bayyit*), so widely practiced in East European communities. This is part of the general decline in home observance.[44] The

[41] The wearing of fabric consisting of a mixture of woolen and linen is forbidden by Mosaic law. See for instance, the advertisement by the Union of Orthodox Rabbis urging the preaching of sermons on this subject in the *Jewish Morning Journal* (Oct., 8, 1948). A free *sha'atnez* laboratory is also in existence in Brooklyn.

[42] Cf. the advertisement by Crawford Clothes "Non-*Shaatnes* Clothes available"; and the advertisement by one, Margolis, "Featuring non-*Shaatnes* Clothes," *The Orthodox Union* (Oct., 1945), p. 25.

[43] William Rosenau in *Jewish Ceremonial Institutions and Customs* (Baltimore, 1903), p. 65, wrote: "Like the phylacteries, the Praying Scarf has fallen into disuse among some Jews." Interestingly, the Chevra Malbish Arumim of Brownsville, Brooklyn, N. Y., offered a free *tzitzit* tying service in an advertisement in the *Jewish Morning Journal* (April 7, 1949).

[44] Jacob S. Golub and Noah Nardi, "A Study in Jewish Observance," *The Reconstructionist*, vol. XI, no. 9 (June 15, 1945). Cf. Louis Katzoff, *Issues in Jewish Education: A Study of the Philosophy of the Conservative Congregational School*, (New York,

use of the *mikveh* (ritual bath) by women has also declined and is a subject of continuous discussion in Orthodox circles.

Other ceremonials, on the other hand, have acquired new significance in this country, particularly the Bar Mitzvah ceremony, which seems to be on its way of readaptation even by the Reform and by the secular Yiddishists.[45] Mention should also be made of the Third Seder, an adaptation of a religious custom by secularists, and now a semi-secular ceremony held on Passover. Introduced by Labor Zionists as a fund raising affair, it was also adopted by the Workmen's Circle as an annual Passover celebration.[46] An interesting innovation is the *taryag* custom, introduced by Jewish educators in 1941. It provides for the entry of the name of the Bar Mitzvah celebrant in a special Jewish National Fund Book.[47] The increasing extravaganza of the Bar Mitzvah celebration will be discussed below. While confirmation of girls is an adaptation by Reform Judaism of a Christian practice, it has been accepted by Conservative Judaism, and we would not be surprised to hear about its practice among the Orthodox.[48] What appears to be purely an American

1949), pp. 107–17. For an interesting plea to women for the retention of the home mores see Betty D. Greenberg and Althea O. Silverman *The Jewish Home Beautiful*, (New York, The Women's League of the United Synagogue of America, 1941).

[45] Cf. Isaac Rivkind *L'Ot ul-Zikkaron* [Bar Mitzvah: A Study in Jewish Cultural History] (New York, 1942), pp. 62–64; 72–73.

[46] L. Feinberg, "Der Dritter Seder fun Arbeter Ring" [The Third Seder of the Workman's Circle], *Der Freind* (New York, June, 1949), pp. 12–13.

[47] Simcha Rubinstein, "Turyag," *Shebile ha-Ḥinuk* vol. I, n. s., no. 4 (1941), pp. 75–77 (cf. Rivkind, *op. cit.*, bibliography, item 48, p. 91). The Union of Orthodox Jewish Congregations also introduced in 1933 the registration of Bar Mitzvah candidates who were given publications and who conducted some joint activities. *The Orthodox Union*, vol. I, no. 4 (Nov., 1933).

[48] On confirmation, cf. David H. Wice, *Universal Jewish Encyclopedia*, vol. III, p. 329. We have not had an opportunity to examine the same author's *Bar Mitzvah and Confirmation in the Light of History and Religious Practice* (1933), a typewritten thesis at the Hebrew Union College. Cf. Rivkind, *op. cit.*, bibliography, item 15, p. 88. See also David Philipson, "Confirmation in the Synagogue," Central Conference of American Rabbis, *Yearbook*, vol. I (1890–91), pp. 43–58, and Louis I. Egelson, "Confirmation Practices in the Jewish Religious School," *ibid.*, vol. XII (1931), pp. 366–399.

development is the *bat mitzvah*, the equivalent of the *bar mitzvah* for girls, the practice of which began in the Conservative Reconstructionist innovations and has been accepted even in some Orthodox synagogues.[49] An interesting new semireligious ceremonial is the *Oneg Shabbat* (Sabbath Delight), a public ceremony held on Friday evenings or on Saturday afternoons, and introduced here following its earlier practice in Jewish Palestine.

Far reaching are also the changes in customs centered about death. Purely American innovations in this area are visits to graves of parents on Father's and Mother's Days. These have become so frequent that the usual contingent of *mole macher* (reciter of *El male raḥamim* prayer) are to be found on these days in the Jewish cemeteries. It would be worthwhile investigating whether this new custom shows signs of replacing the similar practice during the Jewish month of Elul. Certainly, the increasing custom of placing the tombstones in a flat position rather than vertically[50] is due to the new styles in California garden cemeteries rather than to a sudden revival of the ancient Sephardic custom. The custom of placing photographs of the deceased on the tombs is now rarely observed. It would be interesting to trace its rise and decline. The revolution in burial ceremonies and practices, which has resulted in the abandonment of the simple and inexpensive four board box and its replacement by an expensive casket and in the introduction of other luxuries such as flowers and formal dress, is the proper subject not only for investigation but also for remedial action.[51] The abandonment of the

[49] Cf. David H. Wice in *Universal Jewish Encyclopedia*, vol. II (1940), p. 75.

[50] See pictures in advertisements in *New York Post* (Nov. 22 and 30, 1948, and Jan. 17, 1949).

[51] A brief summary of changes is contained in Abraham I. Shinedling's article in the *Universal Jewish Encyclopedia*, vol. IV, pp. 479–480. Cf. also *ibid.*, vol. II, p. 602. For a more elaborate discussion, see Gordon, *op. cit.*, pp. 139 ff. For a compendium of traditional observances and customs with some remarks on changes, see Jekuthiel

traditional shroud and its substitution by the customary clothes
is also taking place. It would also be interesting to find out
to what an extent the practice of having a prayer *minyan* in
the home of the deceased during the first week after death has
been retained.[52] The reduction of the duration of *shiva* (period
of mourning) to three days instead of seven has been noted by
Gordon.[53] The availability of professional reciters of the
kaddish on a commercial basis would seem to indicate that this
practice is not retained as much as it used to be for the first
year following the death.[54] *Kaddish* recitation by professionals
is not restricted to America.[55] The custom of women rising to
recite the *kaddish* prayer with men, even in some Orthodox
synagogues, is probably an American innovation. The use
of the English language for tumular inscriptions parallels a
similar practice of using the vernacular in other countries.
So is probably the memorial *Yahrzeit* certificate. An American
innovation is the repast offered on the cemetery grounds following the unveiling of tombstones. The custom of sending
flowers, candy or fruit baskets to the home of the mourners
has grown in popularity in this country.[56]

Jehudah [Leopold] Greenwald, *Kol Bo al Abelut* (New York, 1947), particularly pp.
13–14. We have witnessed many varieties in ceremonials, including the performance
of Masonic services with distinct Christian connotations, preceding a pseudo-Reform
ceremony by a non-ordained rabbi, who contributed his own variations to the ritual.
On problems raised by "secular" funerals for the non-believers, cf. B. Z. Goldberg,
"Vegn Lvaies" [Concerning Funerals], *The Day*, Feb. 23, 1949.

[52] Paid participants for this purpose were furnished through a leading New York
Orthodox congregation in 1948.

[53] Cf. Gordon, *op. cit.*, p. 144.

[54] The advertisement of a Bronx synagogue offering professional *Kaddish* sayers
was a regular feature in the small advertisement section of the *Jewish Morning Journal*
and *The Day* (1948 and 1949). The transliteration in Latin characters of the *Kaddish*
appears in very many American published prayer books (*Siddurim*). On repasts, see
David Einhorn, "Picnics tsvishn Kvorim oif Yiddishe Cemeteries," [Picnics at the
Graves on Jewish Cemeteries], *Forward*, Nov. 19, 1949.

[55] An interesting suit of a professional *Kaddish* sayer in the State of Israel who
won a $60.00 claim for his services in court was reported in the *Forward* (July 31, 1949).

[56] Memorial Certificate, in Hebrew and English, published in Isaac Leib Judah
Kadushin, *Brit Itzḥak*, part II, *Sefer Tziyon* (New York, 1898), appendix.

Many innovations can be traced back to American mechanical ingenuity and the present progress of the plastics industry. In this category belong the ordinary electric and the more modern fluorescent *Yahrzeit* candles. The latter appear to be similar to illuminations used by Roman Catholics.[57] The old fashioned tallow or paraffin *Yahrzeit* candle that is housed in a drinking glass, with an eye to economy via double utility, appears to be an American product. We are not sure of the origin of the elaborate metal electric commemoration *Yahrzeit* tablet with individual bulbs for individual names that is to be found in the synagogues and usually carries the names of the deceased in English, but we suspect that it is an American innovation. The miniature photographic print Torah is traced to German photographers who, it is said, introduced it in this country at the turn of the century. It became a popular gift for relatives in Europe.[58] Some three years ago we noted the appearance of individual books of the Pentateuch in a similar Torah scroll form, possibly inspired by greater desire for profits. There is also available on the market a photographic reproduction of the *Megillah* (Scroll of the Book of Esther) as well as miniature plastic Torah arks, in addition to similar earlier products made of wood. The plastic Hanukkah *dreidel* (teetotum) that had made its appearance following World War II is but one of the many new products in this line. We have noticed plastic Sabbath and holiday table clothes, probably not older than 1949.[59] Cookie cutters with Jewish symbols

[57] There are several styles of the fluorescent lamps. Prof. Guido Kisch informs me that a leading Orthodox rabbi in Germany had used an electric lamp for Yahrzeit commemoration. The American electric bulbs are equipped with the Star of David. Cf. the illustrated advertisement in *Jewish Morning Journal* (April 1, 1949).

[58] For the information about the origin of the miniature Torah Scrolls, I am indebted to Mr. Menasseh Vaxer of New York.

[59] Cf. the advertisement in the *Hadassah Newsletter* (Sept., 1949), p. 13, in which the manufacturer offers "eight different plastic table clothes with Shabbos, Yomtov and Erez Israel motives in wonderful colors."

were introduced in the same year.[60] A recent innovation is
the musical Hanukkah lamp that plays the traditional hymn
Ma'oz Zur (Rock of Ages) or the *Hatikvah*.[61] The use of the
electric clock to turn the lights and the radios on and off on
Sabbaths and holidays also seems to be an American adaptation. Influences of local commercialism are seen in the trade
mark labels attached to the *tallit* (prayer shawl).

A culture pattern which seems to be more prevalent in this
country than in Europe or in Israel among both the observant
and non-observant is the wearing of the skull-cap, developed
here into what may be called, and not only facetiously at that,
the *yarmulke* cult.[62] The refraining from consumption of meat
on Fridays among Roman Catholics has resulted in at least
one specially prepared "kosher" Catholic product, the "Friday
Franks" made of tuna fish.[63] However, it is only among Jews
that the intimate tie-up of culinary preferences with *kashrut*
requirements have, in this industrial milieu, combined to create
a huge kosher food industry facilitating in many respect the
retention of *kashrut* because of the reduction of work involved
in food preparation in the home.[64] Although Reform Judaism

[60] According to a mail enclosure advertisement the set contains "six cookie cutters
in gleaming, heat-resistant, blue and white plastic." The designs consist of a "Star of
David, Dreidle, Lion of Judea [*sic*!], Sabbath Candle, Holiday Wine and Shofar."
Easy cookie recipes are enclosed for Rosh Hashanah, Purim, Passover, Hanukkah, the
Sabbath.

[61] Cf. the advertisement in *New York Post Home News* (Nov. 30, 1949).

[62] While in European countries and in Israel, the Orthodox customarily wear hats
or caps in public, or even at home, the *yarmulke* (skull-cap) seems to be the more
popular headgear in this country, where it has become the normal gesture of obeisance
to tradition, to the extent that even Gentiles wear it at Jewish gatherings.

[63] "When a group of priests in Boston were served what looked like frankfurters
on a recent Friday, there were instant protests: 'We can't eat meat today.' Then
the surprised priests were told to go ahead and eat them; the frankfurters were actually
made of tuna fish. After other similar test runs on unsuspecting diners, Friday Franks
were put on the market this week by Gloucester's famed old (89 years) Davis Bros.
Canning Company." *Time* (Dec., 5, 1949), pp. 94–95.

[64] An advertisement by a well known business promotion agency in New York
which specializes in the "Jewish market" gives a partial list of advertisers whom the

has almost completely abandoned *kashrut*, many Reform Jews take advantage of products of the kosher food industry. The kosher food industry also serves others who do not observe *kashrut*. Many Conservative and nominally Orthodox Jews maintain the double standard of *kashrut* observance at home and non-observance outside. Here, too, can be noted varied stages in acculturation, or deculturation, depending on the approach.[65] While there is evidence of a decrease in the consumption of kosher meats in some localities, traced to the high prices and inefficient regulation of the industry,[66] the purchase of kosher food does not by itself indicate that the home is a kosher one. In many places the kosher restaurant is being replaced by the "Jewish style" or "kosher style" restaurant.

There is also ample evidence of transculturation in this area. Just as spaghetti has become part and parcel of the menus of many American restaurants, dishes like borsht, potato pancakes and blintzes are served in general restaurants in the larger cities, signifying the Jewish contribution to the general American cuisine as well as the numerical weight of the Jewish middle and upper classes.[67] The Passover season presents a

agency served during a period of twenty-eight years, listing 56 national advertisers. It points to the influence of the Yiddish press as an advertising medium (*New York Herald Tribune* Nov. 11, 1947). Cf. also *Kosher Food Guide. Organized Kashruth*, a periodical published in New York, whose vol. I, no. 1 is dated March, 1935.

[65] Some cynic has observed that "Every Jew carries his own *Shulḥan Aruk*." The process begins with eating vegeterian or dairy foods outside the home. It continues with the eating of fish, later shell-fish, or meat products, though not pork and sometimes ends with fried bacon for breakfast.

[66] On the problem of *kashrut* in this country, see the thorough work by Jeremiah J. Berman, *Sheḥitah: A Study in the Cultural and Social Life of the Jewish People* (New York, 1941). It is a recurrent topic in the press, cf., for example, articles by Dr. A. Klorman, *Jewish Morning Journal*, Nov. 24, 1948; by P. Rubinstein, *ibid.*, April 5, 1949; by David Eidelsberg, *ibid.*, July 22, 1949.

[67] A 1949 menu of a drug store in Cleveland lists, together with the usual dishes "Kosher Salami Sandwiches" and "Hot Kosher Corned Beef de Luxe." Even more interesting is the menu of a Cleveland restaurant, dated June 10, 1949. Not only do "Stuffed Kishke," "Shrimp Cocktail," "Chopped Liver," "Gefilte Fish," "Pickled Herring" and "Creamed Herring" appear on the menu among the appetizers with Baked Virginia Ham Sandwich and Kosher Corned Beef Sandwich on the sandwich

most interesting period in observance and semi-observance, with cafeterias and restaurants in New York serving both Matzah and bread as well as non-kosher dishes in Passover style.[68] An interesting institution is the Jewish dairy cafeteria or restaurant found in New York and possibly also in other very large cities. It is a restaurant *sui generis* and deserves further study, like many other subjects mentioned in this paper.[69] Interestingly enough, delicatessen of the type which

list, but there is also a special *Kosher Korner* in which the following dishes are listed: "Cottage Cheese and Sour Cream; 2 Cheese Blintzes with Sour Cream; Chopped Liver w. Potato Salad; Corned Beef & Eggs; Assorted Cold Cuts with Potato Salad & Sliced Tomato." The reader will note not only the mixture of kosher and non-kosher meats, but also the indiscriminate combination of meat and dairy dishes in the *Kosher Korner*. Clementine Paddleford, the food expert of the *New York Herald Tribune*, in her description of a Viennese Hungarian restaurant in New York mentions the "chicken in the pot with those fluffy matzoth balls" (Dec. 4, 1948). Restaurants run by Jews which feature Jewish dishes together with the customary fare of general restaurants have sprung up in smaller cities and communities where there may be a sizeable Jewish business element.

[68] The elaborate preparations for the Passover are generally well known. In New York some of the largest department stores open up special Passover departments. A leaflet containing Passover recipes was offered for three cents to its readers by the magazine section of the *New York Herald Tribune* (April 10, 1949, p. 48). Passover recipes by Harriet Jean Anderson are listed also in the magazine section of the *New York Herald Tribune, idem*, pp. 38–39. The increasing use of prepared food is seen in the disappearance of *borsht*-making in the home. A questionnaire on Passover Customs and Practices issued by the Yiddish Scientific Institute in 1949, includes a question, "If you generally eat in a non-kosher restaurant, do you patronize that restaurant on Passover, too? If you do, do you omit bread and meat on the Passover days? Do you patronize on Passover only a restaurant that is kosher and in accordance with the special dietary regulations for Passover?" Chocolate "matzo" bars were introduced in 1949. Another interesting aspect of Passover in America is the utilization of the Passover Haggadah for commercial advertising. The first Haggadah of this kind seems to have been the one published by the printery of E. Zunser in 1895, the cover of which bears the advertisement of the bookseller, M. Germansky. See no. 144 in Abraham G. Duker, "Eged Haggadot," *Kiryat Sepher* (Jerusalem), vol. VIII, no. 1 (Nisan, 1931), p. 116. The early advertisers were steamship companies, banks, booksellers and food processors. Of late, many commercial Haggadahs are sponsored by Orthodox institutions. Cf. Isaac Rivkind, "Haggadot Pesaḥ," *Hadoar*, vol. VII, no. 22 (April 15, 1927), p. 341.

[69] Leah W. Leonard, in the preface to her cookbook *Jewish Cookery in accordance with the Jewish Dietary Laws* (New York, 1949), p. viii, interestingly calls attention to the fact that the earliest American Jewish cookbook, Mrs. Esther Levy's, *Jewish Cookery Book, On Principles of Economy adapted for Jewish Housekeepers . . .*, published

is considered as being typically Jewish food, can serve as a good example of American acculturation. Delicatessen was comparatively unknown in the East European milieu. In this country, Jews adopted it from the Germans in such a thorough fashion that it became identified as a Jewish dietary component.[70] The gingerbread Haman is also an evidence of American adaptation.[71]

Culinary habits are influenced in great measure by American conditions, — to the extent that the diet of even the immigrant generation differs greatly from that of the country of origin. Outstanding is the use of citrus fruits and of vegetables. More bizarre adaptations showing strong acculturation influences are the use of "Kosher Bacon," the common term used for "beef frye," parts of beef resembling bacon in appearance and as some would have it also in taste.[72] The kosher Chinese noodles also belong in this category. An American innovation is the substitution of the kosher inscription in Hebrew or in roman letters by the (U) brand,[72a] certifying the product's *kashrut* by the Union of Orthodox Jewish Congregations of America. Worthy of notice is also the innovation of certifying the *kashrut* of mineral and chemical products, such as salt,

in 1871, "contains very few Passover Recipes, and not *one* for *gefilte fish!*" (authoress' italics and exclamation mark). Generally, little is known about the acculturation trends in cooking. While the East European diet predominates, German influence is quite visible in the typical Jewish dishes suggested in Greenberg and Silverman, *op. cit.*, pp. 89–110. In contrast, Leonard's book shows a distinct Rumanian influence. A special section is devoted to recipes in Israel, with distinct Near East influences, perhaps pointing to a new ingredient in this area. Indeed, a comparative study of cookbooks and the evolution of Jewish dishes in this country awaits the scholarly gourmet.

[70] See articles by Jay Grayson in *Forward* (Aug. 22 and 24, 1949); also Ruth Glaser "From the American Scene — The Jewish Delicatessen," *Commentary*, vol. I, no. 5 (March, 1946), pp. 58–63.

[71] Cf. cakes suggested in picture opposite page 54 in Greenberg and Silverman's *The Jewish Home Beautiful, op. cit.*, which contains no description.

[72] There is a host of these prepared foods. We are acquainted with a familiar brand which customers in some localities call "Jewish Bacon," or "Kosher Bacon."

[72a] A small capital U, placed in the center of a large capital letter O.

detergerts and other products which did not require attestation in the Old World milieu.[73]

Important social and religious functions are performed through the catering industry, institutionalized in the hotel and the commercial wedding halls of varying sizes, accommodations and charges. In the metropolitan communities, the neighborhood commercial hall (called wedding temple, wedding salon, wedding chapel), and usually operated by or in collaboration with a cantor, "reverend" or rabbi, and the large catering establishments, operating through hotels, have to a large extent taken the place of the synagogue and community center as the locale for family celebrations, — the major ones being weddings, Bar Mitzvahs, and silver and golden weddings. The custom of baking and cooking by the bride's family and friends in the immigrant days, when only quarters would be rented in the neighborhood ball room, has given way to the caterers, who also supply *yarmulkes* (skull caps) with the name of the bride and groom, and the date and locale of the wedding printed inside. Of late, matchbooks with similar imprints and properly initialled paper napkins have also been supplied. The menu too deserves collection and study. Such supplies are also available for Bar Mitzvahs and other occasions. The celebration of engagements is less frequently heard of, and the signing of the *tena'im* (engagement contract) seems to be practiced only among the extreme Orthodox. A new fashion is the celebration of weddings and Bar-Mitzvahs in resort hotels.

The unsynagogued elements which, together with the large numbers considered nominally Orthodox, outnumber the affili-

[73] Cf. the advertisement of kosher cosmetics for Passover which lists "lipstick (medium, crimson red, gypsy red), cream rouge, face powder, liquid shabbos soap, tooth powder, creams, nail polish, nail polish remover, brilliantine." The advertisement is published in English and Yiddish (*Jewish Morning Journal*, April 8, 1949). There is no historical material at all published dealing with such commercial products. It would be interesting to trace the histories of the firms catering to the Jewish market.

ated, find in the wedding hall or hotel the answer to their religious needs on such occasions. In consequence, the wedding hall has become an important factor in fashioning cultural and religious patterns. Innovations in ritual are assumed by the less informed to be genuine and required by Jewish custom. In our collection of descriptions of ceremonials, we note the trend towards the abandonment of the traditional ritual in favor of substitutions. Some of these are borrowed from non-Jewish practices and from Hollywood sources, while others have evolved in the commercial wedding halls and hotels. Often the innovations are merely interwoven in the traditional ritual. The maid of honor, the best man, the bridesmaids and ushers, the ring bearer, the flower girl — all these are evidences of acculturation which by this time seem to be endowed with the prestige of sanctity. While the ceremonial is performed by a rabbi (ordained or self-termed), cantor, "reverend," or choir leader, major roles have been evolved for the choir, jazz band, and the master of ceremonies, who is not to be confused with the *badḥan* or jester, a rarity in this country. We also note the evolution of bizarre innovations, such as the participation of dancers who dress in abbreviated ballet skirts, scatter flowers in front of the procession. The ritual includes the performance of songs from the stage and motion pictures. One choir leader advertises a ceremonial protected by the copyright laws.[74]

[74] Cf. the advertisement by a choir leader who refers to himself as an *institutzie far zich alein* (an institution by himself), and calls attention to a "new *Huppah* ceremony, a new *Bar Mitzvah* ceremony, with the latest effects." The advertisement also includes the warning that to "copy or to imitate the *Huppah* or *Bar Mitzvah* ceremony without the permission of the author is legally forbidden under the Copyright Law (*Jewish Morning Journal*, Sept. 24, 1948). Another advertisement, in the *New York Post* (Nov. 19, 1948) reads as follows: "Terrific is the expression of all who hear and witness Rev. S. . . . Beautiful Wedding Ceremony. Concisely Addressed. Ritual Arranged in Special Duet Music . . . Glorious Voiced Soprano Singing Latest Wedding Song Remember Dear, By permission of . . ., distributor."

The Minnesota Rabbinical Association restricted the wedding ceremonies to the home and the synagogue because its members felt that "only the sanctuary of the home or the sanctuary of the synagogue is an appropriate setting for so sacred a service" (*National Jewish Post*, Nov. 15, 1948). There is little published material on the various

We have heard of the custom of releasing white doves from cages during the ceremony.[75] The position of the marriage broker (*shadkhan*) has declined in importance also in this country in consequence of modernization. Still the presence of matrimonial bureaus and Lonely Hearts or Friendship social clubs indicates that the need for intermediaries has not been completely eliminated.[76] The commercial *Bar Mitzvah* cere-

types of weddings. Descriptions of more traditional weddings are contained in Daniel Persky's "Ḥatunot li-Yehudei Amerika" [Weddings of American Jews] *Hadoar*, vol. XXVII, no. 17 (Feb. 25, 1949). The use of the song "Oh Promise Me," is mentioned in the *Universal Jewish Encyclopedia*, vol. X, p. 482. The song is borrowed from Robin Hood by Reginald de Koven. Harry Simonhoff in a critique of the use of "Wagner's Bridal Chorus March" from *Lohengrin* in the wedding ceremonial refers to the composer's anti-Semitism and suggests the substitution of the "March of the Priests" from Felix Mendelssohn's oratorio *Athalia*. Citations from the article which appeared in the Miami *Jewish Floridian* are given in the column by Helen Cohen, *The National Jewish Post* (Indianapolis), June 17, 1949, p. 7.

The wedding ceremonials generally include frequent picture taking and sound recording. The ceremony is supervised by a master of ceremonies. Investigation is also needed on the maintenance of the Old World custom such as throwing raisins and candy on the bridegroom upon his being called up to the Torah on the Sabbath preceding the wedding, as well as on the retention of this custom. In New York City, Hassidic wedding ceremonies of rabbinical families are sometimes performed in the open, — more often, however, in wedding halls, where we have witnessed the American innovation of the use of the microphone. The custom of refraining from marrying during the *Sefirah* period between Passover and Shabuot is still widely practiced even among the more affluent. Cf. Werner J. Cahnman, "A Note on Marriage Announcements in the *New York Times*," *American Sociological Review*, vol. XIII, no. 1 (Feb., 1948), pp. 96–97 where Cahnman comments on the conclusion concerning the low proportion of Jewish marriage announcements in the *New York Times* by David L. and Mary A. Hatch in their study of the "Criteria on Social Status as derived from Marriage Announcements in the *New York Times*," *ibid.*, vol. XII, no. 4 (Aug., 1947), pp. 396–403. The authors were unaware of the coincidence at times of the *Sefirah* period with the month that they had selected for their study during the years 1932–1942.

[75] We have heard of this custom being practiced in this country at least twenty years ago. Georg Herlitz and Max Grunwald "Wedding and Wedding Customs," *Universal Jewish Encyclopedia*, vol. X (New York, 1943), p. 482, tell of the "bestrewing of the bridal pair with wheat, a custom practiced along the Rhine and in Hesse, allowing hens to fly over the canopy, a custom which used to be observed in Posen."

[76] Cf. Rose Braunstein, *A Study of Jewish Matrimonial Clubs in New York City, 1936–37* (Typescript Thesis), The Graduate School for Jewish Social Work (New York, 1939). Advertisements of *shadkhanim* and matrimonial bureaus appear regularly in the Yiddish Sunday *Day* (New York).

mony too has evolved its own ritual, resembling closely the extravaganza of the wedding ceremony. There is the march, the bringing in of the *Bar Mitzvah* cake, the lighting of the thirteen candles, or of fourteen — one for luck — the use of the choir, the rendition, sometimes, of "Mein Yiddishe Momme" by the *Bar Mitzvah* celebrant or of "Dos Pintele Yid" by an artist. So much importance is now being attached to this commercial hall ceremonial, that we have heard of cases where it has replaced the synagogue ritual completely, even eliminating the custom of calling up the Bar Mitzvah lad to the reading of the Torah. The *Bar Mitzvah* cake, usually in the form of a Torah scroll, is also an American innovation.[77] We have not had the opportunity to observe the golden or silver wedding anniversary ceremonials. From what we have heard, their observance in the hotels or commercial halls is just as bizarre as that of the others.

Since the elaborate ritual is one of the chief selling points in the competition between the caterers and hall proprietors, the trend in this area of observances is towards increasing

[77] The Bar Mitzvah cake is of course an adaptation of the birthday cake, and one of a galaxy of baking products, which includes the Shabuot cake with the tablets containing the Ten Commandments. Cf. photograph opposite p. 32 in *The Jewish Home Beautiful*, by Betty D. Greenberg and Althea O. Silverman, *op. cit.* We have never seen the East European *Hoshana Rabbah* cake with the customary doves and ladders in this country.

There is little published descriptive material on the commercialized Bar Mitzvah celebration. Most of our information is therefore from oral reports by eye witnesses. A description of several Bar Mitzvah celebrations is included in Bezalel Kantor, "Yiddishe 'Simchos' " (Jewish Joyous Occasions), *Der Yiddisher Kemfer* (New York), Dec. 3, 1948, pp. 8–10. The article also includes a description of a wedding ceremony. It appeared in an abridged form in English under the title "Simchas in America" in *The Jewish Spectator* (New York), March, 1949, pp. 15–17. A plea for order in observances is Isaac Levitats', "Communal Regulation of Bar Mitzvah," *Jewish Social Studies*, vol. XI, no. 2 (April, 1949), pp. 153–162. Of the many publicity seeking stratagems connected with the Bar Mitzvah, we were most impressed by the Philadelphia boy who "solemnly declared" following his speech at the celebration in one "of the richest halls in New York," that he would donate an ambulance for the Red Mogen David in Israel. The picture of the Bar Mitzvah boy, ambulance and proud parents and relatives appeared in *The Day* (March 2, 1949), p. 8.

extravaganza, and as a by-product, also increasing costs. The economic aspects of this culture pattern deserve study. Disastrous is its effect on the status of the poorer and lower middle class people who are forced to spend a great deal of their income on these family occasions in order to keep up with the proverbial Joneses. The continuation of this trend spells ruination to the poorer classes and carries with it threats to communal institutions, since there is little money left once the caterer's bill is paid. These rituals also tend to become accepted as the proper and customary ones, so much so that it is possible to categorize them as local *minhagim* (customs), at least in the largest cities.[78] The effects of these practices in other areas also deserve serious consideration. The same choirs perform in the Orthodox synagogues on the High Holidays and festivals, and also on the Sabbath, in the wealthier ones. The adaptation of the jazz tempo in the synagogue worship, the inclusion of popular melodies in the ritual as symbolized by the common acceptance of the melody of "Misery Lous" for a chief *Selihot* (penitential) theme,[79] are threatening the aesthetic standard of the services and the survival of the traditional modes of Jewish music. The increasing custom of spending the holidays in resorts is also a factor to be studied, with its evolving patterns of behavior, services, etc.

The same influences are to be found on the Yiddish stage and radio, in the entertainment programs in the Jewish hotels in the Catskills and other regions, where the same pattern of entertainment is followed. It has been asserted that the "Borsht Belt" in the Catskills performs a most important function in the artistic life and amusement industry of the country by providing the stage opportunities for new talents.

[78] The importance of the *minhag* in changing Jewish practices cannot be underestimated. For a popular presentation, cf. Solomon Freehof, *Reform Jewish Practice* (Cincinnati, 1944).

[79] The choir leader presumably is the same person who advertised the copyright wedding ceremony. Cf. note 74.

Much of the entertainment in the resorts centers about Jewish "humor" usually of the vulgar type, particularly as presented by the comedian or master of ceremonies.[80] The perpetuation of these motifs through the mixed language phonograph record tends to identify the Yiddish language, Jewish traditional culture, the immigrant culture, and even acculturated Jewish patterns with vulgarity and unacceptability.[81]

There is much to be investigated in the patterns that prevail or are being developed in psychological attitudes as well as scales of status value. Group inferiority is a common phenomenon among immigrant ethnic groups and much of the clash of generations between the immigrant parents and their American-born children revolves about the differences of approach to problems of status. The problem of marginality and self-hate has been the subject of serious study and deserves more attention as it applies to culture patterns.[82] The most

---

[80] These have been the subject of many letters to the editor in the Yiddish press.

[81] As examples, we shall merely list titles of some records: "Ginsberg from Scotland Yard," "Her Husband's Business," "Number 4 Homintosh Lane," "Galitzyaner Rhumba," "Litvak Polka," "Bialystoker Square Dance," "Lefkowitz the Kop," "Oom-Glick Blues," "The Son of Pincus the Peddler," "Calypso Mandelbaum," "Sarah Come Back to the Range," "Senorita from the Bronx," "My Machaya from Hawaii," "Matzoh Balls," "Hershele at the Induction Center," "Basic Yiddish," "Dalang der Schlang, Mr. Butcher." "Shepsel Kanarik fun Poughkeepsie," "Nancy from Delancey," "The Groom Couldn't Get In." A record band is featured under the name "Alte Kockaire and Pat Zell and Shmendrik's Orchestra." There is also a "Mishiginer Hershel with Barrely Pullick and Orchestra."

Another category is the English record interspersed with some Yiddish words, used to convey vulgar meanings. There are also records with mixed Yiddish and Spanish and mixed Yiddish and English vocals in both the vulgar and non-vulgar veins. The student of acculturation and transculturation will find ample material in the contribution of Second Avenue to Broadway. We are acquainted with some twenty-five recorded adaptations of Second Avenue tunes to English words, some of which have attained great popularity. Of course the translation of popular hits from English into Yiddish is a regular feature of Yiddish radio hours with recordings available in many cases. There are no thorough listings of these types of records. We regret the limitation of space prevents us from presenting examples of these types.

[82] On the subject of marginality and alienation, see Everett V. Stonequist, *The Marginal Man* (New York, 1937); *id.,* "The Marginal Character of the Jews," in

obvious acculturation area is that of given names. Mencken has remarked that "of all the immigrant peoples in America, the Jews seem to be most willing to change their names."[83] The adoption of non-Hebraic names has been a common pattern first in countries of emancipation and among the wealthier and more "Europeanized" elements in the Jewish population centers in Eastern Europe, where they came to be increasingly adopted also by the poorer classes, with changes first taking place among women. The common practice in "emancipated" circles in Europe was to give to children two sets of names, one of the majority culture and the other Hebraic or Yiddish, — the latter for use in the synagogue ritual, in the signature on a *ketubah*, or other documents, or for tombstone inscriptions. In Germany and in some other countries no connection seemed to have been required in all cases between the Hebraic and the other name. In the United States it is generally the custom to adjust the "American" name to the Hebraic one by taking care that the initials in both are phonetically the same. A common pattern of this adjustment has been adopted so much so that it is taken for granted that certain Hebrew names are "translated" by their American

Jews in a Gentile World, edited by Isacque Graeber and Steuart H. Britt, *op. cit.*, pp. 296–310. Milton M. Goldberg, "A Qualification of the Marginal Man Theory," *American Sociological Review*, vol. VI, no. 1 (Feb., 1941), pp. 52–58; Jessie Bernard, "Biculturality: A Study in Social Schizophrenia," in *Jews in a Gentile World*, *op. cit.*, pp. 264–293. For material on self-hate, see Kurt Lewin, *Resolving Social Conflicts* (New York, 1948), pp. 145–158 and pp. 186–200; Abraham G. Duker, *Jewish Survival in the World Today* (New York, 1941). Source Book, part II B, pp. 2–6, 10–13, 15–18; Source Book, part III A, pp. 70–98.

For an interesting example, as evidenced by a scholar, see Anonymous, "An Analysis of Jewish Culture," *Jews in a Gentile World*, *op. cit.*, pp. 243–263.

[83] H. L. Mencken, *American Language, Supplement II* (New York, 1948), pp. 415 ff.; and his *American Language* (New York, 1937), pp. 487, 497–502, 506–508. Concerning names, see also Alfred J. Kolatch *These Are the Names* (New York, 1948), pp. 73–81, which contains data on frequency of names and shifting tendencies in naming. Interestingly, Rabbi Aaron Gordon's *Eben Meir* (Piotrkow, 1909), a rabbinical treatise on divorce, reveals a similar concentration on certain name changes. Space prevents us from citing examples from this important hitherto neglected source for the study of American Jewish names.

"counterparts." It would be interesting to study the extent of the awareness and knowledge of the Hebrew names. As a rule Biblical names are avoided among the "American" ones, with the exception of some acceptable ones, which have drifted in via the Christian milieu, such as Michael, Daniel, etc. Of late the tendency can be noted of abandoning this double set of names, and bestowing only up-to-date English ones. While the newspaper announcements, a convenient source for the study of contemporary names, do not seem to indicate much variety, occasionally some unusual names are encountered,[84] including Christopher.[85] The "Judaization" of "American" non-Jewish names and their identification as too "Jewish" has thus far led to their consequent abandonment or modification, as in the cases of Morris and later Maurice, Isadore or Isidor, Max, Sidney, and more recently Irving (the more fashionable revision being that to Irwin).[86] A not too popular reversal of the process, traced to the influence of Zionism and Israel, is the adoption of Biblical or modern Hebrew Israeli names.[87]

Not so far reaching have been the changes in the family names. Still, the National Jewish Welfare Board reported in connection with its study of the participation of Jews in the United States armed forces in World War II, that fifty to sixty per cent of the names in the returned questionnaires were general "American" names, such as Smith or Brown, with the somewhat bizarre sprinkling of appellations such as Doughertys and Flanagans.[88] In some cases, the family names of children are changed upon their birth, while the parents retain their

[84] For example, Ming Toy Goldberg, or Harvard Yale Ginzberg.

[85] Leonard Lyon, "The Lion's Den," *New York Post* (Sept. 2, 1948), reports that the son of Moss Hart and Kitty Carlisle, both Jews, is called Christopher.

[86] Cf. Kolatch, *op. cit.*

[87] We witnessed the naming at a New York synagogue of a girl by the name Israela on Saturday, May 15, 1948, the day after the declaration of Israel's independence.

[88] See Jewish Welfare Board, *Suggested Topics for New Speakers on the Necessity of Compiling War Records for Jewish Men and Women in World War II* (prepared for the Speakers' Bureau in the Philadelphia Jewish War Record Drive, Feb.-March, 1943) [mimeographed].

own names. Often different sets of names for parents and children appear in social announcements, where sometimes the information is added that the name has been legally changed. It would be interesting to investigate the extent of the factors of ethnic immigrant inferiority feelings and the specific Jewish inferiority feelings that operate in such cases.

There is also need to investigate a whole gamut of attitudes, such as the change in the family structure, now that the clash between the immigrant parents and their children seems to be receding into history. The strong Jewish mother person which appears from time to time in fiction, presents a typical research problem in this area.[89]

Ample sources in the fields of case work, psychiatry, rabbinical and newspaper counseling await the researcher in this field. There is also need for investigating the effects of the increasing middle class character of the Jewish population on its ways of living and thinking. A crying need is for investigation of attitudes towards the majority population, the ambivalence of respect and disrespect, fear and faith in goodwill assurances. In our perusal of a series of novels dealing with intermarriage, we were struck by the prevalent authors' choices of characters of the male Jew and female Gentile.[90]

---

[89] As for instance in Delmore Schwartz, *The World is a Wedding* (New York, 1947).

[90] In *Intellectual Trends, Syllabus*, Training Bureau for Jewish Communal Service (1949) [mimeographed], we remarked that "the intermarriage novel bids fair to become the most numerous branch of fiction on Jewish themes . . . The characteristics of this type of literature reflect the cultural milieu of Jews who seek acceptance in Gentile society as well as that of the outside society which is willing to accept them only in part. The male is, in most cases, the Jewish partner of the intermarriage solution. Novels in which a Gentile falls in love with a Jewish woman are rare. The Jewish partner is usually an idealistic person, fairly acceptable, except for occasional racial or cultural quirks which hold fascination at least in the eyes of the general reader. It is usually his Jewish relatives who are portrayed as impossible or unacceptable. The themes are usually autobiographical (p. 8)." Similarly, the war novel too shows the same tendencies of making the Jewish hero more acceptable by endowing him with partly non-Jewish descent (Stefan Heym, *The Crusaders*, New York, 1948) or a Gentile wife or sweetheart (Irwin Shaw, *The Young Lions*, New York, 1948; Ira Wolfert, *An Act of Love*, New York, 1948). For bibliographies on Jewish characters in fiction see Joseph Mersand, *Traditions in American Literature* (New York, 1939); Joshua

Rarely, if ever, is there the process indicated in reverse, as for instance in the case of Ivanhoe and Rebecca in Scott's novel.[91] This would denote greater acceptability of the Jewish male than female, still to be proven in life. It would be interesting to learn the relation of this attitude to the notion of superiority of male in the traditional Jewish milieu. Generally, the feelings of Jewish inferiority and the phenomena of Jewish thinking in terms of Christian concepts also remain to be investigated.

We have indicated some changes in the cultural patterns of American Jews, without any intentions of exhausting the subject, but rather with the purpose of calling attention to the need of research in these areas in which the historian ought to play his part, without abandoning it to the sociologist, anthropologist or psychiatric student. American Jewish history is both Jewish history and American history. It is part of the history of world Jewry. It is also more than peripheral to the history of inter-group relations in this country, a field which is also in need of more investigation.

The specialist in American Jewish history must make his contributions also to this field. His research, however, must be preceded by the collector. The study of culture patterns requires more than a collection of archival and newspaper materials. There is need for collecting the various commercial and art objects mentioned in this paper. There is a need for recording pronunciation and other language data (not only in Yiddish) before these are lost to posterity. There is a need for collecting data, through interviews and questionnaires, as well as through autobiographies. There are also pragmatic values for community planning, education and ideological orientation involved in studying the evolution of the culture patterns. We do not dwell on all these aspects in our present discussion.

Bloch, "Annual Review," in the *Jewish Book Annual* (New York) and Iva Cohen, "American Jewish Bibliography," in the *American Jewish Year Book.*

[91] Cf., for instance, Curtis Carroll Davis, "*Judith Bensaddi* and the Reverend Doctor Henry Ruffner — The Earliest Appearance in American Fiction of the Jewish Problem?" *PAJHS*, no. XXXIX, part 2 (Dec., 1949), pp. 115–142.

BIBLIOGRAPHY FOR FURTHER READING

ADLER, CYRUS, and AARON M. MARGALITH. *With Firmness in the Right: American Diplomatic Action Affecting Jews, 1840-1945.* New York: The American Jewish Committee, 1946. 489 pp.

BISNO, ABRAHAM. *Union Pioneer.* Madison: The University of Wisconsin Press, 1967. xvii+244 pp. illus.

BOGEN, BORIS D. *Jewish Philanthropy: An Exposition of Principles and Methods of Jewish Social Service in the United States.* New York: The Macmillan Company, 1917. 391 pp.

DINNERSTEIN, LEONARD. *The Leo Frank Case.* New York: Columbia University Press, 1968. xiii+248 pp. illus.

DUSHKIN, ALEXANDER M. *Jewish Education in New York City.* New York: The Bureau of Jewish Education, 1918. 596 pp.

EPSTEIN, MELECH. *Jewish Labor in U.S.A.: An Industrial, Political, and Cultural History of the Jewish Movement, 1882-1914.* New York: Trade Union Sponsoring Committee, 1950. 456 pp.

EPSTEIN, MELECH. *Jewish Labor in U.S.A. 1914-1952: An Industrial, Political, and Cultural History of the Jewish Labor Movement.* New York: Trade Union Sponsoring Committee, 1953. 466 pp.

FISHMAN, JOSHUA A. *Yiddish in America: Socio-Linguistic Description and Analysis,* Bloomington: Indiana University, 1965. vii+94 pp.

FUCHS, LAWRENCE H. *The Political Behavior of American Jews.* Glencoe, Ill.: The Free Press, 1956. 220 pp.

GLAZER, NATHAN. *American Judaism.* Chicago: The University of Chicago Press, 1957. 176 pp.

GLAZER, NATHAN and DANIEL PATRICK MOYNIHAN. *Beyond the Melting Pot: The Negroes, Puerto Ricans, Jews, Italians, and Irish of New York City.* Cambridge, Mass.: M.I.T. Press, 1963. vii+360 pp.

GOLDEN, HARRY. *A Little Girl is Dead.* Cleveland: World Publishing Company, 1965. xv+363 pp. illus.

GOLDSTEIN, SIDNEY and CALVIN GOLDSCHEIDER. *Jewish Americans: Three Generations in a Jewish Community.* Englewood Cliffs: Prentice-Hall, 1968. xvii+274 pp. illus.

GORDON, WHITNEY H. *A Community in Stress.* New York: Living Books, 1964. xxiv+269 pp.

HALPERN, BEN. *The American Jew: A Zionist Analysis.* New York: The Theodor Herzl Foundation, 1956. 174 pp.

JANOWSKY, OSCAR I. (Ed.) *The American Jew: A Composite Portrait.* New York: Harper & Brothers, 1942. 332 pp.

JANOWSKY, OSCAR I., (Ed.) *The American Jew: A Reappraisal.* Philadelphia: The Jewish Publication Society of America, 1964. xvi+468 pp.

KRAMER, JUDITH R. and SEYMOUR LEVENTMAN. *Children of the Gilded Ghetto: Conflict Resolutions of Three Generations of American Jews.* New Haven: Yale University Press, 1961. xviii+228 pp.

LEVITAN, TINA. *Islands of Compassion: A History of the Jewish Hospitals of New York.* New York: Twayne, 1964. 304 pp. illus.

LIFSON, DAVID S. *The Yiddish Theatre in America.* New York: T. Yoseloff, 1965. 659 pp. illus.

LIPSKY, LOUIS. *Tales of the Yiddish Rialto: Reminiscences of Playwrights and Players in New York's Jewish Theatre in the Early 1900's.* New York: T. Yoseloff, 1962. 234 pp.

LIPTZIN, SOL. *The Jew in American Literature.* New York: Bloch, 1966. 251 pp.

MALIN, IRVING. *Jews and Americans.* Carbondale: Southern Illinois University Press, 1965. xii+193 pp.

MEYER, ISIDORE S. (Ed.) *Early History of Zionism in America.* New York: The American Jewish Historical Society and the Theodor Herzl Foundation, 1958. 340 pp.

MILLER, JAMES. *The Detroit Yiddish Theater 1920 to 1937.* Detroit: Wayne State University Press, 1967. 195 pp. illus.

MORRIS, ROBERT and MICHAEL FREUND, (Eds.) *Trends and Issues in Jewish Social Service in the United States, 1899-1952.* Philadelphia: The Jewish Publication Society of America, 1966. xxix+642 pp.

PARISH, WILLIAM J. *The Charles Ilfeld Company: A Study of the Rise and Decline of Mercantile Capitalism in New Mexico.* Cambridge: Harvard University Press, 1961. xxi+431 pp. illus.

RIBALOW, HAROLD U., comp. *Autobiographies of American Jews.* Philadelphia: The Jewish Publication Society of America, 1965. xiii+496 pp.

RINGER, BENJAMIN B. *The Edge of Friendliness: A Study of Jewish-Gentile Relations.* New York: Basic Books, 1967. xii+272 pp.

ROSENSTOCK, MORTON. *Louis Marshall: Defender of Jewish Rights.* Detroit: Wayne State University Press, 1965. 334 pp.

SHER, EVA. *Life With Farmer Goldstein.* New York: Funk & Wagnalls, 1967. 247 pp.

SHERMAN, C. BEZALEL. *The Jew within American Society: A Study in Ethnic Individuality.* Detroit: Wayne State University Press, 1961. 260 pp.

SKLARE, MARSHALL. *Conservative Judaism: An American Religious Movement.* Glencoe, Ill.: The Free Press, 1955. 298 pp.

SKLARE, MARSHALL and JOSEPH GREENBLUM. *Jewish Identity on the Suburban Frontier: A Study of Group Survival in the Open Society.* New York: Basic Books, 1967. xv+362 pp.

STEMBER, CHARLES HERBERT and others. *Jews in the Mind of America.* New York: Basic Books, 1966. xiv+413 pp.

WINTER, NATHAN H. *Jewish Education in a Pluralist Society: Samson Benderly and Jewish Education in the United States.* New York: New York University Press, 1966. xvi+262 pp.

INDEX

Abrahams, Lewis, 25
Adams, Charles Follen, 4
Adams, Henry, 8
Adath Israel, Congregation (New
    York City), 132, 139
Addams, Jane, 219
Adee, Alvee A., 56-57
Adler, Cyrus, 29, 63
    Jewish Theological Seminary of
        America and, 122-23
    Schechter and, 111, 112, 113,
        114, 115, 116, 126, 127
    Sulzberger and, 120
Adler, Jacob, 80
Adult School of Jewish Studies
    (Cleveland, Ohio), 304, 306
Agriculture in United States, and
    Russian Jews, 97-101
Agudat Harabbanim (Rabbinical or-
    ganization), 144-45
Alaska, 97, 334
Alien Contract Labor Laws, 34
Alien Enemy Act of 1798, 105n
Alien and Sedition Act of 1798
    (United States), 105n
Amalgamated Clothing Workers of
    America, 332
Amalgamated Men's Clothing Work-
    ers, 234, 238, 243
American Association for Jewish
    Education, 286, 311
American Civil Liberties Union, 338
American Committee for the Protec-
    tion of the Foreign-Born, 329
American Council for Judaism, 182
American Federation of Labor, 46,
    81, 211, 229, 230, 240, 243,
    245
American Federation of Labor—
    Congress of Industrial Organi-
    zation, 245
American Federation for Polish Jews,
    333

American Federation of Zionists,
    133n, 162n, 179
American Hebrew (periodical), 82,
    93, 128, 173, 174n
    on Schechter, 114, 115, 116, 118,
        119, 129
    on Union of Orthodox Jewish Con-
        gregations of America, 143,
        144n
    on World War II refugees, 330
    on Zionism, 181, 182
American Israelite (periodical), 138
    on Schechter, 114
    on Zionism, 156-57, 174, 175, 176,
        180n
American Israelites (organization),
    135
American Jewish Archives, 151n
American Jewish Committee, 29, 38,
    190n, 339n, 349n
    anti-Semitism and, 364
    constituancy of, 333, 345n
    Jewish immigration to America
        and, 30, 35, 36, 43, 44, 57, 58,
        191n, 322, 323, 327, 329, 332
American Jewish Conference (1943),
    347-48
American Jewish Congress, 157, 322,
    325, 332, 333, 334, 338, 342
American Jewish Relief Committee,
    190n
American Party (political party), 105,
    106
Americanization of Jews, 342-45, 347,
    367-68, 385-95, 414-15, 419
    Bar Mitzvah and, 402-10, 412-13
    death ceremonies and, 403-5
    holidays and, 396-98, 402, 405-6
    home customs, 399-402
    Kashrut and, 406-10
    names and, 416-18
    weddings and, 410, 411-12
Anarchism, 17, 29, 127

Howells, William Dean, 187
Hughes, Charles Evans, 202
Hungarian Greek Catholics, 389
Hungarian immigrants, 83, 107
Hungary, 10, 67
  anti-Semitism in, 3
  Jewish immigrants from, 60, 222, 252
Hunter, Robert, 185, 192, 202n
Husband, William Walter, 58

Iddishkeit (Jewishness), influence on businessmen of, 249-84
Illinois, 43
Illiteracy in United States, 108-9
Immigration, 3, 320-21
  American attitudes toward
    from 1870-1891, 23
    from 1891-1924, 23-63
    opposition, 104-10, 184, 191n, 324, 326, 329, 335, 337, 378
  American Jews and, 103-4, 106, 330-31, 332-33, 335, 338, 340, 343-44, 347
  Depression's effect on, 321, 324, 325-26, 327, 340
  Jewish, *see* Immigration, Jewish
  labor and, 25, 29, 46, 47, 54, 107
  literacy test for, 107, 108, 191, 320
  Socialist Party and, 189n, 197-98, 199, 204
Immigration, Jewish, 191n, 329, 341
  agitation for German-Jewish immigration, 322-23, 324, 325, 328-29
  anti-Semitism and, 252, 253, 259, 283, 337, 339, 362, 366
  from Austria, 81n, 222, 252, 328
  Reform Judaism and, 158-59
  studies on, 250-51
    case studies, 261-84
    goals, 252
  Union of Orthodox Congregations of America and, 142
  to United States, 23
    "Brief in the Matter of Hersh Skuratowski," 30-32, 35, 59
    causes, 252-54, 259, 260
    economic status, 66, 68, 69-71, 83, 87, 96, 97, 99-101, 103, 354
    Galveston plan, 26
    Geigow vs Uhl, 40
    immigration laws, 23-25, 26-30, 34, 35-61, 104-10, 320, 326-29, 331, 340, 345

Industrial Removal Office, 26, 96, 97, 99
  of Orthodox Jews, 254
  statistics on, 252n, 340
Immigration Restriction League (Boston, Massachusetts), 43
Independent, Dearborn (periodical), 3, 380
Independent Order of B'nai B'rith, 40, 62, 65, 289, 332n, 334, 337, 339, 344, 346, 363
  constituency of, 333
  Jewish immigration to the United States and, 26, 28, 29, 35, 36, 322
Independent Order Brith Abraham, 191n
Indiana, 153
Indianapolis Conference (1906), 153
Indians, American, 379
Industrial Removal Office, 26, 96, 97, 99
Industrial Trade Commission, 94, 98
Industry
  anti-unionism of, 222-25, 231
  arbitration and mediation in, 230-35
  garment, 69
  immigration and, 106-7
  technology in, 225-29
  unemployment funds and, 235
Ingraham, Rev. Joseph, 14
Institute of Jewish Studies (Cleveland, Ohio), *see* Jewish Teachers Institute
Institute of Labour Management of Great Britain, 234
Intermarriage, 82
International Encyclopedia, 71, 74
International Ladies' Garment Workers' Union, 228, 234, 237, 238, 332n
International Socialist Congress of 1904 (Amsterdam, Holland), 197
Interstate Commerce Commission, United States, 223
Ireland, 27, 106
Irish, 375, 376, 377
  in industry, 81n
  Jewish intermarriage with, 82
  in New York City, 68, 69, 70, 75, 76, 83, 89, 94, 101, 102, 110
  politics and, 108
Isaacs, Abram, 71
Isaacs, Jacob, 17

Schwellenbach, Louis B., 343-44
Scotland, 27
Scotsmen
    immigration and, 108
    in New York City, 75
    stereotype of, 351
Scottish Rite Masonry, 20, 76, 363
Seasongood, Lewis, 356
Segal, Joseph, 202n
Seligman, Edwin R. A., 71
Seligman, Joseph, 1, 356, 359, 360
Seligman, Theodore, 361
Senate Immigration Committee, 326
Separation of Church and State, 147
    Zionism and, 153-54
Sephardic Congregation (Manchester, England), 133n
Sephardic Jews, 391
Servants in Jewish families, 356
Seton Hall University (Newark, New Jersey), 130n
Seventeenth of Tammuz (Jewish holiday), 397
Shalom Aleichem (Rabinowitz, Shalom), 258n
Shalom zakhr (Jewish observance), 400
Shannon, David, 197, 204
Shapiro, Ezra, 297, 302, 315
Shavuot (Jewish holiday), 397
Shearith Israel, Congregation (New York City), 128, 133, 136
Shir ha ma'alot (Psalm 121), 399
Shirtwaist-makers strike (1909), 218, 219
Sholem Aleichem Folk Shul (Jewish school), 296
Siberia, 263, 278, 279, 282
Silver, Rabbi Abba Hillel, 288, 297, 315, 318
Simhat Torah (Jewish holiday), 255, 397
Singer, J., 165n
Skuratowski, Hersh, 30-32, 35, 59
Slobod, Samuel
    life in America
        as a businessman, 268-69
        as a peddler, 262-66
        political, 266-68
    life in Russia, 261
    personality characteristics of, 269-71
Social security, 235-36
Socialism, 86, 127
    Debs and, 185, 186, 192, 201, 202
    See also Socialist Party

Socialist Congress of 1907 (Stuttgart, Germany), 197
Socialist Convention of 1908 (Chicago, Illinois), 198
Socialist Party of United States
    East Side of New York and, 183, 185, 186, 188, 196, 201-2
    endorsers, 187
    ethnic interest, 184, 192-93, 195, 202, 205-7
    immigration and, 189n, 197-98, 199, 204
    labor and, 184-207, 218, 219, 239, 240
Sokolsky, George, 325
Sola, Rev. Meldola De, 118
Solis-Cohen, Dr. Solomon, 144n
    Jewish Theological Seminary of America and, 113, 117
    Schechter and, 111, 112, 120, 126
South, American, 329, 373, 374
    anti-Semitism in, 371-72, 378-79, 380
South Carolina, 281
Spanish Jews, 67
Spanish-American War (1898), 140
Spivak, Chaim, 269
Srole, Leo, 384n
Steffens, Lincoln, 187, 192
Stereotypes, 350, 375,
    of Jews, 351-53, 357-58, 363, 371, 376-77
    of non-Jewish nationalities, 351
Stoddard, Lothrop, 2
Stoeckers and anti-Semitism, 3
Stokes, James Graham Phelps, 185, 194n, 202n, 219
Stokes, Mrs. James Graham Phelps, 194n
Stolz, Joseph, 169
Straus, Isidor, 122
Straus, Nathan, 363
Straus, Oscar S., 77, 221, 232
Sukkot (Jewish holiday), 398
Sullivan, Timothy, 187
Sulzberger, Cyrus, 36
Sulzberger, Mayer, 29, 62, 111, 115, 116, 117, 118, 120, 121, 123, 125, 126, 127
Sulzer, William, 364
Sunday Sabbath Services
    Montefiore on, 124-25
    Reform Judaism and, 142
Survey Report on Jewish Education (1924), 286-87